Global and National Macroeconometric Modelling

Global and National Macroeconometric Modelling: A Long-Run Structural Approach

Anthony Garratt
Department of Economics, Mathematics and Statistics, Birkbeck College, University of London

Kevin Lee
School of Economics, University of Nottingham

M. Hashem Pesaran
University of Southern California, and Trinity College, Cambridge

Yongcheol Shin
Department of Economics and Related Studies, University of York

OXFORD
UNIVERSITY PRESS

OXFORD
UNIVERSITY PRESS

Great Clarendon Street, Oxford OX2 6DP

Oxford University Press is a department of the University of Oxford.
It furthers the University's objective of excellence in research, scholarship, and education by publishing worldwide in

Oxford New York

Auckland Cape Town Dar es Salaam Hong Kong Karachi
Kuala Lumpur Madrid Melbourne Mexico City Nairobi
New Delhi Shanghai Taipei Toronto

With offices in

Argentina Austria Brazil Chile Czech Republic France Greece
Guatemala Hungary Italy Japan Poland Portugal Singapore
South Korea Switzerland Thailand Turkey Ukraine Vietnam

Published in the United States
by Oxford University Press Inc., New York

First published 2006

First published in paperback 2012

British Library Cataloguing in Publication Data
Data available

Library of Congress Cataloging in Publication Data
Data available

Typeset by Newgen Imaging Systems (P) Ltd., Chennai, India
Printed in Great Britain
on acid-free paper by
The MPG Books Group Ltd, Bodmin and King's Lynn

978–0–19–929685–9 (hbk); 978–0–19–965046–0 (pbk)

10 9 8 7 6 5 4 3 2 1

Preface to Paperback Edition

The recent financial crisis and the subsequent widespread economic depression in the industrialised economies and some of the emerging economies have highlighted the increasingly interdependent nature of the world economy and the financial markets in particular. Shocks to one economy or market transmit, often rapidly, to other economies or markets and tend to accentuate the risks of downturns. The repercussions of the recent crisis are still being felt as public sector debt levels have risen rapidly and the sovereign debt crises currently being experienced in many countries are causing financial disruption and are likely to lead to further rounds of macroeconomic adjustments.

Against this background, the validity and usefulness of DSGE modelling, as currently practised and probably representing the predominant approach to macroeconomic modelling today, has come under question. Many of the DSGE models used by central bankers did not include the foreign, financial, and housing variables that proved crucial to the transmission of the crisis. These models also included a very limited treatment of fiscal policy or debt management. DSGE models have provided many theoretical insights but their insistence on a particular type of micro-founded theory and on particular approaches to identification and estimation has been at the expense of adequately representing the data and of being relevant to the central policy issues of concern.

The long-run structural approach to macroeconometric modelling developed in this volume provides a more flexible framework which can be, and has been, successfully used in modelling exercises to take account of interactions between real and financial variables as well as the economic connections across markets and economies. Under this approach, economic theory is used pragmatically to provide lists of variables that interact strongly, flag up crucial constraints of the sort that determine long-run relations, suggest restrictions on the signs of the interaction between variables, and provide guidance on functional forms. The approach emphasises the long-run relationships that exist between variables and recognises the role they play in influencing macroeconomic dynamics, letting the data pin down the transitory dynamics rather than imposing strong prior views on them. The approach reflects the view that short-run interactions are often governed by political and institutional factors rather than specific calculations by a representative agent operating in a stylised environment. In contrast, long-run theoretical relations, driven by arbitrage opportunities, tend to be determined by long-run economic calculations and less by short-term institutional or political constraints. The flexibility of the approach and its pragmatic blend of theory and evidence mean that the long-run structural modelling approach takes the data seriously and provides a means of obtaining an economically meaningful interpretation of the events that show in the data without the theory becoming a straitjacket.

Since the publication of the first edition of this volume in 2006, the long-run structural modelling approach has been applied in a wide range of academic analyses and has informed and been adopted in work by many international agencies including the European Central Bank, the IMF, the Inter-American Development Bank, Banque de France, and Swiss National Bank, among others. The approach has also been associated with a surge of interest in the literature in two important related areas, in particular:

First, the approach has promoted the detailed study of global and regional interactions through the GVAR methodology. Here, economies are tied together through the careful construction of separate measures of 'foreign' variables in each of the separate national models. The GVAR methodology allows one to decouple a model of the world economy into subsystems so that country-specific models can be estimated separately but consistently and then analysed simultaneously taking into account that all the variables in the global model are endogenous and interlinked. The technique, therefore, sidesteps the curse of dimensionality that usually affects the analysis of large interconnected systems and this explains why the techniques have been widely taken up. Recent research in this area has resulted in a range of papers and procedures that have been widely employed in policy analysis and forecasting, brought together in the *GVAR Toolbox* available at http://www-cfap.jbs.cam.ac.uk/research/gvartoolbox/index.html.

Secondly, the approach of the book has prompted new developments in the area of decision-making using macroeconometric models and in particular in the production of forecasts (of point estimates, densities, and event probabilities) for use in decision-making based on the information available in real-time. The VAR methods at the heart of the long-run structural approach provide easy-to-estimate models and can be readily investigated through simulation. For these reasons, the approach can take full advantage of model averaging methods used in forecasting to take into account model and regime uncertainties that surround policy advice and it can be used to present forecasts in a way that is useful for decision-makers. The models can also be easily re-estimated as new information becomes available and so can fully exploit the real-time datasets that are now widely available, containing the entire history of data vintages as they were published (not just the most recent single vintage) and including direct measures of expectations obtained from surveys to reflect agents' beliefs as expressed in real time. Therefore, the approach is extremely useful in understanding and informing real world decision-making. Research in this area has grown rapidly over recent years and is discussed in the research programme described at http://www.nottingham.ac.uk/cfcm/research/decision-making-using-macroeconomic-models-research-programme.aspx.

The research described in the book has proved useful to a range of policy- and decision-makers and has formed the launch pad for subsequent work in many areas of macroeconometric modelling and forecasting. Recent economic developments have once again highlighted the importance of allowing for the complexities of macroeconomic and financial systems and their interactions. The gains from doing so remain as important as ever and we are pleased that the long-run structural approach has proven useful in helping decision-makers to build statistically adequate models that are at the same time useful in policy analysis and forecasting even in testing times.

November 2011

Preface

National and global macroeconometric modelling has had a long and venerable history in the UK, with important implications for macroeconomic policy in general and monetary policy in particular. It is an activity that involves sustained research input of several investigators with a variety of skills. The present work is not an exception and its completion has required the enthusiasm and commitment of a large number of individuals and institutions. It was given initial impetus by funding from the UK's Economic and Social Research Council (Grant no. L116251016) and from the Newton Trust of Trinity College, Cambridge (under Anil Seal), to whom we are very grateful. They funded a project on 'Structural Modelling of the UK Economy within a VAR Framework using Quarterly and Monthly Data', conceived and originally housed in the Department of Applied Economics (DAE) at the University of Cambridge in the mid-1990s. The authors all worked at Cambridge at the time, along with Brian Henry and Martin Weale who were also co-applicants on the project. Although the team dispersed over the years (Garratt to Leicester and then Birkbeck; Henry to LBS and then Oxford; Lee to Leicester; Shin to Edinburgh and Leeds; and Weale to the National Institute), we remain very grateful for the resources and congenial atmosphere provided by co-researchers and colleagues during our time working at and visiting the DAE.

The research associated with the project extended well beyond the original intentions of the funded project, however, and has benefited from the help and expertise of many friends and colleagues. We are particularly grateful to Richard Smith and Ron Smith, who have collaborated with us and made essential contributions to various aspects of the work in the book, and we have received invaluable comments from Manuel Arrelano, Michael Binder, Carlo Favero, Paul Fisher, Clive Granger, David Hendry, Cheng Hsiao, George Kapetanios, Adrian Pagan, Bahram Pesaran, Til Schuermann, James Stock, Ken Wallis and Mike Wickens. The book draws on material from a variety of our published journal articles also, and we are particularly grateful to the constructive and enlightening comments received from the editors and referees of *Econometric Reviews* (especially regarding parts of the material of Chapter 6), *Economic Journal* (Chapters 4 and 9), *Economics Letters* (Chapter 6), *Journal of the American Statistical Association* (Chapters 7 and 11) and *Journal of Econometrics* (Chapter 6). And the project has also been assisted greatly by the contributions of Yoga Affandi, Mutita Akusuwan, Mahid Barakchian, James Mitchell, Dimitrios Papaikonomou and Eduardo Salazar.

While we have been keen to disseminate various aspects of our work in the form of publications in academic journals, it was always our intention to write up the project in the form of a book describing the entire process of model building, including the methodology tying the economics and the econometric techniques together, descriptions of the data collection and analysis, and the use of the model in various decision-making contexts. We hope that our description will increase transparency on the process of model building. In the light of new economic and econometric ideas, and with the advent of fast and readily available computing power, macroeconometric model-building is an activity that can be widely pursued for a better understanding of national and global economies and their interlinkages. We hope this book serves to reduce the investment required in the first stages of the sustained effort required in building and using macroeconometric models.

November 2005

Contents

List of tables

List of figures

1

Introduction

Macroeconometric modelling is at the heart of decision-making by governments, industrial and financial institutions. Models are used to organise and describe our understanding of the workings of the national and global economies, provide a common framework for communication, predict future economic developments under alternative scenarios, and to evaluate potential outcomes of policies and external events. This book aims to contribute to this important literature by providing a detailed description of the 'long-run structural modelling approach' applied to modelling of national economies in a global context. The modelling approach builds on recent developments in macroeconomic theory and in time series econometrics, and provides a transparent framework for forecasting and policy analysis. The book covers theoretical as well as practical considerations involved in the model-building process, and gives an overview of the econometric methods.

The modelling strategy is illustrated through a detailed application to the UK economy. This application is intended to be of interest in its own right, as well as providing a blueprint for long-run structural modelling by potential users of the approach in other contexts. To this end, we also provide the data and computer code employed in the UK modelling exercise to illustrate the steps taken and to facilitate replication of the methods and their application to other datasets. Hence, the book aims to provide a description of the construction and use of the UK macroeconometric model in sufficient detail so that it will be of use to practitioners who might wish to undertake a similar sort of exercise; users are persuaded of the cohesion between the modelling activity and the end uses of the model; and the policy analyses and forecasts that are presented are readily interpretable and of direct use by decision-makers. We also describe various extensions of the modelling exercise, including an explanation of how the modelling approach could be applied to develop a global macroeconometric model, developed from scratch or accommodating the UK model, and an explanation of how the UK model could be used to focus on specific features of the national economy which might be of specific interest to particular decision-makers.

In describing our modelling activities, we address directly the anxieties of those who make use of macroeconomic models but who recognise also the uncertainties and ambiguities involved in modelling and associated forecasting. So, in explaining our strategy, we make an explicit distinction between those elements of economic theory that we believe with some degree of confidence (usually associated with the long-run properties of the economy) and those elements for which economic theory is less clear-cut (on the short-run dynamics arising out of the precise sequencing of decisions, for example). We also compare our views on the working of the macroeconomy with those of alternative modelling approaches, noting the areas in which there is broad agreement and those in which there is less consensus. We note too that, once we have estimated our model, we can test formally the validity of hypotheses implied by our specific economic theory. This discussion aims to place our modelling approach in context, trying to reconcile it with the work of other macromodellers. And it aims to reassure the reader that the modelling approach is securely anchored to a firm and transparent theoretical base.

The distinction drawn between confidently held views and less confidently held beliefs on the underlying economic theory also informs our interpretation of the model and its dynamic properties. Hence, there are some properties of the model which reflect the influence of the views on the long-run relationships between variables implied by economic theory. But other aspects of the dynamic properties of the model are interpretable only if one has a particular view on the short-run processes driving decision-making, and these views may be more contentious. By explicitly drawing these distinctions, we are able to provide more reliable and informed predictions on the outcome of policies and on the reactions of the macroeconomic variables of interest to external events and to relate the model predictions directly to the underlying economic theory.

Most importantly, when considering the use of models in forecasting, we emphasise the needs of decision-makers and other end-users. For this reason, we do not present our forecasts only in the form of point forecasts with confidence intervals, as is usually the case, but provide tables and graphs of 'probability forecasts'. These measures refer to events considered to be of interest to decision-makers (such as 'recession' or 'low inflation' at various forecast horizons, for example) and indicate the likelihood of these events taking place according to the estimated model. The probability forecasts convey the uncertainty surrounding the model's forecasted outcomes in a clear and transparent way.

1.1 Historical background

Macroeconometric modelling in the UK and elsewhere has undergone a number of important changes over the past twenty or thirty years, driven by developments in economic and econometric theory as well as changing economic circumstances. One important impetus in this process was Lucas' (1976) critique of macroeconometric policy evaluation, which resulted in widespread adoption of the rational expectations methodology in macroeconomic models. It also provoked considerable scepticism concerning the use of large-scale macroeconometric models in policy analysis and initiated the emergence of a new generation of econometric models explicitly based on dynamic intertemporal optimisation decisions by firms and households. At the same time, Sims' (1980) critique raised serious doubts about the traditional, Cowles Commission approach to identification of behavioural relations, which had been based on what Sims termed 'incredible' restrictions on the short-run dynamics of the model. This critique generated considerable interest in the use of vector autoregressive (VAR) models in macroeconometric analysis.[1] A third impetus for change in the way in which macroeconometric modelling has been undertaken came from the increased attention paid to the treatment of non-stationarity in macroeconomic variables. The classic study was that by Nelson and Plosser (1982), who showed that the null hypothesis of a unit root could not be rejected in a wide range of macroeconomic time series in the US. This resurrected the spectre of spurious regression noted originally by Yule (1926), Champernowne (1960), and more recently by Granger and Newbold (1974). Subsequently, the work of Engle and Granger (1987), Johansen (1991) and Phillips (1991) on cointegration showed possible ways of dealing with the spurious regression problem in the presence of unit root variables, with important consequences for macroeconometric modelling in particular.

[1] Sims' critique also extends to the identification of rational expectations models.

1.2 Alternative modelling approaches

Different purposes require different models. A purely theoretical model may be adequate for some purposes while, for other purposes, a purely statistical description of the data may be adequate. However, in many cases, we need to combine theoretical coherence with a good description of the data. This synthesis has taken four main forms. *First*, there are large-scale macroeconometric models such as the various vintages of HM Treasury's model of the UK economy and the Federal Reserve Board's model of the US economy. These models can contain hundreds of variables and equations and are typically built on detailed sub-models of the various sectors of the macroeconomy. The large-scale models have made many important innovations over the years but, by their very nature and because of the questions they are designed to address, they have evolved slowly. Hence, they have essentially followed the tradition of the Cowles Commission, making a distinction between exogenous and endogenous variables and imposing restrictions, often on the short-run dynamic properties of the model, in order to achieve identification. The parameters have been typically estimated by least squares or by instrumental variables methods, and full information estimation of the model parameters has rarely been attempted.

Secondly, following the methodology developed by Doan, Litterman and Sims (1984), Litterman (1986), and Blanchard and Quah (1989), there are unrestricted, Bayesian, and 'structural' vector autoregression (VAR) specifications that are used extensively in the literature. VAR and Bayesian VARs (BVAR) are primarily used for forecasting. The structural VAR approach aims to provide the VAR framework with structural content through the imposition of restrictions on the covariance structure of different types of shocks. The basis of the structural VAR analysis is the distinction made between shocks with temporary (transient) effects from those with permanent effects which are then related to economic theory in a rather loose manner by viewing the two types of shocks as demand and supply type shocks, for example. The approach does not attempt to model the structure of the economy in the form of specific behavioural relationships. Its application is also limited to relatively small models where the distinction between the two types of shocks is sufficient to deliver identification. The particular application considered by Blanchard and Quah to illustrate their approach, for example, is based on a bivariate VAR in real output and the rate of unemployment.

The *third* approach is closely associated with the Dynamic Stochastic General Equilibrium (DSGE) methodology originally employed in the Real Business Cycle literature. This approach developed following the seminal work of Kydland and Prescott (1982) and Long and Plosser (1983), and provides an explicit intertemporal general equilibrium model of the economy based on optimising decisions made by households and firms. Originally, the emphasis of these models was on real factors (*e.g.* productivity shocks) but more recently the 'New Keynesian DSGE models' have been developed to allow for monetary policy rules, adjustment costs, heterogeneity, and endogenous technological progress, for example, and also to accommodate nominal rigidities.[2] In consequence, the differences between the DSGE and the most recent incarnations of traditional macroeconometric models have become less pronounced. Also many of the DSGE models can be approximated by restricted VAR models, which also renders them more comparable with other modelling approaches.[3]

The *fourth* approach, and the one which we aim to promote in this book, is the 'structural cointegrating VAR' approach. This approach is based on the desire to develop a macroeconometric model that has transparent theoretical foundations, providing insights on the behavioural relationships that underlie the functioning of the macroeconomy. Implicit in the modelling approach is the belief that economic theory is most informative about the long-run relationships, as compared to the short-run restrictions that are more contentious. The approach allows testing of the over-identifying restrictions on the long-run relations and provides a statistically coherent framework for the analysis of the short run. At the practical level, the approach is based on a log-linear VARX model, where the familiar VAR model is augmented with weakly exogenous variables, such as oil prices, and country-specific foreign variables.[4] On the assumption that the individual macroeconomic series have a unit root, each of the long-run relationships derived from theory is associated with a cointegrating relationship between the variables, and the existence of these cointegrating relationships imposes restrictions on a VAR model of the variables. Hence, the approach provides an estimated structural model of the macroeconomy, in which the only restrictions on the short-run

[2] See Section 2.3 for details.

[3] See, for example, Kim and Pagan (1995), and Christiano *et al.* (1998). New Keynesian versions of the DSGE models have also been developed successfully by Smets and Wouters (2003) and Christiano *et al.* (2005).

[4] The econometrics of VARX models are described in detail in Chapter 6.

dynamics of the model are those which are imposed through the decision to limit attention to log-linear VARX models with a specified maximum lag length.[5] The work of King *et al.* (1991), Gali (1992), Mellander *et al.* (1992) and Crowder *et al.* (1999) is in this vein, although our own work has shown the flexibility of the approach, including the first attempts to use the structural cointegrating VARX modelling approach to build national and global macroeconometric models.[6]

It is worth noting at the outset that, while the approach that we advocate emphasises the importance of long-run restrictions, it is entirely possible to investigate also the validity and implications of specific theories on the short run while still following our modelling strategy. Of course, this would require the imposition of further restrictions on the cointegrating VAR, but these additional short-run restrictions can be imposed without reference to the restrictions imposed on the long run and have no bearing on the influence of the long-run restrictions (or *vice versa*). Indeed, there are many questions of interest that necessitate the use of a macroeconometric model and which require the investigator to take a view on the short-run behaviour of the macroeconomy; investigating the effects of monetary policy, for example. This can be done and, indeed, we shall devote some time in the book to the examination of monetary policy using our estimated model for the UK.

1.3 The long-run modelling approach

The long-run structural modelling approach begins with an explicit statement of a set of long-run relationships between the macroeconomic variables of interest, derived from macroeconomic theory, including key arbitrage and solvency conditions for example. These long-run relationships are then embedded within an otherwise unrestricted VARX model, augmented appropriately with country-specific foreign variables. The VARX model is then estimated, using recently developed econometric

[5] Hence, the approach cannot capture directly the possibility that some of the macroeconomic relationships contain a moving average component or involve important asymmetries in adjusting to shocks, for example. The impact of these influences on the dynamics of the macroeconomy can only be approximated within the context of a *non-linear* dynamic model.

[6] The work of these earlier papers is more limited in scope. The models of King *et al.* (1991), Gali (1992) and Crowder *et al.* (1999) are closed economy models unsuitable for modelling a small open economy such as the UK. The model of Mellander *et al.* (1992) attempts to capture the open nature of the Swedish economy only by adding a terms of trade variable to the consumption–investment–income model analysed by King *et al.* (1991).

methods, to obtain an augmented cointegrating VAR model which incorporates the structural long-run relationships. This direct procedure also yields theory-consistent restrictions on the intercepts and/or the trend coefficients in the VAR, which play an important role in testing for cointegration and co-trending, as well as for testing restrictions on the long-run relations.

The approach shares common features with many applications of cointegration analysis. However, it is distinct because many applications of cointegration analysis start with an unrestricted VAR and then (sometimes) impose restrictions on the cointegrating relations, without a clear *a priori* view of the economy's structural relations. This latter more statistical approach is likely to be applicable when there exists only one cointegrating relationship among the variables in the VAR. When the number of cointegrating relations are two or more, without a clear and comprehensive theoretical understanding of the long-run relations of the macroeconomy, identification of the cointegrating relations and the appropriate choice of intercepts/trends in the underlying VAR model will become a very difficult, if not an impossible, undertaking. By beginning the analysis with an explicit statement of the underlying macroeconomic theory, the structural cointegrating VAR approach that we employ places the macroeconomic theory centre-stage in the development of the macroeconometric model.

The long-run structural approach has a number of other strengths in undertaking national and global macroeconometric modelling too. Being based on a cointegrating VAR with fully specified long-run properties, the estimated model possesses a transparency which is frequently lost in larger macromodels and our approach ensures that the resultant macromodel has a long-run structural interpretation. Further, by clarifying the relationship between economic theory and the short- and long-run restrictions of our model, our approach makes clear the difficulties involved in interpreting the effects of shocks in general, and in the analysis of impulse responses in particular. And our approach allows for a fairly general dynamic specification, and avoids some of the difficulties involved in other modelling approaches where a tight economic theory is used to impose very rigid restrictions on the short-run dynamics at the expense of fit with the data.[7]

The UK model that we present as the detailed illustration of our approach focuses on five domestic variables whose developments are widely regarded

[7] See, for example, Kim and Pagan's (1995) discussion of some of the early DSGE models.

as essential to a basic understanding of the behaviour of the UK macroeconomy; namely, output, prices, the nominal interest rate, the exchange rate and real money balances. It also contains four foreign variables: foreign output, the foreign price level, the foreign interest rate, and oil prices. The analysis gives a forum with which to illustrate further strengths of our modelling approach, providing insights on the UK from at least three perspectives. *First*, the econometric methodology that has been developed provides the means for testing formally the validity of restrictions implied by specific long-run structural relations within a given macromodel. The ability to test rigorously the validity of long-run restrictions implied by economic theory within the context of a small and transparent, but reasonably comprehensive, model of the UK macroeconomy is an important step towards an evaluation of the long-run underpinnings of alternative macrotheories. As such we test and implement an approach standard in theory but rare in practice. *Second*, our approach allows an investigation of the short-run dynamic responses of the model to shocks, while ensuring that the effects of the shocks on the long-run relations eventually vanish. This provides an important insight into the dynamics of cointegrating models where shocks have permanent effects on the levels of individual variables in the model. The methods employed enable us to undertake realistic policy evaluation exercises following one of two routes. The first route imposes no restrictions on the short-run dynamics of the model and investigates the model properties using 'generalised impulse response analysis'. This route avoids the strictures of Sims' critique and provides insights on the macroeconomy's dynamic responses which, unlike the orthogonalised impulse responses, are invariant to the order of the variables in the underlying VAR. The second route supplements the long-run restrictions with additional restrictions based on theorising on the short run. This route is susceptible to the criticisms of Sims and requires strong assumptions to be made on issues which are not uncontentious. But the route allows us to investigate the impact of very specific policy innovations (*e.g.* monetary policy shocks) and other external events (*e.g.* oil price innovations). And *third*, the relative simplicity of the cointegrating VAR model enables us to generate forecasts not just of the most likely outcomes of our macroeconomic variables, but also to generate forecasts of the likelihood of various events taking place and to investigate the sources of uncertainty surrounding these forecast probabilities. Hence, for example, we are able to evaluate the likelihood of the Bank of England hitting its inflation target over the near or longer term, and whether this is compatible with avoiding recession. Hence, our approach relates the forecasts to the underlying properties of the macroeconomic model and presents the forecasts in a way which is helpful to those agents for whom the performance of the UK economy is an important influence on decision-making.

1.4 The organisation of the book

The book can be considered to be in three parts. In the first part, consisting of Chapters 2–7, we discuss the way in which economic theory and econometric analysis can be brought together to construct a macroeconometric model in which the long-run relationships are consistent with economic theory and where the short-run dynamics have an interpretation. The second part, consisting of Chapters 8–9, is devoted to the practical detail of estimating a long-run structural macroeconometric model, illustrated by a detailed description of the estimation of a model of the UK macroeconomy. And in the third part, consisting of Chapters 10–13, we discuss the interpretation and use of long-run structural macroeconometric models, describing the uses of the illustrative UK model along with extensions of the modelling activity to investigate global macroeconometric models and other specified issues in a national macroeconometric context.

In more detail, Chapter 2 briefly describes some alternative approaches to macroeconometric modelling, focusing primarily on their long-run characteristics and the consensus that has developed surrounding desirable long-run properties. Chapter 3 describes a framework for macroeconometric modelling which draws out the links with economic theory relating to the long run and with theory relating to the short run. The chapter elaborates a modelling strategy that can be employed to accommodate directly the theory of the long run and notes the ways in which short-run theory can also be accommodated. It also reviews the recent literature on modelling short-run dynamics, highlighting the difficulties in obtaining consensus on appropriate short-run restrictions and commenting on the approaches taken in the literature in examining policy shocks in general and monetary policy in particular. Chapter 4 describes a specific theoretical framework for macroeconomic modelling of a small open economy that can be embedded within a macroeconometric model, noting the testable restrictions on the long-run relations suggested by the theory. Complementing this, Chapter 5 explores a set of identifying restrictions on the short-run dynamics that might be used to supplement the long-run restrictions if the model is to be used to investigate the effect of economically meaningful shocks. Chapter 6 then briefly reviews the econometric methods needed for the empirical analysis of cointegrating VAR models, including new material (on the conditions under which error correction models are mean-reverting, for example) that are particularly useful in practical macroeconometric modelling. Finally in this part, Chapter 7 provides an introduction to the interpretation and estimation of probability forecasts which we consider to be a particularly useful method for presenting forecasts.

The part of the book concerned with the practical construction of the illustrative model of the UK economy begins with Chapter 8, which provides an overview of the data. Chapter 9 describes the empirical work underlying the construction of the UK model, discusses the results obtained from testing its long-run properties, and compares the model with benchmark univariate models of the variables. This description of the modelling work not only provides one of the first examples of the use of these cointegrating VAR techniques in an applied context, but it also includes a discussion of bootstrap experiments designed to investigate the small sample properties of the tests employed.

The final part of the book is concerned with the use of long-run structural macroeconometric models. It begins with Chapter 10, which discusses the dynamic properties of the estimated model. Chapter 11 is concerned with forecasting and prediction based on the model. Here we elaborate the notion of probability forecasting, which provides a useful means of conveying the uncertainties surrounding forecasts obtained from the model, and illustrate the usefulness of probability forecasts with reference to the Bank of England's inflation targets and the UK's growth prospects. Chapter 12 describes some recent extensions of the model and some other applications, including an introduction to the development of a model of the global macroeconomy using the same modelling approach.

Finally, in the appendices, we provide an account of the construction and sources of the data plus instructions on how to replicate the results presented in the empirical sections of the book. Much of the modelling work described in the book can be undertaken using Pesaran and Pesaran's (1997) econometric package *Microfit*. But for those who prefer to work with a programmable language, to adapt some of the procedures for example, we provide in the appendices also a simple manual for the use of a set of computer programs written in *Gauss* that can be used to replicate or extend the analysis of the book too. The data and code are available through the authors' webpages. It is worth noting that the use of the programs, as described in the manual, is relatively straightforward to follow, although the user will need some familiarity with *Gauss* to implement them.

2

Macroeconometric modelling: Alternative approaches

This chapter provides an overview of the main approaches to macroeconometric modelling, focusing in particular on the implications of the different approaches for modelling the long run. We discuss the 'structural cointegrating VAR' approach to macroeconometric modelling in general terms and compare it to other approaches currently followed in the literature; namely, the large-scale simultaneous equation macroeconometric models, structural VARs, and the dynamic stochastic general equilibrium (DSGE) models. The primary purpose of the review is to ascertain the extent to which there is a consensus on the desired long-run properties of a macroeconometric model and to compare the effectiveness of the different approaches to macroeconomic modelling in their attempts to test and incorporate these long-run properties into models in practice.

2.1 Large-scale simultaneous equation models

Large-scale simultaneous equation macroeconometric models (SEMs) have a long history and can be traced back to Tinbergen and Klein and the subsequent developments at the Cowles Commission. Prominent examples of large-scale models include the first and second generation models developed at the Federal Reserve Board (see, for example, Ando and Modigliani, 1969, Brayton and Mauskopf, 1985, and Brayton and Tinsley, 1996), Fair's (1994) model of the US economy, Murphy's (1988, 1992) model for Australia, and the various vintages of models constructed for the UK at the London Business School (LBS), the National Institute of

Economic and Social Research (NIESR), HM Treasury (HMT), and the Bank of England (BE).[1]

The relatively poor forecasting performance of the large-scale models in the face of the stagflation of the 1970s, in conjunction with the advent of rational expectations and the critiques of Lucas (1976) on policy evaluation and Sims (1980) on identification, brought about a number of important changes in the development and the use of large-scale SEMs throughout the 1980s and subsequently. Important developments have taken place in three major areas.[2] *First*, in response to Sims' criticism of the use of 'incredible' identifying restrictions involving short-run dynamics, and under the influence of developments in cointegration analysis (*e.g.* Engle and Granger, 1987), a consensus has formed that the important aspect of a structural model is its long-run relationships, which must be identified without having to restrict the model's short-run dynamics. *Second*, in response to the criticism that large-scale models paid insufficient attention to the micro-foundations of the underlying relationships and the properties of the macroeconomic system considered as a whole, there is now a greater use made of economic theory in the specification of large-scale models. And *third*, in response to the criticisms of Lucas, considerable work has been undertaken to incorporate rational expectations (RE), or strictly speaking model consistent expectations, into large-scale macromodels.

Under the influence of these developments, more recent generations of large-scale models have shared a number of important features. Almost invariably, the models have comprised of three basic building blocks: equilibrium conditions, expectations formation, and dynamic adjustments. The equilibrium conditions have been typically derived from the steady state properties of a Walrasian general equilibrium model, and there seems to be clear evidence of a developing consensus on what constitutes the appropriate general equilibrium model for characterising the long-run relations built around utility maximising households and profit-maximising firms facing appropriate budget and technology constraints.

[1] Bodkin *et al.* (1991) provide a comprehensive survey of the history of macroeconometric model building. The evolution and the development of macroeconometric modelling at the Federal Reserve Board is reviewed by Brayton *et al.* (1997). For the UK these developments were documented in a series of volumes produced by the ESRC Macroeconomic Modelling Bureau (see, for example, Wallis *et al.* 1987). Further reviews of the modelling in the UK and elsewhere can be found in Smith (1994), Wallis (1995) and Hall (1995).

[2] A detailed discussion of these developments in the case of the UK practice can be found in Hall (1995). Similar arguments have also been advanced by Brayton *et al.* (1997) in the case of the US experience.

This consensus side-steps the Sims critique by focusing on the long run and remaining agnostic on short-run dynamics.

Despite the progress made, and the growing consensus on what constitutes best practice in macroeconometric modelling, large-scale models have continued to be viewed with some scepticism by some, particularly in the area of policy analysis.[3] The complexity of the interactions of different parts of a large dynamic model means that the accumulated response of the macroeconomy to a particular shock or change in a given exogenous variable can be difficult to interpret, particularly as far as their effects on the long-run relations are concerned.[4] It is also difficult to identify and correct for misspecification in large-scale models, as attempts to fix one part of the model can have far reaching (and often unpredictable) consequences for the properties of the overall model.[5] Furthermore, as far as estimation is concerned, full information methods are often not an option given the size of the models. With these difficulties in mind, it has been argued that it is simply not possible for large-scale models to follow a best practice approach because of their size and complexity.

These difficulties are particularly apparent in the modelling exercises undertaken to consider global interactions. One of the first attempts at global linkages was Larry Klein's Project Link adopted by the United Nations which linked up traditional large-scale macroeconometric models developed originally for national economies. Other examples include the IMF's MULTIMOD multi-regional model (Laxton *et al.* (1998)) and the National Institute's Global Econometric Model (NiGEM) which estimates/calibrates a common model structure across OECD countries, China and a number of regional blocks and the IMF's MULTIMOD. The country/region-specific models in NiGEM are still large, each comprised of 60–90 equations with 30 key behavioural relationships.[6] These contributions provide significant insights into the interlinkages that exist among the major world economies and have proved invaluable in global forecasting. However, there are important weaknesses in the models. For example,

[3] See, for example, Whitley (1997).

[4] Innovative methods for characterising and summarising SEM's short-run and long-run properties have been developed to address this problem, however, primarily through stochastic simulation methods. See, for example, Wallis *et al.* (1987), Turner (1991) and Wallis and Whitley (1987). Methods for the analysis of the long-run properties of large macroeconometric models have also been developed by Murphy (1992), Fisher *et al.* (1992), and Wren-Lewis *et al.* (1996).

[5] See, for example, the empirical exercise of Fisher *et al.* (1992) relating to the current account balance reaction to nominal exchange rate changes in the models developed by NIESR, LBS, BE and HMT at that time.

[6] For a recent detailed account, see Barrell *et al.* (2001).

as argued in Pesaran, Schuermann and Weiner (2004), these models do not typically address the financial linkages that exist among the world's major economies. Moreover, they can be rather cumbersome to use in practice and the interlinkages of the different relations in different country models are often difficult to interpret.[7]

To summarise, while important progress has been made in the construction and use of large-scale SEMs, it is still often argued that these models are subject to a number of limitations that arise primarily from their large and complex structure. As Brayton *et al.* (1997) conclude: 'Large-scale macromodels are by their nature slow to evolve.' Simultaneous estimation and evaluation of such models is currently computationally prohibitive and, given the available time series data, may not be even feasible. A full integration of theory and measurement has proved elusive to large-scale model builders. Despite the imaginative attempts made over the past two decades, it remains a formidable undertaking to construct a theory-consistent large-scale macroeconometric model which has transparent long-run properties and fits the data well.

2.2 Unrestricted and structural VARs

2.2.1 *Unrestricted VARs*

The unrestricted VAR approach introduced into macroeconometrics by Sims (1980) stands at the other extreme to large-scale models. It focuses on modelling a relatively small set of core macroeconomic variables using a VAR specification with particular emphasis on the statistical fit of the model to the data possibly at the expense of theoretical consistency, both from a short-run and a long-run perspective. Sims' objective was to investigate the dynamic response of the system to shocks (through impulse response functions) without having to rely on 'incredible' identifying restrictions, or potentially controversial restrictions from economic theory. This strategy eschews the need to impose long-run relationships on the model's variables, and relies exclusively on time series observations to identify such relationships if they happen to exist.

According to the Wold decomposition theorem, all covariance stationary processes can be written as the sum of a deterministic (perfectly predictable) component and a stationary process possessing an infinite order

[7] The global VAR model of Pesaran, Schuermann and Weiner (2004) adopts the structural cointegrating VAR approach to developing a model to analyse global financial and real interactions. As explained in Section 3.4 and illustrated in Section 12.2, this analysis provides the modelling outcome with considerably more transparency.

moving average (MA) representation.[8] Restricting attention to 'invertible' processes,[9] one obtains a unique MA representation, also known as the 'fundamental' representation which fully characterises the sample autocorrelation coefficients. Such a fundamental representation can be approximated by a finite order vector autoregressive moving average (VARMA) process. However, estimation of VARMA models poses important estimation problems, particularly when the number of variables in the VARMA model is relatively large. For this reason, Sims chooses to work with a finite order VAR model which is much simpler to estimate, but involves further approximations. To perform impulse response analysis, Sims' approach then requires the use of a Choleski decomposition of the variance covariance matrix of the model's innovations/shocks. This enables the MA representation to be written in terms of orthogonalised innovations. It is the responses of the macroeconomic variables to these orthogonalised shocks that are described in Sims' orthogonalised impulse responses.

This approach to modelling has been subject to a number of criticisms (see, for example, Pagan, 1987), some of which are worth noting here. First, the approach requires care in the initial stages in the choice of transformation of the data to achieve stationarity. In particular, it is important that economically meaningful, and statistically significant, relations are not excluded from the analysis at this stage by the choice of transformation. For example, a VAR model in the first differences of $I(1)$ variables is mis-specified if there exists a cointegrating relationship between two or more of the $I(1)$ variables. Second, care is needed in the choice of variables to be included in the VAR analysis, and it is difficult to imagine how this choice could be made without reference to some underlying economic theory. And third, since the choice of the Choleski decomposition is not unique, there are a number of alternative sets of orthogonalised impulse responses which can be obtained from any estimated VAR model. A particular choice of orthogonalisation might be suggested by economic theory, and Sims' original approach to choosing an orthogonalisation was to impose a causal ordering on the variables in the VAR. However, such a causal ordering can be difficult to justify in practice. In the absence of a generally accepted casual ordering, the orthogonalised impulse responses are difficult to interpret economically.

[8] See, for example, pages 108–109 of Hamilton (1994).

[9] Limiting attention to the fundamental Wold representation is not uncontentious. As shown in Hansen and Sargent (1991), for example, the MA representation that underlies the VAR model can be non-fundamental (in the sense that one or more of the roots of the MA process fall inside the unit circle) and at the same time be economically meaningful.

Due to their flexibility and ease of use, VAR models are used extensively in forecasting and as benchmarks for evaluation of large-scale and DSGE models. In order to mitigate the curse of dimensionality and the large number of parameters typically estimated in VAR models, Doan, Litterman and Sims (1984) have also proposed Bayesian VARs (BVARs) which combine unrestricted VARs with Bayesian, or what has come to be known as 'Minnesota' priors. Other types of priors have also been considered in the literature; DeJong *et al.* (1993), for example, combine a VAR(1) model with prior probabilities on its parameters derived from a RBC model. This approach represents a coherent attempt to take advantage of the empirical simplicity of the VAR approach while at the same time making use of economic theory and, as discussed later in this chapter, is an approach which has been taken up recently in the context of Dynamic Stochastic General Equilibrium modelling. See also Section 2.3 on the use of Bayesian techniques in DSGE models.

2.2.2 *Structural VARs*

The structural VAR approach builds on Sims' approach but attempts to identify the impulse responses by imposing *a priori* restrictions on the covariance matrix of the structural errors and/or on long-run impulse responses themselves. This approach is developed by Bernanke (1986), Blanchard and Watson (1986) and Sims (1986) who considered *a priori* restrictions on contemporaneous effects of shocks, and subsequently by Blanchard and Quah (1989), Clarida and Gali (1994) and Astley and Garratt (1996) who use restrictions on the long-run impact of shocks to identify the impulse responses. In contrast to the unrestricted VAR approach, structural VARs explicitly attempt to provide some economic rationale behind the covariance restrictions used, and thus aim to avoid the use of arbitrary or implicit identifying restrictions associated with orthogonalised impulse responses. However, while the use of 'theory based' covariance restrictions in small systems allow the impulse responses to be identified under the structural VAR approach, such restrictions still do not enable identification of the long-run relationships among the variables. Furthermore, even the covariance restrictions are not always easy to interpret or motivate from an economic perspective, particularly in the case of VAR models with three or more variables. So, as explained in detail in the following chapters, the number of exactly identifying covariance restrictions required increases rapidly with the number of variables in the VAR. In a system involving m variables and a set of m orthogonalised structural shocks, the required number of such restrictions is equal to $m(m-1)/2$. For example, in the case of the core model of the UK presented in this book, which includes nine endogenous variables, the number of covariance restrictions required to exactly identify the impulse responses will be 36, even if the covariance of the structural shocks is assumed to be diagonal. It is not clear how so many restrictions could be identified within the structural VAR framework, let alone motivated from an appropriate economic theory perspective.

There are also inherent difficulties with the interpretation that are given to the impulse responses obtained under the structural VAR approach. For example, in Blanchard and Quah (1989), a bivariate VAR model of unemployment and output growth is investigated by first solving the two variables in terms of two orthogonalised white-noise shocks, and then estimating impulse responses under the identifying assumption that one of the shocks has no long-run effects on output levels. They then refer to this shock as the 'demand shock', and refer to the other shock as the 'supply shock'.[10] However, while it might be an interesting exercise to consider the effects on output and unemployment of the two different types of shock, and while it might be possible to elaborate a model of the macroeconomy in which demand shocks have the property assumed by Blanchard and Quah, there seems little rationale in referring to these innovations as 'demand' and 'supply' shocks in the context of the purely statistical model used by these authors. The different types of shock considered in this analysis are defined with reference to their statistical properties (*i.e.* whether or not they have a permanent effect on output levels) and not with reference to a model of how consumers and producers behave in a macroeconomy.[11] Also, in the context of VAR models with three or more variables, the possibility of more than one permanent or transitory shock poses a further identification problem since many combinations of stationary shocks will themselves be stationary. For further details see Section 3.2.5.

2.3 Dynamic stochastic general equilibrium models

Unrestricted VARs and the Structural VARs make minimal use of economic theory, while the use of theory in large-scale models is typically modular,

[10] Recall that since $m = 2$, only one covariance restriction is needed to identify the impulse responses.

[11] For a more detailed critical evaluation of the structural VAR approach see Levtchenkova *et al.* (1998).

in the sense that the theory is used in a coherent manner only in specific modules or parts of the model. In contrast, the DSGE models develop a general equilibrium approach to modelling using stochastic intertemporal optimisation techniques applied to decision problems of representative households and firms.[12]

The DSGE model is expressed in terms of 'deep' structural parameters, such as the parameters that enter the preferences, production technologies and the probability distributions of taste and technology shocks. In practice, very simple forms are chosen for these functions (power utility function and Cobb–Douglas production functions, for example). Nevertheless, the resultant optimal decision rules are complicated functions of the macroeconomic variables. These are generally approximated around the deterministic steady-state values of the macroeconomic variables to provide a log-linear system of rational expectations (RE) equations with backward and forward components. The RE solution of this system is obtained assuming certain transversality conditions hold (thus ruling out bubble effects), the DSGE model provides the correct characterisation of economy, the representative agent paradigm is acceptable, and that the underlying processes remain stable into the infinite future. The latter assumption is made implicitly (although rarely acknowledged) in order to derive the expected present value of the discounted future variables that enter the RE solution. Under these assumptions the RE solution can be written as a VAR (or a VARX in the case of open economies) model subject to cross-equation parametric restrictions.[13]

The proponents of the DSGE approach to macroeconomic modelling argue that this approach takes macroeconomic theory seriously in a way that the large-scale SEMs do not. In particular, it is argued that the use of a general equilibrium framework ensures that the DSGE models display stock equilibria, rather than the flow equilibria which are characteristic of the traditional approach to macroeconometric models. The derivation of the model's relationships as solutions to intertemporal optimisation problems of households and firms ensures that the model has an internal consistency and a relationship with economic theory that is lost in traditional large-scale models. However, we have already noted that the proponents

[12] For a survey of early developments in the literature on DSGE models, see the contributions in the volume edited by Cooley (1995), while discussion of the more recent 'New Keynesian' DSGE models is given in Smets and Wouters (2003) and Christiano *et al.* (2005).

[13] A specific illustration of this procedure is given in Chapter 3 below. See also, for example, Binder and Pesaran (1995), Kim and Pagan (1995), Wickens (1995), and Pesaran and Smith (2005) in the case of open economy DSGE models within a global context.

of large-scale models have made considerable progress in relating the structure of their models to economic theory, particularly in relation to the long-run properties of the model. Indeed, we noted that there has developed a consensus on the appropriate theory for the characterisation of the long run, based on Walrasian general equilibrium theory, which has been adopted (at least in part) in many of the current generation of large-scale models. In this respect, therefore, the differences in the theoretical underpinnings of the DSGE models and the large-scale models are less polarised than is sometimes argued.

However, there are important differences between the two approaches both in content and in emphasis. In particular, they differ significantly in their treatment of short-run dynamics. The DSGE models not only provide the form of relationships between economic variables that exist in the long run, but also provide an explicit statement of the dynamic evolution of the macroeconomy in response to shocks. It is argued (for example, in Plosser, 1989) that the foundations of typical Keynesian models are static in nature, and that the dynamics are introduced arbitrarily through accelerator mechanisms for investment and inventory behaviour, or through arbitrary nominal rigidities in wage and price setting, or through partial adjustment mechanisms in various forms, for example. The lack of cohesion in the derivation of the long-run and dynamic properties in the large-scale models represents a fundamental shortcoming of the large-scale SEMs, according to this argument, encouraging the view that the long-run evolution of the macroeconomy can be considered independently of short- and medium-term fluctuations. In contrast, there are no dichotomies between the determinants of long-run growth and short-run fluctuations in DGSE models (though the long run is often not modelled explicitly in its entirety in DSGE models either and actual data are often (arbitrarily) filtered before they are analysed).

In fact, one can distinguish two phases in the development of the DSGE models which have separate implications for modelling macrodynamics. In the first phase, one of the primary motivating ambitions behind the DSGE models was to establish that the dynamic responses of the macroeconomy are consistent with a model in which there are no market failures, the predicted outcomes are Pareto optimal, and intervention by a social planner to force agents to change their actions will be welfare reducing. The 'real business cycle' agenda that lay behind the first phase of the development of the DSGE approach to modelling therefore played down the potential role of monetary policy in generating economic fluctuations and instead placed considerable emphasis on real shocks. Indeed, many of the calibration exercises undertaken in the first phase of the DSGE literature ignored the monetary sector altogether.

It was quickly recognised that this first phase of models required some refinement if it was to provide a satisfactory understanding of economic fluctuations. The first generation of DSGE models were therefore extended to incorporate features such as adjustment costs (*e.g.* Kydland and Prescott, 1982, Christiano and Eichenbaum, 1992a, and Cogley and Nason, 1995); signal extraction and learning (*e.g.* Kydland and Prescott, 1982, and Cooley and Hansen, 1995); aggregation (*e.g.* Christiano, Eichenbaum and Marshall, 1991 on temporal aggregation and Cooley *et al.* 1997 and Ríos-Rull, 1995 on cross-sectional aggregation); endogenous technological progress (*e.g.* Stadler, 1990 and Hercowitz and Sampson, 1991) and information heterogeneities (*e.g.* Kasa, 2000). However, it remained unclear whether a model could be developed that would be capable of simultaneously dealing with all of these factors in a satisfactory manner and, even if it could, whether it would be any more transparent or easy to interpret than the available stock of large-scale models. Moreover, by limiting attention to particular sources of dynamics, the first-phase models following the DSGE approach were likely to be too restrictive. In fact, as it turned out, when the models were confronted with the data, in Litterman and Weiss (1985), King *et al.* (1991), Christiano and Eichenbaum (1992b) or Kim and Pagan (1995), for example, the evidence suggested that this was indeed the case.

The second phase in the development of DSGE models returned to the simpler basic characteristics of the earliest DSGE models, emphasising the micro-foundations of macroeconomic fluctuations, but explicitly incorporating nominal frictions and paying more attention to monetary factors influencing business cycles. There were early attempts to incorporate money in DSGE models (see, for example, Cooley and Hansen, 1989, 1995), but there is now a considerable literature elaborating 'New Keynesian DSGE models', which have price and wage rigidities at their core and which are designed to consider the impact of monetary policy (see Clarida *et al.* (1999) for a review). A simple New Keynesian DSGE model consists of an 'IS curve' relating output to the expected real interest rate, a Phillips curve relating inflation to expected inflation and output (measured as deviations from its trend), and a policy rule relating the nominal interest rate to output and inflation. The IS curve is motivated with reference to optimising behaviour on the part of households, the Phillips curve is based on profit-maximising pricing behaviour on the part of monopolistically competitive firms, and the policy rule is based on a policy-maker that optimises an objective function describing welfare in terms of inflation and output.[14] As in all DSGE models, the decisions made by households, firms and the policy-maker are interrelated and intertemporal, generating explicit dynamic structures. But this class of models also pays particular attention to the rigidities that exist in price setting, frequently incorporating 'Calvo (1983) contracts', in which prices are reset only periodically and with a fixed probability, to motivate both backward- and forward-looking effects in the Phillips curve, for example. These modelling assumptions have important implications for the dynamic properties of the DSGE models, their ability to fit the data and their implications for monetary policy analysis. Indeed, recent modelling exercises by Gali and Gertler (1999), Clarida *et al.* (2000), Smets and Wouters (2003), Favero and Rovelli (2003), Del Negro and Schorfheide (2004), Del Negro *et al.* (2005) and Christiano *et al.* (2005), among others, indicate that these second-generation DSGE models are able to introduce more flexible dynamics, often with the help of Bayesian estimation techniques, and can perform relatively well in explaining various episodes of historical macroexperience and in forecasting.

2.4 The structural cointegrating VAR approach

The structural cointegrating VAR modelling strategy is described in detail in Section 3.1.3 of the next chapter. But, stated briefly, the strategy begins with an explicit statement of the long-run relationships between the variables of the model obtained from macroeconomic theory. These relationships will typically be based on stock-flow and accounting identities, arbitrage (equilibrium) conditions, and long-run solvency requirements that ensure stationary asset–income ratios. The long-run relationships are approximated by log-linear equations, with disturbances that characterise the deviations of the long-run relations from their realised, short-run counterparts. These deviations are referred to as the 'long-run structural shocks'. Not all of the variables contained in the long-run relationships suggested by economic theory are observable, however, and in writing the long-run relationships in terms of observable variables, 'long-run reduced form shocks' are derived as functions of the long-run structural shocks. The long-run, or error correcting, relations are then embedded within an otherwise unrestricted log-linear VAR model of a given order in the

[14] For an open economy version of the New Keynesian DSGE model see, for example, Gali and Monacelli (2005).

variables of interest to obtain a cointegrating VAR model which incorporates the structural long-run relationships as its steady-state solution. This allows testing for the presence of the cointegrating relations and the over-identifying restrictions implied by the long-run economic theory. In this way, the cointegrating VAR model will embody the long-run theory restrictions in a transparent, and an empirically consistent, manner. The theory also imposes restrictions on the intercepts and/or the trend coefficients in the VAR, which play an important role in testing for cointegration as well as co-trending, often ignored in other approaches to macroeconometric modelling.[15]

2.4.1 *Comparisons with the alternative approaches*

COMPARISON WITH LARGE-SCALE SEMS

As the discussion above makes clear, the structural cointegrating VAR approach to macroeconometric modelling begins by describing the relationships which define the long-run structure of the macroeconomy, and embeds these long-run relationships within an otherwise unrestricted VAR model of the macroeconomy. The number of variables chosen to include in the core model is selected to ensure that the system can be estimated simultaneously, taking into account all of the potential feedbacks between the variables captured by the short-run dynamics and suggested by the long-run economic relationships. One of the primary strengths of this approach, therefore, is that the model is developed and estimated in a way that ensures that the long-run relations of the estimated model are data consistent and theoretically coherent. Furthermore, this is accomplished without compromising short-run empirical adequacy as an important criteria by which models in the final analysis must be judged. The transparency of the model's long-run properties would also be important for impulse response analysis and forecasting, particularly over the medium term.

Despite its advantages, the cointegrating VAR model is still highly restrictive and, given the available time series data, it can deal with at most 8–10 variables simultaneously. This clearly precludes addressing many important issues if we were to confine our analysis to a single cointegrating VAR model. Macroeconometric models are used for many different purposes by government, academic and corporate institutions, and no one

[15] See Chapter 6 for a discussion of the relevant econometric issues involved in the analysis of cointegrating VARs.

model will be appropriate for all of these uses (see Whitley, 1997). However, traditional macroeconometric models tend to become large often in response to demands for more disaggregated analysis, and for addressing a wider range of policy questions. For example, a central bank may require a detailed model of the monetary sector, corporate institutions might require forecasts and analysis disaggregated by the main industrial sectors (energy, construction, agriculture, transportation, *etc.*), and government agencies might be required to investigate the effects of a given policy on particular interest groups and/or markets. As will be discussed in more detail in Chapter 3 below, our approach to meeting these model-specific requirements is through the development of appropriate *satellite* models. These are constructed using similar econometric techniques to those employed in the estimation of the core model, and are then linked up to the core model, with the core variables (and the associated error correction terms from the core model) influencing sectoral developments, but not *vice versa* (see Pesaran and Ron Smith, 1997). The distinction between the core and satellite models is made possible by allowing the error correction terms of the core model to enter the relationships of the satellite models but not *vice versa*. This enables consistent estimation of the satellite model by treating the variables of the core model as weakly exogenous. Examples of satellite models include models of the labour market, households' portfolio and expenditure decisions, foreign trade and fiscal policy.[16]

COMPARISON WITH UNRESTRICTED AND STRUCTURAL VAR MODELLING

Unrestricted and restricted VAR modelling places great emphasis on characterising the dynamic behaviour of variables and makes considerable use of impulse response analysis as a means of illustrating the timing of the reactions of various variables to different types of structural shock. The identification of the structural shocks, using the reduced form shocks obtained from the estimated VAR models, requires a well-defined economic theory of the short run, concerned with the sequencing of decisions and information available to different economic agents and with the various rigidities arising in decision-making. This emphasis on identifying the effects of specific economic shocks and the associated short-run dynamics contrasts with that of the structural cointegrating VAR approach.

[16] An illustration of how a satellite model of the household sector might be coupled with the core macroeconomic model is described in Chapter 12.

The structural cointegrating VAR approach to modelling emphasises the long-run relationships that exist between variables. This is based on the view that economic theory is typically more informative on these long-run relationships than it is on the short-run dynamics, noting that theory is frequently silent on the sequencing of decisions, the structure of information sets across agents, and the nature of rigidities that arise from transactions costs. The structural cointegrating VAR approach describes explicitly the nature of the '*long-run* structural errors' that arise from a specific economic theory and that characterise deviations from long-run relationships. It also clarifies the links between these long-run structural errors and the 'long-run reduced form errors' that can be related to the data at hand.

If it is the case that economic theory is insufficiently well-defined to provide credible identifying restrictions on the short-run behaviour of economic agents, then a more general method of analysing impulse responses is required; that is, one that allows an examination of the short-run dynamic interrelations of the model without needing to identify the nature of the shocks. The current literature on impulse response analysis focuses on the effects of identified shocks are often difficult to accomplish in a satisfactory manner, particularly in the case of VAR models with 8–10 variables often encountered in the analysis of small open economies. The source of the difficulty lies in the *unobservable* nature of the shocks of interest such as monetary policy shocks, say, or demand and supply shocks. An alternative, less ambitious approach is to consider the impulse response functions associated with unit shifts in observable variables, such as output, interest rates and inflation. Clearly, a unit shock to the interest rate variable need not be the same as a monetary policy shock, since many different internal and external factors could influence interest rates. But the impulse response associated with a unit (one standard error) shift in interest rates would be informative about the dynamic properties of the model as well as being relevant to private sector decisions that are concerned with the consequences of a rate rise rather than the precise reasons behind its occurrence. The Generalised Impulse Response Function (GIRF), introduced in Koop *et al.* (1996) and developed in Pesaran and Shin (1998), provides such a method. Unlike the more familiar orthogonalised IR functions, the GIRFs are invariant to the ordering of the variables included in the VAR and provide an empirically coherent solution to the analysis of impulse responses so long as the shocks under consideration relate to observed variables. For example the GIRFs can be used to compute the time profile of the effects of a shock to oil prices, output or interest rate without any ambiguities. In many applications, such as the analysis of market interactions or the sensitivity of market or credit risks to changes in the market environment, the GIRFs are sufficient. The effects of system-wide shocks on the variables of the VAR or on the cointegrating relations can also be analysed using the persistence profile methodology advanced in Pesaran and Shin (1996). This type of analysis is also invariant to the ordering of the variables in the VAR and does not require economic identification of the shocks. The identification problem arises when it is further required to decompose the effects of the shocks to the observed variables into unobserved theoretical concepts such as supply, demand, or monetary policy shocks. In such cases, as we shall demonstrate in Chapter 10, the GIRF approach need to be combined with additional *a priori* restrictions from economic theory, preferably within a decision context.[17]

It is worth emphasising that the structural cointegrating VAR approach to modelling is not incompatible with the identification of economically meaningful shocks to the macroeconomy and the application of more standard impulse response analysis. Rather, this is a question of emphasis. The structural cointegrating VAR approach implies that the structural relationships that are suggested by theory for the short run are less robust and can be held with less confidence. But it is perfectly possible to elaborate an economic theory which motivates both short-run and long-run restrictions and the structural cointegrating VAR approach would remain valid (supplemented with the additional restrictions suggested on the short run). These issues are discussed in detail in Chapter 3 below, which concentrates on the identification issues associated with short-run structures, and in Chapter 5, where a specific model of short-run decision-making is elaborated to illustrate the issues involved in showing how monetary policy shocks can be identified without having to identify other types of shocks that might also impinge on the macroeconomy.

COMPARISON WITH DSGE MODELLING

In DSGE modelling, the derivation of the long-run, steady-state relations of the macromodel starts with the intertemporal optimisation problems faced by households and firms and then solves for the long-run relations using the Euler first-order conditions and the stock-flow constraints. Given the invariably non-linear nature of the Euler equations and the linear forms

[17] The econometric issues involved in GIR analysis are discussed in Chapter 6 and their application to the core model of the UK economy is described in Chapter 10.

of the constraints, the resultant relations of the model economy are usually approximated by log-linear relations (the real business cycle literature and the New Keynesian DSGE literature follow this methodology). The long-run relations are then obtained by assuming that the model economy is stationary and ergodic in certain variables, such as growth rates, capital per effective worker and asset–income ratios, and typically ignoring expectational errors. The structural cointegrating VAR approach, on the other hand, works directly with the arbitrage conditions which provide intertemporal links between prices and asset returns in the economy as a whole. The arbitrage conditions, however, must be appropriately modified to allow for the risks associated with market uncertainties.

Clearly, the above two approaches are closely related and yield similar results as far as the long-run relations are concerned. The main difference between the two approaches lies in the empirical validation of the long-run relations and their treatment of short-run dynamics. The strength of the intertemporal optimisation approach lies in the explicit identification of macroeconomic disturbances as shocks to tastes, to technology, to policy, and so on, rendered possible by the explicit statement on the form of the short-run dynamics. However, this is achieved at the expense of often strong assumptions concerning the form of the underlying utility and cost functions, expectations formation process and the related assumption that the DSGE model remains stable into the indefinite future, and the process of technological change. In contrast, the cointegrating VAR approach advanced in this work is silent on short-run dynamics, but is in line with the DSGE model as far as the long-run relations are concerned. Our approach also has the added advantage that particular long-run relations are considered only when adequately supported by the evidence. We test the validity of the long-run relations rather simply imposing them on *a priori* grounds.

Both the DSGE modelling approach and the structural cointegrating VAR approach represent attempts to combine theory and evidence to obtain models that will be useful for policy- and decision-makers. The differences in approach reflect modellers' strength of conviction on different aspects of the theory and evidence. So, the structural cointegrating VAR approach assumes that we understand how the economy works in the long run with some degree of confidence, and allows theory to inform this aspect of modelling. But it is less sure on the short-run dynamics and so turns to the evidence on these. In comparison, the DSGE approach emphasises more the use of theory in the modelling of both the short run and long run.

We shall show, in Chapter 6, that the estimation of our structural cointegrating VAR model is straightforward using estimation techniques developed in Pesaran and Shin (2002) and Pesaran, Shin and Smith (2000). The issue of combining theory and evidence is typically less straightforward in the larger DSGE models where the highly restricted VAR model suggested by the theory cannot be readily reconciled with the data. Kapetanios *et al.* (2005) discuss this issue, outlining the steps taken in the construction of a 'conceptual model' (for example, a restricted VAR derived from a variant of a DSGE model) and its translation into a 'data adjusted model' which can better match the data in policy-oriented macroeconomic modelling. One approach to making this translation is Ireland's (2004) method based on 'tracking shocks'. Here, any observed macroeconomic variable is assumed to differ from its corresponding latent variable (as generated by the conceptual model) by a tracking shock. This shock, in turn, is assumed to follow some known stochastic process. Forecasts are provided as an average reconciliation of the data and the outcome suggested by the conceptual model, with the split between theory and evidence depending on the nature of the tracking errors in the sample.[18] Alternatively, Del Negro and Schorfheide (2004) describe a Bayesian method, along similar lines to that developed by DeJong *et al.* (1993), in which a New Keynesian DSGE is used to provide priors for a VAR and these are updated in the light of the data, where the investigator explicitly chooses the weight to be placed on the theory-based prior relative to the evidence. The paper also shows how the posterior inference on the VAR parameters can be translated into posterior inference for the DSGE parameters so that theory and evidence is combined and summarised in such a way as to retain its economic meaning. A third possible method, advocated by Christiano *et al.* (2005), focuses on matching theoretical and empirical impulse responses.

Kapetanios *et al.* (2005) make the important point that, no matter which method is used to combine theory and evidence, the underlying conceptual model will need to accommodate cointegrating relations if the effects of some shocks are persistent (so that some of the variables are $I(1)$ variables and long-run relations exist between them in levels). This feature will provide its own restrictions on the VAR derived from the conceptual model so that, once the theory-based long-run relations are incorporated

[18] Recent models in various central banks adopt a DSGE structure as their core theoretical components, but also allow for non-core empirically based dynamics. See, for example, the TOTEM model of the Bank of Canada as described in Cayen, Corbett and Perrier (2005) or Adolfson *et al.*'s (2005) description of their model of the Swedish economy.

into the model, it can be written as a VECM (see also Giannone *et al.* (2005)). They note that failing to impose these restrictions (if cointegration exists in the data) will cause difficulties when trying to match the theory with data and will cause considerable problems in forecasting.[19] A related issue arises in many DSGE models in which analysis is carried out using variables measured as deviations from some *ad hoc* trend estimate (*e.g.* the Hodrick–Prescott filter). Of course, the choice of a misspecified trend will generate bias in estimation so the choice of trend is much more significant than many DSGE modellers are prepared to acknowledge. But perhaps even more importantly, the use of this type of de-trending makes it rather difficult to test hypotheses based on long-run theory. In contrast, our approach readily allows the long-run theory to be tested and the equilibrium values to be explicitly identified.

The long-run structural and the DSGE approaches both represent attempts to reconcile theory and data. The differences between the approaches are based on differences in emphasis and practicalities rather than principle. The methods taken in the DSGE models to reconcile theory and data oblige the projected paths of the variable to converge to the equilibrium value suggested by the theory of the core conceptual model. This implicitly places emphasis on the long-run properties of the theory, which are held with some confidence, exactly as in our approach. But this is achieved in a more restricted way than in our long-run structural approach (being based on a single weighting parameter in the Bayesian method described above, for example) and the long-run relations suggested by theory are typically not tested in the DSGE models. The short-run restrictions suggested by the DSGE models (including those implied by the forward-looking expectations involved[20]) can be accommodated, and tested, within the cointegrating VAR framework used in the long-run structural approach.

In short, many economists might accept the view that economic theory is more likely to provide a coherent guide to the long-run characteristics of the macroeconomy than its short-run dynamics, and the mainstream macroeconometric and structural VAR models are based on a pragmatic approach to capturing the dynamics. As we shall demonstrate in the

[19] Christiano, Eichenbaum and Evans's (2005) attempts to tie down model parameters by matching impulse responses will suffer from this shortcoming, for example, since the impulse responses are based on short-run dynamics and are not consistent with the presence of long-run relations in levels.

[20] See Section 3.2 for details on how the expectation effects are accommodated in the long-run structural model.

following chapter, our own approach is to allow the dynamics to be flexibly estimated within a VAR or VARX framework, but to impose restrictions on the system to ensure that the estimated relationships are theory-consistent in the long run. Theory-inspired short-run restrictions can then be considered in the light of their empirical validity, and not adopted blindly since they are implied by a particular macroeconomic theory.

3

National and global structural macroeconometric modelling

The discussion of the previous chapter suggested that there is a degree of consensus surrounding the desirable long-run properties of a macroeconomic model and that most recently developed models will be similar in this regard whether they have been developed following the SEM, VAR or DSGE approaches. There is far less agreement about the way in which short-run dynamic adjustment should be tackled, however, and in this chapter we broaden the discussion to consider this aspect of macroeconomic modelling too. To this end, in the following section, we present a canonical dynamic structural model. This allows us to clarify the distinction between short-run and long-run effects and to illustrate the issues involved in identifying these respective effects. Using the model, we can also provide a general description of the modelling strategy involved in constructing a 'structural cointegrating macroeconomic model' as applied to the UK in the subsequent chapters of the book. We believe that this strategy provides a coherent approach to dealing with both short-run and long-run influences in a way that can reflect the strength of conviction with which we believe the underlying economic theory.

The description of the canonical dynamic structural model also helps explain how the identification of short-run dynamics relates to the identification of economically meaningful shocks and the measurement of their dynamic effects. These issues are important since they lie at the heart of the discussion surrounding the identification of monetary policy shocks and the measurement of their effects. In this chapter, we shall review the attempts that have been made in the literature to impose structure on the short-run dynamics of macroeconomic models and to identify the effects of different types of shock, and particularly monetary policy shocks.

Finally in this chapter, we shall elaborate on the context within which a macroeconomic modelling exercise of this sort might be conducted and describe three ways in which the model might be extended. Specifically, we note *first* that, in any national macroeconomic model, there might be influences that are determined exogenously to the model. While much of the discussion is conducted under the (implicit) assumption that all of the variables in the model are determined endogenously, this section demonstrates that the modelling framework can be readily extended to accommodate exogenous shocks. *Next*, we note that any national macroeconomic model might constitute just one element of a broader examination of the economic behaviour of a number of economies. The UK economy within the world economy, for example, or within the European Community, say. With this in mind, we describe how the modelling strategy elaborated and applied to a national model can be extended to place its behaviour within the global context. *Thirdly*, we note that in any modelling exercise, interest might focus on a particular sector of the national economy rather than the whole. A detailed understanding of the macroeconomy might be an essential element of understanding the behaviour of the particular sector, but is not an end in itself. Thus it is worth considering how the analysis of a particular sector might be developed in these circumstances and the final section of the chapter considers this sectoral dimension.

3.1 Identification in a dynamic structural vector error correction model

A very general dynamic linear structural model of the determination of the $m \times 1$ vector of variables $\mathbf{z}_t$ is given by the Vector Error Correcting Model (VECM):

$$\mathbf{A}\Delta\mathbf{z}_t = \widetilde{\mathbf{a}} + \widetilde{\mathbf{b}}t - \widetilde{\mathbf{\Pi}}\mathbf{z}_{t-1} + \sum_{i=1}^{p-1} \widetilde{\mathbf{\Gamma}}_i \Delta\mathbf{z}_{t-i} + \boldsymbol{\varepsilon}_t. \tag{3.1}$$

The m equations in the model embody what are seen as the relevant autonomous economic relationships.[1] $\mathbf{A}$, $\widetilde{\mathbf{\Pi}}$ and $\widetilde{\mathbf{\Gamma}}_i$ are $m \times m$ matrices, and $\widetilde{\mathbf{a}}$ and $\widetilde{\mathbf{b}}$ are $m \times 1$ vectors of unknown structural coefficients. The matrix $\mathbf{A}$ contains the contemporaneous structural coefficients, while $\widetilde{\mathbf{\Pi}}$ and $\widetilde{\mathbf{\Gamma}}_i$

[1] Here, we assume that all variables of interest are determined endogenously within the system. The modelling framework can be readily extended to VEC models with weakly exogenous $I(1)$ variables, as discussed in Section 3.3.1 below.

contain the dynamic coefficients relating $\Delta \mathbf{z}_t$ to past values of $\mathbf{z}_t$. The term $\boldsymbol{\varepsilon}_t$ is an $m \times 1$ vector of disturbances, assumed to be serially uncorrelated, with zero means and a positive definite variance covariance matrix, $\boldsymbol{\Omega}$. These are the structural shocks relating to the m economic relationships.[2]

The form in (3.1) is particularly useful when the elements of $\mathbf{z}_t$ are stationary in differences, or integrated of order one, $I(1)$. In general, linear combinations of $I(1)$ variables are typically $I(1)$, but when there exist linear combinations of the $\mathbf{z}_t$, say $\boldsymbol{\beta}'\mathbf{z}_t$, that are stationary, or $I(0)$, the $\mathbf{z}_t$ are said to be cointegrated. If $\mathbf{z}_t$ were composed of only stationary variables, then $\widetilde{\boldsymbol{\Pi}}$ would be a matrix of full rank, m. In this case, one cannot meaningfully separate out long-run and short-run effects although a distinction can still be made between level effects and the effects on first differences. Disturbing the system has no long-run impact and the variables eventually return to their unconditional mean (or to a deterministic trend if $\widetilde{\mathbf{b}} \neq 0$). If $\mathbf{z}_t$ were $I(1)$ and not cointegrated, $\widetilde{\boldsymbol{\Pi}}$ would be a null matrix. The system is described by a VAR in differences; all shocks have persistent effects, but there are no equilibrium relationships that exist between the levels that impact on these persistent effects. But suppose there are r cointegrating vectors, $0 < r < m$. Then $\boldsymbol{\beta}$ will be an $m \times r$ matrix and $\widetilde{\boldsymbol{\Pi}}$ will be of rank r, with the form

$$\widetilde{\boldsymbol{\Pi}} = \widetilde{\boldsymbol{\alpha}}\boldsymbol{\beta}'. \tag{3.2}$$

The $I(0)$ variables $\boldsymbol{\beta}'\mathbf{z}_t$ (appropriately adjusted by demeaning and detrending) are often interpreted as errors or deviations from equilibrium. Thus the $m \times r$ matrix, $\widetilde{\boldsymbol{\alpha}}$, has a natural interpretation as a matrix of adjustment coefficients that measure how rapidly deviations from equilibrium feedback onto the variables $\mathbf{z}_t$. Here, the cointegrating relationships act as an attractor for the system and, despite the persistent effect of shocks on the individual variables, shocks to the system have no persistent effect on the equilibrium relations and their effects on such relations will die out eventually.

The reduced form vector error correction model in (3.1) is given by

$$\Delta \mathbf{z}_t = \mathbf{a} + \mathbf{b}t - \boldsymbol{\Pi} z_{t-1} + \sum_{i=1}^{p-1} \boldsymbol{\Gamma}_i \Delta \mathbf{z}_{t-i} + \mathbf{v}_t, \tag{3.3}$$

[2] This form appears backward-looking, in the sense that all variables are dated at time t and earlier. But the model can readily accommodate the solution of forward-looking models of the form associated with SEMs incorporating RE or with DSGE models, for example. See Pesaran (1997) for a discussion.

where $\mathrm{a} = \mathrm{A}^{-1}\widetilde{\mathrm{a}}$, $\mathrm{b} = \mathrm{A}^{-1}\widetilde{\mathrm{b}}$, and $\boldsymbol{\Gamma}_i = \mathrm{A}^{-1}\widetilde{\boldsymbol{\Gamma}}_i$. Further, we have $\boldsymbol{\Pi} = \mathrm{A}^{-1}\widetilde{\boldsymbol{\Pi}} = \mathrm{A}^{-1}\widetilde{\boldsymbol{\alpha}}\boldsymbol{\beta}' = \boldsymbol{\alpha}\boldsymbol{\beta}'$, where $\boldsymbol{\alpha} = \mathrm{A}^{-1}\widetilde{\boldsymbol{\alpha}}$ and $\mathrm{v}_t = \mathrm{A}^{-1}\boldsymbol{\varepsilon}_t$ are the reduced form errors with variance covariance matrix $\boldsymbol{\Sigma}$, where $\boldsymbol{\Omega} = \mathrm{A}\boldsymbol{\Sigma}\mathrm{A}'$. Within this framework, there are two quite distinct questions that we might wish to address. First, how do we identify the r distinct long-run relationships implicit in (3.2)? And second, assuming that the parameters and errors of (3.3) can be estimated, how do we identify the parameters A, $\widetilde{\mathrm{a}}$, $\widetilde{\mathrm{b}}$, $\widetilde{\boldsymbol{\Pi}}$, and $\widetilde{\boldsymbol{\Gamma}}_i$, $i = 1, \ldots, p-1$, and hence obtain measures of the effects of the economically meaningful structural shocks?

3.1.1 *Identifying long-run relationships*

Consideration of (3.3) shows that, even if an estimate of $\boldsymbol{\Pi}$ was available, without further restrictions, neither $\boldsymbol{\alpha}$ nor $\boldsymbol{\beta}'$ are separately identified. We can choose any non-singular $r \times r$ matrix, Q, and write

$$\boldsymbol{\Pi} = \boldsymbol{\alpha}\boldsymbol{\beta}' = (\boldsymbol{\alpha}\, Q'^{-1})(\mathrm{Q}'\boldsymbol{\beta}') = \boldsymbol{\alpha}_*\boldsymbol{\beta}'_*,$$

so that $\boldsymbol{\alpha}_* = \boldsymbol{\alpha}\, Q'^{-1}$ and $\boldsymbol{\beta}_* = \boldsymbol{\beta}\, Q$ constitute observationally equivalent alternative structures. In order to identify the cointegrating vectors, we need to provide r^2 independent pieces of information, formed from r restrictions on each of the r cointegrating relations. Only r restrictions are provided by 'normalisation' conditions and so a further $r^2 - r$ restrictions will be needed to uniquely identify $\boldsymbol{\beta}$ (and hence $\boldsymbol{\alpha}$).[3]

It is important to note that knowledge of the structural coefficients A, $\widetilde{\mathrm{a}}$, $\widetilde{\mathrm{b}}$, $\widetilde{\boldsymbol{\Pi}}$, and $\widetilde{\boldsymbol{\Gamma}}_i$, $i = 1, \ldots, p-1$, does not resolve the problem of identification of the long-run relations when z_t is $I(1)$. Reiterating the fact that $\boldsymbol{\Pi} = A^{-1}\widetilde{\boldsymbol{\Pi}} = \mathrm{A}^{-1}\widetilde{\boldsymbol{\alpha}}\boldsymbol{\beta}' = \boldsymbol{\alpha}\boldsymbol{\beta}'$, it is clear that knowing the value of A would not resolve the issue of how to uniquely factor the rank-deficient matrix $\widetilde{\boldsymbol{\Pi}}$ into the $m \times r$ matrices $\widetilde{\boldsymbol{\alpha}}$ and $\boldsymbol{\beta}$. The structural coefficient matrices determine the short-run responses and on their own do not identify the long-run relations.[4]

Beginning with Johansen (1988), a large and sophisticated literature has developed considering the analysis of cointegrating VAR models of the form in (3.3). Johansen (1988, 1991) provides procedures for testing the rank of $\boldsymbol{\Pi}$ and then estimating $\boldsymbol{\alpha}$ and $\boldsymbol{\beta}'$ using statistically motivated

[3] Wickens (1996) also considers the interpretation of cointegrating vectors, raising the possibility of imposing restrictions on the loading vector $\boldsymbol{\alpha}$ and also concluding that prior, structural information is essential for identification of meaningful cointegrating vectors.

[4] Similarly, identification of the long run relations do not generally help with identification of short-run coefficients.

identifying restrictions that assume the columns of β form an orthogonal set. While mathematically natural given the statistical structure of the problem, these restrictions have no economic meaning since in general there is no reason to expect economic cointegrating relations to be orthogonal. When $r > 1$, economic interpretation of the Johansen estimates of the cointegrating vectors is almost impossible. Similarly, the identification conditions employed by Phillips (1991), in the context of a triangular VECM, are chosen for their mathematical convenience rather than their suitability for economic interpretation.

The obvious alternative means of obtaining the $r^2 - r$ required restrictions is to draw on economic theory and other *a priori* information. Since the restrictions are to be imposed on the r cointegrating vectors, the relevant economic theory is that of the long run. This avoids the criticisms of many that economic theory is insufficiently well-defined to impose restrictions based on the short-run dynamics (*cf.* the Sims critique cited previously); indeed, as the discussion of the previous chapter made clear, in the context of macroeconometric models, there exists a broad consensus on the nature of the restrictions that might be imposed on a macroeconometric model in the long run. Pesaran and Shin (2002) describe precisely this approach to identifying the long-run relationships embedded within the cointegrating VAR. The modelling strategy implied by this approach is elaborated upon at the end of the subsection (and the econometric methods are described in detail in Chapter 6). First, however, we consider the identification issues relating to the short-run parameters and the structural shocks of (3.1).

3.1.2 *Identifying short-run structural parameters and shocks*

Abstracting from the issues relating to the long-run relationships, exact identification of the structural coefficients in (3.1) from the estimated parameters of the reduced form model in (3.3) requires m^2 restrictions to be imposed on the structural parameters. These are typically imposed on $\mathbf{A}$ and/or $\mathbf{\Omega}$. The traditional econometric approach to restricting short-run dynamics was to impose a particular shape (such as a geometrically declining or bell-shaped form), deemed plausible on *a priori* grounds, on the distributed lag functions relating to different components of $\mathbf{z}_t$. Early contributors to this approach include Nerlove (1958), Griliches (1967), and Jorgenson (1966). Dryhmes (1971) provides a comprehensive review of this early literature. A more recent literature on dynamic economic theory has attempted to provide restrictions on the short-run dynamics that are more plausible theoretically. An important example is the short-run restrictions involved in Real Business Cycle models due to the intertemporal nature of decision-making in these models and to the particular specification adopted in characterising technological progress.[5] Another example is given by the restrictions implied by the rational expectations hypothesis in the context of the Linear–Quadratic (LQ) optimisation models involving adjustment costs. Dynamic adjustment cost models have been applied in a number of important areas in applied econometrics with some success and could be an important source of *a priori* restrictions on the short-run dynamics of macroeconometric models. Some recent versions of the DSGE model, based on New Keynesian sticky price models, attempt to integrate intertemporal optimisation and adjustment cost models.

A third approach taken to identify the structural parameters is that promoted by the 'Structural VAR' approach to macroeconometric modelling, discussed in the previous chapter. The identifying restrictions imposed here are typically motivated with reference to some 'tentative' theory on macroeconomic dynamics, expressed with reference to contemporaneous relationships or with reference to the long-run impulse responses. Perhaps the most prominent example of this approach is the familiar recursive structure pioneered by Sims (1980) which requires $\mathbf{A}$ to be a lower or an upper triangular matrix and $\mathbf{\Omega}$ to be a diagonal matrix. This imposes a recursive, Wold-causal ordering on the contemporaneous relationships among the variables in $\mathbf{z}_t$ and can be motivated by 'tentative' economic theory on the timing of decisions and the detailed arrangements of the decision-making context. Such theories can also be used to motivate non-recursive structures on the structural parameters. This approach is particularly prevalent in the literature concerned with identifying monetary policy shocks. We shall discuss these three approaches to imposing structure on the short-run dynamics to identify short-run structural parameters and the structural shocks in more detail below.

Although there is a range of possible sources of theoretical restrictions on the short-run dynamics, in many cases, theory is either silent on the nature of the adjustment process or the theoretical restrictions are overly strong (making all the dynamics a function of a few deep parameters) with the consequence that they are invariably rejected by the data. In such cases, inferences about the long-run parameters and the dynamic properties of

[5] Other types of short-run restrictions could be obtained in the context of learning models.

the macroeconomy need to be conducted using unrestricted short-run parameters.

3.1.3 *A modelling strategy*

The canonical model described above emphasises the distinct contributions of economic theory as it relates to identification of the short-run and long-run relationships. In developing a modelling strategy, we need to consider the different characteristics of these contributions.

Typically, theories relating to the short run are concerned with relationships between variables motivated as the outcome of specific decisions made at a particular moment in time. Each row of the structural model of (3.1) describes the determination of one of the variables in the system and the restrictions imposed on the contemporaneous parameter matrix $\mathbf{A}$ reflect the assumed behaviour of the agent or group of agents setting the variable. Each equation in the model shows the factors taken into account by the decision-makers when they determine the value of a particular variable through their actions. The factors are either included explicitly in the model in the form of the contemporaneous values of the other variables in $\mathbf{z}_t$ or the lagged values of $\mathbf{z}_t$, or implicitly as part of the economically meaningful structural shocks, $\boldsymbol{\varepsilon}_t$.

The long-run relationships identified by economic theory typically do not relate to a specific time period or to particular events or decisions, but reflect the outcome of (potentially numerous) equilibrating pressures exerted over a (typically unspecified) period of time. Economic theory might provide little insight on the means by which a particular disequilibrium feeds back on the system and might involve concepts that are inherently unobservable or are difficult to measure accurately, such as expectations, natural rates or potential output. For example, economic theory might suggest that, in the long run, supply and demand of a good will be equal but might not elaborate on the tatonnement process involved other than to observe that price and quantity will react in an unspecified way to eliminate excess demand or supply (where the excess is itself unobserved). At any time, the system might be out of equilibrium along any of the dimensions suggested by economic theory, but neither these disequilibria nor the corresponding equilibrating pressures will be observable. On the other hand, theory also suggests the existence of long-run equilibrium relationships between the observed variables and the deviations from these will be observed. These deviations from equilibria are more useful for modelling purposes and might be termed *'long-run errors'*, which we denote by ξ_t.[6]

The modelling strategy involved in constructing a structural cointegrating model of the macroeconomy is based on the idea that the long-run errors, ξ_t, can be expressed as a linear combination of the variables in the system, possibly supplemented by appropriate deterministic intercepts and trends; that is,

$$\xi_t = \boldsymbol{\beta}'\mathbf{z}_t - \mathbf{b}_0 - \mathbf{b}_1 t, \tag{3.4}$$

for appropriate parameter vectors $\mathbf{b}_0$ and $\mathbf{b}_1$ and where $\boldsymbol{\beta}'$ is the $r \times m$ matrix of parameters that describes the r equilibrium relationships expected to hold between the m variables in $\mathbf{z}_t$ in the long run. In modelling the short-run dynamics of the variables in $\mathbf{z}_t$, we follow the standard VAR approach established by Sims (1980) and others, and assume that changes in the $\mathbf{z}_t$ can be well-approximated by a linear function of a finite number of past changes in $\mathbf{z}_t$. Assuming that the variables in $\mathbf{z}_t$ are difference-stationary, our modelling strategy is to embody the ξ_t in an otherwise unrestricted VAR(p) model in $\mathbf{z}_t$; that is, we consider the $(p-1)$th order VEC model

$$\Delta\mathbf{z}_t = \mathbf{a}_0 - \boldsymbol{\alpha}\xi_{t-1} + \sum_{i=1}^{p-1}\boldsymbol{\Gamma}_i\Delta\mathbf{z}_{t-i} + \mathbf{v}_t. \tag{3.5}$$

Given the definition of the long-run errors in (3.4), the model in (3.5) can be rewritten as

$$\Delta\mathbf{z}_t = \mathbf{a}_0 - \boldsymbol{\alpha}\left[\boldsymbol{\beta}'\mathbf{z}_{t-1} - \mathbf{b}_0 - \mathbf{b}_1(t-1)\right] + \sum_{i=1}^{p-1}\boldsymbol{\Gamma}_i\Delta\mathbf{z}_{t-i} + \mathbf{v}_t, \tag{3.6}$$

or

$$\Delta\mathbf{z}_t = \mathbf{a} + \mathbf{b}t - \boldsymbol{\alpha\beta}'\mathbf{z}_{t-1} + \sum_{i=1}^{p-1}\boldsymbol{\Gamma}_i\Delta\mathbf{z}_{t-i} + \mathbf{v}_t,$$

which is of the form of (3.3), with $\mathbf{a} = \mathbf{a}_0 + \boldsymbol{\alpha}\left(\mathbf{b}_0 - \mathbf{b}_1\right)$ and $\mathbf{b} = \boldsymbol{\alpha}\mathbf{b}_1$. This model embodies directly the predictions of economic theory, as it relates to the long run. This is in contrast to some cointegrating VAR analysis which starts with an unrestricted VAR and investigates some vague priors about the nature of the long-run relations. Estimation of a model of the

[6] The relationship between economically meaningful but unobservable disequilibria and observable long-run errors is illustrated in the economic theory of the long run elaborated in Chapter 4.

form in (3.6) can be carried out using the long-run structural modelling approach described in Pesaran and Shin (2002) and Pesaran, Shin and Smith (2000). A complete description of the econometric methods is postponed until Chapter 6. However, it is worth noting here that this approach not only provides estimates of the parameters in (3.6), but it can also provide a straightforward test of the long-run theory. Specifically, estimation of a VECM $(p-1)$ of the form in (3.6) can be carried out first imposing just r^2 exact identifying restrictions on the cointegrating relations. This will ensure that there are r cointegrating relations among the series but is not likely to impose the full structure suggested by the economic theory; *i.e.* these are likely to be a subset of the restrictions suggested by economic theory and embedded directly within (3.6). Estimation of the model subject to the full set of restrictions suggested by economic theory provides over-identifying restrictions that can be tested.

3.2 Specifying the dynamic structure of a macroeconomic model

The discussion above makes it clear that estimation of the structural parameters and the structural shocks to the model in (3.1) requires m^2 restrictions to be imposed, typically on $\mathbf{A}$ and/or $\mathbf{\Omega}$. In this section, we elaborate on some of the approaches taken in the literature to motivate such restrictions. We focus on three approaches that are pervasive in the literature. The first approach is that associated with the Dynamic Stochastic General Equilibrium models; the second is a broad class of 'Adjustment Cost' models; and the third class, associated with the Structural VAR approach to macroeconomic modelling, relies on miscellaneous assumptions on the contemporaneous and long-run interactions among variables, including recursiveness and exclusion assumptions, based on 'tentative' economic theory.

3.2.1 *Dynamics of DSGE models*

The strength of the DSGE approach to modelling the macroeconomy is that, in principle at least, it is based on the decisions of all agents in the economy. In this approach, macroeconomic phenomena are the outcome of the decisions made by these agents, driven by individual preferences, subject to constraints and relating to a whole range of variables simultaneously. The different decisions are reconciled to form a general equilibrium through the economy-wide market system. One result of this is that the models designed following this approach have clearly defined steady-state properties built into them automatically. This is the feature of the models discussed at length in the previous chapter. A second important feature of DSGE models arises because the decisions made by agents are usually intertemporal, relating to choices and constraints on economic magnitudes both today and in the future. This means that the dynamic structure of the DSGE model is also specified explicitly.

The derivation of an explicit dynamic structure for DSGE models is both a strength and a weakness. On the positive side, the approach provides very clear predictions on the dynamic responses of variables to different types of innovation impacting on the macroeconomy and these predictions can be tested. The downside is the difficulty of matching these predictions with the data; see, for example, the discussion of Kim and Pagan (1995) below. The DSGE modellers have responded to this challenge by supplementing the 'intrinsic dynamics' generated by the intertemporal optimisation of the DSGE models' agents with 'extrinsic dynamics' of various forms (motivated by the presence of adjustment costs, learning, aggregation issues, and so on).[7]

To illustrate these points, we consider below the DSGE model presented in Christiano and Eichenbaum (1992b) and analysed in some detail in Binder and Pesaran (1995). This model is in the spirit of the 'first phase' of DSGE models which focused on real magnitudes. But the ideas would carry over to the 'New Keynesian DSGE' models discussed in the previous chapter that are based on an IS curve, a Phillips curve and a policy rule (either in their closed economy form or in the open economy version derived in Gali and Monacelli (2005), for example).[8] In particular, the explicit reliance on forward-looking behaviour and rational expectations can be readily accommodated by our VARX modelling structure.

The model we consider here assumes an aggregate constant returns to scale Cobb–Douglas production function in which labour augmenting technology A_t, labour N_t and capital K_t are used to produce output Y_t. This can be used for consumption C_t, investment I_t or government spending G_t. The representative household has a time endowment of N. Capital is assumed to depreciate at rate δ so that

$$K_{t+1} = (1 - \delta)K_t + I_t. \tag{3.7}$$

[7] See the citations provided in Chapter 2.

[8] Pesaran and Smith (2005) provide a formal account of the relationship between the New Keynesian DSGE models and the VARX models that will be discussed below in Section 3.3.1.

Given the Cobb–Douglas production function, the production constraint is

$$C_t + K_{t+1} - (1-\delta)K_t + G_t = K_t^{\alpha}(A_t N_t)^{1-\alpha}. \tag{3.8}$$

The forces outside the control of the representative household are technology and government spending and it is assumed that the laws of motion of these variables can be represented as follows:

$$\Delta \ln(A_t) = \gamma_t = \gamma + \varepsilon_{at}, \qquad \varepsilon_{at} \sim N(0, \sigma_a^2), \tag{3.9}$$

and

$$\ln(G_t/A_t) = \ln(g_t) = \tau_0 + \tau_1 \ln(g_{t-1}) + \varepsilon_{gt}, \qquad \varepsilon_{gt} \sim N(0, \sigma_g^2), \tag{3.10}$$

$|\tau_1| < 1$, so that the logarithm of A_t is represented by a random walk with drift and government expenditure expressed relative to technology, $g_t = G_t/A_t$, follows a simple AR(1) process. As is well known, the competitive equilibrium outcome is the same as that of a Social Planner who acts to maximise the utility of the representative household, which is assumed to be given by

$$\sum_{t=1}^{\infty} \rho^t \left[\ln(C_t) + \theta(N - N_t)\right], \tag{3.11}$$

where ρ is the discount factor and θ reflects the weight given to leisure in the utility function.

The Social Planner maximises the representative household's utility through the choice of C_t, K_{t+1} and N_t for $t = 0, 1, 2, \ldots$, demonstrating the simultaneous and intertemporal nature of the model solution. The source of the dynamics in the solution to this model are also apparent, arising from the forward-looking properties of the utility function and the intertemporal nature of the production constraint arising from capital accumulation. These dynamics are supplemented by the dynamics introduced through the processes assumed to drive technology and government expenditure.

To be more precise, the solution of the model is obtained with the Social Planner maximising the following Lagrangian

$$L_0 = E_0 \left\{ \sum_{t=1}^{\infty} \rho^t \left[\ln(c_t) + \theta(N - N_t) + \ln(A_t) \right] \right\}$$
$$+ E_0 \left\{ \sum_{t=1}^{\infty} \lambda_t \rho^t \left[k_t^{\alpha} N_t^{1-\alpha} \exp(-\alpha \gamma_t) - c_t \right. \right.$$
$$\left. \left. -k_{t+1} + (1-\delta) k_t \exp(-\gamma_t) - g_t \right] \right\},$$

through choice of c_t, k_{t+1} and N_t for $t = 0, 1, 2, \ldots$, where E_0 indicates the expectation formed on the basis of information at time 0 and lower case letters indicate that the variable is expressed as a ratio relative to A_t; *i.e.* $y_t = Y_t/A_t$, $c_t = C_t/A_t$, $k_t = K_t/A_t$ and $i_t = I_t/A_t$. The first-order conditions for this optimisation are non-linear and in general do not lend themselves to an exact solution. However, the non-stochastic steady-state values of y_t, c_t, k_t, i_t and N_t, denoted by $\overline{y}$, $\overline{c}$, $\overline{k}$, $\overline{i}$ and $\overline{N}$, respectively, are given by non-linear equations derived from the first-order conditions as follows:

$$\overline{y} = \overline{k}^{\alpha} \overline{N}^{1-\alpha} \exp(-\alpha\gamma),$$
$$\overline{c} = \overline{y} - \overline{i} - \overline{g},$$
$$\overline{k} = \left[\exp(-\alpha\gamma)\overline{s}_k\right]^{1/(1-\alpha)} \overline{N},$$
$$\overline{i} = \overline{k} - (1-\delta)\exp(-\gamma)\overline{k},$$
$$\overline{N} = \left[\frac{1-\alpha}{\theta} + \frac{\overline{g}}{\overline{s}_k^{\alpha/(1-\alpha)} \exp(-\alpha\gamma/(1-\alpha))} \right] \div \left[(1-\delta)\exp(-\gamma)\overline{s}_k\right],$$

where $\overline{g}$ is the mean of g_t and

$$\overline{s}_k = \frac{\alpha\rho}{1-\rho(1-\delta)\exp(-\gamma)} = \overline{k}/\overline{y}.$$

These non-linear equations illustrate the steady-state properties automatically built into the model, with steady-state labour inputs explained by the 'deep' parameters of the model, α, ρ, δ, γ, θ and $\overline{g}$, and the steady-state growth path of the remaining variables driven by technological progress (recalling from the specification of the labour augmenting technological progress in (3.9) that steady-state growth is γ).

Further, expanding the first-order conditions obtained from the Social Planner's optimisation around the non-stochastic steady-state outcomes above, we obtain a log-linear approximation for the model solution with which to characterise the model dynamics. Specifically, eliminating the shadow prices from the log-linearised first-order conditions, we obtain the following:

$$\mathbf{A}\mathbf{z}_t = \mathbf{B}\mathbf{z}_{t-1} + \mathbf{C}E_t(\mathbf{z}_{t+1}) + \mathbf{u}_t, \tag{3.12}$$

where

$$\mathbf{z}_t = \begin{pmatrix} \widetilde{k}_{t+1} \\ \widetilde{N}_t \\ \widetilde{c}_t \\ \widetilde{y}_t \\ \widetilde{i}_t \end{pmatrix}, \qquad \mathbf{u}_t = \begin{pmatrix} \bar{s}_g \widetilde{g}_t \\ \theta_1 \widetilde{\gamma}_t \\ \alpha \widetilde{\gamma}_t \\ \alpha \widetilde{\gamma}_t \\ \theta_3 \widetilde{\gamma}_t \end{pmatrix}$$

and

$$\mathbf{A} = \begin{pmatrix} 0 & 0 & -\bar{s}_c & 1 & -\bar{s}_i \\ 1 & 0 & 0 & 0 & -(1-\theta_1) \\ 0 & -(1-\alpha) & 0 & 1 & 0 \\ 0 & \alpha & 1 & 0 & 0 \\ \theta_2 & 0 & -1 & 0 & 0 \end{pmatrix},$$

$$\mathbf{B} = \begin{pmatrix} 0 & 0 & 0 & 0 & 0 \\ \theta_1 & 0 & 0 & 0 & 0 \\ \alpha & 0 & 0 & 0 & 0 \\ \alpha & 0 & 0 & 0 & 0 \\ 0 & 0 & 0 & 0 & 0 \end{pmatrix},$$

$$\mathbf{C} = \begin{pmatrix} 0 & 0 & 0 & 0 & 0 \\ 0 & 0 & 0 & 0 & 0 \\ 0 & 0 & 0 & 0 & 0 \\ 0 & 0 & 0 & 0 & 0 \\ 0 & \theta_2 & -1 & 0 & 0 \end{pmatrix},$$

where a variable written with an '$\sim$' overstrike means that it is measured relative to its non-stochastic steady-state value (*i.e.* $\widetilde{k}_t = \ln(k_t/\bar{k}_t)$, for example), where $\bar{s}_c = \bar{c}/\bar{y}$, $\bar{s}_i = \bar{i}/\bar{y}$ and $\bar{s}_g = \bar{g}/\bar{y}$, and where $\theta_1 = (1-\delta)\exp(-\gamma)$, $\theta_2 = \rho\alpha(1-\alpha)\bar{s}_k^{-1}$ and $\theta_3 = \rho\alpha^2\bar{s}_k^{-1} + \rho\theta_1$. Hence, the dynamic specification derived for the DSGE model in (3.7)–(3.11) is summarised by the multivariate linear rational expectations model given in (3.12) which is driven by the exogenous shock to technology and fiscal policy.

There have been many methods proposed for the solution of such models, and these are reviewed in Binder and Pesaran (1995). Clearly, the system is capable of generating very sophisticated dynamics, and the solution depends on whether the quadratic determinantal equation,

$$\det(\mathbf{C}\lambda^2 - \mathbf{A}\lambda + \mathbf{B}) = 0,$$

has pairs of solutions which satisfy the regularity conditions; namely whether, for each pair, one root will fall inside the unit circle and the other outside it. Assuming these conditions are satisfied, then the model has a unique stable solution given by

$$\mathbf{z}_t = \mathbf{b} + \boldsymbol{\lambda}\mathbf{z}_{t-1} + \mathbf{v}_t,$$

where $\boldsymbol{\lambda}$ is the solution with all its roots on or inside the unit circle and $(\mathbf{A} - \mathbf{C}\boldsymbol{\lambda})\mathbf{v}_t = \mathbf{u}_t$, so the DSGE model fits readily into a VARX structure. Denoting the steady-state values with an overbar once more, the long-run structural relations associated with (3.12) will be given by

$$(\mathbf{A} - \mathbf{B} - \mathbf{C})\bar{\mathbf{z}}_t = \eta_t,$$

where the η_t are the long-run errors and

$$(\mathbf{A} - \mathbf{B} - \mathbf{C}) = \begin{pmatrix} 0 & 0 & -\bar{s}_c & 1 & -\bar{s}_i \\ 1-\theta_1 & 0 & 0 & 0 & -(1-\theta_1) \\ -\alpha & -(1-\alpha) & 0 & 1 & 0 \\ -\alpha & \alpha & 1 & 0 & 0 \\ \theta_2 & -\theta_2 & 0 & 0 & 0 \end{pmatrix}.$$

It is also worth emphasising that it is not only the matrix $(\mathbf{A} - \mathbf{B} - \mathbf{C})$ that is subject to restrictions. The elements of $\mathbf{A}, \mathbf{B}$ and $\mathbf{C}$ are themselves subject to a number of restrictions. Given the number of coefficients of zero and unity in the matrices $\mathbf{A}$, $\mathbf{B}$ and $\mathbf{C}$, it is also clear that the solution imposes a large number of restrictions on the system dynamics. These are precisely the restrictions that are tested in Kim and Pagan (1995), for example, and which are easily rejected by the data.

3.2.2 *Dynamics of adjustment cost models*

A second approach in which the dynamic structure of a model is specified is one where there is an explicit intertemporal optimisation problem involving adjustment costs. There are many examples of models of this type found in the applied econometrics literature. Nickell (1985) and Breeson *et al.* (1992) focus on models of labour demand, for example; Blundell *et al.* (1992) focus on capital investment; West (1995) focuses on inventory models; and so on. Hansen and Sargent (1995) also provide a useful overview of linear–quadratic general equilibrium models with adjustment costs. The latter reference works with a familiar but restrictive class of objective function, having the advantage that the optimisation produces a linear decision rule. But the approach is similar if the analysis starts with a general non-linear specification of an objective function and linearises around the resultant first-order conditions.

To briefly review the nature of the dynamic specification arising from these models, consider the following quadratic optimisation problem

$$\min_{(\mathbf{z}_{t+s})} E_t \left\{ \sum_{s=0}^{\infty} \rho^s \left[\left(\mathbf{z}_{t+s} - \mathbf{z}^{\dagger}_{t+s}\right)' \mathbf{H} \left(\mathbf{z}_{t+s} - \mathbf{z}^{\dagger}_{t+s}\right) + \Delta \mathbf{z}_{t+s} \mathbf{G} \Delta \mathbf{z}_{t+s} + \Delta^2 \mathbf{z}_{t+s} \mathbf{K} \Delta^2 \mathbf{z}_{t+s} \right] \right\} \tag{3.13}$$

for given values of $\mathbf{z}^{\dagger}_t$, $\mathbf{z}^{\dagger}_{t+1}$, $\mathbf{z}^{\dagger}_{t+2}, \ldots$, where $\mathbf{z}_t$ is the vector of decision variables, $\mathbf{H}$, $\mathbf{G}$ and $\mathbf{K}$ are symmetric matrices of structural parameters and ρ is a discount factor in $(0, 1)$. $\mathbf{z}^{\dagger}_{t+s}$ represents the corresponding vector of targets, which may be fixed or evolving stochastically. The problem in (3.13) indicates that costs are quadratic and strictly convex in the arguments. Costs are incurred if the decision variables deviate from their targets and if the decision variables are changed from their previous value. The third term allows for the possibility that the *rate* at which the variables are changed also generates an independent cost. The relative importance of the three elements of costs are captured by the parameters in H, G and K. Assuming that the targets are indeed varying stochastically, differentiating (3.13) with respect to $\mathbf{z}_t$ and rearranging the resultant conditions yields the following stochastic Euler equation system:

$$\begin{aligned} \mathbf{z}_t = {} & \mathbf{M}^{-1}[\mathbf{G} + 2(1+\rho)\mathbf{K}]\mathbf{z}_{t-1} - \mathbf{M}^{-1}\mathbf{K}\mathbf{z}_{t-2} \\ & + \rho^{-1}\mathbf{M}^{-1}[\mathbf{G} + 2(1+\rho)\mathbf{K})]\, E_t(\mathbf{z}_{t+1}) \\ & - \rho^2\mathbf{M}^{-1}\mathbf{K}\, E_t(\mathbf{z}_{t+2}) + \mathbf{M}^{-1}\mathbf{H}\mathbf{z}^{\dagger}_t, \end{aligned} \tag{3.14}$$

where $\mathbf{M} = \mathbf{H} + (1+\rho)\mathbf{G} + (1 + 4\rho + \rho^2)\mathbf{K}$. The solution of (3.14) can be obtained in a number of different ways, some of which are reviewed in Binder and Pesaran (1995). However, it is intuitively clear that the solution for $\mathbf{z}_t$ will depend, in general, on $\mathbf{z}_{t-1}$, $\mathbf{z}_{t-2}$ and expressions for $E_t(\mathbf{z}_{t+i})$, $i = 0, 1, 2, \ldots$, so that an explicit solution requires a statement on the process driving the targets. For this purpose, we might describe the process explaining the targets by the vector ARMA specification

$$\theta(L)\mathbf{z}^{\dagger}_{t+s} \equiv \boldsymbol{\phi}(L)\boldsymbol{\epsilon}_{t+s}, \qquad \boldsymbol{\epsilon}_{t+s} \sim i.i.d.\,(\mathbf{0}, \boldsymbol{\Sigma}_{\epsilon}),$$

where $\boldsymbol{\Sigma}_{\epsilon}$ is an $m \times m$ covariance matrix for $\boldsymbol{\epsilon}_t$. The solution for $\mathbf{z}_t$ will therefore depend on $\mathbf{z}_{t-1}$, $\mathbf{z}_{t-2}$, current and lagged values of $\mathbf{z}^{\dagger}_t$ and $\boldsymbol{\epsilon}_t$. The dynamic structure of the solution will be a complicated function of the parameters in H, G, K, $\boldsymbol{\theta}$ and $\boldsymbol{\phi}$ but, given the linearity of the problem, will be readily written in the form of a VAR.[9] Moreover, despite its complexity, the solution will be explicitly derived and the restrictions suggested in the model solution can usually be tested in the context of a straightforward regression exercise.[10]

3.2.3 *Identification of short-run dynamics based on 'tentative' theory on contemporaneous relations*

The Structural VAR approach to macroeconometric modelling described in the previous chapter aims to provide economic meaning to the estimated shocks and associated impulse responses by suggesting restrictions on the contemporaneous relations between variables based on a 'tentative' economic theory. Perhaps the most frequently used form of restriction imposed on the short-run dynamics of a VAR model of the form in (3.1) is that suggested by Sims (1980). This approach assumes a recursive structure among the variables whereby the first variable in the VAR is assumed to be contemporaneously independent of the other variables, the second is contemporaneously influenced by the first but no other, the third by the first two but not the rest, and so on. It is also assumed that the structural shocks are independent of each other. This identification scheme imposes a triangular structure on A and assumes that $\boldsymbol{\Omega}$ is a diagonal matrix, namely:

$$\mathbf{A} = \begin{pmatrix} 1 & 0 & \dots & 0 \\ a_{21} & 1 & \dots & 0 \\ \dots & \dots & \dots & \dots \\ a_{m1} & a_{m2} & \dots & 1 \end{pmatrix}, \quad \text{and} \quad \boldsymbol{\Omega} = \begin{pmatrix} \omega_{11} & 0 & \dots & 0 \\ 0 & \omega_{22} & \dots & 0 \\ \dots & \dots & \dots & \dots \\ 0 & 0 & \dots & \omega_{mm} \end{pmatrix}. \tag{3.15}$$

[9] This point was illustrated in Nickell (1985), who showed that adjustment costs models can frequently be represented by a simple VECM, depending on the nature of the stochastic process characterising the determination of the target variables.

[10] Pesaran (1991) considers these issues explicitly in the context of a univariate model. The paper describes the order conditions necessary for the identification of the structural parameters and the cross-equation restrictions that can be tested (in either the structural equations or the reduced form) in this case.

The zeros on the top right-hand of A, imposed by the recursiveness, provides $\frac{1}{2}m(m-1)$ restrictions; the 'normalising' unit coefficients on the diagonal of A provide a further m restrictions; and the zero off-diagonals in $\boldsymbol{\Omega}$, imposed by the orthogonality assumption, provide a further $\frac{1}{2}m(m-1)$ restrictions. This provides the m^2 restrictions required in total to exactly identify the structural parameters of (3.1).

In fact, the identifying structure of (3.15) described in Sims (1980) was initially suggested as part of a more mechanical, statistical exercise in which the dynamics of an estimated reduced form system could be illustrated by tracing the impact of specific 'orthogonalised' shocks. Starting from an estimated reduced form VECM of the type given in (3.3), orthogonalised impulses can be derived from the estimated reduced form errors, $\mathbf{v}_t$, and associated estimated variance–covariance matrix, $\boldsymbol{\Sigma}$, using the Choleski decomposition $\mathbf{A}\boldsymbol{\Sigma}\mathbf{A}' = \boldsymbol{\Omega}$ where $\mathbf{A}$ is lower triangular and $\boldsymbol{\Omega}$ is a diagonal matrix. Since the errors $\boldsymbol{\varepsilon}_t = \mathbf{A}\mathbf{v}_t$ are orthogonal by construction, it is straightforward to trace out the dynamic effects on the variables in $\mathbf{z}_t$ of an impulse in one of the elements of $\boldsymbol{\varepsilon}_t$. Sims acknowledged that the choice of Choleski decomposition, and associated orthogonalised shocks, was arbitrary and depended on the ordering of the variables and suggested trying various different Choleski decompositions to characterise the dynamic properties of the system (see Sims (1980, 1981) for example). However, Cooley and Leroy (1985) noted that, despite the apparent atheoretic content of the orthogonalisation, the choice of any Choleski decomposition is equivalent to imposing a clearly defined recursive structure on the contemporaneous relationships across the variables in the system.

There are many applied economists who would find a recursive structure of the sort given in (3.15) no more persuasive than the exclusion restrictions used to distinguish between exogenous and endogenous variables in the early Cowles Commission work and described by Sims as 'incredible'. But there are others who embrace this sort of structure, motivating the restrictions imposed through 'tentative' theory on the timing and sequencing of decisions. The theory is 'tentative' in the sense that it is typically not derived from any form of optimising behaviour on the part of agents or given any explicit microeconomic foundations. Rather, the theory reflects the investigator's *a priori* beliefs on the costs involved in making particular decisions, on the consequent frequency of decisions and on the sequencing of these decisions, based on the investigator's understanding of the institutional background and the decision-making context. The difficulty in translating such beliefs into an identifying structure is that there is a degree of judgement involved and it is difficult to formalise the nature of any disagreements that arise between investigators on such restrictions. The approach also relies to a considerable extent on the frequency with which the main variables in the VAR are observed. For example, the degree of contemporaneous dependence in variables measured at an annual frequency might be large as compared to the case when the frequency of observations is monthly or weekly.[11] The challenge facing this approach is, therefore, to choose an identification scheme that is sufficiently well-grounded in theory and sufficiently loosely defined that the restrictions are relatively uncontentious for the dataset available.

Two further examples of the identification of structural shocks through the application of 'tentative' theory are provided by Blanchard (1989) and Gali (1992). Both papers describe a broadly 'Keynesian' IS-LM aggregate demand and aggregate supply model that places restrictions on $\mathbf{A}$ and $\mathbf{\Omega}$. Blanchard considers a five equation system involving output, unemployment, prices, wages and money explained, in turn, by relationships based on aggregate demand, Okun's (1962) Law, wage-setting behaviour, price-setting behaviour and a money rule. These relationships motivate restrictions on the contemporaneous short-run effects of the structural disturbances. For example, given contemporaneous output, (un)employment is determined solely by productivity shocks in the Okun's Law relationship; given wages and output, price-setters decisions are influenced by (only) price-setting innovations and productivity shocks in the price-setting relationship; and so on. The structural innovations are themselves considered to be independent of each other. Gali's (1992) paper is in a similar vein. Restricting attention to output, interest rates, money and prices, Gali describes a four equation system relating to the IS, LM, money supply rule and Phillips curve relationships. The associated structural innovations are 'spending', 'money demand', 'money supply' and 'supply' shocks. Identifying restrictions considered here include that neither money supply nor money demand shocks have a contemporaneous effect on output, and that neither output nor prices enter the money supply rule.

Both Blanchard and Gali provide time series results, analyses of impulse responses and discussion of US macroeconomic fluctuations on the basis of their identifying schemes, arguing that, broadly speaking, the results confirm the usefulness of the Keynesian modelling framework. However, while the results are interesting and informative, their conclusions are

[11] Even in the case of observations sampled at daily frequencies, the presence of common factors can bring about a substantial degree of correlated behaviour and contemporaneous dependence.

only as reliable as the identifying assumptions on which the analysis is based. The exclusion restrictions imposed are very similar in form to those employed in the traditional Cowles Commission work which have been subject to so much scepticism over the past three decades. Moreover, the systems described by Blanchard and Gali work at a level of abstraction that makes it difficult to relate the economic relationships of their systems to specific decision-making by particular agents. This renders the definition of the relationships, and the associated shocks, almost tautological. For example, output in Blanchard's system depends on demand shocks and productivity shocks only. If productivity shocks could be identified from the remaining supply-side relationships of the system, then there is a one-to-one correspondence between output movements and 'demand shocks'. The denomination of these innovations as 'demand' shocks conveys an economic meaning to them, but a description of these as 'output shocks' seems equally justified. In the absence of a more elaborate theory, it is difficult to envisage which agents take the decision to set output and what information is at their disposal when they do so. Seen in this light, this identifying assumption appears rather vacuous and difficult to justify.

3.2.4 *Measuring the effects of monetary policy*

The use of tentative theory on the contemporaneous relations among variables is perhaps most widely used in the study of monetary policy shocks. Christiano, Eichenbaum and Evans (1999, CEE) provide a very useful review of this literature. In their paper, CEE describe three alternative identifying structures in which variables are grouped into three sets: a set including variables for which the contemporaneous values are known when policy is set; a set of policy instruments; and a set of variables for which the contemporaneous values are observed only after the policy decisions are made. The frequency of the observations on the variables is taken to be monthly and the assumed structure imposes a block recursive structure on the matrix **A**.

In the first identifying structure, (s1), the monetary policy instrument (measured by the federal funds rate) is set taking into account information on the contemporaneous values of output, domestic prices and commodity prices, but considering only lagged values of total reserves, of non-borrowed reserves and of the money supply. In the second identifying scheme, (s2), the instrument is the non-borrowed reserves, and the federal funds rate is included only as one of the variables observed after policy is set. And in the third scheme, (s3), the non-borrowed reserves remains the instrument, but total reserves is switched into the set of contemporaneously observed variables. CEE point out that identifying structures of the sort outlined in (s1) and (s2) are widely used; for example, in papers by Christiano and Eichenbaum (1992a), Christiano *et al.* (1996, 1998), Eichenbaum and Evans (1995), Bernanke and Blinder (1992), Bernanke and Mihov (1998) and Gertler and Gilchrist (1994). But the very fact that CEE include in their review three alternative identification schemes is immediate evidence of the lack of consensus that exists on theories of contemporaneous dependence.

The motivation for the three identifying structures considered in CEE is based on two complementary and interrelated arguments: the first argument is concerned with the information available to decision-makers and the second is concerned with the operational procedures followed by the monetary authorities. On the first of these, the motivation given by CEE for the assumption that policy-makers observe the contemporaneous values of output, domestic prices and commodity prices when setting policy is provided as follows:

> The Fed does have at its disposal monthly data on aggregate employment, industrial output and other indicators of real activity. It also has substantial amounts of information regarding the price level. In our view, the assumption that the Fed sees output and prices when they choose the policy instrument seems at least as plausible as assuming that they don't [CEE, p. 83][12]

CEE recognise the relative frailty of this assumption, acknowledging that quarterly measures of output and prices, namely real GDP and the GDP deflator, are actually only known with a lag. This point is elaborated in Brunner (2000) and Rotemberg and Woodford (1999). Brunner notes that information on most broad measures of time-t economic activity and on time-t domestic prices is simply not available until one month after the time-t monetary policy is set (and is indeed subject to considerable subsequent data revision).[13] Rotemberg and Woodford (1999) make the point that the political process of responding to data takes time even if the data is, in principle, reported concurrently. CEE also make reference to Sims and Zha (1998), for example, in which an entirely different sequencing

[12] The argument is further developed in footnote 64 of CEE where the available indicators of prices and output are listed in a little more detail.

[13] Brunner also makes the point that the information available to policy-makers is almost certainly considerably wider than that represented by the variables included in these VAR analyses and persuasively makes the case for the inclusion of direct measures of market participants' expectations in the VAR as a parsimonious means of including additional relevant information.

is adopted, assuming that only contemporaneous commodity prices and money supply are known to policy-makers when setting interest rates. Moreover, this structure is assumed in the context of a model estimated using quarterly data.

Kim and Roubini (2000) also make use of an identification scheme based on information flows. They note that, while price and activity data is published with (at least) a one month lag, monetary data is available within the month and financial data is available daily. This reasoning is used to motivate an identification scheme that is broadly based on the sequencing of decisions, but which is more complex than the usual block recursive structure.

The motivation for the identifying assumptions considered by CEE, Kim and Roubini and others are also based on the perceived institutional arrangements and operational procedures implemented by the US monetary policy-makers. These provide an explanation for the different treatment of the federal funds rate, total reserves, non-borrowed reserves and money supply under the identification schemes (s1)–(s3). This aspect of the tentative theory underlying the identification of the short-run relations is emphasised in Bernanke and Blinder (1992), Bernanke and Mihov (1998), Strongin (1995) and Gordon and Leeper (1994). The latter paper, for example, focuses attention directly on the actions of the Fed in the federal funds market via open market operations and discount window operations. They argue that, at least in the case of the United States, much work in the area incorrectly associates innovations in monetary policy either with movements in the funds rate or with movements in reserves because it fails to fully specify the underlying behavioural relationships in the federal funds market. They argue that identification of monetary policy requires a fully specified model of the market relationships and, to this end, they argue that the demand for reserves will depend on the federal funds rate, prices and output only, while the Fed's decisions on the fund rate will depend on reserves, long-term interest rates and commodity prices only.[14] Imposing the further recursive assumption that financial and goods markets respond to money market disturbances only with a lag, this identifying structure on the supply and demand for reserves allows the short-run structural parameters of the relations of the federal funds market, and hence monetary policy shocks, to be identified (the latter defined as unexplained movements in the rate-setting equation).

[14] There is also an explicit informational assumption here that the Fed's interest rate decisions are based on money and financial market data released at high frequencies but not based on current innovations in goods market variables which are observed only with a lag.

Gordon and Leeper (1994) make the further important point that many empirical studies use broad monetary aggregates as measures of policy variables, as though the separation of policy behaviour from financial sector behaviour is of only secondary importance (failing to distinguish, for example, between the federal funds rate and the Treasury bill rate). Clearly, when the identification of shocks relies on the fine distinctions of timing in decision-making, it is very likely that monetary policy shocks derived from the federal funds market in which the monetary authorities operate will be distinct from money supply shocks derived from the money markets in which financial institutions operate. The authors demonstrate empirically that this is indeed the case.

The literature on identifying monetary policy shocks has produced some important and innovative contributions. But, as the discussion surrounding CEE makes clear, there is little consensus in the literature on the identifying restrictions motivated by the sequencing of decisions or the information flows faced by decision-makers. And, as the work of Gordon and Leeper illustrates, identifying structures motivated by the operational procedures implemented by the monetary authorities requires very detailed knowledge of the money market and financial markets and is also unlikely to deliver uncontentious restrictions. Both of these points illustrate well the general difficulties involved in the identification of contemporaneous dependencies in macroeconomic models.

3.2.5 *Identification using 'tentative' theory on long-run relations*

An alternative approach to identification is to follow the Structural VAR approach and impose restrictions on the model parameters based on 'tentative' theory relating to the long-run properties of the model. This approach was popularised by Blanchard and Quah (1989) who provide a structural interpretation to the shocks by imposing *a priori* restrictions on the covariance matrix of the structural errors and on the long-run responses of variables to the shocks. This approach has been widely employed, including more recent uses of the approach in Gali (1992), Clarida and Gali (1994), Lastrapes and Selgin (1994, 1995), Bullard and Keating (1995), Astley and Garratt (1996), Crowder *et al.* (1999), Gonzalo and Ng (2001). Blanchard and Quah (1989) identify 'demand' and 'supply' shocks in a bivariate VAR in output growth and unemployment on the usual assumption that the two shocks are contemporaneously orthogonal plus the further assumption that 'demand' shocks have no permanent effect on output whilst 'supply' shocks do. In the moving average representation for output growth, this assumption ensures that the *sum* of the coefficients on the current and lagged observations of the demand shock is equal to zero. Inverting the moving average representation to obtain the (approximate) VAR representation, the restriction translates to the imposition of restrictions involving *all* the reduced form parameters. The implications of the transitory/permanent decomposition of the shocks for the structural parameters varies across the structural equations and are discussed in Pagan and Pesaran (2005). Given that these restrictions relate to the long run, this approach does not rely on the precise timing and sequencing of decisions and is less sensitive to the frequency of the observations of the data.

The two-variable example considered by Blanchard and Quah is a rather special case. In more general VAR models, where there are $m-r$ unit roots and r cointegrating relations, the assumption that there are r transitory structural shocks and $m-r$ permanent structural shocks, orthogonal to each other, is equivalent to assuming that $m-r$ of the variables evolve independently of the long-run relations that exist between the variables. This imposes $(m-r)\times r$ restrictions on the matrix of adjustment coefficients, $\widetilde{\boldsymbol{\alpha}}$, in the structural VECM of (3.1).[15] Even if the cointegrating vector $\boldsymbol{\beta}$ is identified, the Blanchard and Quah assumptions on the permanent/transitory nature and orthogonality of the shocks provide only $(m-r)r+\frac{1}{2}(m+1)m$ restrictions (including m normalisation restrictions), fewer than the m^2 restrictions required to fully identify the shocks to the system. The assumption that shocks can be split into those that are permanent and those that are transitory will provide sufficient restrictions to identify the shocks only in the special case where $m=2$ and $r=1$; of course, this is the case in the bivariate model used by Blanchard and Quah (1989) where there is one transitory (demand) shock and one permanent (supply) shock.[16] But generally, further restrictions are required. For example, a further $\frac{1}{2}(m-r)(m-r-1)+\frac{1}{2}(r-1)r$ restrictions, giving m^2 in total, would be provided by using Sims' recursive identification approach applied to the two types of shock (permanent and temporary) separately. This approach is described in Gonzalo and Ng (2001). But such an identification strategy is subject to the same criticisms already levelled against the recursive schemes discussed above.

[15] See Pagan and Pesaran (2005) for details.

[16] Blanchard and Quah trivially identify $\boldsymbol{\beta}$ by assuming unemployment (u) is stationary and output (y) is $I(1)$. Including u as the first variable in their bivariate VAR identifies $\boldsymbol{\beta}$ as $(1,0)$ since u is $I(0)$ by assumption.

3.3 National macroeconomic modelling in a global context

The modelling strategy reviewed in Section 3.1.3 treats all the core variables included in the VAR symmetrically and no distinction has been drawn between endogenous and exogenous variables. However, this modelling strategy, and the associated econometric methods, is not efficient in the case of small open economies, or if one wishes to develop satellite models that are influenced by the core variables but they themselves have little feedback into the core variables (to be made precise below). In the context of most macroeconometric modelling exercises, a natural example of variables that we might choose to treat as exogenous to the domestic economy is the international price of oil which is largely set outside the UK economy.

For most small open economies whose decisions do not significantly influence the rest of the world, including the UK, one might consider macroeconomic events abroad to be exogenously determined. Having said this, however, there may be occasions when movements in macroeconomic variables of a small economy like the UK provide important contemporaneous indicators of movements in world-wide economic variables. For example, news on the threat of war is likely to impact on demand and output across all of the world's economies. In these circumstances, treating domestic output as though it can have no power for explaining contemporaneous movements in foreign output will incorrectly omit these important feedbacks from unobserved external events. Hence, the decision on how to treat a foreign variable can involve a judgement between, on the one hand, treating the variable as exogenous to capture the (obvious) characteristic that foreigners do not look to the domestic variable in their decision-making and, on the other hand, the less direct gain of capturing influences from outside the model which impact jointly and contemporaneously on domestic and foreign variables.

This judgement needs to take into account the statistical implications of the modelling decision. These will typically encourage the treatment of variables as endogenous, as the treatment of an exogenous variable as endogenous involves a loss of efficiency in estimation, which is usually relatively harmless. In contrast, the treatment of an endogenous variable as exogenous will introduce biases in the estimation which can be considerably more damaging. In what follows we consider an intermediate case where the foreign $I(1)$ variables are treated as weakly exogenous, in the sense that they affect the domestic variables contemporaneously (and could be affected by lagged changes of domestic and foreign variables) but are not affected by disequilibria in the domestic economy. In other words, in error correcting regressions of changes in foreign variables none of the lagged error correction terms associated with the domestic economy should be statistically significant. Note that this is not the same as the notion of 'Granger Causality' under which none of the domestic variables are allowed to enter the model for the foreign variables. A weakly exogenous $I(1)$ variable is also referred to as 'long-run' forcing by Granger and Lin (1995).

3.3.1 *VARX models: VAR models with weakly exogenous variables*

To elaborate on the treatment of endogenous and exogenous variables in our modelling framework, denote the m_y variables in $\mathbf{z}_t$ that are endogenously determined by $\mathbf{y}_t$, and denote the m_x variables that are exogenously determined by $\mathbf{x}_t$. In this case, $\mathbf{z}_t = (\mathbf{y}'_t, \mathbf{x}'_t)'$, and the structural model of (3.1) can be rewritten as

$$\begin{pmatrix} \mathbf{A}_{yy} & \mathbf{A}_{yx} \\ 0 & \mathbf{A}_{xx} \end{pmatrix} \begin{pmatrix} \Delta \mathbf{y}_t \\ \Delta \mathbf{x}_t \end{pmatrix} = \tilde{\mathbf{a}} + \tilde{\mathbf{b}}t - \tilde{\mathbf{\Pi}} \begin{pmatrix} \mathbf{y}_{t-1} \\ \mathbf{x}_{t-1} \end{pmatrix} + \sum_{i=1}^{p-1} \tilde{\mathbf{\Gamma}}_i \begin{pmatrix} \Delta \mathbf{y}_{t-i} \\ \Delta \mathbf{x}_{t-i} \end{pmatrix} + \begin{pmatrix} \boldsymbol{\varepsilon}_{yt} \\ \boldsymbol{\varepsilon}_{xt} \end{pmatrix}, \quad (3.16)$$

where

$$\tilde{\mathbf{\Pi}} = \begin{pmatrix} \underset{(m_y \times m)}{\tilde{\mathbf{\Pi}}_y} \\ \underset{(m_x \times m)}{0} \end{pmatrix} = \begin{pmatrix} \underset{(m_y \times r)}{\tilde{\boldsymbol{\alpha}}_y} \\ \underset{(m_x \times r)}{0} \end{pmatrix} \underset{(r \times m)}{\boldsymbol{\beta}'} .$$

The first m_y equations in the system in (3.16) provide the decision-rules explaining the determination of the endogenous variables and, hence, the disturbances $\boldsymbol{\varepsilon}_{yt}$ continue to have a clear structural interpretation. Non-zero values of $\mathbf{A}_{yy}$ and $\mathbf{A}_{yx}$ allow for contemporaneous influences on the variables in $\mathbf{y}_t$ from the other variables in $\mathbf{y}_t$ and from the variables in $\mathbf{x}_t$. Non-zero values of $\tilde{\mathbf{\Pi}}_y$ allow for feedback from long-run reduced form disturbances, $\boldsymbol{\xi}_t$. These are linear combinations of variables which may be endogenously or exogenously determined; *i.e.* we continue to define $\boldsymbol{\xi}_t = \boldsymbol{\beta}'\mathbf{z}_{t-1}$. Given the exogeneity of the variables in $\mathbf{x}_t$ and given that they continue to exert an influence on the long-run outcomes of $\mathbf{y}_t$ via $\boldsymbol{\xi}_t$, the $\mathbf{x}_t$ are often termed 'long-run forcing' variables.

The remaining m_x equations in (3.16) characterise the determination of the exogenously determined variables. A zero matrix in the lower triangle of $\mathbf{A}$ shows that there are no direct contemporaneous feedbacks from the variables in $\mathbf{y}_t$ to those in $\mathbf{x}_t$, and the $m_x \times m$ matrix of zeros in $\widetilde{\mathbf{\Pi}}$ shows that there are no feedbacks from the long-run reduced form disturbances, $\boldsymbol{\xi}_t$, to $\mathbf{x}_t$ either. The structural disturbances, $\boldsymbol{\varepsilon}_{xt}$, have a clear economic meaning in the sense that they relate to unanticipated movements in the exogenous variables but, given that these variables are considered to be determined outside the system under consideration, they do not have the same behavioural content as the $\boldsymbol{\varepsilon}_{yt}$ structural shocks.

Strict exogeneity in the $\mathbf{x}_t$ requires the $\boldsymbol{\varepsilon}_{xt}$ shocks to be uncorrelated with the $\boldsymbol{\varepsilon}_{yt}$ shocks. In the case where they are not, the asymptotically innocuous assumption that $(\boldsymbol{\varepsilon}_{yt}, \boldsymbol{\varepsilon}_{xt})$ are jointly normally distributed provides the linear relationship:

$$\boldsymbol{\varepsilon}_{yt} = \mathbf{\Omega}_{yx}\mathbf{\Omega}_{xx}^{-1}\boldsymbol{\varepsilon}_{xt} + \boldsymbol{\eta}_{yt},$$

where the structural errors have variance covariance matrix

$$\mathbf{\Omega} = \begin{pmatrix} \mathbf{\Omega}_{yy} & \mathbf{\Omega}_{yx} \\ \mathbf{\Omega}_{xy} & \mathbf{\Omega}_{xx} \end{pmatrix}$$

and, by construction, $\boldsymbol{\varepsilon}_{xt}$ and $\boldsymbol{\eta}_{yt}$ are uncorrelated. The first m_y equations of (3.16) can then be rewritten as

$$\mathbf{A}_{yy}\Delta\mathbf{y}_t + \mathbf{A}_{yx}^{*}\Delta\mathbf{x}_t = \widetilde{\mathbf{a}}_y^{*} + \widetilde{\mathbf{b}}_y^{*}t - \widetilde{\mathbf{\Pi}}_y\mathbf{z}_{t-1} + \sum_{i=1}^{p-1}\widetilde{\mathbf{\Gamma}}_{yi}^{*}\Delta\mathbf{z}_{t-i} + \boldsymbol{\eta}_{yt}, \tag{3.17}$$

where $\widetilde{\mathbf{a}}_y^{*} = \widetilde{\mathbf{a}}_y - \mathbf{\Omega}_{yx}\mathbf{\Omega}_{xx}^{-1}\widetilde{\mathbf{a}}_x$, $\widetilde{\mathbf{b}}_y^{*} = \widetilde{\mathbf{b}}_y - \mathbf{\Omega}_{yx}\mathbf{\Omega}_{xx}^{-1}\widetilde{\mathbf{b}}_x$, $\widetilde{\mathbf{\Gamma}}_{yi}^{*} = \widetilde{\mathbf{\Gamma}}_{yi} - \mathbf{\Omega}_{yx}\mathbf{\Omega}_{xx}^{-1}\widetilde{\mathbf{\Gamma}}_{xi}$, and $\mathbf{A}_{yx}^{*} = \mathbf{A}_{yx} - \mathbf{\Omega}_{yx}\mathbf{\Omega}_{xx}^{-1}\mathbf{A}_{xx}$ and where we have used the decomposition, $\widetilde{\mathbf{a}} = \left(\widetilde{\mathbf{a}}_y', \widetilde{\mathbf{a}}_x'\right)'$, $\widetilde{\mathbf{b}} = \left(\widetilde{\mathbf{b}}_y', \widetilde{\mathbf{b}}_x'\right)'$ and $\widetilde{\mathbf{\Gamma}}_{yi} = \left(\widetilde{\mathbf{\Gamma}}_{yi}', \widetilde{\mathbf{\Gamma}}_{xi}'\right)'$. This formulation of the structural equations explaining $\mathbf{y}_t$ allows for the indirect effects of changes in $\mathbf{x}_t$ on $\mathbf{y}_t$, experienced through the contemporaneous dependence between the structural shocks, as well as the direct effects captured through the elements of $\mathbf{A}$.

The above representation decomposes the modelling task into the specification of a 'conditional model' for $\Delta\mathbf{y}_t$ given by (3.17), and a 'marginal model' for $\Delta\mathbf{x}_t$ which under weak exogeneity can be written more generally as

$$\mathbf{A}_{xx}\Delta\mathbf{x}_t = \widetilde{\mathbf{a}}_x + \widetilde{\mathbf{b}}_x t - \mathbf{\Pi}_{xx}\mathbf{x}_{t-1} + \sum_{i=1}^{p-1}\widetilde{\mathbf{\Gamma}}_{xi}\Delta\mathbf{z}_{t-i} + \boldsymbol{\varepsilon}_{xt}. \tag{3.18}$$

Note the absence of error correction terms from the conditional model in the marginal model. In the case where $\mathbf{x}_t$'s are $I(1)$ and not cointegrated amongst themselves we have the further restrictions, $\mathbf{\Pi}_{xx} = \mathbf{0}$. In this set-up $\mathbf{x}_t$ is said to be long-run forcing for the error correcting model in $\Delta\, \mathbf{y}_t$.

The combined model of the structural equations explaining $\Delta\mathbf{y}_t$ in (3.17) and the structural equations explaining $\Delta\mathbf{x}_t$ in (3.18) can now be written as:

$$\mathbf{A}^*\Delta\mathbf{z}_t = \widetilde{\mathbf{a}}^* + \widetilde{\mathbf{b}}^* t - \widetilde{\mathbf{\Pi}}\mathbf{z}_{t-1} + \sum_{i=1}^{p-1} \widetilde{\mathbf{\Gamma}}_i^* \Delta\mathbf{z}_{t-i} + \boldsymbol{\varepsilon}_t^*, \tag{3.19}$$

where

$$\mathbf{A}^* = \begin{pmatrix} \mathbf{A}_{yy} & \mathbf{A}_{yx}^* \\ 0 & \mathbf{A}_{xx} \end{pmatrix}, \quad \widetilde{\mathbf{\Pi}} = \begin{pmatrix} \mathbf{\Pi}_{yy} & \mathbf{\Pi}_{yx} \\ 0 & \mathbf{\Pi}_{xx} \end{pmatrix} \quad \widetilde{\mathbf{a}}^* = \begin{pmatrix} \widetilde{\mathbf{a}}_y^* \\ \widetilde{\mathbf{a}}_x \end{pmatrix},$$

$$\widetilde{\mathbf{b}}^* = \begin{pmatrix} \widetilde{\mathbf{b}}_y^* \\ \widetilde{\mathbf{b}}_x \end{pmatrix}, \quad \widetilde{\mathbf{\Gamma}}_i^* = \begin{pmatrix} \widetilde{\mathbf{\Gamma}}_{yi}^* \\ \widetilde{\mathbf{\Gamma}}_{xi} \end{pmatrix} \text{ and } \quad \boldsymbol{\varepsilon}_t^* = \begin{pmatrix} \boldsymbol{\eta}_{yt} \\ \boldsymbol{\varepsilon}_{xt} \end{pmatrix}.$$

The associated reduced form system is readily obtained, following the arguments surrounding (3.1) and (3.3) but using $\mathbf{A}^*$ in place of $\mathbf{A}$. Estimation of the reduced form system can proceed by the maximum likelihood (ML) method, taking account of the long-run restrictions implied by the economic theory on the elements in $\widetilde{\mathbf{\Pi}}$, as described in Chapter 6; see Pesaran and Shin (2002) and Pesaran, Shin and Smith (2000) for further details. Identification of the structural parameters of (3.19), and the structural errors, requires quite separate identifying restrictions on the short-run dynamics of the sort discussed in the subsections above. These restrictions will clearly need to take account of the structure incorporated into (3.19) to reflect the exogeneity of the $\mathbf{x}_t$ but, otherwise, the modelling framework is unaffected.

3.3.2 *Developing satellite or sectoral models*

The structural modelling strategy advanced here can also be adapted to account for sectoral effects. This can be done by linking the national macroeconomic models to other 'sectoral' models assuming a block recursive structure. The identifying structure imposed on the system assumes that the variables of the sectoral models are influenced by the variables of the national macroeconomic model, but do not exert a corresponding influence on the variables of the national model. Such a set-up would allow analysis to focus on issues of particular interest in the labour market, international trade, or particular sectors or regions in the national economy.

To illustrate the idea, consider a set of sectoral variables, $\mathbf{w}_t$, which are influenced by the variables in the national model, $\mathbf{z}_t$, but have no feedback to the 'core' macroempirical variables. As above, the elements of $\mathbf{z}_t$ can themselves be distinguished according to whether they are endogenously determined within the national model, $\mathbf{y}_t$, or determined exogenously, $\mathbf{x}_t$. For expositional purposes, assume that a simple first-order model is appropriate and that there are only contemporaneous interactions between the different types of variables. To broaden the possible relevance of the model, assume also that anticipated and unanticipated values of the explanatory variables can have different effects. The structure is then

$$\begin{aligned}
\mathbf{x}_t &= \mathbf{D}_1\mathbf{x}_{t-1} + \mathbf{u}_{1t}, \\
\mathbf{y}_t &= \mathbf{F}_1\mathbf{y}_{t-1} + \mathbf{F}_2\mathbf{x}_t + \mathbf{F}_3\left[\mathbf{x}_t - E_{t-1}(\mathbf{x}_t)\right] + \mathbf{u}_{2t}, \\
\mathbf{w}_t &= \mathbf{G}_1\mathbf{w}_{t-1} + \mathbf{G}_2\mathbf{y}_t + \mathbf{G}_3\left[\mathbf{y}_t - E_{t-1}(\mathbf{y}_t)\right] \\
&\quad + \mathbf{G}_4\mathbf{x}_t + \mathbf{G}_5\left[\mathbf{x}_t - E_{t-1}(\mathbf{x}_t)\right] + \mathbf{u}_{3t}.
\end{aligned}$$

Solving for the terms involving expectations, and stacking the relationships in vector form, we have

$$\begin{pmatrix} \mathbf{I} & \mathbf{0} & \mathbf{0} \\ -(\mathbf{F}_2+\mathbf{F}_3) & \mathbf{I} & \mathbf{0} \\ -(\mathbf{G}_4+\mathbf{G}_5) & -(\mathbf{G}_2+\mathbf{G}_3) & \mathbf{I} \end{pmatrix} \begin{pmatrix} \mathbf{x}_t \\ \mathbf{y}_t \\ \mathbf{w}_t \end{pmatrix}$$

$$= \begin{pmatrix} \mathbf{D}_1 & \mathbf{0} & \mathbf{0} \\ -\mathbf{F}_3\mathbf{D}_1 & \mathbf{F}_1 & \mathbf{0} \\ -(\mathbf{G}_3\mathbf{F}_2\mathbf{D}_1+\mathbf{G}_5\mathbf{D}_1) & -\mathbf{G}_3\mathbf{F}_1 & \mathbf{G}_1 \end{pmatrix} \begin{pmatrix} \mathbf{x}_{t-1} \\ \mathbf{y}_{t-1} \\ \mathbf{w}_{t-1} \end{pmatrix} + \begin{pmatrix} \mathbf{u}_{1t} \\ \mathbf{u}_{2t} \\ \mathbf{u}_{3t} \end{pmatrix}. \tag{3.20}$$

The structure of the model is block triangular, as is immediately apparent from the matrix premultiplying the vector of variables on the LHS of (3.20). There is clearly a causal structure from $\mathbf{x}_t$ to $\mathbf{y}_t$; and from $\mathbf{x}_t$ and $\mathbf{y}_t$ to $\mathbf{w}_t$. If we assume that $E(\mathbf{u}_{it}\mathbf{u}_{jt}) = \mathbf{0}$, for $i \neq j$, then the model is block recursive. This structure has the advantage that the analysis of the variables in $\mathbf{z}_t = (\mathbf{x}_t', \mathbf{y}_t')'$ can be carried out without reference to those in $\mathbf{w}_t$, while the variables in $\mathbf{w}_t$ can be studied by means of 'sectoral models', estimated independently of the model for $\mathbf{z}_t$ and taking values of $\mathbf{x}_t$, $\mathbf{y}_t$, $\mathbf{u}_{1t}$ and $\mathbf{u}_{2t}$ as given.

The development of satellite or sectoral models opens up many opportunities for modelling decision-making in the real world. The number of parameters that are estimated in a VAR could confine the approach to the analysis of a relatively small number of variables. This would be a potentially significant limitation of the modelling approach. Further, longer time series do not necessarily resolve the problem because the structural stability of the model might be called into question with very long spans of data. The assumptions described above provide a means of circumventing these problems so long as the block recursive structure of (3.20) corresponds to the decision-making context.

The purpose of this chapter has been to set out a canonical dynamic structural model which demonstrates the distinction between short-run and long-run effects in a model and to highlight the important role of economic theory in identifying these respective effects. Economic theory was shown to be central to the identification of long-run relations and of economically meaningful shocks, and we argued that some of the identifying assumptions used in the literature, especially those relating to the short run and based on the sequencing of decisions or release of data, seem to be relatively frail. On the other hand, our approach to macroeconometric modelling is a pragmatic one; we recognise that it will never be possible to model the economy in its entirety and all models are imperfect and potentially contentious, therefore. For this reason, we emphasise the criterion of model relevance, urging modellers to construct models that are useful for policy analysis and decision-making. We believe our approach to modelling will allow the modeller to capture the properties of the data well while informing the model with economic theory. Our emphasis is on the economic theory of the long run, based on the strength of conviction with which we believe theory as it relates to the long run and the short run, but our modelling approach can readily accommodate the restrictions suggested by theories of the short run as well as the long run. In deciding on the theory to be embedded within the model, the model should consider what is the *minimal structure required for its purpose*. This will include a clear view on the part of the modeller of what can be taken as exogenous and what needs to be modelled endogenously. Hence, for the purposes of monetary or macroeconomic decisions in the UK, for example, it seems entirely reasonable that the world economy might be taken as long-run forcing (weakly exogenous) to the core macroeconomic model of the UK, and that the variables of the core macromodel might be taken as long-run forcing in particular sectors of the economy. The modelling choice on what constitutes the minimal structure is, of course, itself informed by economic theory and, in what follows, we describe in more detail particular models of the long run, in Chapter 4, and of the short run, in Chapter 5, that will inform our modelling choices as they relate to the UK macroeconomy.

3.4 Global vector autoregressive (GVAR) models

The discussion so far has considered the modelling of a single national economy, possibly containing exogenous variables to take into account the effects of variables determined outside the national economy. In many instances, however, one might be interested to model more explicitly the source of the foreign influences on the domestic economy and the contributions of the national economy to the broad global changes that are, in turn, influencing the other economies of the world. One possible example of such an analysis is a model of the UK economy and its interactions with the economies in the euro area. Such an analysis might be used to establish the impact of shocks to the euro area economies on the UK, and *vice versa*, to quantify the likely effects of the UK's entry into the monetary union. Pesaran, Smith and Smith (2005) provide such an exercise. Or, given the increasing globalisation of world financial markets, a second application could be the analysis of the effect of shocks to financial markets on business cycles both within and across economies.

These analyses require the development of a 'global' modelling framework within which the national model can be incorporated, along with equivalent models of the other economies in the rest of the world. The straight application of the modelling framework outlined in Section 3.1.3 is an attractive approach, but is almost certainly constrained by computational limitations. Hence, while it is possible in principle to extend the modelling strategy to cover the same m variables in each of, say, $N+1$ separate economies, in practice this would involve the estimation of a cointegrated VAR involving around $mp(N+1)$ parameters in each equation of the model to be estimated (where p is the order of the VAR). If there are five variables modelled in each economy, 20 economies and a lag-order of 2 is used, this generates at least 210 parameters to be estimated in each equation, which is clearly infeasible for the data series that are available.

The issue of how to overcome this problem is pursued in Pesaran, Schuermann and Weiner (2004, PSW), with further development in Dees, di Mauro, Pesaran and Smith (2005, DdPS), in which a Global VAR (GVAR) model is developed to investigate global interactions and the analysis of regional shocks on the world economy in general. The problem of modelling many economies in a coherent and consistent manner is solved through the careful construction of separate measures of 'foreign' variables for use in each of the separate national models. The country-specific foreign variables are then treated as weakly exogenous (in the sense discussed above) when estimating each of the country models. Specifically, individual country (or region) VEC models are estimated using a range of domestic macroeconomic variables plus corresponding foreign variables constructed from other economies' data using weights to match the international trade pattern of the country under consideration. The individual country models are then combined in a consistent and cohesive manner to generate forecasts for *all* the variables in the world economy simultaneously.

To illustrate these ideas in a little more detail, assume that there are $N+1$ economies in the world, indexed by $i = 0, 1, \ldots, N$, and denote the country-specific variables by the $m \times 1$ vector $\mathbf{y}_{it}$ and the associated country-specific foreign variables by $\mathbf{y}^*_{it}$, then a first-order country-specific model can be written[17]

$$\mathbf{y}_{it} = \mathbf{a}_{i0} + \mathbf{\Phi}_i \mathbf{y}_{i,t-1} + \mathbf{\Lambda}_{i0}\mathbf{y}^*_{it} + \mathbf{\Lambda}_{i1}\mathbf{y}^*_{i,t-1} + \mathbf{u}_{it}, \tag{3.21}$$

$$\mathbf{y}^*_{it} = \sum_{j=0}^{N} w_{ij}\mathbf{y}_{jt}, \tag{3.22}$$

where $w_{ij} \geq 0$ are the weights attached to the foreign variables such that $\sum_{j=0}^{N} w_{ij} = 1$, and $w_{ii} = 0$ for all i. These weights could be based on trade shares, for example (*i.e.* the share of country j in the total trade of country i). The country-specific errors $\mathbf{u}_{it}$ are assumed to be serially uncorrelated with mean zero and a non-singular covariance matrix $\mathbf{\Omega}_{ii}$. For the purpose of estimation and inference, it is worth noting that the model in (3.21) can be readily recast as a cointegrating VARX of the form that we have considered above. Moreover, the country-specific foreign variables $\mathbf{y}^*_{it}$ can be treated as weakly exogenous for most countries so this construction will introduce no extra difficulties in terms of the econometric estimation.[18]

Although the model is estimated on a country by country basis, the shocks are allowed to be weakly correlated across countries. In particular,

[17] The number of variables in the different country models need not be the same. Here we assume all country models are based on the same set of variables to simplify the exposition.

[18] The econometric issues involved are explored in detail in Pesaran (2004b).

it is assumed that

$$E\left(\mathbf{u}_{it}\mathbf{u}'_{jt}\right) = \boldsymbol{\Omega}_{ij} \text{ for } t = t',$$
$$= 0 \text{ for } t \neq t'.$$

Global interactions take place through three distinct, but interrelated channels:

1. Direct dependence of $\mathbf{y}_{it}$ on $\mathbf{y}^*_{it}$ and its lagged values.
2. Dependence of the region-specific variables on common global exogenous variables such as oil prices.
3. Non-zero contemporaneous dependence of shocks in region i on the shocks in region j, measured via the cross-country covariances, $\boldsymbol{\Omega}_{ij}$.

The individual models are estimated allowing for unit roots and cointegration assuming that region-specific foreign variables are weakly exogenous, with the exception of the model for the US economy which is treated as a closed economy model. The US model is linked to the outside world through exchange rates themselves being determined in rest of the region-specific models. While models of the form in equation (3.21) are relatively standard, PSW show that the careful construction of the global variables as weighted averages of the other regional variables leads to a simultaneous system of regional equations that may be solved to form a global system. They also provide theoretical arguments as well as empirical evidence in support of the weak exogeneity assumption that allows the region-specific models to be estimated consistently.

To obtain the global VAR (GVAR) model, define the $(m+m^*)\times 1$ vector as

$$\mathbf{z}_{it} = \begin{pmatrix} \mathbf{y}_{it} \\ \mathbf{y}^*_{it} \end{pmatrix}$$

and rewrite (3.21) as

$$\mathbf{A}_i\mathbf{z}_{it} = \mathbf{a}_{i0} + \mathbf{B}_i\mathbf{z}_{i,t-1} + \mathbf{u}_{it}, \tag{3.23}$$

where $\mathbf{A}_i = (\mathbf{I}_m, -\boldsymbol{\Lambda}_{i0})$ and $\mathbf{B}_i = (\boldsymbol{\Phi}_i, \boldsymbol{\Lambda}_{i1})$. Collecting all the country-specific variables together in a $(N+1)\,m \times 1$ vector $\mathbf{y}_t = (\mathbf{y}'_{0t}, \mathbf{y}'_{1t}, \mathbf{y}'_{2t}, \ldots, \mathbf{y}'_{Nt})'$, it is easily seen that the country-specific variables can all be written in terms of $\mathbf{y}_t$:

$$\mathbf{z}_{it} = \mathbf{W}_i\mathbf{y}_t, \qquad i = 0, 1, \ldots, N, \tag{3.24}$$

where $\mathbf{W}_i$ is a matrix of known weights such that

$$\begin{pmatrix} \mathbf{y}_{it} \\ \mathbf{y}_{it}^{*} \end{pmatrix} = \mathbf{W}_i \mathbf{y}_t.$$

For example, for country $i = 0$ we have

$$\mathbf{W}_0 = \begin{pmatrix} \mathbf{I}_m & \mathbf{0} & \mathbf{0} & \cdots & \mathbf{0} \\ \mathbf{0} & w_{01}\mathbf{I}_m & w_{02}\mathbf{I}_m & \cdots & w_{0N}\mathbf{I}_m \end{pmatrix},$$

where $w_{01} + w_{02} + ... + w_{0N} = 1$. Using (3.24) in (3.23), we have

$$\mathbf{A}_i \mathbf{W}_i \mathbf{y}_t = \mathbf{a}_{i0} + \mathbf{B}_i \mathbf{W}_i \mathbf{y}_{t-1} + \mathbf{u}_{it} \tag{3.25}$$

and stacking these equations yields the model

$$\mathbf{G}\mathbf{y}_t = \mathbf{a}_0 + \mathbf{H}\mathbf{y}_{t-1} + \mathbf{u}_t, \tag{3.26}$$

where

$$\mathbf{a}_0 = \begin{pmatrix} \mathbf{a}_{00} \\ \mathbf{a}_{10} \\ \vdots \\ \mathbf{a}_{N0} \end{pmatrix}, \ \mathbf{u}_t = \begin{pmatrix} \mathbf{u}_{0t} \\ \mathbf{u}_{1t} \\ \vdots \\ \mathbf{u}_{Nt} \end{pmatrix}, \ \mathbf{G} = \begin{pmatrix} \mathbf{A}_0 \mathbf{W}_0 \\ \mathbf{A}_1 \mathbf{W}_1 \\ \vdots \\ \mathbf{A}_N \mathbf{W}_N \end{pmatrix}, \ \mathbf{H} = \begin{pmatrix} \mathbf{B}_0 \mathbf{W}_0 \\ \mathbf{B}_1 \mathbf{W}_1 \\ \vdots \\ \mathbf{B}_N \mathbf{W}_N \end{pmatrix}.$$

Finally, the GVAR model simplifies to a large dimensional VAR model

$$\mathbf{y}_t = \mathbf{G}^{-1}\mathbf{a}_0 + \mathbf{G}^{-1}\mathbf{H}\mathbf{y}_{t-1} + \mathbf{G}^{-1}\mathbf{u}_t. \tag{3.27}$$

Hence, having estimated the separate national models in the form of (3.21), the global model in (3.27) can be solved recursively forward to obtain future values of all the endogenous variables in the global model, $\mathbf{y}_t$, for forecasting multi-step ahead to investigate the dynamic response of the global economy to shocks and in the analysis of international interactions.

The GVAR model allows for cross-country as well as inter-country cointegration. For example, within each country model one could have the Fisher parity that relates domestic nominal short term interest rate to the domestic inflation rate, as well as relating domestic prices and output to their foreign counter parts and exchange rates. As shown in DdPS, the GVAR can also be derived from global factor models where there might be one or more unobserved common factors with differential effects across countries. Finally, it is worth noting that cointegration properties of the individual country models are preserved in the GVAR model, and in general mean-reverting features of the individual economies carry over to the world economy.

4

An economic theory of the long run

As was noted in Chapter 2, there are various theoretical approaches to the derivation of the long-run, steady-state relations of a macroeconometric model. However, we have argued that many of the approaches yield very similar results as far as the long-run relations are concerned and that there is a degree of consensus on these long-run properties across macroeconomic models. In this chapter, we outline the theoretical basis of the long-run relations to be considered for the modelling of a small open economy such as the UK. The analysis emphasises stock-flow equilibria and arbitrage conditions, appropriately modified to allow for the risks associated with market uncertainties. The arbitrage conditions provide intertemporal links between prices, interest rates and asset returns in the economy as a whole. The approach is distinct from the intertemporal optimisation approach underlying the DSGE models, but it is closely related and yields similar results on the long-run relations.

The minimal structure required of any model of the macroeconomy must accommodate a description of the production technology, the role of market forces and a characterisation of the institutional set-up (including financial institutions and the role of money, for example). The model described in this chapter is based on three sectors (namely the private, government and foreign sectors) and, to provide the required minimal economic structure, in what follows we begin with a description of output determination and the technological diffusion process, comment on the important arbitrage conditions arising from market forces, and note the implications of institutional solvency requirements for the long-run relationships in the macroeconomy.

4.1 Production technology and output determination

We assume that, in the long run, aggregate output is determined according to the following constant returns to scale production function in labour (denoted by N_t) and capital stock (denoted by K_t):

$$\frac{\tilde{Y}_t}{P_t} = F(K_t, A_t N_t) = A_t N_t F\left(\frac{K_t}{A_t N_t}, 1\right), \tag{4.1}$$

where $\tilde{Y}_t$ is gross domestic product measured in pounds sterling (with nominal magnitudes denoted with a '$\sim$' throughout), P_t, is a general price index, $\tilde{Y}_t/P_t$ is real aggregate output, and A_t stands for an index of labour-augmenting technological progress, assumed to be composed of a deterministic component, $a_0 + g\,t$, and a stochastic mean-zero component, u_{at} :

$$\ln(A_t) = a_0 + g\,t + u_{at}. \tag{4.2}$$

The process generating u_{at} is likely to be quite complex and there is little direct evidence on its evolution. But a few studies that have used patent data or R&D expenditures to directly analyse the behaviour of u_{at} over the course of the business cycle generally find highly persistent effects of technological disturbances on output (discussed in Fabiani (1996) and the references cited therein). The indirect evidence on u_{at}, obtained from empirical analysis of aggregate output, also corroborates this finding and generally speaking does not reject the hypothesis that u_{at} contains a unit root. (See, for example, Nelson and Plosser (1982) and, for the UK, Mills (1991).)

We further assume that the fraction of the population which is employed at time t, $\lambda_t = N_t/POP_t$, is a stationary process such that

$$N_t = \lambda\, POP_t \exp(\eta_{nt}), \tag{4.3}$$

where POP_t is population at the end of period t and η_{nt} represents a stationary, mean-zero process capturing the cyclical fluctuations of the unemployment rate around its steady-state value, $1 - \lambda$. The presence of, for example, real and nominal wage and price rigidities could generate deviations from the equilibrium, and these might be large and prolonged. However, these influences are captured by the presence of the η_{nt}, and ultimately it is assumed that the long-run equilibrium unemployment rate is re-established. The assumption that the steady-state unemployment rate is constant is by no means innocuous: it requires labour supply to be inelastic with respect to the real wage in the long run, and abstracts from the possibility that there exist factors which might cause permanent changes in labour supply decisions.[1] The first requirement might not be too unrealistic in the very long run, given the absence of a long-term trend increase in unemployment corresponding to the unremitting rise in real wages (when measured over decades rather than years). However, many commentators would point to changes in labour market conditions which persist and which might reasonably be expected to influence the equilibrium unemployment rate; these might include shocks to incentives due to changes in the incidence of direct and indirect taxation; changes in the size and coverage of benefit payments; changes in the extent of union influence and other institutional changes in wage-bargaining arrangements; and so on. Our approach can be justified on the grounds that these institutional changes are by their nature constrained not to change continually and without bounds (so that they can be subsumed into the η_{nt}) or that their effects are small compared to the consequences of technical progress which dominates output determination.[2]

Under the above assumptions and using the relations (4.1), (4.2) and (4.3) it now readily follows that

$$y_t = a_0 + \ln(\lambda) + g\,t + \ln(f(\kappa_t)) + u_{at} + \eta_{nt}, \tag{4.4}$$

where $y_t = \ln[\tilde{Y}_t/(POP_t \times P_t)]$ is the logarithm of real per capita output, $\kappa_t = K_t/A_tN_t$ is the capital stock per effective labour unit, and $f(\kappa_t) = F(\kappa_t, 1)$ is a well-behaved function in the sense that it satisfies the Inada conditions. See, for example, Barro and Sala-i-Martin (1995, p. 16). Assuming the aggregate saving rate is monotonic in κ_t and that certain other mild regularity conditions hold, Binder and Pesaran (1999) show that, irrespective of whether the process generating u_{at} is stationary or contains a unit root, κ_t converges to a steady-state probability distribution with $\kappa_t \to \kappa_\infty$, where κ_∞ is a time-invariant random variable with a non-degenerate probability distribution function. Hence, in the long run the evolution of per capita output will be largely determined by technological process, with $E[\Delta \ln(y_t)] = g$. Also whether y_t contains a unit root crucially depends on whether there is a unit root in the process generating technological progress.[3]

[1] See Nickell (1990) for a review of the literature on unemployment determination.

[2] Notice that the assumption that the unemployment rate is stationary in effect rules out long-run hysteresis effects in the unemployment process.

[3] See Lee *et al.* (1997, 1998) and Pesaran (2004a) for further discussion of the time series properties of output series derived under the stochastic Solow model framework.

Given the small and open nature of the UK economy, it might be reasonable to assume that, in the long run, A_t is determined by the level of technological progress in the rest of the world; namely

$$A_t = \gamma A_t^* \exp(\eta_{at}), \tag{4.5}$$

where A_t^* represents the level of foreign technological progress, γ captures productivity differentials based on fixed, initial technological endowments, and η_{at} represents stationary, mean zero disturbances capturing the effects of information lags or (transitory) legal impediments to technology flows across different countries, for example. Assuming that per capita output in the rest of the world is also determined according to a neoclassical growth model, and using a similar line of reasoning as above, we have

$$y_t - y_t^* = \ln(\gamma) + \ln(\lambda/\lambda^*) + \ln[f(\kappa_t)/f^*(\kappa_t^*)] + \eta_{at} + (\eta_{nt} - \eta_{nt}^*), \tag{4.6}$$

where foreign variables are shown with a 'star'. Similarly to κ_t the foreign capital stock per effective labour unit, κ_t^*, also tends to a time-invariant probability distribution function, and hence under the assumption that A_t^* (or A_t) contain a unit root, (y_t, y_t^*) will be cointegrated with a cointegrating vector equal to $(1, -1)$. (See Lee (1998) and Pesaran (2004a) for further discussion.)

The above stochastic formulation of the neoclassical growth model also has important implications for the determination of the real rate of return, which we denote by ρ_t. Profit maximisation on the part of firms ensures that, in the steady state, ρ_t will be equal to the marginal product of capital, so that

$$\rho_t = f'(\kappa_t), \tag{4.7}$$

where $f'(\kappa_t)$ is the derivative of $f(\kappa_t)$ with respect to κ_t. Since $\kappa_t \to \kappa_\infty$, it therefore follows that $\rho_t \to f'(\kappa_\infty)$; thus establishing that the steady-state distribution of the real rate of return will also be ergodic and stationary. This result allows us to write

$$1 + \rho_{t+1} = (1 + \rho) \exp(\eta_{\rho,t+1}), \tag{4.8}$$

where $\eta_{\rho,t+1}$ is a stationary process normalised so that $E[\exp(\eta_{\rho,t+1}) \mid I_t] = 1$, and where I_t is the publicly available information set at time t. This normalisation ensures that ρ is in fact the mean of the steady-state distribution of real returns, ρ_t, given by $E\,[f'(\kappa_\infty)]$.

4.2 Arbitrage conditions

Market forces in the model motivate a set of arbitrage conditions that are included in many macroeconomic models in one form or another. They are the (relative) Purchasing Power Parity (*PPP*), the Fisher Inflation Parity (*FIP*), and the Uncovered Interest Parity (*UIP*) relationships. We consider each of these in turn.

Purchasing Power Parity is based on the presence of goods market arbitrage, and captures the idea that the price of a common basket of goods will be equal in different countries when measured in a common currency. Information disparities, transportation costs or the effects of tariff and non-tariff barriers are likely to create considerable deviations from (absolute) *PPP* in the short run and, with the likely exception of information disparities, these might persist indefinitely. However, if the size of these influences has a constant mean over time, then the common currency price of the basket of goods in the different countries will rise one-for-one over the longer term, and this is captured by the (weaker) concept of 'relative *PPP*'. The primary explanation of long-run deviations from relative *PPP* is the 'Harrod–Balassa–Samuelson (H–B–S) effect' in which the price of a basket of traded and non-traded goods rises more rapidly in countries with relatively rapid productivity growth in the traded goods sector.[4] Following these arguments, we express relative *PPP* as

$$P_{t+1} = E_{t+1}P^*_{t+1} \exp(\eta_{ppp,t+1}), \tag{4.9}$$

where E_t is the effective exchange rate, defined as the domestic price of a unit of foreign currency at the beginning of period t (so that an increase in the exchange rate represents a depreciation of the home country currency), P^*_t is the foreign price index and the term in brackets captures the deviations from *PPP*. Here, $\eta_{ppp,t+1}$ is assumed to follow a stationary (or possibly trend-stationary) process capturing short-run variations in transport costs, information disparities, and the effects of tariff and non-tariff barriers. The errors $\eta_{ppp,t+1}$ could be conditionally heteroscedastic, although this particular source of variability is unlikely to be very important in quarterly macromodels. The effects of differential productivity growth rates in the traded and non-traded goods sectors at home and abroad, accommodating the H–B–S effect, can be captured by assuming that $\eta_{ppp,t+1}$ contains a trend.

[4] See Obstfeld and Rogoff (1996, Chapter 4) and Rogoff (1996) for further discussion of this effect and alternative modifications to *PPP*.

Deviations from *PPP* might be observed because real exchange rates are measured using price indices which involve different baskets of commodities across countries. In this case, real shocks which cause changes in the relative price of particular commodities will have differential impacts on countries' prices, and deviations from *PPP* remain consistent with goods market arbitrage. In the case of the UK, which is an oil producer, the (potential) direct effect of changes in the relative price of oil on the UK's real exchange rate could be accommodated in the model by including a multiplicative term in the relative oil price variable, say $(P^o_{t+1}/P^*_{t+1})^\theta$ on the right-hand side of (4.9).[5] Of course, one might doubt that changes in relative oil prices would have a permanent effect on real exchange rates over long horizons, in which case $\theta = 0$. However, even in this case, the relative oil price variable could still affect real exchange rates over prolonged periods, given the size of the oil price changes in recent years, because of differential speeds of adjustment to the productivity shock in different economies. Ultimately, this is a matter to be investigated empirically.[6]

The *FIP* relationship captures the equilibrium outcome of the arbitrage process between holding bonds and investing in physical assets. Denoting the expected real rate of return on physical assets over the period t to $t+1$ by ρ^e_{t+1}, and denoting inflation expectations over the same period by $(P^e_{t+1} - P_t)/P_t$, we have

$$
\begin{aligned}
(1 + R_t) &= (1 + \rho^e_{t+1}) \left(1 + \frac{P^e_{t+1} - P_t}{P_t}\right) \exp(\eta_{fip,t+1}) \\
&= (1 + \rho^e_{t+1}) \left(\frac{P^e_{t+1}}{P_{t+1}}\right) \left(1 + \frac{\Delta P_{t+1}}{P_t}\right) \exp(\eta_{fip,t+1}), \qquad (4.10)
\end{aligned}
$$

where R_t is the nominal interest rate on domestic assets held from the beginning to the end of period t and $\eta_{fip,t+1}$ is the risk premium, capturing the effects of money and goods market uncertainties on risk-averse agents. We assume that $\eta_{fip,t+1}$ follows a stationary process with a finite mean and variance. Also recall that in the context of the neoclassical growth model

[5] This approach is advocated in Chauduri and Daniel (1998), for example. The inclusion of the relative oil price term in (4.9) can also be justified with reference to the H–B–S effect. Certainly, (relative) oil price changes have a pervasive effect on productivity, and these might have a differential effect in the traded and non-traded sectors of different economies. See Bruno and Sachs (1984) or Perron (1989), among others, for discussion of the role of the 1973 oil price shock in the worldwide slowdown in productivity.

[6] Distinguishing whether these effects are permanent or transitory is likely to be difficult using available datasets. However, the importance of explicitly taking into account the effects of oil price changes on the dynamics of real exchange rates has been widely acknowledged in applied work; see, for example, Johansen and Juselius (1992).

the real rate of interest (which we take to be the same as the real rate of return on capital) follows a stationary process; see (4.7) and (4.8).

The third arbitrage condition is based on the *UIP* relationship, which captures the equilibrium outcome of the arbitrage process between holding domestic and foreign bonds. In this, any differential in interest rates across countries must be offset by expected exchange rate changes to eliminate the scope for arbitrage. The presence of transactions costs, risk premia and speculative effects provide for the possibility of short-run deviations from *UIP*, and we therefore define the *Interest Rate Parity* (*IRP*) relationship as follows:

$$
\begin{aligned}
(1+R_t) &= (1+R_t^*)\left(1+\frac{E_{t+1}^e - E_t}{E_t}\right)\exp(\eta_{uip,t+1}) \\
&= (1+R_t^*)\left(\frac{E_{t+1}^e}{E_{t+1}}\right)\left(1+\frac{\Delta E_{t+1}}{E_t}\right)\exp(\eta_{uip,t+1}), \qquad (4.11)
\end{aligned}
$$

where R_t^* is the nominal interest rate paid on foreign assets during period t and $\eta_{uip,t+1}$ is the risk premium associated with the effects of bond and foreign exchange uncertainties on risk-averse agents. As before, we shall assume that $\eta_{uip,t+1}$ is stationary and ergodic.[7]

For the purpose of long-run modelling, we assume that the expectations errors $\eta_{i,t+1}^e$, $i = p, e, \rho$, defined by

$$
\begin{aligned}
P_{t+1}^e &= P_{t+1}\exp(\eta_{p,t+1}^e), \\
E_{t+1}^e &= E_{t+1}\exp(\eta_{e,t+1}^e), \\
\text{and } (1+\rho_{t+1}^e) &= (1+\rho_{t+1})\exp(\eta_{\rho,t+1}^e) \qquad (4.12)
\end{aligned}
$$

follow stationary processes. The assumption that the expectation errors are stationary seems quite plausible and is consistent with a wide variety of hypotheses concerning the expectations formation process.[8] In this case, the three arbitrage relationships discussed above can be written in terms of the observables using the expressions in (4.8) and (4.12). Specifically, the *FIP* relation can be written as:

$$
r_t = \ln(1+\rho) + \Delta p_t + \eta_{fip,t+1} + \eta_{\rho,t+1} + \eta_{\Delta\Delta p,t+1} + \eta_{p,t+1}^e + \eta_{\rho,t+1}^e, \qquad (4.13)
$$

[7] As noted earlier, the relationships in (4.10) and (4.11) can also be derived from Euler equations obtained from consumer and producer optimisation in an intertemporal model of an economy with well-behaved preferences and technologies.

[8] This assumption is consistent with the Rational Expectations Hypothesis (REH), for example. However, it is much less restrictive than the REH, and can accommodate the possibility of systematic expectational errors in the short run, possibly due to incomplete learning.

where lower cases denote the logarithm of a variable, so that $r_t = \ln(1+R_t)$ and $p_t = \ln(P_t)$,

$$\Delta p_t = \ln\left(1 + \frac{\Delta P_t}{P_{t-1}}\right)$$

and

$$\eta_{\Delta\Delta p,t+1} = \ln\left(\frac{P_{t+1}}{P_t} \bigg/ \frac{P_t}{P_{t-1}}\right).$$

Similarly, the *IRP* relation can be written as

$$r_t = r_t^* + \eta_{\Delta e,t+1} + \eta_{uip,t+1} + \eta_{e,t+1}^e, \tag{4.14}$$

where $r_t^* = \ln(1 + R_t^*)$ and $\eta_{\Delta e,t+1} = \Delta \ln(E_{t+1})$. And the log-linear version of the *PPP* relationship in (4.9) is given by

$$p_{t+1} = p_{t+1}^* + e_{t+1} + \eta_{ppp,t+1}, \tag{4.15}$$

where $p_{t+1}^* = \ln(P_{t+1}^*)$ and $e_{t+1} = \ln(E_{t+1})$.

4.3 Accounting identities and stock-flow relations

The institutional set-up of the model is captured through the use of the relevant accounting identities and stock-flow relations. We use the following stock identities:

$$\tilde{D}_t = \tilde{H}_t + \tilde{B}_t, \tag{4.16}$$

$$\tilde{F}_t = E_t\tilde{B}_t^* - (\tilde{B}_t - \tilde{B}_t^d), \tag{4.17}$$

$$\tilde{L}_t = \tilde{H}_t + \tilde{B}_t^d + E_t\tilde{B}_t^*, \tag{4.18}$$

where $\tilde{D}_t$ is net government debt, $\tilde{H}_t$ is the stock of high-powered money, $\tilde{B}_t$ is the stock of domestic bonds issued by the government, $\tilde{F}_t$ is the net foreign asset position of the economy, $\tilde{B}_t^*$ is the stock of foreign assets held by domestic residents, $\tilde{B}_t^d$ is the stock of domestic assets held by domestic residents, and $\tilde{L}_t$ $(= \tilde{D}_t + \tilde{F}_t)$ is the stock of financial assets held by the private sector.[9] All the stocks are measured at the beginning of period t. Recall that nominal magnitudes are denoted with a '$\sim$', and these are expressed

[9] It is assumed that foreign asset holdings of domestic residents and domestic holdings of foreign residents are composed of government bonds only.

in pounds sterling, except $\tilde{B}_t^*$ which is expressed in foreign currency. It is assumed that the government holds no foreign assets of its own.

We also have the output–expenditure flow identity:

$$\tilde{Y}_t = \tilde{C}_t + \tilde{I}_t + \tilde{G}_t + (\tilde{X}_t - \tilde{M}_t), \tag{4.19}$$

where $\tilde{C}_t$ is consumption expenditures, $\tilde{I}_t$ investment expenditures, $\tilde{G}_t$ government expenditures, $\tilde{X}_t$ expenditures on exports and $\tilde{M}_t$ expenditures on imports, all are in current market prices and expressed in pounds sterling. The private sector disposable income is defined by

$$\tilde{Y}_t^d = \tilde{Y}_t - \tilde{T}_t + R_t\tilde{B}_t^d + E_tR_t^*\tilde{B}_t^*, \tag{4.20}$$

where $\tilde{T}_t$ represents taxes net of transfers to the private sector.

The model economy's stock-flow relationships are:

$$\Delta\tilde{D}_{t+1} = \tilde{G}_t + R_t\tilde{B}_t - \tilde{T}_t, \tag{4.21}$$

$$\Delta\tilde{L}_{t+1} = \tilde{Y}_t^d - \tilde{C}_t - \tilde{I}_t + (E_{t+1}^e - E_t)\tilde{B}_t^*, \tag{4.22}$$

$$\Delta\tilde{F}_{t+1} = \tilde{X}_t - \tilde{M}_t + \widetilde{NFA}_t + (E_{t+1}^e - E_t)\tilde{B}_t^*, \tag{4.23}$$

where $\widetilde{NFA}_t = E_tR_t^*\tilde{B}_t^* - R_t(\tilde{B}_t - \tilde{B}_t^d)$ is net factor income from abroad, and E_{t+1}^e stands for exchange rate expectations formed on the basis of publicly available information at time t. Hence, the term $(E_{t+1}^e - E_t)\tilde{B}_t^*$ is the (expected) revaluation of foreign assets held by domestic residents accruing through exchange rate appreciation in period t.[10] Note that, since $\tilde{L}_t = \tilde{D}_t + \tilde{F}_t$, any two of (4.21)–(4.23) implies the third.

4.4 Long-run solvency requirements

The assumption that the private sector remains solvent, taken with the stock-flow relationships given by (4.21)–(4.23), provides the motivation for further long-run relationships between macroeconomic variables. In order to ensure the long-run solvency of the private sector asset/liability position, we assume

$$\tilde{L}_{t+1}/\tilde{Y}_t = \mu \exp(\eta_{ly,t+1}), \tag{4.24}$$

[10] In most formulations of stock-flow relationships the asset revaluation term is either ignored or is approximated by an *ex post* counterpart such as $(E_t - E_{t-1})\tilde{B}_t^*$. But for consistency with the arbitrage (equilibrium) conditions to be set out below, we prefer to work with the *ex ante* asset revaluation term.

where $\eta_{ly,t+1}$ is a stationary process, so that the ratio of total financial assets to the nominal income level is stationary and ergodic. Expression (4.24) captures the idea that domestic residents are neither willing nor able to accumulate claims on, or liabilities to, the government and the rest of the world which are out of line with their current and expected future income. This condition, in conjunction with assumptions on the determinants of the equilibrium portfolio balance of the private sector assets, provides additional long-run relations.

In modelling the equilibrium portfolio balance of private sector assets, we follow Branson's (1977) Portfolio Balance Approach. From (4.18), we note that the stock of financial assets held by the private sector consists of the stock of high-powered money plus the stock of domestic and foreign bonds held by domestic residents. Given this adding-up constraint, we specify two independent equilibrium relationships relating to asset demand; namely, those relating to the demand for high-powered money and for foreign assets. These relationships are characterised in our model by the following:

$$\frac{\tilde{H}_{t+1}}{\tilde{L}_t} = F_h\left(\frac{Y_t}{P_t}, \rho^e_{b,t+1}, \rho^{*e}_{b,t+1}, \frac{\Delta P^e_{t+1}}{P_t}, t\right)\exp(\eta_{h,t+1}), \tag{4.25}$$

and

$$\frac{\tilde{F}_{t+1}}{\tilde{L}_t} = F_f\left(\frac{Y_t}{P_t}, \rho^e_{b,t+1}, \rho^{*e}_{b,t+1}, \frac{\Delta P^e_{t+1}}{P_t}, t\right)\exp(\eta_{f,t+1}), \tag{4.26}$$

where $F_{h1} \geq 0, F_{h2} \leq 0, F_{h3} \leq 0, F_{h4} \leq 0$, and $F_{f1} \leq 0, F_{f2} \leq 0, F_{f3} \geq 0$, $F_{f4} \geq 0$, and where

$$Y_t = \frac{\tilde{Y}_t}{POP_{t-1}}, \qquad \rho^e_{b,t+1} = \frac{(1+R_t)}{\left(1+\frac{P^e_{t+1}-P_t}{P_t}\right)} - 1,$$

and

$$\rho^{*e}_{b,t+1} = \frac{(1+R^*_t)\left(1+\frac{E^e_{t+1}-E_t}{E_t}\right)}{\left(1+\frac{P^e_{t+1}-P_t}{P_t}\right)} - 1.$$

The last two terms are the expected real rates of return on domestic and foreign bonds, respectively (both measured in domestic currency), η_{ht} is a stationary process which captures the effects of various factors that contribute to the short-run deviations of the ratio of money balances to total financial assets from its long-run determinants, and η_{ft} is the corresponding stationary process capturing the effects of short-run deviations of the ratio of foreign assets to total financial assets from its long-run position. The determinants of the ratio of money to total financial assets in (4.25) include the real output level, to capture the influence of the transactions demand for money, and the expected real rates of return on the three alternative forms of holding financial assets; namely domestic bonds, foreign bonds and high-powered money. We have also specified a deterministic trend in $F_h(\cdot)$ to allow for the possible effect of the changing nature of financial intermediation, and the increasing use of credit cards in settlement of transactions on the convenience value of money. One would expect a downward trend in H/L, reflecting a trend reduction in the proportion of financial assets held in the form of non-interest bearing high-powered money over time. The determinants of the ratio of foreign assets to total financial assets in (4.26) are the same, with the decision to hold assets in the form of bonds mirroring that relating to holding assets in the form of money.

In view of the *IRP* relationship of (4.11), it is clear that, in the steady state, domestic and foreign bonds become perfect substitutes, and their expected rates of return are equal. Similarly, given the *FIP* relationship of (4.10) the real rates of return on (both) domestic and foreign bonds are equal to the (stationary) real rate of return on physical assets in the steady state. Hence, the asset demand relationships of (4.25) and (4.26) can be written equally as:

$$\frac{\tilde{H}_{t+1}}{\tilde{L}_t} = F_{hl}\left(\frac{Y_t}{P_t}, R_t, t\right)\exp(\eta_{hl,t+1}), \quad F_{hl1} \geq 0, \ F_{hl2} \leq 0, \tag{4.27}$$

and

$$\frac{\tilde{F}_{t+1}}{\tilde{L}_t} = F_{fl}\left(\frac{Y_t}{P_t}, R_t, t\right)\exp(\eta_{fl,t+1}), \quad F_{fl1} \leq 0, \ F_{fl2} \geq 0, \tag{4.28}$$

where the effects of the short-run deviations from *IRP* and *FIP* are now subsumed into the more general stationary processes $\eta_{hl,t+1}$ and $\eta_{fl,t+1}$ and where the effects of the expected real rate of return on non-interest bearing money holdings (*i.e.* minus the expected inflation rate) are captured by the domestic nominal interest rate (again making use of (4.10)). Note that this final effect implies that different rates of inflation, and hence different levels of nominal interest rates, could change the equilibrium portfolio composition, depending on the responsiveness of the asset demands to the relative returns on the three assets, so that changes in nominal rates of interest can potentially have lasting real effects.[11]

4.4.1 *Liquidity (real money balances)*

The solvency condition in (4.24) combined with the asset demand relationship of equation (4.27) now yields

$$\frac{\tilde{H}_{t+1}}{\tilde{Y}_t} = \frac{H_{t+1}}{Y_t} = \mu F_h\left(\frac{Y_t}{P_t}, R_t, t\right)\exp(\eta_{ly,t+1} + \eta_{hl,t+1}), \tag{4.29}$$

where $H_t = \tilde{H}_t/POP_{t-1}$ or, in its approximate log-linear form,

$$(h_t - y_t) = \ln(\mu) + \mu_1 t + \mu_2 r_t + \mu_3 y_t + \eta_{ly,t+1} + \eta_{hl,t+1},$$

where $h_t - y_t = \ln(H_{t+1}/P_t) - \ln(Y_t/P_t) = \ln(H_{t+1}/Y_t)$ and with unknown parameters μ_i, $i = 1, 2, 3$.[12] The equivalent relationship, based on (4.24) and (4.28), yields the following expression for the ratio of net foreign assets (measured in domestic currency) to the nominal output level:

$$\frac{\tilde{F}_{t+1}}{\tilde{Y}_t} = \mu F_f\left(\frac{Y_t}{P_t}, R_t, t\right)\exp(\eta_{fl,t+1} + \eta_{ly,t+1}), \tag{4.30}$$

although foreign asset levels are less frequently the focus of attention in macroeconometric models.[13] Equation (4.29) therefore provides the final long-run relationship to be considered in our model of the UK macroeconomy, along with the other four relationships described in (4.6), (4.13), (4.14) and (4.15).

4.4.2 *Imports and exports*

Before moving on to consider how the five steady-state relationships given in (4.6), (4.13), (4.14), (4.15), and (4.29) can be incorporated into an empirical model, it is worth briefly elaborating on the potential role that might be played by the demand for foreign assets in the domestic economy.

[11] The possibility of the 'super-non-neutrality' of monetary policy arising through this route is discussed in Buiter (1980), for example.

[12] For expositional simplicity, we have chosen to denote $\ln(H_{t+1}/P_t)$ by h_t, rather than h_{t+1}. Recall that H_{t+1} relates to the stock of high-powered money at the beginning of period $t + 1$.

[13] The stock-flow relationship of (4.23) can be used in conjunction with (4.17) to motivate a relationship between net foreign assets, net exports and domestic and foreign interest rates. Assuming that net exports depend on domestic and foreign output and the terms of trade, substitution of these relationships into (4.28) provides the justification for a further possible long-run relationship between Y_t, Y_t^*, R_t, R_t^*, and $E_t P_t^*/P_t$.

Specifically, we can show that the conditions (4.24) and (4.28), when taken with assumptions on import and export determination, provide a further equilibrium condition between the real exchange rate, domestic and foreign outputs and the interest rate. Given the stationarity of the real exchange rate expressed by (4.15) and given the relationship between domestic and foreign outputs in (4.6), it is reasonable to believe that this extra equilibrium relationship will provide little additional explanatory power in a model that incorporates the effects of (4.15) and (4.6) already. Indeed, in the empirical model of the later chapters, we do not include this additional equilibrium relationship. But it is worth elaborating the relationship here both to clarify the potential role of foreign asset demand and to note that, in practice, the equilibrating pressures assigned to deviations from *PPP* and the 'output gap' relationship may in fact confound these effects and those arising from balance of payments outcomes.

To derive the extra equilibrium relationship, we note that the stock-flow relationship (4.23) can be used in conjunction with the definition of the country's net foreign asset position in (4.17) to write

$$
\begin{aligned}
\tilde{F}_{t+1} &= \tilde{X}_t - \tilde{M}_t + \tilde{F}_t + E_t R_t^* \tilde{B}_t^* - R_t(\tilde{B}_t - \tilde{B}_t^d) + (E_{t+1}^e - E_t)\tilde{B}_t^* \\
&= \tilde{X}_t - \tilde{M}_t + (1 + R_t)\tilde{F}_t - E_t \tilde{B}_t^* \left(R_t - R_t^* - \frac{\Delta E_{t+1}^e}{E_t} \right).
\end{aligned}
$$

Dividing through by nominal income, and writing the various ratios in per capita terms, we obtain

$$
\frac{F_{t+1}}{Y_t} = \frac{X_t - M_t}{Y_t} + (1 + R_t)\left(\frac{F_t}{Y_{t-1}} \right)\left(\frac{Y_{t-1}}{Y_t} \right) - \frac{E_t B_t^*}{Y_t}\left(R_t - R_t^* - \frac{\Delta E_{t+1}^e}{E_t} \right),
$$

where $Y_t = \tilde{Y}_t / POP_{t-1}$, $X_t = \tilde{X}_t / POP_{t-1}$ and $F_t = \tilde{F}_t / POP_{t-1}$. Let g_t denote the growth of per capita output and note that $Y_t / Y_{t-1} = (1 + g_t)(1 + \Delta P_t / P_{t-1})$. Hence

$$
\begin{aligned}
\frac{F_{t+1}}{Y_t} = \frac{X_t - M_t}{Y_t} &+ \frac{(1 + R_t)}{(1 + g_t)(1 + \Delta P_t / P_{t-1})}\left(\frac{F_t}{Y_{t-1}} \right) \\
&- \frac{E_t B_t^*}{Y_t}\left(R_t - R_t^* - \frac{\Delta E_{t+1}^e}{E_t} \right).
\end{aligned}
\tag{4.31}
$$

Now, under our assumptions, $(1+g_t)$ and $(1+R_t)/(1+\Delta P_t/P_{t-1})$ both tend to stationary processes with constant means, $1+g$ and $1+\rho$, respectively, and the term in $R_t - R_t^* - (\Delta E_{t+1}^e/E_t)$ itself tends to a stationary process. Recalling from (4.30) that the value of $\tilde{F}_{t+1}/\tilde{Y}_t$ depends on $Y_t/P_t, R_t$ and t, the solvency condition and the relationships describing the determinants of the ratio of foreign to total financial assets provides, through (4.31), a long-run relationship between $(X_t - M_t)/Y_t$, Y_t/P_t and R_t. We represent this relationship by the following:

$$\frac{X_t - M_t}{Y_t} = F_b\left(\frac{Y_t}{P_t}, R_t, t\right)\exp(\eta_{b,t+1}), \quad F_{b1} \leq 0,\ F_{b2} \geq 0, \tag{4.32}$$

where $\eta_{b,t+1}$ is a stationary process.

To complete our derivations, we further assume that real per capita imports (M_t/P_t) and exports (X_t/P_t) are determined according to the following relations:

$$\frac{X_t}{P_t} = F_x\left(\frac{Y_t^*}{P_t^*}, \frac{E_tP_t^*}{P_t}\right)\exp(\eta_{xt}), \qquad F_{x1} > 0,\ F_{x2} > 0, \tag{4.33}$$

$$\frac{M_t}{E_tP_t^*} = F_m\left(\frac{Y_t}{P_t}, \frac{E_tP_t^*}{P_t}\right)\exp(\eta_{mt}), \qquad F_{m1} > 0,\ F_{m2} < 0,$$

where η_{xt} and η_{mt} are stationary processes with zero means. In the long run, real per capita exports are assumed to depend on real activity levels abroad, Y_t^*/P_t^*, and on the relative price of goods abroad compared to those at home, while real per capita imports depend on domestic real per capita output and relative prices. The stationary processes η_{xt} and η_{mt} characterise the short-run departure of exports and imports from their long-term determinants. Using (4.32) and (4.33), we obtain

$$F_x\left(\frac{Y_t^*}{P_t^*}, \frac{E_tP_t^*}{P_t}, \frac{P_t^o}{P_t^*}\right)\exp(\eta_{xt}) - \frac{E_tP_t^*}{P_t}F_m\left(\frac{Y_t}{P_t}, \frac{E_tP_t^*}{P_t}, \frac{P_t^o}{P_t^*}\right)\exp(\eta_{mt})$$
$$= \frac{Y_t}{P_t}F_b\left(\frac{Y_t}{P_t}, R_t, t\right)\exp(\eta_{b,t+1}), \tag{4.34}$$

or, in its approximate log-linear form,

$$(e_t + p_t^* - p_t) = \mu_4 + \mu_5 t + \mu_6 y_t + \mu_7 y_t^* + \mu_8 r_t + \eta_{xt} + \eta_{mt} + \eta_{b,t+1},$$

with unknown parameters μ_i, $i = 4, \ldots, 8$. In summary, then, the interplay between the stock-flow equilibria, the demand for foreign assets, the solvency condition, and simple assumptions on the determinants of import and export demand generates a further long-run relationship between the real exchange rate, domestic and foreign outputs and the interest rate. In principle, this 'trade balance' relationship could be investigated alongside the five steady-state relationships in (4.6), (4.13), (4.14), (4.15) and (4.29). However, comparison of the log-linear version of (4.34) with those of the *PPP* relationship of (4.15) and the output relationship of (4.6) shows that it is likely to be difficult to distinguish the separate contributions of the trade balance relationship empirically. For these reasons, we do not pursue the effects of the trade balance relationship in what follows.

4.5 Econometric formulation of the model

In this section, we adopt the modelling strategy elaborated in Section 3.1.3 to derive an econometric formulation for our model based on the economic theory of the long run elaborated above. For empirical purposes, we employ a log-linear approximation of the five long-run equilibrium relationships set out in the previous section in (4.15), (4.14), (4.6), (4.29) and (4.13).[14] These constitute the theory-based long-run relationships of the model and take the following form:

$$p_t - p_t^* - e_t = b_{10} + b_{11}t + \xi_{1,t+1}, \tag{4.35}$$

$$r_t - r_t^* = b_{20} + \xi_{2,t+1}, \tag{4.36}$$

$$y_t - y_t^* = b_{30} + \xi_{3,t+1}, \tag{4.37}$$

$$h_t - y_t = b_{40} + b_{41}t + \beta_{44}r_t + \beta_{46}y_t + \xi_{4,t+1}, \tag{4.38}$$

$$r_t - \Delta p_t = b_{50} + \xi_{5,t+1}, \tag{4.39}$$

recalling that $p_t = \ln(P_t)$, $p_t^* = \ln(P_t^*)$, $e_t = \ln(E_t)$, $y_t = \ln(Y_t/P_t)$, $y_t^* = \ln(Y_t^*/P_t^*)$, $r_t = \ln(1+R_t)$, $r_t^* = \ln(1+R_t^*)$, $h_t - y_t = \ln(H_{t+1}/P_t) - \ln(Y_t/P_t) = \ln(H_{t+1}/Y_t)$ and $b_{50} = \ln(1+\rho)$. We have allowed for intercept and trend terms (when appropriate) in order to ensure that (long-run) reduced form disturbances, $\xi_{i,t+1}$, $i = 1, 2, ..., 5$, have zero means. These disturbances are

[14] We assume a trend term enters the log-linear *PPP* relationship, as mentioned earlier.

related to the long-run structural disturbances, the η_i's, in the following manner:[15]

$$\xi_{1,t+1} = \eta_{ppp,t} - b_{10} - b_{11}t,$$
$$\xi_{2,t+1} = \eta_{uip,t+1} + \eta^{e}_{e,t+1} + \eta_{\Delta e,t+1} - b_{20},$$
$$\xi_{3,t+1} = \eta_{at} + (\eta_{nt} - \eta^{*}_{nt}) + (\eta_{kt} - \eta^{*}_{kt}), \qquad (4.40)$$
$$\xi_{4,t+1} = \eta_{ly,t} + \eta_{hl,t},$$
$$\xi_{5,t+1} = \eta_{fip,t+1} + \eta_{\rho,t+1} + \eta_{\Delta\Delta p,t+1} + \eta^{e}_{p,t+1} + \eta^{e}_{\rho,t+1}.$$

The above relationships between the long-run structural disturbances, η_i's, and the long-run reduced form disturbances, ξ_i's, clearly show the difficulties involved in identifying the effects of changes in particular structural disturbances on the dynamic behaviour of the macroeconomy. For example, $\xi_{5,t+1}$ is composed of the five structural disturbances, $\eta_{fip,t+1}$, $\eta_{\rho,t+1}$, $\eta_{\Delta\Delta p,t+1}$, $\eta^{e}_{p,t+1}$, $\eta_{\rho,t+1}$, representing the different factors that could be responsible for disequilibria between inflation and interest rates. In general, without further *a priori* restrictions, the effect of particular structural disturbances, η_i's, cannot be identified: firstly, there are many more long-run structural disturbances than there are long-run reduced form disturbances; and, secondly, there is no reason to believe that the η_i's are not themselves contemporaneously correlated. Empirical analysis at best enables us to identify the effect of changes in the long-run reduced form disturbances on the evolution of the macroeconomy towards its long-run equilibrium, although, as we discuss below, even identification of the effects of specific changes in these long-run reduced form disturbances will typically require further identifying restrictions based on an explicit model of short-run decision-making.

The five long-run relations of the model, (4.35)–(4.39), can be written more compactly as

$$\boldsymbol{\xi}_t = \boldsymbol{\beta}'\mathbf{z}_{t-1} - \mathbf{b}_0 - \mathbf{b}_1(t-1), \qquad (4.41)$$

where

$$\mathbf{z}_t = \left(p^{o}_{t}, e_t, r^{*}_{t}, r_t, \Delta p_t, y_t, p_t - p^{*}_{t}, h_t - y_t, y^{*}_{t}\right)'. \qquad (4.42)$$
$$\mathbf{b}_0 = (b_{10}, b_{20}, b_{30}, b_{40}, b_{50})', \ \mathbf{b}_1 = (b_{11}, 0, 0, b_{41}, 0)',$$
$$\boldsymbol{\xi}_t = (\xi_{1t}, \xi_{2t}, \xi_{3t}, \xi_{4t}, \xi_{5t})',$$

[15] In the case of $\xi_{2,t+1}$, we have taken account of the effect of exchange rate depreciation on the interest rate differential since, as we shall see below, the hypothesis that $\eta_{\Delta e,t+1}$ is stationary cannot be rejected.

and

$$\beta' = \begin{pmatrix} 0 & -1 & 0 & 0 & 0 & 0 & 1 & 0 & 0 \\ 0 & 0 & -1 & 1 & 0 & 0 & 0 & 0 & 0 \\ 0 & 0 & 0 & 0 & 0 & 1 & 0 & 0 & -1 \\ 0 & 0 & 0 & -\beta_{44} & 0 & -\beta_{46} & 0 & 1 & 0 \\ 0 & 0 & 0 & 1 & -1 & 0 & 0 & 0 & 0 \end{pmatrix}. \quad (4.43)$$

The description of the long-run disturbances in (4.41) is, of course, of precisely the form of (3.4) introduced in the outline of our modelling strategy in Section 3.1.3.

For estimation purposes, we choose to partition $\mathbf{z}_t = (p_t^o, \mathbf{y}_t')'$ where $\mathbf{y}_t = (e_t, r_t^*, r_t, \Delta p_t, y_t, p_t - p_t^*, h_t - y_t, y_t^*)'$. Here, p_t^o (the logarithm of oil prices) is considered to be a 'long-run forcing' variable for the determination of $\mathbf{y}_t$, in the sense that changes in p_t^o have a direct influence on $\mathbf{y}_t$, but changes in p_t^o are not affected by the presence of ξ_t, which measure the extent of disequilibria in the UK economy. The treatment of oil prices as 'long-run forcing' represents a generalisation of the approach to modelling oil price effects in some previous applications of cointegrating VAR analyses (*e.g.* Johansen and Juselius, 1992, or Pesaran and Shin, 1996), where the change in the oil price is treated as a strictly exogenous $I(0)$ variable. The approach taken in the previous literature excludes the possibility that there might exist cointegrating relationships involving oil prices, while the approach taken here allows the validity of the hypothesised restriction to be tested and for the restriction to be imposed if it is not rejected.

We choose to treat foreign output and interest rates as endogenous for pragmatic reasons. As the discussion of Section 3.4 makes clear, the natural modelling choice for a small open economy like the UK would be to treat y_t^* and r_t^* as long-run forcing. However, we shall want to use our model for forecasting purposes and therefore require a world model with which to forecast future values of y_t^* and r_t^*. Rather than build a world model, we have implemented the model by treating these variables as endogenous (effectively supplementing simple autoregressive models of foreign output and interest rates with the lagged values of the UK variables as a substitute for the world model). It is worth noting that the endogenous treatment of foreign output and interest rates involves loss of efficiency in estimation if they were in fact long-run forcing or strictly exogenous, but this is clearly less serious than treating these variables as exogenous if this turned out to be false, for example.

Under the assumption that oil prices are long-run forcing for $\mathbf{y}_t$, the cointegrating properties of the model can be investigated without having to specify the oil price equation.[16] However, specification of an oil price equation is required in the analysis of the short-run dynamics and forecasting. For this purpose we shall adopt the following general specification for the evolution of oil prices:

$$\Delta p_t^o = \delta_o + \sum_{i=1}^{p-1} \delta_{oi} \Delta \mathbf{z}_{t-i} + u_{ot}, \tag{4.44}$$

where u_{ot} represents a serially uncorrelated oil price shock with a zero mean and a constant variance. The above specification ensures oil prices are long-run forcing for $\mathbf{y}_t$ since it allows lagged changes in the endogenous and exogenous variables of the model to influence current oil prices but rules out the possibility that the error correction terms, ξ_t, have any effects on oil price changes. These assumptions are weaker than the requirement of 'Granger non-causality' often invoked in the literature.

Assuming that the variables in $\mathbf{z}_t$ are difference-stationary (as discussed in Chapter 8), our modelling strategy is now to embody ξ_t in an otherwise unrestricted VAR($p-1$) in $\mathbf{z}_t$. Under the assumption that oil prices are long-run forcing, it is efficient (for estimation purposes) to base our analysis on the following *conditional* error correction model

$$\Delta \mathbf{y}_t = \mathbf{a}_y - \boldsymbol{\alpha}_y \boldsymbol{\xi}_t + \sum_{i=1}^{p-1} \boldsymbol{\Gamma}_{yi} \Delta \mathbf{z}_{t-i} + \boldsymbol{\psi}_{yo} \Delta p_t^o + \mathbf{u}_{yt}, \tag{4.45}$$

where $\mathbf{a}_y$ is an 8×1 vector of fixed intercepts, $\boldsymbol{\alpha}_y$ is an 8×5 matrix of error correction coefficients (also known as the loading coefficient matrix), $\{\boldsymbol{\Gamma}_{yi}, i = 1, 2, ..., p-1\}$ are 8×9 matrices of short-run coefficients, $\boldsymbol{\psi}_{yo}$ is an 8×1 vector representing the impact effects of changes in oil prices on $\Delta \mathbf{y}_t$, and $\mathbf{u}_{yt}$ is an 8×1 vector of disturbances assumed to be *i.i.d.*$(0, \boldsymbol{\Sigma}_y)$, with $\boldsymbol{\Sigma}_y$ being a positive definite matrix, and by construction uncorrelated with u_{ot}. Using equation (4.41), we now have

$$\Delta \mathbf{y}_t = \mathbf{a}_y + \boldsymbol{\alpha}_y \mathbf{b}_0 - \boldsymbol{\alpha}_y \left[\boldsymbol{\beta}' z_{t-1} - \boldsymbol{b}_1 (t-1) \right] + \sum_{i=1}^{p-1} \boldsymbol{\Gamma}_{yi} \Delta \mathbf{z}_{t-i} + \boldsymbol{\psi}_{yo} \Delta p_t^o + \mathbf{u}_{yt}, \tag{4.46}$$

where $\boldsymbol{\beta}' z_{t-1} - \mathbf{b}_1 (t-1)$ is a 5×1 vector of error correction terms. The above specification embodies the economic theory's long-run predictions by construction.

[16] See, for example, Pesaran, Shin and Smith (2000).

Estimation of the parameters of the model, (4.46), can be carried out using the long-run structural modelling approach described in Pesaran and Shin (2002) and Pesaran, Shin and Smith (2000). It is based on a modified and generalised version of Johansen's (1991, 1995) maximum likelihood approach to the problem of estimation and hypothesis testing in the context of vector autoregressive error correction models. With this approach, having selected the order of the underlying VAR model (using model selection criteria such as the Akaike Information Criterion (AIC) or the Schwarz Bayesian Criterion (SBC)), we test for the number of cointegrating relations among the nine variables in $\mathbf{z}_t$. When performing this task, and in all the subsequent empirical analysis, we work in the context of a VAR model with unrestricted intercepts and restricted trend coefficients.[17] In terms of (4.46), we allow the intercepts to be freely estimated but restrict the trend coefficients so that $\boldsymbol{\alpha}_y\mathbf{b}_1 = \boldsymbol{\Pi}_y\boldsymbol{\gamma}$, where $\boldsymbol{\Pi}_y = \boldsymbol{\alpha}_y\boldsymbol{\beta}'$ and $\boldsymbol{\gamma}$ is a 9×1 vector of unknown coefficients. These restrictions ensure that the solution of the model in levels of $\mathbf{z}_t$ will not contain quadratic trends. We then compute Maximum Likelihood (ML) estimates of the model's parameters subject to exact and over-identifying restrictions on the long-run coefficients. Assuming that there is empirical support for the existence of five long-run relationships, as suggested by theory, exact identification in our model requires five restrictions on each of the five cointegrating vectors (each row of $\boldsymbol{\beta}$), or a total of 25 restrictions on $\boldsymbol{\beta}$. These represent only a subset of the restrictions suggested by economic theory as characterised in (4.43), however. Estimation of the model subject to all the (exact- and over-identifying) restrictions given in (4.43) enables a test of the validity of the over-identifying restrictions, and hence the long-run implications of the economic theory, to be carried out.

[17] This is referred to as Case IV in Pesaran, Shin and Smith (2000), see Subsection 6.2.1 below.

5

An economic theory of the short run

The modelling strategy described in the previous chapter has the two-fold advantage that it is capable of accommodating the relationships that exist between variables in the long run as suggested by an explicit macroeconomic theory, and that the estimated model reflects parsimoniously the complex dynamic relationships that exist between variables at shorter horizons. In this chapter, we consider the problem of identification of contemporaneous relationships, and in particular discuss the identification of the monetary policy shocks and the associated impulse responses.

Our view is that the economic theory of the long run described in the previous chapter can be held with some degree of confidence (and, as we shall see, we can judge whether this confidence is justifiable through a formal statistical test of the over-identifying restrictions suggested by the theory). We are less confident in the economic theory of the short run that we shall present. The theory that is described is 'tentative' in the sense described in Section 3.2.3 of Chapter 3, relying to a large extent on *a priori* views on the sequencing of decisions and the institutional detail of the decision-making process. As we noted in that discussion, there is no consensus on the appropriate form of short-run restrictions in macroeconometric models, and we recognise the frailty of the theory elaborated here. On the other hand, some identifying restrictions are essential if we are to investigate specific types of shock (*e.g.* monetary policy shocks) and we present a theory which seems the most reasonable to us and which involves the imposition of the minimum possible identifying structure.

Before describing the proposed theory of the short run, it is worth briefly summarising the specification of the macromodel derived in the previous chapter. Combining the oil price equation (4.44) and the conditional model explaining the remaining eight variables of interest (4.46), we obtain the reduced form specification

$$\Delta \mathbf{z}_t = \begin{pmatrix} \Delta p_t^o \\ \Delta \mathbf{y}_t \end{pmatrix} = \mathbf{a} - \boldsymbol{\alpha}\left[\boldsymbol{\beta}' z_{t-1} - b_1(t-1)\right] + \sum_{i=1}^{p-1} \boldsymbol{\Gamma}_i \Delta \mathbf{z}_{t-i} + \mathbf{v}_t, \qquad (5.1)$$

where

$$\mathbf{z}_t = \left(p_t^o, e_t, r_t^*, r_t, \Delta p_t, y_t, p_t - p_t^*, h_t - y_t, y_t^*\right)'.$$

and

$$\mathbf{a} = \begin{pmatrix} \delta_o \\ \psi_{yo}\delta_o + a_y - \alpha_y b_0 \end{pmatrix}, \boldsymbol{\alpha} = \begin{pmatrix} 0 \\ \boldsymbol{\alpha}_y \end{pmatrix}, \boldsymbol{\Gamma}_i = \begin{pmatrix} \delta_{oi} \\ \boldsymbol{\psi}_{yo}\delta_{oi} + \boldsymbol{\Gamma}_{yi} \end{pmatrix},$$

$$\mathbf{v}_t = \begin{pmatrix} 1 & 0 \\ \boldsymbol{\psi}_{yo} & \mathbf{I}_8 \end{pmatrix} \begin{pmatrix} u_{ot} \\ \mathbf{u}_{yt} \end{pmatrix} = \begin{pmatrix} u_{ot} \\ \boldsymbol{\psi}_{yo} u_{ot} + \mathbf{u}_{yt} \end{pmatrix}.$$

Under standard assumptions, all the reduced form coefficients can be consistently estimated from the ML estimates of the parameters of the conditional model (4.46), and the OLS regression of the oil price equation (4.44). In particular, the vector of the reduced form errors $\mathbf{v}_t$, and its covariance matrix, $\boldsymbol{\Sigma}$, can be estimated consistently from the reduced form parameters. The 'structural' VECM associated with the *long-run structural* macroeconometric model defined by (4.44) and (4.46) can be written as:

$$\mathbf{A}\ \Delta \mathbf{z}_t = \widetilde{\mathbf{a}} - \widetilde{\boldsymbol{\alpha}}\left[\boldsymbol{\beta}' z_{t-1} - \mathbf{b}_1(t-1)\right] + \sum_{i=1}^{p-1} \widetilde{\boldsymbol{\Gamma}}_i \Delta \mathbf{z}_{t-i} + \boldsymbol{\varepsilon}_t, \qquad (5.2)$$

where $\mathbf{A}$ represents the 9×9 matrix of contemporaneous structural coefficients, $\widetilde{\mathbf{a}} = \mathbf{A}\mathbf{a}$, $\widetilde{\boldsymbol{\alpha}} = \mathbf{A}\boldsymbol{\alpha}$, $\widetilde{\boldsymbol{\Gamma}}_i = \mathbf{A}\boldsymbol{\Gamma}_i$, and $\boldsymbol{\varepsilon}_t = \mathbf{A}\mathbf{v}_t$ are the associated structural shocks which are serially uncorrelated and have zero means and the positive definite variance covariance matrix, $\boldsymbol{\Omega} = \mathbf{A}\boldsymbol{\Sigma}\mathbf{A}'$. So far, the only restrictions relating to the contemporaneous dependencies in (5.2) are those imposed on the first row of $\mathbf{A}$ through the assumption that oil prices are long-run forcing.

This is precisely the set-up described in Chapter 3. For exact identification of *all* the structural coefficients in our model, $9^2 = 81$ restrictions are required to be imposed on $\mathbf{A}$, $\boldsymbol{\Omega}$, or, more unusually, on $\widetilde{\boldsymbol{\Pi}}$ or the $\widetilde{\boldsymbol{\Gamma}}_i$, $i = 1, \ldots, p-1$. Alternatively, it might be possible to identify a specific subset of the structural parameters and/or shocks imposing fewer than

81 restrictions. The restrictions might be motivated by a fully articulated DSGE model of the entire economy; or they might be motivated via a more limited linear–quadratic optimisation model involving adjustment costs; or they might be motivated by a less formal theory.

In our macroeconometric modelling, we do not address the problem of the identification of all the structural shocks. This is because such an exercise would require a detailed specification of all the structural relations and the underlying decisions as well as the mechanisms by which expectations are formed. Rather, we focus on the identification of the effects of oil and monetary policy shocks only, concentrating on the decisions made by monetary authorities and agents in the financial sector. These decisions are discussed with reference to the optimisation problem faced by the monetary authorities (modelled as an LQ model with adjustment costs) combined with 'tentative' theory on the sequencing of decisions and the institutional context. The decisions of the monetary authorities and agents in the financial sector are made taking as given the decision rules of the private agents as embodied in the structural relations bearing on output and inflation in the structural VECM, (5.2). Whilst it might be desirable to consider the identification of other shocks, such as technology or demand shocks, this does not seem to be necessary for the analysis of monetary shocks. As we shall show, the identification of other shocks in the economy can be dealt with using the generalised impulse response approach developed in Pesaran and Shin (1998).

5.1 Modelling monetary policy

5.1.1 *The monetary authority's decision problem*

For identification of the monetary policy shocks, we first need to formally articulate the decision problem of the monetary authorities. We assume that, at the start of each period, the monetary authorities try to influence the market interest rate, r_t, by setting the base rate, r_t^b that they have under their direct control.[1] We then impose a structure on the sequencing of decisions, assuming that the difference between the market rate and the base rate, the term premium, is determined by unanticipated factors such as oil

[1] In the case of the UK, it is reasonable to assume that the Bank of England determines r_t^b, the price of liquidity. This is a characteristic of the institutional framework in the UK and contrasts with the US (as described in Gordon and Leeper (1994), for example).

price shocks, unexpected changes in foreign interest rates and exchange rates. This is justified on the grounds that these four variables, *i.e.* p_t^o, e_t, r_t^*, and $r_t - r_t^b$, are likely to be contemporaneously determined in the market place on a daily (even intra-daily) basis. The remaining variables, y_t, y_t^*, Δp_t, $p_t - p_t^*$, and $h_t - p_t$, are much less frequently observed, often with relatively long delays, and their contemporaneous values can be reasonably excluded from the determination of the term premium, $r_t - r_t^b$. However, as we shall see below, lagged values of these variables can still affect the term premium.

To help explain the structure imposed by the sequencing of decisions described above, and to aid the subsequent exposition, it is worth introducing some notation to explicitly denote the structural parameters of interest. So, let us distinguish between three sets of variables: the first set consists of the four variables determined contemporaneously with r_t^b, namely, p_t^o, e_t, r_t^*, and r_t; the second set, denoted $\mathbf{w}_t$, contains output and inflation, which we shall assume are the variables of direct concern to the monetary authorities; and the third set, denoted $\mathbf{q}_t$, consists of the remaining variable in the model. Hence, we have the following partitioning of the variables:

$$\mathbf{z}_t = \begin{pmatrix} p_t^o \\ \mathbf{y}_t \end{pmatrix}, \quad \mathbf{y}_t = \begin{pmatrix} e_t \\ r_t^* \\ r_t \\ \mathbf{w}_t \\ \mathbf{q}_t \end{pmatrix}, \quad \mathbf{w}_t = \begin{pmatrix} y_t \\ \Delta p_t \end{pmatrix}, \quad \mathbf{q}_t = \begin{pmatrix} p_t - p_t^* \\ h_t - y_t \\ y_t^* \end{pmatrix}.$$

The assumption that oil prices are determined as in (4.44) and that e_t, r_t^*, and r_t are determined prior to the variables in $\mathbf{w}_t$ and $\mathbf{q}_t$ imposes a structure on the parameter matrices of (5.2) as follows:[2]

$$\widetilde{\mathbf{a}} = \begin{pmatrix} \delta_0 \\ \widetilde{a}_e \\ \widetilde{a}_{r^*} \\ \widetilde{a}_r \\ \widetilde{\mathbf{a}}_w \\ \widetilde{\mathbf{a}}_q \end{pmatrix}, \quad \widetilde{\boldsymbol{\alpha}} = \begin{pmatrix} 0 \\ \widetilde{\alpha}_e \\ \widetilde{\alpha}_{r^*} \\ \widetilde{\alpha}_r \\ \widetilde{\boldsymbol{\alpha}}_w \\ \widetilde{\boldsymbol{\alpha}}_q \end{pmatrix}, \quad \widetilde{\boldsymbol{\Gamma}}_i = \begin{pmatrix} \delta_i \\ \widetilde{\boldsymbol{\Gamma}}_{e,i} \\ \widetilde{\boldsymbol{\Gamma}}_{r^*,i} \\ \widetilde{\boldsymbol{\Gamma}}_{r,i} \\ \widetilde{\boldsymbol{\Gamma}}_{w,i} \\ \widetilde{\boldsymbol{\Gamma}}_{q,i} \end{pmatrix}, \quad \boldsymbol{\varepsilon}_t = \begin{pmatrix} \varepsilon_{o,t} \\ \varepsilon_{e,t} \\ \varepsilon_{r^*,t} \\ \varepsilon_{r,t} \\ \boldsymbol{\varepsilon}_{w,t} \\ \boldsymbol{\varepsilon}_{q,t} \end{pmatrix},$$

[2] In fact, for expositional purposes, we make the further assumption that exchange rates are determined prior to foreign interest rates in what follows.

and

$$\mathbf{A} = \begin{pmatrix} 1 & 0 & 0 & 0 & 0 & 0 \\ -\widetilde{\psi}_e & 1 & 0 & 0 & 0 & 0 \\ -\widetilde{\psi}_{r^*} & a_{r^*e} & 1 & 0 & 0 & 0 \\ -\widetilde{\psi}_r & a_{re} & a_{rr^*} & 1 & 0 & 0 \\ -\widetilde{\boldsymbol{\psi}}_w & \mathbf{A}_{we} & \mathbf{A}_{wr^*} & \mathbf{A}_{wr} & \mathbf{A}_{ww} & \mathbf{A}_{wq} \\ -\widetilde{\boldsymbol{\psi}}_q & \mathbf{A}_{qe} & \mathbf{A}_{qr^*} & \mathbf{A}_{qr} & \mathbf{A}_{qw} & \mathbf{A}_{qq} \end{pmatrix}.$$

Note that $\mathbf{A}$ has a lower triangular structure only in the case of the variables, p_{ot}, e_t, r_t^* and r_t that are primarily market determined on a daily basis. However, $\mathbf{A}$ taken as a whole is not triangular. The parameters of the corresponding reduced form equations given in (5.1) can be similarly defined, using

$$\mathbf{a} = \begin{pmatrix} \delta_0 \\ a_e \\ a_{r^*} \\ a_r \\ \mathbf{a}_w \\ \mathbf{a}_q \end{pmatrix}, \quad \boldsymbol{\alpha} = \begin{pmatrix} 0 \\ \alpha_e \\ \alpha_{r^*} \\ \alpha_r \\ \boldsymbol{\alpha}_w \\ \boldsymbol{\alpha}_q \end{pmatrix}, \quad \boldsymbol{\Gamma}_i = \begin{pmatrix} \delta_i \\ \boldsymbol{\Gamma}_{e,i} \\ \boldsymbol{\Gamma}_{r^*,i} \\ \boldsymbol{\Gamma}_{r,i} \\ \boldsymbol{\Gamma}_{w,i} \\ \boldsymbol{\Gamma}_{q,i} \end{pmatrix}, \quad \mathbf{v}_t = \begin{pmatrix} v_{o,t} \\ v_{e,t} \\ v_{r^*,t} \\ v_{r,t} \\ \mathbf{v}_{w,t} \\ \mathbf{v}_{q,t} \end{pmatrix}.$$

Given the above relationships between the structural and reduced form parameters, we can return to the monetary authorities' decision problem. The sequencing of decisions assumes that the term premium equation has the following form:

$$\begin{aligned} r_t - r_t^b &= \rho_{b,t-1} + a_{rr^*}\left[r_t^* - E\left(r_t^* \mid \Im_{t-1}\right)\right] \\ &\quad + a_{re}\left[e_t - E\left(e_t \mid \Im_{t-1}\right)\right] \\ &\quad + \widetilde{\psi}_r\left[p_t^o - E\left(p_t^o \mid \Im_{t-1}\right)\right] + \varepsilon_{rt}, \end{aligned} \tag{5.3}$$

where $\Im_{t-1}$ is the information set of the monetary authorities at the end of $t-1$, $\rho_{b,t-1}$ is the predictable component of the term premium, which could be a general function of one or more elements in the information set $\Im_{t-1}$, r_t^b is the systematic component of monetary policy, and ε_{rt} is the monetary policy shock.[3] Hence, in addition to ε_{rt}, the unexpected component of the term premium is assumed to vary linearly with the

[3] In the absence of a fully specified model of the markets which link the monetary authorities with other financial markets, we associate monetary policy shocks with innovations to short-term interest rates. It is worth noting that several researchers, including Sims (1992) and Bernanke *et al.* (1997), have argued that, within this context, innovations to short-term interest rates are preferable to using innovations in monetary aggregates.

unanticipated changes in oil prices, the exchange rate, and the foreign interest rate. We shall assume that the monetary policy shocks, ε_{rt}, satisfy the following standard orthogonality condition:

$$E\left(\varepsilon_{rt} \mid \Im_{t-1}\right) = 0,$$

and the associated time-varying expected term premium is given by

$$E\left(r_t - r_t^b \mid \Im_{t-1}\right) = \rho_{b,t-1}.$$

The term premium equation of (5.3) can be written equivalently as

$$\Delta r_t = r_t^b - r_{t-1} + \rho_{b,t-1} + a_{rr^*}\left[\Delta r_t^* - E\left(\Delta r_t^* \mid \Im_{t-1}\right)\right] + a_{re}\left[\Delta e_t - E\left(\Delta e_t \mid \Im_{t-1}\right)\right] + \widetilde{\psi}_r\left[\Delta p_t^o - E\left(\Delta p_t^o \mid \Im_{t-1}\right)\right] + \varepsilon_{rt}. \quad (5.4)$$

Under expectations formation mechanisms consistent with the reduced form VECM (5.1), the expectational variables $E\left(\Delta r_t^* \mid \Im_{t-1}\right)$, $E\left(\Delta e_t \mid \Im_{t-1}\right)$, and $E\left(\Delta p_t^o \mid \Im_{t-1}\right)$ can be solved in terms of the error correction terms, $\boldsymbol{\beta}' \mathbf{z}_{t-1} - \mathbf{b}_1 (t-1)$, and $\Delta \mathbf{z}_{t-i}$, $i = 1, 2, \ldots, p-1$, to yield:

$$\Delta r_t - a_{rr^*}\Delta r_t^* - a_{re}\Delta e_t - \widetilde{\psi}_r \Delta p_t^o = r_t^b - r_{t-1} + \rho_{b,t-1} + \boldsymbol{\phi}_r^*\left[\boldsymbol{\beta}'\mathbf{z}_{t-1} - \mathbf{b}_1(t-1)\right] + \sum_{i=1}^{p-1} \boldsymbol{\phi}_{zi}^* \Delta \mathbf{z}_{t-i} + \varepsilon_{rt}, \quad (5.5)$$

where the parameters $\boldsymbol{\phi}_r^*$ and $\boldsymbol{\phi}_{zi}^*$ are functions of a_{rr^*}, a_{re}, a_{ro} and the coefficients in the rows of (5.1) associated with the equations for Δr_t^*, Δe_t and Δp_t^o. This relates the change in the market rate to the base rate, to changes in the contemporaneously determined variables r_t^*, e_t and p_t^o, and to past information. We turn now to the determination of the base rate.

5.1.2 *The derivation of the base rate*

For the derivation of r_t^b, we follow the literature on inflation targeting and assume that it is derived as the solution to the following optimisation problem:[4]

$$\min_{r_t^b} \left\{E\left[C(\mathbf{w}_t, r_t) \mid \Im_{t-1}\right]\right\}, \quad (5.6)$$

[4] For recent accounts, see Blinder (1998), Bernanke *et al.* (1999) and Svensson (1999), for example.

where $C(\mathbf{w}_t, r_t)$ is the loss function of the monetary authorities, assumed to be quadratic so that

$$C(\mathbf{w}_t, r_t) = \frac{1}{2}(\mathbf{w}_t - \mathbf{w}_t^{\dagger})'\mathbf{Q}(\mathbf{w}_t - \mathbf{w}_t^{\dagger}) + \frac{1}{2}\theta(r_t - r_{t-1})^2, \tag{5.7}$$

where $\mathbf{w}_t = (y_t, \Delta p_t)'$ and $\mathbf{w}_t^{\dagger} = (y_t^{\dagger}, \pi_t^{\dagger})'$ are the target variables and their desired values, respectively. Since the target variables are both assumed to be $I(1)$ in our model, the desired target values, $\mathbf{w}_t^{\dagger}$ also need to be $I(1)$ and cointegrated with $\mathbf{w}_t$ for the optimisation problem to be controllable; otherwise the solution to the control problem will not be consistent with the assumed structural model. The 2×2 matrix $\mathbf{Q}$ characterises the authorities' short term trade-off between output growth and a reduction in the rate of inflation. The final term in (5.7) is intended to capture the institutional and political costs of changes to the interest rate.

The solution to the above optimisation problem requires the specification of a model linking the target variables, $\mathbf{w}_t$, to the policy instrument, r_t^b. Within our framework, such a model can be derived as a sub-system of the general long-run structural model specified in (5.2), with (5.5) as its structural interest rate equation. Subject to this sub-model, we can derive the first-order condition for the minimisation of (5.6), which is easily seen to be given by[5]

$$E\left[\left(\frac{\partial \mathbf{w}_t}{\partial r_t^b}\right)' \mathbf{Q}(\mathbf{w}_t - \mathbf{w}_t^{\dagger}) + \theta\left(\frac{\partial r_t}{\partial r_t^b}\right)\Delta r_t \mid \Im_{t-1}\right] = 0. \tag{5.8}$$

The outcome of this optimisation is a feedback rule (or reaction function) explaining the determination of r_t^b given the information available to the authorities. The parameters of the feedback rule depend on the preference parameters and the parameters of the econometric model. A complete description of the optimisation and the relationship between the parameters of the feedback rule is given in Appendix A. Stated simply, though, the feedback rule is of the following form:

$$r_t^b = r_{t-1} - \rho_{b,t-1} + \boldsymbol{\Upsilon}'\left[E(\mathbf{w}_t \mid \Im_{t-1}, \Delta r_t^b = 0) - \mathbf{w}_t^{\dagger}\right] \tag{5.9}$$

where $\boldsymbol{\Upsilon}'$ is a function of the parameters of the econometric model and of the preference parameters of the monetary authorities, $\mathbf{Q}$ and θ. Here,

[5] The problem of the credibility of the monetary policy, discussed in the literature by Barro and Gordon (1983), Rogoff (1985) and, more recently, by Svensson (1997), for example, is resolved in our application by the common knowledge assumption and the information symmetry. It is also worth noting that the extension of the decision problem to an intertemporal setting will complicate the analysis but does not materially alter our main conclusions.

$E(\mathbf{w}_t|\Im_{t-1}, \Delta r_t^b = 0)$ indicates the value of the target variables that would occur in time t in the absence of any interest rate adjustment and in the absence of any structural innovations to the economic system. The expression $E(\mathbf{w}_t \mid \Im_{t-1}, \Delta r_t^b = 0)$ is a function of information available to the monetary authorities and, as demonstrated in Appendix A, (5.9) can be written in more detail as:

$$r_t^b = r_{t-1} - \rho_{b,t-1} + \boldsymbol{\phi}^{\diamond} - \boldsymbol{\Upsilon}' \left(\mathbf{w}_t^{\dagger} - \mathbf{w}_{t-1}\right)$$
$$+ \boldsymbol{\phi}_r^{\diamond}\left[\boldsymbol{\beta}'\mathbf{z}_{t-1} - \mathbf{b}_1(t-1)\right] + \sum_{i=1}^{p-1} \boldsymbol{\phi}_{zi}^{\diamond}\Delta\mathbf{z}_{t-i}, \tag{5.10}$$

where $\boldsymbol{\phi}^{\diamond}$, $\boldsymbol{\phi}_r^{\diamond}$, and $\boldsymbol{\phi}_{zi}^{\diamond}$ are again functions of the parameters of the econometric model and of the preference parameters of the monetary authorities.

INFLATION TARGETING AND THE BASE RATE REACTION FUNCTION

The term $E(\mathbf{w}_t \mid \Im_{t-1}, \Delta r_t^b = 0)$ expresses the monetary authorities' conditional forecast of the target variables in time t assuming that they leave the base rate unchanged. The term $\left[E(\mathbf{w}_t|\Im_{t-1}, \Delta r_t^b = 0) - \mathbf{w}_t^{\dagger}\right]$ therefore has a natural interpretation as the *gap* between the desired level of the target variables and the authorities' forecast of the target variables in the absence of policy intervention. Written in this way, the reaction function of (5.9) clarifies the link between 'instrument rules' and 'target rules' in guiding monetary policy, as discussed recently in Svensson (2001, 2002), for example.

Svensson defines a 'target rule' as a commitment to set a policy instrument so as to achieve specific criteria for target variables. He contrasts this with an 'instrument rule' in which the central bank mechanically sets its instrument as a simple function of a small subset of the information available to the central bank, via a reaction function. He notes that, while most of the literature discusses central banks' behaviour in terms of reaction functions and instrument rules, few central banks have committed to mechanical instrument rate rules in practice. Rather, *inflation targeting* has been adopted as a strategy for implementing monetary policy by various countries in recent years, meaning that: (i) there is a numerical inflation target announced (either as a point target or as an acceptable range); (ii) monetary instruments are set such that the inflation forecasts of the authorities, conditional on the instrument setting, are consistent with the target (so that the decision process can be described as 'inflation-forecast targeting'); and (iii) the authorities provide transparent and explicit policy reports presenting forecasts and are held accountable for achieving the target. Svensson argues that inflation targeting is better described and prescribed as a commitment to a targeting rule than a commitment to an instrument rule.

As it is written in (5.10), the base rate reaction function derived above could clearly form the basis of an instrument rule, linking the authorities' base interest rate decision to known information on lagged variables in a complex but mechanical formula. However, the form in (5.9) shows that, despite the complexity, the reaction function has a relatively straightforward form based on the authorities' view of conditional forecasts of the target variables expressed relative to their desired levels. Moreover, as is demonstrated in detail in Appendix A, the reaction function can readily provide the motivation for a target rule.

To demonstrate this idea in Appendix A, we substitute the base rate reaction function into the structural relationships explaining the determination of the target variables in (5.2). This shows that, when the monetary authorities are following the reaction function derived above, the target variable outcome can be written as

$$\mathbf{w}_t = (\mathbf{I}_2 - \mathbf{\Lambda})E(\mathbf{w}_t \mid \Im_{t-1}, \Delta r_t^b = 0) + \Lambda \mathbf{w}_t^{\dagger} + \mathbf{v}_{ww,t}^{\diamond}$$

where $\mathbf{\Lambda}$ is a 2×2 matrix of fixed parameters and $\mathbf{v}_{ww,t}^{\diamond}$ is a composite shock generated by the structural shocks impacting on the p_t^o, e_t, r_t^* and target variables in time t. Hence, the target variable outcomes are a weighted average of the expected levels that would be achieved if the base rate is left unchanged and their desired levels, plus a random component, $\mathbf{v}_{ww,t}^{\diamond}$. The weights on the expected target variables and the desired target variables, $(\mathbf{I}_2 - \mathbf{\Lambda})$ and $\mathbf{\Lambda}$ respectively, depend on the preference parameters and the parameters of the econometric model. In particular, they reflect the relative importance of deviations of the target variables from their desired levels and the costs of changing the base rate in the monetary authorities' objective function in (5.6). Hence, in the simple case where there is only one target variable (say inflation), so that $\mathbf{A}_{wr}'$, $\mathbf{A}_{ww}'$ and $\mathbf{Q}$ in (5.2) and (5.7) are scalars, and equal to a_{wr}, 1, and q, respectively, say; then the weight is simply given by

$$\Lambda = \frac{a_{wr}^2 q}{a_{wr}^2 q + \theta}.$$

As $q/\theta \rightarrow \infty$, so that the cost of deviations of inflation from its desired level rises relative to the cost of changing the base rate, we have $\frac{a_{wr}^2 q}{a_{wr}^2 q+\theta} \rightarrow 1$ and

$$\mathbf{w}_t = \mathbf{w}_t^{\dagger} + \mathbf{v}_{ww,t}^{\diamond}. \tag{5.11}$$

Abstracting from the unpredictable structural shocks, the target variable would track the desired level precisely therefore. Hence, in the case where the costs of changing the base rate are small,[6] a commitment to an instrument rule of the form in (5.9), based on the gap between the inflation rate expected in the absence of a policy response and the desired inflation rate, is operationally equivalent to a commitment to a target rule in which policy is undertaken so as to achieve a specific desired inflation target.[7]

5.1.3 *The structural interest rate equation*

The final stage in deriving the structural interest rate equation is made in two further steps. First, we require a specification for $\mathbf{w}_t^{\dagger}$. Given that the desired target values need to be $I(1)$ and cointegrated with $\mathbf{w}_t$, a simple specification for $\mathbf{w}_t^{\dagger}$ that satisfies these requirements is given by

$$\mathbf{w}_t^{\dagger} = \begin{pmatrix} y_{t-1} + g_y^{\dagger} \\ \Delta p_{t-1} - g_{\pi}^{\dagger} \end{pmatrix} = \mathbf{w}_{t-1} + \mathbf{g}^{\dagger}, \tag{5.12}$$

where $\mathbf{g}^{\dagger} = (g_y^{\dagger}, -g_{\pi}^{\dagger})'$, $g_y^{\dagger} > 0$ is the fixed target level for output growth, and $g_{\pi}^{\dagger} > 0$ is the desired reduction in the rate of inflation. This specification is realistic and provides a reasonable working hypothesis with which to complete an empirical model. A discussion of alternative specifications for $\mathbf{w}_t^{\dagger}$ is considered below.

[6] Svensson, for example, is sceptical about the importance of these issues; see Section 5.6 of Svensson (2002).

[7] This is a desired time-t inflation target, given that it is contemporaneous time-t inflation that enters into the objective function. We consider the case where future inflation enters into the objective function below.

Finally, substitution of (5.9) in (5.5) yields the following structural interest rate equation

$$
\begin{aligned}
&\Delta r_t - a_{rr*}\Delta r_t^* - a_{re}\Delta e_t - \widetilde{\psi}_r \Delta p_t^o \\
&\quad = \boldsymbol{\Upsilon}'\left[E(\mathbf{w}_t \mid \Im_{t-1}, \Delta r_t^b = 0)\right] - \mathbf{w}_t^{\dagger} \\
&\quad + \boldsymbol{\phi}_r^*\left[\boldsymbol{\beta}'\mathbf{z}_{t-1} - \mathbf{b}_1(t-1)\right] + \sum_{i=1}^{p-1} \boldsymbol{\phi}_{z,i}^* \Delta \mathbf{z}_{t-i} + \varepsilon_{rt},
\end{aligned} \tag{5.13}
$$

which illustrates clearly the need for $\mathbf{w}_t$ and $\mathbf{w}_t^{\dagger}$ to be cointegrated.[8] Further, using (5.12) and (5.10), we obtain

$$
\begin{aligned}
&\Delta r_t - a_{rr*}\Delta r_t^* - a_{re}\Delta e_t - \widetilde{\psi}_r \Delta p_t^o \\
&\quad = \left(\phi^{\diamond} - \boldsymbol{\Upsilon}'\mathbf{g}^{\dagger}\right) + (\boldsymbol{\phi}_r^{\diamond} + \boldsymbol{\phi}_r^*)\left[\boldsymbol{\beta}'\mathbf{z}_{t-1} - \mathbf{b}_1(t-1)\right] \\
&\quad + \sum_{i=1}^{p-1} (\boldsymbol{\phi}_{zi}^{\diamond} + \boldsymbol{\phi}_{z,i}^*)\Delta \mathbf{z}_{t-i} + \varepsilon_{rt},
\end{aligned} \tag{5.14}
$$

where ε_{rt} is the monetary policy shock, as discussed above. Note that this structural equation is consistent with the long-run properties of the general structural model specified in (5.2). In particular, although changes in the preference parameters of the monetary authorities affect the magnitude and the speed with which interest rates respond to economic disequilibria, such changes have no effect on the long-run coefficients, $\boldsymbol{\beta}$, that are determined by general arbitrage conditions. It is also easily shown that, while changes in the trade-off parameter matrix, $\mathbf{Q}$, affect all the short-run coefficients of the interest rate equation, changes to the desired target values, $g_y^{\dagger}$ and $g_{\pi}^{\dagger}$, affect only the intercept term, $\phi^{\diamond} - \boldsymbol{\Upsilon}'\mathbf{g}^{\dagger}$.[9]

[8] For example, the interest rate decision would not have been consistent with the assumed underlying structural model if a fixed inflation rate target were specified; *i.e.* if it was required that $\pi_t^{\dagger} = g_{\pi}^{\dagger}$ as opposed to our specification where $\pi_t^{\dagger} = \Delta p_{t-1} - g_{\pi}^{\dagger}$.

[9] These properties could form the basis of an empirical test of recent developments in the conduct of monetary policy in the UK. But such an analysis is beyond the scope of the present work.

5.2 Alternative model specifications

The model derived above provides a sufficiently complete description of the context within which the monetary authorities' make their decisions to explicitly identify monetary policy shocks. But, as has been noted already, the identifying structure is based on assumptions on the sequencing of decisions and on the information sets available to agents when making decisions which may be contentious. Identification also relies on an assumed structure for the authorities' objective function and assumptions on how desired values for target variables are formed. In this section, we briefly comment on alternative assumptions that could be made on these latter two issues and consider the impact these alternative assumptions would have on the identification of the monetary policy shocks.

5.2.1 *Forecast-inflation targeting*

The model above makes use of an objective function in which it is the *current* values of the variables in $\mathbf{w}_t$ that are assumed of importance to the monetary authorities. In contrast, King (1994) argues that *future* values of target variables should also be of interest to monetary authorities. Certainly in the UK, for example, the Bank of England overtly follows a targeting rule in which there is a commitment to set policy so that the inflation rate for about two years ahead is on target. The decision to focus attention on future values of target variables is reasonable if there is a significant delay between the implementation of the monetary policy decision and the time the effects are felt. In this case, the authorities' objective function might be written as

$$\min_{r_t^b} \left\{ E\left[\sum_{h=0}^{\infty} \delta^h C(\mathbf{w}_{t+h}, r_t) \mid \mathfrak{I}_{t-1} \right] \right\}, \tag{5.15}$$

where $C(\mathbf{w}_{t+h}, r_t)$ might continue to have the quadratic form of (5.7) and δ is a discount rate. This complicates the authorities' decision-rule and focuses attention on forecasts of future target variables. However, the identification of monetary policy shocks is unaffected by this complexity and the impulse responses obtained on the basis of the identification scheme of the previous section remains unchanged here.

To see this, consider the simple case in which the monetary authorities care about just one particular period ahead, $t + h$ say, and face the optimisation problem

$$\min_{r_t^b} \left\{ E\left[C(\mathbf{w}_{t+h}, r_t) \mid \Im_{t-1}\right]\right\}, \tag{5.16}$$

with

$$C(\mathbf{w}_{t+h}, r_t) = \frac{1}{2}(\mathbf{w}_{t+h} - \mathbf{w}_{t+h}^{\dagger})'\mathbf{Q}(\mathbf{w}_{t+h} - \mathbf{w}_{t+h}^{\dagger}) + \frac{1}{2}\theta(r_t - r_{t-1})^2. \tag{5.17}$$

Identification of the monetary policy shocks can be achieved following the steps described in the previous section. Hence, as explained in more detail in Appendix A, minimisation of (5.16) provides a reaction function of the form

$$r_t^b = r_{t-1} - \rho_{b,t-1} + \boldsymbol{\Upsilon}_h'\left[E(\mathbf{w}_{t+h} \mid \Im_{t-1}, \Delta r_t^b = 0) - \mathbf{w}_{t+h}^{\dagger}\right] \tag{5.18}$$

where $\boldsymbol{\Upsilon}_h'$ is a function of the parameters of the econometric model and of the preference parameters of the monetary authorities (and $\mathbf{w}_{t+h}^{\dagger}$ is assumed known at time $t-1$). Assuming that the derived reaction function is followed, the target variable outcome, $\mathbf{w}_{t+h}$, will be a weighted average of $E(\mathbf{w}_{t+h} \mid \Im_{t-1}, \Delta r_t^b = 0)$ and $\mathbf{w}_{t+h}^{\dagger}$ plus the effects of structural shocks experienced between t and $t+h$. In the case where the costs of adjusting the base rate are small relative to the costs of deviating from the desired level, $\mathbf{w}_{t+h}$ will track $\mathbf{w}_{t+h}^{\dagger}$ closely (abstracting from the effects of the unknown structural innovations that occur between t and $t+h$) and the commitment to the instrument rule in (5.18) is equivalent to pursuing a target rule where policy attempts to achieve a specified forecast-inflation target. Moreover, having derived the base rate reaction function in (5.18), the structural interest rate equation is derived exactly as in Section 5.1.3 above. Hence, the form of the structural model for $\mathbf{z}_t$ is exactly as in (5.2) and monetary policy shocks are once more identified as changes in the interest rate not explained by unanticipated movements in oil prices, exchange rates and foreign interest rates.

5.2.2 *Choice of targets and their desired levels*

The form of the monetary authorities' objective function played a central role in the short-run economic theory that underlies the identification of monetary policy shocks in the previous section. There has been a lively debate in the literature in recent years over the terms that should enter into the authorities' objective function and over their desired levels. In this section, we briefly comment on this discussion and relate the arguments to our identification scheme.

The objective function described in the previous section is consistent with monetary authorities' statements about their objectives. The maintenance of low and stable inflation is an explicitly stated objective for the independent central banks that now implement monetary policy in many countries. And many policy-makers are also encouraged to consider the output consequences of monetary policy.[10] However, despite the general consensus among practitioners, there remains considerable controversy over certain aspects of the objectives of monetary policy in the academic community.

Among those who believe that inflation should be stabilised around a fixed target level, there is long-standing disagreement on whether this should be at zero or a small positive figure (see King (1999) for a review). Some argue that non-zero inflation is damaging because of the distortions to money demand that arise and because of the relative price distortions that are created in a world with less than instantaneous or asynchronised price adjustment.[11] Others argue that a low but positive inflation rate is optimal on the basis of the presence of downward nominal rigidities (*e.g.* Akerlof *et al.* (1996)) or on the basis of the dangers of a liquidity trap given a zero bound to nominal interest rates (*e.g.* Summers (1991)). Still others believe that monetary policy should aim at price *level* targeting rather than inflation targeting (*e.g.* Svensson (1999)).

The debate regarding the role of output in monetary authorities' objective functions is also unresolved. There is now a broad consensus within macroeconomics that there is relatively little scope for manipulating real magnitudes through monetary policy in the long run and attention focuses on the role of monetary policy in minimising short-run variation of output around its 'long-run level'. Hence, desired output levels found in the literature typically refer to 'potential output' and the 'output gap' between actual and potential output. The term is used in the sense introduced by Okun (1962) and refers to the level of output potentially available at full employment and given the level of technological knowledge, the capital stock, natural resources, skill of the labour force and so on. In practice, this desired level is frequently measured as a trend in actual output

[10] In the UK, for example, the Bank of England's remit is to achieve an annual rate of consumer price inflation of 2.0% (over an unspecified time horizon) and, insofar as it does not compromise the targeting of inflation, the Bank is to support the policy of the government including its objectives for growth and employment.

[11] See Feldstein (1998), Bakhshi *et al.* (1997) and Woodford (2002, 2003), for example.

data, obtained as a simple exponential trend or through the Hodrick–Prescott filter. These empirical measures are simple statistical constructs, however, and have little economic motivation. Indeed, if potential output is difference-stationary, as the evidence seems to suggest, these measures are unlikely to be satisfactory. Woodford (2002, 2003) provides a more detailed discussion of the appropriate measure of desired output based on an explicit model of private sector behaviour in which welfare can be considered explicitly. He demonstrates that a socially optimal desired level of output is the 'natural level' of output, defined as the equilibrium level of output that would obtain in the event of perfectly flexible prices. But again, an adequate measure of such a concept will require a relatively complete macroeconomic model to be developed.

In the model of the previous section, we assumed in expression (5.12) that there are fixed desired *growth rates* for output and inflation, so that desired levels of output and inflation in each period are a fixed markup over last period's level. The advantage of such a specification is that it ensures that the desired levels are $I(1)$ and this is necessary to generate $I(1)$ values for the target variable outcomes. The disadvantage is that this form for the desired target variables does not correspond to the economic concepts discussed above any better than the standard use of trends. However, while the form of the variables in (5.12) is the simplest that will ensure difference-stationarity, it is not the only assumption that will generate $I(1)$ variables. In particular, an alternative approach to motivating measures of desired target variables is suggested by the idea that it would be unreasonable to choose desired targets which are inconsistent with the long-run relationships outlined by economic theory. Hence, we might make use of the long-run relationships involving the target variables to suggest sensible measures of their desired levels which will be $I(1)$ by construction. In this, a balance is struck between the integration properties of the observed variables such as real output and inflation and their desired target values.

For example, following this approach in the case of output determination, we recall that the economic theory of the long run elaborated in Chapter 4 suggested a long-run relationship between domestic and foreign output. The relationship was based on a stochastic Solow growth model, a simple model of technological progress and an assumption that, subject to transitory impediments to information flows and legal impediments, technology flows across national boundaries. This view provided the long-run 'output gap' relationship in (4.37) that was embedded within our macroeconometric model, *i.e.* $y_t = y_t^* + b_{30} + \xi_{3,t+1}$, with stationary zero-mean long-run reduced form disturbance ξ_{3t}. Given this theory of the long run, and the acknowledgement that domestic and foreign outputs are being driven by an underlying (and unobserved) common measure of technological progress, a reasonable measure of potential output might be given by the value of foreign output at time t expected when policy is set. This also provides a natural alternative measure of desired UK output; *i.e.*

$$y_t^{\dagger} = E(y_t^* \mid \Im_{t-1}).$$

This alternative measure of target output has the required property that it is $I(1)$. Moreover, an expression for $E(y_t^* \mid \Im_{t-1})$ can be obtained, in terms of $\boldsymbol{\beta}' \mathbf{z}_{t-1}$and $\Delta \mathbf{z}_{t-i}$, $i = 1, \ldots, p-1$, from the reduced form expression y_t^* in (5.1). Inclusion of this expression in (5.13) would provide a structural interest rate equation of precisely the same form as in (5.14). The coefficients of the associated reduced form model would have a different interpretation, but *the identified monetary policy shocks obtained on the basis of the estimated reduced form model would be the same and any impulse response analysis undertaken would be unchanged.*

In a similar vein, the description of the Fisher equation of Chapter 4 motivated a long-run relationship between nominal interest rates and inflation that might be used to motivate an alternative measure of the desired inflation rate. Specifically, the long-run theory provided a stationary real interest rate equation in (4.39) of the form $r_t - \Delta p_t = b_{50} + \xi_{5,t+1}$, with stationary zero-mean long-run reduced form disturbance ξ_{5t}. Simply rewriting the long-run relationship and abstracting from the long-run disturbances, we might consider $\Delta p_t^{\dagger} = E[r_t - b_{50} \mid \Im_{t-1}]$, so that the desired interest rate is that which would ensure the real interest rate is at its long-run level for any expected value of r_t. Further, given that the nominal interest rate is, via the base rate, the instrument under the control of the monetary authorities, and given that interest rate movements are intrinsically costly in the authorities' cost function in (5.7), the desired level might reasonably be defined under the assumption of no change in the base rate,[12] so that we might amend the above to give

$$\begin{aligned}\Delta p_t^{\dagger} &= E[r_t - b_{50} \mid \Im_{t-1}, \Delta r_t^b = 0] \\ &= r_{t-1} - b_{50}.\end{aligned}$$

[12] Even if the cost of adjusting the instrument rate is considered close to zero, the authorities might consider the desired level of inflation to be such that, if the economy is in equilibrium, no instrument rate adjustment is required. The definition of desired inflation would build in the assumption that $\Delta r_t^b = 0$ in this case.

Again, this alternative measure of the target inflation rate has the required property that it is $I(1)$.[13] And, once more, inclusion of this expression in (5.13) would provide a structural interest rate equation of precisely the same form as in (5.14), the identified monetary policy shocks would be the same, and any impulse response analysis undertaken on the basis of the model would be unchanged.

[13] Note that the Taylor (1993) rule is typically written as

$$r_t = (1-\lambda)\left[\rho + \Delta p_t + \gamma_1(\Delta p_t - \Delta p_t^{\dagger}) + \gamma_2(y_t - y_t^{\dagger})\right] + \lambda r_{t-1},$$

with ρ being the average real interest rate. Now, when Δp_t and y_t are at their desired levels in this expression, then

$$r_t - r_{t-1} = (1-\lambda)\left[\rho + \Delta p_t^{\dagger} - r_{t-1}\right]$$

and we again have $\Delta p_t^{\dagger} = r_{t-1} - \rho$ when $\Delta r_t = 0$.

6

Econometric methods: A review

In this chapter, we provide an overview of the econometric methods used in long-run structural macroeconometric modelling. The aim is to place in context the methods employed, to describe the steps taken in the estimation and development of the model, to help explain the various econometric tools used in interpreting the empirical results, and to explore some of the ways in which a long-run structural macroeconometric model can be used.

The long-run structural VARX modelling approach adopted in our work is described in Pesaran and Shin (2002) and Pesaran, Shin and Smith (2000), jointly denoted PSS, and is based on a modified and generalised version of Johansen's (1988, 1991, 1995) maximum likelihood approach to the problem of estimation and hypothesis testing in the context of augmented vector autoregressive error correction models. Of course, the analysis of economic time series containing unit roots has a long history, traceable to Yule's seminal (1926) paper on the potential pitfalls of interpreting regressions based on such data.[1] Granger and Newbold (1974) revived the issue when they showed that spurious regressions could result from the regression of one independent random walk on another.[2] The theoretical rationale behind the Granger–Newbold spurious regression result was set out in Phillips (1986) who showed that the R^2 of the regressions involving $I(1)$ variables tend to one and the t-ratios grow without bound as the sample size increases, even if the underlying $I(1)$ variables

[1] Excellent surveys of the literature on cointegration are provided in Banerjee *et al.* (1993), Watson (1994), Hamilton (1994), and in the papers in the *Special Issue of the Journal of Economic Surveys* edited by Oxley and McAleer (1998). The material of this chapter draws on Pesaran and Smith (1998) in that *Special Issue*.

[2] The problem of spurious regression in the case of stationary but *highly* serially correlated regressors was demonstrated earlier by Champernowne (1960), also using Monte Carlo techniques.

are statistically independent. The possibility of spurious regression and the growing availability of tests for unit roots, *e.g.* Dickey and Fuller (1979), led to a proliferation of testing for the order of integration of economic time series in the 1980s. The classic study is Nelson and Plosser (1982) who raised the possibility that the null hypothesis of a unit root could not be rejected for most US economic time series. At the same time, Granger (1981, 1986) and Engle and Granger (1987) were developing the analysis of cointegrated systems, explaining the links with the (relatively well-established) error correction models used for example in Sargan (1964) and subsequently popularised through the work of Davidson *et al.* (1978). Johansen's maximum likelihood approach popularised the use of cointegration analysis, allowing for symmetric treatment of all the variables in the cointegrated system and for an analysis of the number of cointegrating relations. Our own approach, elaborated in PSS, builds on this to allow economic theory to motivate the exact and over-identifying restrictions studied in the cointegration analysis in place of the type of statistical identification used by Johansen. PSS also develop the econometric analysis of vector error correction models with weakly exogenous $I(1)$ variables.

In what follows, we provide a brief statement of the econometric issues involved in the modelling approach advanced in PSS. We start by describing a general structural VARX model, allowing for the possibility of drawing a distinction between endogenous and exogenous variables. We use this general model to place in context the identification issues raised in Chapter 3 and to introduce the ideas behind impulse response analysis. We then turn our attention to cointegrating VARX models, contrasting the PSS approach to the Johansen approach, commenting on the small sample properties of some of the test statistics and broadening the discussion of the impulse response analysis to a more general analysis of system dynamics in the cointegrated VARX context. We end the chapter with comments on the small sample properties of some of the test statistics discussed in the chapter and on the distributional properties of the impulse response function. These statistical properties can be readily investigated through simulation methods and we explain how simulation methods can be used in this regard. This sets the scene for the use of structural VARX models in forecasting discussed in Chapter 7. Throughout the chapter, our description of the econometric techniques is informed by how they are used in practice and we relate the discussion to the choices that an applied econometrician has to make in the practical application of cointegrating VARX techniques.

6.1 Augmented VAR or VARX models

6.1.1 *The structural VARX model*

The general structural VARX model for an $m_y \times 1$ vector of endogenous variables $\mathbf{y}_t$, is given by:[3]

$$\mathbf{A}\mathbf{y}_t = \mathbf{A}_1\mathbf{y}_{t-1} + \cdots + \mathbf{A}_p\mathbf{y}_{t-p} + \mathbf{B}_0\mathbf{x}_t + \mathbf{B}_1\mathbf{x}_{t-1} + \cdots + \mathbf{B}_p\mathbf{x}_{t-p} + \mathbf{D}\mathbf{d}_t + \boldsymbol{\varepsilon}_t, \tag{6.1}$$

for $t = 1, 2, \ldots, T$, where $\mathbf{d}_t$ is a $q \times 1$ vector of deterministic variables (*e.g.* intercept, trend and seasonal variables), $\mathbf{x}_t$ is an $m_x \times 1$ vector of exogenous variables, $\boldsymbol{\varepsilon}_t = (\varepsilon_{1t}, \varepsilon_{2t}, \ldots, \varepsilon_{m_y t})'$ is an $m_y \times 1$ vector of serially uncorrelated errors distributed independently of $\mathbf{x}_t$ with a zero mean and a constant positive definite variance–covariance matrix, $\boldsymbol{\Omega} = (\omega_{ij})$, where ω_{ij} is the (i, j)th element of $\boldsymbol{\Omega}$. For given values of $\mathbf{d}_t$ and $\mathbf{x}_t$, the above dynamic system is stable if all the roots of the determinantal equation

$$\left|\mathbf{A} - \mathbf{A}_1\lambda - \mathbf{A}_2\lambda^2 - \cdots - \mathbf{A}_p\lambda^p\right| = 0, \tag{6.2}$$

lie strictly outside the unit circle. This stability condition ensures the existence of long-run relationships between $\mathbf{y}_t$ and $\mathbf{x}_t$, which will be cointegrating when one or more elements of $\mathbf{x}_t$ are integrated, namely contain unit roots. The assumption, however, rules out the possibility that the endogenous variables, $\mathbf{y}_t$, will themselves be cointegrating when the model contains no exogenous variables.

The above VARX model is structural in the sense that it explicitly allows for instantaneous interactions between the endogenous variables through the contemporaneous coefficient matrix, $\mathbf{A}$. It can also be written as

$$\mathbf{A}(L)\mathbf{y}_t = \mathbf{B}(L)\mathbf{x}_t + \mathbf{D}\mathbf{d}_t + \boldsymbol{\varepsilon}_t, \tag{6.3}$$

where L is the lag operator such that $L\mathbf{y}_t = \mathbf{y}_{t-1}$, and

$$\mathbf{A}(L) = \mathbf{A} - \mathbf{A}_1 L - \cdots - \mathbf{A}_p L^p; \quad \mathbf{B}(L) = \mathbf{B}_0 + \mathbf{B}_1 L + \cdots + \mathbf{B}_p L^p.$$

Of particular interest are the system long-run effects of the exogenous variables which are given by:

$$\mathbf{A}(1)^{-1}\mathbf{B}(1) = \left(\mathbf{A} - \sum_{i=1}^{p} \mathbf{A}_i\right)^{-1} \sum_{i=0}^{p} \mathbf{B}_i.$$

[3] In general, different orders can be assumed for the distributed lag functions associated with the endogenous and exogenous variables. Alternatively, p can be viewed as the maximum lag order of the distributed lag functions on $\mathbf{y}_t$ and $\mathbf{x}_t$.

Notice that, since all the roots of (6.2) fall outside the unit circle by assumption, the inverse of $\mathbf{A}(1)$, which we denote by $\mathbf{A}(1)^{-1}$, exists.

INITIAL MODELLING CHOICES

The decision to work with a model of the type described above presents the applied econometrician with a number of important choices, namely:

1. The number and list of the endogenous variables to be included, $(m_y, \mathbf{y}_t)$.
2. The number and list of the exogenous variables (if any) to be included, $(m_x, \mathbf{x}_t)$.
3. The nature of the deterministic variables (intercepts, trends, seasonals) and whether the intercepts and/or the trend coefficients need to be restricted.
4. The lag orders of the VARX (the lag order of the $\mathbf{y}_t$ and $\mathbf{x}_t$ components of the VARX need not be the same).
5. The order of integration of the variables.

These choices change the maximised value of the log-likelihood (MLL) so that, in principle, they could be made on the basis of either hypothesis testing exercises or by means of model selection criteria such as the Akaike Information Criterion (AIC), or the Schwarz Bayesian Criterion (SBC). However, different significance levels, different forms of the tests and different model selection criteria invariably can lead to different model specifications. In many cases, little is known about the small sample properties of these procedures and what is known is often not reassuring. Little is also known about the properties of the tests or model selection criteria when the range of models considered does not include the data generation process. These choices are often closely related and the outcomes are sensitive to initial choices. The combination of these choices gives us a very large space of possible models and there is no reason to expect a series of sequential choices (*e.g.* fix m_y and m_x, then choose p conditional on m_y and m_x, *etc.*) to adequately explore the possible model space. Joint tests may lead to different inferences from a sequence of individual tests. Sequential procedures are likely to suffer from pre-test bias, while general to specific searches face the difficulty that the unrestricted models are profligate with parameters.

While data-dependent decision procedures are extremely important, they have to be supplemented with other considerations given the complexity of most applied modelling problems. In particular, choices will be informed by the purpose of the exercise and by prior information from economic theory; theory being interpreted widely. In principle, this combination could be done formally by embodying the purpose of the exercise in an explicit loss function and the theory information in a prior probability distribution for the parameters, and then applying Bayesian techniques. In practice, the difficulty of formalising the loss function and prior probability distributions makes a formal use of these other considerations attractive only for relatively simple problems. Often, the applied econometrician will make use of a range of informal procedures for integrating economic and statistical information. For example, statistically insignificant variables may be retained when they are economically important, and statistically significant variables may be deleted when they are likely to be economically unimportant, since misleading statistical significance can arise for many reasons. For example, chance correlations with omitted variables, like cold winters or policy announcements, can make variables significant. It is a matter of judgement whether these variables or lags are regarded as economically important.

Given the size of the potential model space, defined by the choices discussed above, it is important to investigate a range of specifications and allow for model uncertainty in forecasting and policy analysis. At present full exploration of the model space is likely to be highly data-intensive and computationally burdensome, if not infeasible. Even much simpler problems, like determining the lag order in a single-equation autoregressive distributed lag model, as discussed in Pesaran and Shin (1999), require many hundred regressions. As full exploration is not feasible, organised sensitivity analysis plays an important role. This sensitivity analysis should investigate both the statistical significance and the economic importance of the restrictions.

6.1.2 *The reduced form VARX model*

The reduced form of the structural model (6.1), which expresses the endogenous variables in terms of the predetermined and exogenous variables, is given by

$$\mathbf{y}_t = \mathbf{\Phi}_1\mathbf{y}_{t-1} + \cdots + \mathbf{\Phi}_p\mathbf{y}_{t-p} + \mathbf{\Psi}_0\mathbf{x}_t + \mathbf{\Psi}_1\mathbf{x}_{t-1} + \cdots + \mathbf{\Psi}_p\mathbf{x}_{t-p} + \mathbf{\Upsilon}\mathbf{d}_t + \mathbf{u}_t, \tag{6.4}$$

where $\mathbf{\Phi}_i = \mathbf{A}^{-1}\mathbf{A}_i$, $\mathbf{\Psi}_i = \mathbf{A}^{-1}\mathbf{B}_i$, $\mathbf{\Upsilon} = \mathbf{A}^{-1}\mathbf{D}$, $\mathbf{u}_t = \mathbf{A}^{-1}\boldsymbol{\varepsilon}_t$ is *i.i.d.* $(0, \mathbf{\Sigma})$ with $\mathbf{\Sigma} = \mathbf{A}^{-1}\mathbf{\Omega}\mathbf{A}'^{-1} = (\sigma_{ij})$. The classical identification problem is how to recover the structural form parameters

$$(\mathbf{A}, \mathbf{A}_{i+1}, \mathbf{B}_i, i = 0, 1, \ldots, p; \ \mathbf{D} \text{ and } \boldsymbol{\Omega}),$$

from the reduced form parameters,

$$(\boldsymbol{\Phi}_i, \boldsymbol{\Psi}_i, i = 0, 1, \ldots, p, \boldsymbol{\Upsilon}, \text{ and } \boldsymbol{\Sigma}).$$

This is the identification issue raised in the discussion of Section 3.1, and Section 3.1.2 in particular. The resolution of this identification problem formed the basis of the Cowles Commission approach to structural modelling in econometrics. Exact identification of the structural parameters requires m_y^2 *a priori* restrictions, of which m_y restrictions would be provided by normalisation conditions. The restrictions typically involve setting certain elements of the structural coefficient matrices to zero. These were the *a priori* restrictions criticised by Sims (1980), particularly when such identifying restrictions were obtained by restricting the short-run dynamics. Most of the traditional macromodels were heavily over-identified and while, in principle, these over-identifying restrictions could be tested, in practice the number of exogenous and predetermined variables was so large that it was impossible to estimate the reduced form. There are a variety of other ways of imposing identifying restrictions. For instance, if after a suitable ordering, it is assumed that $\mathbf{A}$ is triangular *and* $\boldsymbol{\Omega}$ diagonal (though there is no general theoretical reason to expect it to be so), the structural system becomes a recursive causal chain, each equation of which can be consistently estimated by OLS. The assumptions that $\mathbf{A}$ is triangular and $\boldsymbol{\Omega}$ is diagonal each provide $m_y(m_y - 1)/2 + m_y(m_y - 1)/2$ restrictions respectively, which together with the m_y normalisation restrictions just identify the system. As we shall see below these assumptions are also equivalent to the use of the Choleski decomposition of $\boldsymbol{\Sigma}$ originally advocated by Sims for identification of impulse responses.

6.1.3 *Impulse response analysis*

One of the main features of the traditional macromodels was their dynamic multipliers, which measured the effect of a shock to an exogenous variable, *e.g.* a policy change, or a shock to one of the structural errors, $\boldsymbol{\varepsilon}_t$, on the (expected) future values of the endogenous variables. Here, we shall briefly review how one can measure the dynamic effects of shocks or impulse response functions.

Under the stability assumption (namely that the roots of (6.2) lie strictly outside the unit circle), $\mathbf{A}(L)$ is invertible and the time profile of the effect of a shock can be calculated from the 'final form' of the structural model:

$$\mathbf{y}_t = \mathbf{A}(L)^{-1}\mathbf{B}(L)\mathbf{x}_t + \mathbf{A}(L)^{-1}\mathbf{D}\mathbf{d}_t + \mathbf{A}(L)^{-1}\boldsymbol{\varepsilon}_t. \tag{6.5}$$

This expresses each endogenous variable in terms of an infinite distributed lag on the exogenous variables and an infinite moving average process on the structural errors. Notice that the dynamic multipliers, the effects of a shock to $\mathbf{x}_t$, can be derived from the reduced form coefficients, but to measure the dynamic effect of a shock to the structural errors we have to identify the structural coefficients. The equivalent final form representation of the reduced form model is:

$$\mathbf{y}_t = \boldsymbol{\Phi}(L)^{-1}\boldsymbol{\Psi}(L)\mathbf{x}_t + \boldsymbol{\Phi}(L)^{-1}\boldsymbol{\Upsilon}\mathbf{d}_t + \boldsymbol{\Phi}(L)^{-1}\mathbf{u}_t, \tag{6.6}$$

where[4]

$$\boldsymbol{\Phi}(L) = \mathbf{I}_{m_y} - \boldsymbol{\Phi}_1 L - \cdots - \boldsymbol{\Phi}_p L^p, \quad \boldsymbol{\Psi}(L) = \boldsymbol{\Psi}_0 + \boldsymbol{\Psi}_1 L + \cdots + \boldsymbol{\Psi}_p L^p,$$

and $\mathbf{I}_{m_y}$ is an identity matrix of order m_y. Since $\boldsymbol{\Phi}(L)$ is invertible, we have the following moving-average representation of the structural errors:

$$\boldsymbol{\Phi}(L)^{-1}\mathbf{u}_t = \sum_{i=0}^{\infty} \boldsymbol{\Theta}_i \mathbf{u}_{t-i} = \sum_{i=0}^{\infty} \boldsymbol{\Theta}_i \mathbf{A}^{-1}\boldsymbol{\varepsilon}_{t-i}, \tag{6.7}$$

where the $\boldsymbol{\Theta}_i$'s can be calculated from the following recursive relations:

$$\boldsymbol{\Theta}_i = \boldsymbol{\Phi}_1\boldsymbol{\Theta}_{i-1} + \boldsymbol{\Phi}_2\boldsymbol{\Theta}_{i-2} + \cdots + \boldsymbol{\Phi}_p\boldsymbol{\Theta}_{i-p}, \quad \text{for } i = 0, 1, 2, \ldots, \tag{6.8}$$

where $\boldsymbol{\Theta}_i = 0$, for $i < 0$ and $\boldsymbol{\Theta}_0 = \mathbf{I}_{m_y}$.

Although this *infinite* moving average representation exists only when the model is stable, it turns out that similar results can be obtained even in the unstable case where one or more roots of (6.2) are on the unit circle. Irrespective of whether the model is stationary or contains unit roots, one can derive impulse response functions for the responses of the endogenous variables to a 'unit' displacement in the particular elements of either the exogenous variables, $\mathbf{x}_t$, or the errors ($\mathbf{u}_t$ or $\boldsymbol{\varepsilon}_t$). The former represents the time profile of the response of the system to changes in the observed forcing variables of the system, while the latter examines the responses of

[4] Since A is non-singular and the roots of $|\mathbf{A} - \mathbf{A}_1\lambda - \mathbf{A}_2\lambda^2 - \cdots - \mathbf{A}_p\lambda^p| = 0$ are assumed to fall outside the unit circle, it follows that the roots of $\left|\mathbf{I}_{m_y} - \boldsymbol{\Phi}_1\lambda - \boldsymbol{\Phi}_2\lambda^2 - \cdots - \boldsymbol{\Phi}_p\lambda^p\right| = 0$ will also fall outside the unit circle.

the system to changes in the unobserved forcing variables. The impulse response functions for the errors can be defined either with respect to the 'structural' errors, $\boldsymbol{\varepsilon}_t$, or with respect to the reduced form errors, $\mathbf{u}_t$. All these impulse responses can be obtained using the generalised impulse response approach advanced in Koop *et al.* (1996) for non-linear models and discussed in more detail for linear models in Pesaran and Shin (1998). The generalised impulse response function GIRF measures the change to the n period ahead forecast of each of the variables that would be caused by a shock to the exogenous variable, structural or reduced form disturbance.

GENERALISED IMPULSE RESPONSE FUNCTIONS

To formally define the generalised impulse response functions, denote the information set containing current and all lagged values of $\mathbf{y}_t$ and $\mathbf{x}_t$ by $\Im_t = (\mathbf{y}_t, \mathbf{y}_{t-1}, \ldots; \mathbf{x}_t, \mathbf{x}_{t-1}, \ldots)$. Consider a shock to the ith structural error, ε_{it}, and let $\mathfrak{g}(n, \mathbf{z} : \varepsilon_i)$ be the generalised impulse responses of $\mathbf{z}_{t+n} = (\mathbf{y}'_{t+n}, \mathbf{x}'_{t+n})'$ to a unit change in ε_{it}, measured by one standard deviation, namely $\sqrt{\omega_{ii}}$. At horizon n the GIRF is defined by the point forecast of $\mathbf{z}_{t+n}$ conditional on the information $\Im_{t-1}$ and the one standard error shock of the ith structural error, ε_{it}, relative to the baseline conditional forecasts. Namely,

$$\mathfrak{g}(n, \mathbf{z} : \varepsilon_i) = E(\mathbf{z}_{t+n} \mid \varepsilon_{it} = \sqrt{\omega_{ii}}, \Im_{t-1}) - E(\mathbf{z}_{t+n} \mid \Im_{t-1}).$$

Clearly, since the $\mathbf{x}_t$ are assumed to be strictly exogenous, the effects of shocking ε_{it} on $\mathbf{x}_{t+h}$ will be zero, *i.e.* $\mathfrak{g}(n, \mathbf{x} : \varepsilon_i) = \mathbf{0}$ for all n and i.[5] Since the ε_{it} are serially uncorrelated then their impulse response functions are non-zero only at horizon zero when $\mathfrak{g}(n, \boldsymbol{\varepsilon} : \varepsilon_i) = E(\boldsymbol{\varepsilon}_t \mid \varepsilon_{it} = \sqrt{\omega_{ii}})$ for $n = 0$, but for all other horizons $n > 0$ we have $\mathfrak{g}(n, \boldsymbol{\varepsilon} : \varepsilon_i) = 0$.

If the structural errors are correlated, a shock to one error will be associated with changes in the other errors. As shown by Koop *et al.* (1996), in the Gaussian case where $\boldsymbol{\varepsilon}_t \backsim i.i.d.N(\mathbf{0}, \boldsymbol{\Omega})$, $(\boldsymbol{\varepsilon}_t, \varepsilon_{it})$ are also normally distributed

$$\begin{pmatrix} \boldsymbol{\varepsilon}_t \\ \varepsilon_{it} \end{pmatrix} \sim i.i.d.N\left[\begin{pmatrix} 0 \\ 0 \end{pmatrix}, \begin{pmatrix} \boldsymbol{\Omega} & \mathrm{Cov}(\boldsymbol{\varepsilon}_t, \varepsilon_{it}) \\ \mathrm{Cov}(\varepsilon_{it}, \boldsymbol{\varepsilon}_t) & V(\varepsilon_{it}) \end{pmatrix}\right],$$

[5] This would not of course be the case if $\mathbf{x}_t$ was only weakly exogenous.

then noting that $V(\varepsilon_{it}) = \omega_{ii}$

$$E(\boldsymbol{\varepsilon}_t|\varepsilon_{it} = \sqrt{\omega_{ii}}) = E(\boldsymbol{\varepsilon}_t) + \frac{\text{Cov}(\boldsymbol{\varepsilon}_t, \varepsilon_{it})}{V(\varepsilon_{it})}(\sqrt{\omega_{ii}} - 0)$$
$$= \frac{1}{\sqrt{\omega_{ii}}}\text{Cov}(\boldsymbol{\varepsilon}_t, \varepsilon_{it})$$
$$= \frac{1}{\sqrt{\omega_{ii}}}\begin{pmatrix} \omega_{1i} \\ \omega_{2i} \\ \vdots \\ \omega_{m_y i} \end{pmatrix}. \tag{6.9}$$

which can be written more compactly as

$$E(\boldsymbol{\varepsilon}_t|\varepsilon_{it} = \sqrt{\omega_{ii}}) = \left(\frac{1}{\sqrt{\omega_{ii}}}\right)\boldsymbol{\Omega}\mathbf{e}_i,$$

where $\mathbf{e}_i$ is an $m_y \times 1$ selection vector of zeros except for its ith element which is set to unity.[6] This gives the predicted shocks in each structural error given a shock to ε_{it}, based on the typical correlation observed historically between the structural errors. In the special case where the structural errors are orthogonal, the shock only changes the ith error and we have

$$E\left(\boldsymbol{\varepsilon}_t \mid \varepsilon_{it} = \sqrt{\omega_{ii}}\right) = \sqrt{\omega_{ii}}\mathbf{e}_i.$$

Application of the generalised impulse response analysis to the VARX specification, (6.1), now yields

$$\mathbf{A}\mathfrak{g}\left(n, \mathbf{y} : \varepsilon_i\right) = \mathbf{A}_1\mathfrak{g}\left(n-1, \mathbf{y} : \varepsilon_i\right) + \cdots + \mathbf{A}_p\mathfrak{g}\left(n-p, \mathbf{y} : \varepsilon_i\right) + \mathfrak{g}\left(n, \boldsymbol{\varepsilon} : \varepsilon_i\right),$$

for $n = 0, 1, 2, \ldots,$ with the initial values $\mathfrak{g}\left(n, \mathbf{y} : \varepsilon_i\right) = 0$ for $n < 0$ and as we saw above the last term is non-zero only for $n = 0$. The identification of $\mathfrak{g}\left(n, \mathbf{y} : \varepsilon_i\right)$ requires the identification of the structural coefficients $\mathbf{A}$ and $\mathbf{A}_i$, $i = 1, \ldots, p$, and the covariance matrix $\boldsymbol{\Omega}$. It is also possible to identify $\mathfrak{g}\left(n, \mathbf{y} : \varepsilon_i\right)$ by a mixture of identification restrictions on $\mathbf{A}$ and $\boldsymbol{\Omega}$. To see this we premultiply both sides of the above relationship by $\mathbf{A}^{-1}$ and obtain

$$\mathfrak{g}\left(n, \mathbf{y} : \varepsilon_i\right) = \boldsymbol{\Phi}_1\mathfrak{g}\left(n-1, \mathbf{y} : \varepsilon_i\right) + \cdots + \boldsymbol{\Phi}_p\mathfrak{g}\left(n-p, \mathbf{y} : \varepsilon_i\right)$$
$$+ \mathbf{A}^{-1}\mathfrak{g}\left(n, \boldsymbol{\varepsilon} : \varepsilon_i\right), \tag{6.10}$$

[6] This result also holds in non-Gaussian but linear settings where the conditional expectations $E\left(\boldsymbol{\varepsilon}_t \mid \varepsilon_{it} = \sqrt{\omega_{ii}}\right)$ can be assumed to be linear.

where as before $\mathbf{\Phi}_i = \mathrm{A}^{-1}\mathrm{A}_i\ i = 1, 2, \ldots, p$, and the last term is non-zero only for $n = 0$. The $\mathbf{\Phi}_i$ can be estimated from the reduced form, thus the indeterminacy is confined to the contemporaneous interaction of the structural errors through the expression $\mathrm{A}^{-1}\mathfrak{g}\,(0, \boldsymbol{\varepsilon} : \varepsilon_i)$, and is resolved up to a scalar multiplication if $\mathrm{A}^{-1}\mathbf{\Omega}$ can be estimated consistently. However, to identify (or consistently estimate) $\mathrm{A}^{-1}\mathbf{\Omega}$ involves the imposition of m_y^2 *a priori* restrictions on the elements of A and/or $\mathbf{\Omega}$. Evidently, the identification of the structural impulse responses does not require A and $\mathbf{\Omega}$ to be separately identified, and it is possible to trade off restrictions across A and $\mathbf{\Omega}$. But in cases where there are no *a priori* grounds for restricting $\mathbf{\Omega}$, since $\mathrm{A}^{-1}\mathbf{\Omega}\mathrm{A}^{'-1} = \Sigma$, then $\mathrm{A}^{-1}\mathbf{\Omega} = \mathbf{\Sigma}\mathrm{A}^{'}$, and the identification of the impulse responses with respect to structural errors requires complete knowledge of the contemporaneous effects, A.

ORTHOGONALISED IMPULSE RESPONSES

The standard approach to deriving impulse response functions is to start from the moving average representations of the final form, (6.6). The reduced form disturbances are correlated and the covariance matrix of $\mathbf{u}_t$, which can be consistently estimated, is given by $\mathbf{\Sigma} = \mathrm{A}^{-1}\mathbf{\Omega}\mathrm{A}^{'-1}$. Orthogonalised impulse response function advanced by Sims (1980) makes use of the Choleski decomposition of $\mathbf{\Sigma} = \mathbf{P}\mathbf{P}'$, where $\mathbf{P}$ is a lower triangular matrix. This can be used to create a new sequence of errors, $\mathbf{u}_t^* = \mathbf{P}^{-1}\mathbf{u}_t$, $t = 1, 2, \ldots, T$, which are orthogonal to each other contemporaneously with unit standard errors, namely $E\left(\mathbf{u}_t^*\mathbf{u}_t^{*\prime}\right) = \mathbf{I}_{m_y}$. Thus the effect of a shock to one of these orthogonalised errors, $\mathbf{u}_t^* = \left(u_{1t}^*, u_{2t}^*, \ldots, u_{m_y t}^*\right)'$, say u_{1t}^*, on the remaining shocks is unambiguous, because it is not correlated with the other orthogonalised errors. The impulse response analysis is also often supplemented by the forecast error variance decomposition where the error variance of forecasting the ith variable n periods ahead is decomposed into the components accounted for by innovations in different variables in the VAR.

There are two problems with orthogonalised impulse response functions and the forecast error variance decomposition. *First,* the impulse responses obtained refer to the effects on the endogenous variables, y_{it}, of a unit displacement (measured by one standard error) in the orthogonalised error, u_{jt}^*, and not in the structural or even the reduced form errors, ε_{jt} and u_{jt}. *Second,* notice that the choice of $\mathbf{P}$ is unique only for a particular ordering of the variables in the VAR. Unless $\mathbf{\Sigma}$ is diagonal, or close to diagonal, different orderings of the variables will give different estimates of the impulse response functions. In fact, the particular ordering of the variables in the VAR and the Choleski decomposition procedure used constitute an implicit identification assumption, equivalent to the recursive identifying restrictions discussed in Section 3.2.3. Orthogonalised impulse response functions, therefore, actually employ traditional identification assumptions, typically motivated by what we termed 'tentative' theory on contemporaneous relations. Other identification schemes based on similarly tentative theory were discussed in Section 3.2.3 in the context of the Structural VAR models. The interpretation of the impulse responses obtained on the basis of these is only as robust as the underlying identifying assumptions and, as the discussion of Section 3.2.3 showed, our view is that economic theory only rarely provides justification for robust short-run identifying restrictions (although it is more capable of providing justification for identifying restrictions on the long-run coefficients).

When plausible *a priori* information to identify the effects of structural shocks is not available, it would still be of some interest to examine the effect of shocks to the reduced form errors, $\mathbf{u}_t = \mathbf{A}^{-1}\boldsymbol{\varepsilon}_t$. The generalised impulse response function provides a natural way to do this since it measures the effect on the endogenous variables of a typical shock to the system, based on the estimated covariances of the reduced form shocks computed using the historical data. Recall from (6.9) that the generalised impulse responses of $\mathbf{y}_{t+n}$ with respect to u_{it} (the ith element of $\mathbf{u}_t$) are given by

$$\mathfrak{g}\left(n, \mathbf{y} : u_i\right) = \boldsymbol{\Phi}_1 \mathfrak{g}\left(n-1, \mathbf{y} : u_i\right) + \cdots + \boldsymbol{\Phi}_p \mathfrak{g}\left(n-p, \mathbf{y} : u_i\right) + \mathfrak{g}\left(n, \mathbf{u} : u_i\right), \tag{6.11}$$

where the last term is non-zero only for $n = 0$, when it is

$$\mathfrak{g}(n, \mathbf{u} : u_i) = \left(\frac{1}{\sqrt{\sigma_{ii}}}\right) \boldsymbol{\Sigma}\mathbf{e}_i \text{ for } n = 0. \tag{6.12}$$

These impulse responses can be uniquely estimated from the parameters of the reduced form and unlike the orthogonalised impulse responses are invariant to the ordering of the variables in the VAR. One can also construct a comparable forecast error variance decomposition.

In the case of stationary variables the generalised impulse response function, as defined by (6.10) or (6.11), will tend to zero as n tends to infinity.

In the case of $I(1)$ variables it will tend to a non-zero constant as n goes to infinity. When the variables are $I(1)$ and cointegrated, there will be linear combinations of the generalised impulse response function that tend to zero and we discuss this further below.[7]

Note that an alternative methodology used to investigate the dynamic properties of large-scale systems, often employed by macromodellers, is to consider the effect of a displacement in the intercept of one of the model's equations. This is equivalent to shocking the innovation in the equation and implicitly assumes that changes in one equation's intercept has no effect on the intercepts of the other equations in the system. Of course, this is one possible counter-factual exercise that might be of interest. But in interrelated systems, it is not likely that one could change the parameters of one part of the system without initiating changes elsewhere. The interpretation of dynamics based on innovations of the type captured by generalised impulse responses is, in our opinion, a much more plausible type of counter-factual than the *ad hoc* once-and-for-all changes in parameter values considered by many macromodellers.

PERSISTENCE PROFILES

The above impulse responses consider the effect of a shock to a *particular* exogenous variable, x_{it}, or an error term, ε_{it} or u_{it}. An alternative approach, developed in Lee and Pesaran (1993), would be to consider the effect of system-wide shocks at time t on the evolution of the system at time $t+n$. Under this approach, the generalised impulse responses are derived with respect to the whole vector of shocks, $\boldsymbol{\varepsilon}_t$ or $\mathbf{u}_t$, and viewed as random variables. The probability distribution function of these random variables is then examined as a function of n. In the case where $\boldsymbol{\varepsilon}_t$ (or $\mathbf{u}_t$) are Gaussian, the generalised impulse responses with respect to the system-wide shocks are also Gaussian with a zero mean and the covariance matrix $\boldsymbol{\Theta}_n\boldsymbol{\Sigma}\boldsymbol{\Theta}_n'$ (see (6.8)). The diagonal elements of $\boldsymbol{\Theta}_n\boldsymbol{\Sigma}\boldsymbol{\Theta}_n'$ (appropriately scaled) are called the persistence profiles by Lee and Pesaran (1993). It is easily seen that the same persistence profiles are obtained for the structural as well as the reduced form errors. For a stationary VAR, the persistence profiles tend to zero as $n \to \infty$. For VARs with unit roots, the persistence profiles tend to the spectral density function (apart from a scalar constant) of $\Delta\mathbf{y}_t$ at zero frequency.

[7] The relationships between the generalised impulse response functions and the orthogonalised impulse responses are discussed in Pesaran and Shin (1998).

6.2 Cointegrating VAR models

Much of the econometric analysis of cointegration has been done in the context of a VAR(p), where all the variables are regarded as endogenous. Initially, we follow the literature and assume that the VAR model *only* contains endogenous $I(1)$ variables and linear deterministic trends. Setting $\mathbf{B}_i = \mathbf{0}$ in (6.1), we have:

$$\mathbf{y}_t = \mathbf{\Phi}_1 \mathbf{y}_{t-1} + \cdots + \mathbf{\Phi}_p \mathbf{y}_{t-p} + \mathbf{a}_0 + \mathbf{a}_1 t + \mathbf{u}_t, \tag{6.13}$$

where $\mathbf{a}_0$ and $\mathbf{a}_1$ are $m \times 1$ vectors of unknown coefficients.[8] To cover the unit root case we allow for the roots of

$$\left| \mathbf{I}_m - \mathbf{\Phi}_1 \lambda - \mathbf{\Phi}_2 \lambda^2 - \cdots - \mathbf{\Phi}_p \lambda^p \right| = 0, \tag{6.14}$$

to fall on and/or outside the unit circle, but rule out the possibility that one or more elements of $\mathbf{y}_t$ be $I(2)$.[9] We shall return to the case where the model also contains exogenous $I(1)$ variables below. The model can be re-parameterised as a Vector Error Correction Model (VECM)

$$\Delta y_t = -\mathbf{\Pi} \mathbf{y}_{t-1} + \sum_{i=1}^{p-1} \mathbf{\Gamma}_i \Delta \mathbf{y}_{t-i} + \mathbf{a}_0 + \mathbf{a}_1 t + \mathbf{u}_t, \tag{6.15}$$

where

$$\mathbf{\Pi} = \mathbf{I}_m - \sum_{i=1}^{p} \mathbf{\Phi}_i, \quad \mathbf{\Gamma}_i = -\sum_{j=i+1}^{p} \mathbf{\Phi}_j, \; i = 1, \ldots, p-1. \tag{6.16}$$

If the elements of $\mathbf{y}_t$ were $I(0)$, $\mathbf{\Pi}$ will be a full rank $m \times m$ matrix. If the elements of $\mathbf{y}_t$ are $I(1)$ and not cointegrated then it must be that $\mathbf{\Pi} = \mathbf{0}$ and a VAR model in first differences will be appropriate. If the elements of $\mathbf{y}_t$ are $I(1)$ and cointegrated with rank($\mathbf{\Pi}$) $= r$, then $\mathbf{\Pi} = \boldsymbol{\alpha}\boldsymbol{\beta}'$, where $\boldsymbol{\alpha}$ and $\boldsymbol{\beta}$ are $m \times r$ full column rank matrices, and there will be $r < m$ linear combinations of $\mathbf{y}_t$, the cointegrating relations, $\boldsymbol{\xi}_t = \boldsymbol{\beta}' \mathbf{y}_t$, which are $I(0)$. The variables $\boldsymbol{\xi}_t$ are often interpreted as the deviations from equilibrium, an interpretation that is at the heart of the long-run structural modelling strategy elaborated in Section 3.1.3.

Under cointegration, (6.15) can be written as:

$$\Delta \mathbf{y}_t = -\boldsymbol{\alpha}\boldsymbol{\beta}' \mathbf{y}_{t-1} + \sum_{i=1}^{p-1} \mathbf{\Gamma}_i \Delta \mathbf{y}_{t-i} + \mathbf{a}_0 + \mathbf{a}_1 t + \mathbf{u}_t, \tag{6.17}$$

[8] To simplify the notations in this section we denote the dimension of $\mathbf{y}_t$ by $m_y = m$.
[9] A review of the econometric analysis of $I(2)$ variables is provided in Haldrup (1998).

where α is the matrix of adjustment or feedback coefficients, which measure how strongly the deviations from equilibrium, the r stationary variables $\beta' \mathbf{y}_{t-1}$, feedback onto the system. If there are $0 < r < m$ cointegrating vectors, then some of the elements of α must be non-zero, *i.e.* there must be some Granger causality involving the levels of the variables in the system to keep the elements of $\mathbf{y}_t$ from diverging.

The unrestricted estimate of Π can be obtained using (6.15). In the restricted model, (6.17), which accommodates $r < m$ cointegrating vectors, we need to estimate the two $m \times r$ coefficient matrices, α and β. This rank reduction therefore imposes $m^2 - 2mr$ restrictions to be imposed on Π. Further, as noted in Section 3.1.1, α and β are not separately identified without some additional restrictions since, for any non-singular matrix Q, we have $\Pi = \alpha QQ^{-1}\beta'$, and the new coefficient matrices $\alpha^* = \alpha Q$ and $\beta^{*\prime} = Q^{-1}\beta'$ would be *observationally equivalent* to using α and β' respectively. Put differently, any linear combination of the $I(0)$ variables, $\xi_t = \beta' \mathbf{y}_t$, are also $I(0)$ variables. To avoid this indeterminacy, we require r independent restrictions on each of the r cointegrating relations, a total of r^2 further restrictions (r of which are provided by normalisation conditions). Thus in the restricted model, we impose $(m^2 - 2mr) + r^2 = (m - r)^2$, namely $m^2 - 2mr$ restrictions imposed by the rank restrictions on Π, and r^2 exact identifying restrictions.

6.2.1 *Treatment of the deterministic components*

If there are unrestricted linear trends in the unrestricted VAR, in general there will be quadratic trends in the level of the variables when the model contains unit roots. To avoid quadratic trends, the linear trend coefficients must be restricted. As shown, for example, in Pesaran, Shin and Smith (2000), using (6.13), $\Delta \mathbf{y}_t$ can be represented by an infinite moving average[10]

$$\Delta \mathbf{y}_t = \mathbf{C}(L)\left(\mathbf{a}_0 + \mathbf{a}_1 t + \mathbf{u}_t\right), \tag{6.18}$$

where

$$\mathbf{C}(L) = \sum_{j=0}^{\infty} \mathbf{C}_j L^j = \mathbf{C}(1) + (1 - L)\mathbf{C}^*(L), \tag{6.19}$$

[10] This 'first-difference MA representation' was originally given in Engle and Granger (1987) for VAR models without linear trends.

$$\mathbf{C}^*(L) = \sum_{j=0}^{\infty} \mathbf{C}_j^* L^j,\ \mathbf{C}_j^* = \mathbf{C}_{j-1}^* + \mathbf{C}_j, \text{ or } \mathbf{C}_j^* = -\sum_{i=j+1}^{\infty} \mathbf{C}_i. \tag{6.20}$$

Consider now the relationship between $\mathbf{C}_i$ and $\mathbf{\Phi}_1, \mathbf{\Phi}_2, \ldots, \mathbf{\Phi}_p$, the parameter matrices of the underlying VAR specification in (6.13), and note that since $\mathbf{C}(L)$ is invertible, we must also have[11]

$$\mathbf{C}^{-1}(L)\Delta\mathbf{y}_t = \mathbf{\Phi}(L)\mathbf{y}_t,$$

where as before

$$\mathbf{\Phi}(L) = \mathbf{I}_m - \mathbf{\Phi}_1 L - \mathbf{\Phi}_2 L^2 - \cdots - \mathbf{\Phi}_p L^p.$$

Hence, we also have

$$\left[\mathbf{C}^{-1}(L)(1-L) - \mathbf{\Phi}(L)\right]\mathbf{y}_t = \mathbf{0},$$

or

$$(1-L)\,\mathbf{I}_m = \mathbf{\Phi}(L)\mathbf{C}(L) = \mathbf{C}(L)\mathbf{\Phi}(L).$$

Therefore

$$\mathbf{C}_i = \mathbf{\Phi}_1\mathbf{C}_{i-1} + \mathbf{\Phi}_2\mathbf{C}_{i-2} + \cdots + \mathbf{\Phi}_p\mathbf{C}_{i-p}, \quad \text{for } i = 2, 3, \ldots, \tag{6.21}$$

where $\mathbf{C}_0 = \mathbf{I}_m$, $\mathbf{C}_1 = \mathbf{\Phi}_1 - \mathbf{I}_m$, and $\mathbf{C}_i = \mathbf{0}$, for $i < 0$.

Using (6.19) in (6.18), it is now easily seen that

$$\Delta\mathbf{y}_t = \mathbf{b}_0 + \mathbf{b}_1 t + \mathbf{C}(1)\mathbf{u}_t + \mathbf{C}^*(L)\Delta\mathbf{u}_t, \tag{6.22}$$

where

$$\mathbf{b}_0 = \mathbf{C}(1)\mathbf{a}_0 + \mathbf{C}^*(1)\mathbf{a}_1, \quad \mathbf{b}_1 = \mathbf{C}(1)\mathbf{a}_1.$$

Cumulating (6.22) forward, we obtain the 'level MA representation'

$$\mathbf{y}_t = \mathbf{y}_0 + \mathbf{b}_0 t + \mathbf{b}_1 \frac{t(t+1)}{2} + \mathbf{C}(1)\mathbf{s}_t + \mathbf{C}^*(L)(\mathbf{u}_t - \mathbf{u}_0),$$

where $\mathbf{s}_t$ denotes the partial sum $\mathbf{s}_t = \sum_{j=1}^{t}\mathbf{u}_j$, $t = 1, 2, \ldots,$ and $\text{rank}\,[\mathbf{C}(1)] = m - r$. It is immediately seen that, since $\mathbf{b}_1 = \mathbf{C}(1)\mathbf{a}_1$, in general $\mathbf{y}_t$ will contain m different linear deterministic trends, $\mathbf{b}_0 t$, $m - r$ different (independent) deterministic quadratic trends given by $\frac{1}{2}t(t+1)\mathbf{C}(1)\mathbf{a}_1$, $m - r$ unit root (or permanent) components given by

[11] Recall that by assumption $\Delta\mathbf{y}_t$ is covariance stationary.

$C(1)s_t$, and m stationary components given by $C^*(L)(u_t - u_0)$.[12] With a_1 unrestricted, the quadratic trend term disappears only in the full rank stationary case where there are no unit roots, namely if rank$(\Pi) = m$.

To remove the quadratic trends and ensure that the trend in the deterministic part of y_t is linear for all values of r, we need to restrict the trend coefficients such that

$$a_1 = \Pi\gamma, \tag{6.23}$$

where γ is an arbitrary $m \times 1$ vector of fixed constants. Note that γ is unrestricted only if Π is full rank. In this case $\gamma = \Pi^{-1}a_1$. But where Π is rank deficient, all elements of γ can be estimated from the reduced form coefficients. In this case the reduced form trend coefficients are restricted.

For the above choice of a_1, it is easily seen that $b_1 = C(1)\Pi\gamma = 0$.[13] Under this restriction on the trend coefficients, we have

$$y_t = y_0 + b_0 t + C(1)s_t + C^*(L)(u_t - u_0), \tag{6.24}$$

and its associated vector error correction formulation is given by

$$\begin{aligned}\Delta y_t &= -\alpha\beta'\left(y_{t-1} - \gamma t\right) + \sum_{i=1}^{p-1} \Gamma_i \Delta y_{t-i} + a_0 + u_t \\ &= -\Pi_* y^*_{t-1} + \sum_{i=1}^{p-1} \Gamma_i \Delta y_{t-i} + a_0 + u_t,\end{aligned} \tag{6.25}$$

where $\Pi_* = \alpha\beta'_*$, $\beta'_* = (\beta', -\beta'\gamma)$, $y^*_{t-1} = (y'_{t-1}, t)'$, and the deterministic trend is now specified to be a part of the cointegrating relations, $\beta'\left(y_{t-1} - \gamma t\right) = \beta'_* y^*_{t-1}$. This ensures that the y_t contains only linear and not quadratic deterministic trends. This result also shows that in general the cointegration relations could contain linear trends if y_t is trended. In the absence of a time trend term in the cointegrating relations we must have $\beta'\gamma = 0$. These provide r further restrictions, known as 'co-trending' restrictions which are testable.

A similar conclusion also follows from the 'level MA representation', (6.24). Premultiplying both sides of (6.24) by β' we have

$$\beta' y_t = \beta' y_0 + \left(\beta' b_0\right) t + \beta' C(1) s_t + \beta' C^*(L)(u_t - u_0).$$

[12] This decomposition of the stochastic part of y_t into permanent and transitory components is not unique and raises a number of identification problems discussed by Levtchenkova *et al.* (1998).

[13] Notice from (6.13) and (6.18) that since $C(L)\Phi(L) = (1 - L)I_m$, then $C(1)\Phi(1) = C(1)\Pi = 0$.

But $\boldsymbol{\beta}'\mathbf{C}(1) = \mathbf{0}$, and it is also easily established that

$$\boldsymbol{\beta}'\mathbf{b}_0 = \boldsymbol{\beta}'\mathbf{C}(1)\mathbf{a}_0 + \boldsymbol{\beta}'\mathbf{C}^*(1)\mathbf{a}_1 = \boldsymbol{\beta}'\mathbf{C}^*(1)\boldsymbol{\Pi}\boldsymbol{\gamma} = \boldsymbol{\beta}'\boldsymbol{\gamma}.$$

Hence

$$\boldsymbol{\beta}'\mathbf{y}_t = \boldsymbol{\beta}'\mathbf{y}_0 + \left(\boldsymbol{\beta}'\boldsymbol{\gamma}\right)t + \boldsymbol{\beta}'\mathbf{C}^*(L)(\mathbf{u}_t - \mathbf{u}_0), \tag{6.26}$$

and in the case of VAR models with linear trends, the cointegrating relations will generally contain deterministic trends, unless the co-trending restrictions $\boldsymbol{\beta}'\boldsymbol{\gamma} = 0$ are imposed. The hypothesis of co-trending is particularly relevant in the output convergence literature where 'convergence' involves both cointegration and co-trending. See, for example, Pesaran (2004a) for a pairwise approach to testing for output and growth convergence.

So far we have focused on cointegrating VAR models with linear deterministic trends. A similar consideration also applies to cointegrating VAR models that contain intercepts only. Once again to ensure that the level variables do not contain different numbers of independent linear deterministic trends as the cointegrating rank changes, the intercepts in these models must be restricted accordingly. It is also possible that different elements of $\mathbf{y}_t$ may have different trend characteristics. For example, output and interest rates are often included in the same VAR, while it is clear that these variables have different trend characteristics. Although there are a large number of possible treatments of the deterministic elements, it will be convenient to distinguish between five different cases often encountered in practice:

- **Case I:** (No intercepts; no trends.) $\mathbf{a}_0 = \mathbf{0}$ and $\mathbf{a}_1 = \mathbf{0}$. Hence, the VECM (6.17) becomes

$$\Delta\mathbf{y}_t = -\boldsymbol{\Pi}\mathbf{y}_{t-1} + \sum_{i=1}^{p-1}\boldsymbol{\Gamma}_i\Delta\mathbf{y}_{t-i} + \mathbf{u}_t. \tag{6.27}$$

- **Case II:** (Restricted intercepts; no trends.) $\mathbf{a}_0 = \boldsymbol{\Pi}\boldsymbol{\mu}$ and $\mathbf{a}_1 = \mathbf{0}$. The VECM (6.17) is

$$\Delta\mathbf{y}_t = \boldsymbol{\Pi}\boldsymbol{\mu} - \boldsymbol{\Pi}\mathbf{y}_{t-1} + \sum_{i=1}^{p-1}\boldsymbol{\Gamma}_i\Delta\mathbf{y}_{t-i} + \mathbf{u}_t. \tag{6.28}$$

- **Case III:** (Unrestricted intercepts; no trends.) $\mathbf{a}_0 \neq \mathbf{0}$ and $\mathbf{a}_1 = \mathbf{0}$. In this case, the intercept restriction $\mathbf{a}_0 = \boldsymbol{\Pi}\boldsymbol{\mu}$ is ignored and the structural

VECM estimated is

$$\Delta \mathbf{y}_t = \mathbf{a}_0 - \boldsymbol{\Pi} \mathbf{y}_{t-1} + \sum_{i=1}^{p-1} \boldsymbol{\Gamma}_i \Delta \mathbf{y}_{t-i} + \mathbf{u}_t. \tag{6.29}$$

- **Case IV:** (Unrestricted intercepts; restricted trends.) $\mathbf{a}_0 \neq \mathbf{0}$ and $\mathbf{a}_1 = \boldsymbol{\Pi}\boldsymbol{\gamma}$. Thus

$$\Delta \mathbf{y}_t = \mathbf{a}_0 + (\boldsymbol{\Pi}\boldsymbol{\gamma})t - \boldsymbol{\Pi} \mathbf{y}_{t-1} + \sum_{i=1}^{p-1} \boldsymbol{\Gamma}_i \Delta \mathbf{y}_{t-i} + \mathbf{u}_t. \tag{6.30}$$

- **Case V:** (Unrestricted intercepts; unrestricted trends.) $\mathbf{a}_0 \neq \mathbf{0}$ and $\mathbf{a}_1 \neq \mathbf{0}$. Here, the VECM estimated is

$$\Delta \mathbf{y}_t = \mathbf{a}_0 + \mathbf{a}_1 t - \boldsymbol{\Pi} \mathbf{y}_{t-1} + \sum_{i=1}^{p-1} \boldsymbol{\Gamma}_i \Delta \mathbf{y}_{t-i} + \mathbf{u}_t. \tag{6.31}$$

It should be emphasised that the DGPs for Cases II and III are identical as are those for Cases IV and V. However, as in the test for a unit root proposed by Dickey and Fuller (1979) compared with that of Dickey and Fuller (1981) for univariate models, estimation and hypothesis testing in Cases III and V proceed ignoring the constraints linking, respectively, the intercept and trend coefficient vectors, $\mathbf{a}_0$ and $\mathbf{a}_1$, to the parameter matrix $\boldsymbol{\Pi}$ whereas Cases II and IV fully incorporate these restrictions. As argued in Pesaran, Shin and Smith (2000), Cases II and IV are likely to be particularly relevant in practice and are preferable to the corresponding unrestricted Cases III and V.

6.2.2 *Trace and maximum eigenvalue tests of cointegration*

If the sole purpose of the cointegration analysis is simply to test for cointegration (or select the appropriate number of cointegrating relations), the nature of the r^2 restrictions employed to ensure there are r identified cointegrating relations is not important since the maximised log-likelihood values will be invariant to how the long-run relations are exactly identified. This was shown by Johansen (1988, 1991) who established an algorithm for maximising the likelihood of (6.25) subject to the constraint that $\boldsymbol{\Pi}_* = \boldsymbol{\alpha\beta}'_*$ and under the assumption that the disturbances are Gaussian. The algorithm involves two steps. In the first, $\Delta \mathbf{y}_t$ and $\mathbf{y}^*_{t-1} = (\mathbf{y}'_{t-1}, \mathbf{t})'$ are regressed in turn on $\Delta \mathbf{y}_{t-1}, \Delta \mathbf{y}_{t-2}, \ldots, \Delta \mathbf{y}_{t-p+1}$ and 1 to generate residuals $\mathbf{r}_{0t}$ and $\mathbf{r}_{1t}$, respectively. Then, defining

$$\mathbf{S}_{00} = T^{-1} \sum_{t=1}^{T} \mathbf{r}_{0t}\mathbf{r}'_{0t}, \ \mathbf{S}_{01} = T^{-1} \sum_{t=1}^{T} \mathbf{r}_{0t}\mathbf{r}'_{1t}, \ \mathbf{S}_{11} = T^{-1} \sum_{t=1}^{T} \mathbf{r}_{1t}\mathbf{r}'_{1t}, \tag{6.32}$$

the m ordered eigenvalues of $\mathbf{S}_{11}^{-1}\mathbf{S}_{10}\mathbf{S}_{00}^{-1}\mathbf{S}_{01}$ namely $\lambda_1 > \lambda_2 > \cdots > \lambda_m$, are computed. The maximum value of the log-likelihood function subject to the constraint that there are r cointegrating relations is given by

$$\ell_T(\widehat{\boldsymbol{\beta}}_T) = -\frac{Tm}{2}\left(1 + \log(2\pi)\right) - \frac{T}{2}\log|\mathbf{S}_{00}| - \frac{T}{2}\sum_{i=1}^{r}\log\left(1 - \lambda_i\right), \qquad (6.33)$$

where $\widehat{\boldsymbol{\beta}}_T$ is the ML estimate of the $m \times r$ cointegrating coefficient matrix (see also the discussion below). This expression can be calculated irrespective of the form of the r^2 independent restrictions on the cointegrating relations. In fact it is easily established that $\ell_T\left(\widehat{\boldsymbol{\beta}}_T'\right) = \ell_T\left(\mathbf{Q}\widehat{\boldsymbol{\beta}}_T'\right)$, for any choice of a $r \times r$ non-singular matrix, $\mathbf{Q}$.

If the applied econometrician is simply interested in testing the null hypothesis of r cointegrating relations in (6.15):

$$H_0 : \text{Rank}(\boldsymbol{\Pi}) = r, \qquad (6.34)$$

there are two types of the log-likelihood ratio statistics that can be used for this purpose. The 'trace' statistic is intended for testing the null hypothesis (6.34) against the full rank hypothesis,

$$H_{1a} : \text{Rank}(\boldsymbol{\Pi}) = m, \qquad (6.35)$$

and the 'maximum eigenvalue' statistic is intended for testing the null against

$$H_{1b} : \text{Rank}(\boldsymbol{\Pi}) = r + 1. \qquad (6.36)$$

These statistics are computed as

$$\lambda_{\text{trace}} = -T\sum_{i=r+1}^{m}\ln(1 - \lambda_i), \qquad (6.37)$$

$$\lambda_{\max} = -T\ln(1 - \lambda_{r+1}). \qquad (6.38)$$

Given the presence of unit roots, the asymptotic distributions of both statistics are non-standard (and depend on the nature of the deterministic processes involved), but Johansen (1991) provided the appropriate critical values based on Monte Carlo simulations, and Pesaran, Shin and Smith (2000) provided the corresponding statistics under Cases I–V above.

6.2.3 *Identifying long-run relationships in a cointegrating VAR*

Typically, the applied econometrician will be interested not only in the number of cointegrating relations that might exist among the variables but also the specification of the identifying (and possibly over-identifying) restrictions on the cointegrating relations. Indeed, Johansen (1988, 1991) have provided procedures for estimating $\boldsymbol{\alpha}$ and $\boldsymbol{\beta}$, using 'statistical' over-identifying restrictions. He computed the ML estimates of $\boldsymbol{\beta}$ as the r eigenvectors corresponding to the first r largest eigenvalues of the canonical correlation matrix, $\mathbf{S}_{11}^{-1}\mathbf{S}_{10}\mathbf{S}_{00}^{-1}\mathbf{S}_{01}$, where $\mathbf{S}_{00}$, $\mathbf{S}_{01}$, and $\mathbf{S}_{11}$ are defined in (6.32). These are often referred to as 'empirical' or 'statistical' identifying restrictions, and together impose the r^2 restrictions needed for exact identification of $\boldsymbol{\beta}$. However, while mathematically natural given the statistical structure of the problem, these restrictions have no economic meaning since there is no reason to expect economic cointegrating vectors to be orthogonal. When $r > 1$, the economic interpretation of the Johansen estimates of the cointegrating vectors is almost impossible. See also Phillips (1991) for an alternative non-economic identification adopting a triangular structure.

The more satisfactory approach promoted in Pesaran and Shin (2002) is to estimate the cointegrating relations under a general set of structural long-run restrictions provided by *a priori* economic theory. Suppose that we are considering an example of a model with unrestricted intercepts and restricted trends (Case IV), and the cointegrating vectors, $\boldsymbol{\beta}_*$, are subject to the following k general linear restrictions, including cross-equation restrictions:[14]

$$\mathbf{R}\,\text{vec}(\boldsymbol{\beta}_*) = \mathbf{f}, \tag{6.39}$$

where $\mathbf{R}$ and $\mathbf{f}$ are a $k \times (m+1)r$ matrix of full row rank and a $k \times 1$ vector of known constants, respectively, and $\text{vec}(\boldsymbol{\beta}_*)$ is the $(m+1)r \times 1$ vector of long-run coefficients, which stacks the r columns of $\boldsymbol{\beta}_*$ into a vector. Three cases can be distinguished: (i) $k < r^2$: the under-identified case; (ii) $k = r^2$: the exactly identified case; and (iii) $k > r^2$: the over-identified case.

ESTIMATION OF THE LONG-RUN COINTEGRATING VECTORS SUBJECT TO IDENTIFYING RESTRICTIONS

Following Pesaran and Shin (2002), we will describe the ML estimation of the long-run parameters $\boldsymbol{\beta}$ of the *VEC* model (6.25) subject to the k identifying restrictions on $\boldsymbol{\beta}$ given by (6.39). We first note that the concentrated

[14] Pesaran and Shin (2002) also consider the more general case where the restrictions on the cointegrating coefficients may be non-linear.

log-likelihood function for the cointegrated model is given by:[15]

$$\ell_T(\boldsymbol{\beta}) = \text{constant} \; - \frac{T}{2}\left\{\ln|\boldsymbol{\beta}'\mathbf{A}_T\boldsymbol{\beta}| - \ln|\boldsymbol{\beta}'\mathbf{B}_T\boldsymbol{\beta}|\right\}. \tag{6.40}$$

where

$$\mathbf{A}_T = \mathbf{S}_{11} - \mathbf{S}_{10}\mathbf{S}_{00}^{-1}\mathbf{S}_{01}, \quad \mathbf{B}_T = \mathbf{S}_{11}, \tag{6.41}$$

and $\mathbf{S}_{00}, \mathbf{S}_{10}, \mathbf{S}_{11}$ are defined in (6.32). Then, the ML estimator of $\boldsymbol{\theta} = \text{vec}(\boldsymbol{\beta})$ is obtained by solving

$$\max_{\theta,\lambda} \Lambda\left(\boldsymbol{\theta}, \boldsymbol{\lambda}\right),$$

where $\Lambda\left(\boldsymbol{\theta}, \boldsymbol{\lambda}\right)$ is the Lagrangian function for this constrained ML estimation problem and given by

$$\begin{aligned}\Lambda\left(\boldsymbol{\theta}, \boldsymbol{\lambda}\right) &= \frac{1}{T}\ell_T\left(\boldsymbol{\theta}\right) - \frac{1}{2}\boldsymbol{\lambda}'\mathbf{h}\left(\boldsymbol{\theta}\right) \\ &= \text{constant} - \frac{1}{2}\left\{\ln\left|\boldsymbol{\beta}'\mathbf{A}_T\boldsymbol{\beta}\right| - \ln\left|\boldsymbol{\beta}'\mathbf{B}_T\boldsymbol{\beta}\right| - \boldsymbol{\lambda}'\left(\mathbf{R}\boldsymbol{\theta} - \mathbf{f}\right)\right\},\end{aligned} \tag{6.42}$$

where $\mathbf{h}\left(\boldsymbol{\theta}\right) = \mathbf{R}\boldsymbol{\theta} - \mathbf{f}$ and $\boldsymbol{\lambda}$ is a $k \times 1$ vector of Lagrange multipliers.

We distinguish between two cases: when the cointegrating vectors are exactly identified ($k = r^2$), and when they are subject to over-identifying restrictions ($k > r^2$). In both cases it is convenient to start with the exactly identified ML estimator of $\boldsymbol{\beta}$ obtained by Johansen's eigenvalue routine, *i.e.* the r eigenvectors corresponding to the first r largest eigenvalues of $\mathbf{S}_{11}^{-1}\mathbf{S}_{10}\mathbf{S}_{00}^{-1}\mathbf{S}_{01}$, which we denote by $\hat{\boldsymbol{\beta}}_J$.

Exactly identified case ($k = r^2$)

In the exactly identified case, the ML estimator of $\boldsymbol{\beta}$ is obtained simply by

$$\hat{\boldsymbol{\theta}} = \left(\mathbf{I}_r \otimes \hat{\boldsymbol{\beta}}_J\right)\left[\mathbf{R}\left(\mathbf{I}_r \otimes \hat{\boldsymbol{\beta}}_J\right)\right]^{-1}\mathbf{f}, \tag{6.43}$$

where $\mathbf{I}_r$ is an $r \times r$ identity matrix and $\mathbf{R}$ and $\mathbf{f}$ are defined by (6.39). Note that by construction $\hat{\boldsymbol{\beta}}_J'\mathbf{B}_T\hat{\boldsymbol{\beta}}_J = \mathbf{I}_r$ and $\hat{\boldsymbol{\beta}}_{Ji}'\left(\mathbf{B}_T - \mathbf{A}_T\right)\hat{\boldsymbol{\beta}}_{Jj} = 0$ for $i \neq j$, $i, j = 1, 2, \ldots, r$ and $\hat{\boldsymbol{\beta}}_{Ji}$ is the ith column of $\hat{\boldsymbol{\beta}}_J$.

[15] Since the main focus is on the long-run parameters, $\boldsymbol{\beta}$, we can concentrate out all the short-run parameters from the log-likelihood function.

Over-identified case ($k > r^2$)

Now there are $k - r^2$ additional restrictions that need to be taken into account at the estimation stage. This can be done by explicitly maximising the Lagrangian function (6.42). We assume that the normalisation restrictions on each of the r cointegrating vectors are also included in $\mathbf{h}(\boldsymbol{\theta}) = \mathbf{R}\boldsymbol{\theta} - \mathbf{f} = \mathbf{0}$.

The first-order conditions are given by

$$\mathbf{d}_T(\hat{\boldsymbol{\theta}}) - \mathbf{R}'\hat{\boldsymbol{\lambda}} = \mathbf{0}, \tag{6.44}$$

$$\mathbf{R}\hat{\boldsymbol{\theta}} - \mathbf{f} = \mathbf{0}, \tag{6.45}$$

where $\mathbf{d}_T(\boldsymbol{\theta}) = T^{-1}[\partial \ell_T(\boldsymbol{\theta})/\partial \boldsymbol{\theta}]$. Let $\hat{\boldsymbol{\theta}}^{(0)}$ and $\hat{\boldsymbol{\lambda}}^{(0)}$ be the initial estimates of the ML estimators of $\boldsymbol{\theta}$ and $\boldsymbol{\lambda}$. Taking the Taylor series expansion of (6.44) and (6.45) around $\hat{\boldsymbol{\theta}}^{(0)}$ and $\hat{\boldsymbol{\lambda}}^{(0)}$, we obtain[16]

$$\begin{bmatrix} \mathbf{G}_T\left(\hat{\boldsymbol{\theta}}^{(0)}\right) & \mathbf{R}' \\ \mathbf{R} & \mathbf{0} \end{bmatrix} \begin{bmatrix} T\left(\hat{\boldsymbol{\theta}} - \hat{\boldsymbol{\theta}}^{(0)}\right) \\ \hat{\boldsymbol{\lambda}} - \hat{\boldsymbol{\lambda}}^{(0)} \end{bmatrix} = \begin{bmatrix} \mathbf{d}_T\left(\hat{\boldsymbol{\theta}}^{(0)}\right) - \mathbf{R}'\hat{\boldsymbol{\lambda}}^{(0)} \\ -T\left(\mathbf{R}\hat{\boldsymbol{\theta}}^{(0)} - \mathbf{f}\right) \end{bmatrix} + o_p(1), \tag{6.46}$$

where $\mathbf{G}_T(\hat{\boldsymbol{\theta}}) = T^{-2}[-\partial^2 \ell_T(\hat{\boldsymbol{\theta}})/\partial\boldsymbol{\theta}\partial\boldsymbol{\theta}']$. To deal with the singularity of the normalised Hessian matrix, $\mathbf{G}_T(\hat{\boldsymbol{\theta}})$ in the case of cointegration, we let

$$\mathbf{J}_T(\boldsymbol{\theta}) = \mathbf{G}_T(\boldsymbol{\theta}) + \mathbf{R}'\mathbf{R}.$$

Then, the solution of (6.46) using a generalised inverse based on $\mathbf{J}_T(\hat{\boldsymbol{\theta}})$ is given by

$$\begin{bmatrix} T\left(\hat{\boldsymbol{\theta}} - \hat{\boldsymbol{\theta}}^{(0)}\right) \\ \hat{\boldsymbol{\lambda}} - \hat{\boldsymbol{\lambda}}^{(0)} \end{bmatrix} = \begin{bmatrix} \mathbf{V}_{\theta\theta}\left(\hat{\boldsymbol{\theta}}^{(0)}\right) & \mathbf{V}_{\theta\lambda}\left(\hat{\boldsymbol{\theta}}^{(0)}\right) \\ \mathbf{V}'_{\theta\lambda}\left(\hat{\boldsymbol{\theta}}^{(0)}\right) & \mathbf{V}_{\lambda\lambda}\left(\hat{\boldsymbol{\theta}}^{(0)}\right) \end{bmatrix}$$
$$\times \begin{bmatrix} \mathbf{d}_T\left(\hat{\boldsymbol{\theta}}^{(0)}\right) - \mathbf{R}'\hat{\boldsymbol{\lambda}}^{(0)} \\ -T\left(\mathbf{R}\hat{\boldsymbol{\theta}}^{(0)} - \mathbf{f}\right) \end{bmatrix} + o_p(1), \tag{6.47}$$

[16] The detailed derivations for $\mathbf{d}_T(\boldsymbol{\theta})$ and $\mathbf{G}_T(\boldsymbol{\theta})$ can be found in the DAE Working Paper version of Pesaran and Shin (2002).

where

$$\mathbf{V}_{\theta\theta}(\hat{\boldsymbol{\theta}}) = \mathbf{J}_T^{-1}(\hat{\boldsymbol{\theta}}) - \mathbf{J}_T^{-1}(\hat{\boldsymbol{\theta}})\mathbf{R}'\left[\mathbf{R}\mathbf{J}_T^{-1}(\hat{\boldsymbol{\theta}})\mathbf{R}'\right]^{-1}\mathbf{R}\mathbf{J}_T^{-1}(\hat{\boldsymbol{\theta}}), \tag{6.48}$$

$$\mathbf{V}_{\theta\lambda}(\hat{\boldsymbol{\theta}}) = \mathbf{J}_T^{-1}(\hat{\boldsymbol{\theta}})\mathbf{R}'\left[\mathbf{R}\mathbf{J}_T^{-1}(\hat{\boldsymbol{\theta}})\mathbf{R}'\right]^{-1}, \quad \mathbf{V}_{\lambda\lambda}(\hat{\boldsymbol{\theta}}) = \left[\mathbf{R}\mathbf{J}_T^{-1}(\hat{\boldsymbol{\theta}})\mathbf{R}'\right]^{-1}.$$

Hence, we obtain the following generalised version of the Newton–Raphson algorithm:[17]

$$\begin{pmatrix} \hat{\boldsymbol{\theta}}^{(i)} \\ \hat{\boldsymbol{\lambda}}^{(i)} \end{pmatrix} = \begin{pmatrix} \hat{\boldsymbol{\theta}}^{(i-1)} \\ \hat{\boldsymbol{\lambda}}^{(i-1)} \end{pmatrix} \begin{bmatrix} \mathbf{V}_{\theta\theta}\left(\hat{\boldsymbol{\theta}}^{(i-1)}\right) & \mathbf{V}_{\theta\lambda}\left(\hat{\boldsymbol{\theta}}^{(i-1)}\right) \\ \mathbf{V}'_{\theta\lambda}\left(\hat{\boldsymbol{\theta}}^{(i-1)}\right) & \mathbf{V}_{\lambda\lambda}\left(\hat{\boldsymbol{\theta}}^{(i-1)}\right) \end{bmatrix}$$
$$\times \begin{bmatrix} T^{-1}\left\{\mathbf{d}_T\left(\hat{\boldsymbol{\theta}}^{(i-1)}\right) - \mathbf{R}'\hat{\boldsymbol{\lambda}}^{(i-1)}\right\} \\ -T\left(\mathbf{R}\hat{\boldsymbol{\theta}}^{(i-1)} - \mathbf{f}\right) \end{bmatrix}. \tag{6.49}$$

From (6.47) we also find that

$$T\left(\hat{\boldsymbol{\theta}} - \boldsymbol{\theta}\right) \overset{a}{\sim} MN\left[0, \mathbf{V}_{\theta\theta}(\boldsymbol{\theta})\right], \tag{6.50}$$

which shows that the cointegrating parameters are super-consistent and have an asymptotic (mixture) normal distribution. It also shows that a consistent estimator of the asymptotic variance of $\hat{\boldsymbol{\theta}}$ is given by (6.48). See also Pesaran and Shin (2002) for a proof, and Pesaran and Pesaran's (1997) *Microfit 4.0* for more details of the numerical algorithms and other computational considerations.

For the initial estimates, $\hat{\boldsymbol{\theta}}^{(0)}$, we suggest using the linearised exactly identified estimators given by (6.43). One important aspect of this methodology is the fact that we begin with the exactly identifying restrictions from economic theory, rather than the type of statistical identification favoured by Johansen. This is particularly important for models with a relatively large number of long-run relations. Clearly, without some guidance from theory it would be extremely difficult to advance an exactly identified model with meaningful and understandable properties.

[17] See Magnus and Neudecker (1988, pp. 57–60) for the algebra about the bordered Gramian matrix.

TESTING THE VALIDITY OF OVER-IDENTIFYING RESTRICTIONS

Consider the general $k \geq r^2$ restrictions on $\boldsymbol{\theta}$ given by (6.39), and partition these restrictions as

$$\begin{pmatrix} \mathbf{R}_A\boldsymbol{\theta} \\ \mathbf{R}_B\boldsymbol{\theta} \end{pmatrix} = \begin{pmatrix} \mathbf{f}_A \\ \mathbf{f}_B \end{pmatrix}, \tag{6.51}$$

where $\mathbf{R}_A$, $\mathbf{R}_B$ are $r^2 \times (m+1)r$, and $(k - r^2) \times (m+1)r$ known matrices, and $\mathbf{f}_A$, $\mathbf{f}_B$ are $r^2 \times 1$ and $(k - r^2) \times 1$ known vectors, respectively. Since we need r^2 independent restrictions to just identify $\boldsymbol{\theta}$, without loss of generality, $\mathbf{R}_A\boldsymbol{\theta} = \mathbf{f}_A$ can be regarded as such r^2 just-identifying restrictions. The remaining restrictions, $\mathbf{R}_B\boldsymbol{\theta} = \mathbf{f}_B$, will then constitute the $k - r^2$ over-identifying restrictions.

Let $\hat{\boldsymbol{\theta}}_1$ be the (unrestricted) ML estimators of $\boldsymbol{\theta}$ obtained subject to the r^2 exactly identifying restrictions (say, $\mathbf{R}_A\boldsymbol{\theta} = \mathbf{f}_A$), and $\hat{\boldsymbol{\theta}}_0$ be the restricted ML estimators of $\boldsymbol{\theta}$ obtained subject to the full k restrictions (namely, $\mathbf{R}\boldsymbol{\theta} = \mathbf{f}$), respectively. Then, the $k-r^2$ over-identifying restrictions on $\boldsymbol{\theta}$ can be tested using the log-likelihood ratio statistic given by

$$LR = 2\left[\ell_T\left(\hat{\boldsymbol{\theta}}_1\right) - \ell_T\left(\hat{\boldsymbol{\theta}}_0\right)\right], \tag{6.52}$$

where $\ell_T\left(\hat{\boldsymbol{\theta}}_1\right)$ and $\ell_T\left(\hat{\boldsymbol{\theta}}_0\right)$ represent the maximised values of the log-likelihood function obtained under $\mathbf{R}_A\boldsymbol{\theta} = \mathbf{f}_A$ and $\mathbf{R}\boldsymbol{\theta} = \mathbf{f}$, respectively. Pesaran and Shin (2002) prove that the log-likelihood ratio statistic for testing $\mathbf{R}\boldsymbol{\theta} = \mathbf{f}$ given by (6.52) has a χ^2 distribution with $k - r^2$ degrees of freedom, asymptotically. Small sample properties of the tests of over-identifying restrictions on the cointegrating vectors are described in Section 6.4 below.

6.2.4 *Estimation of the short-run parameters of the conditional VEC model*

Having computed the ML estimates of the cointegrating vectors $\hat{\boldsymbol{\beta}}_*' = \left(\hat{\boldsymbol{\beta}}', -\hat{\boldsymbol{\beta}}\boldsymbol{\gamma}'\right)'$, obtained under the exact and/or over-identifying restrictions given by (6.39), the ML estimates of the short-run parameters $(\boldsymbol{\alpha}, \boldsymbol{\Gamma}_1, \ldots, \boldsymbol{\Gamma}_{p-1}, \mathbf{a}_0)$ in (6.25) can be computed by the OLS regressions of $\Delta\mathbf{y}_t$ on

$$\hat{\boldsymbol{\xi}}_t^*, \Delta\mathbf{y}_{t-1}, \ldots, \Delta\mathbf{y}_{t-p+1} \text{ and } 1,$$

where $\hat{\xi}_t^* = \hat{\beta}_*' \mathbf{y}_{t-1}^*$ is the ML estimate of $\xi_t^* = \beta_*' \mathbf{y}_{t-1}^*$. Notice that $\hat{\beta}$ is super-consistent, while the ML estimators of the short-run parameters are $\sqrt{T}$-consistent. The ML estimate of the (restricted) trend coefficients are then obtained by $\widehat{\mathbf{a}}_1 = \hat{\alpha}_y \hat{\beta}' \gamma$.

It is worth emphasising that, having established the form of the long-run relations, then standard OLS regression methods and standard testing procedures can be applied. All of the right-hand side variables in the error correction regression models are stationary and are either dated at time $t-1$ or earlier. In these circumstances, OLS is the appropriate estimation procedure and diagnostic statistics for residual serial correlation, normality, heteroscedasticity and functional form misspecifications can be readily computed, based on these OLS regressions, in the usual manner.[18] This is an important observation because it simplifies estimation and diagnostic testing procedures. Moreover, it makes it clear that the modelling procedure is robust to uncertainties surrounding the order of integration of particular variables. It is frequently difficult to establish the order of integration of particular variables using the techniques and samples of data which are available, and it would be worrying if the modelling procedure relied on assumptions that variables were integrated of a particular order. However, the observations above indicate that, so long as the $\hat{\xi}_t^* = \hat{\beta}_*' \mathbf{y}_{t-1}^*$ are stationary, the conditional VEC model, estimated and interpreted in the usual manner, will be valid even if it turns out that some or all of the variables in $\mathbf{y}_{t-1}^*$ are $I(0)$ and not $I(1)$ after all. A related discussion with mathematical proofs is given in Pesaran and Shin (1999) for cases where $r = 1$.

6.2.5 *Analysis of stability of the cointegrated system*

Having estimated the system of equations in the cointegrating VAR, we will typically need to check on the stability of the system as a whole, and more particularly to check that the disequilibria from the cointegrating relations are in fact mean-reverting. Although such a mean-reverting property is intrinsic to the modelling framework when the cointegration restrictions are not rejected, it is possible that the estimated model does not display this property in practice or that, if it does, the speed with which the system

[18] Further discussion of the validity of standard diagnostic test procedures when different estimation procedures are adopted in models involving unit roots and cointegrating relations is provided in Gerrard and Godfrey (1998), and the importance of the use of predicted values in the tests is discussed in Pesaran and Taylor (1999).

reverts back to its equilibrium is very slow. Summary statistics that shed light on the convergence property of the error correction terms, $\hat{\boldsymbol{\xi}}_t$, will therefore be of some interest.

In the empirical applications of cointegration analysis where $r = 1$, the rate of convergence of $\hat{\boldsymbol{\xi}}_t$ to its equilibrium is ascertained from the estimates of the error correction coefficients, $\boldsymbol{\alpha}$. However, as we shall demonstrate below, this procedure is not generally applicable. Consider the simple two variable error correction model

$$\begin{pmatrix} \Delta y_{1t} \\ \Delta y_{2t} \end{pmatrix} = -\begin{pmatrix} \alpha_1 \\ \alpha_2 \end{pmatrix} (\beta_1 y_{1,t-1} + \beta_2 y_{2,t-1}) + \begin{pmatrix} u_{1t} \\ u_{2t} \end{pmatrix}, \tag{6.53}$$

in which the variables y_{1t} and y_{2t} are cointegrated with cointegrating vector $\boldsymbol{\beta} = (\beta_1, \beta_2)'$. Denoting $\xi_{t+1} = \beta_1 y_{1t} + \beta_2 y_{2t}$, and premultiplying both sides of (6.53) by $\boldsymbol{\beta}'$, we obtain

$$\Delta\xi_{t+1} = -(\boldsymbol{\beta}'\boldsymbol{\alpha})\xi_t + \boldsymbol{\beta}'\mathbf{u}_t,$$

where $\boldsymbol{\alpha} = (\alpha_1, \alpha_2)'$ and $\mathbf{u}_t = (u_{1t}, u_{2t})'$, or

$$\xi_{t+1} = (1 - \boldsymbol{\beta}'\boldsymbol{\alpha})\xi_t + \boldsymbol{\beta}'\mathbf{u}_t. \tag{6.54}$$

Since $\boldsymbol{\beta}'\mathbf{u}_t$ is I(0), then, the stability of this equation requires $|1 - \boldsymbol{\beta}'\boldsymbol{\alpha}\ | = |1 - \beta_1\alpha_1 - \beta_2\alpha_2| < 1$, or $\beta_1\alpha_1 + \beta_2\alpha_2 > 0$, and $\beta_1\alpha_1 + \beta_2\alpha_2 < 2$. It is clear that these conditions depend on the adjustment parameters from both equations (α_1 and α_2) as well as the parameters of the cointegrating vector, and the estimate of α_1 alone will not allow us to sign the expressions $\beta_1\alpha_1 + \beta_2\alpha_2$ and $\beta_1\alpha_1 + \beta_2\alpha_2 - 2$. Hence, for example, restricting α_1 to lie in the range (0, 2) ensures the stability of (6.54) only under the normalisation $\beta_1 = 1$, and in the simple case where $\alpha_2 = 0$.[19]

More generally, we can rewrite (6.17) as an infinite order difference equation in an $r \times 1$ vector of (stochastic) disequilibrium terms, $\boldsymbol{\xi}_t = \boldsymbol{\beta}'\mathbf{y}_{t-1}$. Under our assumption that all the variables in $\mathbf{y}_t$ are $I(1)$, and all the roots of $\left|\mathbf{I}_m - \sum_{i=1}^{p-1} \boldsymbol{\Gamma}_i \mathbf{y}^i\right| = 0$ fall outside the unit circle, we have the following expression for $\Delta\mathbf{y}_t$:

$$\Delta\mathbf{y}_t = \boldsymbol{\Gamma}(L)^{-1}\left(-\boldsymbol{\alpha}\boldsymbol{\xi}_t + \mathbf{a}_0 + \mathbf{a}_1 t + \mathbf{u}_t\right), \quad t = 1, 2, \ldots, T, \tag{6.55}$$

where $\boldsymbol{\Gamma}(L) = \mathbf{I}_m - \sum_{i=1}^{p-1} \boldsymbol{\Gamma}_i L^i$. Defining $\boldsymbol{\Theta}(L) = \boldsymbol{\Gamma}(L)^{-1} = \sum_{i=0}^{\infty} \boldsymbol{\Theta}_i L^i$, then it is easily seen that the following recursive relations hold:

$$\boldsymbol{\Theta}_n = \boldsymbol{\Gamma}_1\boldsymbol{\Theta}_{n-1} + \boldsymbol{\Gamma}_2\boldsymbol{\Theta}_{n-2} + \cdots + \boldsymbol{\Gamma}_{p-1}\boldsymbol{\Theta}_{n-p+1}, \quad n = 1, 2, \ldots,$$

[19] When $\alpha_2 = 0$, y_{2t} is said to be 'long-run forcing' for y_{1t}.

where $\Theta_0 = I_m$, and $\Theta_n = 0$ for $n < 0$. Premultiplying (6.55) by β', then we have

$$\Delta\xi_{t+1} = -\beta'\left(I_m + \sum_{i=1}^{\infty}\Theta_i L^i\right)\alpha\xi_t + \beta'\left(I_m + \sum_{i=1}^{\infty}\Theta_i L^i\right)(a_0 + a_1 t + u_t), \tag{6.56}$$

or

$$\xi_{t+1} = \left[(I_r - \beta'\alpha) - \sum_{i=1}^{\infty}(\beta'\Theta_i\alpha)L^i\right]\xi_t + \left(\beta' + \sum_{i=1}^{\infty}\beta'\Theta_i L^i\right)(a_0 + a_1 t + u_t). \tag{6.57}$$

This shows that, in general, when $p \geq 2$, the error correction variables, ξ_{t+1}, follow infinite order VARMA processes, and there exists no simple rule involving α alone that could ensure the stability of the dynamic processes in ξ_{t+1}.[20]

However, given the assumption that none of the roots of $\left|I_m - \sum_{i=1}^{p-1}\Gamma_i z^i\right| = 0$ fall on or inside the unit circle, it is easily seen that the matrices Θ_i, $i = 0, 1, 2, \ldots$ are absolutely summable,[21] and therefore a suitably truncated version of $\sum_{i=1}^{\infty}(\beta'\Theta_i\alpha)L^i$ can provide us with an adequate approximation in practice. Using an ℓ-order truncation we have

$$\xi_{t+1} \approx \sum_{i=1}^{\ell} D_i\xi_{t-i+1} + v_t, \quad t = 1, 2, \ldots, T, \tag{6.58}$$

where

$$D_1 = I_r - \beta'\alpha, \quad D_i = -\beta'\Theta_{i-1}\alpha, \; i = 2, 3, \ldots, \ell, \tag{6.59}$$

$$v_t = \left(\beta' + \sum_{i=1}^{\ell}\beta'\Theta_i L^i\right)(a_0 + a_1 t + u_t).$$

To explicitly evaluate the stability of the cointegrated system, we rewrite (6.58) more compactly as

$$\check{\xi}_{t+1} = \boldsymbol{D}\check{\xi}_t + \check{v}_t, \quad t = 1, 2, \ldots, T, \tag{6.60}$$

[20] This result also highlights the deficiency of residual-based approaches to testing for cointegration, where finite-order ADF regressions are fitted to the residuals even if the order of the underlying VAR is 2 or more.

[21] The matrix sequence, $\{\Theta_i, i = 0, 1, 2, \ldots\}$ is said to be absolutely summable if $\sum_{i=0}^{\infty}\left[tr(\Theta_i\Theta_i')\right]^{1/2} < \infty$, which is satisfied since $\Gamma(L)$ is invertible. See, for example, Lütkepohl (1991), Section C3, pp. 488–491.

where

$$\underset{r\ell\times 1}{\check{\boldsymbol{\xi}}_t} = \begin{pmatrix} \boldsymbol{\xi}_t \\ \boldsymbol{\xi}_{t-1} \\ \boldsymbol{\xi}_{t-2} \\ \vdots \\ \boldsymbol{\xi}_{t-\ell+1} \end{pmatrix},$$

$$\underset{r\ell\times r\ell}{\mathbf{D}} = \begin{pmatrix} \mathbf{D}_1 & \mathbf{D}_2 & \mathbf{D}_3 & \cdots & \mathbf{D}_{\ell-1} & \mathbf{D}_\ell \\ \mathbf{I}_r & \mathbf{0} & \mathbf{0} & \cdots & \mathbf{0} & \mathbf{0} \\ \mathbf{0} & \mathbf{I}_r & \mathbf{0} & \cdots & \mathbf{0} & \mathbf{0} \\ & & & \vdots & & \\ \mathbf{0} & \mathbf{0} & \mathbf{0} & \cdots & \mathbf{I}_r & \mathbf{0} \end{pmatrix},$$

$$\underset{r\ell\times 1}{\check{\mathbf{v}}_t} = \begin{pmatrix} \mathbf{v}_t \\ \mathbf{0} \\ \mathbf{0} \\ \vdots \\ \mathbf{0} \end{pmatrix}. \tag{6.61}$$

The above cointegrated system is stable if all the roots of

$$\left|\mathbf{I}_r - \mathbf{D}_1 z - \cdots - \mathbf{D}_\ell z^\ell\right| = 0$$

lie outside the unit circle, or if all the eigenvalues of $\mathbf{D}$ have modulus less than unity.[22]

6.2.6 *Impulse response analysis in cointegrating VARs*

Using the level MA representation, (6.24), generalised impulse response functions can be calculated for the cointegrating VAR model (6.25) in a way similar to the VAR discussed above. Now, it is easily seen that the effect of a unit shock to the ith reduced form error, u_{it}, is given by[23]

$$\mathfrak{g}\left(n, \mathbf{y} : u_i\right) = \frac{1}{\sqrt{\sigma_{ii}}}\tilde{\mathbf{C}}_n \boldsymbol{\Sigma}\mathbf{e}_i, \quad n = 0, 1, \ldots, \quad i = 1, \ldots, m, \tag{6.62}$$

where $\mathbf{u}_t$ is *i.i.d.* $(\mathbf{0}, \boldsymbol{\Sigma})$, $\tilde{\mathbf{C}}_n = \sum_{j=0}^{n} \mathbf{C}_j$, $\mathbf{C}_j$'s are given by the recursive relations (6.21), and $\mathbf{e}_i$ is a selection vector of zeros with unity as its ith

[22] Notice that the stability analysis is not affected by the presence of deterministic and stationary exogenous variables in the system.

[23] Combining (6.11) and (6.24) together, we obtain $\mathfrak{g}\left(n, \mathbf{y} : u_i\right) = \sigma_{ii}^{-1/2}\left\{\mathbf{C}(1) + \mathbf{C}_n^*\right\} \boldsymbol{\Sigma}\mathbf{e}_i$. Then, using (6.20), we find that $\mathbf{C}(1) + \mathbf{C}_n^* = \sum_{j=0}^{n} \mathbf{C}_j = \tilde{\mathbf{C}}_n$.

element. For the effect of a unit shock to the ith structural form error, ε_{it}, we notice that (6.24) can be written as

$$\mathbf{y}_t = \mathbf{y}_0 + \mathbf{b}_0 t + \mathbf{C}(1)\mathbf{s}_t + \mathbf{C}^*(L)\mathbf{A}^{-1}(\boldsymbol{\varepsilon}_t - \boldsymbol{\varepsilon}_0), \tag{6.63}$$

where we use $\mathbf{u}_t = \mathbf{A}^{-1}\boldsymbol{\varepsilon}_t$, and therefore we have

$$\mathfrak{g}(n, \mathbf{y} : \varepsilon_i) = \frac{1}{\sqrt{\omega_{ii}}}\tilde{\mathbf{C}}_n\mathbf{A}^{-1}\boldsymbol{\Omega}\mathbf{e}_i, \quad n = 0, 1, \ldots, \quad i = 1, \ldots, m, \tag{6.64}$$

where $\boldsymbol{\varepsilon}_t$ is $i.i.d.$ $(\mathbf{0},\boldsymbol{\Omega})$ with $\boldsymbol{\Sigma} = \mathbf{A}^{-1}\boldsymbol{\Omega}\mathbf{A}'^{-1}$. In particular,

$$\mathfrak{g}(\infty, \mathbf{y} : \varepsilon_i) = \omega_{ii}^{-1/2}\mathbf{C}(1)\mathbf{A}^{-1}\boldsymbol{\Omega}\mathbf{e}_i, \; \mathfrak{g}(\infty, \mathbf{y} : u_i) = \sigma_{ii}^{-1/2}\mathbf{C}(1)\boldsymbol{\Sigma}\mathbf{e}_i,$$

which shows that shocks will have permanent effects on the $I(1)$ variables, unlike the stationary case.

Shocks will have only a temporary effect on the cointegrating relations though. Hence, the generalised impulse response function for the cointegrating relations $\boldsymbol{\xi}_t = \boldsymbol{\beta}'\mathbf{y}_{t-1}$ with respect to a unit shock to the structural errors is given by

$$\mathfrak{g}(n, \boldsymbol{\xi} : \varepsilon_i) = \frac{1}{\sqrt{\omega_{ii}}}\boldsymbol{\beta}'\tilde{\mathbf{C}}_n\mathbf{A}^{-1}\boldsymbol{\Omega}\mathbf{e}_i, \quad n = 0, 1, \ldots, \quad i = 1, \ldots, m. \tag{6.65}$$

Since $\boldsymbol{\beta}'\tilde{\mathbf{C}}_\infty = \boldsymbol{\beta}'\mathbf{C}(1) = \mathbf{0}$, it follows that $\mathfrak{g}(\infty, \boldsymbol{\xi} : \varepsilon_i) = \mathbf{0}$, and ultimately the effects of shocks on the cointegrating relations will disappear. Nevertheless, estimation of $\mathfrak{g}(n, \boldsymbol{\xi} : \varepsilon_i)$ for a finite n still requires *a priori* identification of $\mathbf{A}^{-1}\boldsymbol{\Omega}$. Once again, a variety of identification schemes can be used for this purpose. Alternatively, we could focus on the impulse response functions of $\boldsymbol{\xi}_t = \boldsymbol{\beta}'\mathbf{y}_{t-1}$ with respect to the ith reduced form shock, u_{it}. In this case

$$\mathfrak{g}(n, \boldsymbol{\xi} : u_i) = \frac{1}{\sqrt{\sigma_{ii}}}\boldsymbol{\beta}'\tilde{\mathbf{C}}_n\boldsymbol{\Sigma}\mathbf{e}_i, \quad n = 0, 1, \ldots, \quad i = 1, \ldots, m. \tag{6.66}$$

which is uniquely determined from the knowledge of the reduced form parameters.

Furthermore, generalised forecast error variance decompositions for the cointegrating VAR model (6.25) can be computed as follow:

$$\psi_{ij,n} = \frac{\sigma_{ii}^{-1}\sum_{\ell=0}^{n}\left(\mathbf{e}_i'\tilde{\mathbf{C}}_\ell\boldsymbol{\Sigma}\mathbf{e}_j\right)^2}{\sum_{\ell=0}^{n}\mathbf{e}_i'\tilde{\mathbf{C}}_\ell\boldsymbol{\Sigma}\tilde{\mathbf{C}}_\ell'\mathbf{e}_i}, \quad n = 0, 1, \ldots; \text{ and } i, j = 1, \ldots, m. \tag{6.67}$$

The $\psi_{ij,n}$ in (6.67) measures the proportion of the n-step ahead forecast error variance of variable i accounted for by the reduced form error in the jth equation in the system unlike the orthogonalised forecast error variance decomposition, which due to non-zero correlations across the shocks, cause the different proportions not necessarily to add up to unity.

Corresponding orthogonalised impulse response functions and forecast error variance decompositions for the cointegrating VAR model (6.25) are given by:

$$o\left(n, \mathbf{y} : u_i^*\right) = \tilde{\mathbf{C}}_n \mathbf{P} \mathbf{e}_i, \quad n = 0, 1, \ldots, \quad i = 1, \ldots, m, \tag{6.68}$$

$$o\left(n, \boldsymbol{\xi} : u_i^*\right) = \boldsymbol{\beta}' \tilde{\mathbf{C}}_n \mathbf{P} \mathbf{e}_i, \quad n = 0, 1, \ldots, \quad i = 1, \ldots, m, \tag{6.69}$$

$$o_{ij,n} = \frac{\sigma_{ii}^{-1} \sum_{\ell=0}^{n} \left(\mathbf{e}_i' \tilde{\mathbf{C}}_\ell \mathbf{P} \mathbf{e}_j\right)^2}{\sum_{\ell=0}^{n} \mathbf{e}_i' \tilde{\mathbf{C}}_\ell \boldsymbol{\Sigma} \tilde{\mathbf{C}}_\ell' \mathbf{e}_i}, \quad n = 0, 1, 2, \ldots, \quad i, j = 1, \ldots, m, \tag{6.70}$$

where u_{it}^* is an orthogonalised residual and $\mathbf{P}$ is a lower triangular matrix obtained by the Choleski decomposition of $\boldsymbol{\Sigma} = \mathbf{P}\mathbf{P}'$.

Finally, we could examine the effect of system-wide shocks on the cointegrating relations using the persistence profiles discussed above in Section 6.1.3. Pesaran and Shin (1996) suggest using the persistence profiles to measure the speed of convergence of the cointegrating relations to equilibrium. The scaled persistence profiles of the jth cointegrating relation is given by

$$h\left(\boldsymbol{\beta}_j' \mathbf{y}_t, n\right) = \frac{\boldsymbol{\beta}_j' \tilde{\mathbf{C}}_n \boldsymbol{\Sigma} \tilde{\mathbf{C}}_n' \boldsymbol{\beta}_j}{\boldsymbol{\beta}_j' \boldsymbol{\Sigma} \boldsymbol{\beta}_j}, \quad n = 0, 1, \ldots, \quad j = 1, \ldots, r, \tag{6.71}$$

which is scaled to have a value of unity on impact. The profiles tend to zero as $n \to \infty$, and provide a useful graphical representation of the extent to which the cointegrating (equilibrium) relations adjust to system-wide shocks. Once again, the main attraction of persistence profiles lies in the fact that they are uniquely determined from the reduced form parameters and do not depend on the nature of the system-wide shocks considered. Using (6.26), the cointegrating relations in terms of the structural errors may be written as

$$\boldsymbol{\beta}_j' \mathbf{y}_t = \boldsymbol{\beta}_j' \mathbf{y}_0 + \left(\boldsymbol{\beta}_j' \boldsymbol{\gamma}\right) t + \boldsymbol{\beta}_j' \mathbf{C}^*(L) \mathbf{A}^{-1} \left(\boldsymbol{\varepsilon}_t - \boldsymbol{\varepsilon}_0\right),$$

and the persistence profile of $\boldsymbol{\beta}_j'\mathbf{y}_t$ with respect to the structural errors, $\boldsymbol{\varepsilon}_t$, is given by

$$\frac{\boldsymbol{\beta}_j'\left(\tilde{\mathbf{C}}_n\mathbf{A}^{-1}\right)\boldsymbol{\Omega}\left(\tilde{\mathbf{C}}_n\mathbf{A}^{-1}\right)'\boldsymbol{\beta}_j}{\boldsymbol{\beta}_j'\mathbf{A}^{-1}\boldsymbol{\Omega}\mathbf{A}'^{-1}\boldsymbol{\beta}_j}, \quad n = 0, 1, \ldots, \quad j = 1, \ldots, r.$$

But, since $\boldsymbol{\Sigma} = \mathbf{A}^{-1}\boldsymbol{\Omega}\mathbf{A}'^{-1}$, this persistence profile is in fact identical to the one derived using the reduced form errors, $\mathbf{u}_t$, given by (6.71).

6.3 The cointegrated VAR model with $I(1)$ exogenous variables

The most complete econometric model that we might wish to consider is the case in which there are both endogenous and exogenous variables and linear deterministic trends. This is the model discussed in Pesaran, Shin and Smith (2000), where we distinguish between an $m_y \times 1$ vector of endogenous variables $\mathbf{y}_t$ and an $m_x \times 1$ vector of exogenous $I(1)$ variables $\mathbf{x}_t$ among the core variables in $\mathbf{z}_t = (\mathbf{y}_t', \mathbf{x}_t')'$, with $m = m_y + m_x$.

We begin with the extended *vector error correction* model (VECM) in $\mathbf{z}_t$ (*cf.* (6.17)),

$$\Delta\mathbf{z}_t = -\boldsymbol{\Pi}\mathbf{z}_{t-1} + \sum_{i=1}^{p-1}\boldsymbol{\Gamma}_i\Delta\mathbf{z}_{t-i} + \mathbf{a}_0 + \mathbf{a}_1 t + \mathbf{u}_t, \tag{6.72}$$

where the short-run response matrices $\{\boldsymbol{\Gamma}_i\}_{i=1}^{p-1}$ and the long-run multiplier matrix $\boldsymbol{\Pi}$ are similarly defined to those below (6.17).

By partitioning the error term $\mathbf{u}_t$ conformably with $\mathbf{z}_t = \left(\mathbf{y}_t', \mathbf{x}_t'\right)'$ as $\mathbf{u}_t = \left(\mathbf{u}_{yt}', \mathbf{u}_{xt}'\right)'$ and its variance matrix as

$$\boldsymbol{\Sigma} = \begin{pmatrix} \boldsymbol{\Sigma}_{yy} & \boldsymbol{\Sigma}_{yx} \\ \boldsymbol{\Sigma}_{xy} & \boldsymbol{\Sigma}_{xx} \end{pmatrix},$$

we are able to express $\mathbf{u}_{yt}$ conditionally in terms of $\mathbf{u}_{xt}$ as

$$\mathbf{u}_{yt} = \boldsymbol{\Sigma}_{yx}\boldsymbol{\Sigma}_{xx}^{-1}\mathbf{u}_{xt} + \boldsymbol{\upsilon}_t, \tag{6.73}$$

where $\boldsymbol{\upsilon}_t \sim i.i.d.\,(\mathbf{0}, \boldsymbol{\Sigma}_{\upsilon\upsilon})$, $\boldsymbol{\Sigma}_{\upsilon\upsilon} \equiv \boldsymbol{\Sigma}_{yy} - \boldsymbol{\Sigma}_{yx}\boldsymbol{\Sigma}_{xx}^{-1}\boldsymbol{\Sigma}_{xy}$ and $\boldsymbol{\upsilon}_t$ is uncorrelated with $\mathbf{u}_{xt}$ by construction. Substitution of (6.73) into (6.72) together with a similar partitioning of the parameter vectors and matrices $\mathbf{a}_0 = \left(\mathbf{a}_{y0}', \mathbf{a}_{x0}'\right)'$,

$\mathbf{a}_1 = \left(\mathbf{a}'_{y1}, \mathbf{a}'_{x1}\right)'$, $\mathbf{\Pi} = \left(\mathbf{\Pi}'_y, \mathbf{\Pi}'_x\right)'$, $\mathbf{\Gamma}_i = \left(\mathbf{\Gamma}'_{yi}, \mathbf{\Gamma}'_{xi}\right)'$, $i = 1, \ldots, p-1$, provides a conditional model for $\Delta \mathbf{y}_t$ in terms of $\mathbf{z}_{t-1}, \Delta \mathbf{x}_t, \Delta \mathbf{z}_{t-1}, \Delta \mathbf{z}_{t-2}, \ldots$; *viz.*

$$\Delta \mathbf{y}_t = -\mathbf{\Pi}_{yy.x} \mathbf{z}_{t-1} + \mathbf{\Lambda} \Delta \mathbf{x}_t + \sum_{i=1}^{p-1} \mathbf{\Psi}_i \Delta \mathbf{z}_{t-i} + \mathbf{c}_0 + \mathbf{c}_1 t + \boldsymbol{v}_t, \tag{6.74}$$

where $\mathbf{\Pi}_{yy.x} \equiv \mathbf{\Pi}_y - \mathbf{\Sigma}_{yx}\mathbf{\Sigma}_{xx}^{-1}\mathbf{\Pi}_x$, $\mathbf{\Lambda} = \mathbf{\Sigma}_{yx}\mathbf{\Sigma}_{xx}^{-1}$, $\mathbf{\Psi}_i \equiv \mathbf{\Gamma}_{yi} - \mathbf{\Sigma}_{yx}\mathbf{\Sigma}_{xx}^{-1}\mathbf{\Gamma}_{xi}$, $i = 1, \ldots, p-1$, $\mathbf{c}_0 \equiv \mathbf{a}_{y0} - \mathbf{\Sigma}_{yx}\mathbf{\Sigma}_{xx}^{-1}\mathbf{a}_{x0}$ and $\mathbf{c}_1 \equiv \mathbf{a}_{y1} - \mathbf{\Sigma}_{yx}\mathbf{\Sigma}_{xx}^{-1}\mathbf{a}_{x1}$,

Following Johansen (1995), we assume that the process $\{\mathbf{x}_t\}_{t=1}^{\infty}$ is weakly exogenous with respect to the matrix of long-run multiplier parameters $\mathbf{\Pi}$, namely,

$$\mathbf{\Pi}_x = \mathbf{0}. \tag{6.75}$$

Therefore,

$$\mathbf{\Pi}_{yy.x} = \mathbf{\Pi}_y. \tag{6.76}$$

Consequently, from (6.72) and (6.74), the system of equations is rendered as

$$\Delta \mathbf{y}_t = -\mathbf{\Pi}_y \mathbf{z}_{t-1} + \mathbf{\Lambda} \Delta \mathbf{x}_t + \sum_{i=1}^{p-1} \mathbf{\Psi}_i \Delta \mathbf{z}_{t-i} + \mathbf{c}_0 + \mathbf{c}_1 t + \boldsymbol{v}_t, \tag{6.77}$$

$$\Delta \mathbf{x}_t = \sum_{i=1}^{p-1} \mathbf{\Gamma}_{xi} \Delta \mathbf{z}_{t-i} + \mathbf{a}_{x0} + \mathbf{u}_{xt}, \tag{6.78}$$

where now the restrictions on trend coefficients (6.23) are modified to

$$\mathbf{c}_1 = \mathbf{\Pi}_y \boldsymbol{\gamma}. \tag{6.79}$$

The restriction $\mathbf{\Pi}_x = \mathbf{0}$ in (6.75) implies that the elements of the vector process $\{\mathbf{x}_t\}_{t=1}^{\infty}$ are not cointegrated among themselves as is evident from (6.78). Moreover, the information available from the differenced VAR($p-1$) model (6.78) for $\{\mathbf{x}_t\}_{t=1}^{\infty}$ is redundant for efficient conditional estimation and inference concerning the long-run parameters $\mathbf{\Pi}_y$ as well as the deterministic and short-run parameters $\mathbf{c}_0$, $\mathbf{c}_1$, $\mathbf{\Lambda}$ and $\mathbf{\Psi}_i$, $i = 1, \ldots, p-1$, of (6.77).[24] Furthermore, we may regard $\{\mathbf{x}_t\}_{t=1}^{\infty}$ as *long-run forcing* for $\{\mathbf{y}_t\}_{t=1}^{\infty}$; see Granger and Lin (1995). Note that this restriction does not preclude $\{\mathbf{y}_t\}_{t=1}^{\infty}$ being *Granger-causal* for $\{\mathbf{x}_t\}_{t=1}^{\infty}$ in the *short run*.

[24] In general the variance of $\boldsymbol{v}_t$ will be smaller than that of $\mathbf{u}_{yt}$ because it is easily seen that

$$\mathbf{\Sigma}_{vv} - \mathbf{\Sigma}_{yy} = -\mathbf{\Sigma}_{yx}\mathbf{\Sigma}_{xx}^{-1}\mathbf{\Sigma}_{xy} \leq 0.$$

When there are r cointegrating relations among $\mathbf{z}_t$, then we may express

$$\boldsymbol{\Pi}_y = \boldsymbol{\alpha}_y \boldsymbol{\beta}', \tag{6.80}$$

where $\boldsymbol{\alpha}_y$ $(m_y \times r)$ and $\boldsymbol{\beta}$ $(m \times r)$ are matrices of error correction coefficients and of the long-run (or cointegrating) coefficients, both of which are of full column rank, r. For the purpose of empirical analysis, we assume that the lag order p is large enough so that $\mathbf{u}_t$ and $\boldsymbol{v}_t$ are serially uncorrelated, and have zero mean and positive definite covariance matrices, $\boldsymbol{\Sigma}$ and $\boldsymbol{\Sigma}_{vv}$, respectively. For the purpose of the ML estimation, we also assume that $\mathbf{u}_t$ and $\boldsymbol{v}_t$ are normally distributed, although this is not binding if the number of the time series observations available is large enough.[25]

To a large extent, the analysis of a cointegrated VAR model containing exogenous $I(1)$ variables follows very similar lines to that described in Section 6.2 above. Hence, to avoid the unsatisfactory possibility that there exist quadratic trends in the level solution of the data generating process for $\mathbf{z}_t$ when there is no cointegration, we can again assume that there are restrictions on the intercepts and/or time trends corresponding to Cases I–V in Section 6.2.1 above. We delineate five cases of interest; *viz.*

- **Case I:** (No intercepts; no trends.) $\mathbf{c}_0 = \mathbf{0}$ and $\mathbf{c}_1 = \mathbf{0}$. Hence, the structural VECM (6.77) becomes

$$\Delta \mathbf{y}_t = -\boldsymbol{\Pi}_y \mathbf{z}_{t-1} + \boldsymbol{\Lambda} \Delta \mathbf{x}_t + \sum_{i=1}^{p-1} \boldsymbol{\Psi}_i \Delta \mathbf{z}_{t-i} + \boldsymbol{v}_t. \tag{6.81}$$

- **Case II:** (Restricted intercepts; no trends.) $\mathbf{c}_0 = \boldsymbol{\Pi}_y \boldsymbol{\mu}$ and $\mathbf{c}_1 = \mathbf{0}$. The structural VECM (6.77) is

$$\Delta \mathbf{y}_t = \boldsymbol{\Pi}_y \boldsymbol{\mu} - \boldsymbol{\Pi}_y \mathbf{z}_{t-1} + \boldsymbol{\Lambda} \Delta \mathbf{x}_t + \sum_{i=1}^{p-1} \boldsymbol{\Psi}_i \Delta \mathbf{z}_{t-i} + \boldsymbol{v}_t. \tag{6.82}$$

- **Case III:** (Unrestricted intercepts; no trends.) $\mathbf{c}_0 \neq \mathbf{0}$ and $\mathbf{c}_1 = \mathbf{0}$. In this case, the intercept restriction $\mathbf{c}_0 = \boldsymbol{\Pi}_y \boldsymbol{\mu}$ is ignored and the structural

Therefore, the parameters in the conditional model (6.77) are likely to be estimated more precisely than the parameters of the unconditional model. Whether this is an advantage depends on what the economic parameters of interest are. If the parameters of interest are $\boldsymbol{\Pi}_y = (\boldsymbol{\Pi}_{yy}, \boldsymbol{\Pi}_{yx})$, it is clear from the above equation that $\Delta \mathbf{x}_t$ will be weakly exogenous for $\boldsymbol{\Pi}_y$ only if either $\boldsymbol{\Sigma}_{yx} = 0$ so that $\boldsymbol{\Theta} = 0$ or if $\boldsymbol{\Pi}_x = (\boldsymbol{\Pi}_{xy}, \boldsymbol{\Pi}_{xx}) = 0$. In either of these cases the coefficient matrix on $(\mathbf{y}_{t-1}, \mathbf{x}_{t-1})$ in the conditional model will provide an estimate of $\boldsymbol{\Pi}_y$. In other cases the economic parameter of interest may be simply the long-run effects of $\mathbf{x}_t$ on $\mathbf{y}_t$ so one might be interested in $\boldsymbol{\Pi}_y - \boldsymbol{\Theta}\boldsymbol{\Pi}_x$ directly, in which case the model conditional on $\mathbf{x}_t$ is appropriate whether or not $\boldsymbol{\Pi}_x = 0$.

[25] For a more precise statement of these assumptions see Johansen (1995), and Pesaran, Shin and Smith (2000).

VECM estimated is

$$\Delta \mathbf{y}_t = \mathbf{c}_0 - \mathbf{\Pi}_y \mathbf{z}_{t-1} + \mathbf{\Lambda}\Delta \mathbf{x}_t + \sum_{i=1}^{p-1} \mathbf{\Psi}_i \Delta \mathbf{z}_{t-i} + \boldsymbol{v}_t. \tag{6.83}$$

- **Case IV:** (Unrestricted intercepts; restricted trends.) $\mathbf{c}_0 \neq \mathbf{0}$ and $\mathbf{c}_1 = \mathbf{\Pi}_y \boldsymbol{\gamma}$. Thus,

$$\Delta \mathbf{y}_t = \mathbf{c}_0 + \left(\mathbf{\Pi}_y \boldsymbol{\gamma}\right) t - \mathbf{\Pi}_y \mathbf{z}_{t-1} + \mathbf{\Lambda}\Delta \mathbf{x}_t + \sum_{i=1}^{p-1} \mathbf{\Psi}_i \Delta \mathbf{z}_{t-i} + \boldsymbol{v}_t. \tag{6.84}$$

- **Case V:** (Unrestricted intercepts; unrestricted trends.) $\mathbf{c}_0 \neq \mathbf{0}$ and $\mathbf{c}_1 \neq \mathbf{0}$. Here, the deterministic trend restriction $\mathbf{c}_1 = \mathbf{\Pi}_y \boldsymbol{\gamma}$ is ignored and the structural VECM estimated is

$$\Delta \mathbf{y}_t = \mathbf{c}_0 + \mathbf{c}_1 t - \mathbf{\Pi}_y \mathbf{z}_{t-1} + \mathbf{\Lambda}\Delta \mathbf{x}_t + \sum_{i=1}^{p-1} \mathbf{\Psi}_i \Delta \mathbf{z}_{t-i} + \boldsymbol{v}_t. \tag{6.85}$$

Tests of the cointegrating rank are obtained along exactly the same lines as those in Section 6.2.2, with the first step in the algorithm generating residuals $\mathbf{r}_{0t}$ and $\mathbf{r}_{1t}$ from the regression of, in turn, $\Delta \mathbf{y}_t$ and $\mathbf{z}^*_{t-1} = \left(\mathbf{z}'_{t-1}, t\right)'$ on $\Delta \mathbf{x}_t, \Delta \mathbf{z}_{t-1}, \Delta \mathbf{z}_{t-2}, \ldots, \Delta \mathbf{z}_{t-p+1}$ and 1.[26] Estimation of the VECM subject to exactly and over-identifying long-run restrictions can be carried out using maximum likelihood methods as in Section 6.2.3 applied to (6.77) subject to the appropriate restrictions on the intercepts and trends, subject to Rank$(\mathbf{\Pi}_y) = r$, and subject to k general linear restrictions of the form in (6.39). And, having computed ML estimates of the cointegrating vectors, estimation of the short-run parameters of the conditional VECM can be computed using OLS regressions exactly as in Section 6.2.4.

The investigation of the dynamic properties of the system including exogenous $I(1)$ variables does require a little care, however. For this, we require the full-system VECM, obtained by augmenting the conditional model for $\Delta \mathbf{y}_t$, (6.77), with the marginal model for $\Delta \mathbf{x}_t$, (6.78). This is written as

$$\Delta \mathbf{z}_t = -\boldsymbol{\alpha}\boldsymbol{\beta}' \mathbf{z}_{t-1} + \sum_{i=1}^{p-1} \mathbf{\Gamma}_i \Delta \mathbf{z}_{t-i} + \mathbf{a}_0 + \mathbf{a}_1 t + \mathbf{H}\boldsymbol{\zeta}_t, \tag{6.86}$$

[26] Asymptotic distributions of the trace and maximum eigenvalue statistics are again non-standard, and depend on whether the intercepts and/or the coefficients on the deterministic trends are restricted or unrestricted. Pesaran, Shin and Smith (2000) have tabulated the upper 5% and 10% quantiles of the asymptotic critical values of both statistics via stochastic simulations with $T = 500$ and $10,000$ replications. See also Mackinnon (1996).

where $\boldsymbol{\beta}$ is defined by (6.80),

$$\boldsymbol{\alpha} = \begin{pmatrix} \boldsymbol{\alpha}_y \\ 0 \end{pmatrix}, \ \boldsymbol{\Gamma}_i = \begin{pmatrix} \boldsymbol{\Psi}_i + \boldsymbol{\Lambda}\boldsymbol{\Gamma}_{xi} \\ \boldsymbol{\Gamma}_{xi} \end{pmatrix}, \ \mathbf{a}_0 = \begin{pmatrix} \mathbf{c}_0 + \boldsymbol{\Lambda}\boldsymbol{a}_{x0} \\ \mathbf{a}_{x0} \end{pmatrix}, \ \mathbf{a}_1 = \begin{pmatrix} \mathbf{c}_1 \\ 0 \end{pmatrix}, \tag{6.87}$$

$$\boldsymbol{\zeta}_t = \begin{pmatrix} \boldsymbol{v}_t \\ \mathbf{u}_{xt} \end{pmatrix}, \ \mathbf{H} = \begin{pmatrix} \mathbf{I}_{m_y} & \boldsymbol{\Lambda} \\ 0 & \mathbf{I}_{m_x} \end{pmatrix}, \ \mathrm{Cov}(\boldsymbol{\zeta}_t) = \boldsymbol{\Sigma}_{\zeta\zeta} = \begin{pmatrix} \boldsymbol{\Sigma}_{vv} & 0 \\ 0 & \boldsymbol{\Sigma}_{xx} \end{pmatrix}. \tag{6.88}$$

Analysis of the stability of the cointegrated system follows the arguments of Section 6.2.5, and impulse response analysis follows the arguments in Section 6.2.6, but *applied to the full system in* (6.86). While efficient conditional estimation of, and inference on, the parameters of (6.77) can be conducted without reference to the marginal model (6.78), the dynamic properties of the system have to accommodate the influence of the processes driving the exogenous variables.

This last point is worth emphasising and applies to any analysis involving counter-factuals, including impulse response analysis and forecasting exercises, for example. Macromodellers frequently consider the dynamic response of a system to a change in an exogenous variable by considering the effects of a once-and-for-all increase in the variable.[27] This (implicitly) imposes restrictions on the processes generating the exogenous variable, assuming that there is no serial correlation in the variable and that a shock to one exogenous variable can be considered without having to take into account changes in other exogenous variables. These counter-factual exercises might be of interest. But, generally speaking, one needs to take into account the possibility that changes in one exogenous variable will have an impact on other exogenous variables and that these effects might continue and interact over time. This requires an explicit analysis of the dynamic processes driving the exogenous variables, as captured by the marginal model in (6.78). The whole point of the approach to investigating model dynamics reflected in the model of (6.86) and incorporated in the idea of generalised impulse response analysis is to explicitly allow for the conditional correlation structure in errors and the interactions between endogenous and exogenous variables to provide a 'realistic' counter-factual exercise based on the contemporaneous covariances and interactions observed historically in the data.

[27] This corresponds to our earlier discussion of the dynamic impact of a once-and-for-all shock to an equation in a system captured as an intercept shift.

6.4 Small sample properties of test statistics

The distributions of the trace and maximal eigenvalue statistics used to test the number of cointegrating relationships (see (6.37) and (6.38)) and of the log-likelihood ratio statistic used to test the validity of the over-identifying restrictions (see (6.52)) are appropriate only asymptotically. Moreover, recent work has shown that the asymptotic results are valid only when relatively large samples of data are available if the cointegrating VAR model is of even modest size (in terms of the number of parameters involved); that is, when the order of the VAR or the number of variables in the VAR exceeds three or four, say.[28] This suggests that care should be taken in interpreting the test statistics obtained.

In some cases, it is possible to undertake bootstrapping exercises to investigate directly the small sample properties of the estimated statistics. For example, suppose that the VEC model of (6.77) and (6.78) has been estimated subject to the just- or over-identifying restrictions suggested by economic theory. Using the observed initial values for each variable, it is possible to generate S new samples of data (of the same size as the original) under the hypothesis that the estimated version of (6.77) and (6.78) is the true data generating process. For each of the S replications of the data, the tests of the cointegrating rank and of the over-identifying restrictions can be carried out and, hence, distributions of the test statistics are obtained which take into account the small sample of data available when calculating the statistics. Working at the $\alpha\%$ level of significance, critical values which take into account the small sample properties of the tests can be obtained by observing, from the right tails of the simulated distributions, the value of the statistics which would ensure that the probability that the null is not rejected when it is true is $(1-\alpha)$.

More specifically, suppose that the model in (6.77) has been estimated under the exactly or over-identifying restrictions given by (6.39). We therefore have estimates of the cointegrating vectors, $\hat{\boldsymbol{\beta}}_*$, of the short-run parameters, $\left(\hat{\boldsymbol{\alpha}}_y, \hat{\boldsymbol{\Psi}}_1, \ldots, \hat{\boldsymbol{\Psi}}_{p-1}, \hat{\boldsymbol{\Lambda}}, \hat{\boldsymbol{c}}_0\right)$, and of the covariance matrix, $\hat{\boldsymbol{\Sigma}}_{vv}$. Taking the observed values of $\Delta\mathbf{x}_t$ as fixed or re-sampled using (6.78) over the whole sample, and taking the p lagged values of the $\mathbf{y}_t$ observed just prior to the sample as fixed also, for the sth replication, we can recursively

[28] See, for example, Abadir *et al.* (1999), Gonzalo (1994) and Muscatelli and Hurn (1995).

simulate the values of $\Delta \mathbf{y}_t^{(s)}$, $s = 1, 2, \ldots, S$, using

$$\Delta \mathbf{y}_t^{(s)} = -\hat{\boldsymbol{\alpha}}_y \hat{\boldsymbol{\beta}}_*' \mathbf{z}_{t-1}^{*(s)} + \sum_{i=1}^{p-1} \hat{\boldsymbol{\Psi}}_i \Delta \mathbf{z}_{t-i}^{(s)} + \hat{\boldsymbol{\Lambda}} \Delta \mathbf{x}_t + \hat{\mathbf{c}}_0 + \boldsymbol{v}_t^{(s)}, \quad t = 1, 2, \ldots, T. \tag{6.89}$$

To obtain $\boldsymbol{v}_t^{(s)}$, allowing for the observed correlation of shocks across the $\Delta \mathbf{y}_t$, we can generate draws from a multivariate normal distribution chosen to match the observed correlation of the estimated reduced form errors, $\hat{\boldsymbol{\Sigma}}_{vv}$, (termed a *parametric* bootstrap) or we can re-sample with replacement from the estimated residuals (a *non-parametric* bootstrap).[29]

Having generated the $\Delta \mathbf{y}_t^{(s)}$, $t = 1, \ldots, T$, and making use of the observed $\Delta \mathbf{x}_t$, it is straightforward to estimate the VECM of (6.77) subject to just-identifying restrictions and then subject to the over-identifying restrictions of (6.39) to obtain a sequence of log-likelihood ratio test statistics, $LR^{(s)}$, each testing the validity of the over-identifying restrictions in the s-th simulated dataset, $s = 1, \ldots, S$.[30] These statistics can be sorted into ascending order and, given that the data has been generated by the model at (6.77) incorporating the over-identifying restrictions of $\hat{\boldsymbol{\beta}}_*$, critical values can be identified which are relevant to this particular model and which take into account the sample size. Hence, for example, the value of $LR^{(s)}$ which exceeds 95% of the observed statistics represents the appropriate 95% critical value for the test of the validity of the over-identifying restrictions.[31]

6.5 Empirical distribution of impulse response functions and persistence profiles

The simulation methods described above are relatively easy to implement in the context of a VAR and can be applied in various contexts.

[29] More detailed discussion on generating simulated errors in bootstrap procedures is provided in Section 7.3.3.

[30] The maximum likelihood estimation of the VECM can be time-consuming, especially if one is to be sure that all of the estimates relate to global and not local maxima. Practically, the choice of an optimisation algorithm is likely to be important in this exercise, and the simulated annealing algorithm discussed in Goffe *et al.* (1994) can prove useful in this respect.

[31] Simulation here is used to find the probability of rejection for one point in the space covered by the null (that the over-identifying restrictions are valid). The classical significance level is the *maximum* of the rejection probabilities over the null space. By using a single point, the observed critical values potentially understate the true rejection level.

An important example is in examining the distributional properties of the various statistics used to investigate the dynamic properties of the estimated models we have discussed in the chapter. Specifically, in this section, we describe the steps involved in the calculation of empirical distribution of generalised (orthogonalised) impulse response functions and persistence profiles based on a vector error correction model using stochastic simulation techniques.

Consider the underlying vector error correction model, (6.86), which can be rewritten as

$$\mathbf{z}_t = \sum_{i=1}^{p} \mathbf{\Phi}_i \mathbf{z}_{t-i} + \mathbf{a}_0 + \mathbf{a}_1 t + \mathbf{H}\boldsymbol{\zeta}_t, \quad t = 1, 2, \ldots, T, \tag{6.90}$$

where $\mathbf{\Phi}_1 = \mathbf{I}_m - \boldsymbol{\alpha\beta}' + \mathbf{\Gamma}_1$, $\mathbf{\Phi}_i = \mathbf{\Gamma}_i - \mathbf{\Gamma}_{i-1}$, $i = 2, \ldots, p-1$, $\mathbf{\Phi}_p = -\mathbf{\Gamma}_{p-1}$. In what follows, we take into account parameter uncertainty and describe how to evaluate the empirical distributions of generalised (orthogonalised) impulse response functions of both individual variables and cointegrating relations and persistence profiles. In the presence of exogenous $I(1)$ variables, they are given, respectively, by

$$\mathfrak{g}\left(n, \mathbf{z} : \zeta_i\right) = \frac{1}{\sqrt{\sigma_{\zeta,ii}}} \tilde{\mathbf{C}}_n \mathbf{H} \mathbf{\Sigma}_{\zeta\zeta} \mathbf{e}_i, \quad n = 0, 1, \ldots, \quad i = 1, \ldots, m, \tag{6.91}$$

$$\mathfrak{g}\left(n, \boldsymbol{\xi} : \zeta_i\right) = \frac{1}{\sqrt{\sigma_{\zeta,ii}}} \boldsymbol{\beta}' \tilde{\mathbf{C}}_n \mathbf{H} \mathbf{\Sigma}_{\zeta\zeta} \mathbf{e}_i, \quad n = 0, 1, \ldots, \quad i = 1, \ldots, m, \tag{6.92}$$

$$\mathfrak{o}\left(n, \mathbf{z} : \zeta_i^*\right) = \tilde{\mathbf{C}}_n \mathbf{H} \mathbf{P}_\zeta \mathbf{e}_i, \quad n = 0, 1, \ldots, \quad i = 1, \ldots, m, \tag{6.93}$$

$$\mathfrak{o}\left(n, \boldsymbol{\xi} : \zeta_i^*\right) = \boldsymbol{\beta}' \tilde{\mathbf{C}}_n \mathbf{H} \mathbf{P}_\zeta \mathbf{e}_i, \quad n = 0, 1, \ldots, \quad i = 1, \ldots, m, \tag{6.94}$$

$$h\left(\boldsymbol{\beta}_j' \mathbf{z}, n\right) = \frac{\boldsymbol{\beta}_j' \tilde{\mathbf{C}}_n \mathbf{H} \mathbf{\Sigma}_{\zeta\zeta} \mathbf{H}' \tilde{\mathbf{C}}_n' \boldsymbol{\beta}_j}{\boldsymbol{\beta}_j' \mathbf{H} \mathbf{\Sigma}_{\zeta\zeta} \mathbf{H}' \boldsymbol{\beta}_j}, \quad n = 0, 1, \ldots, \quad j = 1, \ldots, r, \tag{6.95}$$

where $\boldsymbol{\zeta}_t$ is *i.i.d.* $\left(\mathbf{0}, \mathbf{\Sigma}_{\zeta\zeta}\right)$, $\sigma_{\zeta,ij}$ is (i,j)th element of $\mathbf{\Sigma}_{\zeta\zeta}$, $\tilde{\mathbf{C}}_n = \mathbf{\Sigma}_{j=0}^{n} \mathbf{C}_j$, with $\mathbf{C}_j$'s given by the recursive relations (6.21), $\mathbf{H}$ and $\mathbf{\Sigma}_{\zeta\zeta}$ are given in (6.88), $\boldsymbol{\xi}_t = \boldsymbol{\beta}' \mathbf{z}_{t-1}$, $\mathbf{e}_i$ is a selection vector of zeros with unity as its ith element, $\mathbf{P}_\zeta$ is a lower triangular matrix obtained by the Choleski decomposition of $\mathbf{\Sigma}_{\zeta\zeta} = \mathbf{P}_\zeta \mathbf{P}_\zeta'$, and $m = m_x + m_y$.

Suppose that the ML estimators of $\mathbf{\Phi}_i$, $i = 1, \ldots, p$, $\mathbf{a}_0$, $\mathbf{a}_1$, $\mathbf{H}$ and $\mathbf{\Sigma}_{\zeta\zeta}$ are given and denoted by $\hat{\mathbf{\Phi}}_i$, $i = 1, \ldots, p$, $\hat{\mathbf{a}}_0$, $\hat{\mathbf{a}}_1$, $\hat{\mathbf{H}}$ and $\hat{\mathbf{\Sigma}}_{\zeta\zeta}$, respectively.

To allow for parameter uncertainty, we use the bootstrap procedure and simulate S (*in-sample*) values of $\mathbf{z}_t$, $t = 1, 2, \ldots, T$, denoted by $\mathbf{z}_t^{(s)}$, $s = 1, \ldots, S$, where

$$\mathbf{z}_t^{(s)} = \sum_{i=1}^{p} \hat{\mathbf{\Phi}}_i \mathbf{z}_{t-i}^{(s)} + \hat{\mathbf{a}}_0 + \hat{\mathbf{a}}_1 t + \hat{\mathbf{H}} \zeta_t^{(s)}, \quad t = 1, 2, \ldots, T, \tag{6.96}$$

realisations are used for the initial values, $\mathbf{z}_{-1}, \ldots, \mathbf{z}_{-p}$, and $\boldsymbol{\zeta}_t^{(s)}$'s can be drawn either by parametric or non-parametric methods (see 7.3.3).

Having obtained the S sets of simulated in-sample values,

$$\left(\mathbf{z}_1^{(s)}, \mathbf{z}_2^{(s)}, \ldots, \mathbf{z}_T^{(s)}\right),$$

the VAR(p) model, (6.90), is re-estimated S times to obtain the ML estimates, $\hat{\mathbf{\Phi}}_i^{(s)}$, $\hat{\mathbf{a}}_0^{(s)}$, $\hat{\mathbf{a}}_1^{(s)}$, $\hat{\mathbf{H}}^{(s)}$ and $\hat{\mathbf{\Sigma}}_{\zeta\zeta}^{(s)}$, for $i = 1, 2, \ldots, p$, and $s = 1, 2, \ldots, S$. For each of these bootstrap replications, we then obtain the estimates of $\mathfrak{g}^{(s)}\left(n, \mathbf{z}^{(s)} : \zeta_i^{(s)}\right)$, $\mathfrak{g}^{(s)}\left(n, \boldsymbol{\xi}^{(s)} : \zeta_i^{(s)}\right)$, $\mathfrak{o}^{(s)}\left(n, \mathbf{z}^{(s)} : \zeta_i^{*(s)}\right)$, $\mathfrak{o}^{(s)}\left(n, \boldsymbol{\xi}^{(s)} : \zeta_i^{*(s)}\right)$, $h^{(s)}\left(\boldsymbol{\beta}_j' \mathbf{z}^{(s)}, n\right)$. Therefore, using these S sets of simulated estimates, we will obtain both empirical mean and confidence intervals of impulse response functions and persistence profiles.

7

Probability forecasting: Concepts and analysis

Having considered the econometric issues involved in the estimation, testing and interpretation of a long-run structural VAR model, in this chapter we turn attention to the use of the model in probability forecasting. Much of the material would be relevant to forecasts based on any type of model. However, the material is particularly relevant here since VARs are frequently employed in forecasting. Moreover, given the size and simplicity of the structure of most VAR models, these models are particularly well-suited to an investigation of the various types of uncertainty that influence forecasts, and their use in decision-making.

7.1 Probability forecasting

In much of what follows, we are concerned with the notion of *probability forecasting*, arguing that these convey the uncertainties surrounding forecasts from a macroeconomic model in a very straightforward way and one that is most useful in decision-making. A probability forecast is a statement of the likelihood of a specified event taking place conditional on the available information and can be estimated on the basis of any macroeconomic model. The event can be defined with respect to the values of a single variable or a set of variables, measured at a particular time, or at a sequence of times, or over a particular interval of time in the future.

For example, in a macroeconomic context, suppose that the focus of interest is inflation, Δp_t, and output growth, Δy_t. Then events that might be of interest include

$$\begin{aligned}
\pi_{1t} &= \Pr\left(\Delta p_{t+1} < a_1 \mid \mathfrak{I}_t\right), \\
\pi_{2t} &= \Pr\left(\Delta p_{t+1} < a_1, \Delta y_{t+1} > a_2 \mid \mathfrak{I}_t\right), \\
\pi_{3t} &= \Pr\left(\Delta p_{t+h} < a_1, \Delta y_{t+h} > a_2 \mid \mathfrak{I}_t\right), \; h \geq 1, \\
\pi_{4t} &= \Pr\left(\Delta p_{t+1} < a_1, \Delta p_{t+2} < a_1, \Delta p_{t+3} < a_1, \Delta p_{t+4} < a_1 \mid \mathfrak{I}_t\right),
\end{aligned} \tag{7.1}$$

where $\mathfrak{I}_t$ denotes a non-decreasing information set up to time t. The first example illustrates a *single* event while the others relate to *joint* events involving either more than one variable or a variable considered at more than one time horizon. Examples one and two are concerned with the *one-step ahead* forecast horizon, example three is concerned with an *h-step ahead* forecast horizon, and the fourth example relates to a *multiple-step ahead* forecast horizon. The probability of all events are conditional on $\mathfrak{I}_t$.

The calculation of probability forecasts remains relatively unusual, however. Macroeconomic forecasts are typically presented in the form of point forecasts and their uncertainty is characterised (if at all) by forecast confidence intervals. Focusing on point forecasts is justified when the underlying decision problems faced by agents and the government are linear in constraints and quadratic in the loss function; the so-called LQ problem. But for most decision problems, reliance on point forecasts will not be sufficient and probability forecasts will be needed (see, for example Granger and Pesaran, 2000a,b).

The need for probability forecasts is also acknowledged by a variety of researchers and institutions. In the statistics literature, for example, Dawid (1984) has been advocating the use of probability forecasting in a sequential approach to the statistical analysis of data; the so-called 'prequential approach'. In the macroeconometric modelling literature, Fair (1980) was one of the first to compute probability forecasts using a macroeconometric model of the US economy. For example, in a macroeconomic context, the motivation for the current monetary policy arrangements in the UK is that it provides for transparency in policy-making and an economic environment in which firms and individuals are better able to make investment and consumption decisions. The range of possible decisions that a firm can make regarding an investment plan represents the firm's action space. The 'states of nature' in this case are defined by all of the possible future out-turns for the macroeconomy. For example, referring to the illustrative events above, the investment decision might rely on inflation in the next period, or the average rate of inflation over some longer period, remaining below a target level; or interest might focus on the future path of inflation and output growth considered together. In making a decision, the firm should define a loss function which evaluates the profits or losses associated with each point in the action space and given any 'state of nature'. Except for LQ decision problems, decision rules by individual households and firms will generally require probability forecasts with respect to different threshold values reflecting their specific cost–benefit ratios. For this purpose, we need to provide estimates of the whole probability distribution function of the events of interest, rather than point forecasts or particular forecast intervals which are likely to be relevant only to the decision problem of a few. Probability event forecasts can also convey important information on the properties of a model. For example, long-run neutrality of output growth to inflation (or *vice versa*) would imply that

$$\lim_{h\to\infty} \Pr\left(\Delta p_{t+h} < a_1, \Delta y_{t+h} > a_2 \mid \Im_t\right)$$
$$= \left[\lim_{h\to\infty} \Pr\left(\Delta p_{t+h} < a_1 \mid \Im_t\right)\right] \times \left[\lim_{h\to\infty} \Pr\left(\Delta y_{t+h} > a_2 \mid \Im_t\right)\right]. \tag{7.2}$$

7.1.1 *Probability forecasts in a simple univariate AR(1) model*

As an illustration we first consider probability forecasts in the case of a simple univariate AR(1) model. This serves to illustrate the use of the concept in a simple context, but also demonstrates some of the (perhaps surprising) features of probability forecasts and highlights the problems involved in calculating probability forecasts analytically (as opposed to the use of the simulation methods described below).

Consider the following AR(1) model for the log of real output y_t:

$$y_t = \mu + (1-\rho)\gamma t + \rho y_{t-1} + u_t, \quad t = 1, 2, \ldots, T, T+1, \ldots, T+H, \tag{7.3}$$

where u_t's are independently and identically distributed random variables with a zero mean and variance σ^2. In the case where output can be assumed to be trend stationary (*i.e.* $|\rho| < 1$), the trend growth rate of y_t is given by γ. In the case where y_t is difference stationary (*i.e.* $\rho = 1$), the average growth rate will be given by μ. The restricted specification of the trend coefficient in (7.3) ensures that irrespective of whether y_t is trend stationary or first difference stationary its deterministic trend component is linear.

Defining the lag polynomial

$$\rho_h(L) = 1 + \rho L + \rho^2 L^2 + \cdots + \rho^{h-1} L^{h-1},$$

then, by successive substitution in (7.3), we can obtain

$$y_{T+h} = \rho^h y_T + \rho_h(L)\left[\mu + (1-\rho)\gamma(T+h) + u_{T+h}\right], \; h = 1, 2, \ldots H,$$

which after some algebra yields

$$y_{T+h} = \rho^h y_T + \delta(h, T) + h\gamma + v_{T+h}, \tag{7.4}$$

where

$$\delta(h, T) = \left(\frac{1-\rho^h}{1-\rho}\right)\mu - \left(\frac{1-\rho^h}{1-\rho}\right)\rho\gamma + T(1-\rho^h)\gamma,$$

$$v_{T+h} = \sum_{i=0}^{h-1} \rho^i u_{T+h-i}.$$

For a given initial value and the sample size, T, the sum of the terms $\rho^h y_T$ and $\delta(h, T)$ is of $O(1)$ in h and will be dominated by $h\gamma$ as the forecast horizon, h, is extended. Note that

$$\lim_{h\to\infty} \delta(h, T) = \frac{\mu - \rho\gamma}{1-\rho} + T\gamma, \quad \text{if } |\rho| < 1,$$

and $\delta(h, T) = h(\mu - \gamma)$ if $\rho = 1$. Therefore, for sufficiently large h, the deterministic component of y_{T+h} will be given by $h\gamma + T\gamma + (\mu - \rho\gamma)/(1-\rho)$ if $|\rho| < 1$, and by $y_T + h\mu$ if $\rho = 1$. It is interesting to note that irrespective of whether y_t has a unit root or not, the mean of the h-step ahead forecast will be of the same order of magnitude.

Also, for reasonably long forecast horizons, the composite error term v_{T+h} will be approximately distributed as a normal variate even if the underlying errors, u_t, were not normally distributed. In particular, for sufficiently large h we have

$$v_{T+h} \backsimeq N\left[0, \sigma^2\left(\sum_{j=1}^{h} \rho^{2(j-1)}\right)\right]. \tag{7.5}$$

Unlike the point forecasts, the orders of the variance of the h-step ahead forecasts differ depending on whether $|\rho| < 1$ or $\rho = 1$. Under the former $V(y_{T+h}|\Im_t) = V(v_{T+h}) = O(1)$, whilst under the latter $V(v_{T+h}) = O(h)$. But as we shall see, the probability forecasts have similar limit properties under $|\rho| < 1$ or $\rho = 1$, when y_t contains deterministic trends.

FORECASTING GROWTH PROBABILITIES: AN ANALYTIC SOLUTION

To illustrate the nature of probability forecasts in the univariate AR(1) model, we present below expressions for forecasts of output growth over different horizons. Specifically, we consider the four-period average growth rate over the period $T + h - 4$ to $T + h$, for any arbitrary horizon h, and also the average growth rate in y_t over the period T to $T + h$, for horizon h. The four-period average growth rate is given by

$$\frac{y_{T+h} - y_{T+h-4}}{4} = f_1\left(\rho, y_T, \delta\left(4, T\right)\right) + \gamma + \frac{v_{T+h} - v_{T+h-1}}{4}, \quad h = 4, 5, \ldots H, \tag{7.6}$$

where $f_1\left(\rho, y_T, \delta\left(4, T\right)\right) = \rho^{h-4}\left\{-(1-\rho^4)y_T + \delta\left(4, T\right)\right\}/4$, while the average growth rate of y_t over the period T to $T + h$ is given by

$$\frac{y_{T+h} - y_T}{h} = f_2\left(\rho, y_T, \delta\left(h, T\right)\right) + \gamma + h^{-1}v_{T+h}, \quad h = 1, 2, \ldots H, \tag{7.7}$$

where $f_2\left(\rho, y_T, \delta\left(h, T\right)\right) = \left\{-\left(1-\rho^h\right)y_T + \delta(h, T)\right\}/h$. The four-period average given by (7.6) provides a good example of a typical event of interest; setting $h = 4$, for example, we would have the annual growth rate over the coming year if quarterly data were used. Given the trended nature of the y_t process, the 'long average' in (7.7) provides useful insights on the long-run properties of the probability forecasts. In what follows, we examine probability forecasts of $\left(y_{T+h} - y_T\right)/h$ in both the stationary and unit root cases, but we focus on the case where parameters are known, so that the only source of uncertainty relates to the future shocks.

Case 1: y_t is trend stationary ($|\rho| < 1$)

If y_t is trend stationary, then (7.5) provides

$$\frac{v_{T+h} - v_{T+h-4}}{4} \sim N\left[0, \frac{\sigma^2}{4^2}\left(1+\rho^2\right)\left(2-(1-\rho^4)\rho^{2(h-4)}\right)\right], \tag{7.8}$$

while

$$\frac{1}{h}v_{T+h} \sim N\left[0, \frac{\sigma^2}{h^2}\left(\frac{1-\rho^{2h}}{1-\rho^2}\right)\right]. \tag{7.9}$$

From (7.6) and using (7.8), we have

$$\Pr\left(\frac{y_{T+h} - y_{T+h-4}}{4} < a \mid \Im_T\right)$$
$$= \Pr\left\{\frac{v_{T+h} - v_{T+h-4}}{4} < \left[a - \gamma - f_1\left(\rho, y_T, \delta\left(4, T\right)\right)\right] \mid \Im_T\right\}$$
$$= \Phi\left\{\frac{4\left[a - \gamma - f_1\left(\rho, y_T, \delta\left(4, T\right)\right)\right]}{\sigma\sqrt{\left(1+\rho^2\right)\left(2 - (1-\rho^4)\rho^{2(h-4)}\right)}}\right\},$$

while from (7.7)

$$\Pr\left(\frac{y_{T+h} - y_T}{h} < a \mid \Im_T\right)$$
$$= \Pr\left\{h^{-1}v_{T+h} < \left[a - \gamma - f_2\left(\rho, y_T, \delta\left(h, T\right)\right)\right] \mid \Im_T\right\},$$
$$= \Phi\left\{\frac{h\sqrt{1-\rho^2}\left[a - \gamma - f_2\left(\rho, y_T, \delta\left(h, T\right)\right)\right]}{\sigma\sqrt{1-\rho^{2h}}}\right\}, \qquad (7.10)$$

where $\Phi(\cdot)$ denotes the cumulative distribution function of a standard normal variate. For sufficiently large h we now have

$$\lim_{h\to\infty}\left[\Pr\left(\frac{y_{T+h} - y_{T+h-4}}{4} < a \mid \Im_T\right)\right] = \Phi\left(\frac{4\left(a-\gamma\right)}{\sigma\sqrt{2\left(1+\rho^2\right)}}\right),$$

and the probability of the four-period average falling below a given threshold converges to a constant.

For the long average, as $h \to \infty$ we have

$$\lim_{h\to\infty}\left[\Pr\left(\frac{y_{T+h} - y_T}{h} < a \mid \Im_T\right) - \Phi\left(\frac{h\sqrt{1-\rho^2}\left(a-\gamma\right)}{\sigma}\right)\right] = 0, \qquad (7.11)$$

and hence

$$\lim_{h\to\infty}\Pr\left(\frac{y_{T+h} - y_T}{h} < a \mid \Im_t\right) = \left\{\begin{array}{ll} 1 & \text{if } a > \gamma \\ 0.5 & \text{if } a = \gamma \\ 0 & \text{if } a < \gamma \end{array}\right\}.$$

This shows that, at the infinite horizon, the probability of events relating to the long average will typically degenerate to values of zero or one, depending on the value of the trend growth rate, γ, relative to the selected threshold value. This property follows directly from the fact that y_t tends (mean-reverts) to its deterministic trend path as $h \to \infty$. In addition this result also explains why the long-run forecasts of trend stationary models are not affected by intercept adjustments.

Case 2: y_t has a unit root ($\rho = 1$).

In this case, the analysis simplifies considerably and we have

$$\Pr\left(\frac{y_{T+h} - y_{T+h-4}}{4} < a \mid \Im_T\right) = \Phi\left[\frac{\sqrt{4}\,(a-\mu)}{\sigma}\right], \tag{7.12}$$

and

$$\Pr\left(\frac{y_{T+h} - y_T}{h} < a \mid \Im_T\right) = \Phi\left[\frac{\sqrt{h}\,(a-\mu)}{\sigma}\right]. \tag{7.13}$$

For the long average case

$$\lim_{h\to\infty} \Pr\left(\frac{y_{T+h} - y_T}{h} < a \mid \Im_T\right) = \left\{\begin{array}{cc} 1 & \text{if } a > \mu \\ 0.5 & \text{if } a = \mu \\ 0 & \text{if } a < \mu \end{array}\right\}, \tag{7.14}$$

which is the same as the result obtained for the trend stationary case.

The above discussion highlights an extremely important property of the probability forecasts, showing that the probability of the long-run average growth rate, $(y_{T+h} - y_T)/h$, will take a value of zero or one at the infinite horizon whether or not there exists a unit root in the series. Comparison of (7.10) and (7.13) shows that the speeds with which the probability forecasts degenerate are given by $h\sqrt{(1-\rho^2)}$ and $\sqrt{h}$ for the trend stationary and the unit root processes, respectively. Thus, the main distinction between the stationary and unit root case is the speed with which the zero/unity boundary is reached.

Consider now the effect of parameter uncertainty on the probability forecasts, and for simplicity assume that $\rho = 1, \sigma^2$ is given and that the unknown mean growth rate, μ, is estimated by the sample mean, $\widehat{\mu} = T^{-1}\sum_{t=1}^{T} \Delta y_t$. To allow for parameter uncertainty, we first write (7.7) for $\rho = 1$ as

$$\frac{y_{T+h} - y_T}{h} = \widehat{\mu} + (\mu - \widehat{\mu}) + h^{-1} v_{T+h}, \tag{7.15}$$

and let μ to be unknown conditional on the past observations given by the information set, $\Im_T = \{y_{1,}y_2, \ldots, y_T\}$. The uncertainty associated with

μ can be characterised by[1]

$$\mu - \widehat{\mu}|\Im_T \sim N\left(0, \frac{\sigma^2}{T}\right). \tag{7.16}$$

This result can be viewed as the posterior distribution of μ with respect to diffuse priors for μ. Using (7.16) in conjunction with (7.15), we have

$$h^{-1}\left(y_{T+h} - y_T\right) \sim N\left(\widehat{\mu}, \frac{\sigma^2}{T} + \frac{\rho^2}{h}\right),$$

and therefore,

$$\Pr\left(\frac{y_{T+h} - y_T}{h} < a \mid \Im_T\right) = \Phi\left(\frac{a - \widehat{\mu}}{\sigma\sqrt{\frac{1}{T} + \frac{1}{h}}}\right).$$

The result in this case depends on the relative size of T and h. For a fixed T and as $h \to \infty$,

$$\lim_{h\to\infty} \Pr\left(\frac{y_{T+h} - y_T}{h} < a \mid \Im_T\right) = \Phi\left(\frac{\sqrt{T}[a - \hat{\mu}]}{\sigma}\right),$$

which differ from the limit result given by (7.14) when μ is known. Clearly, result (7.14) follows if T and $h \to \infty$, jointly. In this case the uncertainty surrounding the value of μ vanishes as $T \to \infty$ and we return to the case of known μ. In the case where h is relatively small, the effect of parameter uncertainty on the probability estimates is of order T^{-1}. To establish this result we first write $\pi_t = \Pr[h^{-1}\left(y_{T+h} - y_T\right) < a \mid \Im_T\,]$ as

$$\pi_t(x) = \Phi\left[\theta\,(1 + x)^{-1/2}\right],$$

where $\theta = \sqrt{h}\,(a - \widehat{\mu})\,/\sigma$ and $x = h/T$. Expanding $\pi_t(x)$ around $x = 0$, we have[2]

$$\pi_t(x) = \pi_t\,(0) - \left[\frac{\theta}{2}\phi(\theta)\right]x + O(x^2),$$

where $\pi_t\,(0)$ corresponds to the probability estimate that ignores parameter uncertainty. Hence, for finite h we have

$$\pi_t(x) = \pi_t\,(0) + O\left(\frac{h}{T}\right),$$

[1] It is also assumed that conditional on $\Im_T$, μ and v_{T+h} are i.i.d. normal variables.
[2] Such an expansion is sensible since h is assumed to be small relative to T.

as required. This result holds more generally and in practice the effect of parameter uncertainty on probability forecasts would be of second-order importance when h is small and T relatively large.

7.2 Modelling forecast uncertainties

Returning to a more general setting, model-based forecasts are subject to five different types of uncertainties:

- future uncertainty
- parameter uncertainty (for a given model)
- model uncertainty
- policy uncertainty
- measurement uncertainty (data inadequacies and measurement errors).

Here, we focus on the first three and consider how to allow for them in the computation of probability forecasts. Policy and measurement uncertainties pose special problems of their own and will not be addressed here. Future uncertainty refers to the effects of unobserved future shocks on forecasts, while parameter and model uncertainties are concerned with the robustness of forecasts to the choice of parameter values (for a given model) and more generally the alternative models under consideration.[3]

7.2.1 *Future and parameter uncertainties*

The standard textbook approach to taking account of future and parameter uncertainties is through the use of confidence intervals around point forecasts. Instead of a point forecast, an interval forecast is provided. Although such forecast intervals may contain important information about probability forecasts of interest to a particular decision-maker, they do not allow for a full recovery of the forecast probability distribution function which is needed in decision-making contexts where the decision problem is not of the LQ type. The relationships between forecast intervals and probability forecasts become even more tenuous when forecasts of *joint* events or forecasts from multiple models are considered. For example, it would be impossible to infer the probability of the joint event of a positive output growth and an inflation rate falling within a pre-specified range from

[3] For a discussion on the problem of model uncertainty, see Draper (1995) and Chatfield (1995).

given variable-specific forecast intervals. In fact, even if the primary object of interest is a point forecast, as we shall see below, consideration of probability forecasts can help clarify how best to pool point mean and volatility forecasts in the presence of model uncertainty.

For the purpose of exposition, initially we abstract from parameter uncertainty and consider the following simple linear regression model:

$$y_t = \mathbf{x}'_{t-1}\boldsymbol{\beta} + u_t, \qquad t = 1, 2, \ldots, T,$$

where $\mathbf{x}_{t-1}$ is a $k \times 1$ vector of predetermined regressors, $\boldsymbol{\beta}$ is a $k \times 1$ vector of fixed but unknown coefficients, and $u_t \sim N(0, \sigma^2)$. The optimal forecast of y_{T+1} at time T (in the mean squared error sense) is given by $\mathbf{x}'_T\boldsymbol{\beta}$. In the absence of parameter uncertainty, the calculation of a probability forecast for a specified event is closely related to the more familiar concept of forecast confidence interval. For example, suppose that we are interested in the probability that the value of y_{T+1} lies below a specified threshold, say a, conditional on $\Im_T = (y_T, \mathbf{x}_T, y_{T-1}, \mathbf{x}_{T-1}, \ldots .)$, the information available at time T. For given values of $\boldsymbol{\beta}$ and σ^2, we have

$$\Pr\left(y_{T+1} < a \mid \Im_T\right) = \Phi\left(\frac{a - \mathbf{x}'_T\boldsymbol{\beta}}{\sigma}\right),$$

where as before $\Phi(\cdot)$ is the standard Normal cumulative distribution function while the $(1 - \alpha)\%$ forecast interval for y_{T+1} (conditional on $\Im_T$) is given by $\mathbf{x}'_T\boldsymbol{\beta} \pm \sigma\Phi^{-1}(1 - (\alpha/2))$.

The two approaches, although related, are motivated by different considerations. The point forecast provides the threshold value $a = \mathbf{x}'_T\boldsymbol{\beta}$ for which $\Pr\left(y_{T+1} < a \mid \Im_T\right) = 0.5$, while the forecast interval provides the threshold values $c_L = \mathbf{x}'_T\boldsymbol{\beta} - \sigma\Phi^{-1}(1 - (\alpha/2))$, and $c_U = \mathbf{x}'_T\boldsymbol{\beta} + \sigma\Phi^{-1}(1 - (\alpha/2))$ for which $\Pr\left(y_{T+1} < c_L \mid \Im_T\right) = \alpha/2$ and $\Pr\left(y_{T+1} < c_U \mid \Im_T\right) = 1 - (\alpha/2)$. Clearly, the threshold values, c_L and c_U, associated with the $(1 - \alpha)\%$ forecast interval may or may not be of interest.[4] Only by chance will the forecast interval calculations provide information in a way which is directly useful in specific decision-making contexts.

The relationship between probability forecasts and interval forecasts becomes even more obscure when parameter uncertainty is also taken into account. In the context of the above regression model, the point estimate

[4] The association between probability forecasts and interval forecasts is even weaker when one considers *joint* events. Many different such intervals will be needed for the purpose of characterising the probability forecasts of joint events.

of the forecast is given by $\widehat{y}_{T+1} = \mathbf{x}_T'\widehat{\boldsymbol{\beta}}_T$, where

$$\widehat{\boldsymbol{\beta}}_T = \mathbf{Q}_{T-1}^{-1}\mathbf{q}_T,$$

is the Ordinary Least Squares (OLS) estimate of $\boldsymbol{\beta}$, with

$$\mathbf{Q}_{T-1} = \sum_{t=1}^{T} \mathbf{x}_{t-1}\mathbf{x}_{t-1}', \quad \text{and} \quad \mathbf{q}_T = \sum_{t=1}^{T} \mathbf{x}_{t-1}y_t.$$

The relationship between the actual value of y_{T+1} and its time T predictor can be written as

$$\begin{aligned} y_{T+1} &= \mathbf{x}_T'\boldsymbol{\beta} + u_{T+1} \\ &= \mathbf{x}_T'\widehat{\boldsymbol{\beta}}_T + \mathbf{x}_T'(\boldsymbol{\beta} - \widehat{\boldsymbol{\beta}}_T) + u_{T+1}, \end{aligned} \tag{7.17}$$

so that the forecast error, ξ_{T+1}, is given by

$$\xi_{T+1} = y_{T+1} - \widehat{y}_{T+1} = \mathbf{x}_T'(\boldsymbol{\beta} - \widehat{\boldsymbol{\beta}}_T) + u_{T+1}.$$

This example shows that the point forecasts, $\mathbf{x}_T'\widehat{\boldsymbol{\beta}}_T$, are subject to two types of uncertainties, namely that relating to $\boldsymbol{\beta}$ and that relating to the distribution of u_{T+1}. For any given sample of data, $\Im_T$, $\widehat{\boldsymbol{\beta}}_T$ is known and can be treated as fixed. On the other hand, although $\boldsymbol{\beta}$ is assumed fixed at the estimation stage, it is unknown to the forecaster and, from this perspective, it is best viewed as a random variable at the forecasting stage. Hence, in order to compute probability forecasts which account for future as well as parameter uncertainties, we need to specify the joint probability distribution of $\boldsymbol{\beta}$ and u_{T+1}, conditional on $\Im_T$. As far as u_{T+1} is concerned, we continue to assume that

$$u_{T+1}|\Im_T \sim N(0, \sigma^2),$$

and to keep the exposition simple, for the time being we shall assume that σ^2 is known and that u_{T+1} is distributed independently of $\boldsymbol{\beta}$. For $\boldsymbol{\beta}$, noting that

$$\left(\widehat{\boldsymbol{\beta}}_T - \boldsymbol{\beta}\right)|\Im_T \sim N\left(0, \sigma^2\mathbf{Q}_{T-1}^{-1}\right), \tag{7.18}$$

we assume that

$$\boldsymbol{\beta} \mid \Im_T \sim N\left(\widehat{\boldsymbol{\beta}}_T, \sigma^2\mathbf{Q}_{T-1}^{-1}\right), \tag{7.19}$$

which is akin to a Bayesian approach with non-informative priors for $\boldsymbol{\beta}$. Hence

$$\xi_{T+1} \mid \Im_T \sim N\left[0, \sigma^2\left(1 + \mathbf{x}_T'\mathbf{Q}_{T-1}^{-1}\mathbf{x}_T\right)\right].$$

The $(1-\alpha)\%$ forecast interval in this case is given by

$$c_{LT} = \mathbf{x}_T'\widehat{\boldsymbol{\beta}}_T - \sigma\left\{1 + \mathbf{x}_T'\mathbf{Q}_{T-1}^{-1}\mathbf{x}_T\right\}^{1/2}\Phi^{-1}\left(1-\frac{\alpha}{2}\right), \tag{7.20}$$

and

$$c_{UT} = \mathbf{x}_T'\widehat{\boldsymbol{\beta}}_T + \sigma\left\{1 + \mathbf{x}_T'\mathbf{Q}_{T-1}^{-1}\mathbf{x}_T\right\}^{1/2}\Phi^{-1}\left(1-\frac{\alpha}{2}\right). \tag{7.21}$$

When σ^2 is unknown, under the standard non-informative Bayesian priors on $(\boldsymbol{\beta},\sigma^2)$, the appropriate forecast interval can be obtained by replacing σ^2 by its unbiased estimator, $\hat{\sigma}_T^2 = (T-k)^{-1}\sum_{t=1}^{T}(y_t - \mathbf{x}_{t-1}'\widehat{\boldsymbol{\beta}}_T)'(y_t - \mathbf{x}_{t-1}'\widehat{\boldsymbol{\beta}}_T)$, and $\Phi^{-1}(1-(\alpha/2))$ by the $(1-(\alpha/2))\%$ critical value of the standard t-distribution with $T-k$ degrees of freedom. Although such interval forecasts have been discussed in the econometrics literature, the particular assumptions that underlie them are not often fully recognised.

Using this interpretation, the effect of parameter uncertainty on forecasts can also be obtained via stochastic simulations, by generating alternative forecasts of y_{T+1} for different values of $\boldsymbol{\beta}$ (and σ^2) drawn from the conditional probability distribution of $\boldsymbol{\beta}$ given by (7.19). Alternatively, one could estimate probability forecasts by focusing directly on the probability distribution of y_{T+1} for a given value of $\mathbf{x}_T$, simultaneously taking into account both parameter and future uncertainties. For example, in the simple case where σ^2 is known, this can be achieved by simulating $y_{T+1}^{(j,s)}$, where

$$y_{T+1}^{(j,s)} = \mathbf{x}_T'\widehat{\boldsymbol{\beta}}^{(j)} + u_{T+1}^{(s)}, \qquad j = 1,2,\ldots,J,\ \ s = 1,2,\ldots,S,$$

$\widehat{\boldsymbol{\beta}}^{(j)}$ is the jth random draw from $N\left(\widehat{\boldsymbol{\beta}}_T, \sigma^2\mathbf{Q}_{T-1}^{-1}\right)$, and $u_{T+1}^{(s)}$ is the sth random draw from $N\left(0,\sigma^2\right)$, which is independant of the drawing $\widehat{\boldsymbol{\beta}}^{(j)}$.[5] This is an example of the parametric 'bootstrap predictive density' discussed in Harris (1989). In large samples, the stochastic simulation approach will be equivalent to the analytical methods discussed above, as J and $S \to \infty$. However, as argued below, it is more generally applicable and will be used in our empirical application.

An alternative approach to allowing for the effects of future and parameter uncertainties on prediction of y_{T+1} would be to follow the literature on 'predictive likelihoods', where a predictive density for y_{T+1} conditional on $\Im_T$ is derived directly.[6] In the case of the regression example, the problem

[5] In the realistic case where σ^2 is unknown it is replaced by $\hat{\sigma}_T^2$.

[6] A large number of different predictive likelihoods have been suggested in the statistics literature. Bjørnstad (1990) provides a review.

has been studied by Levy and Perng (1986) who show that the optimal prediction density for y_{T+1}, in the Kullback–Leibler information-theoretic sense, is the Student t-distribution with $T - k$ degrees of freedom, having the location $\hat{y}_{T+1} = \mathbf{x}'_T\widehat{\boldsymbol{\beta}}_T$ and the dispersion $\hat{\sigma}^2_T\left(1 + \mathbf{x}'_T\mathbf{Q}^{-1}_{T-1}\mathbf{x}_T\right)$. This is the same as the Bayes predictive density of $y_{T+1} \mid \Im_T$ with a non-informative prior on $(\boldsymbol{\beta},\sigma^2)$. In this way Levy and Perng provide a non-Bayesian interpretation of Bayes predictive density in the context of linear regression models.

7.2.2 *Model uncertainty: Combining probability forecasts*

Suppose we are interested in a decision problem that requires probability forecasts of an event defined in terms of one or more elements of $\mathbf{z}_t$, over the period $t = T+1, T+2, \ldots, T+h$, where $\mathbf{z}_t = (z_{1t}, z_{2t}, \ldots, z_{nt})'$ is an $n\times 1$ vector of the variables of interest and h is the forecast (decision) horizon. Assume also that the data generating process (DGP) is unknown and the forecasts are made considering m different models indexed by i (that could be nested or non-nested). Each model, M_i, $i = 1, 2, \ldots, m$, is characterised by a probability density function of $\mathbf{z}_t$ defined over the estimation period $t = 1, 2, \ldots, T$, as well as the forecast period $t = T+1, T+2, \ldots, T+h$, in terms of a $k_i \times 1$ vector of unknown parameters, $\boldsymbol{\theta}_i$, assumed to lie in the compact parameter space, $\boldsymbol{\Theta}_i$. Model M_i is then defined by

$$M_i : \left\{f_i\left(\mathbf{z}_1, \mathbf{z}_2, \ldots, \mathbf{z}_T, \mathbf{z}_{T+1}, \mathbf{z}_{T+2}, \ldots, \mathbf{z}_{T+h}; \boldsymbol{\theta}_i\right), \boldsymbol{\theta}_i \in \boldsymbol{\Theta}_i\right\}, \qquad (7.22)$$

where $f_i(\cdot)$ is the joint probability density function of past and future values of $\mathbf{z}_t$. Conditional on each model, M_i, being true we shall assume that the true value of $\boldsymbol{\theta}_i$, which we denote by $\boldsymbol{\theta}_{i0}$, is fixed and remains constant across the estimation and the prediction periods and lies in the interior of $\boldsymbol{\Theta}_i$. We denote the maximum likelihood estimator of $\boldsymbol{\theta}_{i0}$ by $\widehat{\boldsymbol{\theta}}_{iT}$, and assume that it satisfies the usual regularity conditions so that

$$\sqrt{T}\left(\widehat{\boldsymbol{\theta}}_{iT} - \boldsymbol{\theta}_{i0}\right)|M_i \overset{a}{\backsim} N\left(0, \mathbf{V}_{\theta_i}\right),$$

where $\overset{a}{\backsim}$ stands for 'asymptotically distributed as', $\mathbf{V}_{\theta_i}$ is a positive definite matrix, and $T^{-1}\mathbf{V}_{\theta_i}$ is the asymptotic covariance matrix of $\widehat{\boldsymbol{\theta}}_{iT}$ conditional on M_i, with $\mathbf{V}_{\theta_i}$ being a positive definite matrix.[7] Under these assumptions, parameter uncertainty only arises when T is finite and $\widehat{\boldsymbol{\theta}}_{iT} \overset{a}{\rightarrow} \boldsymbol{\theta}_{i0}$ as $T \rightarrow \infty$.

[7] In the case of cointegrating VAR models, a more general version of this result is needed. This is because the cointegrating coefficients converge to their asymptotic distribution at a faster rate than the other parameters in the model. However, the general results of this section are not affected by this complication.

The case where $\boldsymbol{\theta}_{i0}$ could differ across the estimation and forecast periods poses new difficulties and can be resolved in a satisfactory manner if one is prepared to formalise how $\boldsymbol{\theta}_{i0}$ changes over time. See, for example, Pesaran, Timmermann and Pettenuzzo (2004).[8]

7.2.3 *Bayesian model averaging*

The object of interest is the probability density function of $\mathbf{Z}_{T+1,h} = (\mathbf{z}_{T+1}, \ldots, \mathbf{z}_{T+h})$ conditional on the available observations at the end of period T, $\mathbf{Z}_T = (\mathbf{z}_1, \mathbf{z}_2, \ldots, \mathbf{z}_T)$, denoted by $\Pr(\mathbf{Z}_{T+1,h} | \mathbf{Z}_T)$. For this purpose, models and their parameters serve as intermediate inputs in the process of characterisation and estimation of $\Pr(\mathbf{Z}_{T+1,h} | \mathbf{Z}_T)$. The Bayesian approach provides an elegant and logically coherent solution to this problem, with a full solution given by the so-called 'Bayesian model averaging' formula (*e.g.* Draper (1995) and Hoeting *et al.* (1999)):

$$\Pr(\mathbf{Z}_{T+1,h} | \mathbf{Z}_T) = \sum_{i=1}^{m} \Pr(M_i | \mathbf{Z}_T) \Pr(\mathbf{Z}_{T+1,h} | \mathbf{Z}_T, M_i), \tag{7.23}$$

where $\Pr(M_i | \mathbf{Z}_T)$ is the posterior probability of model M_i,

$$\Pr(M_i | \mathbf{Z}_T) = \frac{\Pr(M_i) \Pr(\mathbf{Z}_T | M_i)}{\sum_{j=1}^{m} \Pr(M_j) \Pr(\mathbf{Z}_T | M_j)}. \tag{7.24}$$

$\Pr(M_i)$ is the prior probability of model M_i, $\Pr(\mathbf{Z}_T | M_i)$ is the integrated likelihood,

$$\Pr(\mathbf{Z}_T | M_i) = \int_{\boldsymbol{\theta}_i} \Pr(\boldsymbol{\theta}_i | M_i) \Pr(\mathbf{Z}_T | M_i, \boldsymbol{\theta}_i) \, d\boldsymbol{\theta}_i. \tag{7.25}$$

$\Pr(\boldsymbol{\theta}_i | M_i)$ is the prior on $\boldsymbol{\theta}_i$ conditional on M_i, $\Pr(\mathbf{Z}_T | M_i, \boldsymbol{\theta}_i)$ is the likelihood function of model M_i, and $\Pr(\mathbf{Z}_{T+1,h} | \mathbf{Z}_T, M_i)$ is the posterior predictive density of model M_i defined by

$$\Pr(\mathbf{Z}_{T+1,h} | \mathbf{Z}_T, M_i) = \int_{\boldsymbol{\theta}_i} \Pr(\boldsymbol{\theta}_i | \mathbf{Z}_T, M_i) \Pr(\mathbf{Z}_{T+1,h} | \mathbf{Z}_T, M_i, \boldsymbol{\theta}_i) \, d\boldsymbol{\theta}_i, \tag{7.26}$$

in which $\Pr(\boldsymbol{\theta}_i | \mathbf{Z}_T, M_i)$ is the posterior probability of $\boldsymbol{\theta}_i$ given model M_i:

$$\Pr(\boldsymbol{\theta}_i | \mathbf{Z}_T, M_i) = \frac{\Pr(\boldsymbol{\theta}_i | M_i) \Pr(\mathbf{Z}_T | M_i, \boldsymbol{\theta}_i)}{\sum_{j=1}^{m} \Pr(M_j) \Pr(\mathbf{Z}_T | M_j)}. \tag{7.27}$$

[8] Pesaran, Timmermann and Pettenuzzo (2004) propose a Bayesian procedure that allows for the possibility of new breaks over the forecast horizon, taking account of the size and duration of past breaks (if any) by means of a hierarchical hidden Markov chain model. Predictions are formed by integrating over the hyper parameters from the meta distributions that characterise the stochastic break point process.

The Bayesian approach requires *a priori* specifications of $\Pr(M_i)$ and $\Pr(\boldsymbol{\theta}_i \,|M_i)$ for $i = 1, 2, \ldots, m$, and further assumes that one of the m models being considered is the DGP so that $\Pr\left(\mathbf{Z}_{T+1,h} \,|\mathbf{Z}_T\right)$ defined by (7.23) is proper.

7.2.4 *Pooling of forecasts*

The Bayesian model averaging formula also provides a simple 'optimal' solution to the problem of *pooling* of the point and volatility forecasts. In the context of the above set-up the point forecasts are given by $E\left(\mathbf{Z}_{T+1,h} \,|\mathbf{Z}_T, M_i\right)$, $i = 1, 2, \ldots, m$, and can be combined in a variety of ways as discussed extensively in the literature. For reviews of the forecast combination literature see Clemen (1989), Granger (1989), Diebold and Lopez (1996) and Newbold and Harvey (2002).

In general the combined or pooled point forecasts can be written as

$$E_w\left(\mathbf{Z}_{T+1,h} \,|\mathbf{Z}_T\right) = \sum_{i=1}^{m} w_{iT} E\left(\mathbf{Z}_{T+1,h} \,|\mathbf{Z}_T, M_i\right),$$

where w_{iT}, $i = 1, 2, \ldots, m$ are the weights attached to the individual point forecasts. The main issues are: Should the weights be non-negative and add up to unity? Should they be based on past relative performance of the alternative models and hence be time varying? How should the relative performance of the various models be measured, namely should we be using in-sample criteria of fit and parsimony or out-of-sample realised performance?

In situations where the models under consideration are thought to be exhaustive (and hence the true data generating process is thought to lie in the set of models under consideration), the Bayesian approach can be used to provide a coherent answer to these questions. Under Bayesian model averaging (BMA) the weights, w_{iT}, are set to the posterior probability of model M_i and hence are non-negative and satisfy the additivity condition, $\sum_{i=1}^{m} w_{iT} = 1$. Using the Bayesain weights the combined point forecast is given by

$$E\left(\mathbf{Z}_{T+1,h} \,|\mathbf{Z}_T\right) = \sum_{i=1}^{m} \Pr\left(M_i \,|\mathbf{Z}_T\right) E\left(\mathbf{Z}_{T+1,h} \,|\mathbf{Z}_T, M_i\right).$$

In practice the derivation of the model-specific probability weights pose a number of conceptual and computations issues that will be briefly addressed below.

In cases where the models under consideration are not exhaustive and the underlying data generation process could be time varying, non-Bayesian weights might be more appropriate. Many alternatives have been proposed in the literature. Amongst these the simple average rule where equal weights are attached to the alternative forecasts tends to perform surprisingly well, as noted originally by Clemen (1989).[9] Recently, Granger and Jeon (2004) have proposed a modification of this procedure where the average rule is applied to a subset of best performing models. This modification, referred to as 'thick' modelling, is particularly relevant when there are many forecasts under consideration.

Pooling of forecast variances can also be considered. Under BMA we have (*e.g.* Draper, 1995)

$$\begin{aligned}\mathrm{Var}\left(\mathbf{z}_{T+1,h}\,|\mathbf{Z}_T\right) &= \sum_{i=1}^{m} \Pr\left(M_i\,|\mathbf{Z}_T\right)\mathrm{Var}\left(\mathbf{z}_{T+1,h}\,|\mathbf{Z}_T, M_i\right) \\ &+ \sum_{i=1}^{m} \Pr\left(M_i\,|\mathbf{Z}_T\right)\left[E\left(\mathbf{z}_{T+1,h}\,|\mathbf{Z}_T, M_i\right)\right. \\ &\left.- E\left(\mathbf{z}_{T+1,h}\,|\mathbf{Z}_T\right)\right]^2,\end{aligned}$$

Once again, more generally, we could have

$$\begin{aligned}\mathrm{Var}_w\left(\mathbf{z}_{T+1,h}\,|\mathbf{Z}_T\right) &= \sum_{i=1}^{m} w_{iT}\mathrm{Var}\left(\mathbf{z}_{T+1,h}\,|\mathbf{Z}_T, M_i\right) \\ &+ \sum_{i=1}^{m} w_{iT}\left[E\left(\mathbf{z}_{T+1,h}\,|\mathbf{Z}_T, M_i\right) - E\left(\mathbf{z}_{T+1,h}\,|\mathbf{Z}_T\right)\right]^2,\end{aligned}$$

where the weights w_{iT} could be obtained using Bayesian or non-Bayesian procedures. The first term in the above expression accounts for within model variability and the second term for between model variability. Clearly, a procedure that only combines the forecast variances will not be correct unless all models have the same point forecasts. Pooling of predictive densities clearly does not imply using averages of the moments of the underlying distributions except for the first moments.

There is no doubt that the Bayesian model averaging provides an attractive solution to the problem of accounting for model uncertainty. But its strict application can be problematic particularly in the case of high-dimensional models such as the vector error correction model of the UK economy considered in our empirical work. The major difficulties lie in

[9] Recent Monte Carlo evidence that attempts to explain this empirical finding is provided by Hendry and Clements (2004) and Smith and Wallis (2005).

the choice of the space of models to be considered, the model priors $\Pr(M_i)$, and the specification of meaningful priors for the unknown parameters, $\Pr(\boldsymbol{\theta}_i | M_i)$. The computational issues, while still considerable, are partly overcome by Monte Carlo integration techniques. For an excellent overview of the issues involved in the application of BMA approach to forecasting, see Hoeting *et al.* (1999). See also Fernandez *et al.* (2001a,b) and Pesaran and Zaffaroni (2005) for specific applications.

Putting the problem of model specification to one side, the two important components of BMA formula are the posterior probability of the models, $\Pr(M_i | \mathbf{Z}_T)$, and the posterior density functions of the parameters, $\Pr(\boldsymbol{\theta}_i | \mathbf{Z}_T, M_i)$, for $i = 1, \ldots, m$. In what follows we therefore consider different approximations of $\Pr(M_i | \mathbf{Z}_T)$ and $\Pr(\boldsymbol{\theta}_i | \mathbf{Z}_T, M_i)$, assuming that T is sufficiently large that the sample observations dominate the choice of the priors; in essence adopting a classical stance within an otherwise Bayesian framework. See also Garratt *et al.* (2003b).

7.3 Computation of probability forecasts: Some practical issues

Suppose the *joint event* of interest is defined by $\boldsymbol{\varphi}\left(\mathbf{Z}_{T+1,h}\right) < \mathbf{a}$, where $\boldsymbol{\varphi}(\cdot)$ and $\mathbf{a}$ are the $L \times 1$ vectors $\boldsymbol{\varphi}(\cdot) = (\varphi_1(\cdot), \varphi_2(\cdot), \ldots, \varphi_L(\cdot))'$, $\mathbf{a} = (a_1, a_2, \ldots, a_L)'$, $\varphi_j(\mathbf{Z}_{T+1,h})$ is a scalar function of the variables over the forecast horizon $T+1, \ldots, T+h$, and a_j is the 'threshold' value associated with $\varphi_j(\cdot)$. To simplify the exposition, we denote this joint event by $\mathfrak{A}_{\varphi}$. The (conditional) probability forecast associated with this event assuming that model M_i holds is given by

$$\pi_i\left(\mathbf{a}, h; \boldsymbol{\varphi}(\cdot), \boldsymbol{\theta}_i\right) = \Pr\left[\boldsymbol{\varphi}\left(\mathbf{Z}_{T+1,h}\right) < \mathbf{a} \,|\mathbf{Z}_T, M_i, \boldsymbol{\theta}_i\right]. \tag{7.28}$$

In practice, we might be interested in computing probability forecasts for a number of alternative threshold values over the range $a_j \in [a_{\min}, a_{\max}]$.

With future uncertainty only

If the model is known to be M_i defined by (7.22) but the value of $\boldsymbol{\theta}_i$ is not known, a *point estimate* of $\pi_i\left(\mathbf{a}, h; \boldsymbol{\varphi}(\cdot), \boldsymbol{\theta}_i\right)$ can be obtained by

$$\pi_i\left(\mathbf{a}, h; \boldsymbol{\varphi}(\cdot), \widehat{\boldsymbol{\theta}}_{iT}\right) = \int_{\mathfrak{A}_{\varphi}} f_i\left(\mathbf{Z}_{T+1,h} \,|\mathbf{Z}_T, M_i, \widehat{\boldsymbol{\theta}}_{iT}\right) d\mathbf{Z}_{T+1,h}. \tag{7.29}$$

This probability distribution function only takes account of future uncertainties that arise from the model's stochastic structure, as it is computed for a given density function, M_i, and a given value of $\boldsymbol{\theta}_i$, namely $\widehat{\boldsymbol{\theta}}_{iT}$. It is also known as the 'profile predictive likelihood'. See, for example, Bjørnstad (1990).

With future and parameter uncertainty

To allow for parameter uncertainty, we assume that conditional on $\mathbf{Z}_T$, the probability distribution function of $\boldsymbol{\theta}_i$ is given by $g(\boldsymbol{\theta}_i | \mathbf{Z}_T, M_i)$. Then,

$$\tilde{\pi}_i(\mathbf{a}, h; \varphi(\cdot)) = \int_{\boldsymbol{\theta}_i \in \boldsymbol{\Theta}_i} \pi_i(\mathbf{a}, h; \varphi(\cdot), \boldsymbol{\theta}_i)\; g(\boldsymbol{\theta}_i | \mathbf{Z}_T, M_i)\, d\boldsymbol{\theta}_i, \tag{7.30}$$

or equivalently,

$$\tilde{\pi}_i(\mathbf{a}, h; \varphi(\cdot)) = \int_{\boldsymbol{\theta}_i \in \boldsymbol{\Theta}_i} \int_{\mathfrak{A}_\varphi} f_i(\mathbf{Z}_{T+1,h} | \mathbf{Z}_T, M_i, \boldsymbol{\theta}_i)\; g(\boldsymbol{\theta}_i | \mathbf{Z}_T, M_i)\, d\mathbf{Z}_{T+1,h} d\boldsymbol{\theta}_i. \tag{7.31}$$

Computation of (7.31) requires the knowledge of $g(\boldsymbol{\theta}_i | \mathbf{Z}_T, M_i)$. In the absence of model priors $\Pr(M_i)$ or priors for the unknown parameters, $\Pr(\boldsymbol{\theta}_i | M_i)$, we might assume

$$\boldsymbol{\theta}_i | \mathbf{Z}_T, M_i \overset{a}{\backsim} N\left(\widehat{\boldsymbol{\theta}}_{iT}, T^{-1}\widehat{\mathbf{V}}_{\boldsymbol{\theta}_i}\right). \tag{7.32}$$

In this case, the point estimate of the probability forecast, $\pi_i\left(\mathbf{a}, h; \varphi(\cdot), \widehat{\boldsymbol{\theta}}_{iT}\right)$, and the alternative estimate, $\tilde{\pi}_i(\mathbf{a}, h; \varphi(\cdot))$, that allows for parameter uncertainty are asymptotically equivalent as $T \to \infty$. The latter is the 'bootstrap predictive density' described in Harris (1989), who demonstrates that it performs well in a number of important cases. Also, both of these estimates under M_i tend to $\pi_i(\mathbf{a}, h; \varphi(\cdot), \boldsymbol{\theta}_{i0})$, which is the profile predictive likelihood evaluated at the true value $\boldsymbol{\theta}_{i0}$. In practice, computations of $\pi_i\left(\mathbf{a}, h; \varphi(\cdot), \widehat{\boldsymbol{\theta}}_{iT}\right)$ and $\tilde{\pi}_i(\mathbf{a}, h; \varphi(\cdot))$ are typically carried out by stochastic simulations (see Section 7.3.2 below), and the two estimates will differ by terms that are $O(h/T)$ and will be very close when h is small and T large.[10]

With future and model uncertainty

The probability estimates that allow for model uncertainty can now be obtained using the Bayesian averaging procedure. Abstracting from parameter uncertainty we have

$$\pi\left(\mathbf{a}, h; \varphi(\cdot), \widehat{\boldsymbol{\theta}}_T\right) = \sum_{i=1}^{m} w_{iT} \pi_i\left(\mathbf{a}, h; \varphi(\cdot), \widehat{\boldsymbol{\theta}}_{iT}\right), \tag{7.33}$$

[10] See Bjørnstad (1990, 1998) for reviews of the literature on predictive likelihood analysis.

where $\widehat{\boldsymbol{\theta}}_T = \left(\widehat{\boldsymbol{\theta}}'_{1T}, \ldots, \widehat{\boldsymbol{\theta}}'_{mT}\right)'$, and the weights, $w_{iT} \geq 0$ can be derived by approximating the posterior probability of model M_i by[11]

$$\ln \Pr\left(M_i \,|\mathbf{Z}_T\right) = LL_{iT} - \left(\frac{k_i}{2}\right) \ln(T) + O(1), \tag{7.34}$$

where LL_{iT} is the maximised value of the log-likelihood function for model M_i. This is the familiar Schwarz (1978) Bayesian information criterion for model selection. The use of this approximation leads to the following choice for w_{iT}:

$$w_{iT} = \frac{\exp\left(\Delta_{iT}\right)}{\sum_{j=1}^{m} \exp\left(\Delta_{jT}\right)}, \tag{7.35}$$

where $\Delta_{iT} = SBC_{iT} - \max_j \left(SBC_{jT}\right)$ and $SBC_{iT} = LL_{iT} - \left(\frac{k_i}{2}\right)\ln(T)$. Alternatively, following Burnham and Anderson (1998), one could use Akaike weights defined by $\Delta_{iT} = AIC_{iT} - \max_j \left(AIC_{jT}\right)$, $AIC_{iT} = LL_{iT} - k_i$. While the Schwarz weights are asymptotically optimal if the DGP lies in the set of models under consideration, the Akaike weights are likely to perform better when the true model does not lie in the set of models under consideration, that are viewed as approximations to a complex and (possibly) unknown DGP.

With future, parameter and model uncertainty

When parameter uncertainty is also taken into account, we have

$$\tilde{\pi}\left(\mathbf{a}, h; \varphi(\cdot)\right) = \sum_{i=1}^{m} w_{iT} \tilde{\pi}_i\left(\mathbf{a}, h; \varphi(\cdot)\right), \tag{7.36}$$

where $\tilde{\pi}_i\left(\mathbf{a}, h; \varphi(\cdot)\right)$ is the bootstrap predictive density defined by (7.31) that makes use of the normal approximation given by (7.32). Again, in practice, computations of $\pi_i\left(\mathbf{a}, h; \varphi(\cdot)\right)$and $\tilde{\pi}_i\left(\mathbf{a}, h; \varphi(\cdot)\right)$ are typically carried out by stochastic simulations (see Section 7.3.2 below).

7.3.1 *Computation of probability forecasts using analytic methods*

In this subsection, we outline the computational difficulties that typically will be encountered in the calculation of probability forecasts. We illustrate this using the simpler case in which it is assumed that the parameters of

[11] See also Draper (1995) for approximate posterior probability forecasts, conditional on the model M_i being true.

the model are known, so that only stochastic uncertainty is considered, and the probability forecast is evaluated according to (7.29).

In this case there is generally no conceptual difficulty in evaluating the probability of an event taking place using (7.29) for known $\widehat{\boldsymbol{\theta}}$. However, the computation can become complicated because of the form of the functions φ or due to the difficulties arising from the selection of appropriate limits of integration for the expression, or because of the complexity of the event to be forecast even if the functions φ are reasonably simple.

Consider, for example, the linear case in which the joint event of interest $\varphi\left(\mathbf{z}_{T+1},\ldots,\mathbf{z}_{T+h}\right)$ can be expressed by

$$\varphi\left(\mathbf{z}_{T+1},\ldots,\mathbf{z}_{T+h}\right)=\varphi\left(\hat{\mathbf{z}}_{T+1},\ldots,\hat{\mathbf{z}}_{T+h}\right)+\boldsymbol{\nu}_{T+h}, \tag{7.37}$$

where $\varphi\left(\hat{\mathbf{z}}_{T+1},\ldots,\hat{\mathbf{z}}_{T+h}\right)$ represents a (consistent) estimate of $\varphi\left(\mathbf{z}_{T+1},\ldots,\mathbf{z}_{T+h}\right)$, based on estimated model parameter values $\widehat{\boldsymbol{\theta}}_T$, and the stochastic uncertainty surrounding the estimate is captured by an $L\times 1$ vector of the corresponding forecast errors, $\boldsymbol{\nu}_{T+h}$, which is assumed to be normally distributed with zero means and an $L\times L$ positive covariance matrix, $\boldsymbol{\Sigma}_{\nu}$. In this case, the probability forecast defined by (7.29) is given by

$$\begin{aligned}
&\widehat{\pi}\left(\mathbf{a},h;\varphi(.),\widehat{\boldsymbol{\theta}}_T\right)\\
&\quad=\Pr\left(\varphi\left(\mathbf{z}_{T+1},\ldots,\mathbf{z}_{T+h}\right)<\mathbf{a}\right)=\Pr\left(\boldsymbol{\nu}_{T+h}<\mathbf{a}-\varphi\left(\hat{\mathbf{z}}_{T+1},\ldots,\hat{\mathbf{z}}_{T+h}\right)\right)\\
&\quad=\int_{-\infty}^{a_L^*}\cdots\int_{-\infty}^{a_1^*}\left[(2\pi)^{-\frac{1}{2}L}\left|\boldsymbol{\Sigma}_{\nu}\right|^{-\frac{1}{2}}\exp\left(-\frac{1}{2}\boldsymbol{\nu}_{T+h}'\boldsymbol{\Sigma}_{\nu}^{-1}\boldsymbol{\nu}_{T+h}\right)\right]d\nu_{T+h,1}\cdots d\nu_{T+h,L},
\end{aligned}$$

where

$$a_j^*=a_j-\varphi_j\left(\hat{z}_{T+1},\ldots,\hat{z}_{T+h}\right),\quad j=1,2,\ldots,L.$$

Even in this relatively simple case, the evaluation of the probability involves L multiple integrals and, unless L is small (1 or 2), its computation would be quite demanding.

7.3.2 *Computation of probability forecasts based on VAR models by stochastic simulation*

In this subsection, we describe the steps involved in the calculation of probability forecasts based on a vector error correction model described in Section 6.3, using stochastic simulation techniques. Consider the underlying vector error correction model, (6.86), which can be rewritten as

$$\mathbf{z}_t = \sum_{i=1}^{p} \mathbf{\Phi}_i \mathbf{z}_{t-i} + \mathbf{a}_0 + \mathbf{a}_1 t + \mathbf{H}\boldsymbol{\zeta}_{t}, \quad t = 1, 2, \ldots, T, \tag{7.38}$$

where $\mathbf{\Phi}_1 = \mathbf{I}_m - \boldsymbol{\alpha\beta}' + \mathbf{\Gamma}_1$, $\mathbf{\Phi}_i = \mathbf{\Gamma}_i - \mathbf{\Gamma}_{i-1}$, $i = 2, \ldots, p-1$, $\mathbf{\Phi}_p = -\mathbf{\Gamma}_{p-1}$, and $\boldsymbol{\zeta}_t$ is assumed to be a serially uncorrelated *i.i.d.* vector of shocks with zero means and a positive definite covariance matrix, $\mathbf{\Sigma}_{\zeta\zeta}$ given by (6.88). In what follows, we consider the calculation of probability forecasts first for given values of the parameters, and then taking into account parameter uncertainty.

FORECASTS IN THE ABSENCE OF PARAMETER UNCERTAINTY

Suppose that the ML estimators of $\mathbf{\Phi}_i$, $i = 1, \ldots, p$, $\mathbf{a}_0$, $\mathbf{a}_1$, $\mathbf{H}$ and $\mathbf{\Sigma}_{\zeta\zeta}$ are given and denoted by $\hat{\mathbf{\Phi}}_i$, $i = 1, \ldots, p$, $\hat{\mathbf{a}}_0$, $\hat{\mathbf{a}}_1$, $\hat{\mathbf{H}}$ and $\hat{\mathbf{\Sigma}}_{\zeta\zeta}$, respectively. Then, the point estimates of the h-step ahead forecasts of $\mathbf{z}_{T+h}$ conditional on $\Im_T$, denoted by $\hat{\mathbf{z}}_{T+h}$, can be obtained recursively as

$$\hat{\mathbf{z}}_{T+h} = \sum_{i=1}^{p} \hat{\mathbf{\Phi}}_i \hat{\mathbf{z}}_{T+h-i} + \hat{\mathbf{a}}_0 + \hat{\mathbf{a}}_1 (t+h), \quad h = 1, 2, \ldots, \tag{7.39}$$

where the initial values, $\mathbf{z}_T, \mathbf{z}_{T-1}, \ldots, \mathbf{z}_{T-p+1}$, are given. To obtain probability forecasts by stochastic simulation, we simulate the values of $\mathbf{z}_{T+h}$ by

$$\mathbf{z}_{T+h}^{(r)} = \sum_{i=1}^{p} \hat{\mathbf{\Phi}}_i \mathbf{z}_{T+h-i}^{(r)} + \hat{\mathbf{a}}_0 + \hat{\mathbf{a}}_1 (t+h) + \hat{\mathbf{H}}\boldsymbol{\zeta}_{T+h}^{(r)},$$
$$h = 1, 2, \ldots; \ r = 1, 2, \ldots, R, \tag{7.40}$$

where superscript '(r)' refers to the rth replication of the simulation algorithm, and $\mathbf{z}_T^{(r)} = \mathbf{z}_T$, $\mathbf{z}_{T-1}^{(r)} = \mathbf{z}_{T-1}, \ldots, \mathbf{z}_{T-p+1}^{(r)} = \mathbf{z}_{T-p+1}$ for all r. The $\boldsymbol{\zeta}_{T+h}^{(r)}$'s can be drawn either by parametric or non-parametric methods as described in Section 7.3.3 below. The probability that $\varphi_\ell\left(\mathbf{z}_{T+1}^{(r)}, \ldots, \mathbf{z}_{T+h}^{(r)}\right) < \mathbf{a}_\ell$, is computed as

$$\pi_R\left(\mathbf{a}_\ell, h; \varphi_\ell(\cdot), \widehat{\boldsymbol{\theta}}\right) = \frac{1}{R}\sum_{r=1}^{R} I\left(\mathbf{a}_\ell - \varphi_\ell\left(\mathbf{z}_{T+1}^{(r)}, \ldots, \mathbf{z}_{T+h}^{(r)}\right)\right),$$

where $\widehat{\boldsymbol{\theta}}$ is a vector containing estimates of all the parameters, and $I(A)$ is an indicator function which takes the value of unity if $A > 0$, and zero otherwise. To simplify the notation we denote $\pi_R\left(\mathbf{a}_\ell, h; \varphi_\ell(\cdot), \widehat{\boldsymbol{\theta}}\right)$ by $\pi_R(\mathbf{a}_\ell)$. The predictive probability distribution function is now given by $\pi_R(\mathbf{a}_\ell)$ as the threshold values, $\mathbf{a}_\ell$, are varied over the relevant regions.

FORECASTS IN THE PRESENCE OF PARAMETER UNCERTAINTY

To allow for parameter uncertainty, we use the bootstrap procedure and first simulate S (*in-sample*) values of $\mathbf{z}_t$, $t = 1, 2, \ldots, T$, denoted by $\mathbf{z}_t^{(s)}$, $s = 1, \ldots, S$, where

$$\mathbf{z}_t^{(s)} = \sum_{i=1}^{p} \hat{\boldsymbol{\Phi}}_i \mathbf{z}_{t-i}^{(s)} + \hat{\mathbf{a}}_0 + \hat{\mathbf{a}}_1 t + \mathbf{H}\zeta_t^{(s)}, \quad t = 1, 2, \ldots, T, \tag{7.41}$$

realisations are used for the initial values, $\mathbf{z}_{-1}, \ldots, \mathbf{z}_{-p}$, and $\zeta_t^{(s)}$'s can be drawn either by parametric or non-parametric methods (see Section 7.3.3 below). Having obtained the S set of simulated in-sample values, $\left(\mathbf{z}_1^{(s)}, \mathbf{z}_2^{(s)}, \ldots, \mathbf{z}_T^{(s)}\right)$, the VAR($p$) model (7.38) is estimated S times to obtain the ML estimates, $\hat{\boldsymbol{\Phi}}_i^{(s)}$, $\hat{\mathbf{a}}_0^{(s)}$, $\hat{\mathbf{a}}_1^{(s)}$, $\hat{\mathbf{H}}^{(s)}$ and $\hat{\boldsymbol{\Sigma}}_{\zeta\zeta}^{(s)}$, for $i = 1, 2, \ldots, p$, and $s = 1, 2, \ldots, S$.

For each of these bootstrap replications, R replications of the h-step ahead point forecasts are computed as

$$\mathbf{z}_{T+h}^{(r,s)} = \sum_{i=1}^{p} \hat{\boldsymbol{\Phi}}_i^{(s)} \mathbf{z}_{T+h-i}^{(r,s)} + \hat{\mathbf{a}}_0^{(s)} + \hat{\mathbf{a}}_1^{(s)}(t+h) + \hat{\mathbf{H}}^{(s)} \boldsymbol{\zeta}_{T+h}^{(r,s)}, \tag{7.42}$$

for $h = 1, 2, \ldots H$; $r = 1, 2, \ldots, R$ and $s = 1, 2, \ldots, S$, and the predictive distribution function is then computed as

$$\pi_{R,S}(\mathbf{a}_\ell) = \frac{1}{SR} \sum_{r=1}^{R} \sum_{s=1}^{S} I\left[\mathbf{a}_\ell - \varphi_\ell\left(\mathbf{z}_{T+1}^{(r,s)}, \ldots, \mathbf{z}_{T+h}^{(r,s)}\right)\right].$$

Bootstrapping cointegrating models can be done either for a fixed number of cointegrating relations (obtained from estimates based on the actual time series), or the cointegrating relations could be re-estimated for each bootstrap replication. In our empirical applications we follow the former, but allow for the uncertainty surrounding the number of cointegrating vectors by means of model averaging techniques; namely different choices of the number of cointegrating relations are regarded as different models.

7.3.3 *Generating simulated errors*

We now provide more details on the mechanism by which shocks are generated in stochastic simulation methods described above. There are two basic ways that the in-sample and future errors, $\boldsymbol{\zeta}_t^{(s)}$ and $\boldsymbol{\zeta}_{T+h}^{(r,s)}$ respectively, can be simulated so that the contemporaneous correlations that exist across the errors in the different equations of the VAR model are taken into account and maintained. The first is a *parametric* method where the errors are drawn from an assumed probability distribution function. Alternatively, one could employ a *non-parametric* procedure. The latter is slightly more complicated and is based on re-sampling techniques in which the simulated errors are obtained by a random draw from the in-sample estimated residuals (*e.g.* Hall, 1992).

Parametric approach

Under this approach the errors are drawn for example, from a multivariate distribution with zero means and the covariance matrix, $\hat{\boldsymbol{\Sigma}}^{(s)}_{\zeta\zeta}$. To obtain the simulated errors for m variables over h periods we first generate mh draws from an assumed *i.i.d.* distribution which we denote by $\epsilon^{(r,s)}_{T+i}$, $i = 1, 2, \ldots, h$. These are then used to obtain $\left\{\zeta^{(r,s)}_{T+i}, i = 1, 2, \ldots h\right\}$ computed as $\zeta^{(r,s)}_{T+h} = \hat{\mathbf{P}}^{(s)}\epsilon^{(r,s)}_{T+h}$ for $r = 1, 2, \ldots, R$ and $s = 1, 2, \ldots, S$, where $\hat{\mathbf{P}}^{(s)}$ is the lower triangular Choleski factor of $\hat{\boldsymbol{\Sigma}}^{(s)}_{\zeta\zeta}$ such that $\hat{\boldsymbol{\Sigma}}^{(s)}_{\zeta\zeta} = \hat{\mathbf{P}}^{(s)}\hat{\mathbf{P}}^{(s)\prime}$, and $\hat{\boldsymbol{\Sigma}}^{(s)}_{\zeta\zeta}$ is the estimate of $\boldsymbol{\Sigma}_{\zeta\zeta}$ in the sth replication of the bootstrap procedure set out above. In the absence of parameter uncertainty, we obtain $\zeta^{(r)}_{T+h} = \hat{\mathbf{P}}\epsilon^{(r)}_{T+h}$ with $\hat{\mathbf{P}}$ being the lower triangular Choleski factor of $\hat{\boldsymbol{\Sigma}}_{\zeta\zeta}$. In our applications, reported in Chapter 11, for each r and s, we generate $\epsilon^{(r,s)}_{T+i}$ as $i.i.d.N(0, \mathbf{I}_m)$, although other parametric distributions such as the multivariate Student t-distribution can also be used.

Non-parametric approaches

The most obvious non-parametric approach to generating the simulated errors, $\zeta^{(r,s)}_{T+h}$, which we denote 'Method 1', is simply to take h random draws with replacements from the in-sample residual vectors $\left\{\hat{\zeta}^{(s)}_1, \ldots, \hat{\zeta}^{(s)}_T\right\}$. The simulated errors thus obtained clearly have the same distribution and covariance structure as that observed in the original sample. However, this procedure is subject to the criticism that it could introduce serial dependence at longer forecast horizons since the pseudo-random draws are made from the same set of relatively small T vector of residuals.

An alternative non-parametric method for generating simulated errors, 'Method 2', makes use of the Choleski decomposition of the estimated covariance employed in the parametric approach. For a given choice of $\hat{\mathbf{P}}^{(s)}$ a set of mT transformed error terms $\left\{\hat{\epsilon}^{(s)}_1, \ldots, \hat{\epsilon}^{(s)}_T\right\}$ are computed such that $\hat{\epsilon}^{(s)}_t = \hat{\mathbf{P}}^{(s)-1}\hat{\zeta}^{(s)}_t$, $t = 1, 2, \ldots, T$. The mT individual error terms are uncorrelated with each other, but retain the distributional information contained in the original observed errors. A set of mh simulated errors are then obtained by drawing with replacement from these transformed residuals, denoted by $\left\{\epsilon_{T+1}^{(r,s)}, \ldots, \epsilon_{T+h}^{(r,s)}\right\}$. These are then used to obtain $\left\{\zeta_{T+1}^{(r,s)}, \ldots, \zeta_{T+h}^{(r,s)}\right\}$, using the transformations $\zeta_{T+h}^{(r,s)} = \hat{\mathbf{P}}^{(s)}\epsilon_{T+h}^{(r,s)}$ for $r = 1, 2, \ldots, R$ and $s = 1, 2, \ldots, S$. Given that the $\hat{\mathbf{P}}^{(s)}$ matrix is used to generate the simulated errors, it is clear that $\zeta_{T+h}^{(r,s)}$ again has the same covariance structure as the original estimated errors. And being based on errors drawn at random from the transformed residuals, these simulated errors will also display the same distributional features. Further, given that the re-sampling occurs from the mT transformed error terms, Method 2 also has the advantage over Method 1 that the serial dependence introduced through sampling with replacement is likely to be less problematic.

Choice of approach

The two non-parametric approaches described above have the advantage over the parametric approach that they make no distributional assumptions on the error terms, and are better able to capture the uncertainties arising from (possibly rare) extreme observations. However, they suffer from the fact that they require random sampling *with replacement*. Replacement is essential as otherwise the draws at longer forecast horizons are effectively 'truncated' and unrepresentative. On the other hand, for a given sample size, it is clear that re-sampling from the observed errors with replacement inevitably introduces serial dependence in the simulated forecast errors at longer horizons as the same residuals are drawn repeatedly. When generating simulated errors over forecast horizons, therefore, this provides an argument for the use of non-parametric methods over shorter forecast horizons, but suggests that a greater reliance might be placed on the parametric approach for the generation of probability forecasts at longer time horizons.

7.4 Estimation and forecasting with conditional models

The density function $f_i(\cdot)$ given in (7.22) can be decomposed in two ways. First, a sequential conditioning decomposition can be employed to write $f_i(\cdot)$ as the product of the conditional distributions on successive observations on the $\mathbf{z}_t$,

$$f_i(\mathbf{Z}_t; \mathbf{z}_0, \boldsymbol{\theta}) = \prod_{s=1}^{t} f_i\left(\mathbf{z}_s \mid \mathbf{Z}_{s-1}; \mathbf{z}_0, \boldsymbol{\theta}_i\right),$$

where $\mathbf{Z}_s = (\mathbf{z}_0, \mathbf{z}_1, \ldots, \mathbf{z}_s)$ for given initial values $\mathbf{z}_0$. Second, since we frequently wish to distinguish between variables which are endogenous, denoted by $\mathbf{y}_t$, and those which are exogenous, denoted by $\mathbf{x}_t$, we can write $\mathbf{z}_t = \left(\mathbf{y}_t', \mathbf{x}_t'\right)'$ and use the factorisation:

$$f_i\left(\mathbf{z}_t \mid \mathbf{Z}_{t-1}; \mathbf{z}_0, \boldsymbol{\theta}\right) = f_{iy}\left(\mathbf{y}_t \mid \mathbf{x}_t, \mathbf{Z}_{t-1}; \mathbf{z}_0, \boldsymbol{\theta}_{iy}\right) \times f_{ix}\left(\mathbf{x}_t \mid \mathbf{Z}_{t-1}; \mathbf{z}_0, \boldsymbol{\theta}_{ix}\right), \quad (7.43)$$

where $f_{iy}\left(\mathbf{y}_t \mid \mathbf{x}_t, \mathbf{Z}_{t-1}; \mathbf{z}_0, \boldsymbol{\theta}_{iy}\right)$ is the conditional distribution of $\mathbf{y}_t$ given $\mathbf{x}_t$ under model M_i and the information available at time $t-1$, $\mathbf{Z}_{t-1}$, and $f_{ix}\left(\mathbf{x}_t \mid \mathbf{Z}_{t-1}; \mathbf{z}_0, \boldsymbol{\theta}_{ix}\right)$ is the marginal density of $\mathbf{x}_t$ conditional on $\mathbf{Z}_{t-1}$. Note that the unknown parameters $\boldsymbol{\theta}_i$ are decomposed into the parameters of interest, $\boldsymbol{\theta}_{iy}$, and the parameters of the marginal density of the exogenous variables, $\boldsymbol{\theta}_{ix}$. In the case where $\mathbf{x}_t$ is strictly exogenous, knowledge of the marginal distribution of $\mathbf{x}_t$ does not help with the estimation of $\boldsymbol{\theta}_{iy}$, and estimation of these parameters can therefore be based entirely on the conditional distribution, $f_{iy}\left(\mathbf{y}_t \mid \mathbf{x}_t, \mathbf{Z}_{t-1}; \mathbf{z}_0, \boldsymbol{\theta}_{iy}\right)$.

Despite this, parameter uncertainty relating to $\boldsymbol{\theta}_{ix}$ can continue to be relevant for probability forecasts of the endogenous variables, $\mathbf{y}_t$, and forecast uncertainty surrounding the endogenous variables is affected by the way the uncertainty associated with the future path of the exogenous variables is resolved. In practice, the future values of $\mathbf{x}_t$ are often treated as known and fixed at pre-specified values. The resultant forecasts for $\mathbf{y}_t$ are then referred to as *scenario (or conditional) forecasts*, with each scenario representing a different set of assumed future values of the exogenous variables. This approach underestimates the degree of forecast uncertainties. A more plausible approach would be to treat $\mathbf{x}_t$ as strongly or weakly exogenous (as appropriate) at the estimation stage, but to allow for the forecast uncertainties of the endogenous and the exogenous variables jointly. The exogeneity assumption will simplify the estimation process but does not eliminate the need for a joint treatment of future and model uncertainties associated with the exogenous variables and the endogenous variables.

8

The UK macroeconomy

In this part of the book, we provide a description of the construction of a quarterly long-run structural macroeconometric model for the UK using the framework and the techniques set out in Chapters 3–7. The econometric methods employed are relatively straightforward to implement and our intention is to give a detailed account of the different steps involved in the modelling process, covering the specification, estimation and evaluation stages.

The model will be estimated over the period 1965q1–1999q4. This is a sample of data which is relatively reliable in the sense that it is now unlikely to be revised. We also consider some results obtained over a longer sample of data covering the period 1965q1–2001q1. This provides a useful means of investigating the robustness of the model to changes in the sample period and enables us to produce forecasts, in Chapter 11, which are relevant to policy-makers at the time of going to print. A postscript evaluation of point and event forecasts is also provided in Section 11.3. Before undertaking this analysis, however, in the remainder of this chapter, we provide an overview of the time series properties of the macrovariables included in the model.

The theory outlined in Chapter 4 motivates our choice of the variables to be included in the core model and suggests the appropriate measurements to be used. Hence, y_t is measured as the natural logarithm of UK real per capita GDP; p_t is the logarithm of domestic producer prices; $\widetilde{p}_t$ is the logarithm of domestic retail prices; p_t^* is the logarithm of the producer prices of the OECD countries; e_t is the logarithm of the UK effective nominal exchange rate (defined as the domestic price of a unit of foreign currency, so that an increase in e_t represents a depreciation of the home currency); r_t is the domestic nominal interest rate, computed as $r_t = 0.25\ln(1+R_t/100)$, where R_t is the 90 day Treasury Bill average discount rate per annum; r_t^* is the foreign nominal interest rate, computed as $r_t^* = 0.25\ln(1 + R_t^*/100)$, where R_t^* is a weighted average of 90 day interest rates per annum in the US, Germany, Japan and France and weights are provided by the International Monetary Fund Special Drawing Right (SDR); y_t^* is the logarithm of real per capita GDP of the OECD countries; h_t is the logarithm of (end-of-period) real per capita money stock ($M0$); and p_t^o is the logarithm of oil prices, measured by the average crude oil price published by the IMF. Details of the construction and sources of the data are provided in Appendix C.

Considerable care has been exercised in choosing the appropriate measure for the macroeconomic variables of interest described above, ensuring that the various measures correspond as closely as possible to the theoretical concepts discussed in Chapter 4. For example, to ensure a more satisfactory match between theoretical and empirical concepts, producer price indices are used to construct deviations between the domestic and foreign price levels in the *PPP* relationship, while the retail price index is used to measure domestic inflation in the *FIP* relationship.[1] To check on the robustness of our results, we also considered various alternative measures of y_t^*, p_t^* and r_t^*, but we found that these have relatively little impact on the estimation results.[2] For example, the use of a weighted average of the logarithm of the price indices of UK's 42 largest trading partners, where the weights are given by the share of UK imports from these countries and the use of an export-weighted average of foreign output, including countries both inside and outside of the OECD, appears to have only marginal effects on the results. Similarly, the results were hardly affected when we used the US nominal interest rate as an alternative to the SDR-weighted rate.

The data used in the applied work are quarterly, seasonally adjusted series covering the period 1964q1–1999q4. To ensure that all regressions are comparable (irrespective of the order chosen for the underlying VAR model, for example), all estimation results reported in the book are carried out over the period 1965q1–1999q4 (140 observations) or the slightly extended period 1965q1–2001q1 (145 observations). Plots of the core macroeconomic series are provided in Figures 8.1–8.7. In what follows, we summarise the main statistical characteristics of the series and provide

[1] There is considerable evidence, both on the basis of our own analysis and elsewhere, that the various alternative measures of inflation that are available are pairwise cointegrated with a cointegrating vector of $(1, -1)$ and a zero constant. The use of two measures of prices, p_t and $\widetilde{p}_t$, in the analysis has no impact on the long-run properties of the model, therefore, but is likely to capture the short-run dynamics more accurately.

[2] Other approaches to the construction of foreign variables are discussed in Pesaran, Schuermann and Weiner (2004).

a brief account of their history, considering, in turn, the series of outputs, prices, exchange rates, interest rates and money.

8.1 Domestic and foreign output

Figures 8.1a and 8.1b show the level and first differences of the logarithm of domestic output y_t over our sample period, and Figures 8.1c and 8.1d show the corresponding plots for foreign (OECD) output y_t^*.

Both variables show clear upward trends and appear stationary in first differences. Over the whole of the sample period 1965q1–1999q4, y_t and y_t^* grew at similar rates, at 1.97% and 2.10% per annum, respectively. But this obscures quite different experiences over different sub-periods, with foreign output growing very rapidly at the beginning of the sample before slowing at the end while the UK achieved relatively stable rates of growth over these horizons. So, for example, the UK achieved a growth rate of 1.86% per annum during the second half of the 1960s, 1965q1–1969q4, rising to 2.15% over the 1970s, before falling slightly to 1.91% per annum over the period 1980q1–1999q4. Foreign output, by way of contrast, achieved very high levels of growth, of 3.9% per annum, during

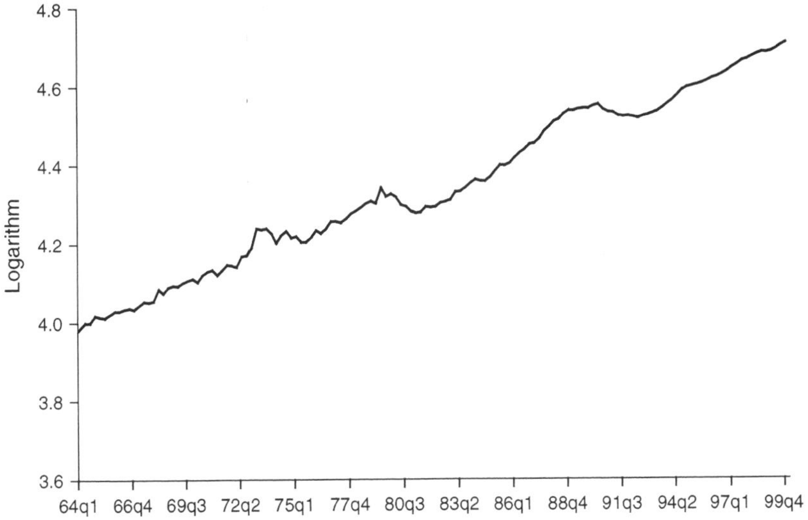

Figure 8.1a UK output, y_t.

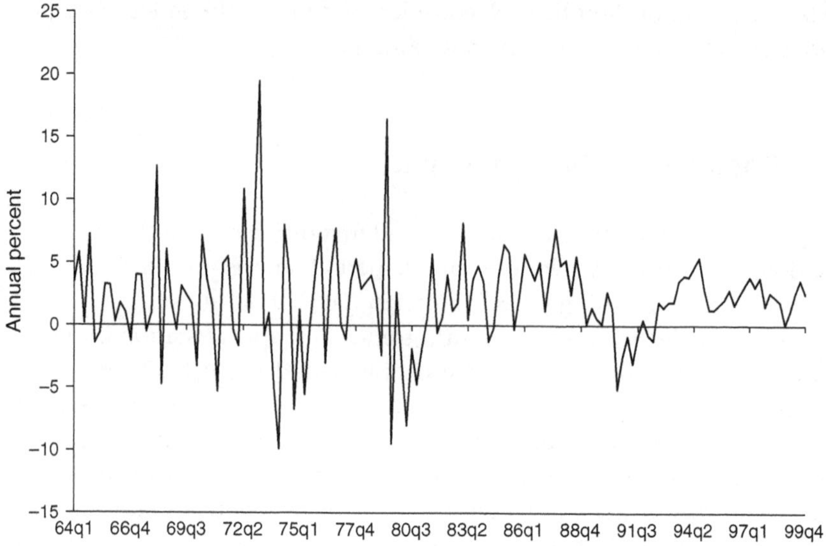

Figure 8.1b First difference of UK output, Δy_t.

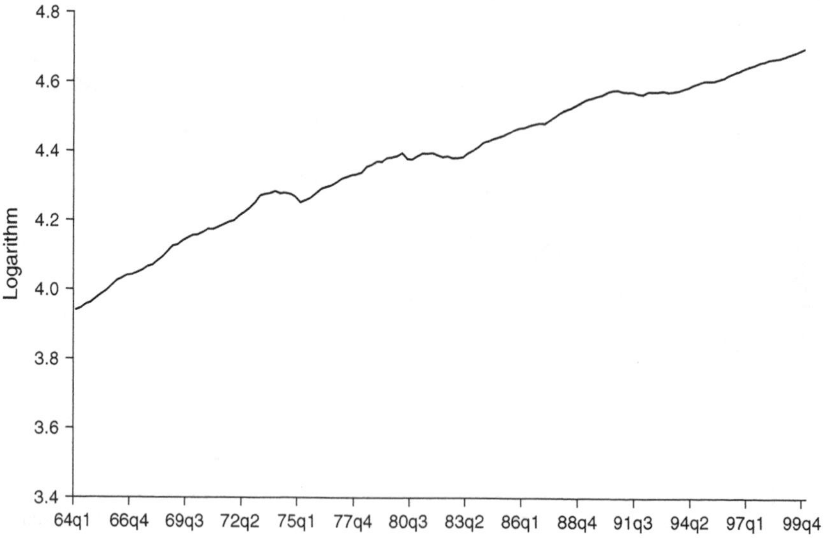

Figure 8.1c Foreign output, y_t^*.

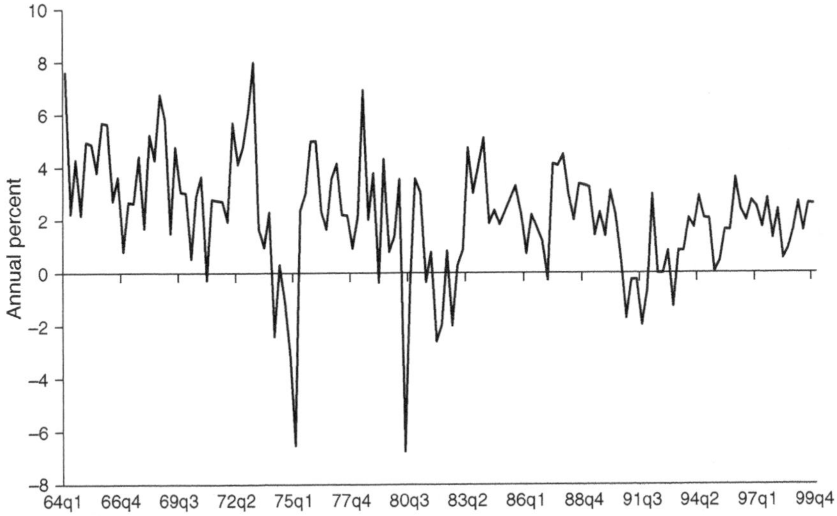

Figure 8.1d First difference of foreign output, Δy_t^*.

1965q1–1969q4, compared to an average growth rate of 2.29% per annum over the period 1970q1–1979q4, and an average rate of 1.56% per annum for the period 1980q1–1999q4.

These differences in growth rates across extended periods are demonstrated in Figures 8.1e and 8.1f, which show clearly the UK's relative decline over the first half of the sample period and relative recovery over the second half of the sample.

Of course, the growth rates achieved over the decades were influenced by some particular, and remarkable, episodes of output change in the UK. For example, y_t fell by around 2.47% in 1974q1 and this was followed by a period of low growth that persisted throughout the mid-1970s. A similar, although less pronounced, slowdown in growth was observed in y_t^* also, and the timing of the slowdown provides some support for the view discussed in Chapter 3 that the oil price shock could be an important factor in bringing about such sharp declines. In the early 1980s, domestic output fell for five consecutive quarters between the periods 1980q1–1981q1, including a fall of 2.00% in 1980q2. There was an associated rise in unemployment from 1.37 million to 2.37 million and this contributed to a growth rate in y_t of just 0.85% per annum over the period 1980q1–1984q4 (compared to 1.1% per annum in y_t^*). However, in terms of international

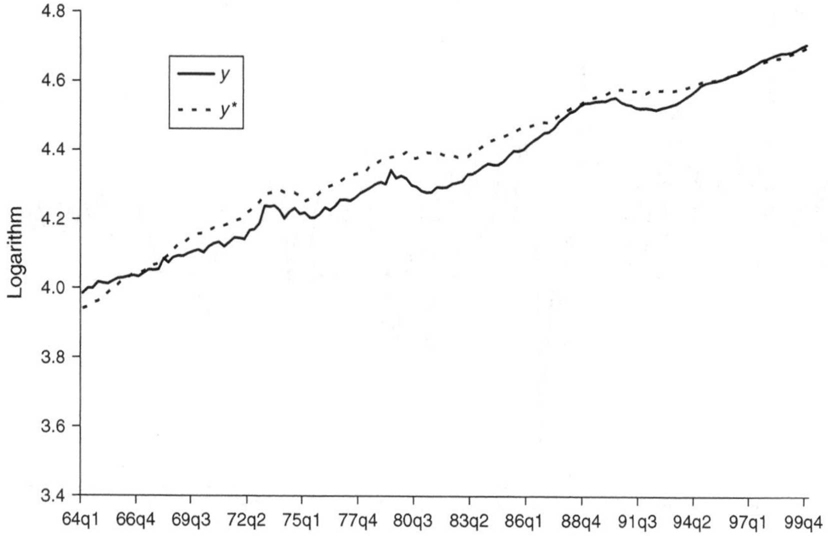

Figure 8.1e UK and foreign output, y_t and y_t^*.

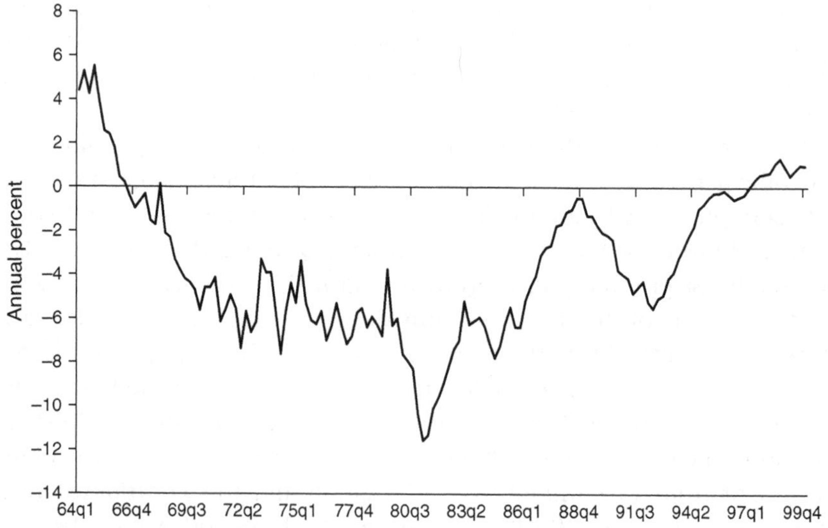

Figure 8.1f Difference of UK and foreign output, $y_t - y_t^*$.

comparisons, this was more than offset during 1985q1–1989q4 by the rapid growth associated with the 'Lawson boom': unemployment fell from 3.34 million to 1.64 million, and output growth reached 3.49% per annum in the UK (compared to 2.45% per annum abroad).

These episodes, among others, have contributed to a relatively volatile output growth series for the UK considered quarter-on-quarter, with the UK output growth series having a standard deviation of 4.1% compared to 2.3% for foreign output growth over the whole sample. However, an additional feature, which is readily apparent in Figures 8.1b in particular, is the large time-variation in the volatility of output growth. For the period 1965q1–1979q4, the standard deviation of Δy_t was 5.33% per annum (compared to 2.51% per annum for Δy_t^*), but these fell dramatically during the second half of the sample to 2.84% per annum for the UK during 1980q1–1999q4 (and to 1.90% per annum for foreign output growth). Output growth in the UK was at its most volatile during the 1970s, during which time there were industrial disputes in the Mining and Energy sectors in 1972 and 1974,[3] and the effects of the oil price rises of the early 1970s were apparent. But the reduction in volatility is not just associated with these particular episodes and it is worth noting here that a decline in the volatility of domestic and foreign prices and interest rates has also been apparent since the mid-1980s, as we shall discuss below.[4]

Finally, an alternative and complementary way of considering the variation in output growth is provided in Table 8.1. This table gives information for the four-quarter moving average of output growth showing the proportion of observations in which this average has fallen below various thresholds during the extended sample 1965q1–2001q1 and during three sub-periods 1970q1–1979q4, 1980q1–1989q4 and 1990q1–2001q1.

For example, we might be interested in the occurrence of a 'recession', which we define as an event where the four-quarter moving average of output growth falls below zero. Table 8.1 shows that the proportion of times in which according to this definition recession occurred over the whole sample was 13.1%, but that this proportion was higher through the

[3] The miners' strike of January–February 1971 resulted in the government declaring a state of emergency, power cuts and fuel rationing, and much of British industry went on a three-day working week. Industrial action by the miners and power engineers in the final months of 1973 resulted in the declaration of a further state of emergency, the imposition of prohibitions on space heating in industrial and commercial premises and the imposition of a reduced working week in January–February 1974.

[4] The decline in the volatility is not thought to be sufficiently large that it will have much effect on the unit root tests. See, for example, Busetti and Taylor (2005) and, for the testing of cointegrating rank in the presence of GARCH error terms, see Garratt, Lee and Pesaran (2005b).

Table 8.1 Historical unconditional probabilities for output growth (4-quarter moving average).

Sample period	Thresholds (per cent)									
	−2.0	−1.0	−0.5	0	1	2	2.5	3	4	5
1970q1–1979q4	5.00	10.00	12.50	15.00	17.50	37.50	57.50	70.00	80.00	90.00
1980q1–1989q4	10.00	12.50	12.50	12.50	17.50	35.00	40.00	47.50	72.50	95.00
1990q1–2001q1	2.22	6.67	13.33	17.78	22.22	42.22	60.00	77.79	93.33	100.00
1965q1–2001q1	4.83	8.28	11.03	13.10	17.93	40.00	55.86	67.59	83.45	95.86

Note: Output growth here is computed as: $(\Delta y_t \times 400) + 0.22236$ where y_t is the logarithm of real per capita output and 0.22236 is the annualised population growth rate.

period 1990q1–2001q1 at 17.8%. Of course, this information is already implicitly provided in Figures 8.1a and 8.1c. But these proportions convey the information on the mean values and the volatility of the series during the sub-samples in a particularly useful and meaningful way and in much the same way as the probability forecasts convey information on expected future events compared to the more usual point forecasts (as discussed in Chapter 7). Certainly the values in Table 8.1 provide useful reference points, showing the unconditional probability of the various events occurring based on the various sub-samples, and can be readily used in the interpretation of the probability forecasts that we shall describe in Chapter 11.

8.2 Domestic and foreign prices

Figures 8.2, 8.3 and 8.4 plot the time paths of the levels and first differences of the various price series considered in our model $p_t, \widetilde{p}_t, p_t^*, p_t - p_t^*, p_t^o$ (plus the second difference of p_t and $\widetilde{p}_t$) over the sample period 1964q1–1999q4. We focus mostly on the price changes, but make the observation that the levels of the price series are clearly non-stationary and upward trended.

Domestic price inflation, measured either by producer price inflation Δp_t or retail price inflation $\Delta \widetilde{p}_t$, was relatively low through the early part of the sample, averaging 4.46% per annum and 5.22% per annum, respectively, over the period 1965q1–1972q2. But it rose to very high levels through the mid-1970s, averaging in excess of 15% per annum during 1972q3–1976q4 and peaking at 25.95% per annum for Δp_t and 33.03% per annum for $\Delta \widetilde{p}_t$ in 1974q1 and 1975q2, respectively.

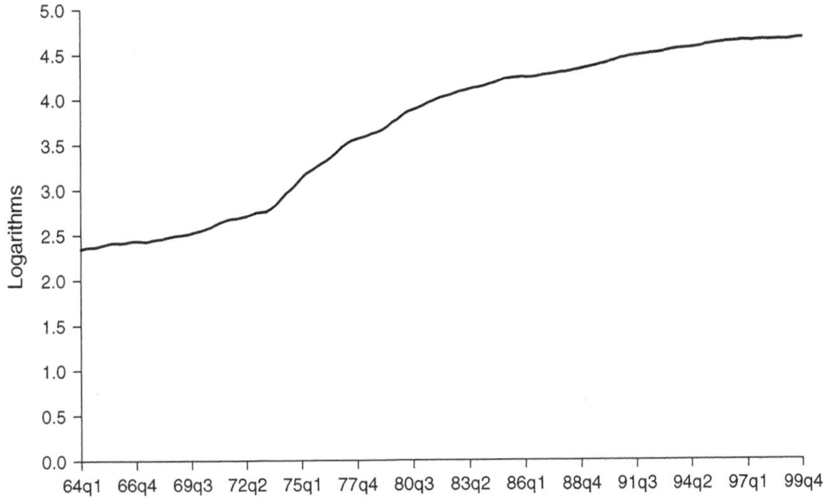

Figure 8.2a UK producer prices, p_t.

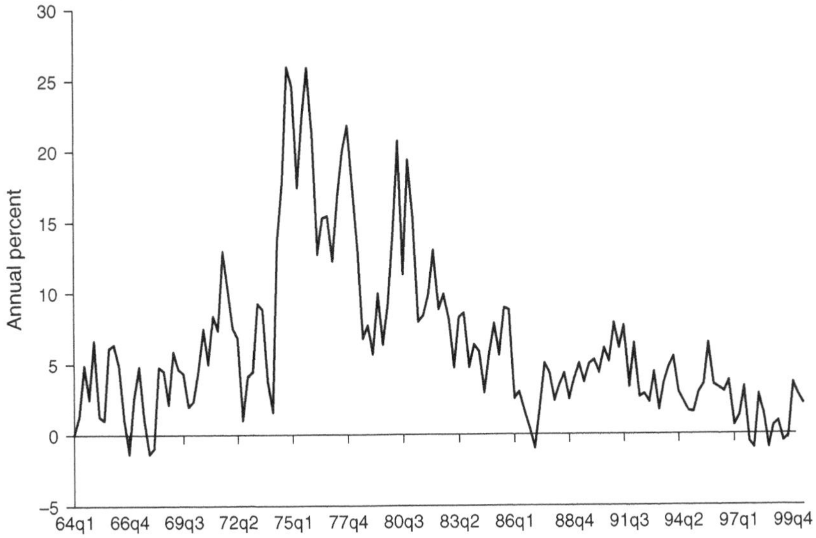

Figure 8.2b First difference of UK producer prices, Δp_t.

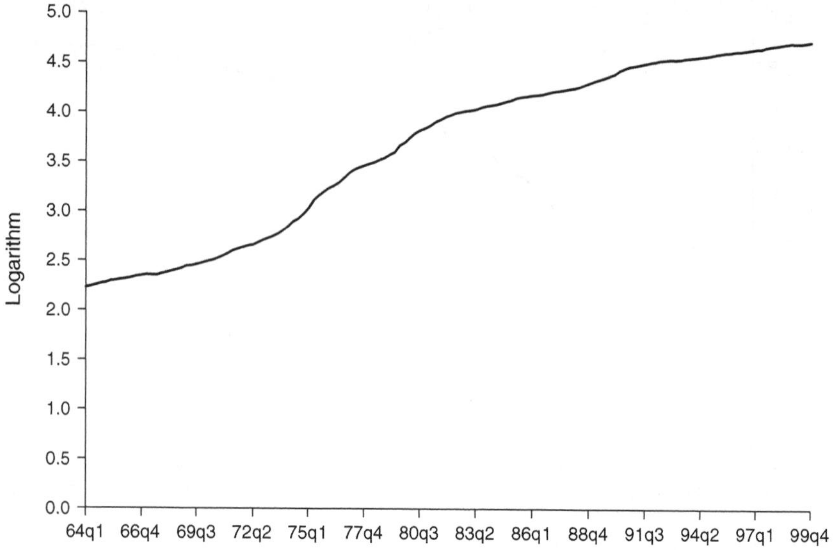

Figure 8.2c UK retail prices, $\widetilde{p}_t$.

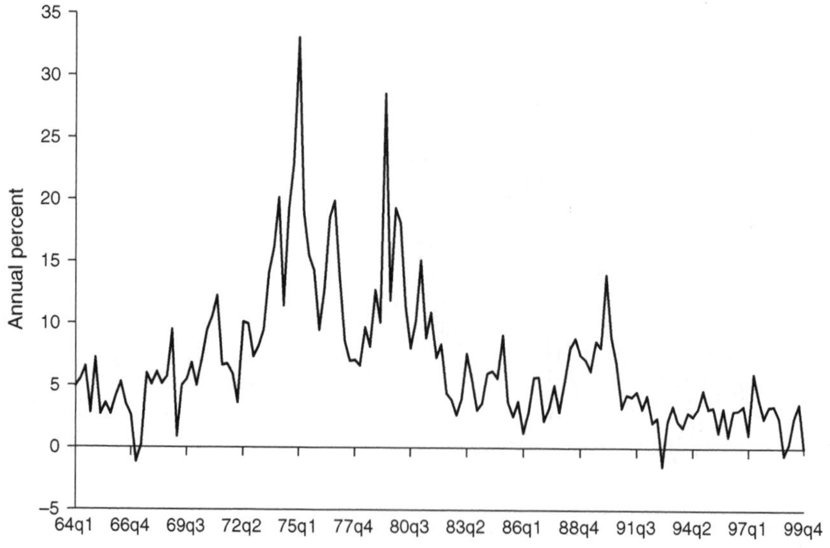

Figure 8.2d First difference of UK retail prices, $\Delta\widetilde{p}_t$.

Focusing on Δp_t, a significant part of these price movements are associated with rapidly rising oil prices and exchange rate depreciations. However, other domestic factors were also associated with the high inflation of this period. The implementation of various forms of incomes policy in this period can also help explain the volatility of the Δp_t series: sharp reductions in the series are observed in 1967q1, 1967q2 and 1973q2, following the statutory period of zero wage increases during the 'Wage Freeze' and 'Severe Restraint' of the Wilson administration (covering two six-month periods beginning June 1966) and the wage and price 'Standstill' of the Heath administration (lasting from November 1972 to March 1993); and the effects of the statutory ceilings on pay increases imposed during 1968q2–1969q2 and 1973q2–1974q3 help account for falls in Δp_t observed at the end of these two sub-periods. The Callaghan government's 'Social Contract' with the Trade Unions, beginning in July 1976, saw a reduction in wage inflation from 27% per annum in 1975 to 9% per annum in 1977, and there was a corresponding reduction in price inflation. But the breakdown of this policy in the 'Winter of Discontent' of 1978/79, the oil price rises of 1978 and 1979 and the increase in VAT from 8% to 15% in June 1979 generated upward pressure on prices, so that producer price inflation averaged 12.07% per annum over the period 1977q1–1981q1. Since that time, Δp_t and $\Delta \widetilde{p}_t$ have achieved relatively low levels once more, averaging 3.97% and 4.53% per annum over the period 1981q2–1998q2. Particularly low levels of inflation, of 2.24% and 2.54% per annum, were observed during the later period 1992q4–1999q4, which largely coincides with the period over which the British government adopted an explicit policy of inflation targeting (a strategy followed in the aftermath of the UK's exit from the ERM in 1992 and implemented both before and after central bank independence was announced in 1997).[5]

In view of the various policy stances taken on inflation over the sample, it is interesting to consider the proportion of times that the (four-quarter moving average of) domestic inflation, as measured by the Retail Price Index has fallen below various thresholds, as shown in Table 8.2.

[5] Inflation targets relating to the Retail Price Index (excluding mortgage payments) were first set explicitly in the UK in October 1992, specifying that inflation should be in the lower half of the range 1–4% per annum by Spring 1997. The policy was formalised further in May 1997 when the Bank of England was given operational independence with the remit to aim for an average annual inflation rate of 2.5%, with the rate falling in the target range 1.5–3.5%. The current target is consumer price inflation of 2.0%, with bands of 1% either side. If these bands are exceeded then a letter is required to be sent to the Chancellor explaining why this has occurred.

These show that realisations of the annual rate of inflation below 6% were rare in the 1970s, but occurred quite frequently during in the 1980s and were experienced in almost 90% of cases in the 1990s. The proportion of occasions on which inflation has been within the acceptable range of [1.5%, 3.5%] over the sample 1965q1–2001q1 is just 24.14%. However, over the low inflation period after 1990q1, inflation was within this band 60% of the time.

The apparently distinct episodes of high and low inflation influence the statistical characterisation of the data since the persistence of shocks in the inflation series suggests that inflation might not be stationary. In contrast,

Table 8.2 Historical unconditional probabilities for inflation (4-quarter moving average).

Sample period	Thresholds (per cent)										
	1.5	2.5	3.5	5.0	6.0	7.0	8.0	9.0	10.0	15.0	20.0
1970q1–1979q4	0.00	0.00	0.00	2.50	7.50	12.50	30.00	37.50	52.50	72.50	90.00
1980q1–1989q4	0.00	0.00	10.00	40.00	55.50	62.50	75.00	77.50	77.50	92.50	100.00
1990q1–2001q1	8.89	28.89	68.89	86.67	88.89	88.89	91.11	93.33	100.00	100.00	100.00
1965q1–2001q1	3.45	10.35	27.59	48.28	57.93	62.01	71.03	74.48	80.69	90.35	97.24

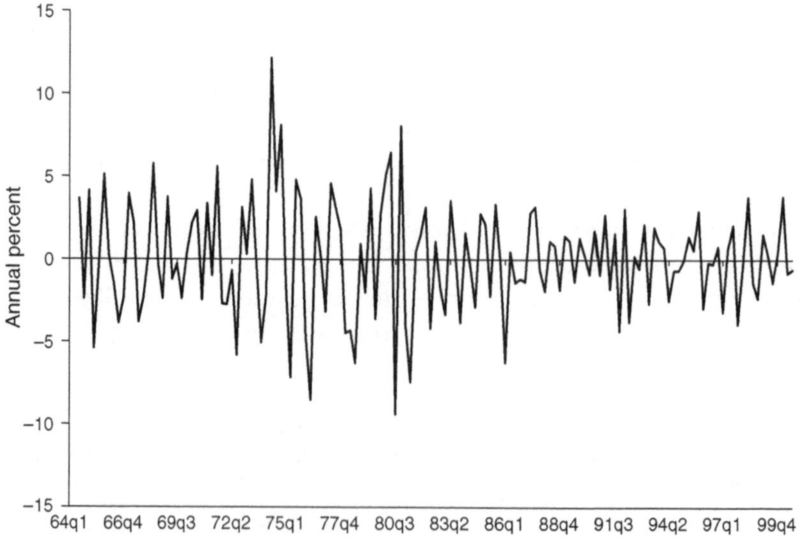

Figure 8.2e Second difference of UK producer prices, $\Delta^2 p_t$.

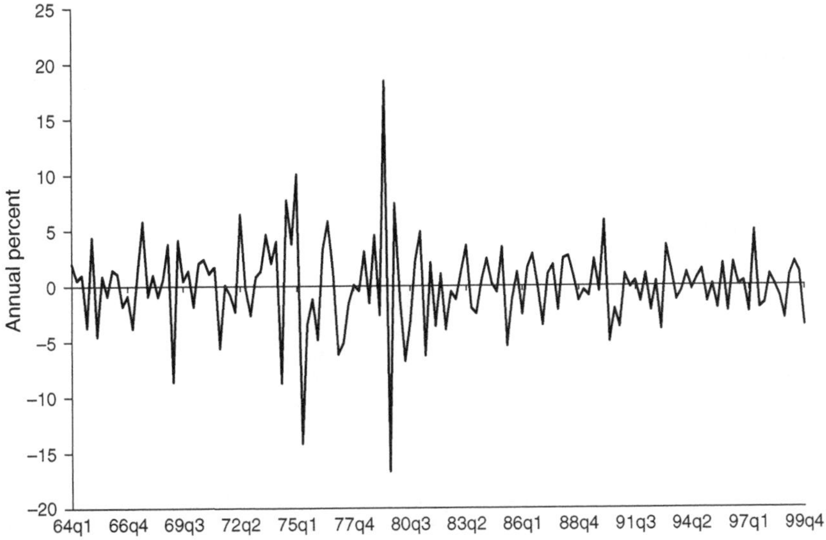

Figure 8.2f Second difference of UK retail prices, $\Delta^2\widetilde{p}_t$.

changes in the rate of inflation (illustrated in Figures 8.2e–f) appear clearly stationary. We discuss this feature of the data more formally in Section 9.2.

The effects of the oil price hikes can also be seen in the Δp_t^* series, with high inflation observed worldwide during the 1970s. There are, however, clear periods during which UK and world inflation diverge.

For example, Figure 8.3c shows the UK price index rose very rapidly relative to world prices around the mid- to late-1970s. In particular, we see that during the period 1972q3 to 1976q4, $(p_t - p_t^*)$ rose at an average rate of 5.05% per annum, and this compares to average growth of 0.55% per annum over the sample period up to 1972q3, and of 0.13% per annum during the sample period after 1976q4.

Finally, to be quite clear on the timing and size of the effects of oil prices on domestic and foreign price inflation, Figures 8.4a and 8.4b plot the level and first difference of oil prices themselves. These are obviously dominated by the effects of the various large oil price shocks.

Over the period 1965q1–1973q4, the price of oil was essentially flat, but quadrupled in 1974q1 as a result of the Yom Kippur War and its aftermath. Oil prices remained relatively stable until the second increase in the price of oil in 1979q2, which was brought about largely due to the Iranian Revolution in February 1979. In 1986q1, the oil price fell sharply, largely

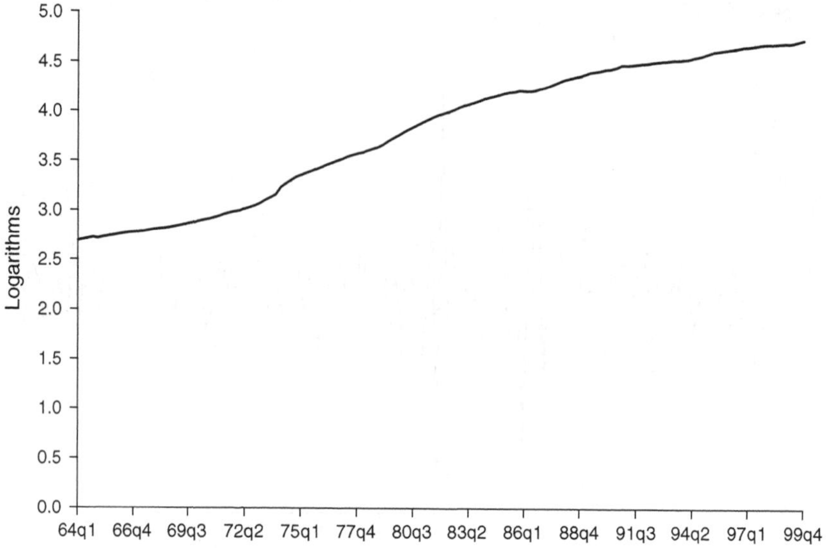

Figure 8.3a Foreign producer prices, p_t^*.

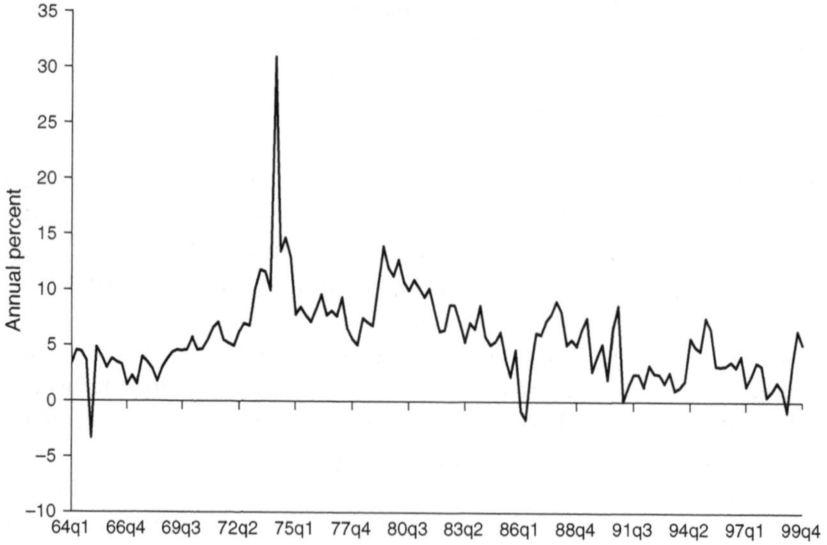

Figure 8.3b First difference of foreign producer prices, Δp_t^*.

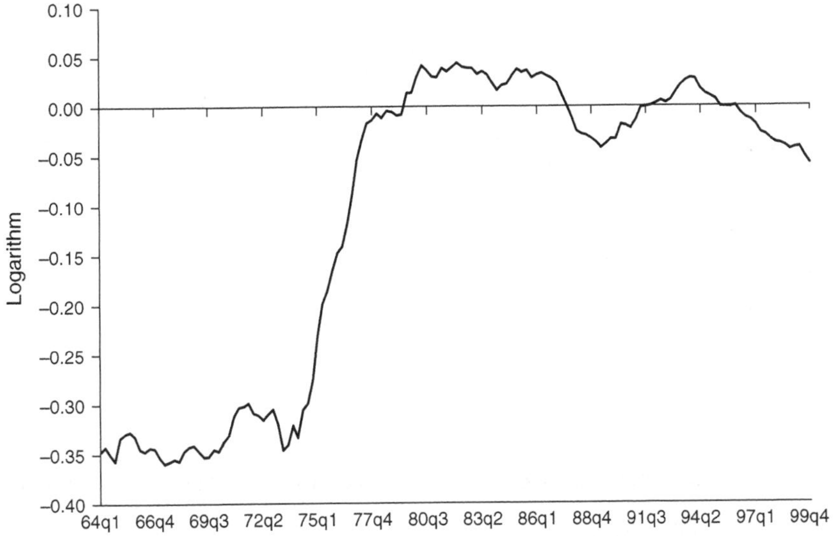

Figure 8.3c Relative prices, $p_t - p_t^*$.

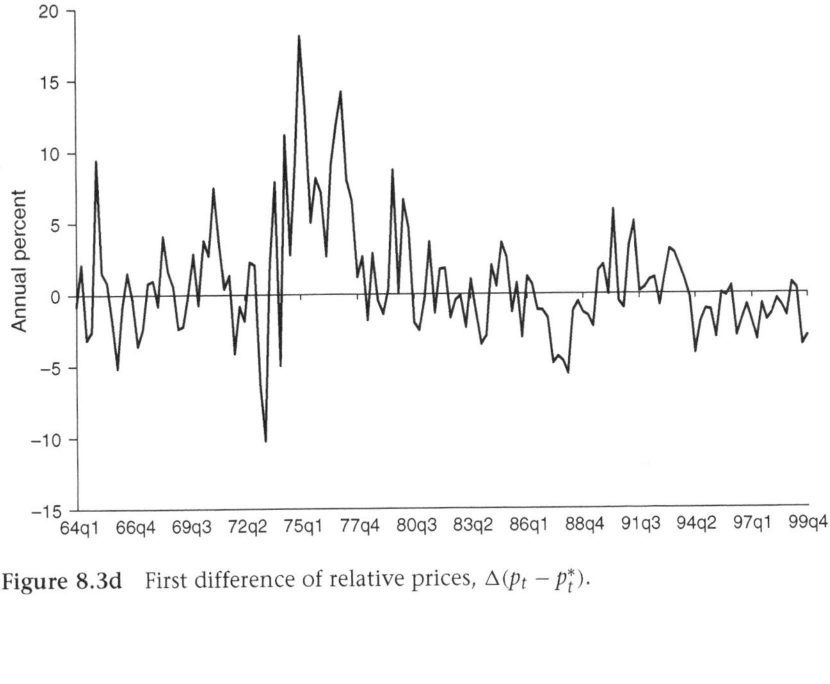

Figure 8.3d First difference of relative prices, $\Delta(p_t - p_t^*)$.

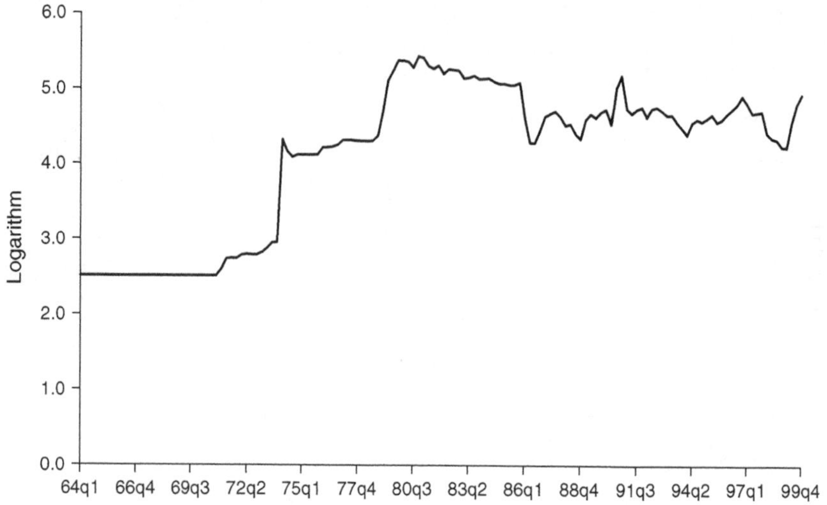

Figure 8.4a Oil price, p_t^o.

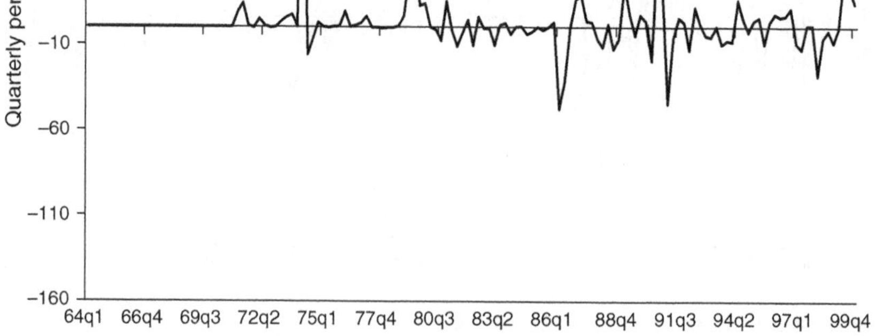

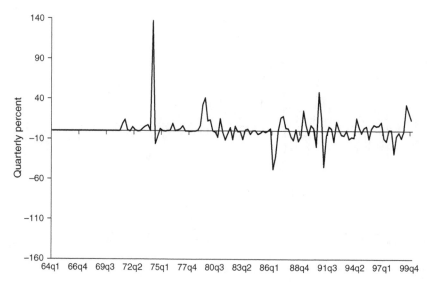

Figure 8.4b First difference of the oil price, Δp_t^o.

instigated by Saudi Arabia, and there followed a period where the level was considerably lower than previously, but where the volatility was high. Large increases in the price of oil were experienced in 1990q3 and 1990q4 during the Persian Gulf War in the aftermath of the invasion of Kuwait by Iraq, but these were reversed in 1991q1. Over the remaining part of our sample, 1991q2–1999q4, real oil prices fell slightly relative to domestic as well as foreign prices.

8.3 Exchange rates

Figures 8.5a and 8.5b plot the level and first differences of the UK effective exchange rate, e_t. When considering exchange rate movements, the sample can conveniently be split into four main episodes, namely: (i) the period of fixed exchange rate upto June 1972; (ii) the high inflation period of 1972q3–1976q4; (iii) the period between 1977q1 and 1981q1; and (iv) 1981q2–1999q4.

During the first of these episodes, e_t depreciated by 2.08% per annum, although this depreciation came about almost entirely through the 14% devaluation of November 1967. The flotation of sterling in June 1972 was

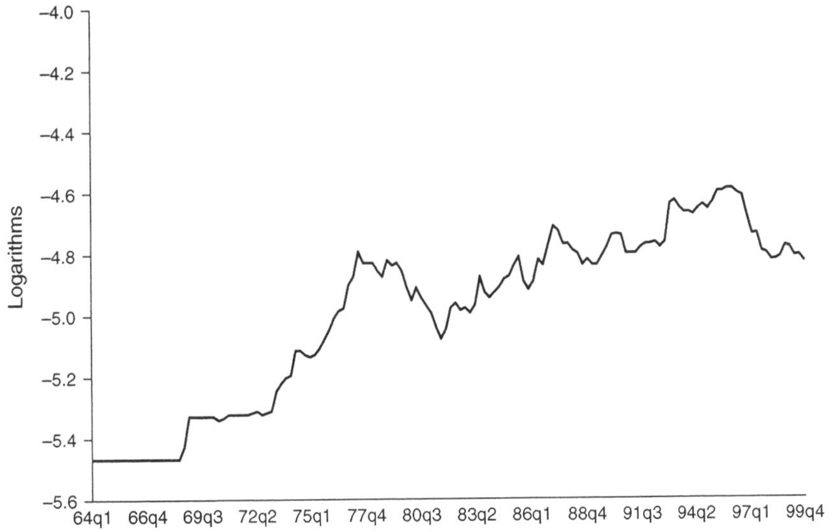

Figure 8.5a Effective exchange rate, e_t.

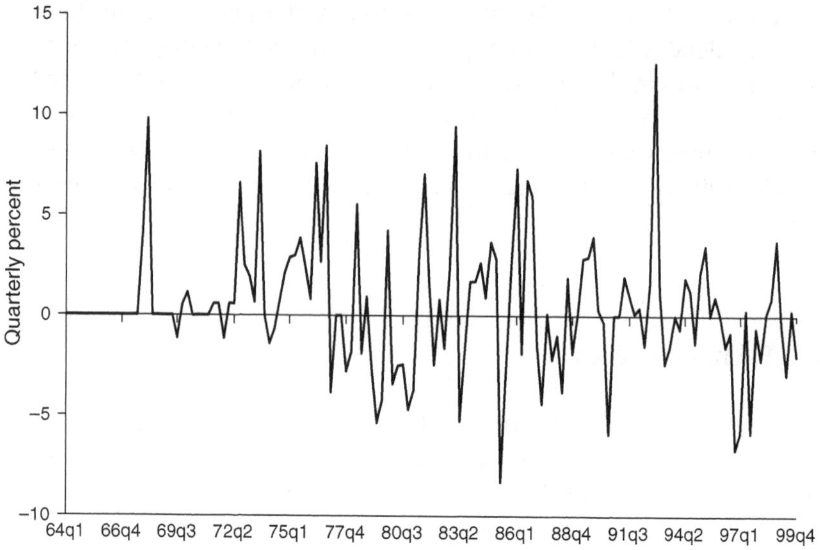

Figure 8.5b First difference of effective exchange rate, Δe_t.

accompanied by a sharp depreciation. And the worsening of the UK's trade balance, associated with its accession to the EC in January 1973 and with the oil price shock of 1973q4, was followed by a sequence of further depreciations. Hence, the average rate of increase in e_t over the second episode, covering 1972q3–1976q4, was 11.61% per annum (substantially outstripping the rise in $(p_t - p_t^*)$ over the same period). The third period, covering 1977q1–1981q1, saw the UK become a net exporter of oil at a time when oil prices rose once more and when the Thatcher administration started to implement its Medium Term Financial Strategy (both in 1979). Over this period, e_t appreciated at a rate of 6.77% per annum, reversing (and overshooting) the trend reduction in the terms of trade that had occurred over the first two periods. Finally, the fourth period is characterised once more by moderate depreciation, averaging 1.33% per annum over 1981q2–1999q4, although this has been subject to a certain degree of exchange rate volatility and there have been a number of episodes during the period which particularly stand out. For example, the rise in e_t of 18.2% during 1986, associated with the fall in oil prices of that year; the period of exchange rate appreciation observed during the pound's shadowing of the Deutschemark during 1987–88; the sharp appreciation of sterling following entry into the ERM in October 1990; the sharp depreciation of sterling in the aftermath of the pound's exit from the ERM in September 1992; and the almost continuous appreciation of sterling from 1996q1 to the end of the sample in 1999q4.

8.4 Domestic and foreign interest rates

Figures 8.6a–8.6d display the time series for r_t, r_t^* and their first differences. Again the series can be considered in four broad episodes, defined according to the movements in r_t^*.

Episode 1 is defined over the period 1965q1–1970q1, during which time r_t^* gradually rose, largely reflecting the rising budget deficit in the US emerging as a result of financing the Vietnam War, rising US inflation and the contractionary monetary policy of the Nixon administration through 1969.[6] The second episode, over the 1970q2–1974q3 period, sees r_t^* first falling and then rising as the US Federal Reserve pursued

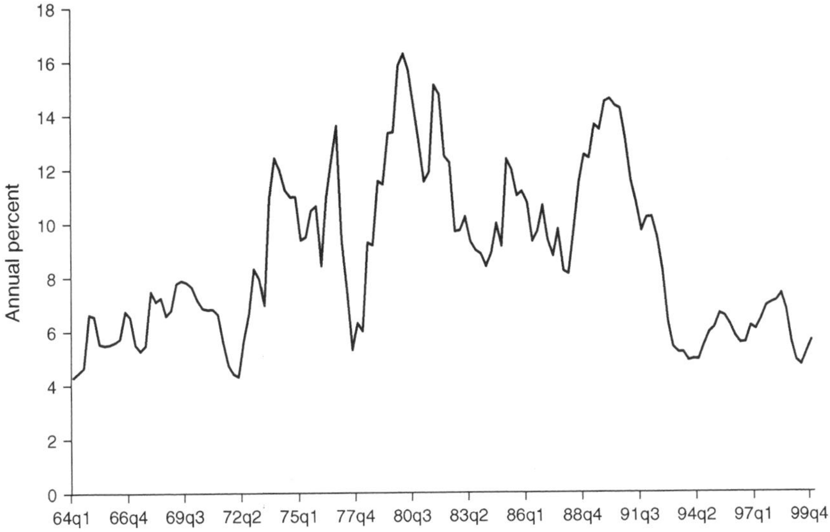

Figure 8.6a UK interest rates, r_t.

[6] This discussion is based on the assumption that the primary driving force in r_t^* is the US short-term interest rate whose weight when computing r_t^* is 0.4382, compared with the next largest weight of 0.2360 for Germany.

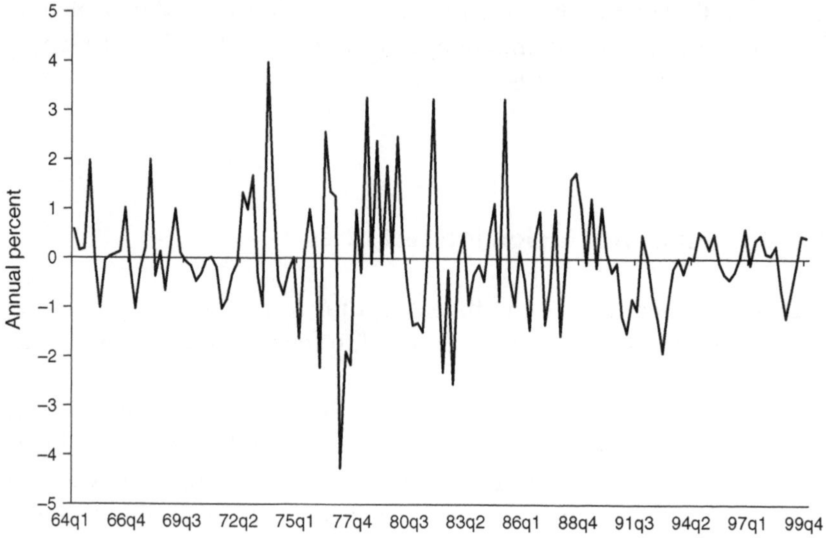

Figure 8.6b First difference of UK interest rates, Δr_t.

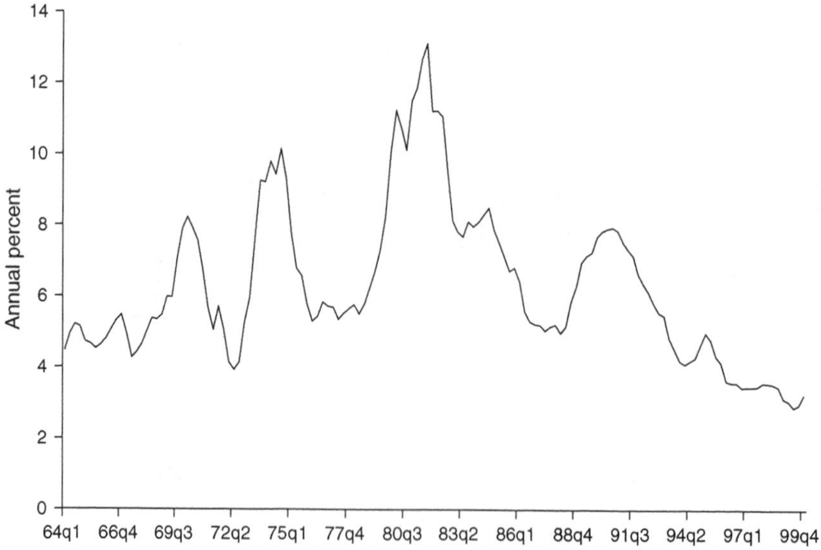

Figure 8.6c Foreign interest rates, r_t^*.

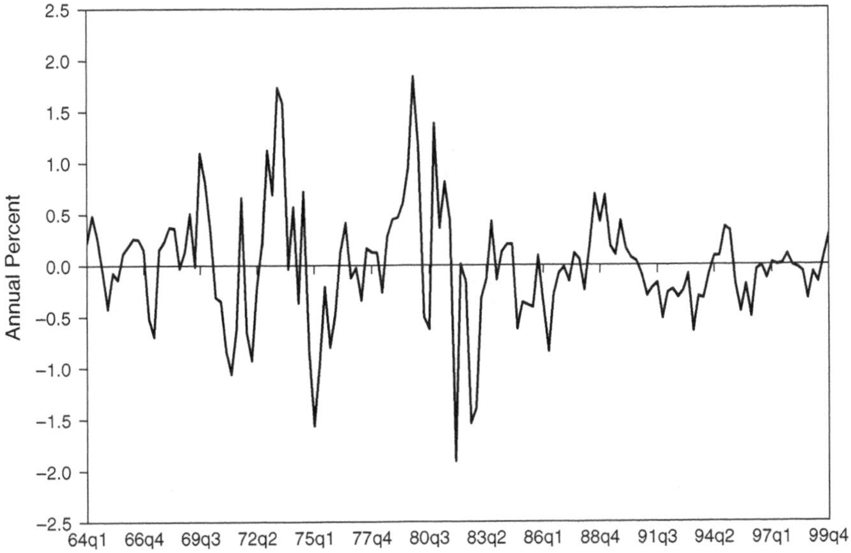

Figure 8.6d First difference of foreign interest rates, Δr_t^*.

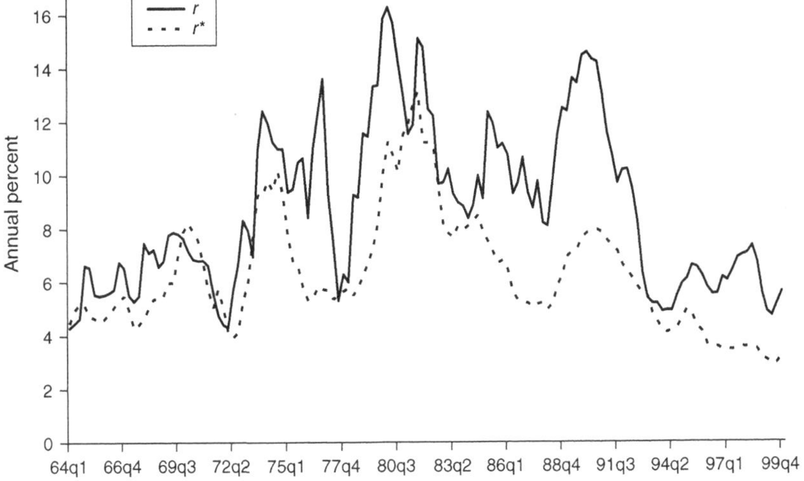

Figure 8.6e UK and foreign interest rates, r_t and r_t^*.

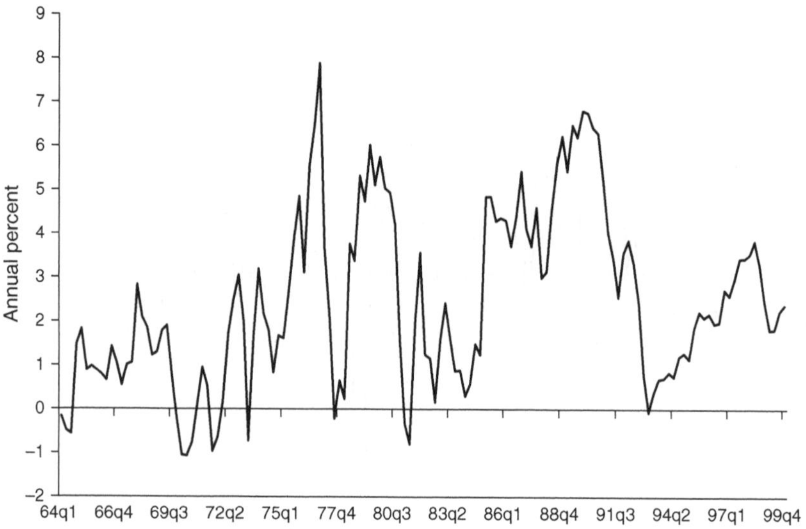

Figure 8.6f Difference of UK and foreign interest rates, $r_t - r_t^*$.

a non-accommodating monetary policy following the OPEC oil price shock. The third episode, 1974q4–1981q3, ends with US rates achieving unprecedentedly high levels following the Reagan administration's anti-inflationary policy and the US monetary authorities' pursuit of tight money through 1980/81, and the fourth episode, lasting to the end of the sample, is characterised by generally falling foreign nominal rates. Rates reached their lowest levels since 1972 at the end of 1987 when the monetary authorities loosened policy following the Wall Street Crash of October 1987, but rose through 1990 in response to the effects of monetary unification of Germany in July 1990.

Over the first of these episodes, r_t corresponds quite closely to movements in r_t^*, although r_t appears relatively high in 1967q4 (at which time Harold Wilson's government in the UK was implementing deflationary measures to support the devaluation of the exchange rate) and r_t fell relatively rapidly through 1971 in reaction to the changes in monetary control outlined in the Bank of England's publication on 'Competition and Credit Control'. In the second episode, the UK and worldwide experience of inflation through the early and mid-1970s coincided with high nominal interest rates at home and abroad. Although r_t rose substantially higher than r_t^* during this period, UK nominal rates did not keep pace with the very high inflation of the time and real rates of interest in the UK were negative for most of the 1970s. During the third episode, while r_t^* fell through 1974q4–1976q2 and then remained low until 1978q2, r_t rose sharply during 1976 following the implementation of monetary targets by the Callaghan administration from mid-1975 and the administration's loan negotiations with the IMF at the end of 1976. UK rates rose throughout 1978/79, preceding the rises abroad, and remained high until international rates began to fall at the end of 1981. Finally, during the fourth episode, UK rates fell through to the end of 1987, although even during this period they remained high by international standards. The UK policy of shadowing the Deutschemark through 1988 and sterling's membership of the ERM between October 1990 and September 1992 saw r_t high relative to r_t^* although, by the end of the sample, r_t was at a level comparable with those of the early 1960s.

8.5 Real money balances relative to income

Figures 8.7a and 8.7b show the time series for $h_t - y_t$ and their first difference. The variable $h_t - y_t$ measures the inverse of the per capita real narrow money velocity and what is very clear is the almost uninterrupted downward trend since the beginning of our period (a trend which goes back as far as the late 1940s; see Janssen, 1996).

This trend is usually explained by progress in payments technology. The increased use of alternative means of payments has caused the proportion of expenditure financed by cash to fall almost continuously. However, since 1990, the trend has flattened out. Explanations given for this are that the payments technology growth has slowed down to a point of no longer having an effect and that a shift to a low inflation environment has led agents to voluntarily hold a larger proportion of their portfolios in cash. Evidence on these hypothesis are presented in Janssen (1996).

This concludes our overview of the UK macroeconomic experiences as reflected in the variables to be included in the core UK macroeconomic

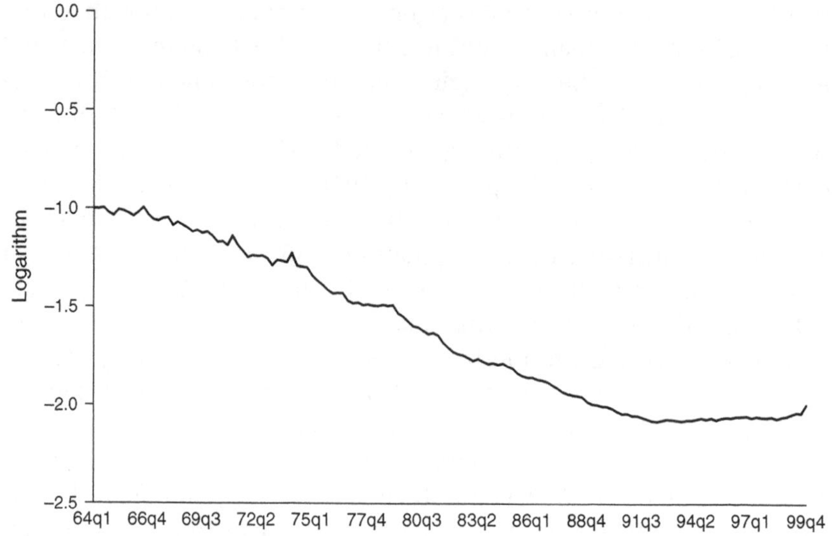

Figure 8.7a Money income ratio, $h_t - y_t$.

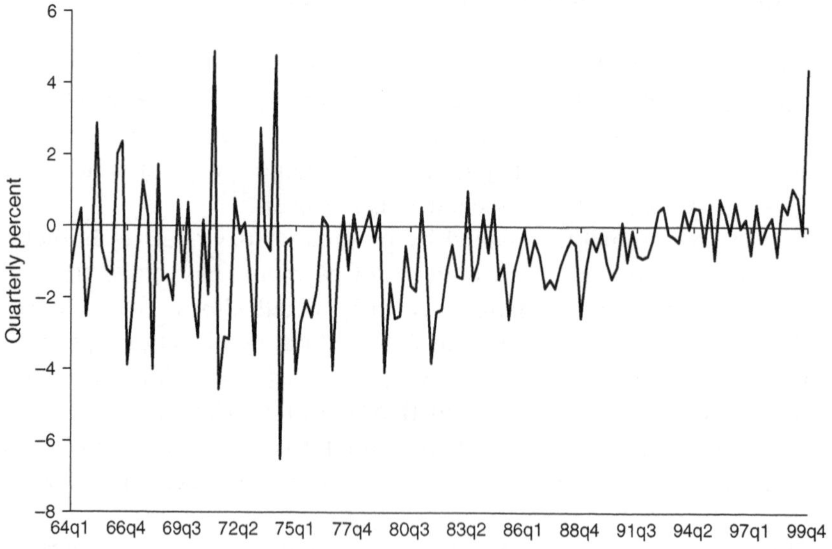

Figure 8.7b First difference of the money income ratio, $\Delta(h_t - y_t)$.

model. The overview is not intended to provide a comprehensive economic history of the UK economy over the last three decades, but provides a useful statement of some of the major events that lie behind the data presented to place the econometric analysis in context. This formal econometric analysis follows in the next chapter.

9

A long-run structural model of the UK

In this chapter, we describe the estimation and testing of the core long-run model of the UK economy set out in Chapter 4. This involves the estimation of a VECM of the form defined in equation (4.46) which for convenience we reproduce here:

$$\Delta \mathbf{y}_t = \mathbf{a}_y + \boldsymbol{\alpha}_y \mathbf{b}_0 - \boldsymbol{\alpha}_y \boldsymbol{\beta}' \left[\mathbf{z}_{t-1} - \boldsymbol{\gamma}(t-1) \right] + \sum_{i=1}^{p-1} \boldsymbol{\Gamma}_{yi} \Delta \mathbf{z}_{t-i} + \boldsymbol{\psi}_{yo} \Delta p_t^o + \mathbf{u}_{yt}, \tag{9.1}$$

where $\boldsymbol{\beta}'\boldsymbol{\gamma} = \mathbf{b}_1$ in (4.46). In this specification, $\mathbf{z}_t$ is partitioned as $\mathbf{z}_t = (p_t^o, \mathbf{y}_t')'$, where $\mathbf{y}_t = (e_t, r_t^*, r_t, \Delta\widetilde{p}_t, y_t, p_t - p_t^*, h_t - y_t, y_t^*)'$, $\mathbf{a}_y$ is an 8×1 vector of fixed intercepts, $\boldsymbol{\alpha}_y$ is an 8×5 matrix of error correction coefficients (also known as the loading coefficient matrix), $\boldsymbol{\Gamma}_{yi}$, $i = 1, 2, \ldots, p-1$, are 8×9 matrices of short-run coefficients, $\boldsymbol{\psi}_{yo}$ is an 8×1 vector representing the impact effects of changes in oil prices on $\Delta \mathbf{y}_t$, $\mathbf{u}_{yt}$ is an 8×1 vector of disturbances assumed to be $i.i.d.(0, \boldsymbol{\Sigma}_y)$, with $\boldsymbol{\Sigma}_y$ being a positive definite matrix, and by construction uncorrelated with u_{ot}, and $\boldsymbol{\beta}'(\mathbf{z}_{t-1} - \boldsymbol{\gamma}(t-1))$ is an $r \times 1$ vector of error correction terms. The long-run theory suggests that $r = 5$, but our approach tests the hypothesis of $r = 5$ against alternative values for r.

The above specification embodies the economic theory's long-run predictions by construction, in contrast to the more usual approach where the starting point is an unrestricted VAR model, with some vague priors about the nature of the long-run relations. By including the trend inside the error correction term, the deterministic trend properties of the model do not change with the number of cointegrating vectors, r.

9.1 The different stages of estimation and testing

As a general guide to the application of the econometric techniques described in Chapter 6, and as a precursor to our own analysis of the core model, we now describe the sequence of steps we followed in our empirical work. Note that in order to incorporate the long-run relationships into a suitable model, as defined above, it is important that the variables used in the empirical analysis can be reasonably argued to be $I(1)$. Hence the preliminary stage in any analysis is to establish the orders of integration of the variables in the vector $\mathbf{z}_t$ and we do this in the next section.[1] Following on from this, we can identify five stages of the estimation procedure.

First, a sequence of unrestricted VAR(p), $p = 0, 1, 2, \ldots, 6$ models are estimated over the same sample period, 1965q1–1999q4. The maximum lag order, 6, is in some sense arbitrary, but is chosen *a priori* bearing in mind the quarterly nature of the observations, and the size of the available sample (namely, 140 quarterly observations). The order of VAR model to be used in the analysis is then selected in the light of the Akaike Information Criterion (AIC) and the Schwarz Bayesian Criterion (SBC).

Second, having established the appropriate order of the VAR model, cointegration tests are carried out using the trace and the maximum eigenvalue statistics, reviewed in Chapter 6. The results of these tests can be inconclusive. So the test results need to be carefully interpreted in conjunction with the theory's prediction described in Chapter 4, before a decision is made concerning the number of the cointegrating relations that are most likely to exist among the variables under investigation.

Third, having decided that there exist, say, r cointegrating vectors among the variables, we are in a position to estimate an exactly identified set of long-run relations, in which r^2 restrictions are imposed on the cointegrating vectors (r restrictions on each of the r vectors). In one sense, the choice of the exactly identifying restrictions is arbitrary: the maximised value of the log-likelihood of the system will be the same irrespective of how the long-run relations are exactly identified. In another sense, however, the choice of exactly identifying restrictions is crucial, as it provides the basis for the development of an econometric model with economically meaningful long-run properties. It is therefore important that the cointegrating

[1] It is, however, important to note that in testing the rank of the cointegrating space, it is not necessary that the underlying variables should all be $I(1)$. The problem arises in interpreting the long-run relations; since an $I(0)$ variable can be viewed trivially as forming a cointegrating relationship with the other variables using $\beta = (0, \ldots, 0, 1, 0, \ldots, 0)$ as a cointegrating vector, with the non-zero element attached to the $I(0)$ variable in question.

relations are exactly identified by imposing restrictions that are a subset of those suggested by economic theory. It is also a good practice to avoid using doubtful theory restrictions as exact identifying restrictions. Estimation of the parameters of the core model, (9.1), can be carried out using the long-run structural modelling approach in described in Chapter 6.

The *fourth* step in the analysis considers the imposition and testing of over-identifying restrictions on the cointegrating vectors, as predicted by economic theory. This analysis is carried out along the lines set out in Pesaran and Shin (2002) and Pesaran, Shin and Smith (2000) and involves the ML estimation of the model subject to the exactly and over-identifying restrictions. The tests of over-identifying restrictions will now be in the form of the familiar χ^2 tests with degrees of freedom equal to the number of the over-identifying restrictions. It is worth noting that this is a system-estimation procedure, and the likelihood function in terms of the cointegrating vectors can be quite complicated, so that the existence of local maxima cannot be ruled out, and the search for the global maximum might be difficult. To avoid convergence problems, it is often advisable to impose over-identifying restrictions one-at-a-time and, as far as possible, in a sequence that can be meaningfully interpreted so that information can be obtained on which of the restrictions is more or less likely to be accepted by the data.[2] Another possibility would be to start from fully specified long-run relationships and then relax some of the theory restrictions one at a time.

The *fifth* step in the analysis concerns the interpretation of the results. The imposition of long-run, theory-based restrictions yield error correction terms that can be interpreted as characterising disequilibria in particular markets, and the associated error correction regressions show the short-run evolution of the variables in the model in response to deviations from equilibrium and to past changes in the variables of the model. The error correction regressions are also subjected to diagnostic tests for residual serial correlation, non-normal errors, functional form misspecification, and heteroscedasticity as is usual in the case of standard regression analysis. The magnitudes of some of the estimated regression coefficients provide useful information on the dynamics of the system, highlighting which of the variables have large and statistically significant effects on each other, although care needs to be exercised in the interpretation of

[2] The interpretation of this sequence of restriction tests should also be sensitive to the fact that asymptotic critical values of over-identifying restrictions tend to over-reject when applied to small samples, and in some cases by a large amount, as discussed earlier in Section 6.4.

the coefficients on the error correction terms as far as the stability of the system as a whole is concerned (as discussed in Chapter 6).

As part of assessing the model we would also need to analyse its dynamics. This involves the use of persistence profiles, impulse responses and probability forecasting which we discuss in Chapters 10 and 11.

9.2 Unit root properties of the core variables

Before the estimation of the model can begin, it is important that the unit root properties of the variables under investigation are established to enable sensible interpretation of the long-run relations. The limitations of the standard tests for unit roots (such as the Dickey and Fuller (1979) or the Phillips and Perron (1988) tests) are well-known, but they nevertheless provide important information on the nature of the persistence of the time series under investigation. For example, it might be difficult to come to a clear-cut conclusion over whether the effects of a shock to a particular variable take a long while to die away (for an $I(0)$ variable) or whether they will never die away (for an $I(1)$ variable) using existing tests and given the limited data available. Even such an ambiguous conclusion can be helpful, however, as it suggests that certain variables are on the borderline of being $I(0)/I(1)$ or $I(1)/I(2)$. For example, one might assume that a given variable is $I(1)$, perhaps on the basis of *a priori* economic reasoning, and subsequently carry out tests to establish the number of cointegrating relations between this and other $I(1)$ variables. The knowledge that this variable is close to being stationary, when considered in isolation, means that the tests of the number of cointegrating relationships are likely to support the presence of a higher number of cointegrating relations than would be the case if the variable in question was clearly $I(1)$.

The results of the Augmented Dickey–Fuller (ADF) and Phillips–Perron (PP) tests, computed over the sample period for the levels and first differences of the core variables, are reported in Tables 9.1a and 9.1b.

Both sets of tests provide relatively strong support for the view that y_t, y_t^*,r_t, r_t^*, e_t, $(h_t - y_t)$ and p_t^o are $I(1)$ series. The unit root hypothesis is clearly rejected when applied to the first differences of these variables, but there is no evidence with which to reject the unit root hypothesis when the tests are applied to the levels. There is, however, some ambiguity regarding the order of integration of the price variables. Application of the ADF test to Δp_t, $\Delta \widetilde{p}_t$ and Δp_t^* yields mixed results: the hypothesis that there is a unit root in the domestic and foreign inflation rates

Table 9.1a Augmented Dickey–Fuller unit root tests applied to variables in the core model, 1965q1–1999q4.

Variable	ADF(0)	ADF(1)	ADF(2)	ADF(3)	ADF(4)
(i) For the first differences					
Δy_t	−11.94	−8.06	−5.40[a]	−5.18	−4.81
Δy_t^*	−7.43	−5.28[a]	−4.53	−4.22	−4.11
Δr_t	−10.54	−7.79	−7.49	−6.08	−6.30[a]
Δr_t^*	−7.06[a]	−6.19	−4.89	−4.85	−4.54
Δe_t	−9.81[a]	−7.89	−6.45	−5.52	−5.39
$\Delta(h_t - y_t)$	−12.21[a]	−8.16	−5.79	−4.82	−3.13
Δp_t	−3.50[a]	−3.19	−2.67	−2.44	−2.43
$\Delta \tilde{p}_t$	−4.41	−3.05[a]	−2.97	−2.42	−2.23
Δp_t^*	−5.06	−3.47	−2.73[a]	−2.75	−2.90
Δp_t^o	−11.05[a]	−8.71	−6.41	−5.68	−5.71
$\Delta^2 p_t$	−13.32	−10.74[a]	−8.80	−7.15	−6.95
$\Delta^2 \tilde{p}_t$	−17.37	−10.22	−9.48	−8.06	−7.43
$\Delta^2 p_t^*$	−17.82	−12.75[a]	−8.63	−6.65	−6.43
$\Delta(p_t - p_t^*)$	−6.69	−4.91	−3.72[a]	−3.60	−3.32
(ii) For the levels					
y_t	−2.32	−2.33	−2.46	−3.14[a]	−3.06
y_t^*	−3.37	−3.18	−3.22[a]	−3.24	−3.22
r_t	−2.23	−2.57[a]	−2.65	−2.32	−2.46
r_t^*	−1.24	−2.47[a]	−2.46	−2.86	−2.71
e_t	−1.03	−1.45[a]	−1.32	−1.33	−1.37
$h_t - y_t$	1.41	1.82[a]	2.00	1.83	1.86
p_t	2.21	−0.39[a]	−0.48	−0.76	−0.90
$\tilde{p}_t$	2.12	−0.03	−0.61[a]	−0.57	−0.88
p_t^*	1.83	−0.07	−0.73	−1.20[a]	−1.13
p_t^o	−1.43[a]	−1.53	−1.38	−1.49	−1.44
$p_t - p_t^*$	0.47	−0.40	−0.66	−1.01[a]	−0.96

Note: When applied to the first differences, augmented Dickey–Fuller (1979, ADF) test statistics are computed using ADF regressions with an intercept and p lagged first differences of dependent variable, while when applied to the levels, ADF statistics are computed using ADF regressions with an intercept, a linear time trend and p lagged first differences of dependent variable, with the exception of the following variables: r_t and r_t^* where only an intercept was included in the underlying ADF regressions. The relevant lower 5% critical values for the ADF tests are −2.88 for the former and −3.45 for the latter. The symbol '*a*' denotes the order of augmentation in the Dickey–Fuller regressions chosen using the Akaike Information Criterion, with a maximum lag order of four.

is rejected for low orders of augmentation (namely, for $p = 0$ and 1), but not for higher orders. The application of the PP test rejects the unit root hypothesis when applied to Δp_t^*, Δp_t and $\Delta \tilde{p}_t$. Overall the available data is not informative as to whether domestic and foreign prices are $I(1)$ or $I(2)$.

These preliminary results regarding the unit roots properties of the core variables raise interesting issues concerning the use of economic theory

Table 9.1b Phillips and Perron unit root tests applied to variables in the core model, 1965q1–1999q4.

Variable	PP(0)	PP(5)	PP(10)	PP(15)	PP(20)
(i) For the first differences					
Δy_t	−11.94	−12.00	−12.02	−11.95	−11.98
Δy_t^*	−7.43	−7.68	−7.73	−7.72	−7.80
Δr_t	−10.54	−10.50	−10.51	−10.67	−11.41
Δr_t^*	−7.06	−7.14	−6.84	−6.43	−6.27
Δe_t	−9.81	−9.75	−9.76	−9.81	−9.73
$\Delta(h_t - y_t)$	−12.21	−12.28	−12.55	−12.86	−13.22
Δp_t	−3.05	−3.30	−3.38	−3.64	−3.78
$\Delta \tilde{p}_t$	−4.41	−4.22	−4.70	−5.04	−5.32
Δp_t^*	−5.06	−5.07	−5.52	−5.91	−6.16
Δp_t^o	−11.05	−11.03	−11.03	−11.03	−11.03
$\Delta^2 p_t$	−13.32	−5.99	−4.49	−4.03	−2.76
$\Delta^2 \tilde{p}_t$	−17.37	−19.84	−21.27	−23.83	−25.96
$\Delta^2 p_t^*$	−17.82	−20.07	−22.92	−24.82	−28.66
$\Delta(p_t - p_t^*)$	−6.69	−6.96	−7.53	−7.87	−8.01
(ii) For the levels					
y_t	−2.32	−2.70	−2.84	−2.70	−2.47
y_t^*	−3.37	−3.07	−3.08	−3.14	−3.22
r_t	−2.23	−2.45	−2.37	−2.24	−2.02
r_t^*	−1.24	−2.13	−2.03	−1.72	−1.54
e_t	−1.03	−1.29	−1.29	−1.35	−1.17
$h_t - y_t$	1.41	1.90	1.85	1.87	1.83
p_t	2.21	0.43	0.01	−0.22	−0.36
$\tilde{p}_t$	2.12	0.45	0.02	−0.18	−0.31
p_t^*	1.83	−1.45	−1.43	−1.46	−1.45
p_t^o	−1.43	−1.45	−1.43	−1.46	−1.45
$p_t - p_t^*$	0.47	−0.43	−0.69	−0.78	−0.79

Note: $PP(\ell)$ represents Phillips and Perron (1988) unit root statistic based on the Bartlett window of size ℓ. In the first difference equations, *PP* test statistics are obtained including only an intercept in the underlying *DF* regressions; in the levels equations, *PP* test statistics are obtained including an intercept and a time trend in the underlying *DF* regressions, with the exception of the following variables; r_t and r_t^* where no trend is included. The relevant lower 5% critical values are −2.88 for the first difference equations, and −3.45 for the levels equations.

and statistical evidence in macroeconometric modelling. Starting from the long-run theory set out in Chapter 4, the validity of the Fisher equation requires that inflation and interest rates have the same order of integration. The theoretical literature generally assumes that these series are $I(0)$, but as we have seen above the empirical evidence is mixed with the interest rate behaving as an $I(1)$ variable and the inflation rate being a borderline case.[3] There is, therefore, a trade-off between the demands of

[3] In this book we are confining the modelling exercise to log-linear specifications and a more complicated non-linear model might be needed for interest rates and inflation, as argued,

theory and econometrics. Our approach to this dilemma is a pragmatic one, aiming to adequately capture the statistical properties of the data in a modelling framework which, at the same time, is coherent with our underlying analytic account of how the economy operates. For these reasons, in our work, we treat r_t, r_t^*, Δp_t, $\Delta \widetilde{p}_t$ and Δp_t^* as $I(1)$ variables. This allows the empirical model to adequately represent the statistical features of the series over the sample period and provides the scope for accommodating in the model the long-run relationships described in Chapter 4.

Of course, domestic and foreign prices appear in their *level* in the PPP relationship of (4.35) and this raises the potential difficulty of mixing $I(1)$ and $I(2)$ variables. Haldrup's (1998) review of the econometric analysis of $I(2)$ variables warns of the dangers of the inappropriate application of econometric methods designed for use with $I(1)$ variables and suggests that it is often useful to transform time series *a priori* to obtain variables that are unambiguously $I(1)$ rather than dealing with mixtures of $I(1)$ and $I(2)$ variables directly. In the case of the core variables under consideration, this is achieved by working with the relative price variables $p_t - p_t^*$ rather than the two price levels p_t and p_t^* separately. As shown in Table 9.1a, the relative price term is unambiguously $I(1)$ according to the ADF statistics.

The decision to include domestic prices in the model in two forms, $(p_t - p_t^*)$ and $\Delta \widetilde{p}_t$ does not create difficulties of inconsistency either algebraically or economically (and would not do so even if we used Δp_t in place of $\Delta \widetilde{p}_t$ in the model). Ignoring the distinction between p_t and $\widetilde{p}_t$ for the moment, we note that the associated structural model of (5.2) contains nine equations in eight endogenous variables. One of the nine equations corresponds to the determination of domestic prices p_t and one corresponds to the determination of foreign prices p_t^* and this is entirely consistent with the fact that the domestic price variable influences the relative price variable and the inflation variable when the model is estimated. Further, there is considerable evidence, both on the basis of our own analysis and elsewhere, that the various alternative measures of inflation that are available are pairwise cointegrated with a cointegrating vector of $(1, -1)$ and a zero constant. The use of two measures of prices, p_t and $\widetilde{p}_t$, in the analysis has no impact on the long-run properties of the

for example, in Pesaran, Timmermann and Pettenuzzo (2004). Such an approach is worth considering but lies outside the scope of the present work.

model, therefore, but is likely to capture the short-run dynamics more accurately.

In summary, then, we can say that it seems appropriate to view all nine variables of $z_t = (p^o_t, e_t, r^*_t, r_t, \Delta\widetilde{p}_t, y_t, p_t - p^*_t, h_t - y_t, y^*_t)'$ as approximately $I(1)$ on the basis of the unit root statistics reported. We therefore conducted our analysis on this basis, although the ambiguity regarding the $\Delta\widetilde{p}_t$ variable needs to be borne in mind in interpreting the subsequent results.

9.3 Testing and estimating of the long-run relations

The first stage of our modelling sequence is to select the order of the underlying VAR using AIC and SBC reported in Table 9.2.

Here we find that a VAR of order two appears to be appropriate when using the AIC as the model selection criterion, but not surprisingly that the SBC favours a VAR of order one. We proceed with the cointegration analysis using a VAR(2), on the grounds that the consequences of overestimation of the order of the VAR are much less serious than underestimating it; see Kilian (2002).[4]

Using a VAR(2) model with unrestricted intercepts and restricted trend coefficients, and treating the oil price variable, p^o_t, as a weakly exogenous $I(1)$, or long-run forcing, variable, we computed Johansen's 'trace'

Table 9.2 Akaike and Schwarz Information Criteria for lag order selection.

Lag length	Log likelihood	AIC	SBC
6	4641.2	4155.2	3440.4
5	4538.7	4133.7	3538.0
4	4459.0	4135.0	3658.4
3	4389.0	4146.0	3788.5
2	4326.0	4164.0	3925.7
1	4222.3	4141.3	4022.2
0	1775.6	1775.6	1775.6

[4] Note that, if the dimension of the VAR is large, then a relatively low lag order can be selected and still accommodate rich dynamic specifications at the level of individual series. Specifically, if the $m \times 1$ vector z_t follows a p-order autoregression, then in general the individual elements follow an $ARMA\,(mp, mp - p)$ process. See Hamilton (1994, p. 349). In our application where $m = 9$ and $p = 2$, the univariate representation of the individual series could be $ARMA(18, 16)$.

Table 9.3 Cointegration rank test statistics for the core model, $(p_t - p_t^*, e_t, r_t, r_t^*, y_t, y_t^*, h_t - y_t, \Delta\widetilde{p}_t, p_t^o)$.

H_0	H_1	Test statistic	95% Critical values	90% Critical values
(a) Trace statistic				
$r = 0$	$r = 1$	324.75	199.12	192.80
$r \leq 1$	$r = 2$	221.16	163.01	157.02
$r \leq 2$	$r = 3$	161.88	128.79	123.33
$r \leq 3$	$r = 4$	116.14	97.83	93.13
$r \leq 4$	$r = 5$	78.94	72.10	68.04
$r \leq 5$	$r = 6$	48.71	49.36	46.00
$r \leq 6$	$r = 7$	22.46	30.77	27.96
$r \leq 7$	$r = 8$	6.70	15.44	13.31
(b) Maximum eigenvalue statistic				
$r = 0$	$r = 1$	103.59	58.08	55.25
$r \leq 1$	$r = 2$	59.27	52.62	49.70
$r \leq 2$	$r = 3$	45.75	46.97	44.01
$r \leq 3$	$r = 4$	37.20	40.89	37.92
$r \leq 4$	$r = 5$	30.23	34.70	32.12
$r \leq 5$	$r = 6$	26.25	28.72	26.10
$r \leq 6$	$r = 7$	15.76	22.16	19.79
$r \leq 7$	$r = 8$	6.70	15.44	13.31

Note: The underlying VAR model is of order 2 and contains unrestricted intercepts and restricted trend coefficients, with p_t^o treated as an exogenous $I(1)$ variable. The statistics refer to Johansen's log-likelihood-based trace and maximal eigenvalue statistics and are computed using 140 observations for the period 1965q1–1999q4. The asymptotic critical values are taken from Pesaran, Shin and Smith (2000).

and 'maximal eigenvalue' statistics.[5] These statistics, together with their associated 90% and 95% critical values, are reported in Table 9.3.

The maximal eigenvalue statistic indicates the presence of just two cointegrating relationships at the 5% significance level, which does not support our *a priori* expectations of five cointegrating vectors. However, as shown by Cheung and Lai (1993), the maximum eigenvalue test is generally less robust to the presence of skewness and excess kurtosis in the errors than the trace test. Given that we have evidence of non-normality in the residuals of the VAR model used to compute the test statistics, we therefore believe it is more appropriate to base our cointegration tests on the trace statistics. As it happens the trace statistics reject the null hypotheses that $r = 0, 1, 2, 3$ and 4 at the 5% level of significance but cannot reject the null hypothesis that $r = 5$. This is in line with our *a priori* expectations based on the long-run theory of Chapter 4, which suggests the

[5] An account of the algorithms used for the computation of cointegration test statistics in the presence of $I(1)$ exogenous variables can be found, for example, in Pesaran, Shin and Smith (2000).

existence of five possible long-run relations, reproduced below for ease of exposition:

$$p_t - p_t^* - e_t = b_{10} + b_{11}t + \xi_{1,t+1} \tag{9.2}$$

$$r_t - r_t^* = b_{20} + \xi_{2,t+1} \tag{9.3}$$

$$y_t - y_t^* = b_{30} + \xi_{3,t+1} \tag{9.4}$$

$$h_t - y_t = b_{40} + b_{41}t + \beta_{44}r_t + \beta_{46}y_t + \xi_{4,t+1} \tag{9.5}$$

$$r_t - \Delta p_t = b_{50} + \xi_{5,t+1}. \tag{9.6}$$

Proceeding under the assumption that there are five cointegrating vectors, the five long-run relations of the core model, (9.2)–(9.6), can be written more compactly as

$$\boldsymbol{\xi}_t = \boldsymbol{\beta}'_{TH}\mathbf{z}_{t-1} - \mathbf{b}_0 - \mathbf{b}_1(t-1), \tag{9.7}$$

where

$$\mathbf{b}_0 = (b_{10}, b_{20}, b_{30}, b_{40}, b_{50})',$$
$$\mathbf{b}_1 = (b_{11}, 0, 0, b_{41}, 0)',$$
$$\boldsymbol{\xi}_t = (\xi_{1t}, \xi_{2t}, \xi_{3t}, \xi_{4t}, \xi_{5t})',$$

and

$$\boldsymbol{\beta}'_{TH} = \begin{pmatrix} 0 & -1 & 0 & 0 & 0 & 0 & 1 & 0 & 0 \\ 0 & 0 & -1 & 1 & 0 & 0 & 0 & 0 & 0 \\ 0 & 0 & 0 & 0 & 0 & 1 & 0 & 0 & -1 \\ 0 & 0 & 0 & -\beta_{44} & 0 & -\beta_{46} & 0 & 1 & 0 \\ 0 & 0 & 0 & 1 & -1 & 0 & 0 & 0 & 0 \end{pmatrix}. \tag{9.8}$$

The matrix $\boldsymbol{\beta}'_{TH}$, as described in equation (9.8), imposes all the restrictions necessary to correspond to the long-run relationships and as such is *over-identified*. However, the first step in the estimation is to exactly identify the long run, which with five cointegrating relations requires five restrictions on each relationship. In view of the underlying long-run theory as encapsulated in the relations (9.2)–(9.6), we impose 25 *exactly* identifying restrictions on the cointegrating matrix (in the form of five restrictions on each of the five cointegrating vectors) so that the exactly identified cointegrating matrix is given by:

$$\beta'_{EX} = \begin{pmatrix} \beta_{11} & \beta_{12} & 0 & 0 & \beta_{15} & 0 & 1 & \beta_{18} & 0 \\ \beta_{21} & 0 & \beta_{23} & 1 & \beta_{25} & 0 & 0 & 0 & \beta_{29} \\ \beta_{31} & 0 & 0 & 0 & 0 & 1 & \beta_{37} & \beta_{38} & \beta_{39} \\ \beta_{41} & 0 & 0 & -\beta_{44} & \beta_{45} & -\beta_{46} & 0 & 1 & 0 \\ \beta_{51} & 0 & 0 & \beta_{54} & -1 & 0 & 0 & \beta_{58} & \beta_{59} \end{pmatrix}. \quad (9.9)$$

The first vector (the first row of β'_{EX}) relates to the purchasing power parity (*PPP*) relationship defined by (9.2) and is normalised on $p_t - p_t^*$; the second relates to the interest rate parity (*IRP*) relationship defined by (9.3) and is normalised on r_t; the third relates to the 'output gap' (*OG*) relationship defined by (9.4) and is normalised on y_t;[6] the fourth is the money market equilibrium condition (*MME*) defined by (9.5) and is normalised on $h_t - y_t$.; and the fifth is the real interest rate relationship (*FIP*) defined by (9.6), normalised on $\Delta\widetilde{p}_t$.

Having exactly identified the long-run relations, we then tested the over-identifying restrictions predicted by the long-run theory. There are 20 unrestricted parameters in (9.9) and, based on the theory restrictions as set out in (9.8), there are 18 theory-based over-identifying restrictions that could be tested. Note that the theory does not restrict two of the parameters of the money demand equation (β_{44} and β_{46}) in the fourth row of β_{TH} defined by (9.8). In addition, working with a cointegrating VAR with restricted trend coefficients (as described in Sections 6.2.1 and 6.2.3), there are potentially five further parameters on the trend terms in the five co-integrating relationships. There is no economic rationale for including time trends in the *IRP*, *FIP* or *OG* relationships, and the imposition of zeros on the trend coefficients in these relationships provides a further three over-identifying restrictions. The absence of a trend in the *PPP* relationship is also consistent with the theory of Chapter 4, as is the restriction that $\beta_{46} = 0$ (so that equation (9.5) is effectively a relationship explaining the velocity of circulation of money). Hence, once the long-run theory is fully imposed, there are just two parameters to be freely estimated in the cointegrating relationships, and there are a total of 23 over-identifying restrictions on which the core model is based and with which the validity of the long-run economic theory can be tested.

[6] Our use of the term 'output gap relationship' to describe (9.4) should not be confused with the more usual use of the term which relates more specifically to the difference between a country's actual and potential output levels (although clearly the two uses of the term are related and, for some open economies, the foreign output variable might provide a good proxy for potential output).

9.3.1 *Small sample properties of the tests of restrictions on the cointegrating vectors*

When testing the linear restrictions implied by our long-run theory, we need to take account of the relatively small sample size available. This issue arises in our example despite having 140 quarterly observations as we are investigating the properties of a large dimensioned VARX model subject to a large number of over-identifying restrictions. In order to deal with the small sample bias, we apply the methods described in Section 6.4. These methods involve a bootstrapping exercise to investigate and accommodate the small sample properties of the log-likelihood ratio (LR) test of over-identifying restrictions, generating a simulated distribution for the test statistic when only a small sample is available and using this to derive appropriate critical values against which to compare the estimated test statistic.

Specifically, the LR test for jointly testing the 23 over-identifying restrictions described above and implied by our long-run theory takes the value 71.49. To compute appropriate small sample critical values, we adopt a bootstrap procedure based on 3000 replications of the LR statistic testing the 23 restrictions. For each replication, an artificial dataset is generated (of the same length as the original dataset) on the assumption that the estimated version of the core model is the true data-generating process, using the observed initial values of each variable, the estimated model, and a set of random innovations. These innovations can be obtained as draws from a multivariate normal distribution chosen to match the observed correlation of the estimated reduced form errors (termed a 'parametric bootstrap') or by re-sampling with replacement from the estimated residuals (a 'non-parametric bootstrap'). In the light of the evidence of non-normality of residuals that we found in estimation, we apply the non-parametric bootstrap in this exercise (see Chapter 7 for further details). For each simulated dataset, the cointegrating VAR is estimated first subject to the exactly identifying restrictions of (9.9) and then subject to the over-identifying restrictions of (9.8).[7] The LR test of the over-identifying

[7] Given the complexity of the likelihood in the over-identified case, the choice of the optimisation algorithm to be used in maximising the likelihood may be important in this exercise. We found the Simulated Annealing routine by Goffe *et al.* (1994) to be useful. The simulated annealing algorithm explores a function's entire surface and tries to optimise the function while moving both uphill and downhill. It is therefore largely independent of starting values, and it can escape local minima and go on to find the global optimum by the uphill and downhill moves. Simulated annealing also makes less stringent assumptions on the form of the function than conventional algorithms and can therefore deal more easily with functions that have ridges and plateaux. Hence it is less likely to fail on difficult functions and is more robust than conventional Newton–Raphson and David–Fletcher–Powell uphill-only algorithms.

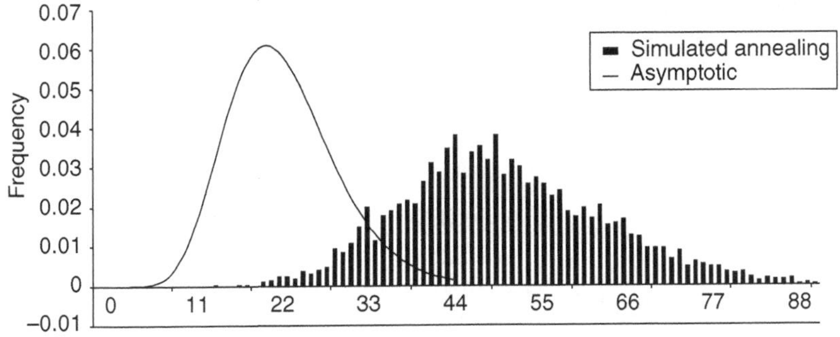

Figure 9.1 Asymptotic and empirical distribution generated by the simulated annealing algorithm of the test of the long-run over-identifying restrictions.

restrictions is carried out on each of the replicated datasets and the empirical distribution of the test statistic is derived across all replications.

Figure 9.1 illustrates the empirical distribution obtained in this way, plotting this alongside the corresponding asymptotic χ^2_{23} distribution. The figure shows the empirical distribution of the test statistic lies substantially to the right of its asymptotic counterpart, demonstrating clearly the need for taking into account the small sample in this instance.

The bootstrapped critical values for the joint tests of the 23 over-identifying restrictions are 67.51 at the 10% significance level and 73.19 at the 5% level. Using these bootstrapped critical values, the 23 theory restrictions cannot be rejected at the conventional 5% level. Moreover, it is worth noting that the simulation is used to find the probability of rejection for one point in H_0, taking the estimated parameters of the core model as given. The classical significance level is the *maximum* of the rejection probabilities over H_0. So, by using a single point, the observed critical values potentially understate the true rejection level. The fact that we (almost) fail to reject at the 5% level might provide more compelling evidence to support the validity of the restrictions than it first appears therefore.

9.4 The vector error correction model

9.4.1 *The long-run estimates*

The estimates of the long-run relations and the reduced form error correction specification are provided in Table 9.4 below. The long-run relations, which incorporate all the restrictions suggested by the theory in Chapter 4, are summarised below:

$$(p_t - p_t^*) - e_t = 4.588 + \widehat{\xi}_{1,t+1} \tag{9.10}$$

$$r_t - r_t^* = 0.0058 + \widehat{\xi}_{2,t+1} \tag{9.11}$$

$$y_t - y_t^* = -0.0377 + \widehat{\xi}_{3,t+1} \tag{9.12}$$

$$h_t - y_t = -0.0538 - \underset{(22.2844)}{56.0975}\, r_t - \underset{(0.0012)}{0.0073}\, t + \widehat{\xi}_{4,t+1} \tag{9.13}$$

$$r_t - \Delta\widetilde{p}_t = 0.0036 + \widehat{\xi}_{5,t+1}. \tag{9.14}$$

The bracketed figures are asymptotic standard errors. The first equation, (9.10), describes the *PPP* relationship and the failure to reject this in the context of our core model provides an interesting empirical finding. Of course, there has been considerable interest in the literature examining the co-movements of exchange rates and relative prices, and the empirical evidence on *PPP* appears to be sensitive to the dataset used and the way in which the analysis is conducted. For example, the evidence of a unit root in the real exchange rate found by Darby (1983) and Huizinga (1988) contradicts *PPP* as a long-run relationship, while Grilli and Kaminsky (1991) and Lothian and Taylor (1996) have obtained evidence in favour of rejecting the unit root hypothesis in real exchange rates using longer annual series. In work investigating *PPP* using cointegration analysis, the results seem to be sensitive to whether the model is a trivariate one (including e_t, p_t and p_t^* in the VAR as separate variables) or a bivariate one (including e_t and $(p_t - p_t^*)$ as two separate variables). The null of no cointegration is rejected more frequently in trivariate than in bivariate analyses.[8] The finding here that *PPP* can be readily incorporated into the model is a useful contribution to this literature, indicating that the empirical evidence to support the relationship is stronger in a more complete model of the macroeconomy incorporating feedbacks and interactions omitted from more partial analyses.

The second cointegrating relation, defined by (9.11), is the *IRP* condition. This includes an intercept, which can be interpreted as the deterministic component of the risk premia associated with bonds and foreign exchange uncertainties. Its value is estimated at 0.0058, implying a risk premium of approximately 2.3% per annum. The empirical support we find for the *IRP* condition is in accordance with the results obtained in the literature, and is compatible with *UIP*, defined by (4.14). However, under

[8] See Taylor (1988) and Mark (1990) for illustrations of further work in this area, and Froot and Rogoff (1995) and MacDonald (1995) for a review of the literature.

the *UIP* hypothesis it is also required that a regression of $r_t - r_t^*$ on $\Delta \ln(E_{t+1})$ has a unit coefficient, but this is not supported by the data.

The third long-run relationship, given by (9.12), is the *OG* relationship with per capita domestic and foreign output (measured by the total OECD output) levels moving in tandem in the long run. It is noteworthy that the co-trending hypothesis cannot be rejected; *i.e.* the coefficient of the deterministic trend in the output gap equation is zero. This suggests that average long-run growth rate for the UK is the same as that in the rest of the OECD. This finding seems, in the first instance, to contradict some of the results obtained in the literature on the cointegrating properties of real output across countries. Campbell and Mankiw (1989), Cogley (1990) and Bernard and Durlauf (1995), for example, consider cointegration among international output series and find little evidence that outputs of different *pairs* of countries are cointegrated. However, our empirical analysis, being based on a single foreign output index, does not necessarily contradict this literature, which focuses on pairwise cointegration of output levels. The hypothesis advanced here, that y_t and y_t^* are cointegrated, is much less restrictive than the hypothesis considered in the literature that *all* pairs of output variables in the OECD are cointegrated.[9]

For the *MME* condition, given by (9.13), we could not reject the hypothesis that the elasticity of real money balances with respect to real output is equal to unity, and therefore (9.13) in fact represents an M0 velocity equation. The *MME* condition, however, contains a deterministic downward trend, representing the steady decline in the money–income ratio experienced in the UK over most of the period 1965–1999, arising primarily from the technological innovations in financial intermediation. There is also strong statistical evidence of a negative interest rate effect on real money balances. This long-run specification is comparable to recent research on the determinants of the UK narrow money velocity reported in, for example, Breedon and Fisher (1996).

Finally, the fifth equation, (9.14), defines the *FIP* relationship, where the estimated constant implies an annual real rate of return of approximately 1.44%. While the presence of this relationship might appear relatively uncontentious, there is empirical work in which the relationship does not seem to be supported by the empirical evidence; see, for example MacDonald and Murphy (1989) and Mishkin (1992). In La Cour and

[9] See Lee (1998) for further discussion of cross-country interdependence in growth dynamics. Pesaran (2004a) also provides an analysis of pairwise output gaps, showing that output convergence is not generally supported by the time series observations.

MacDonald (2000), evidence of a cointegrating relationship between interest rates and inflation was obtained in an analysis of financial data series from the euro area and US. However, the *FIP* relationship itself, with coefficients of $(1, -1)$ on the interest rate and inflation, was observed in the two zones only when the financial variables were incorporated into a larger macrosystem. Our results support the *FIP* relationship and again highlight the important role played by the *FIP* relationship in a model of the macroeconomy which can incorporate interactions between variables omitted from more partial analyses.

9.4.2 *Error correction specifications*

The short-run dynamics of the model are characterised by the eight error correction specifications given in Table 9.4.

The estimates of the error correction coefficients show that the long-run relations make an important contribution in most equations and that the error correction terms provide for a complex and statistically significant set of interactions and feedbacks across commodity, money and foreign exchange markets. The results in Table 9.4 also show that the core model fits the historical data well and has satisfactory diagnostic statistics. The diagnostic statistics of the equations in Table 9.4 are generally satisfactory as far as the tests of the residual serial correlation, functional form and heteroscedasticity are concerned. The assumption of normally distributed errors is rejected in all the error correction equations which is understandable if we consider the three major hikes in oil prices experienced during the estimation period and the special events that have afflicted the UK economy such as the three-day week, coal miners' strikes, the stock market crash of 1987 just to mention a few.

Figures 9.2a–9.2h plot the actual and fitted values for the reduced form error correction equations reported in Table 9.4.

These figures illustrate the extent to which the model fit the historical series. As might be expected, the exchange rate and domestic interest rate equations appear to have least explanatory power, with $\bar{R}^2$ of 0.07 and 0.12 respectively, and the model struggles to fit the observations of variables associated with the unusual events described above and during the volatile periods of the 1970s. But significant equilibrating pressures are found even in the Δe_t and Δr_t equations and, by-and-large, the fitted values seem to perform well in terms of tracking the main movements of all the dependent variables, reflecting the fact that the remaining $\bar{R}^2$ are relatively high and

Table 9.4 Reduced form error correction specification for the core model.

Equation	$\Delta(p_t - p_t^*)$	Δe_t	Δr_t	Δr_t^*	Δy_t	Δy_t^*	$\Delta(h_t - y_t)$	$\Delta(\Delta\tilde{p}_t)$
$\widehat{\xi}_{1,t}$	−0.015†	0.060†	0.002	0.002	0.017†	0.021†	−0.024*	−0.005
	(0.007)	(0.029)	(0.002)	(0.001)	(0.008)	(0.004)	(0.013)	(0.004)
$\widehat{\xi}_{2,t}$	−0.840†	1.42	0.049	0.130*	1.34†	0.891†	−0.721	−0.811†
	(0.301)	(1.28)	(0.107)	(0.043)	(0.353)	(0.181)	(0.576)	(0.297)
$\widehat{\xi}_{3,t}$	0.062†	−0.210*	−0.013	−0.006	−0.165†	−0.021	0.106*	0.034
	(0.029)	(0.121)	(0.010)	(0.004)	(0.034)	(0.017)	(0.055)	(0.028)
$\widehat{\xi}_{4,t}$	0.018†	−0.029	−0.003*	−0.001*	−0.027†	−0.016†	−0.003	0.009*
	(0.005)	(0.020)	(0.002)	(0.001)	(0.005)	(0.003)	(0.009)	(0.005)
$\widehat{\xi}_{5,t}$	−0.149*	−0.244	−0.054*	−0.024†	−0.099	−0.119†	0.408†	0.451†
	(0.083)	(0.353)	(0.028)	(0.012)	(0.098)	(0.050)	(0.159)	(0.082)
$\Delta(p_{t-1} - p_{t-1}^*)$	0.459†	0.150	−0.039	−0.028†	−0.136	−0.013	0.046	0.436†
	(0.095)	(0.404)	(0.032)	(0.014)	(0.111)	(0.057)	(0.182)	(0.094)
Δe_{t-1}	0.051†	0.216†	−0.005	−0.001	0.021	0.013	0.007	−0.022
	(0.022)	(0.092)	(0.007)	(0.003)	(0.025)	(0.013)	(0.042)	(0.021)
Δr_{t-1}	0.416†	−1.31	0.125	−0.067	0.467	0.204	−0.677	0.974†
	(0.294)	(1.25)	(0.098)	(0.042)	(0.345)	(0.177)	(0.562)	(0.290)
Δr_{t-1}^*	−0.810	2.75	−0.606†	0.430†	0.306	0.573	−0.267	0.166
	(0.617)	(2.62)	(0.205)	(0.088)	(0.723)	(0.371)	(1.18)	(0.606)
Δy_{t-1}	0.083	0.072	0.017	0.015	−0.044	0.031	−0.168	0.356†
	(0.089)	(0.381)	(0.030)	(0.013)	(0.105)	(0.053)	(0.172)	(0.089)
Δy_{t-1}^*	0.010	−0.630	−0.050	0.040*	−0.073	0.069	0.602*	−0.010
	(0.161)	(0.683)	(0.054)	(0.023)	(0.188)	(0.097)	(0.307)	(0.158)
$\Delta(h_{t-1} - y_{t-1})$	0.116	0.331	0.026	0.006	0.069	−0.014	−0.253†	0.140†
	(0.054)	(0.228)	(0.018)	(0.008)	(0.063)	(0.032)	(0.103)	(0.053)
$\Delta(\Delta\tilde{p}_{t-1})$	−0.151†	0.321	0.016	0.010	0.125	−0.082*	0.012	−0.244†
	(0.073)	(0.302)	(0.024)	(0.011)	(0.086)	(0.044)	(0.140)	(0.072)
Δp_t^o	−0.018†	−0.024	0.001	0.001†	−0.010†	0.0001	0.024†	0.003
	(0.004)	(0.018)	(0.001)	(0.0005)	(0.005)	(0.002)	(0.008)	(0.004)
Δp_{t-1}^o	0.010†	−0.013	−0.002	−0.0001	0.006	0.002	−0.011	0.016†
	(0.005)	(0.019)	(0.002)	(0.0001)	(0.005)	(0.003)	(0.009)	(0.004)
$\overline{R}^2$	0.484	0.070	0.115	0.345	0.260	0.367	0.257	0.445
Benchmark $\overline{R}^2$	0.316	0.026	0.007	0.213	0.022	0.194	0.00	0.191
$\hat{\sigma}$	0.007	0.032	0.002	0.001	0.009	0.004	0.014	0.007
$\chi^2_{SC}[4]$	2.79	0.96	2.43	17.13†	6.71	0.79	8.37†	5.63
$\chi^2_{FF}[1]$	8.57†	0.13	4.34†	6.70†	0.04	5.28†	0.033	0.01
$\chi^2_{N}[2]$	12.53†	13.98†	17.15†	19.9†	112.4†	10.84	31.45†	118.9†
$\chi^2_{H}[1]$	6.13†	1.97	4.53†	5.2†	0.88	0.93	0.19	4.55†

Note: The five error correction terms are given by

$$\widehat{\xi}_{1,t+1} = p_t - p_t^* - e_t - 4.588,$$

$$\widehat{\xi}_{2,t+1} = r_t - r_t^* - 0.0058,$$

$$\widehat{\xi}_{3,t+1} = y_t - y_t^* + 0.0377,$$

$$\widehat{\xi}_{4,t+1} = h_t - y_t + \underset{(22.2844)}{56.0975} r_t + \underset{(0.0012)}{0.0073} t + 0.05379,$$

$$\widehat{\xi}_{5,t+1} = r_t - \Delta\tilde{p}_t - 0.0036.$$

Standard errors are given in parentheses. '*' indicates significance at the 10% level, and '†' indicates significance at the 5% level. The diagnostics are chi-squared statistics for serial correlation (SC), functional form (FF), normality (N) and heteroscedasticity (H). The benchmark $\overline{R}^2$ statistics are computed based on univariate ARMA(s, q), $s, q = 0, 1, \ldots, 4$ specifications with the s and q orders selected by AIC; see text for details.

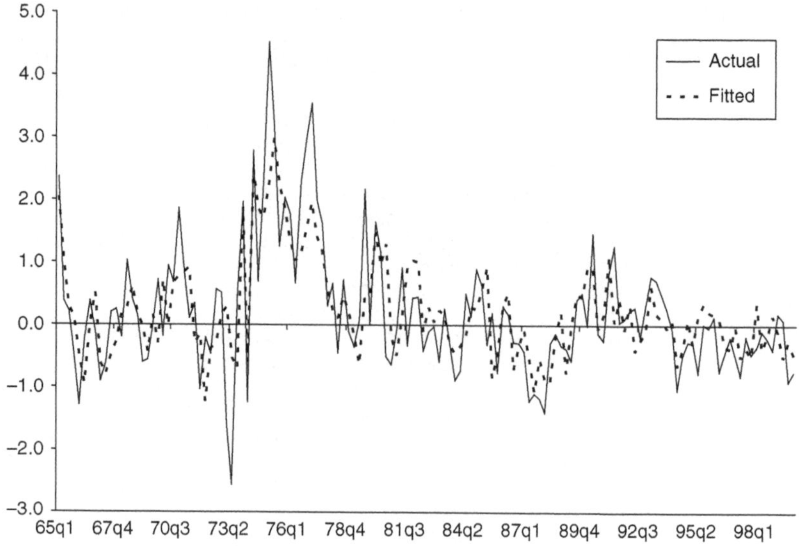

Figure 9.2a Actual and fitted values for the $\Delta(p_t - p_t^*)$ reduced form ECM equation.

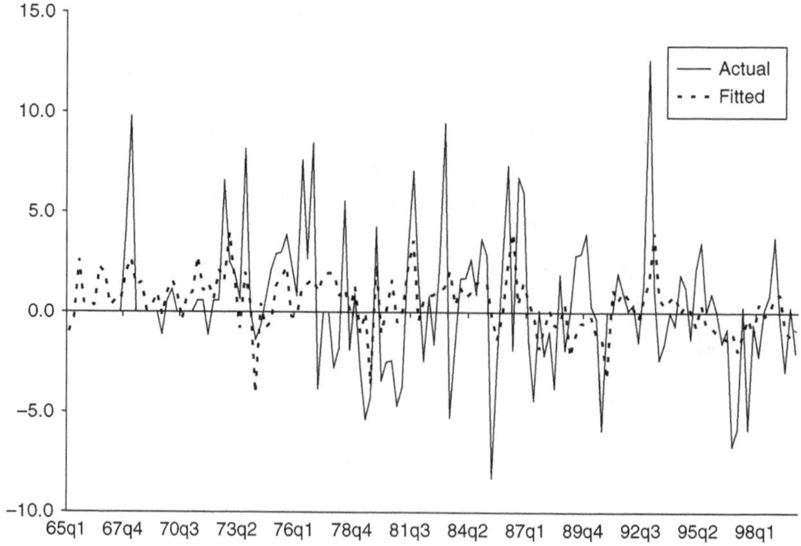

Figure 9.2b Actual and fitted values for the Δe_t reduced form ECM equation.

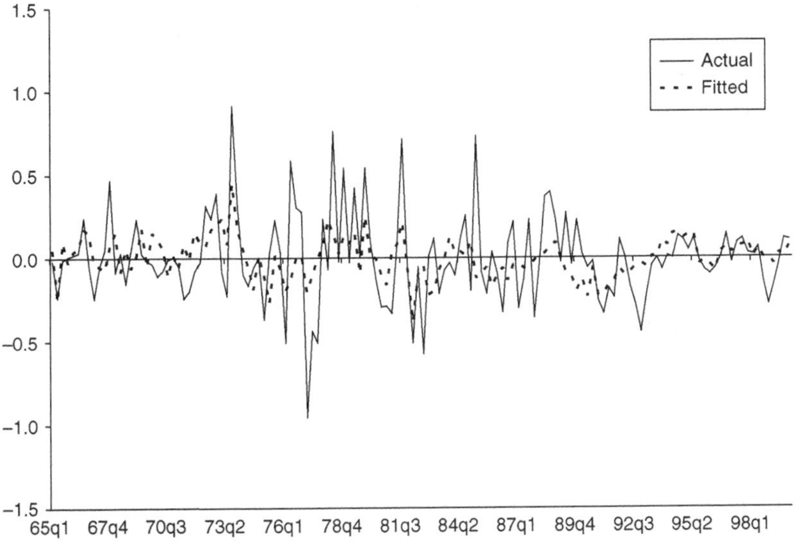

Figure 9.2c Actual and fitted values for the Δr_t reduced form ECM equation.

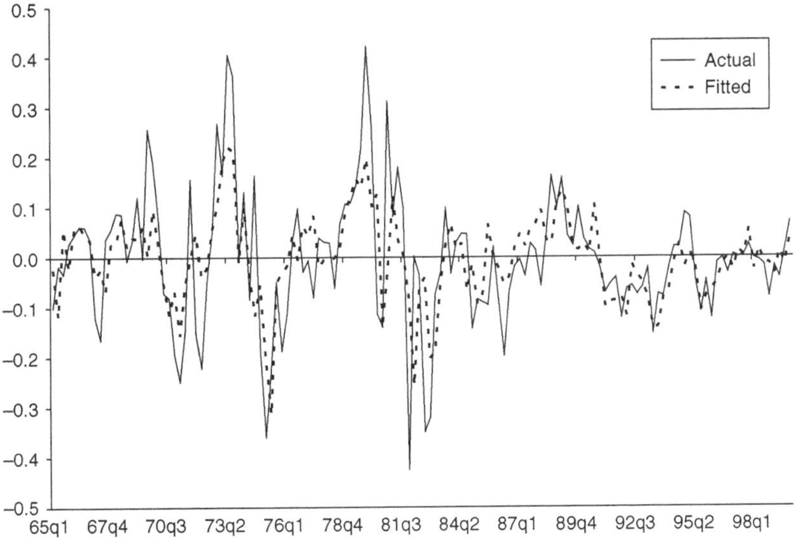

Figure 9.2d Actual and fitted values for the Δr_t^* reduced form ECM equation.

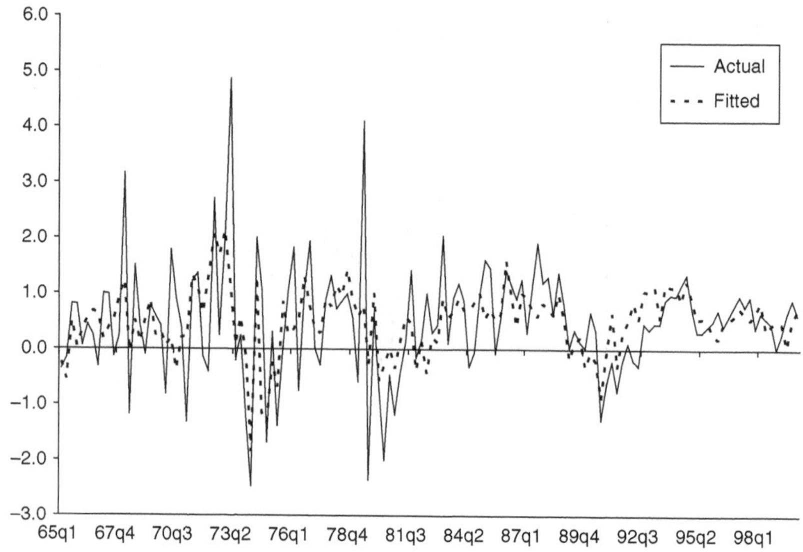

Figure 9.2e Actual and fitted values for the Δy_t reduced form ECM equation.

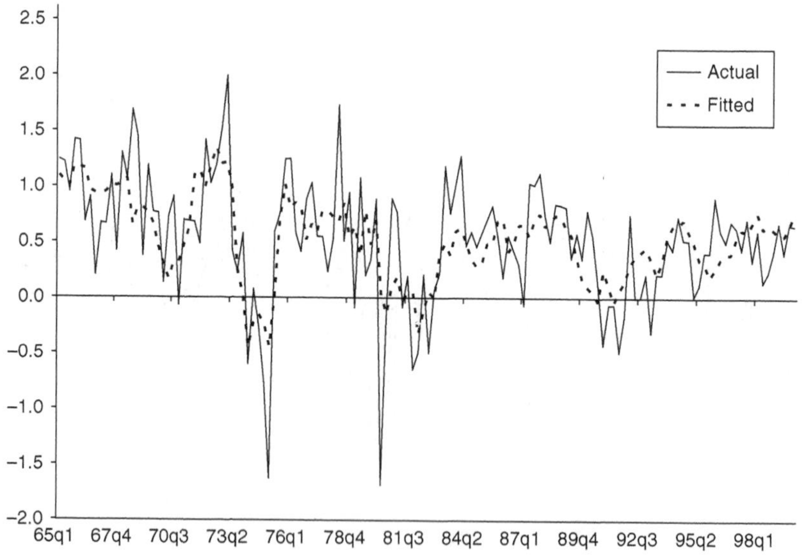

Figure 9.2f Actual and fitted values for the Δy_t^* reduced form ECM equation.

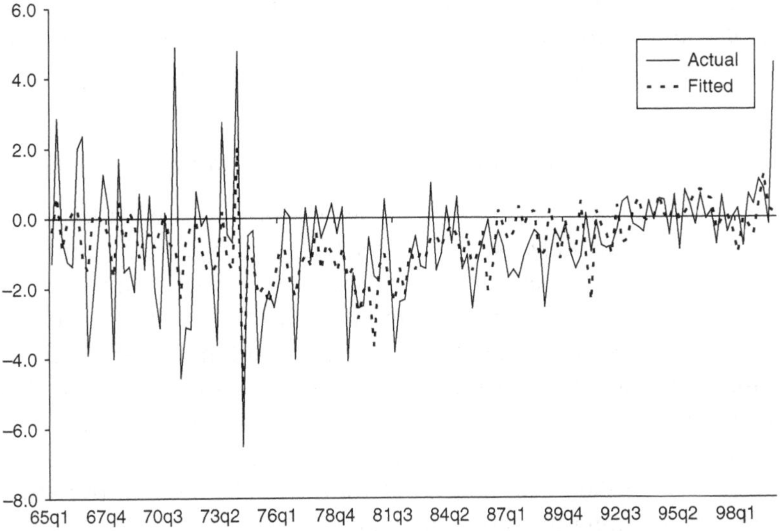

Figure 9.2g Actual and fitted values for the $\Delta(h_t - y_t)$ reduced form ECM equation.

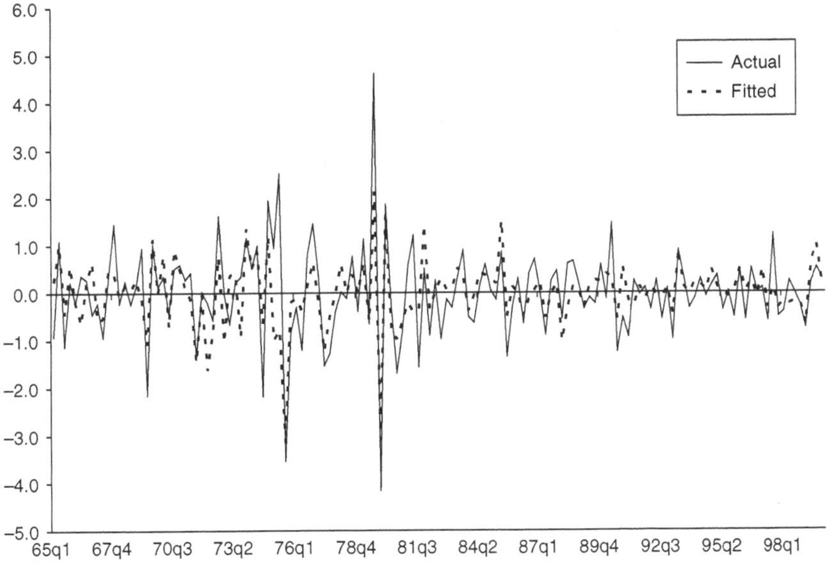

Figure 9.2h Actual and fitted values for the $\Delta(\Delta\widetilde{p}_t)$ reduced form ECM equation.

lie in the range [0.25, 0.49]. Generally speaking, then, the equations of Table 9.4 appear to capture well the time series properties of the main macroeconomic aggregates in the UK over the period since the mid-1960s.

9.4.3 *Comparing the core model with benchmark univariate models*

In order to evaluate the in-sample fit of the individual equations in the core long-run structural model a little more rigorously, we can compare the ECM specifications in Table 9.4 with a set of 'benchmark' univariate time series representations. To this end, and in view of the unit root properties of the variables, we estimate ARMA(p, q) specifications applied to the first differences of each of the eight core endogenous variables in turn. These benchmark models are selected following the Box–Jenkins methodology and allow us to address the question of how much, if at all, the explanatory power and potential forecasting ability of the model has improved by the adoption of the long-run structural modelling approach.[10]

We examine a range of ARMA models for each core endogenous variable. For example, in the case of the real output variable, y_t, the ARMA(p, q) specification can be written as:

$$\Delta y_t = \alpha + \sum_{i=1}^{p} \beta_i \Delta y_{t-i} + \sum_{i=1}^{q} \gamma_i \epsilon_{t-i} + \epsilon_t, \quad t = 1, \ldots, T. \tag{9.15}$$

The first requirement in the construction of the benchmark model is the selection of an *a priori* maximum lag order for the autoregressive and moving average processes, p and q, respectively. Here we choose 4, in light of the quarterly nature of the data, the number of available observations (140 observations for the sample period 1965q1–1999q4) and considering that the degree of serial correlation in the first difference of the macrovariables is not very high. We then examine the full set of model combinations that are spanned by all $p = 0, 1, \ldots, 4$ and $q = 0, 1, \ldots, 4$, providing 25 different combinations. Our preferred benchmark model is then selected on the basis of the Akaike Information Criterion (AIC).

The choice of AIC for model selection, compared with the Schwarz Bayesian Criterion (SBC) for example, relates to various practical and theoretical issues involved in the use of AIC and SBC. For example, choosing the SBC over AIC as a tool of model selection may be reasonable if we are

[10] Of course, these comparisons do not measure the usefulness of the more structural interpretation and understanding which the use of a long-run structural model, based on economic theory, can entail.

confident that the true model lies in the set of models under consideration. Only in these circumstances (and assuming certain other regularity conditions are met) is SBC a consistent model selection criterion. In contrast, AIC is a more appropriate selection criterion if the aim is to select the best approximating model (in the information-theoretic sense), as we believe to be the case in our particular application. We certainly do not claim that the 'true model' lies in the set of models that we are considering (univariate or vector error correcting), so this suggests the use of AIC in model selection. Moreover, the theoretical grounds for the use of SBC in the case of models involving unit roots and cointegration has not been fully developed; there remains no clear practical guidance on how one would allocate degrees of freedom across the equations in a cointegrating system in calculating SBC; and there is evidence that SBC can seriously underestimate the lag order in these circumstances. Moreover, the AIC is designed for minimising the forecast error variance (see Lütkepohl (1991), Chapter 4). This is a feature that might be thought to be important since one of the key uses of our model will be in probability event forecasting (see Chapter 11).[11]

The results of the estimation and selection of the univariate ARMA models are summarised in Table 9.5, providing details of the AIC, SBC and $\overline{R}^2$ statistics calculated for different models estimated for each of the eight endogenous variables.

The first two columns of Table 9.5 relate to the unrestricted 'ARMA(4, 4)' specifications for each variable and to the error correction specification of the core model discussed above and reported in Table 9.4 (described as 'unrestricted' in the sense that the short-run dynamics are unconstrained). The third column relates to our preferred benchmark ARMA model chosen by AIC, and imposing restrictions on the short-run dynamics as discussed above. Comparison across these three columns show that the error correction specifications of our core model outperform the preferred ARMA(p, q) model for 7/8 of the variables, Δe_t being the exception, in terms of the AIC (and in all eight in terms of the estimated $\overline{R}^2$'s). For example, the preferred benchmark ARMA model selected for the relative price variable, $\Delta(p_t - p_t^*)$, in the third column is the ARMA(4, 3) process. This model explains as much as 31.6% of the total variation in $\Delta(p_t - p_t^*)$ but this compares unfavourably with the error correction specification for this variable in the core model, which explains 48.4% of the variation. The preferred benchmark ARMA model for the change in domestic inflation

[11] Note that the use of the same criterion for model selection and model evaluation can lead to misleading results. For model evaluation, we prefer to use out-of-sample forecast evaluation procedures as illustrated in Chapter 11.

Table 9.5 Model selection criteria for the core model and alternative time series specifications.

Variable		Unrestricted		Restricted		
		ARMA(4,4)	ECM	ARMA(p,q) order selected by AIC	ARMA(p,q) order selected by SBC	ECM with short-run restrictions
$\Delta(p-p^*)$						
	AIC	416.62	479.27	463.43	462.37	480.67
	SBC	448.38	455.74	453.43	457.96	460.08
	$\bar{R}^2$	0.308	0.484	0.316	0.277	0.487
	$(\hat{p},\hat{q})$	–	–	(4,3)	(1,1)	–
	$\chi^2(m)$	–	–	–	–	1.18 (2)
Δe						
	AIC	276.37	276.45	280.03	280.03	282.54
	SBC	263.13	253.21	277.09	277.09	270.00
	$\bar{R}^2$	0.028	0.070	0.026	0.026	0.098
	$(\hat{p},\hat{q})$	–	–	(0,1)	(0,1)	–
	$\chi^2(m)$	–	–	–	–	4.35 (8)
Δr^*						
	AIC	741.36	750.80	744.56	744.46	754.29
	SBC	728.12	727.27	741.52	741.52	738.11
	$\bar{R}^2$	0.218	0.345	0.213	0.213	0.356
	$(\hat{p},\hat{q})$	–	–	(1,0)	(1,0)	–
	$\chi^2(m)$	–	–	–	–	3.00 (5)
Δr						
	AIC	632.37	633.17	631.67	631.66	638.55
	SBC	619.14	609.63	628.73	630.19	625.31
	$\bar{R}^2$	0.090	0.115	0.007	0.000	0.142
	$(\hat{p},\hat{q})$	–	–	(1,0)	(0,0)	–
	$\chi^2(m)$	–	–	–	–	3.20 (7)
Δy						
	AIC	442.80	456.97	442.95	442.85	460.72
	SBC	429.54	433.44	437.07	441.38	444.54
	$\bar{R}^2$	−0.130	0.260	0.022	0.000	0.276
	$(\hat{p},\hat{q})$	–	–	(3,0)	(0,0)	–
	$\chi^2(m)$	–	–	–	–	2.47 (5)
Δy^*						
	AIC	540.46	550.45	539.70	538.71	555.17
	SBC	527.22	526.92	535.29	535.77	540.46
	$\bar{R}^2$	0.102	0.367	0.194	0.178	0.385
	$(\hat{p},\hat{q})$	–	–	(1,1)	(1,0)	–
	$\chi^2(m)$	–	–	–	–	0.38 (6)
$\Delta(h-y)$						
	AIC	379.53	388.49	374.68	374.68	393.73
	SBC	366.29	364.96	373.22	373.22	379.02
	$\bar{R}^2$	0.186	0.257	0.000	0.000	0.284
	$(\hat{p},\hat{q})$	–	–	(0,0)	(0,0)	–
	$\chi^2(m)$	–	–	–	–	2.51 (8)
$\Delta^2 p$						
	AIC	456.05	481.16	458.88	457.94	484.53
	SBC	422.81	457.63	448.59	454.99	468.35
	$\bar{R}^2$	0.199	0.445	0.191	0.152	0.454
	$(\hat{p},\hat{q})$	–	–	(3,3)	(0,1)	–
	$\chi^2(m)$	–	–	–	–	3.23 (5)

Note: The unrestricted ECM equations are those reported in Table 9.4. The restricted ARMA(p, q) models are obtained using AIC and SBC searching over all possible orders $p, q = 0, 1, 2, 3, 4$. The restricted ECM equations are obtained using a general-to-specific search procedure that begins with the unrestricted single equation ECM and takes the form of dropping, one at a time, the lagged change and cointegrating terms, starting with the variable with the largest p-value (assuming it is greater than 0.25). The search process ends when all the terms that remain in the equation have p-values of 0.25 or less. The $\chi^2(m)$ statistic is the Lagrange multiplier joint test of m zero restrictions on coefficients of the deleted variables.

is an ARMA(3, 3) process which explains 19.1% of the total variation in $\Delta^2\widetilde{p}_t$. But this compares with 44.5% for the long-run structural error correction specification. The preferred ARMA benchmark model for domestic output growth is an ARMA(3, 0) process, whose explanatory power is low and accounts for 2.2% of the movement in Δy_t. This compares with 26% for the long-run structural error correction specification. This pattern is repeated for all variables as far as the $\overline{R}^2$ is concerned.

The conclusion to be drawn from these results is that the error correction model of the core model does indeed perform well in comparison to univariate time series models chosen according to our preferred AIC. For completion, though, the table also provides details of the SBC statistics, including in the fourth column of Table 9.5 details of the ARMA specification that would be chosen according to this criterion. The SBC statistic places greater weight on parsimony in model selection, and this is reflected by the fact that relatively simple models are chosen in the fourth column. Moreover, comparison of the SBC of the error correction specifications of the core model and that of the ARMA models of the fourth column suggests that the ARMA models outperform the core model (since the SBC shows the ARMA(p, q) model to be preferred for 7/8 variables by this criterion). However, this is not an even-handed comparison. The error correction specifications of the core model were obtained without imposing restrictions on the short-run dynamics and are bound to be disadvantaged relative to the ARMA models when parsimony is given more weight. For a more balanced comparison, therefore, we calculated the SBC statistics associated with a 'restricted ECM' in which a specification search was conducted, starting from the 'unrestricted' ECMs of the core model but dropping terms when the p-values of the estimates coefficient were greater than 0.25. As the results in the final column of Table 9.5 shows, the resultant 'restricted' ECM model outperforms the restricted univariate model in 8/8 cases according to AIC and in 5/8 of the cases according to SBC. So any criticism of our model for not adopting SBC as a selection mechanism for a benchmark comparison effectively disappears when the criteria are employed in a comparable manner.

9.5 An alternative model specification

The core model presented in the sections above fits the short-run dynamics well and embodies the economic theory's long-run relations in a transparent manner and in a way that is consistent with the data. Before moving on to discuss the use of the model, however, it is worth checking its robustness to alternative specifications. This also allows us to illustrate the types of choices typically encountered when performing empirical work of this sort. In what follows, we comment on one possible alternative model, which is similar in many respects to our preferred core model, but which is based on a different interpretation of the preliminary statistical analysis and one that places emphasis on the different aspects of the theoretical arguments.

Specifically, recall from the earlier discussion on the tests of unit roots in the variables that there is some ambiguity in the data regarding the order of integration of the price variables. The application of the ADF(s) tests to Δp_t and Δp_t^* yields mixed results. The hypothesis that there is a unit root in the domestic and foreign inflation rates is rejected for low orders of augmentation (namely, for $p = 0$ and 1), but not for higher orders. Overall the available data is not informative as to whether domestic and foreign prices are $I(1)$ or $I(2)$.

In our preferred model described in the previous section, we chose to follow Haldrup's (1998) advice on the analysis of $I(2)$ variables by working with the inflation series Δp_t and the relative price variable $p_t - p_t^*$ rather than the price levels p_t and p_t^* separately. The statistical evidence supports the view that $p_t - p_t^*$ is $I(1)$ and, on balance, the same is true for Δp_t. So we have some reassurance that our empirical work is statistically sound. However, this is not the only choice available. Investigation shows that the transformed series $p_t - p_t^o$ and $p_t^* - p_t^o$ are also unambiguously $I(1)$ according to the tests available. An alternative model might therefore be obtained employing exactly our modelling procedure, working instead with the vector of variables $\mathbf{z}_t^{ALT} = (p_t - p_t^o, e_t, r_t^*, r_t, y_t, p_t^* - p_t^o, h_t - y_t, y_t^*)'$ and in which the long-run relationships suggested by economic theory are captured by the vector

$$\beta'_{ALT} = \begin{pmatrix} 1 & -1 & 0 & 0 & 0 & -1 & 0 & 0 \\ 0 & 0 & -1 & 1 & 0 & 0 & 0 & 0 \\ 0 & 0 & 0 & 0 & 1 & 0 & 0 & -1 \\ 0 & 0 & 0 & -\beta_{44}^a & -\beta_{46}^a & 0 & 1 & 0 \end{pmatrix}.$$

The vector β_{ALT} incorporates the *PPP*, *IRP*, *OG*, and *MME* relationships of our preferred model (but not *FIP*) and, in terms of its treatment of the ambiguity on the order of integration of the price variables, the model is as justifiable as our preferred model. As shown in the empirical exercise of Garratt *et al.* (2000), this alternative model also performs well in terms of the fit of the data, with the associated test of the long-run relations accepted and with satisfactory diagnostics for the associated error correction equations.

In these circumstances, the judgement on which of the two models is preferred has to be based on economic as well as statistical analysis. The use of the variables $p_t - p_t^o$ and $p_t^* - p_t^o$ in the alternative model has at its base the view that, once the effects of oil price movements are taken into account, the price series are $I(1)$. This is appealing to those who point out that inflation rates are unlikely to grow without bounds and are therefore best modelled as being stationary. However, the statistical evidence indicates unambiguously that nominal interest rates are $I(1)$. If prices are treated as $I(1)$, then the modeller can only maintain the long-run *FIP* relationship if the interest rate is excluded from the cointegrating analysis (assuming nominal rates are $I(0)$ despite the statistical evidence). Or interest rates can be retained in the analysis as $I(1)$ variables, but then the long-run *FIP* relationship cannot be accommodated within the model (as is the case with $\boldsymbol{\beta}_{ALT}$ above). We preferred to work with the relative price variable, $p_t - p_t^*$ and the inflation rate Δp_t, since this allows us to accommodate the *FIP* relationship in the model in a straightforward way. While we recognise the difficulties in the view that price inflation and nominal interest rate series are $I(1)$, we also note the importance of capturing the statistical properties of the sample of data available and of accommodating the *FIP* relationship in the long-run model. We have, therefore, decided to continue with the model described in the earlier section, but we understand that others may make a different judgement. This highlights the importance of taking into account model uncertainty when making decisions on the basis of models. This is an issue that we explore in the work of Chapter 11 below.

10

Impulse response and trend/cycle properties of the UK model

One important use of macroeconometric models is to conduct counter-factual experiments in order to interpret previous historical episodes and to help with policy analysis. For example, it is important to learn about the possible impacts of changes in interest rates or oil prices on output and inflation over one or more years into the future. And our understanding of the macroeconomy will be enhanced if we are able to characterise past observations on economic activity as being related to 'trend' growth or as 'cyclical' movements around the trend. In this chapter, we focus on these uses of an estimated macroeconometric model, noting that we need to supplement the model with additional *a priori* assumptions in order to undertake these counter-factual exercises in many cases.

For example, an analysis of the dynamic impact of shocks is typically carried out using impulse response functions that focus on the evolution of the conditional means of the target variables in response to different types of shocks.[1] The estimation of impulse response functions, with respect to shocks applied to observables such as the oil price, does not pose any new technical difficulties and can be conducted using the generalised impulse response approach described in Section 6.1.3. In the case of monetary policy shocks or shocks to technology or tastes, the analysis of dynamic impulses is complicated due to the fact that such shocks are rarely observed directly and must be identified indirectly through a fully articulated macroeconomic model.

In the context of the core model of the UK economy developed in Chapters 4 and 5, we have made a clear distinction between the long-run

[1] Pesaran, Smith and Smith (2005) argue that a probabilistic approach to the analysis of counter-factuals might be more appropriate. Such an analysis is, however, beyond the scope of the present chapter.

structural and long-run reduced form disturbances, denoted by η_{it} and ξ_{it}, respectively, and between the reduced form shocks associated with the reduced form vector error correction model of (5.1) and the structural shocks associated with the structural macroeconomic model of (5.2), denoted u_{it} and ε_{it}, $i = 1, 2, \ldots, 5$. It is the structural innovations that have a clear economic interpretation: the η_{it} measure the deviations from long-run relationships in which the equilibrating pressures are identified by economic theory,[2] while the u_{it} measure the (typically white noise) deviations of target variables from the value suggested by the corresponding decision rule.

The analysis of the dynamic response of the macroeconomy to reduced form shocks provides important insights with which to interpret recent episodes in the UK economy and with which to consider the potential effects of changes abroad or of moderate changes in policy. Such an analysis illustrates and summarises the complex macrodynamics that can be captured by a cointegrating VAR model. The analysis does not rely on identifying assumptions other than those that relate to the long-run properties of the model (about which there is a relatively high degree of consensus) and so is not subject to the Sims critique. Moreover, the use of the Generalised Impulse Responses (GIR) analysis described in Chapter 6 ensures that the analysis is invariant to the ordering of the variables in the VAR. These impulse responses are relatively robust, therefore, and represent our preferred means of illustrating the dynamic properties of the model. In this chapter, we provide impulse responses of this sort relating to foreign output and to foreign interest rates to illustrate the dynamic properties of the macroeconomy.

If we wish to identify the effects of monetary policy shocks, or structural shocks more generally, we require a much more detailed *a priori* modelling of expectations, production and consumption lags, and the short-run dynamics of the technological process and its diffusion across the countries in the international economy. That is, we require further restrictions to be placed on the contemporaneous relationships amongst the variables. This relates to the 'structural' VECM given in equation (5.2) associated with the long-run structural macroeconometric model:

$$\mathrm{A}\,\Delta \mathbf{z}_t = \widetilde{\mathbf{a}} - \widetilde{\boldsymbol{\alpha}}\left[\boldsymbol{\beta}' \mathbf{z}_{t-1} - \mathbf{b}_1(t-1)\right] + \sum_{i=1}^{p-1} \widetilde{\boldsymbol{\Gamma}}_i \Delta \mathbf{z}_{t-i} + \boldsymbol{\varepsilon}_t, \qquad (10.1)$$

[2] The mechanics of the equilibrating processes are not necessarily described by economic theory (involving unspecified adjustment costs, rigidities, coordination issues and so on), but theory explains why the long-run structural disturbances are stationary.

where A represents the 9×9 matrix of contemporaneous structural coefficients, $\widetilde{\mathbf{a}} = \mathbf{A}\mathbf{a}$, $\widetilde{\alpha} = \mathbf{A}\alpha$, $\widetilde{\mathbf{\Gamma}}_i = \mathbf{A}\mathbf{\Gamma}_i$, and $\boldsymbol{\varepsilon}_t = \mathbf{A}\mathbf{u}_t$ are the associated structural shocks which are serially uncorrelated and have zero means and the positive definite variance covariance matrix, $\mathbf{\Omega} = \mathbf{A}\mathbf{\Sigma}\mathbf{A}'$. As highlighted in Chapter 5, without *a priori* restrictions on A and/or $\mathbf{\Omega}$, it is not possible to give economic meanings to the estimates of the loading coefficients, $\widetilde{\alpha}$, or to identify economically meaningful impulse response functions to shocks. The simplest example of such restrictions is obtained if a variable is considered weakly exogenous. Here, for example, because the oil price is assumed to be an $I(1)$ weakly exogenous variable, with no contemporaneous feedbacks from the endogenous variables to the oil price, identification of the impulse responses of the shock to oil prices does not pose any new problems. More generally, however, the restrictions on A that are necessary for identification of these structural effects require a tight description of the decision-rules followed by the public and private economic agents, incorporating information on agents' use of information and the exact timing of the information flows. An example of a set of short-run restrictions of this type was given in Chapter 5, based on a decision-theoretic model intended to capture the behaviour of the monetary authorities, and these would allow us to examine the short-run dynamic responses of the system to an economically meaningful monetary policy shock. In the section below, we describe in detail the steps taken to obtain the impulse response functions under these short-run restrictions. Subsequently, the impulse responses of these monetary policy shocks are presented alongside those obtained in response to a reduced form shock to the interest rate equation to illustrate the differences between the two approaches.

10.1 Identification of monetary policy shocks

The decision problem of the monetary authorities that underlies the identification scheme we adopt here to analyse monetary policy shocks has already been articulated in Section 5.1. The aim is to derive the impulse response functions of the monetary policy shocks, ε_{rt}, of the structural interest rate equation (5.14) described in Section 5.1. This requires the use of certain *a priori* restrictions based on the timing of the availability of information on the variables of interest. Recall from Section 5.1 that the aim of the monetary authorities is to set the market interest rate r_t by setting the base rate r_t^b. The difference between the two, the term premium, is influenced by the unanticipated factors such as oil price shocks, unexpected changes in foreign interest rates and exchange rates. We assume the market interest rate, r_t, and these three variables are determined on a daily basis, whereas the remaining variables are assumed to be much less frequently observed. Hence, we decompose $\mathbf{z}_t = (\mathbf{z}'_{1t}, \mathbf{z}'_{2t})'$, where $\mathbf{z}_{1t} = (p^o_t, e_t, r^*_t, r_t)'$ and $\mathbf{z}_{2t} = (\Delta p_t, y_t, p_t - p^*_t, h_t - y_t, y^*_t)'$, and partition the structural model (10.1) accordingly:

$$\begin{pmatrix} \mathbf{A}_{11} & \mathbf{A}_{12} \\ \mathbf{A}_{21} & \mathbf{A}_{22} \end{pmatrix} \begin{pmatrix} \Delta \mathbf{z}_{1t} \\ \Delta \mathbf{z}_{2t} \end{pmatrix} = \boldsymbol{\mu}_{t-1} + \begin{pmatrix} \boldsymbol{\varepsilon}_{1t} \\ \boldsymbol{\varepsilon}_{2t} \end{pmatrix},$$

where

$$\boldsymbol{\mu}_{t-1} = \tilde{\mathbf{a}} - \tilde{\boldsymbol{\alpha}} \left[\boldsymbol{\beta}' \mathbf{z}_{t-1} - \mathbf{b}_1 (t-1) \right] + \sum_{i=1}^{p-1} \tilde{\boldsymbol{\Gamma}}_i \Delta \mathbf{z}_{t-i},$$

and

$$\begin{pmatrix} \boldsymbol{\varepsilon}_{1t} \\ \boldsymbol{\varepsilon}_{2t} \end{pmatrix} \backsim i.i.d. \left[\mathbf{0}, \begin{pmatrix} \boldsymbol{\Omega}_{11} & \boldsymbol{\Omega}_{12} \\ \boldsymbol{\Omega}_{21} & \boldsymbol{\Omega}_{22} \end{pmatrix} \right].$$

Our primary concern is with identification of the impulse responses associated with the structural equations explaining the four variables in $\mathbf{z}_{1t}$, namely, p^o_t, e_t, r^*_t, r_t. For this purpose, we adopt the following sets of restrictions:

$$\mathbf{A}_{12} = \mathbf{0}, \tag{10.2}$$

$$\mathbf{A}_{11} = \begin{pmatrix} 1 & 0 & 0 & 0 \\ -a_{eo} & 1 & 0 & 0 \\ -a_{r^*o} & -a_{r^*e} & 1 & 0 \\ -a_{ro} & -a_{re} & -a_{rr^*} & 1 \end{pmatrix}, \tag{10.3}$$

and assume that the covariance matrix of the structural shocks, $\boldsymbol{\varepsilon}_{1t}$, is diagonal:

$$\boldsymbol{\Omega}_{11} = \begin{pmatrix} \omega_{oo} & 0 & 0 & 0 \\ 0 & \omega_{ee} & 0 & 0 \\ 0 & 0 & \omega_{r^*r^*} & 0 \\ 0 & 0 & 0 & \omega_{rr} \end{pmatrix}. \tag{10.4}$$

The first set of restrictions, (10.2), are justified on the grounds that the variables in $\mathbf{z}_{2t}$ are much less frequently observed than those in $\mathbf{z}_{1t}$, and hence are unlikely to contemporaneously affect them. The lower triangular form of $\mathbf{A}_{11}$ is motivated by our theoretical derivation of the structural interest rate equation in Section 5.1, plus the assumption that the UK exchange rate has a contemporaneous impact on foreign interest rates and not *vice versa*.[3] The final set of restrictions, (10.4), imposes further identifying restrictions on the structural shocks corresponding to $\mathbf{z}_{1t}$ by assuming that these shocks are orthogonal to each other. For the sub-system containing $\mathbf{z}_{1t}$, the assumptions (10.3) and (10.4) are the familiar type of exact identifying restrictions employed in the literature, and together impose 4^2 restrictions needed for the exact identification of the impulse responses of the shocks to $\boldsymbol{\varepsilon}_{1t}$. However, as demonstrated in Appendix B, the impulse responses associated with $\boldsymbol{\varepsilon}_{1t}$ are invariant to the identification of the rest of the system and, in particular, do not require $\boldsymbol{\Omega}_{12} = 0$, or $\mathbf{A}$ to be a lower-triangular matrix.[4] It is also possible to show that in our set-up the impulse responses of the monetary policy shocks are invariant to a re-ordering of the variables p_t^o, e_t and r_t^* in $\mathbf{z}_{1t}$. Hence, once the position of the monetary policy variable in $\mathbf{z}_t$ is fixed (in our application after p_t^o, e_t and r_t^*), the impulse response functions of the monetary policy shocks will be invariant to the re-ordering of the variables before and after r_t in $\mathbf{z}_t$. (A proof is provided in Appendix B.)

To derive the impulse responses, first recall that the reduced form equation associated with (10.1) is given by:

$$\Delta \mathbf{z}_t = \mathbf{a} - \boldsymbol{\alpha}\left[\boldsymbol{\beta}' \mathbf{z}_{t-1} - \mathbf{b}_1(t-1)\right] + \sum_{i=1}^{p-1} \boldsymbol{\Gamma}_i \Delta \mathbf{z}_{t-i} + \mathbf{u}_t, \tag{10.5}$$

where the reduced form errors can be partitioned as $\mathbf{u}_t = \left(\mathbf{u}_{1t}', \mathbf{u}_{2t}'\right)'$ conformably with $\mathbf{z}_t = \left(\mathbf{z}_{1t}', \mathbf{z}_{2t}'\right)'$, and note that

$$\boldsymbol{\Omega}_{11} = \mathrm{Cov}\,(\boldsymbol{\varepsilon}_{1t}), \; \boldsymbol{\Sigma}_{11} = \mathrm{Cov}\,(\mathbf{u}_{1t}), \; \mathbf{u}_{1t} = \mathbf{A}_{11}^{-1}\boldsymbol{\varepsilon}_{1t}.$$

Then, under (10.2), $\boldsymbol{\Sigma}_{11} = \mathbf{A}_{11}^{-1}\boldsymbol{\Omega}_{11}\mathbf{A}_{11}'^{-1}$ and the 10 unknown coefficients in $\mathbf{A}_{11}$ and $\boldsymbol{\Omega}_{11}$ can be obtained uniquely from the 10 distinct elements of $\boldsymbol{\Sigma}_{11}$. A consistent estimate of $\boldsymbol{\Sigma}_{11}$ can be computed from the reduced form residuals, $\hat{\mathbf{u}}_{1t}$, namely $\hat{\boldsymbol{\Sigma}}_{11} = T^{-1}\sum_{t=1}^{T}\hat{\mathbf{u}}_{1t}\hat{\mathbf{u}}_{1t}'$. Under the identification scheme in (10.3)–(10.4), the impulse response functions of the effects of a unit shock to the structural errors on $\mathbf{z}_t$ can now be obtained following the approach set out in Koop *et al.* (1996), and discussed further

[3] Recall that we are also assuming that the oil price can contemporaneously affect the macroeconomic variables, but is not itself contemporaneously affected by them.

[4] Note also that the impulse response functions of the monetary policy shocks are invariant to the ordering of the variables in $\mathbf{z}_{2t}$.

in Pesaran and Shin (1998).[5] Let $\mathfrak{g}(n, \mathbf{z} : \varepsilon_i)$, $i = o, e, r^*, r$, be the generalised impulse responses of $\mathbf{z}_{t+n}$ to a unit change in ε_{it}, measured by one standard deviation, namely $\sqrt{\omega_{ii}}$. Then, at horizon n we have

$$\mathfrak{g}(n, \mathbf{z} : \varepsilon_i) = E\left(\mathbf{z}_{t+n} \mid \varepsilon_{it} = \sqrt{\omega_{ii}}, \Im_{t-1}\right) - E\left(\mathbf{z}_{t+n} \mid \Im_{t-1}\right), \quad i = o, e, r^*, r,$$

where $\Im_{t-1}$ is the information set available at time $t-1$. Since all the shocks are assumed to be serially uncorrelated with zero means, (10.5) provides the following recursive relations in $\mathfrak{g}(n, \mathbf{z} : \varepsilon_i)$:

$$\Delta\mathfrak{g}(n, \mathbf{z} : \varepsilon_i) = -\mathbf{\Pi}\mathfrak{g}(n-1, \mathbf{z} : \varepsilon_i) + \sum_{i=1}^{p-1} \mathbf{\Gamma}_i \Delta\mathfrak{g}(n-1, \mathbf{z} : \varepsilon_i) \quad \text{for } n = 1, 2, \ldots, \tag{10.6}$$

with the initialisation $\mathfrak{g}(n, \mathbf{z} : \varepsilon_i) = 0$ for $n < 0$, where $\mathbf{\Pi} = \boldsymbol{\alpha}\boldsymbol{\beta}'$ and $\Delta\mathfrak{g}(n, \mathbf{z} : \varepsilon_i) = \mathfrak{g}(n, \mathbf{z} : \varepsilon_i) - \mathfrak{g}(n-1, \mathbf{z} : \varepsilon_i)$. In the case of $n = 0$ (*i.e.* the impact effects), we have

$$\mathfrak{g}(0, \mathbf{z} : \varepsilon_i) = E\left(\Delta\mathbf{z}_t \mid \varepsilon_{it} = \sqrt{\omega_{ii}}, \Im_{t-1}\right) - E\left(\Delta\mathbf{z}_t \mid \Im_{t-1}\right). \tag{10.7}$$

Under (10.1) and conditional on $\Im_{t-1}$, $\left(\varepsilon_{it}, \Delta\mathbf{z}_t'\right)'$ is distributed with mean

$$\begin{pmatrix} 0 \\ \mathbf{A}^{-1}\boldsymbol{\mu}_{t-1} \end{pmatrix},$$

and the covariance matrix

$$\begin{pmatrix} \omega_{ii} & E\left(\varepsilon_{it}\mathbf{u}_t'\right) \\ E\left(\varepsilon_{it}\mathbf{u}_t\right) & E\left(\mathbf{u}_t\mathbf{u}_t'\right) \end{pmatrix}.$$

In the case where, conditional on $\Im_{t-1}$, $\Delta\mathbf{z}_t$ is normally distributed, using familiar results on conditional expectations of multivariate normal densities, we have[6]

$$E\left(\Delta\mathbf{z}_t \mid \varepsilon_{it} = \sqrt{\omega_{ii}}, \Im_{t-1}\right) = \mathbf{A}^{-1}\boldsymbol{\mu}_{t-1} + \frac{E(\varepsilon_{it}\mathbf{u}_t)}{\omega_{ii}}\sqrt{\omega_{ii}}.$$

But under (10.2),

$$\mathbf{u}_t = \begin{pmatrix} \mathbf{A}_{11}^{-1}\boldsymbol{\varepsilon}_{1t} \\ \mathbf{u}_{2t} \end{pmatrix},$$

[5] For more details and the application of the approach to structural simultaneous equation models see Pesaran and Smith (1998).

[6] This result provides an optimal linear approximation when the errors are not normally distributed.

and hence, using (10.7), we have

$$\mathfrak{g}(0, \mathbf{z} : \varepsilon_i) = \frac{E(\varepsilon_{it}\mathbf{u}_t)}{\sqrt{\omega_{ii}}} = \frac{1}{\sqrt{\omega_{ii}}}\begin{bmatrix} \mathbf{A}_{11}^{-1}E(\varepsilon_{it}\boldsymbol{\varepsilon}_{1t}) \\ E(\varepsilon_{it}\mathbf{u}_{2t}) \end{bmatrix} = \begin{bmatrix} \mathbf{A}_{11}^{-1}\boldsymbol{\Omega}_{11}^{\frac{1}{2}}\boldsymbol{\tau}_i \\ E\left(\frac{\varepsilon_{it}\mathbf{u}_{2t}}{\sqrt{\omega_{ii}}}\right) \end{bmatrix}, \quad (10.8)$$

where $\boldsymbol{\tau}_i$ is a 4×1 selection vector for $i = o, e, r^*, r$. For the oil price shock $\boldsymbol{\tau}_o = (1, 0, 0, 0)'$, and for the monetary policy shock the selection vector is defined by $\boldsymbol{\tau}_r = (0, 0, 0, 1)'$. Under the identification restrictions (10.3) and (10.4), a consistent estimate of $\mathbf{A}_{11}^{-1}\boldsymbol{\Omega}_{11}^{\frac{1}{2}}$ can be obtained by the lower triangular Choleski factor of $\hat{\boldsymbol{\Sigma}}_{11}$. To consistently estimate $E\left(\frac{\varepsilon_{it}\mathbf{u}_{2t}}{\sqrt{\omega_{ii}}}\right)$, we note that, under the same restrictions, ω_{ii}, $i = o, e, r^*, r$, and the unknown elements of $\mathbf{A}_{11}$ can also be consistently estimated using $\hat{\boldsymbol{\Sigma}}_{11}$. It, therefore, remains to obtain a consistent estimate of $E(\varepsilon_{it}\mathbf{u}_{2t})$. Recall that $\boldsymbol{\varepsilon}_{1t} = \mathbf{A}_{11}\mathbf{u}_{1t}$. Hence $E(\varepsilon_{it}\mathbf{u}_{2t})$ can be consistently estimated by the ith row of

$$T^{-1}\sum_{t=1}^{T}\hat{\mathbf{A}}_{11}\hat{\mathbf{u}}_{1t}\hat{\mathbf{u}}_{2t}',$$

where $\hat{\mathbf{A}}_{11}$ is a consistent estimate of $\mathbf{A}_{11}$. It is clear that the impulse response functions of shocks to the structural errors, ε_{it}, $i = o, e, r^*$, and r, are invariant to the way the structural coefficients associated with the second block, $\mathbf{z}_{2t}$, in (10.1) are identified.

10.2 Estimates of impulse response functions

We now report the estimates of impulse response functions of the endogenous variables of the core model. We begin by describing the impulse responses to an oil price shock, which is obtained on the relatively uncontentious assumption that oil prices are weakly exogenous. We then present the impulse responses to a foreign output and foreign interest equation shock, illustrating the use of the GIR techniques. And we then present the impulse responses to a monetary policy shock, obtained under the short-run identifying restrictions and using the method described in Section 10.1 above. We also compare the responses to monetary policy shocks directly with those to an interest rate equation shock. The macroeconomic analyses of the effects of these shocks have been of special interest and help provide further insights into the short-run dynamic properties of our model. We shall also consider the time profile of the effects of shocks on the long-run relationships. Recall that despite the integrated properties of the underlying variables, the effects of shocks on the long-run relations can only be temporary and should eventually disappear. But it is interesting to see how long such effects are likely to last. These types of impulse response functions are referred to as 'persistence profiles' and, as shown in Pesaran and Shin (1996), they shed light on the equilibrating mechanisms embedded within the model.

To compute all the impulse response functions analysed, we need an estimate of the oil price equation.[7] We decided to exclude domestic variables from the equation since we would not expect a small open economy such as the UK to have any significant influence on oil prices. The resultant oil price equation, estimated over the period 1965q1–1999q4, is given by:

$$\Delta p_t^o = \underset{(0.0352)}{-0.0039} + \underset{(0.1070)}{0.04787}\Delta p_{t-1}^o + \underset{(2.6818)}{2.7731}\Delta y_{t-1}^* + \underset{(1.8572)}{0.4199}\Delta p_{t-1}^* + \underset{(11.635)}{2.4855}\Delta r_{t-1}^* + \hat{\varepsilon}_{ot}, \tag{10.9}$$

$$\sqrt{\widehat{\omega}_{oo}} = 0.1661,\ \chi_{SC}^2[4] = 1.86,\ \chi_N^2[2] = 6558.9.$$

where standard errors are in brackets, $\omega_{oo} = \text{var}(\varepsilon_{ot})$ and χ_{SC}^2 and χ_N^2 are chi-squared statistics for serial correlation and normality, respectively. None of the coefficients are statistically significant at the conventional levels, although there is some evidence of a positive effect from past changes in foreign output. The hypothesis that the residuals are serially uncorrelated cannot be rejected either. But, not surprisingly, there is a clear evidence of non-normal errors, primarily reflecting the three major oil price shocks experienced during the period under consideration. These results are in line with the widely held view that oil prices follow a geometric random walk, possibly with a drift. Therefore, we base our computations of impulse responses on the following simple model:

$$\Delta p_t^o = \underset{(0.0139)}{0.0173} + \hat{\varepsilon}_{ot}, \tag{10.10}$$

$$\sqrt{\widehat{\omega}_{oo}} = 0.16485,\ \chi_{SC}^2[4] = 2.19,\ \chi_N^2[2] = 6399.$$

10.2.1 *Effects of an oil price shock*

Over the past three decades, oil price changes have had a significant impact on the conduct of monetary policy in the UK and elsewhere. Increases in oil prices have often been associated with rising prices, falling output and

[7] This relates to the discussion surrounding (4.44) in Chapter 4.

a tightening of monetary policy which has in turn contributed to further output falls. It is important that special care is taken to separate the output and inflation effects of an oil price shock from those of a monetary shock as they are likely to be positively correlated. In our framework, this is achieved by treating oil prices as long-run forcing, and by explicitly modelling the contemporaneous dependence of monetary policy shocks on the oil price shocks, as well as on shocks to exchange rates and foreign interest rates.[8]

Figure 10.1 provides the persistence profiles of the effects of a one standard error increase in oil prices (around 16.5% per quarter) on the five long-run relationships. Figure 10.2 gives the impulse responses of the oil price shock on the levels of all the eight endogenous variables in the model. Both figures also provide bootstrapped 95% confidence error bands (see Section 6.5 for more details).[9] All the persistence profiles converge towards zero, thus confirming the cointegrating properties of the long-run relations. In addition, the persistence profiles provide useful information on the speed with which the different relations in the model, once shocked, will return to their long-run equilibria. The results are generally in line with those found in the literature, with *PPP* and output gap relations showing much slower rates of adjustments to shocks. The effect of the oil price shock on the output gap takes some ten years to complete. This is rather slow, but is comparable to those implied by Barro and Sala-i-Martin's (1995) analyses of international output series.[10] Similarly, deviations from *PPP* are relatively long lived, but the slow speed of convergence towards equilibrium in this relationship is again consistent with existing results which put the half life of deviations from *PPP* at about four years for the major industrialised countries.[11] Convergence to the *FIP*, *IRP* and *MME* relationships is much more rapid, reflecting the standard view that arbitrage in asset markets functions much faster than in the goods markets in restoring equilibria.

[8] For an alternative identification scheme applied to the US economy, see Bernanke *et al.* (1997).

[9] Point estimates and 95% confidence intervals are plotted in Figures 10.1–10.10. We also calculated the empirical means and medians of the bootstrap estimates and generally found them to be close to the point estimates.

The calculations were performed using *GAUSS* and the programs are described in Appendix D. A forthcoming version of Microfit, *Microfit 5.0,* may also be used to calculate the impulse responses and persistence profiles reported here. See Pesaran and Pesaran (2006).

[10] However, Barro and Sala-i-Martin (1995) assume that output series are trend stationary and study convergence to a common trend growth rate. The present study assumes the output series are difference stationary and tests for cointegration between UK and OECD output series. For further discussion, see Lee *et al.* (1997, 1998).

[11] See, for example, Johansen and Juselius (1992), Pesaran and Shin (1996), or Rogoff (1996).

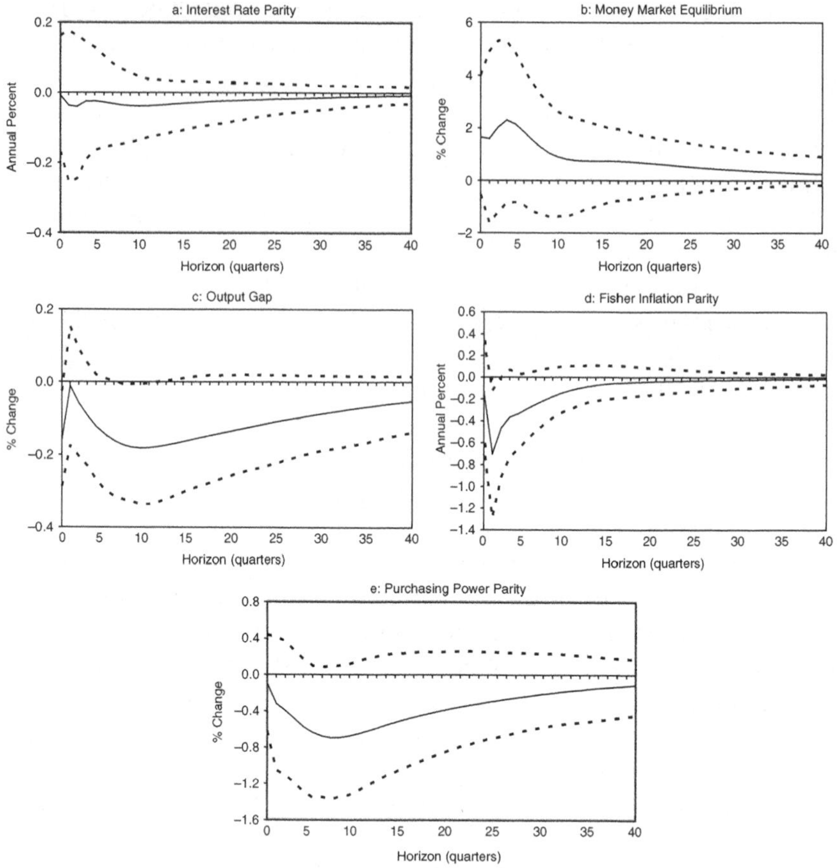

Note: The graphs define the long-run relationships as follows: Interest Rate Parity: $r_t - r_t^*$, Money Market Equilibrium Condition: $h_t - y_t + 56.1r_t + 0.0073t$, the Output Gap: $y_t - y_t^*$, Fisher Inflation Parity: $r_t - \Delta p_t$ and the *PPP* (real exchange rate): $e_t + p_t^* - p_t$. The size of the shock is equal to the standard deviation of the selected equation error. The solid and dashed lines plot the point estimates and 95% confidence intervals, respectively, of the impulse responses. The confidence intervals are generated from a bootstrap procedure using 2000 replications.

Figure 10.1 Persistence profiles of the long-run relations of a positive unit shock to the oil price.

Turning to the impulse response functions in Figure 10.2, the oil price shock has a permanent effect on the level of the individual series, reflecting their unit root properties. Its effect on output has the expected negative sign, reducing domestic output by approximately 0.24% below its base after 2.5 years. Foreign output also declines to the same long-run value but at a much slower speed. On impact, the oil price shock raises the

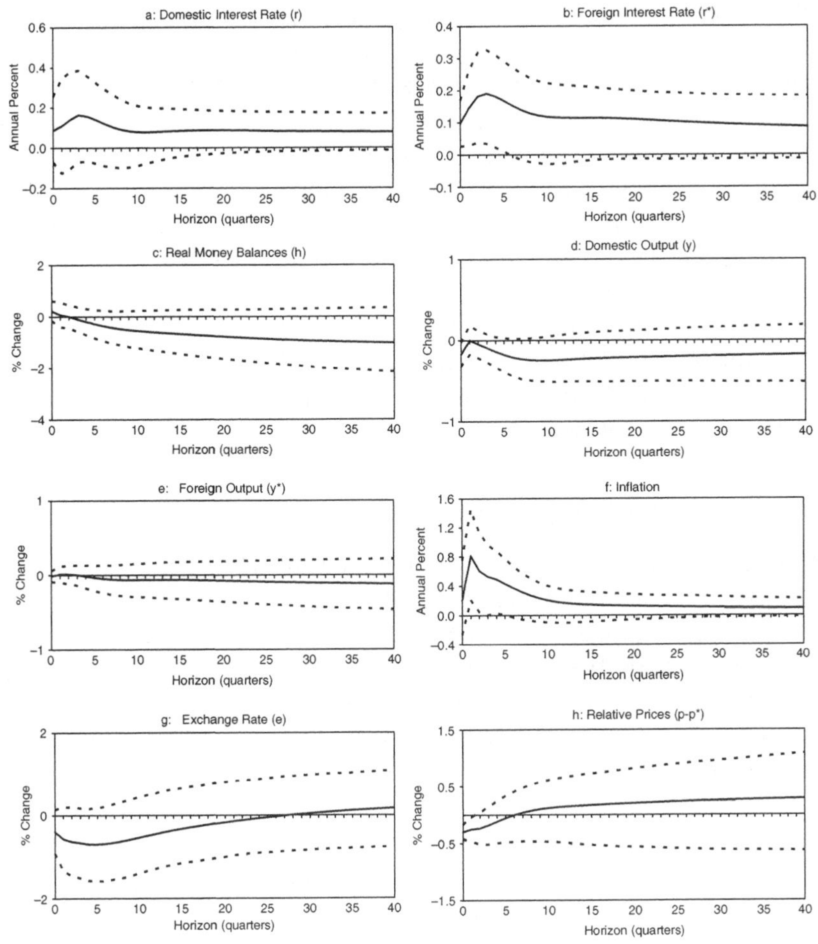

Note: The solid and dashed lines plot the point estimates and 95% confidence intervals, respectively, of the impulse responses. The confidence intervals are generated from a bootstrap procedure using 2000 replications.

Figure 10.2 Generalised impulse responses of a positive unit shock to the oil price.

domestic rate of inflation by 0.20%, and by 0.82% after one quarter, before gradually falling back close to zero after approximately three years. Despite the higher domestic prices, the oil price shock generates a small appreciation of the nominal exchange rate, as can be seen from Figure 10.2g. This initial movement is then followed by further appreciations, although the process starts to reverse after approximately one year. In the long run, the nominal exchange rate fully adjusts to the change in relative prices with

PPP restored but, as noted above, the speed of adjustment is relatively slow. The oil price shock is accompanied by increases in both domestic and foreign interest rates, suggesting a possible tightening of the monetary policy in response to the rise in oil prices. Domestic interest rates increase by some nine basis points on impact, rising to 16 basis points after approximately three quarters, and then falling to a long-run values of eight basis points above its pre-shock level. The oil price shock affects real money balances both directly and indirectly through its impact on interest rates. The overall outcome is to reduce real money balances by around 1% in the long run. This is indicative of the presence of a strong liquidity effect in our model. The oil price shock also causes the real rate of interest to fall, initially by 0.1% and then by 0.7%, before gradually returning to its equilibrium value of zero.

10.2.2 *Effects of a foreign output equation shock*

The Generalised Impulse Responses (GIR), outlined in Chapter 6, describe the time profile of the effect of a unit shock to a *particular equation* on all the model's endogenous variables. The dynamics which result from the shock will embody the contemporaneous interactions of all the endogenous variables of the system. These are captured by the elements of the estimated covariance matrix of the shocks to the endogenous variables which reflects the historical patterns of correlations across the shocks in the sample period under consideration. There are many issues that could be analysed through the GIR analysis and here we focus on the effects of shocks to the foreign output equation. As was noted earlier, unlike the orthogonalised impulse responses, the GIRs are invariant to the ordering of the variables in the VAR, and only require that the particular shock under consideration does not significantly alter the parameters of the model (see Section 6.1.3).[12]

Figure 10.3 plots the persistence profiles of the effects of a unit shock to the foreign output equation for the five long-run relations. The size of the deviations from equilibrium are much smaller than those compared to the oil price shock but the pattern is similar. Hence, the *PPP* and output gap relations show much slower rates of adjustments to shocks, whilst the convergence to the *FIP*, *IRP* and *MME* relationships is much more rapid.

Figure 10.4 gives the impulse responses of the foreign output shock on the levels of all the eight endogenous variables in the model. Given

[12] Here we mean policy changes that do not result in significant changes in the covariance structure of the shocks and/or the coefficients of the underlying VAR model.

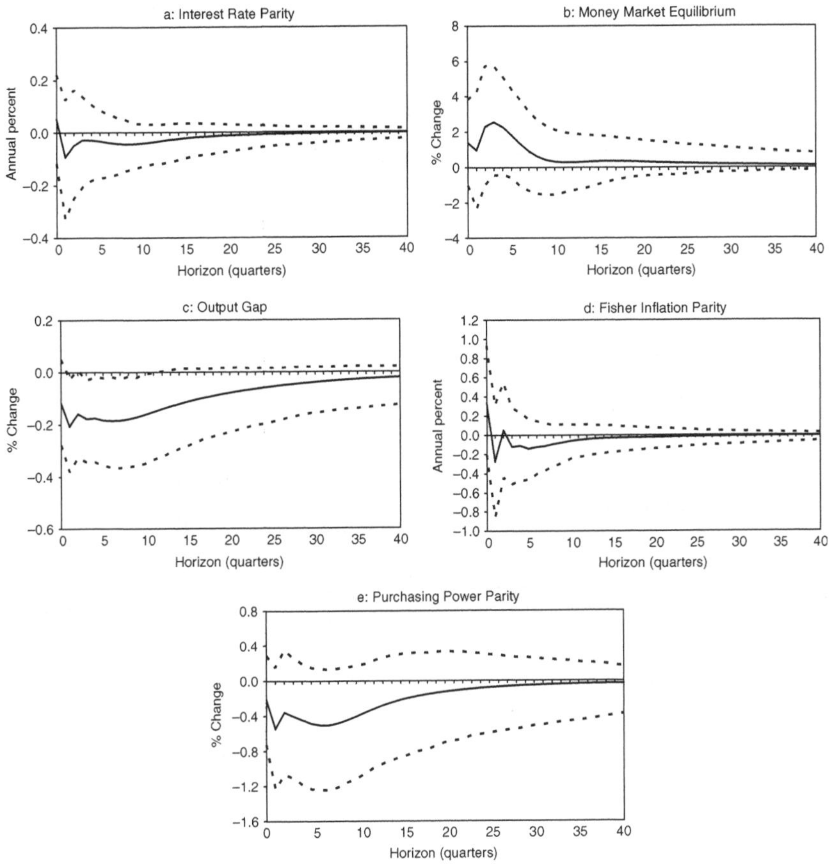

Note: The graphs define the long-run relationships as follows: Interest Rate Parity: $r_t - r_t^*$, Money Market Equilibrium Condition: $h_t - y_t + 56.1r_t + 0.0073t$, the Output Gap: $y_t - y_t^*$, Fisher Inflation Parity: $r_t - \Delta p_t$ and the *PPP* (real exchange rate): $e_t + p_t^* - p_t$. The size of the shock is equal to the standard deviation of the selected equation error. The solid and dashed lines plot the point estimates and 95% confidence intervals, respectively, of the impulse responses. The confidence intervals are generated from a bootstrap procedure using 2000 replications.

Figure 10.3 Persistence profiles of the long-run relations of a positive unit shock to the foreign output equation.

the strong positive correlation that exists between foreign and domestic output innovations, the effect of the foreign output shock on impact is to cause domestic output to increase by approximately 0.3% (see Figure 10.4d).[13] These effects continue to persist over the subsequent quarters. In the long run, the effect of a unit shock to the foreign output

[13] All percentage changes quoted in this section are computed at annual rates.

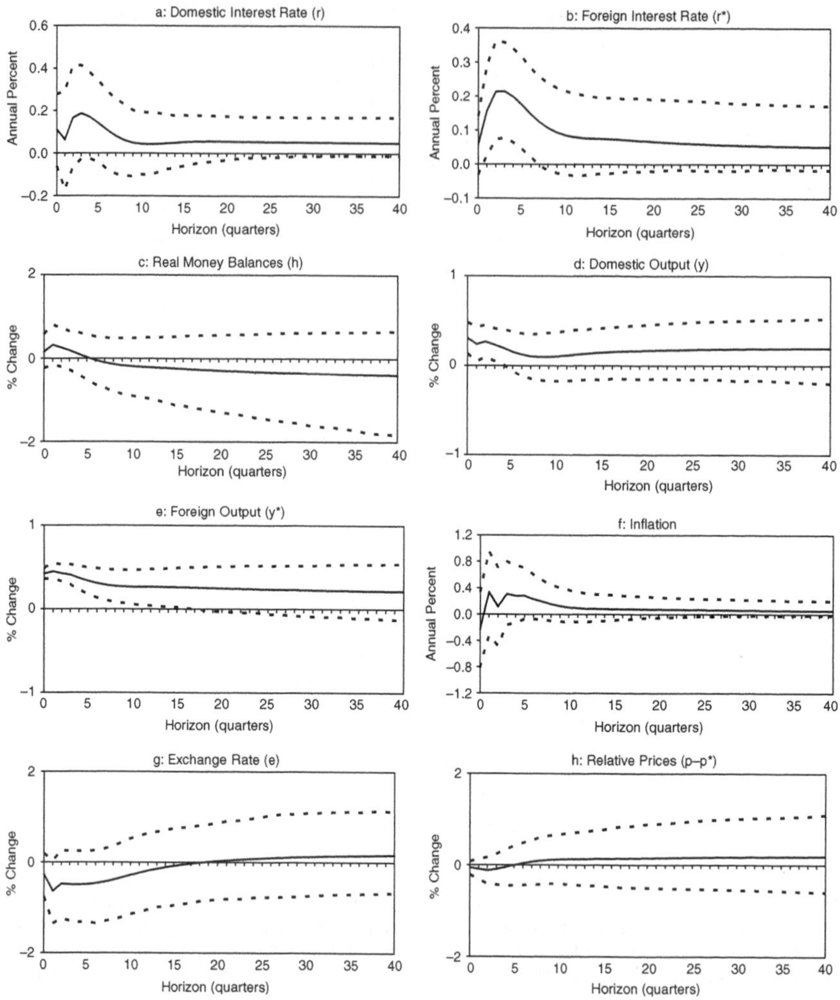

Note: The solid and dashed lines plot the point estimates and 95% confidence intervals, respectively, of the impulse responses. The confidence intervals are generated from a bootstrap procedure using 2000 replications.

Figure 10.4 Generalised impulse responses of a positive unit shock to the foreign output equation.

equation is to increase both domestic and foreign output by 0.2% above their baseline values. However, it is important to note that the gap between domestic and foreign output growths persists even after 20 quarters, with the foreign output level remaining considerably higher than domestic output through this time.

The GIRs for the foreign output shock on the domestic inflation and the nominal exchange rates are displayed in Figures 10.4f and 10.4g. The shock initially reduces domestic prices by 0.23% and appreciates the nominal exchange rate on impact by 0.27%. The fall in inflation is reversed in the following quarter, though, returning to near its baseline value after about 12 quarters. In the long run, the effect of the foreign output shock on the domestic inflation rate is zero, so that the effects are purely temporary.

The effects of the shock on domestic and foreign interest rates are displayed in Figures 10.4a and 10.4b. The initial response to the shock is to increase domestic and foreign interest rates by 11 and six basis points, respectively. Subsequently the foreign interest rate rises above the domestic interest rate, but eventually this gap disappears, as predicted by the long-run interest parity relation embodied in the core model.

10.2.3 *Effects of a foreign interest rate equation shock*

In Figures 10.5 and 10.6, we report the GIRs for a shock to the foreign interest rate equation, where the size of the shock is scaled to ensure that the foreign interest rate rises by one standard deviation of the error variance on impact. Figure 10.5 again confirms the varying speeds of adjustments of the long-run relationships as before.

Figure 10.6 shows the impact effect of the shock to the foreign interest rate equation is to increase the domestic interest rate by 23 basis points whilst domestic output is unchanged. Domestic output falls thereafter, down by 0.37% after four quarters and reaching 0.5% below its baseline value after approximately 16 quarters. This suggests a complicated relationship between interest rate and output changes over the course of the business cycle. The shock to the foreign interest rate equation depreciates the nominal exchange rate on impact by 0.14% and by approximately 0.5% in the long run.

The effects of the shock on domestic interest rates, foreign interest rates, and domestic inflation are displayed in Figures 10.6a–b and 10.6f. The fact that the impulse response function for the foreign interest initially slopes upwards reflects the highly persistent nature of the interest rate movements in the short run. Perhaps not surprisingly, the domestic interest rate is much less affected by the shock with the result that, during the first three years following the shock, the foreign interest rate tends to rise above the domestic interest rate. This interest rate gap (relative to its baseline value)

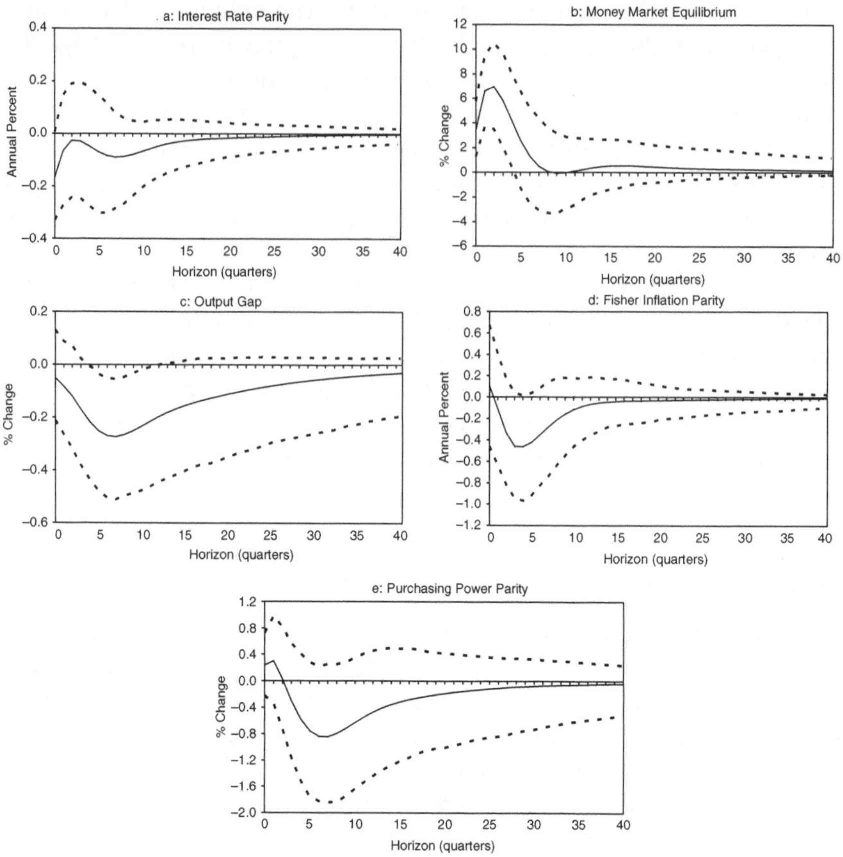

Note: The graphs define the long-run relationships as follows: Interest Rate Parity: $r_t - r_t^*$, Money Market Equilibrium Condition: $h_t - y_t + 56.1r_t + 0.0073t$, the Output Gap: $y_t - y_t^*$, Fisher Inflation Parity: $r_t - \Delta p_t$ and the *PPP* (real exchange rate): $e_t + p_t^* - p_t$. The size of the shock is equal to the standard deviation of the selected equation error. The solid and dashed lines plot the point estimates and 95% confidence intervals, respectively, of the impulse responses. The confidence intervals are generated from a bootstrap procedure using 2000 replications.

Figure 10.5 Persistence profiles of the long-run relations of a positive unit shock to the foreign interest rate equation.

will eventually disappear, however, as predicted by the long-run interest parity relation embodied in the core model.

The initial effect of the interest rate shock on domestic inflation is to increase the rate of inflation by 0.13% followed by 0.57% after one quarter, and 0.88% after four quarters. This effect is reversed from this point onwards, with the inflation rate falling to be approximately 0.1% above its baseline value after about 14 quarters. In the long run, the effect of

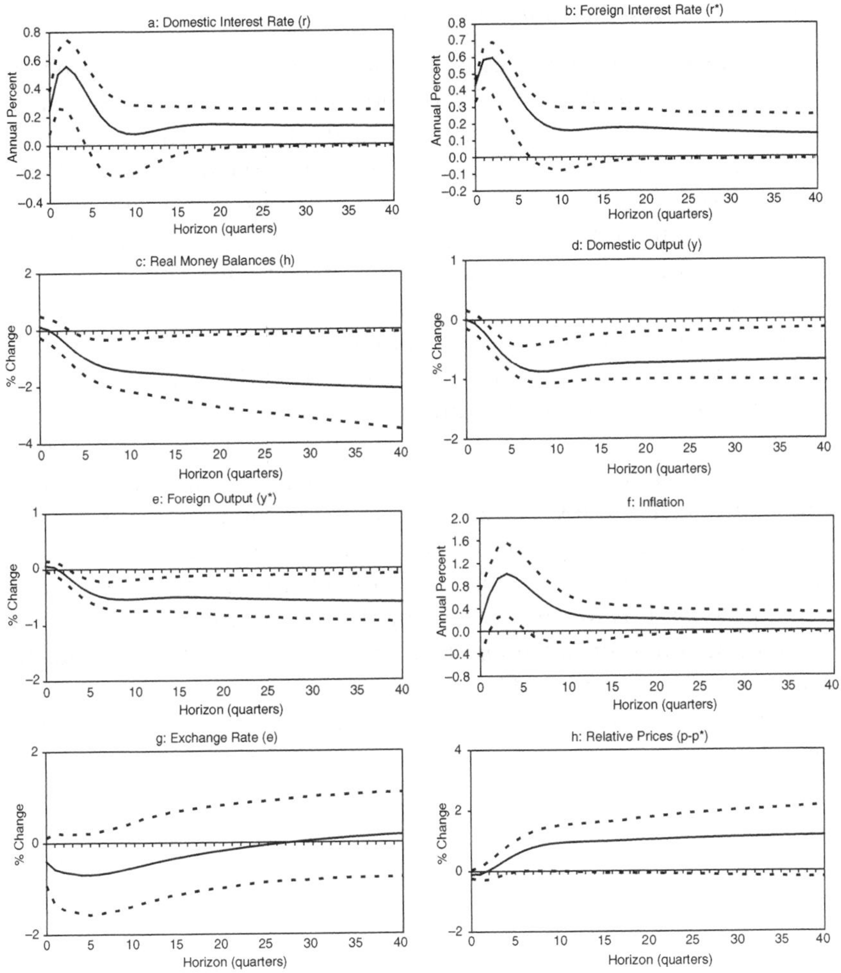

Note: The solid and dashed lines plot the point estimates and 95% confidence intervals, respectively, of the impulse responses. The confidence intervals are generated from a bootstrap procedure using 2000 replications.

Figure 10.6 Generalised impulse responses of a positive unit shock to the foreign interest rate equation.

the interest rate shock on the domestic inflation rate is zero. Throughout, the effects of the shock to the foreign interest rate equation on real money balances are negative, which is in line with the strong negative effect of interest rates on real money balances obtained at the estimation stage.

10.2.4 *Effects of a monetary policy shock*

We turn now to the more economically meaningful monetary policy shocks or, more precisely under our identification scheme set out in Chapter 5, the non-systematic (or unanticipated) component of the policy. Recall that the shock is defined by ε_{rt}, the shock in the structural equation for the market interest rate, and allows oil prices, exchange rates and foreign interest rates to have contemporaneous effects on r_t. The algorithms necessary for the computation of the associated impulse responses are set out above in Section 10.1.

Figure 10.7 presents the persistence profiles of the effects of one standard error unexpected increase in the interest rate (*i.e.* a rise of 91 basis points) on the five long-run relations of the model.

As with the previous shocks, the effects of the monetary policy shock on these relations disappear eventually, but the speed with which this occurs varies considerably across the different arbitrage conditions. The interest parity condition is the quickest to adjust followed by the Fisher inflation parity, the monetary equilibrium condition, purchasing power parity and the output gap. It is worth emphasising that, in our model, the long-run equilibrium condition for interest rate parity rules out the phenomena observed in Eichenbaum and Evans (1995), where a contractionary monetary policy shock could result in a permanent shift in the interest rate differential.

On impact, the effect of the monetary policy shock is most pronounced on the money market equilibrium condition, resulting in a 12.7% unexpected excess supply of money. With foreign interest rates unchanged on impact (by construction), the shock raises the domestic interest rate above the foreign interest rate by 91 basis points, but it also raises the real interest rate by 59 basis points while leaving the real exchange rate unchanged. The output gap is initially left intact, reflecting a lagged response of real output to interest rate changes. However, the contractionary impact of the shock on domestic output (relative to the foreign output) begins to be seen after the second quarter, with domestic output falling below foreign output by 0.29% after two years.

The impulse response functions for the effects of the monetary shock on the various endogenous variables in the model are given in Figure 10.8.

Most of these plots exhibit familiar patterns. After the initial impact, the domestic interest rate declines at a steady rate settling down after approximately four years at an equilibrium value of five basis points above the

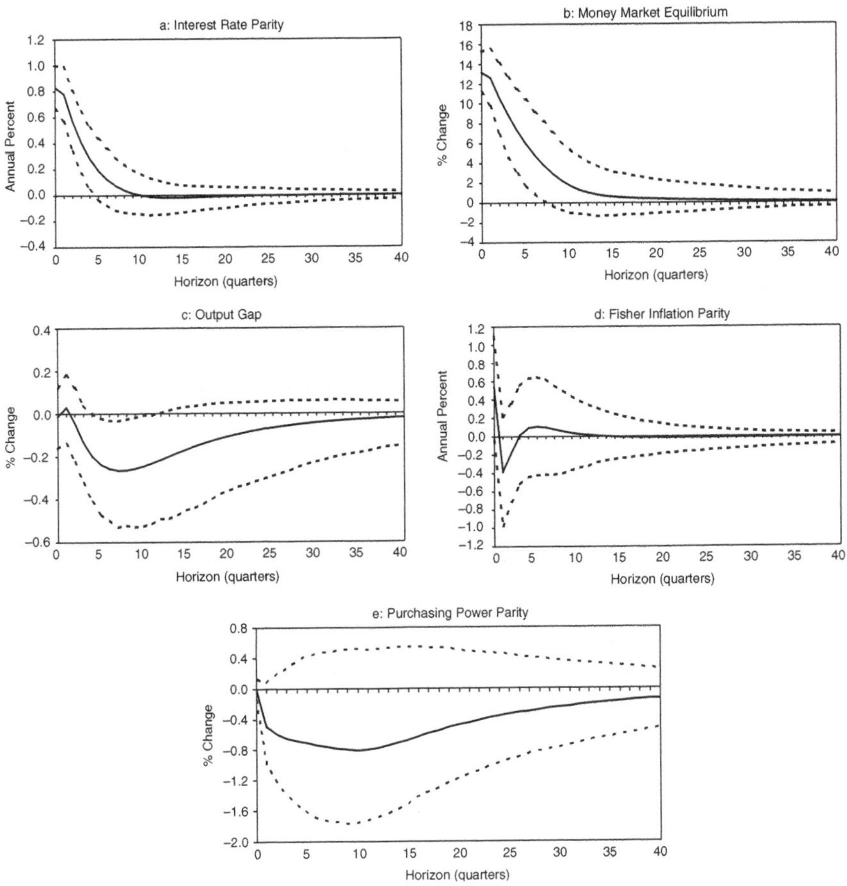

Note: The graphs define the long-run relationships as follows: Interest Rate Parity: $r_t - r_t^*$, Money Market Equilibrium Condition: $h_t - y_t + 56.1r_t + 0.0073t$, the Output Gap: $y_t - y_t^*$, Fisher Inflation Parity: $r_t - \Delta p_t$ and the *PPP* (real exchange rate): $e_t + p_t^* - p_t$. The size of the shock is equal to the standard deviation of the selected equation error. The solid and dashed lines plot the point estimates and 95% confidence intervals, respectively, of the impulse responses. The confidence intervals are generated from a bootstrap procedure using 2000 replications.

Figure 10.7 Persistence profiles of the long-run relations of a positive unit shock to monetary policy.

baseline value. In tandem with the fall in the interest rate, the excess supply of money declines to approximately 8.6% after one year, then to 5.0% after two years, reaching its equilibrium after approximately five years. These results clearly show the presence of a sizeable 'liquidity effect' in our model following the unexpected tightening of the monetary policy.[14]

[14] See, for example, the analysis of liquidity effects in Pagan and Robertson (1998).

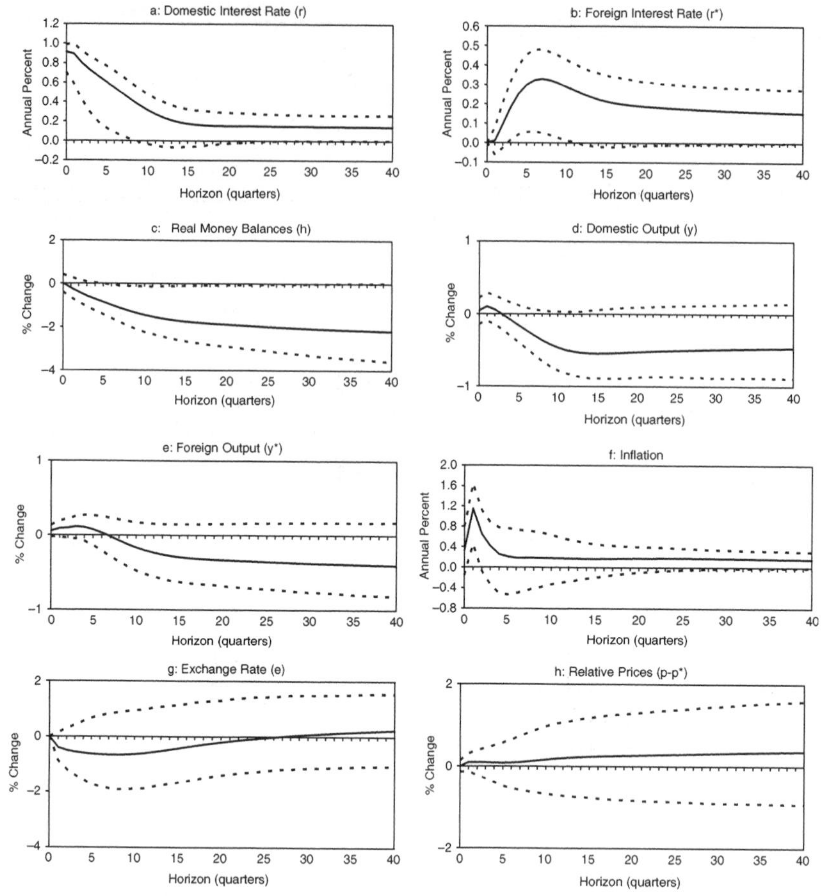

Note: The solid and dashed lines plot the point estimates and 95% confidence intervals, respectively, of the impulse responses. The confidence intervals are generated from a bootstrap procedure using 2000 replications.

Figure 10.8 Generalised impulse responses of a positive unit shock to monetary policy.

The monetary policy shock has little immediate effects on the real side of the economy. The contractionary effects of the policy begin to be felt on output and real money balances after one quarter. The impulse responses of domestic and foreign output are given in Figures 10.8d and 10.8e, each showing a relatively smooth decline to around 0.46% and 0.17%, respectively, below base after two and half years. The speed of adjustments of the two series differ, however, as was seen clearly from the persistence profile of the output gap presented in Figure 10.7c. Figure 10.8f provides evidence of the well-known 'price puzzle', as inflation increases in immediate response to the contractionary monetary shock, falling back to close to zero after three years. Note, however, that with the exception of the first few quarters the inflation responses are insignificantly different from zero so that, insofar as the puzzle is apparent, the underlying long-run relations ensure that the anomaly are observed in the short run only.

The impact effect of the monetary policy shock on the nominal exchange rate is zero by construction but, as can be seen from Figure 10.8g, the shock causes the exchange rate to appreciate by around 0.5% in the following period. The exchange rate remains roughly constant for the subsequent year and then depreciates back to close to its original level after 20 quarters. This pattern is reasonably consistent with the Dornbusch (1976) overshooting model which would predict a large initial appreciation in the exchange rate in response to a monetary contraction, followed by subsequent depreciation to its long-run level. Certainly it matches well the broader view of overshooting discussed in Eichenbaum and Evans (1995) in which there might be a *sequence of periods* of appreciation followed by depreciation because of secondary effects of the shock on risk premia, speculative behaviour and information imperfections relating to the permanence of the shock. Moreover, this time profile for the exchange rate is observed in a set of responses in which interest rate parity is re-established relatively quickly and in which a positive differential of domestic over foreign interest rates is associated with a constant or depreciating exchange rate as suggested by UIP. This accords well with theory, therefore, and is in contrast to the ' exchange rate puzzle' observed by Eichenbaum and Evans (1995) in which the interest rate differential is maintained indefinitely and is associated with a persistently appreciating exchange rate.[15]

By way of comparison, we also provide here the time profiles of the effects of shocks to a unit (one standard error) increase in the domestic interest rate equation. Figure 10.9 provides the persistence profiles of the effects of a unit shock to domestic interest rates (the size of the shock is scaled to ensure domestic interest rates rise by one standard error on impact) on the five long-run relationships. Figure 10.10 gives the

[15] See Gali and Monacelli (2005) for a small open economy model which shows the key difference between alternative rule-based policy regimes as being one of the relative amount of exchange rate volatility.

generalised impulse responses of a unit shock to the interest rate on the levels of all the eight endogenous variables in the model.

As is immediately apparent, the time profiles of the impulse responses of Figures 10.9 and 10.10 are very similar, in both size and shape, to those plotted in Figures 10.7 and 10.8 resulting from the identified monetary policy shock. This may not be too surprising as the impulses in the two experiments are clearly related and the long-run properties of the systems are the same. However, there are differences between the two which are

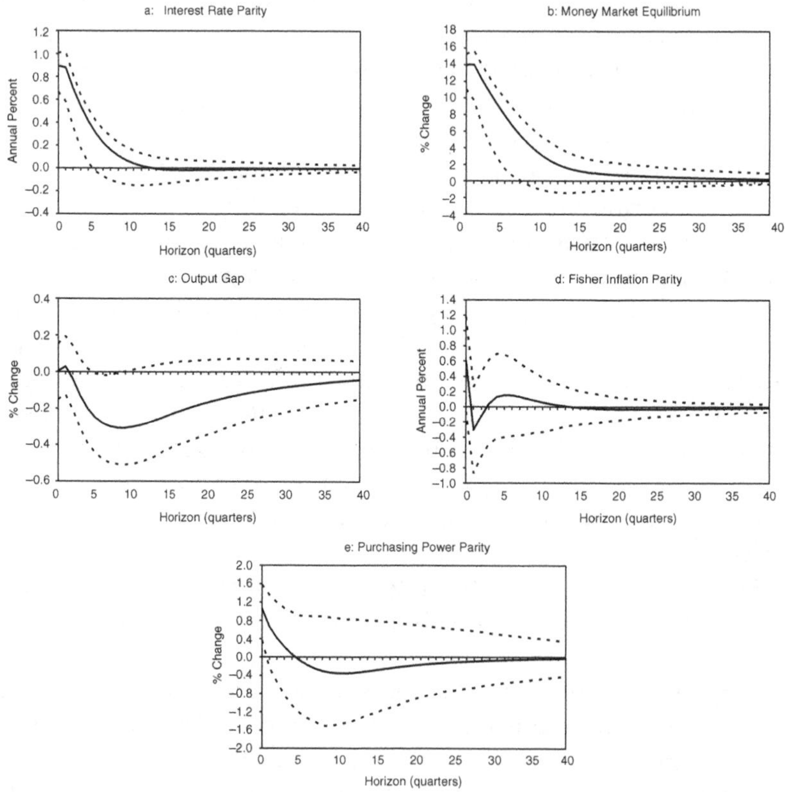

Note: The graphs define the long-run relationships as follows: Interest Rate Parity: $r_t - r_t^*$, Money Market Equilibrium Condition: $h_t - y_t + 56.1r_t + 0.0073t$, the Output Gap: $y_t - y_t^*$, Fisher Inflation Parity: $r_t - \Delta p_t$ and the *PPP* (real exchange rate): $e_t + p_t^* - p_t$. The size of the shock is equal to the standard deviation of the selected equation error. The solid and dashed lines plot the point estimates and 95% confidence intervals, respectively, of the impulse responses. The confidence intervals are generated from a bootstrap procedure using 2000 replications.

Figure 10.9 Persistence profiles of the long-run relations of a positive unit shock to the UK interest rate equation.

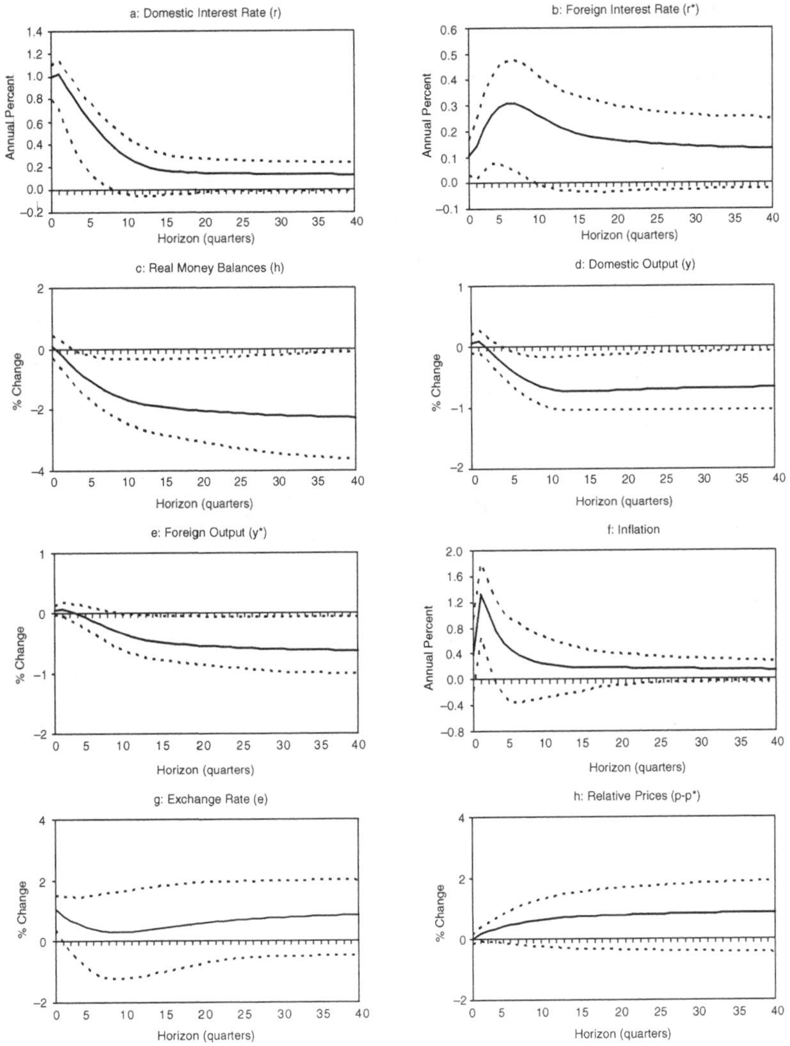

Note: The solid and dashed lines plot the point estimates and 95% confidence intervals, respectively, of the impulse responses. The confidence intervals are generated from a bootstrap procedure using 2000 replications.

Figure 10.10 Generalised impulse responses of a positive unit shock to the UK interest rate equation.

important in terms of interpretation of the responses. In particular, the response of the exchange rate in Figure 10.10g shows important differences to those in Figure 10.8g, indicating a *depreciation* of the exchange rate on impact in response to the positive shock to interest rates. Moreover, the positive differential of domestic over foreign interest rates observed over the first ten quarters is associated in Figure 10.10g with an *appreciating* exchange rate. It is worth emphasising that the GIRs obtained for the shock to the interest rate equation in Figure 10.10 take into account the contemporaneous innovations in the other variables typically observed when the interest rate is shocked. It does not have the interpretation of a monetary policy shock and one should not expect to be able to relate the profile of responses to economically motivated dynamics as we could those for Figure 10.8. But the comparison with the responses of Figure 10.8, which do have this reasonable match with an economically motivated interpretation, illustrates well both the strengths of the GIR analysis of reduced form shocks and its limitations.

10.3 Trend/cycle decomposition in cointegrating VARs

In this section, we consider a decomposition of the variables in the UK model into trends and cycles, with the former further decomposed into deterministic and stochastic components, following Garratt, Robertson and Wright (2005, GRW). As we shall see, the stochastic components will be present only if the underlying VAR contains a unit root. The decomposition can be viewed as a multivariate version of the well-known Beveridge–Nelson (BN) permanent/transitory decomposition, but has the advantage that it is characterised fully in terms of the observables.[16] We illustrate the analysis with an empirical example, highlighting the permanent components of selected variables of the core VEC model of the UK economy developed in the earlier chapters.

It is worth noting that the choice of a permanent trend/transitory cycle decomposition relies on *a priori* assumptions on the extent of the correlation between permanent and transitory innovations. In the literature, views have ranged from the assumption that the innovations arise from the same sources (so that the correlation is perfect) to the assumption that they are entirely unrelated (so that the correlation is zero). Decompositions in the spirit of BN assume that shocks to the transitory component and to the stochastic permanent component have a correlation of one. This is in contrast to the unobserved component's approach to permanent and

[16] Beveridge and Nelson (1981) describe the decomposition in the case of a univariate specification. For a multivariate version of the BN decomposition, see Stock and Watson (1988) and Evans and Reichlin (1994). Other decompositions are provided by Gonzalo and Granger (1995), Proietti (1997), Hecq, Palm and Urbain (2000), and Gonzalo and Ng (2001).

transitory decomposition, for example, which assumes the correlation is zero.[17]

To explain our proposed decomposition scheme, suppose we take any arbitrary partitioning of $\mathbf{z}_t = (\mathbf{y}_t', \mathbf{x}_t')'$ into permanent trend, $\mathbf{z}_t^P$, and transitory cycle, $\mathbf{z}_t^C$ components of the form:

$$\mathbf{z}_t = \mathbf{z}_t^P + \mathbf{z}_t^C, \tag{10.11}$$

where the permanent component may be further subdivided into deterministic and stochastic components

$$\mathbf{z}_t^P = \mathbf{z}_{dt}^P + \mathbf{z}_{st}^P.$$

Following GRW, we define the deterministic and the stochastic trend components of $\mathbf{z}_t$, respectively, by

$$\mathbf{z}_{dt}^P = \mathbf{g}_0 + \mathbf{g}t,$$

$$\mathbf{z}_{st}^P = \lim_{h\to\infty} E_t\left(\mathbf{z}_{t+h} - \mathbf{z}_{d,t+h}^P\right) = \lim_{h\to\infty} E_t\left[\mathbf{z}_{t+h} - \mathbf{g}_0 - \mathbf{g}(t+h)\right], \tag{10.12}$$

where $\mathbf{g}_0$ is an $m \times 1$ vector of fixed intercepts, $\mathbf{g}$ is an $m \times 1$ vector of (restricted) trend growth rates, t is a deterministic trend term, and $E_t(\cdot)$ denotes the expectations operator conditional on the information at time t, taken to be $\{\mathbf{z}_t, \mathbf{z}_{t-1}, \ldots, \mathbf{z}_0\}$. Then we have

$$\mathbf{z}_t^P = \lim_{h\to\infty} E_t\left(\mathbf{z}_{t+h} - \mathbf{g}h\right). \tag{10.13}$$

This definition of permanent trend has a number of important features that are worth emphasising

Remark 1 *Even if we are interested in the permanent/transitory decomposition of the endogenous variables, $\mathbf{y}_t$, we would still need to work with the VECM in $\mathbf{z}_t$ since this allows for long-run restrictions as well as for the short-term interactions that might exist between $\mathbf{y}_t$ and $\mathbf{x}_t$, under which the permanent/transitory properties of $\mathbf{x}_t$ would have a direct bearing on those of $\mathbf{y}_t$. This point reaffirms the desirability of multivariate approaches to trend/cycle decomposition over the univariate such as the Hodrick and Prescott (1997) and the original Beveridge–Nelson decompositions.*

[17] For a description of this alternative approach, see Harvey (1985), Watson (1986), Clarke (1987) and Harvey and Jaeger (1993). A review is provided in Canova (1998). Recently, Morley *et al.* (2003) have shown in a univariate context that when the (identifying) restriction in the unobserved components model that trend and cycle innovations are uncorrelated is relaxed, both decompositions will be identical.

Remark 2 *The stochastic permanent component of $\mathbf{z}_t^P$, namely $\mathbf{z}_{st}^P$, satisfies the property:*[18]

$$\lim_{h \to \infty} E_t\left(\mathbf{z}_{s,t+h}^P\right) = \mathbf{z}_{st}^P, \tag{10.14}$$

which is a limiting martingale property shared by the random walk models. Recall that a process X_t is said to follow a martingale process if $E_t\left(X_{t+h}\right) = X_t$ for all h. In the context of cointegrating VAR models, $\mathbf{z}_{st}^P$ satisfy the martingale property in the limit, whilst the permanent component of the BN decomposition is a martingale process and satisfy the property for all h. To establish the limit martingale property, (10.14), we first note that

$$E_t\left(\mathbf{z}_{t+h} - \mathbf{z}_{d,t+h}^P\right) = E_t\left(\mathbf{z}_{s,t+h}^P\right) + E_t\left(\mathbf{z}_{t+h}^C\right).$$

Since $\mathbf{z}_{t+h}^C$ is transitory, $\lim_{h \to \infty} E_t\left(\mathbf{z}_{t+h}^C\right) = 0$, and therefore

$$\lim_{h \to \infty} E_t\left(\mathbf{z}_{t+h} - \mathbf{z}_{d,t+h}^P\right) = \lim_{h \to \infty} E_t\left(\mathbf{z}_{s,t+h}^P\right).$$

Then, the result in (10.14) follows using (10.12).

Remark 3 *As pointed out earlier the definition of the permanent component given by (10.13) has the advantage that it is defined directly in terms of the observables $\{\mathbf{z}_t, \mathbf{z}_{t-1}, \ldots, \mathbf{z}_0\}$. But this does not render it unique. For example, suppose that $\mathbf{z}_t$ is cointegrated and co-trended such that $\boldsymbol{\beta}'\mathbf{z}_t + \mathbf{c}_0$ is a stationary process with zero mean, and set $\mathbf{z}_{st}^{PP} = \mathbf{z}_{st}^P + \boldsymbol{\beta}'\mathbf{z}_t + \mathbf{c}_0$. Then it readily follows that*

$$\lim_{h \to \infty} E_t\left(\mathbf{z}_{s,t+h}^{PP}\right) = \lim_{h \to \infty} E_t\left(\mathbf{z}_{s,t+h}^P\right) = \mathbf{z}_{st}^P.$$

Therefore, $\mathbf{z}_{st}^{PP}$ is also a stochastic permanent component with the same limiting martingale property as $\mathbf{z}_{st}^P$.

10.3.1 *Relationship of GRW and BN Decompositions*

For a comparison of the BN and GRW decompositions, it is instructive to consider the UK model, which is given by the following vector error correction specification with restricted (deterministic) trend coefficients:[19]

$$\Delta \mathbf{z}_t = \mathbf{a} - \boldsymbol{\alpha}\boldsymbol{\beta}' \left[\mathbf{z}_{t-1} - \boldsymbol{\gamma}(t-1)\right] + \sum_{i=1}^{p-1} \boldsymbol{\Gamma}_i \Delta \mathbf{z}_{t-i} + \mathbf{u}_t. \tag{10.15}$$

[18] The deterministic permanent components are the same for GRW and BN.

[19] See, for example, equation (10.5) and note that under case IV, $\mathbf{b}_1 = \boldsymbol{\beta}'\boldsymbol{\gamma}$, where $\boldsymbol{\gamma}$ is an $m \times 1$ vector of restricted trend coefficients.

Denote the deviation of the variables in $\mathbf{z}_t$ from their deterministic components as $\widetilde{\mathbf{z}}_t$, namely

$$\widetilde{\mathbf{z}}_t = \mathbf{z}_t - \mathbf{g}_0 - \mathbf{g}t.$$

Then in terms of $\widetilde{\mathbf{z}}_t$ we have

$$\Delta\widetilde{\mathbf{z}}_t = \mathbf{a} - \boldsymbol{\alpha}\boldsymbol{\beta}' g_0 - \left(\mathbf{I}_m - \sum_{i=1}^{p-1}\boldsymbol{\Gamma}_i\right)\mathbf{g} - \boldsymbol{\alpha}\boldsymbol{\beta}'(\mathbf{g}-\boldsymbol{\gamma})(t-1)$$
$$- \boldsymbol{\alpha}\boldsymbol{\beta}'\widetilde{\mathbf{z}}_{t-1} + \sum_{i=1}^{p-1}\boldsymbol{\Gamma}_i\Delta\tilde{\mathbf{z}}_{t-i} + \mathbf{u}_t.$$

Since $\widetilde{\mathbf{z}}_t$ has no deterministic components by construction, it must be that

$$\mathbf{a} = \boldsymbol{\alpha}\boldsymbol{\beta}'\mathbf{g}_0 + \left(\mathbf{I}_m - \sum_{i=1}^{p-1}\boldsymbol{\Gamma}_i\right)\mathbf{g}, \tag{10.16}$$

and

$$\boldsymbol{\beta}'\mathbf{g} = \boldsymbol{\beta}'\boldsymbol{\gamma}. \tag{10.17}$$

Hence

$$\Delta\widetilde{\mathbf{z}}_t = -\boldsymbol{\alpha}\boldsymbol{\beta}'\widetilde{\mathbf{z}}_{t-1} + \sum_{i=1}^{p-1}\boldsymbol{\Gamma}_i\Delta\tilde{\mathbf{z}}_{t-i} + \mathbf{u}_t, \tag{10.18}$$

or, equivalently,

$$\widetilde{\mathbf{z}}_t = \sum_{i=1}^{p}\boldsymbol{\Phi}_i\widetilde{\mathbf{z}}_{t-i} + \mathbf{u}_t, \tag{10.19}$$

where

$$\boldsymbol{\Phi}_1 = \mathbf{I}_m + \boldsymbol{\Gamma}_1 - \boldsymbol{\alpha}\boldsymbol{\beta}',\ \boldsymbol{\Phi}_i = \boldsymbol{\Gamma}_i - \boldsymbol{\Gamma}_{i-1},\ i = 2,\ldots,p-1,\ \boldsymbol{\Phi}_p = -\boldsymbol{\Gamma}_{p-1}.$$

The BN decomposition of $\mathbf{z}_t$ can now be written as[20]

$$\mathbf{z}_t = \mathbf{z}_0 + \mathbf{g}t + \mathbf{C}(1)\,\mathbf{s}_{ut} + \mathbf{C}^*(L)(\mathbf{u}_t - \mathbf{u}_0), \tag{10.20}$$

[20] See also Stock and Watson (1988) and Evans and Reichlin (1994), and the discussion in Section 6.2.1.

where

$$\mathbf{s}_{ut} = \sum_{i=1}^{t} \mathbf{u}_i, \; \mathbf{C}^*(L) = \sum_{i=0}^{\infty} \mathbf{C}_i^* L^i,$$

$$\mathbf{C}_i = \mathbf{C}_{i-1}\mathbf{\Phi}_1 + \mathbf{C}_{i-2}\mathbf{\Phi}_2 + \cdots + \mathbf{C}_{i-p}\mathbf{\Phi}_p, \quad \text{for } i = 1, 2, \ldots,$$

with $\mathbf{C}_0 = \mathbf{I}_m$, $\mathbf{C}_1 = -(\mathbf{I}_m - \mathbf{\Phi}_1)$, and $\mathbf{C}_i = \mathbf{0}$ for $i < 0$; $\mathbf{C}_i^* = \mathbf{C}_{i-1}^* + \mathbf{C}_i$, for $i = 1, 2, \ldots$, with $\mathbf{C}_0^* = \mathbf{C}_0 - \mathbf{C}(1)$, and $\mathbf{C}(1) = \sum_{i=0}^{\infty} \mathbf{C}_i$. Hence, the stochastic trend in this approach is defined by

$$\mathbf{z}_{st}^{BN} = \mathbf{C}(1) \sum_{i=1}^{t} \mathbf{u}_i, \tag{10.21}$$

and satisfies the martingale property

$$E_t\left(\mathbf{z}_{s,t+h}^{BN}\right) = \mathbf{z}_{st}^{BN}, \quad \text{for all } h.$$

The two decompositions differ in the way the permanent stochastic components are defined and yield identical results only in the case where $\mathbf{z}_t$ follows a random walk model, possibly with a drift. This arises in the case of univariate models, or in the case of multivariate models without cointegration.[21] For example, considering univariate models, Morley et al. (2003, p. 3) also define $\mathbf{z}_{st}^{BN}$ by

$$z_{st}^{BN} = \lim_{h\to\infty} E_t\left(z_{t+h} - gh\right),$$

and show that it reduces to $z_{st}^{BN} = c(1)\sum_{i=1}^{t} u_i$. Therefore, at first it appears that the two definitions, $\mathbf{z}_{st}^{P} = \lim_{h\to\infty} E_t\left(\mathbf{z}_{t+h} - \mathbf{g}h\right)$ and $\mathbf{z}_{st}^{BN} = \mathbf{C}(1)\sum_{i=1}^{t} \mathbf{u}_i$ are the same in general. But as noted above and the applications below illustrate this is not true in the multivariate case where $\mathbf{z}_t$ is cointegrated.

10.3.2 *Computation of the GRW decomposition*

As noted earlier, the GRW decomposition also has the advantage that it can be computed directly from the error correction or the VAR representation in terms of $\mathbf{z}_t, \mathbf{z}_{t-1}, \ldots, \mathbf{z}_{t-p+1}$. For computational purposes it is convenient to use the companion form of (10.19) given by

$$\widetilde{\mathbf{Z}}_t = \mathbf{F}\widetilde{\mathbf{Z}}_{t-1} + \mathbf{U}_t, \quad t = 1, \ldots, T,$$

[21] Note, however, that the two decompositions are based on the same deterministic trend specifications, with the restrictions on $\mathbf{g}$, defined by (10.17), applicable to both.

where

$$\underset{mp\times 1}{\widetilde{\mathbf{Z}}_t} = \begin{bmatrix} \widetilde{\mathbf{z}}_t \\ \widetilde{\mathbf{z}}_{t-1} \\ \vdots \\ \widetilde{\mathbf{z}}_{t-p+1} \end{bmatrix}, \quad \underset{mp\times 1}{\widetilde{\mathbf{Z}}_t} = \begin{bmatrix} \widetilde{\mathbf{z}}_{t-1} \\ \widetilde{\mathbf{z}}_{t-2} \\ \vdots \\ \widetilde{\mathbf{z}}_{t-p} \end{bmatrix}, \quad \underset{mp\times 1}{\mathbf{U}_t} = \begin{bmatrix} \mathbf{u}_t \\ 0 \\ \vdots \\ 0 \end{bmatrix},$$

$$\underset{mp\times mp}{\mathbf{F}} = \begin{bmatrix} \mathbf{\Phi}_1 & \mathbf{\Phi}_2 & \mathbf{\Phi}_3 & \cdots & \mathbf{\Phi}_{p-1} & \mathbf{\Phi}_p \\ \mathbf{I}_m & 0 & 0 & \cdots & 0 & 0 \\ 0 & \mathbf{I}_m & 0 & \cdots & 0 & 0 \\ \vdots & \vdots & \vdots & \vdots & \vdots & \vdots \\ 0 & 0 & 0 & \cdots & 0 & 0 \\ 0 & 0 & 0 & \cdots & \mathbf{I}_m & 0 \end{bmatrix}.$$

It is easily seen that

$$\widetilde{\mathbf{Z}}_{t+h} = \mathbf{F}^h\widetilde{\mathbf{Z}}_t + \sum_{j=0}^{h-1} \mathbf{F}^j\mathbf{U}_{t+h-j}.$$

Therefore, we have

$$\widetilde{\mathbf{z}}_{t+h} = \mathbf{J}\mathbf{F}^h\widetilde{\mathbf{Z}}_t + \sum_{j=0}^{h-1} \mathbf{J}\mathbf{F}^j\mathbf{U}_{t+h-j} = \mathbf{J}\mathbf{F}^h\widetilde{\mathbf{Z}}_t + \sum_{j=0}^{h-1} \left(\mathbf{J}\mathbf{F}^j\mathbf{J}'\right)\mathbf{u}_{t+h-j},$$

and

$$E_t\left(\widetilde{\mathbf{z}}_{t+h}\right) = \mathbf{J}\mathbf{F}^h\widetilde{\mathbf{Z}}_t,$$

where $\underset{m\times mp}{\mathbf{J}} = (\mathbf{I}_m, \mathbf{0}, \ldots, \mathbf{0})$ is a selection matrix.

In the case of the cointegrating VAR system with $I(1)$ variables, the eigenvalues of the underlying VAR model are either on or inside of the unit circle, and thus we have

$$\mathbf{z}_{st}^P = \lim_{h\to\infty} E_t\left(\widetilde{\mathbf{z}}_{t+h}\right) = \mathbf{J}\mathbf{F}^{\infty}\widetilde{\mathbf{Z}}_t, \tag{10.22}$$

where $\mathbf{F}^{\infty}$ is the limit of $\mathbf{F}^h$ as $h \to \infty$. In the case where all the variables in the VAR are stationary, $\mathbf{F}^{\infty} = \mathbf{0}$ and $\mathbf{z}_t$ will have no stochastic trend components. But in the general case where $\mathbf{z}_t$ contains $I(1)$ variables (and possibly cointegrated), $\mathbf{F}^{\infty}$ tends to a finite non-zero matrix and the overall trend component of $\mathbf{z}_t$ will be given by

$$\mathbf{z}_t^P = \lim_{h\to\infty} E_t\left(\mathbf{z}_{t+h} - \mathbf{g}h\right) = \mathbf{g}_0 + \mathbf{g}t + \mathbf{J}\mathbf{F}^{\infty}\widetilde{\mathbf{Z}}_t. \tag{10.23}$$

The cycle or the transitory component of $\mathbf{z}_t$ is then defined simply as

$$\mathbf{z}_t^C = \mathbf{z}_t - \mathbf{z}_t^P.$$

In the applications below we set the vector of intercepts, $\mathbf{g}_0$, so that the cyclical components have mean zero.

10.3.3 *An application to the UK model*

To compute the decomposition described above, all the required parameters can be estimated from the maximum likelihood estimates of the underlying VEC model, except for $\mathbf{g}$. Note that under Case IV, the estimation of the cointegrating VAR yields an estimate of $\boldsymbol{\beta}'\boldsymbol{\gamma}$, and $\boldsymbol{\gamma}$ cannot be separately identified from $\boldsymbol{\beta}$ in the presence of cointegration. But, noting that $\Delta\mathbf{z}_t$ is stationary with mean $\mathbf{g}$, we can estimate $\mathbf{g}$ by estimating

$$\Delta\mathbf{z}_t = \mathbf{g} + \boldsymbol{\vartheta}_t, \tag{10.24}$$

subject to the restrictions $\boldsymbol{\beta}'\mathbf{g} = \boldsymbol{\beta}'\boldsymbol{\gamma}$ with $\boldsymbol{\beta}'\boldsymbol{\gamma}$ given by the maximum likelihood estimates, say $\widehat{\boldsymbol{\beta}'\boldsymbol{\gamma}}$. A consistent estimate of $\mathbf{g}$ can be obtained by application of the SURE procedure to (10.24) subject to the restrictions, $\boldsymbol{\beta}'\mathbf{g} = \widehat{\boldsymbol{\beta}'\boldsymbol{\gamma}}$. A more efficient estimator can be obtained by exploiting the serial correlation properties of $\boldsymbol{\vartheta}_t$ as well.

In the case of the UK model where

$$\mathbf{z}_t = \left(p_t^o, e_t, r_t^*, r_t, \Delta p_t, y_t, p_t - p_t^*, h_t - y_t, y_t^*\right)',$$
$$\mathbf{g} = \left(g_o, g_e, g_{r^*}, g_r, g_{\Delta p}, g_y, g_{p-p^*}, g_{h-y}, g_{y^*}\right)'$$

and

$$\hat{\boldsymbol{\beta}}'\mathbf{g} = \begin{pmatrix} 0 & -1 & 0 & 0 & 0 & 0 & 1 & 0 & 0 \\ 0 & 0 & -1 & 1 & 0 & 0 & 0 & 0 & 0 \\ 0 & 0 & 0 & 0 & 0 & 1 & 0 & 0 & -1 \\ 0 & 0 & 0 & -56.098 & 0 & 0 & 0 & 1 & 0 \\ 0 & 0 & 0 & 1 & -1 & 0 & 0 & 0 & 0 \end{pmatrix} \begin{pmatrix} g_o \\ g_e \\ g_{r^*} \\ g_r \\ g_{\Delta p} \\ g_y \\ g_{p-p^*} \\ g_{h-y} \\ g_{y^*} \end{pmatrix}$$

$$= \begin{pmatrix} g_e - g_{p-p^*} \\ g_{r^*} - g_r \\ g_y - g_{y^*} \\ -56.098 g_r \\ g_r - g_{\Delta p} \end{pmatrix}.$$

Also, the estimated version of the model yields

$$\widehat{\beta'\gamma} = \begin{pmatrix} 0 \\ 0 \\ 0 \\ -0.007300 \\ 0 \end{pmatrix}.$$

This yields the following restrictions

$$g_e = g_{p-p^*},\, g_{r^*} = g_r,\, g_y = g_{y^*},\, g_r = 0.007300/56.098, \text{ and } g_r = g_{\Delta p}.$$

The presence of a linear trend in the money demand equation implies a very small but a non-zero value for g_r (= 0.00013). We decided to set $g_r = 0$ as it is unlikely that the trend in the money demand equation could prevail in the very long run. Therefore, we estimate **g** subject to the following restrictions:

$$g_e = g_{p-p^*},\, g_y = g_{y^*} \quad \text{and} \quad g_{\Delta p} = g_r = g_{r^*} = 0,$$

and obtained the estimate,

$$\hat{\mathbf{g}} = (0.018557, 0.002179, 0, 0, 0, 0.005256, 0.002179, -0.007287, 0.005256)'.$$

Using these estimates together with the estimated parameters from equation (10.15), we can construct a permanent/transitory or trend/cycle decomposition.

To illustrate the decomposition, Figures 10.11–10.18 plot a range of transitory and permanent components for some selected endogenous variables of the model. Figure 10.11 plots the actual series and the GRW permanent component of domestic output y_t. The GRW permanent component of UK GDP is not as smooth as other trend estimates and it is also subject to some fairly significant downward, as well as upward, shifts at various points in the sample. However, the important point here is that, by construction, the permanent component of y_t is perfectly correlated with the permanent component of y_t^*. This interesting feature, that the permanent stochastic components of the variables that cointegrate and co-trend should be perfectly correlated, also applies to the pairs r_t and r_t^*; and r_t and Δp_t (once the long-run theory restrictions are imposed).

In Figure 10.12, we plot the transitory component of the UK output alongside the transitory component of inflation so that we might look at the cyclical movements in the inflation–output trade-off.[22] Given our

[22] To provide a clearer picture of the relationships we have normalised all the transitory components so that they have mean zero over the sample period under consideration.

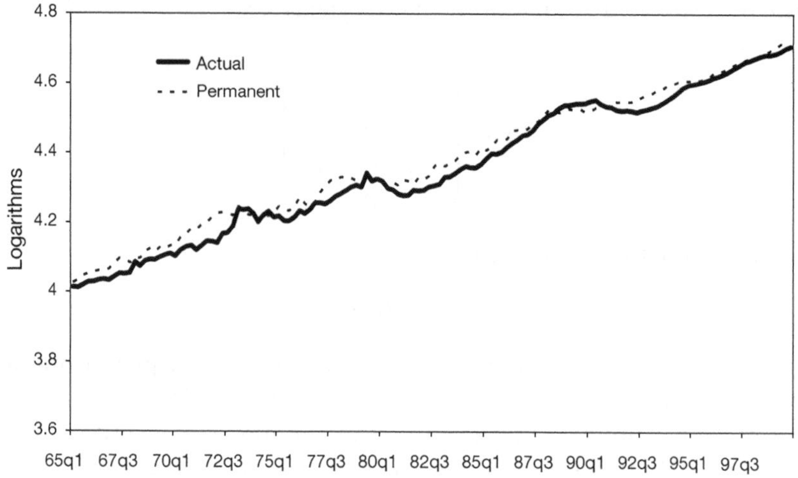

Figure 10.11 Actual UK output (y_t) and the GRW permanent component.

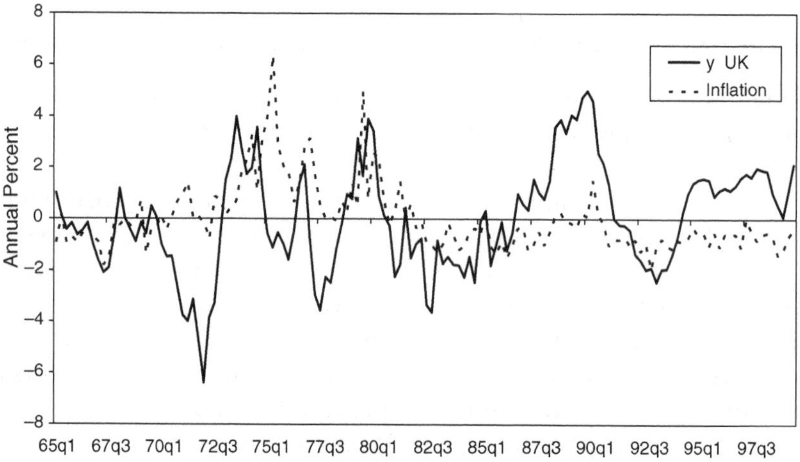

Figure 10.12 GRW transitory components of UK output and inflation: y_t and Δp_t.

explicit multivariate approach to detrending, the figure automatically takes account of the interactions between the variables when analysing the nature of the relationship between output and inflation. As the figure shows, there is a limited degree of positive co-movement between inflation and output, with a correlation coefficient of just 0.14, which is

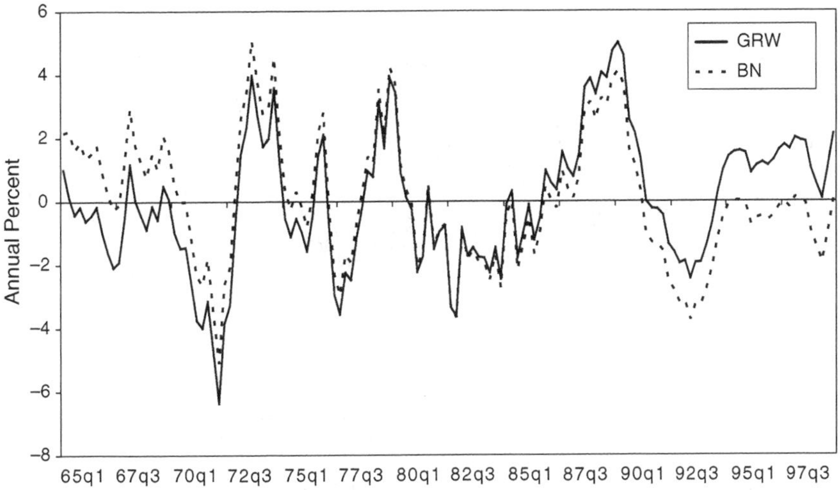

Figure 10.13 GRW and BN transitory components of UK output: y_t.

consistent with a demand-shock view of the business cycle, but the cyclical dependence seems rather weak. A sub-sample analysis could well be more revealing here.

Figure 10.13 plots the GRW and BN transitory components for y_t. There is a clear degree of consensus between the two series, reflected in a correlation coefficient of 0.827, although the BN transitory component suggests higher growth in the early 1960s but lower growth in the late 1990s. In fact, there is a high degree of co-movement between the GRW and BN transitory components for all the endogenous variables, with correlation coefficients of 1.00, 0.965, 0.980, 0.997, 0.999, 0.901 and 0.929 for $e_t, r_t^*, r_t, \Delta p_t, p_t - p_t^*, h_t - y_t$ and y_t^*, respectively. The two decompositions yield the same result for the exchange rate due to its random walk property.

Figure 10.14 plots the GRW transitory components of y_t and y_t^*.[23] The most noticeable feature is the limited degree of co-movement exhibited by the two series, with a correlation coefficient of 0.28, particularly in the late 1960s, early 1980s and late 1990s. For a comparison, Figures 10.15 and 10.16 plot the BN and Hodrick–Prescott (HP) transitory components of the same two series.[24] Both the GRW and BN decompositions show

[23] To make any meaningful comparison between the transitory components of variables with different levels we require that each variable be mean zero and hence we first de-mean (using the sample mean) the transitory components.

[24] The HP filter uses a smoothing parameter value of 1600.

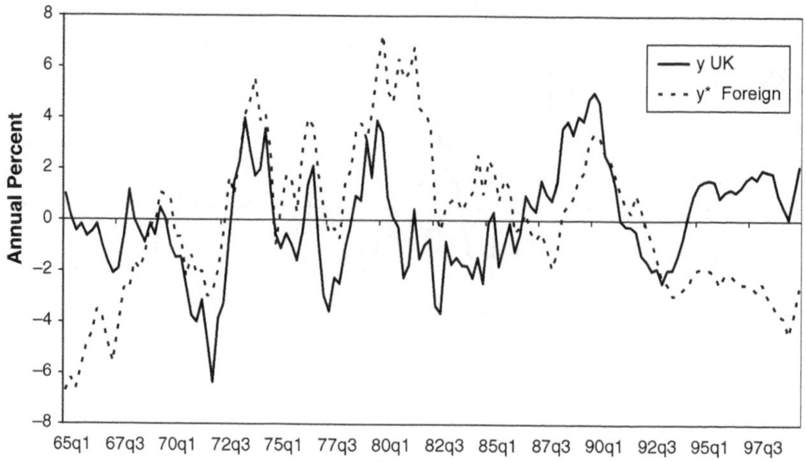

Figure 10.14 GRW transitory components of UK and foreign output: y_t and y_t^*.

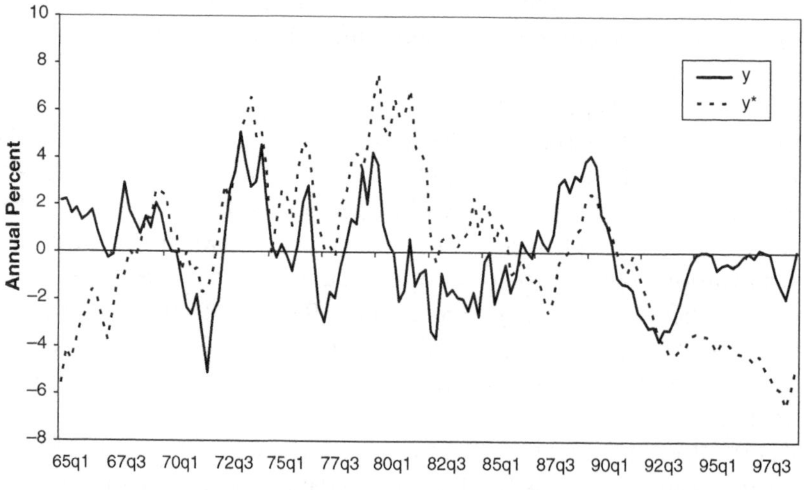

Figure 10.15 BN transitory components of UK and foreign output: y_t and y_t^*.

a low degree of co-movement between the transitory components of UK and foreign output, although the correlation coefficient is slightly higher at 0.38 (as compared to 0.28) in the case of the BN decomposition. The degree of co-movement between the HP transitory y_t and y_t^* components is noticeably higher, yielding a correlation coefficient of

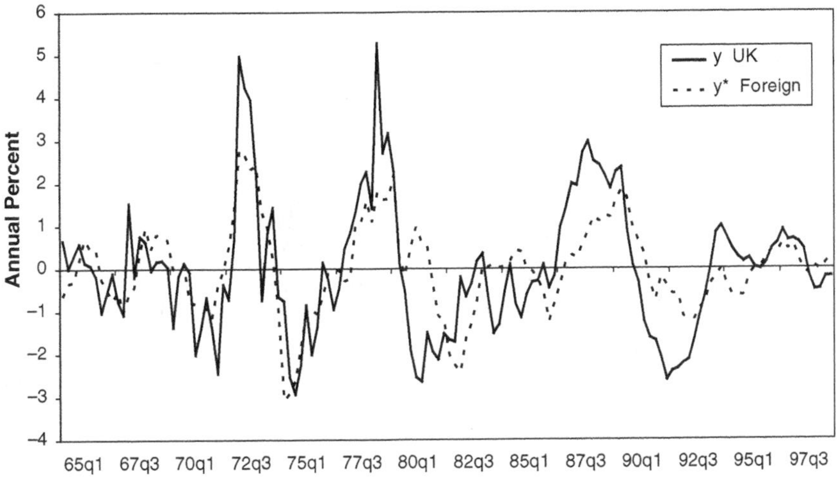

Figure 10.16 Hodrick–Prescott transitory components of UK and foreign output: y_t and y_t^*.

0.69. A tentative implication therefore is that the univariate HP filter overstates the degree of co-movement between the transitory components (*i.e.* induces highly synchronised business cycle for the UK relative to the rest of the world); the multivariate VECM, which imposes the long-run restrictions, does not support such a high degree of short-run synchronisations.

Figure 10.17 plots the transitory components of r_t and r_t^*. As in the case of y_t and y_t^*, the restriction that the permanent components are perfectly correlated is imposed. Here, our zero growth rate assumption on r_t and r_t^* implies that the change in the permanent component of these series is determined purely by the stochastic part (where the deterministic part is fixed at its initial value, see Figure 10.6). The co-movement between domestic and foreign interest rates is positive and reasonably strong, with a correlation coefficient of 0.5. The transitory component of domestic interest rates is more volatile but part of this difference reflects the fact that foreign interest rates are measured as the average of interest rates in a number of countries and hence is likely to be relatively smooth. Figure 10.18 plots the actual r_t series alongside its permanent component. We see here that a large part of movements in r_t could be defined as transitory, with the permanent component showing little variations.

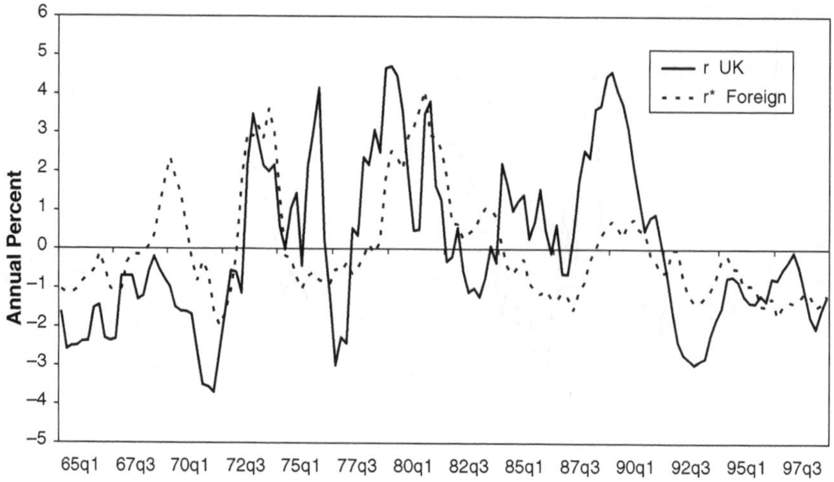

Figure 10.17 GRW transitory components of UK and foreign interest rates: r_t and r_t^*.

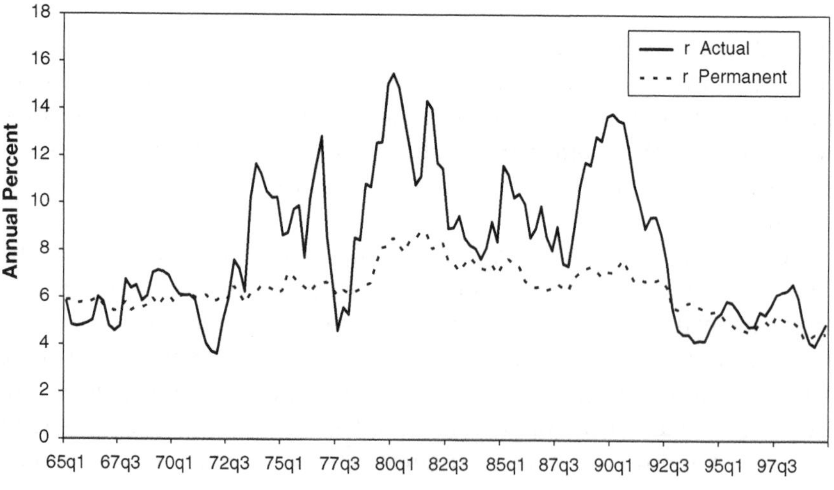

Figure 10.18 Actual and GRW permanent component of UK interest rates: r_t.

10.4 Concluding remarks

In this chapter, we have illustrated how we might use our modelling approach in the analysis of shocks through the use of both GIR and structural identified impulse responses. The cointegrating VAR model is not only able to provide a reasonably flexible characterisation of the short-run dynamics of the macroeconomy but, by making explicit the link with the long-run relationships suggested by economic theory, it also enables us to consider explicitly the links between 'structural' and 'observable' shocks and provides an appropriate treatment of the analysis of the model's dynamic properties. Our use of Persistence Profiles show directly the dynamic effects of system-wide shocks to the equilibrium relations. Hence, for example, the estimated profiles illustrate clearly the differential speeds of response to the disequilibria involving financial variables compared to those involving real magnitudes. Our use of the Generalised Impulse Response functions allows us to investigate the effects of specific shocks to particular equations in the model, gaining insight on the dynamic response to particular events without the use of arbitrary orthogonalisation assumptions and without losing sight of the relationships that exist between the innovations and the underlying economic model.

There are, of course, a variety of other impulse response analyses that can be conducted using our model. Bernanke *et al.* (1997) and Cochrane (1998), for example, suggest counter-factual exercises aimed at distinguishing the effects of systematic changes to monetary policy rules from those that influence the economy's intrinsic propagation mechanisms. As a second example, one might consider impulse response functions associated with a once-and-for-all shift in the intercept of the interest rate equation.[25] This would help, for example, identify the time profile of the effects of shifts in the target variables for output growth or inflation reduction, *i.e.* $\Delta\mathbf{w}^{\dagger}$ in (5.12) of Chapter 5. The model presented in this book provides a potentially fruitful framework with which to investigate these and other counter-factual policy exercises.

Our discussion of the trend/cycle decomposition also highlights the importance of allowing for the long-run restrictions in identification and estimation of the transitory components. For example, by abstracting from the long-run relations that might exist in cross-country outputs, the use of univariate approaches such as the Hodrick–Prescott filter is likely to over state the degree of business cycle synchronisations that exist across countries.

[25] This is equivalent to a GIR function with certain zero restrictions on the error correction covariances.

11

Probability event forecasting with the UK model

In this chapter, we consider the application of the probability forecasting techniques introduced in Chapter 7 to our model of the UK economy. A number of macroeconomic modelling teams in the UK have recently begun to provide further information on the uncertainties surrounding their forecasts of key macroeconomic variables. It is widely acknowledged that it is important to provide this information on the precision of the forecasts in order to enable policy-makers to motivate and justify actions based on the forecasts, and to help a more balanced evaluation of the forecasts by the public.[1] However, it remains rare for forecasters, policy-makers or private, to provide the detailed information on the range of potential outcomes that agents might find useful in decision-making and policy analysis. One explanation of this relates to the difficulty in measuring the uncertainties associated with forecasts in the large mainstream macroeconomic models typically employed. A second explanation is the perceived difficulty in conveying the outcomes of complicated macroeconomic models in a simple and easily understood form.

Our compact modelling approach, however, provides a practical framework for probability forecasting. The model is theoretically coherent, fits the UK historical aggregate time series data reasonably well (as argued in earlier Chapters) and yet the model is small enough to allow for a large variety of probability forecasting problems of interest to be analysed without encountering difficult computational problems. In what follows we shall

[1] For example, the Bank of England now routinely publishes a range of outcomes for its inflation and output growth forecasts (see Britton *et al.* (1998), or Wallis (1999)); the National Institute use their model to produce probability statements alongside their central forecasts (their methods are described in Blake (1996), and Poulizac *et al.* (1996)); and in the financial sector, J.P. Morgan presents 'Event Risk Indicators' in its analysis of foreign exchange markets.

focus on events that particularly interest the monetary authorities namely the inflation rate remaining within a given target band and the economy going into recession over various time frames. We consider these events both individually and jointly. Although only a small number of events are considered, we shall show that these probability event forecasts can convey a considerable amount of information on the uncertainties surrounding a forecast, and correspond with those which the public uses in judging policy-makers' performance.

11.1 An updated version of the core model

In principle, probability forecasts can be computed using any macroeconometric model, although the necessary computations would become prohibitive in the case of most large-scale macroeconometric models, particularly if the objective of the exercise is to compute the probabilities of joint events at long forecast horizons. At the other extreme, the use of small unrestricted VAR models, while computationally feasible, may not be satisfactory for the analysis of forecast probabilities over the medium term. Our VAR model of order 2, involving nine variables, represents an intermediate alternative that is well suited to the generation of probability forecasts. In what follows, therefore we work with a model of the same form as that presented in Chapter 9. However, in order to evaluate the forecasting performance of the model, we extend the dataset, so that it covers the period 1965q1–2001q1, as compared to 1965q1–1999q4 discussed in the earlier chapters and work with updated versions of the core model.[2]

As a reminder we reproduce the model specification below. Under the assumption that oil prices are 'long-run forcing', efficient estimation of the parameters can be based on the following *conditional* error correction model:

$$\Delta \mathbf{y}_t = \mathbf{a}_y - \boldsymbol{\alpha}_y \left[\boldsymbol{\beta}' \mathbf{z}_{t-1} - \mathbf{b}_1 (t-1) \right] + \sum_{i=1}^{p-1} \boldsymbol{\Gamma}_{yi} \Delta \mathbf{z}_{t-i} + \boldsymbol{\psi}_{yo} \Delta p_t^o + \mathbf{u}_{yt}, \quad (11.1)$$

where $\mathbf{y}_t = \left(e_t, r_t^*, r_t, \Delta p_t, y_t, p_t - p_t^*, h_t - y_t, y_t^*\right)'$, $\mathbf{a}_y$ is an 8×1 vector of fixed intercepts, $\boldsymbol{\alpha}_y$ is an 8×5 matrix of error correction coefficients, $\{\boldsymbol{\Gamma}_{yi}, i = 1, 2, \ldots, p-1\}$ are 8×9 matrices of short-run coefficients, $\boldsymbol{\psi}_{yo}$ is an 8×1 vector representing the impact effects of changes in oil prices on $\Delta \mathbf{y}_t$, and

[2] The description of the empirical work of this chapter elaborates that provided in Garratt *et al.* (2003b).

$\mathbf{u}_{yt}$ is an 8×1 vector of disturbances assumed to be $i.i.d.(0, \boldsymbol{\Sigma}_y)$, with $\boldsymbol{\Sigma}_y$ being a positive definite matrix. For forecasting purposes, we specify the process for the change in the oil price to be:

$$\Delta p_t^o = \delta_o + \sum_{i=1}^{p-1} \boldsymbol{\delta}_{oi} \Delta \mathbf{z}_{t-i} + u_{ot}, \tag{11.2}$$

where $\boldsymbol{\delta}_{oi}$ is a 1×9 vector of fixed coefficients and u_{ot} is a serially uncorrelated error term distributed independently of $\mathbf{u}_{yt}$. This specification encompasses the familiar random walk model used in the impulse response analysis in Chapter 10 as a special case and seems quite general for our purposes. Combining (11.1) and (11.2), and solving for $\Delta \mathbf{z}_t$ yields the following reduced form equation which will be used in forecasting:

$$\Delta \mathbf{z}_t = \mathbf{a} - \boldsymbol{\alpha} \left[\boldsymbol{\beta}' \mathbf{z}_{t-1} - \mathbf{b}_1 (t-1) \right] + \sum_{i=1}^{p-1} \boldsymbol{\Gamma}_i \Delta \mathbf{z}_{t-i} + \mathbf{v}_t, \tag{11.3}$$

where $\mathbf{a} = \left(\delta_o, \mathbf{a}_y' - a_o \boldsymbol{\psi}_{yo}' \right)'$, $\boldsymbol{\alpha} = \left(0, \boldsymbol{\alpha}_y' \right)'$, $\boldsymbol{\Gamma}_i = \left(\delta_{oi}', \boldsymbol{\Gamma}_{yi}' - \delta_{oi}' \boldsymbol{\psi}_{yo}' \right)'$ and $\mathbf{v}_t = \left(u_{ot}, \mathbf{u}_{yt}' - u_{ot} \boldsymbol{\psi}_{yo}' \right)'$ is the vector of reduced form errors assumed to be $i.i.d.(0, \boldsymbol{\Sigma})$, where $\boldsymbol{\Sigma}$ is a positive definite matrix.

11.1.1 *Estimation results and in-sample diagnostics*

Chapter 9 documents the empirical exercise with respect to the core model using data over the period 1965q1–1999q4. The results showed that: (i) a VAR(2) model can adequately capture the dynamic properties of the data; (ii) there are five cointegrating relationships amongst the nine macroeconomic variables; and (iii) the over-identifying restrictions suggested by economic theory, and described in Chapter 9 above, cannot be rejected. For the present exercise, we re-estimated the model on the more up-to-date sample, 1965q1–2001q1. The results continue to support the existence of five cointegrating relations, and are qualitatively very similar to those described in Garratt *et al.* (2003a). For example, the interest rate coefficient in the real money balance equation is estimated to be 75.68 (standard error 35.34), compared to 56.10 (22.28) in the original work, while the coefficient on the time trend is estimated to be 0.0068 (0.0010), compared to 0.0073 (0.0012).

Since the modelling exercise here is primarily for the purpose of forecasting, we next re-estimated the model over the shorter period of 1985q1–2001q1, taking the long-run relations as given. The inclusion of the long-run relations estimated over the period 1965q1–2001q1 in a cointegrating VAR model estimated over the shorter sample period 1985q1–2001q1, is justified on two grounds: (i) as argued by Barassi *et al.* (2001) and Clements and Hendry (2002), the short-run coefficients are more likely to be subject to structural change as compared to the long-run coefficients; and (ii) the application of Johansen's cointegration tests is likely to be unreliable in small samples. Following this procedure, we are able to base the forecasts on a model with well-specified long-run relations, but which is also data-consistent, capturing the complex dynamic relationships that hold across the macroeconomic variables over recent years.

Table 11.1 gives the estimates of the individual error correcting relations of the benchmark model estimated over the 1985q1–2001q1 period.

These estimates show that the error correction terms are important in most equations and provide for a complex and statistically significant set of interactions and feedbacks across commodity, money and foreign exchange markets. The estimated error correction equations pass most of the diagnostic tests and compared to standard benchmarks, fit the historical observations relatively well. In particular, the $\bar{R}^2$ of the domestic output and inflation equations, computed at 0.549 and 0.603, respectively, are quite high. The diagnostic statistics for tests of residual serial correlation, functional form and heteroscedasticity are well within the 90% critical values, although there is evidence of non-normal errors in the case of some of the error correcting equations. Non-normal errors is not a serious problem at the estimation and inference stage, but can be important in Value-at-Risk analysis, for example, where tail probabilities are the main objects of interest. In such cases non-parametric techniques for computation of forecast probabilities might be used. See Chapter 7 for further details.

11.1.2 *Model uncertainty*

The theory-based cointegrating model is clearly one amongst many possible models that could be used to provide probability forecasts of the main UK macroeconomic variables. In order to address the issue of model uncertainty in the analysis that follows we adopt the Bayesian Model Averaging (BMA) framework described in Chapter 7.[3]

[3] The role of model uncertainty in explaining historical inflation data and the various monetary policy stances held in post-war US and UK has been highlighted recently by the work of Cogley and Sargent (2001, 2005) and Cogley *et al.* (2005).

Table 11.1 Error correction specification for the over-identified model, 1985q1–2001q1.

Equation	$\Delta(p_t - p_t^*)$	Δe_t	Δr_t	Δr_t^*	Δy_t	Δy_t^*	$\Delta(h_t - y_t)$	$\Delta^2 \tilde{p}_t$
$\hat{\xi}_{1t}$	−0.020*	0.136*	0.003	0.0006	0.010	0.002	0.031*	−0.014*
	(0.010)	(0.071)	(0.004)	(0.001)	(0.009)	(0.006)	(0.017)	(0.008)
$\hat{\xi}_{2t}$	−0.775	−2.59	−593†	0.117	0.541	0.063	−1.31	−1.05†
	(0.664)	(4.63)	(0.281)	(0.075)	(0.592)	(0.418)	(1.09)	(0.508)
$\hat{\xi}_{3t}$	0.022	0.073	0.029	−0.003	−0.061	0.057	0.271†	0.087*
	(0.060)	(0.414)	(0.025)	(0.007)	(0.050)	(0.037)	(0.098)	(0.045)
$\hat{\xi}_{4t}$	0.010*	0.003	0.004	−0.001	−0.012†	0.0004	−0.003	0.005
	(0.006)	(0.043)	(0.003)	(0.0007)	(0.005)	(0.004)	(0.010)	(0.005)
$\hat{\xi}_{5t}$	0.131	2.04	0.007	−0.014	0.315	0.060	0.257	1.26
	(0.239)	(1.67)	(0.101)	(0.027)	(0.203)	(0.150)	(0.393)	(0.183)
$\Delta(p_{t-1} - p_{t-1}^*)$	0.275	−0.588	−0.030	0.007	0.136	0.031	−0.066	0.163
	(0.176)	(1.23)	(0.074)	(0.020)	(0.149)	(0.111)	(0.289)	(0.134)
Δe_{t-1}	0.020	0.210	−0.0001	0.0004	0.019	−0.012	0.059	−0.025
	(0.022)	(0.155)	(0.009)	(0.003)	(0.029)	(0.014)	(0.037)	(0.017)
Δr_{t-1}	−0.025	−3.90	0.214	0.053	0.190	0.025	−0.296	0.960†
	(0.404)	(2.81)	(0.171)	(0.046)	(0.342)	(0.254)	(0.665)	(0.309)
Δr_{t-1}^*	−0.839	5.74	−0.120	0.407†	0.784	−0.732	−2.42	1.15
	(1.23)	(8.59)	(0.522)	(0.139)	(1.05)	(0.775)	(2.03)	(0.943)
Δy_{t-1}	−0.090	−1.47	0.009	−0.017	0.439†	0.343†	−0.782†	0.252*
	(0.177)	(1.23)	(0.075)	(0.020)	(0.150)	(0.111)	(0.291)	(0.135)
Δy_{t-1}^*	−0.052	0.489	0.131	0.072†	0.351*	0.184	0.386	0.147
	(0.229)	(1.51)	(0.097)	(0.026)	(0.194)	(0.053)	(0.377)	(0.175)
$\Delta(h_{t-1} - y_{t-1})$	0.023	−0.081	−0.029	−0.001	−0.057	−0.007	−0.255*	−0.023
	(0.086)	(0.588)	(0.036)	(0.010)	(0.073)	(0.053)	(0.141)	(0.066)
$\Delta^2 \tilde{p}_{t-1}$	−0.064	0.860	−0.012	−0.008	−0.019	−0.049	−0.194	0.017
	(0.171)	(1.19)	(0.072)	(0.019)	(0.145)	(0.107)	(0.281)	(0.131)
Δp_{t-1}^o	−0.005	0.006	−0.0001	−0.0009	0.012†	0.005	0.006	0.003
	(0.005)	(0.036)	(0.002)	(0.0006)	(0.004)	(0.003)	(0.009)	(0.004)
Δp_t^o	−0.010†	−0.019	0.002	−0.0007	−0.010†	−0.001	−0.001	0.004
	(0.005)	(0.032)	(0.002)	(0.0005)	(0.004)	(0.003)	(0.007)	(0.003)
$\bar{R}^2$	0.365	0.089	0.017	0.476	0.549	0.371	0.378	0.603
$\hat{\sigma}$	0.005	0.032	0.002	0.001	0.004	0.003	0.008	0.003
$\chi^2_{SC}[4]$	4.31	3.16	9.40*	1.91	5.74	7.29	7.40	5.89
$\chi^2_{FF}[1]$	3.04	0.76	3.49*	2.26	0.86	2.31	0.02	0.98
$\chi^2_{N}[2]$	3.53	11.2†	7.13†	0.27	1.91	1.47	33.9†	26.0†
$\chi^2_{H}[1]$	0.01	0.01	1.08	0.01	0.83	0.84	0.17	0.057

Note: The five error correction terms, estimated over the period 1965q1–2001q1, are given by

$$\hat{\xi}_{1,t+1} = p_t - p_t^* - e_t - 4.8566,$$

$$\hat{\xi}_{2,t+1} = r_t - r_t^* - 0.0057,$$

$$\hat{\xi}_{3,t+1} = y_t - y_t^* + 0.0366,$$

$$\hat{\xi}_{4,t+1} = h_t - y_t + \underset{(35.34)}{75.68} r_t + \underset{(0.001)}{0.0068} t + 0.1283,$$

$$\hat{\xi}_{5,t+1} = r_t - \Delta\tilde{p}_t - 0.0037.$$

Standard errors are given in parentheses. '*' indicates significance at the 10% level, and '†' indicates significance at the 5% level. The diagnostics are chi-squared statistics for serial correlation (SC), functional form (FF), normality (N) and heteroscedasticity (H).

We confine our analysis to the class of VAR(p) models, which nonetheless allows for the existence of range of important sources of uncertainties. The most important sources of uncertainty in this context are the order of the VAR, p, the number of the long-run (or cointegrating) relations, r, the validity of the over-identifying restrictions imposed on the long-run coefficients, and the specification of the oil price equation. Given the limited time series data available, consideration of models with $p = 3$ or more did not seem advisable. We also thought it would not be worthwhile to consider $p = 1$ on the grounds that the resultant equations would most likely suffer from residual serial correlation. Therefore, we confined the choice of the models to be considered in the BMA procedure to exactly identified VAR(2) models with $r = 0, 1, \ldots, 5$, and two alternative specifications of the oil price equation, namely (11.2), and its random walk counterpart,

$$\Delta p_t^o = \delta_o + u_{ot}. \tag{11.4}$$

Naturally, we also included our benchmark model in the set (for both specifications of the oil price equation), thus yielding a total of 14 models to be considered. We shall use these models in the forecast evaluation exercise below investigating the robustness of probability forecasts from the benchmark model to model uncertainty.

To allow for the effect of model uncertainty, we employed the BMA formulae, (7.33) and (7.36), with the weights, w_{iT}, set according to the following three schemes: Akaike, Schwarz and equal weights ($w_{iT} = 1/14$). The first two are computed using (7.35). In the event, only five of the 14 models appeared as plausible candidates according to the AIC and SBC criteria. Using the AIC, only two candidate models were considered plausible: namely, the exactly identifed five cointegrating vector (CV) models with the two alternative oil price specifications. For the estimation period 1985q1–1998q4, the two models had estimated weights of 0.93 and 0.07 (for the model containing the oil equation in (11.2) and that containing the random walk model, respectively). These weights gradually changed to 0.60:0.40 for the estimation period 1985q1–2000q4, following our recursive forecasting procedure, but all other models had zero weights throughout. Using the SBC, the exactly identified models with 5, 4, 3 and 2 cointegrating vectors, each supplemented by the random walk model for oil prices, were chosen as plausible candidates. For the estimation period 1985q1–1998q4, the weights of these four models were 0.07:0.86:0.06:0.01, respectively, but these also changed gradually to

0.00:0.01:0.22:0.77 for the estimation period 1985q1–2000q4. The number of candidate models considered 'best' is relatively small, therefore, according to AIC and SBC, but there is considerable variability in the estimated posterior probabilities of these chosen models with relatively minor changes in the sample sizes.

11.1.3 *Evaluation and comparisons of probability forecasts*

In the evaluation exercise, each of the 14 alternative models was used to generate probability forecasts for a number of simple events over the period 1999q1–2001q1. This was undertaken in a recursive manner, whereby we first estimated all the 14 models over the period 1985q1–1998q4 and computed one-step-ahead probability forecasts for 1999q1, then repeated the process moving forward one quarter at a time, ending with forecasts for 2001q1 based on models estimated over the period 1985q1–2000q4. The probability forecasts were computed for directional events of interest. In the case of $p_t - p_t^*$, e_t, r_t, r_t^* and $\Delta\widetilde{p}_t$, we computed the probability that these variables rise next period, namely $\Pr\left[\Delta(p_t - p_t^*) > 0 \mid \Im_{t-1}\right]$, $\Pr\left[\Delta e_t > 0 \mid \Im_{t-1}\right])$, and so on, where $\Im_{t-1}$ is the information available at the end of quarter $t-1$. For the remaining variables, ($y_t, y_t^*, h_t - y_t$ and p_t^o) which are trended, we considered the event that the rate of change of these variables rise from one period to the next, namely $\Pr\left[\Delta^2 y_t > 0 \mid \Im_{t-1}\right]$, $\Pr\left[\Delta^2 y_t^* > 0 \mid \Im_{t-1}\right])$, and so on. The probability forecasts are computed recursively using the parametric stochastic simulation technique which allows for future uncertainty and the non-parametric bootstrap technique which allows for parameter uncertainty, as detailed in Chapter 7. Model uncertainty, as highlighted in the previous section, is allowed for through the three weighting schemes: Akaike, Schwarz and equal weights. The probability forecasts were then evaluated using a number of different statistical techniques.

To evaluate the probability forecasts, we adopted a statistical approach, using a threshold probability of 0.5, so that an event was forecast to be realised if its probability forecast exceeded 0.5.[4] Formal statistical comparisons of forecasts and realisations were made using Kuipers score (KS), Pesaran and Timmermann (PT) (1992) directional (market timing) statistic and the probability integral transform as proposed by Dawid (1984) and

[4] As an alternative, we could conduct a decision-theoretic approach to forecast evaluation as advocated in Granger and Pesaran (2000a,b) and reviewed in Pesaran and Skouris (2001), which bases the evaluation of the probability forecasts on their implied economic value in a specific decision-making context. However, this demands a complete specification of the decision problem and this has been rather rare in macroeconomic policy evaluation.

Table 11.2 Forecast evaluation of the benchmark model.

Variable	Threshold	Future uncertainty				Future and parameter uncertainty			
		UD	DD	DU	UU	UD	DD	DU	UU
p_t^o	$\Delta^2 p_t^o > 0$	0	6	1	2	1	5	1	2
e_t	$\Delta e_t > 0$	5	0	0	4	5	0	0	4
r_t^*	$\Delta r_t^* > 0$	0	3	2	4	2	1	2	4
r_t	$\Delta r_t > 0$	5	0	0	4	5	0	0	4
$\Delta \tilde{p}_t$	$\Delta^2 \tilde{p}_t > 0$	1	3	0	5	2	2	0	5
y_t	$\Delta y_t > 0$	2	2	1	4	2	2	1	4
$p_t - p_t^*$	$\Delta(p_t - p_t^*) > 0$	2	5	2	0	3	4	2	0
$h_t - y_t$	$\Delta^2(h_t - y_t) > 0$	0	4	1	4	0	4	1	4
y_t^*	$\Delta^2 y_t^* > 0$	2	3	2	2	2	3	2	2
Total		17	26	9	29	22	21	9	29
Hit rate		$55/81 = 0.679$				$50/81 = 0.617$			

Note: The forecast evaluation statistics are based on one-step-ahead forecasts obtained from models estimated recursively, starting with the forecast of events in 1999q1 based on models estimated over 1985q1–1998q4 and ending with forecasts of events in 2001q1. The events of interest are described in Section 11.1.3. In the column headings the first letter denotes the direction of the forecast (U=up, D=down) and the second letter the direction of the outcome (U=up, D=down). For example, UU indicates an upward movement was correctly forecast. Hit rate is defined as (DD + UU)/(UD + DD + DU + UU).

developed further in Diebold, Gunther and Tay (1998). Table 11.2 reports the incidence of the four possible combinations of our directional forecasts based on the benchmark model. For each variable, nine event forecasts are generated over the period 1999q1–2001q1 (nine quarters), thus providing 81 forecasts for evaluation purposes. These event forecasts are compared with their realisations and grouped under the headings, 'UU', indicating forecasts and realisations are in the same upward direction, 'UD' indicating an upward forecast with a realised downward movement, and so on. High values for UU and DD indicate an ability of the model to forecast upward and downward movements correctly, while high values of UD and DU suggest poor forecasting ability.

The information in Table 11.2 documents the forecasting performance of the benchmark model, and comparable tables of results can be generated based on the probability forecasts obtained from the equal-weighted, AIC-weighted and SBC-weighted averages of the 14 candidate models. Briefly, Table 11.2 shows that for the case of future uncertainty the hit rate is 0.68 versus 0.62 when both parameter uncertainty and future uncertainty are considered. The forecasting performance of these is summarised by KS, defined by $H - F$, where H is the proportion of ups that were

Table 11.3 Diagnostic statistics for the evaluation of benchmark and average model probability forecasts.

Model	Future uncertainty				Future and parameter uncertainty			
	KS	Hit rate	PT	D_n	KS	Hit rate	PT	D_n
Benchmark with (11.2)	0.373	0.679	3.356	0.111	0.269	0.617	2.354	0.136
Benchmark with (11.4)	0.302	0.642	2.701	0.123	0.237	0.605	2.094	0.136
Equal Weights Average	0.259	0.630	2.346	0.062	0.256	0.630	2.322	0.111
AIC Weighted Average	0.302	0.642	2.701	0.160	0.273	0.630	2.451	0.136
SBC Weighted Average	0.207	0.605	1.873	0.111	0.233	0.617	2.109	0.099

Note: The forecast evaluation statistics are based on one-step-ahead forecasts obtained from models estimated recursively, starting with the forecast of events in 1999q1 based on models estimated over 1985q1–1998q4 and ending with forecasts of events in 2001q1. The events of interest are described in Section 11.1.3. The hit rate is defined as is the proportion of ups and downs that were correctly forecast to occur. The KS statistic is the Kuipers score statistic, PT statistic is the Pesaran and Timmermann (1992) test which under the null hypothesis has a standard normal distribution. Finally, D_n is the Kolmogorov–Smirnov statistic where the 5% critical value of D_n for $n = 81$ is equal to 0.149.

correctly forecast to occur, and F is the proportion of downs that were incorrectly forecast.[5] This statistic provides a measure of the accuracy of directional forecasts of the model, with high positive numbers indicating high predictive accuracy. In Table 11.3, we report the KS along with the other forecast evaluation statistics listed above, for the benchmark model, the three average models and the benchmark model replacing the oil equation of (11.2) with the random walk model. Where the probability forecasts take account of future uncertainty only, the KS suggests that the most accurate forecasts are provided by the benchmark model. Allowing for parameter uncertainty in the computation of probability forecasts, however, the KS suggests the benchmark model and the AIC average model produce the most accurate forecasts, although these forecasts perform less well than when just considering future uncertainty.[6]

The Kuipers score is a useful summary measure but does not provide a statistical test of the directional forecasting performance. Pesaran and Timmermann (1992) provide a formal statistical test which, as shown in Granger and Pesaran (2000b), turns out to be equivalent to a test based on

[5] These two proportions are known as the 'hit rate' and 'false alarm rate', respectively. In the case where the outcome is symmetric, in the sense that we value the ability to forecast ups and downs equally, then the score statistic of zero means no accuracy, whilst high positive and negative values indicate high and low predictive power.

[6] These statistics are based on probability forecasts where future uncertainty is taken into account using a parametric procedure. The results are hardly affected if a non-parametric procedure is used instead.

the Kuipers score. The PT statistic is defined by

$$PT = \frac{\widehat{P} - \widehat{P}^*}{\left\{\widehat{V}(\widehat{P}) - \widehat{V}(\widehat{P}^*)\right\}^{\frac{1}{2}}},$$

where $\widehat{P}$ is the proportion of correctly predicted upward movements, $\widehat{P}^*$ is the estimate of the probability of correctly predicting the events under the null hypothesis that forecasts and realisations are independently distributed, and $\widehat{V}(\widehat{P})$ and $\widehat{V}(\widehat{P}^*)$ are the consistent estimates of the variances of $\widehat{P}$ and $\widehat{P}^*$, respectively. Under the null hypothesis, the PT statistic has a standard normal distribution. For the forecasts based on the benchmark model in combination with the estimated oil price equation, (11.2), we obtained PT = 3.356 when only future uncertainty was allowed for, and PT = 2.354 when both future and parameter uncertainties were taken into account. Both of these statistics are statistically significant. The alternative oil price specification of (11.4) yielded corresponding PT test statistics of 2.701 and 2.094, which are significant but marginally less so. The probability forecast results based on the average models were marginally less convincing, with the AIC average having the highest PT of 2.701 for future uncertainty only, but when considering parameter uncertainty as well gives the highest PT of all models of 2.451. These results suggest that the benchmark model performs well under future uncertainty, suggesting the importance of imposing theory-based long-run restrictions for probability forecasting, but that this distinction is removed when both future and parameter uncertainty are considered.

An alternative approach to probability forecast evaluation would be to use the probability integral transforms

$$u(\mathbf{z}_t) = \int_{-\infty}^{\mathbf{z}_t} p_t(\mathbf{x})\, d\mathbf{x}, \qquad t = T+1, T+2, \ldots, T+n,$$

where $p_t(\mathbf{x})$ is the forecast probability density function, and $\mathbf{z}_t$, $t = T+1, T+2, \ldots, T+n$, the associated realisations. Under the null hypothesis that $p_t(\mathbf{x})$ coincides with the true density function of the underlying process, the probability integral transforms will be distributed as $i.i.d.U[0,1]$. This result is due to Rosenblatt (1952), and has been recently applied in time series econometrics by Diebold, Gunther and Tay (1998).[7] In our application, we first computed a sequence of one step ahead probability

[7] Also see Diebold, Hahn and Tay (1999) and Berkowitz (1999).

forecasts (with and without allowing for parameter uncertainty) from the over-identified and exactly identified models for the nine simple events set out above over the nine quarters 1999q1, 1999q2, ..., 2001q1, and hence the associated probability integral transforms, $u(\mathbf{z}_t)$. To test the hypothesis that these probability integral transforms are random draws from $U[0, 1]$, we calculated the Kolmogorov–Smirnov statistic,

$$D_n = \sup_x |F_n(x) - U(x)|,$$

where $F_n(x)$ is the empirical cumulative distribution function (CDF) of the probability integral transforms, and $U(x) = x$, is the CDF of $i.i.d.U[0, 1]$. Large values of the Kolmogorov–Smirnov statistic, D_n, indicate that the sample CDF is not similar to the hypothesised uniform CDF.[8] For the over-identified benchmark specification, we obtained the value of 0.111 for the Kolmogorov–Smirnov statistic when only future uncertainty was allowed for, and the larger value of 0.136 when the underlying probability forecasts took account of both future and parameter uncertainties. The corresponding statistics for the benchmark model with the alternative oil price specification of (11.4) were 0.123 and 0.136, respectively. All these statistics are well below the 5% critical value of Kolmogorov–Smirnov statistic (which for $n = 81$ is equal to 0.149), and the hypothesis that the forecast probability density functions coincide with the true ones cannot be rejected. We cannot reject the same hypothesis for the average models either but with the noticeable exception of the AIC model. The AIC average model obtains a value of 0.160 for the Kolmogorov–Smirnov statistic when only future uncertainty was allowed for and 0.136 when we include parameter uncertainty. Hence we reject the null that the forecast probability density functions coincide with the true ones when considering future uncertainty but not when we consider both future and parameter uncertainty. This is an interesting results in light of the support given to the AIC from the hit rate, the KS and PT statistics. Overall results do not reject any one model but do provide some evidence, in particular when considering future uncertainty, for supporting the use of the over-identified specification in forecasting. With this in mind, we now proceed to the generation of out-of-sample forecast probabilities of interest using the over-identified benchmark model.

[8] For details of the Kolmogorov–Smirnov test and its critical values see, for example, Neave and Worthington (1992, pp. 89–93).

11.2 Probability forecasts of inflation and output growth

Here we apply the techniques described in Chapter 7 to the updated core model of the UK economy to compute out-of-sample probability forecasts of events relating to inflation targeting and output growth which are of particular interest for the analysis of macroeconomic policy in the UK. Inflation targets have been set explicitly in the UK since October 1992, following the UK's exit from the European Exchange Rate Mechanism (ERM). The Chancellor's stated objective at the time was to achieve an average annual rate of inflation of 2%, while keeping the underlying rate of inflation within the 1–4% range. In May 1997, the policy of targeting inflation was formalised further by the setting up of the Monetary Policy Committee (MPC), whose main objective is to meet inflation targets primarily by influencing the market interest rate through fixing the base rate at regular intervals. Its current remit, as set annually by the Chancellor, is to achieve an average annual inflation rate of 2.0%, based on the Harmonised Index of Consumer Prices (HICP), renamed the Consumer Price Index. In this application we have used the RPI index (as an approximation to the measure previously used by the MPC, the Retail Price Index, excluding mortgage interest payments, RPI-x), where the previous target of 2.5% is argued to be equivalent to the new 2.0% target, as the method of constructing the consumer price index will produce a lower measure of inflation than the RPI method. The previous target range of 1.5–3.5% therefore also remains of interest and constitutes one of the events analysed. Note a feature of the policy framework is that the time horizon over which the inflation objective is to be achieved is not stated.

Inflation rates outside the target range act as a trigger, requiring the Governor of the Bank of England to write an open letter to the Chancellor explaining why inflation had deviated from the target, the policies being undertaken to correct the deviation, and how long it is expected before inflation is back on target. The Bank is also expected to conduct monetary policy so as to support the general economic policies of the government, so far as this does not compromise its commitment to its inflation target.

Since October 1992, the Bank of England has produced a quarterly *Inflation Report* which describes the Bank's assessment of likely inflation outcomes over a two-year forecast horizon. In addition to reviewing the various economic indicators necessary to place the inflation assessment into context, the *Report* provides forecasts of inflation over two year horizons, with bands presented around the central forecast to illustrate the range of inflation outcomes that are considered possible (the so-called fan charts). The forecasts are based on the assumption that the base rate is left unchanged. Since November 1997, a similar forecast of output growth has also been provided in the *Report*, providing insights on the Bank's perception of the likely outcome for the government's general economic policies beyond the maintenance of price stability. For a critical assessment of the Bank's approach to allowing for model and parameter uncertainties, see Wallis (1999).

The fan charts produced by the Bank of England are an important step towards acknowledging the significance of forecast uncertainties in the decision-making process and this is clearly a welcome innovation. However, the approach suffers from two major shortcomings. First, it seems unlikely that the fan charts can be replicated by independent researchers. This is largely due to the subjective manner in which uncertainty is taken into account by the Bank, which may be justified from a real-time decision-making perspective but does not readily lend itself to independent analysis. Second, the use of fan charts is limited for the analysis of uncertainty associated with joint events. Currently, the Bank provides separate fan charts for inflation and output growth forecasts, but in reality one may also be interested in joint events involving both inflation and output growth, and it is not clear how the two separate fan charts could be used for such a purpose. Here, we address both of these issues using the benchmark long-run structural model and the various alternative models discussed.

In what follows, we present plots of estimated predictive distribution functions for inflation and output growth at a number of selected forecast horizons. These plots provide us with the necessary information with which to compute probabilities of a variety of events, and demonstrate the usefulness of probability forecasts in conveying the future and parameter uncertainties that surround the point forecasts. But our substantive discussion of the probability forecasts focuses on two central events of interest; namely, keeping the rate of inflation within the announced target range of 1.5–3.5% and avoiding a recession. Following the literature, we define a recession as the occurrence of two successive negative quarterly growth rates. See, for example, Harding and Pagan (2002).

11.2.1 *Point and interval forecasts*

Before reporting the probability forecasts, it is worth briefly summarising the point and interval forecasts to help place the probability forecasts in context. Tables 11.4a and 11.4b provide the point forecasts for domestic

Table 11.4a Point and interval forecasts of inflation and output growth (four quarterly moving averages, per cent, per annum).

Forecast horizon	Output growth		Inflation	
	Forecast	Actual	Forecast	Actual
2001q2	1.84 (1.02, 2.65)	2.33	1.80 (1.11, 2.49)	1.92
2001q3	1.30 (−0.13, 2.73)	2.12	1.61 (0.34, 2.88)	1.80
2001q4	1.28 (−0.62, 3.18)	2.11	1.37 (−0.36, 3.11)	1.04
2002q1	1.27 (−1.05, 3.51)	1.60	1.69 (−0.44, 3.82)	1.21
2002q2	1.42 (−1.10, 3.94)	1.49	2.08 (−0.31, 4.47)	1.20
2002q3	1.65 (−1.08, 4.37)	1.88	2.01 (−0.51, 4.52)	1.48
2002q4	1.89 (−1.04, 4.81)	1.97	1.92 (−0.69, 4.52)	2.50
2003q1	2.02 (−1.08, 5.12)	2.06	1.93 (−0.75, 4.60)	3.00

Note: Forecasts are based on the model reported in Table 11.1, combined with an estimate of the oil price equation (11.2). The figures in parentheses are the lower and upper 95% confidence intervals. The four quarterly moving average output growth is defined as $100 \times \ln(GDP_{T+h}/GDP_{T+h-4})$, where GDP_T is the real Gross Domestic Product in 2001q1, which is computed from the forecasts of per capita output, y_{T+h}, assuming a population growth of 0.22% per annum. The four quarterly moving average inflation rate is defined as $100 \times (p_{T+h} - p_{T+h-4})$ where p_T is the natural logarithm of the retail price index in 2001q1.

Table 11.4b Point and interval forecasts of inflation and output growth (quarter on quarter changes, per cent, per annum).

Forecast horizon	Output growth		Inflation	
	Forecast	Actual	Forecast	Actual
2001q2	1.30 (−1.96, 4.55)	2.01	0.28 (−2.49, 3.06)	4.86
2001q3	1.16 (−2.61, 4.91)	2.00	2.22 (−2.05, 6.50)	0.23
2001q4	1.12 (−2.83, 5.07)	1.19	2.31 (−2.40, 7.04)	−0.46
2002q1	1.53 (−2.59, 5.64)	1.19	1.93 (−3.01, 6.87)	0.23
2002q2	1.89 (−2.37, 6.15)	1.58	1.86 (−3.28, 7.00)	4.80
2002q3	2.05 (−2.36, 6.45)	3.54	1.91 (−3.39, 7.21)	1.36
2002q4	2.08 (−2.45, 6.61)	1.56	1.95 (−3.47, 7.37)	3.61
2003q1	2.08 (−2.56, 6.71)	1.56	1.97 (−3.54, 7.49)	2.24

Note: See Notes to Table 11.4a. Output growth is defined as $400 \times \ln(GDP_{T+h}/GDP_{T+h-1})$, while inflation is defined as $400 \times (p_{T+h} - p_{T+h-1})$.

inflation rates and output growth over the period 2001q1–2003q1 together with their 95% confidence intervals.

Table 11.4a presents the four quarterly growth rate forecasts, while Table 11.4b gives the forecasts of annualised quarter-on-quarter growth rates.[9]

[9] It is worth noting that the inflation target is expressed in terms of RPI-x while our model provides forecasts of RPI.

The model predicts the average annual rate of inflation to fall from 2.5% in 2001q1 to 1.8% in 2001q2. This is followed by further falls for the rest of 2001 before returning to approximately 2% to the end of the forecast horizon, 2003q1. These point forecasts are lower than the inflation rates realised during 2000, as illustrated by the historical data on inflation presented in Figure 11.1a. Output growth is predicted to be positive throughout the forecast horizon, falling from an average annual rate of 2.8% in 2000 to 1.3% by the end of 2001, before rising to around 2.0% thereafter (see Table 11.4a). Therefore, based on these point forecasts, we may be tempted to rule out the possibility of a recession occurring in the UK over the 2001–2003 period.

However, these point forecasts are subject to a high degree of uncertainty, particularly when longer forecast horizons are considered. For example, at the two year forecast horizon the point forecast of annual inflation in 2003q1 is predicted to be 1.9%, which is well within the announced inflation target range. But the 95% confidence interval covers the range −0.8% to +4.6%. For the quarter on quarter definition, the uncertainty is even larger, with a range of −3.5% to 7.5% around a point forecast of approximately 2.0%. Similarly, the point forecast of the quarter on quarter annual rate of output growth in 2003q1 is 2.1%, but its 95% confidence

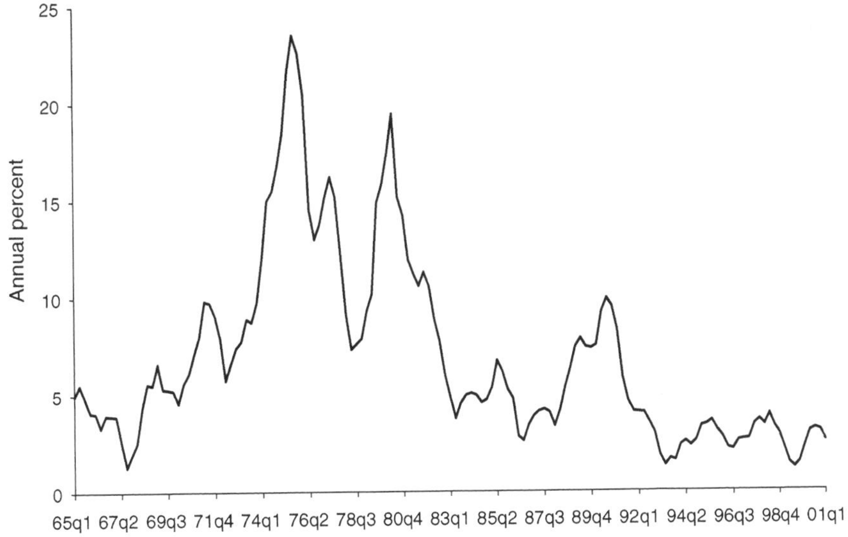

Figure 11.1a Inflation (four-quarter moving average).

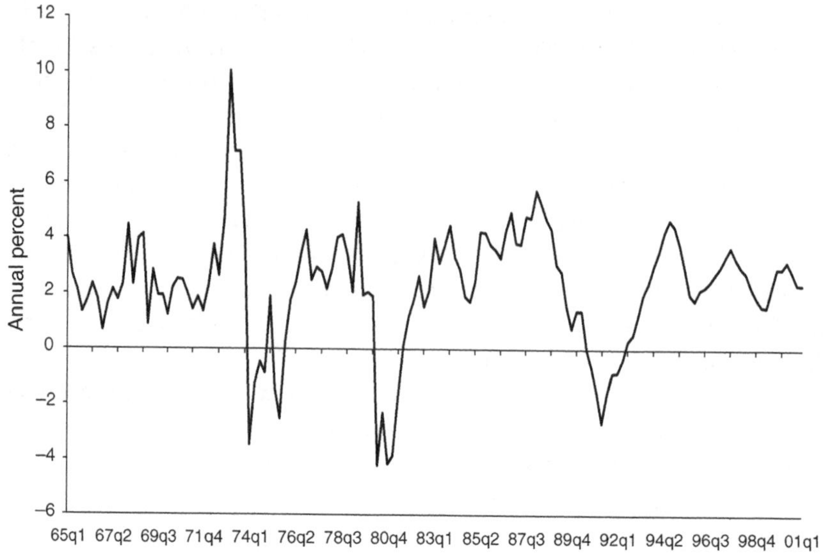

Figure 11.1b Output growth (four-quarter moving average).

interval covers the range −2.6% to +6.7%. As we have noted, it is difficult to evaluate the significance of these forecast intervals for policy analysis and a more appropriate approach is to directly focus on probability forecasts as a method of characterising the various uncertainties that are associated with events of interest. This is the topic that we shall turn to now.

11.2.2 *Predictive distribution functions*

In the case of single events, probability forecasts are best represented by means of probability distribution functions. Figures 11.2a and 11.2b give the estimates of these functions for the four-quarter moving averages of inflation and output growth for the one-quarter, one- and two-year ahead forecast horizons based on the benchmark model (*i.e.* the over-identified version of the cointegrating model, (11.1), augmented with the oil price equation, (11.2)). These estimates are computed using the simulation techniques described in detail in Section 7.3 and take account of both future and parameter uncertainties.

Figure 11.2a presents the estimated predictive distribution function for inflation for the threshold values ranging from 0% to 5% per annum at

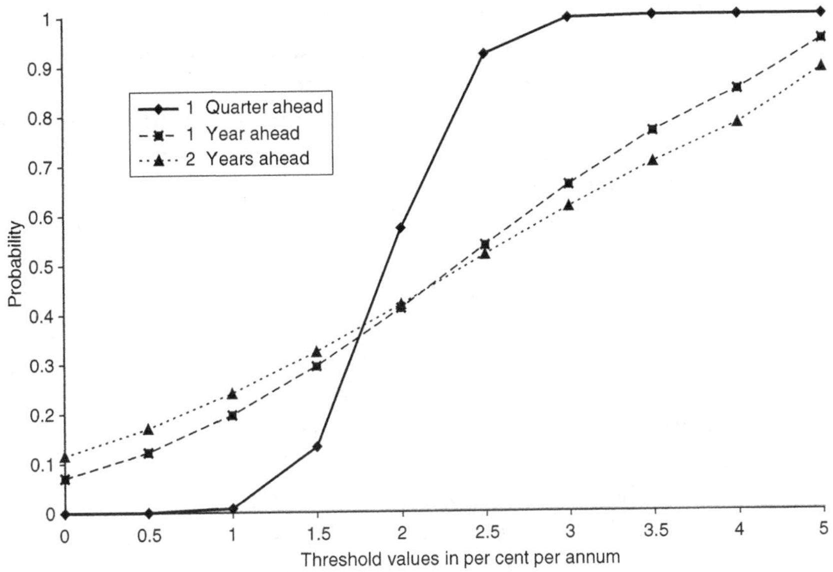

Figure 11.2a Predictive distribution functions for inflation (benchmark model with parameter uncertainty).

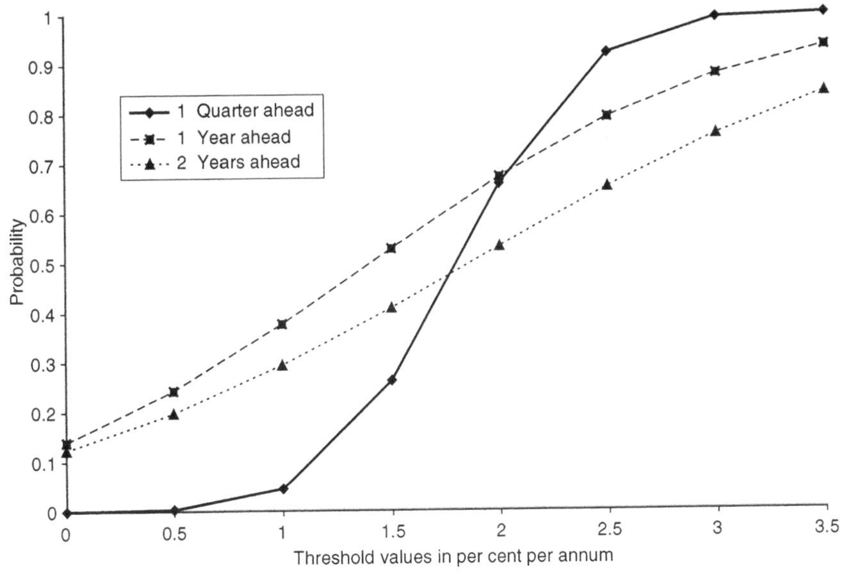

Figure 11.2b Predictive distribution functions for output growth (benchmark model with parameter uncertainty).

the three selected forecast horizons. Perhaps not surprisingly, the function for the one-quarter ahead forecast horizon is quite steep, but it becomes flatter as the forecast horizon is increased. Above the threshold value of 2.0%, the estimated probability distribution functions shift to the right as longer forecast horizons are considered, showing that the probability of inflation falling below thresholds greater than 2.0% declines with the forecast horizon. For example, the forecast probability that inflation lies below 3.5% becomes smaller at longer forecast horizons, falling from close to 100% one quarter ahead (2001q2) to 70% eight quarters ahead (2003q1). These forecast probabilities are in line with the recent historical experience: over the period 1985q1–2001q1, the average annual rate of inflation fell below 3.5% for 53.9% of the quarters, but were below this threshold value throughout the last two years of the sample, 1999q1–2001q1.

Figure 11.2b plots the estimated predictive distribution functions for output growth. These functions also become flatter as the forecast horizon is increased, reflecting the greater uncertainty associated with growth outcomes at longer forecast horizons. These plots also suggest a weakening of the growth prospects in 2001 before recovering a little at longer horizons. For example, the probability of a negative output growth one quarter ahead (2001q2) is estimated to be almost zero, but rises to 14% four quarters ahead (2002q1) before falling back to 12% after eight quarters (2003q1). Therefore, a rise in the probability of a recession is predicted, but the estimate is not sufficiently high for it to be much of a policy concern (at least viewed from the end of our sample period 2001q1).

11.2.3 *Event probability forecasts*

Here we consider three single events of particular interest:

A : achievement of inflation target, defined as the four-quarterly moving average rate of inflation falling within the range 1.5–3.5%;

B : recession, defined as the occurrence of two consecutive quarters of negative output growth;

C : poor growth prospects, defined to mean that the four-quarterly moving average of output growth is less than 1%;

and the joint events $A \cap \overline{B}$ (inflation target is met *and* recession is avoided), and $A \cap \overline{C}$ (inflation target is met *combined* with reasonable growth prospects), where $\overline{B}$ and $\overline{C}$ are complements of B and C.

INFLATION AND THE TARGET RANGE

Two sets of estimates of $\Pr(A_{T+h} \mid \Im_T)$ are provided in Table 11.5a (for $h = 1, 2, \ldots, 8$) and depicted in Figure 11.3 over the longer forecast horizons $h = 1, 2, \ldots, 24$.

The first set relates to π, which only take account of future uncertainty, and the second set relates to $\tilde{\pi}$ which allow for both future and parameter uncertainties. Both π and $\tilde{\pi}$ convey a similar message, but there are nevertheless some differences between them, at least at some forecast horizons, so that it is important that both estimates are considered in practice.

Based on these estimates, and conditional on the information available at the end of 2001q1, the probability that the Bank of England will be able to achieve the government inflation target is estimated to be high in the short run but falls in the longer run, reflecting the considerable uncertainty surrounding the inflation forecasts at longer horizons. Specifically, the probability estimate is high in 2001q2, at 0.87 (0.80) for $\tilde{\pi}$ (π), but it falls rapidly to nearer 0.45 by the end of 2001/early 2002. This fall in the first quarters of the forecast reflects the increasing likelihood of inflation falling below the 1.5% lower threshold (since the probability of observing inflation above the 3.5% upper threshold is close to zero through this

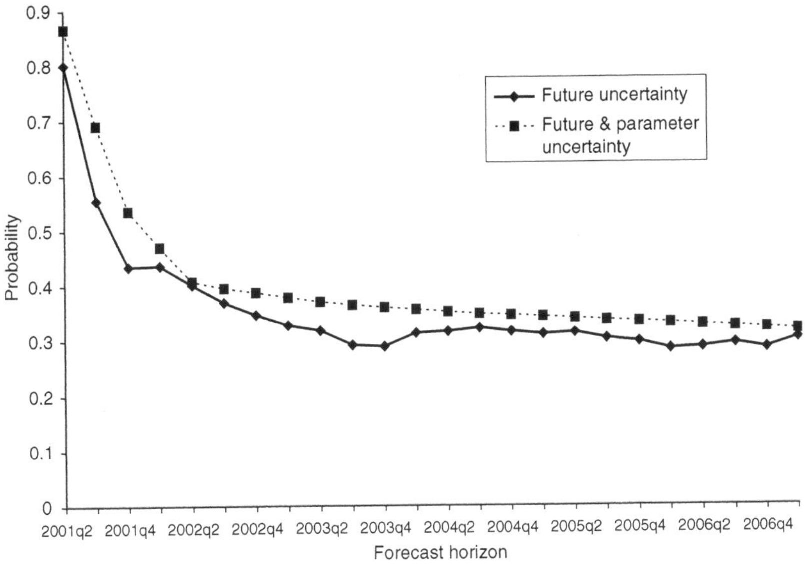

Figure 11.3 Probability estimates of inflation falling within the target range using the benchmark model.

period). Ultimately, though, the estimated probability of achieving inflation within the target range settles to 0.38 (0.35) for $\tilde{\pi}$ (π) in 2003q1. At this longer forecast horizon, the probabilities of inflation falling below and above the target range are 0.32 and 0.30, respectively, using $\tilde{\pi}$ (or 0.42 and 0.23 using π), so these figures reflect the relatively high degree of uncertainty associated with inflation forecasts even at moderate forecast horizons. Hence, while the likely inflation outcomes are low by historical standards and there is a reasonable probability of hitting the target range, there are also comparable likelihoods of undershooting and overshooting the inflation target range at longer horizons.

RECESSION AND GROWTH PROSPECTS

Figure 11.4 shows the estimates of the recession probability, $\Pr(B_{T+h} \mid \Im_T)$ over the forecast horizons $h = 1, 2, \ldots, 24$. For this event, the probability estimates that allow for parameter uncertainty (*i.e.* $\tilde{\pi}$) exceed those that do not (*i.e.* π) at shorter horizons, but the opposite is true at longer horizons. Having said this, however, π and $\tilde{\pi}$ are very similar in size across the different forecast horizons and suggest a very low probability of a recession: based on the $\tilde{\pi}$ estimate, for example, the probability of a recession occurring in 2001q2 is estimated to be around zero, rising to 0.09 in

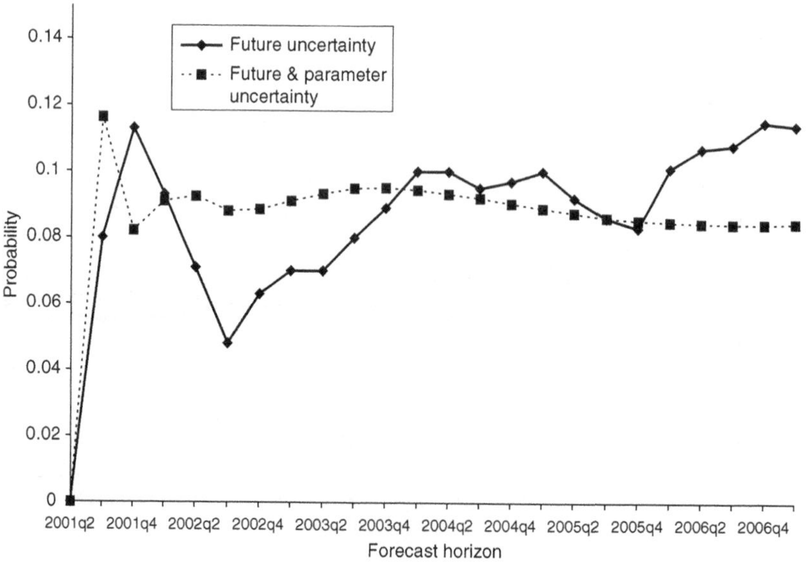

Figure 11.4 Probability estimates of a recession using the benchmark model.

2002q1. However, as shown in Table 11.5b, the probability that the UK faces poor growth prospects is much higher, in the region of 0.35 at the end of 2001, falling to 0.3 in 2003q1 according to the $\tilde{\pi}$ estimates.

Single events are clearly of interest but very often decision-makers are concerned with joint events involving, for example, both inflation and output growth outcomes. As examples here, we consider the probability estimates of the two joint events, $A_{T+h} \cap \overline{B}_{T+h}$, and $A_{T+h} \cap \overline{C}_{T+h}$ over

Table 11.5a Probability forecasts of single events involving inflation.

Forecast horizon	Pr(Inf < 1.5%)		Pr(Inf < 2.5%)		Pr(Inf < 3.5%)		Pr(1.5% < Inf < 3.5%)	
	π	$\tilde{\pi}$	π	$\tilde{\pi}$	π	$\tilde{\pi}$	π	$\tilde{\pi}$
2001q2	0.206	0.135	0.978	0.920	1.000	1.000	0.795	0.865
2001q3	0.437	0.275	0.884	0.732	0.996	0.963	0.560	0.688
2001q4	0.541	0.364	0.849	0.682	0.974	0.899	0.433	0.535
2002q1	0.451	0.292	0.721	0.533	0.893	0.761	0.442	0.469
2002q2	0.367	0.244	0.597	0.441	0.801	0.652	0.434	0.408
2002q3	0.405	0.285	0.611	0.484	0.785	0.683	0.381	0.398
2002q4	0.424	0.315	0.625	0.514	0.792	0.705	0.368	0.390
2003q1	0.422	0.321	0.607	0.515	0.772	0.702	0.351	0.381

Note: The probability estimates for inflation relate to the four quarterly moving average of inflation defined by $400 \times (p_{T+h} - p_{T+h-4})$, where p is the natural logarithm of the retail price index. The probability estimates (π and $\tilde{\pi}$) are computed using the model reported in Table 11.1, where π is the 'Profile Predictive Likelihood' that only takes account of future uncertainty, whereas $\tilde{\pi}$ is the 'Bootstrap Predictive Distribution' function and accounts for both future and parameter uncertainties. The computations are carried out using 2000 replications. See Chapter 7 for computational details.

Table 11.5b Probability forecasts of events involving output growth and inflation.

Forecast horizon	Pr(Recession)	Pr(output growth < 1%)	Pr(1.5% < Inf < 3.5%, No recession)	Pr(1.5% < Inf <3.5%, output growth > 1%)
	$\tilde{\pi}$	$\tilde{\pi}$	$\tilde{\pi}$	$\tilde{\pi}$
2001q2	0.000	0.040	0.865	0.832
2001q3	0.111	0.319	0.629	0.500
2001q4	0.084	0.343	0.499	0.381
2002q1	0.092	0.371	0.426	0.300
2002q2	0.092	0.312	0.373	0.278
2002q3	0.088	0.314	0.365	0.273
2002q4	0.090	0.305	0.358	0.272
2003q1	0.092	0.295	0.350	0.270

Note: The probability estimates for output growth are computed from the forecasts of per capita output, assuming a population growth of 0.22% per annum. Recession is said to have occurred when output growth (measured, quarter on quarter, by $400 \times \ln(GDP_{T+h}/GDP_{T+h-1})$) becomes negative in two consecutive quarters. Also see the notes to Tables 11.4a and 11.5a.

the forecast horizons $h = 1, 2, \ldots, 24$. Probability estimates of these events (based on $\widetilde{\pi}$) are presented in Table 11.5b. Both events are of policy interest as they combine the achievement of the inflation target with alternative growth objectives. For the event $A_{T+h} \cap \overline{B}_{T+h}$, the joint probability forecasts are similar in magnitude to those for $\Pr\left(A_{T+h} \mid \Im_T\right)$ alone at every time horizon. This is not surprising since the probability of a recession is estimated to be small at most forecast horizons and therefore the probability of avoiding recession is close to one. Nevertheless, the differences might be important since even relatively minor differences in probabilities can have an important impact on decisions if there are large, discontinuous differences in the net benefits of different outcomes. The probability forecasts for $A_{T+h} \cap \overline{C}_{T+h}$ are, of course, considerably less than those for $\Pr\left(A_{T+h} \mid \Im_T\right)$ alone.

Figure 11.5 plots the values of the joint event probability over the forecast horizon alongside a plot of the product of the single event probabilities; that is $\Pr\left(A_{T+h} \mid \Im_T\right) \times \Pr\left(\overline{B}_{T+h} \mid \Im_T\right)$, $h = 1, 2, \ldots, 24$. This comparison provides an indication of the degree of dependence/independence of the two events. As it turns out, there is a gap between these of just under 0.1

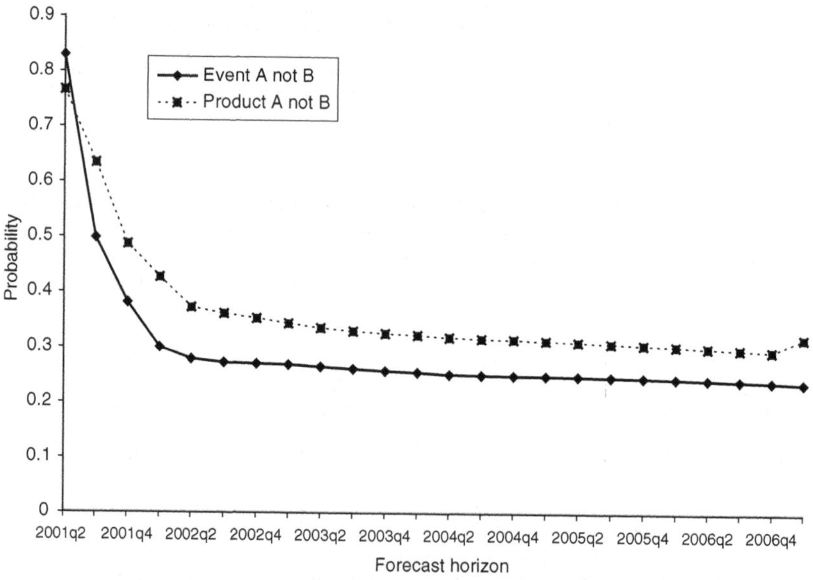

Figure 11.5 Probability estimates of meeting the inflation target without a recession (future and parameter uncertainty).

at most forecast horizons. But the probabilities are relatively close, indicating little dependence between output growth prospects and inflation outcomes. This result is compatible with the long-term neutrality hypothesis that postulates independence of inflation outcomes from output growth outcomes in the long run.

Figure 11.6 also plots the probability estimates of the joint event $A_{T+h} \cap \overline{B}_{T+h}$, but illustrates the effects of taking into account model uncertainty. The figure shows three values of the probability of the joint event over the forecast horizon, each calculated without taking account of parameter uncertainty. One value is based on the benchmark model, but the other two show the weighted average of the probability estimates obtained from the 14 alternative models described in the model evaluation exercise of the previous section. The weights in the latter two probability estimates are set equal in one of the estimates and are the in-sample posterior probabilities of the models approximated by the Akaike weights in the other. The plots show that estimated probabilities from the benchmark model are, by and large, quite close to the 'equal weights' estimate, but these are both lower than the AIC-weighted average, by more than 0.1 at some forecast horizons. Again, the extent to which these differences are considered large or important will depend on the nature of the underlying decision problem.

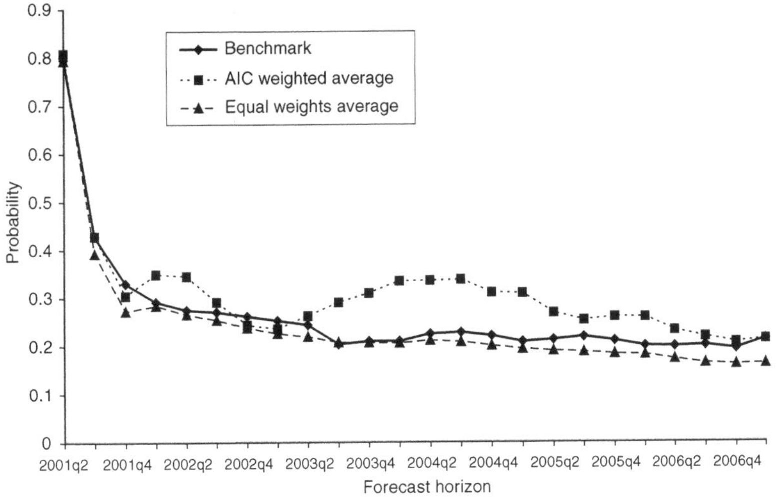

Figure 11.6 Probability estimates of meeting the inflation target without a recession (future uncertainty only).

11.3 A postscript

The elapse of time since the publication of the above forecasts in Garratt *et al.* (2003b) presents us with an opportunity for a real-time out-of-sample forecast evaluation, albeit over a rather short period. In what follows we compare the point and probability forecasts, reported in Tables 11.4a and 11.4b with the realised values of output growth and inflation for the eight quarters 2001q2–2003q1.

The difficulty of producing accurate point forecasts is reflected in the size of the forecast errors but the uncertainty surrounding the point forecasts is so large that in only one case does the realised value exceed the 95% confidence intervals. The less volatile four quarterly moving average changes perform reasonably, with root mean square errors (RMSE) of 0.47 and 0.60 percentage points for output growth and inflation, respectively. The quarter on quarter annual realisations exhibit high volatility, particularly for inflation and as such have larger and more volatile forecast errors. This is reflected in the RMSEs which take the values of 0.72 and 2.43 for output growth and inflation, respectively. On this definition inflation forecasts perform badly. For example, the realised value was 4.86% in 2001q2 as compared to the forecast value of 0.28%.

The probability event forecasts, which use the same distributions as the point and interval forecasts, perform well in terms of predicting specific events and as such convey useful information, not always apparent when using the point forecasts. If we evaluate the probability event forecasts using the threshold probability of 0.5, so that an event was forecast to be realised if its probability forecast exceeded 0.5, then the 'hit rate' (see footnote 5 of this chapter) or percentage of correctly forecasting events, for all the 32 events regarding inflation defined in Table 11.5a is 84% (27 out of 32) for future uncertainty only and 75% (24 out of 32) for future and parameter uncertainty. The hit rate for events associated with output growth (*i.e.* recession defined as two consecutive quarters of negative growth and output growth of $<1\%$) exhibits a hit rate of 100% (16 out of 16). Joint event probability event predictions also perform well with a hit rate of 69% (11 out of 16).

11.4 Concluding remarks

One of the many problems economic forecasters and policy-makers face is conveying to the public the degree of uncertainty associated with point forecasts. Policy-makers recognise that their announcements, in addition to providing information on policy objectives, can themselves initiate responses which affect the macroeconomic outcome. This means that Central Bank Governors are reluctant to discuss either pessimistic possibilities, as this might induce recession, or more optimistic possibilities, since this might induce inflationary pressures. There is therefore an incentive for policy-makers to seek ways of making clear statements regarding the range of potential macroeconomic outcomes for a given policy, and the likelihood of the occurrence of these outcomes, in a manner which avoids these difficulties.

Here we have argued for the use of probability forecasts as a method of characterising the uncertainties that surround forecasts from a macroeconomic model believing this to be superior to the conventional way of trying to deal with this problem through the use of confidence intervals. We argue that the use of probability forecasts has an intuitive appeal, enabling the forecaster (or users of forecasts) to specify the relevant 'threshold values' which define the event of interest (*e.g.* a threshold value corresponding to an inflation target range 1.5–3.5%). This is in contrast to the use of confidence intervals which define threshold values only implicitly, through the specification of the confidence interval widths, and these values may or may not represent thresholds of interest. A further advantage of the use of probability forecasts compared with the use of confidence intervals and over other more popular methods is the flexibility of probability forecasts, as illustrated by the ease with which the probability of joint events can be computed and analysed. Hence, for example, we can consider the likelihood of achieving a stated inflation target range whilst simultaneously achieving a given level of output growth, with the result being conveyed in a single number. In situations where utility or loss functions are non-quadratic and/or the constraints are nonlinear the whole predictive probability distribution function rather than its mean is required for decision-making. This chapter shows how such predictive distribution functions can be obtained in the case of long-run structural models, and illustrates its feasibility in the case of a small macroeconometric model of the UK.

The empirical exercise provides a concrete example of the usefulness of event probability forecasting both as a tool for model evaluation and as a means for conveying the uncertainties surrounding the forecasts of specific events of interest. The model used represents a small but comprehensive model of the UK macroeconomy which incorporates long-run relationships suggested by economic theory so that it has a transparent and theoretically coherent foundation. The model evaluation exercise not only demonstrates the statistical adequacy of the forecasts generated by the model but also highlights the considerable improvements in forecasts obtained through the imposition of the theory-based long-run restrictions. The predictive distribution functions relating to single events and the various joint event probabilities presented illustrate the flexibility of the functions in conveying forecast uncertainties and, from the observed independence of probability forecasts of events involving inflation and growth, in conveying information on the properties of the model. The model averaging approach also provides a coherent procedure to take account of parameter and model uncertainties as well as the future uncertainty.

12

Global modelling and other applications

The modelling approach described in Chapters 2–7, and adopted in the detailed description of the UK macroeconometric model of Chapters 8–11, is widely applicable and has been recently employed in a variety of studies investigating important macroeconomic issues. We conclude the book with a brief description of a number of these applications. The applications have been chosen to illustrate the flexibility of the modelling approach and the range of topics that can be addressed using these techniques. The *first* group of applications are concerned with the widespread use of the Structural Cointegrating VAR modelling approach, and provides a brief description of a global VAR (GVAR) model, which is aimed at capturing regional interdependencies in the world economy. The GVAR illustrates how the modelling approach advanced in the book can be generalised to build a global model within which the core UK model could, in principle, be subsumed. The *second* area focuses on the increasing use of impulse responses and the ways in which the VAR estimates can be interpreted, commenting on the construction of a high-frequency (monthly) version of the core model which is of particular use in identifying monetary policy shocks. Finally, a *third* area of applications focuses on recent use of probability forecasts, including a description of a measure of 'financial distress' that provides probabilistic statements on events in the UK unsecured credit market, investigated as a 'satellite' of the core UK model.

12.1 Recent applications of the structural cointegrating VAR approach

There has been considerable interest and activity in the application of the Structural Cointegrating VAR approach to macroeconometric modelling within academia, and from central bankers, government and industry in recent years. The flexibility of the modelling techniques is evidenced by the sheer variety of studies employing the techniques in the academic literature. So for example, recent applications have investigated monetary policy transmission mechanisms in Australia and New Zealand (Haug *et al.*, 2005), the link between wage setting, minimum wages and inflation in France (L'horty and Rault, 2004), the determinants of the demand for electricity in Greece (Hondroyianis, 2004), the demand for exports in Hong Kong (Abbott and De Vita, 2002), employment dynamics in India (Roy, 2004), the link between financial variables and import demand in Japan (Tang, 2004), the *PPP* hypothesis and the relationship between macroeconomic stability and growth in Turkey (Yazgan, 2003; Ismihan, Metin-Ozcan and Tansel, 2005), and the demand for calories in Zimbabwe (Tiffin and Dawson, 2003).

The approach to modelling the macroeconomy, as opposed to particular macroeconomic relationships, has also been illustrated in models of the US economy, in Anderson *et al.* (2002), the Canadian economy, in Crowder and Wohar (2004), and for the euro area in Brand and Cassola (2004). In the US model, a six-variable cointegrating VAR is obtained (including the CPI, the GDP deflator, real money balances, the federal funds rate, the yield on long-term bonds, and output), and anchored by four long-run relationships suggested by economic theory: namely, a money demand relationship, the Fisher inflation parity relationship, a term-structure relationship, and a relationship linking the two measures of prices. In the Canadian case, the six variables under consideration include disposable income, consumption, wealth, the interest rate, real money balances and the GDP deflator, while the long-run relationships include consumption–income and consumption-wealth relationships, the money demand relationship and the *FIP* relationship. For the euro area, Brand and Cassola's model describes real money balances, inflation, short-term and long-term interest rates and GDP, taking into account a demand for money relationship, a term-structure relationship and the *FIP*, again motivated with reference to the economic theory of the long run.

In each case, the models perform well by various statistical criteria and against alternative models and uncover important policy-relevant features. Hence, the US study concludes that the model provides forecasts that are very similar to those published by government agencies and so could provide a useful tool on which to base policy recommendations, accommodating the steady-state growth model of the economy implicitly shared by many government agencies and private forecasters. The Canadian and euro area studies both focus on the impact of monetary policy change: the Bank of Canada's shift to a stable price level target in the early 1980s was associated with a once-and-for-all shift in the long-run relationships, while no major distortions were found with the advent of Stage Three of Economic and Monetary Union in the euro area model. In all cases, there is no doubt that practitioners, who need manageable and interpretable models to answer specific questions, appreciate the transparency and pragmatism of this modelling approach and that these methods are already in increasingly widespread use in the policy-making and decision-making communities.

In the case of the emerging market economies, in an interesting and thorough application of the long-run structural modelling, Akusuwan (2005) develops a small quarterly macroeconometric model for the Thai economy over the period 1980q1–2002q4, and establishes the existence of three long-run relations, namely the Fisher interest parity, the uncovered interest parity, and the long-run money demand. By allowing for a possible break in the domestic variables following the 1997 Asian crisis, she finds that the crisis has significant effects on the short-run structure of the model, but not on its long-run relationships.

The merits of the application of the approach to macroeconometric modelling are investigated recently by Jacobs and Wallis (2005). In their study, the core model of the previous chapters is compared and contrasted with COMPACT, a large-scale simultaneous equation model of the UK of the type described in Chapter 2 and elaborated in Wren-Lewis *et al.* (1996). It is noted that, with approximately ten times more variables and around 20 behavioural relations, the SEM is able to address a broader set of issues than the core model, but requires the use of single-equation and small sub-system estimation techniques. However, focusing on the main macroeconomic variables that are common to both models, Jacobs and Wallis compare the dynamic responses of the two models to a foreign output shock and to an oil price shock. They find that the core model performs well on the former exercise, compared to the unrealistically slow response of COMPACT, but fails to properly take into account the UK's changing response to oil price changes (given that the UK started and ended the period as a net importer of oil, but was a net exporter mid-sample). These findings, of course, reflect the VAR's power in fitting complicated dynamics and also its relatively simple form. Jacob and Wallis also use simulation methods to uncover the long-run relationships implicit in COMPACT and to compare these to the immediately apparent long-run relationships of the core model. This analysis shows a reassuring degree of consensus, with the interest rate parity (*IRP*), output gap (*OG*) and *FIP* relationships all holding in both models, and a further relationship described as a 'small deviation from the *PPP* relationship' also present in COMPACT's long-run properties.[1] The paper concludes that further research is required to investigate the effects of how best to treat the foreign variables (and in particular whether these are best treated as endogenous or exogenous variables), but highlights the strengths of these modelling approaches and illustrates well the emerging consensus between SEMs and our own approach that was anticipated and described in the discussion of Chapter 2.

Finally, in an exercise related to our analysis conducted in Chapter 11, Strachan and van Dijk (2004) use the UK model as one of three examples to investigate the uncertainty associated with structural features. Using a Bayesian approach they consider cointegration, exogeneity, deterministic processes and over-identification. Posterior probabilities of these features are then used in a model averaging approach to forecasting and impulse response analysis.

12.2 Regional interdependencies and credit risk modelling

The Jacobs and Wallis (2005) paper also raises the important issue of how national macroeconomic models, obtained using the Structural Cointegrating VAR modelling approach, relate to outside factors. This issue is explored in detail in the global vector error correction model of regional interdependencies advanced in Pesaran, Schuermann and Weiner (2004, PSW). The GVAR is used to examine a variety of problems including the effects of foreign shocks on the euro area in Dees, di Mauro, Pesaran and Smith (2005, DdPS), the modelling of credit risk in Pesaran, Schuermann, Treutler and Weiner (2005), and the counter-factual problem of a quantitative analysis of the possible effects of UK or Sweden joining the euro area in Pesaran, Smith and Smith (2005).

Global modelling is subject to a number of important constraints, including the quantity and quality of data available, the curse of dimensionality that arises out of the many between- and within-country channels of interactions and transmissions, our knowledge of economic theory and institutions and the availability of human and computing resources.

[1] Since money is not included as a variable in COMPACT, the fifth long-run relationship in our core model could not be considered in that model. This is likely to limit the use of COMPACT in analysis of liquidity effects and the possible disquilibrium effects of money markets on output and inflation.

The Global VAR approach developed and applied in the above papers and outlined in Section 3.4 provides a coherent solution by treating the foreign variables as weakly exogenous. This assumption is plausible for small open economies and can be tested empirically for medium size economies such as Japan and the euro area. A different modelling set-up would be needed for the US. In PSW the US economy is modelled as a closed economy except for the effective exchange rate which is treated as weakly exogenous. In extending and updating the GVAR, DdPS also experiment with a US model that includes foreign inflation and output variables as weakly exogenous and find that this is not rejected by the data.

Under the weak exogeneity of the foreign variables, country- (or region-) specific vector error correcting models (VECMs) can be estimated consistently, thus obviating the need for estimating the global model as a whole, which would not be feasible in any case. Despite this the variables in each economy are potentially related to all the variables in other economies. This is accomplished by relating the domestic variables of each economy to corresponding foreign variables constructed to match the international trade pattern of the country under consideration. The trade weights can be either fixed or time varying. The key assumption is that they are predetermined. In principle, different types of weights can also be used in constructing different types of foreign variables. But the limited experiments carried out in DdPS suggest that the GVAR results are likely to be reasonably robust to the choice of the weights. Once the estimates of the individual country models are obtained, they are combined in a consistent and cohesive manner to generate forecasts or impulse response functions for *all* the variables in the world economy simultaneously. See also Section 3.4.

Specifically, PSW consider country/region-specific quarterly models estimated over the period 1979q1–1999q1 for seven countries (namely USA, Germany, France, Italy, UK, Japan, China) along with four broader regions (namely, Western Europe, South East Asia, Middle East, and Latin America).[2] For these eleven regions, domestic variables of interest include real output for area i (y_{it}), the rate of price inflation (Δp_{it}), a real equity price index (q_{it}), the real exchange rate ($e_{it} - p_{it}$), where e_{it} is the log of nominal exchange rate in terms of a reference currency (US dollar), an interest rate (r_{it}), and real money balances (m_{it}), with $i = 0$ (US), $1, \ldots, 10$. So, in terms of the domestic variables, we have the vector $\mathbf{y}_{it}$ defined in

[2] The data for the four regions was itself constructed from data for 18 countries. The output of the 25 countries incorporated in the model covers more than 80% of total world output.

(3.21) set as $\mathbf{y}_{it} = (y_{it}, \Delta p_{it}, q_{it}, e_{it} - p_{it}, r_{it}, m_{it})'$, with $k_i = 6$.[3] The vector of foreign variables (indices), denoted by $\mathbf{y}_{it}^*$, is a $k_i^* \times 1$ vector are constructed as weighted averages, with region-specific weights:

$$\left.\begin{aligned} \mathbf{y}_{it}^* &= (y_{it}^*, \Delta p_{it}^*, q_{it}^*, e_{it}^*, r_{it}^*, m_{it}^*)', \\ y_{it}^* &= \textstyle\sum_{j=0}^{10} w_{ij} y_{jt}, \quad p_{it}^* = \sum_{j=0}^{10} w_{ij} p_{jt}, \\ q_{it}^* &= \textstyle\sum_{j=0}^{10} w_{ij} q_{jt}, \quad e_{it}^* = \sum_{j=1}^{10} w_{ij} e_{jt}, \\ r_{it}^* &= \textstyle\sum_{j=0}^{10} w_{ij} r_{jt}, \quad m_{it}^* = \sum_{j=0}^{10} w_{ij} m_{jt}, \end{aligned}\right\} \tag{12.1}$$

where the weights w_{ij}, for $i,j = 0,1,\ldots,10$, are based on trade shares (namely the share of region j in the total trade of region i measured in US dollars). Note that $w_{ii} = 0$, for all i.

Region-specific cointegrating VAR models are estimated treating the relevant foreign variables, along with the price of oil, as exogenous in each case. As noted earlier the only foreign variable included by PSW in the US model was e_{it}^*. A VAR of order 1 is assumed across the regions given the small amount of data available, and careful analysis of the cointegrating properties of the data is employed to choose the cointegrating rank of each regional model. The underlying exogeneity assumptions are confirmed to be acceptable and the adequacy of the dynamic properties of the regional models is established, both taking the regions one at a time and when taken together. In the latter case, the regional models are brought together to form a global model following the steps outlined in expressions (3.23)–(3.27) in Section 3.4. To be more specific, each of the individual region-specific cointegrating VAR models is written in terms of the variables from all other regions, using the definitions in (12.1), and these are then stacked in a large global system accommodating all the contemporaneous and lagged interactions across the 60 plus variables of the system. The corresponding reduced form representation provides the vehicle for forecasting and impulse response analysis.

DdPS, building on the work of PSW, develop a global model covering 33 countries grouped into 25 countries and a single euro area economy comprising eight of the 11 countries that joined the euro in 1999. To deal with the modelling issues that arise from the creation of the euro area (a single exchange rate and a single short-term interest rate post 1999), the GVAR model is estimated with the euro area being treated as a single economy. This turns out to be econometrically justified and allows DdPS to

[3] Asset prices were excluded from the models for China and the Middle East on the grounds that the capital markets are less well-developed.

consider the impact of external shocks on the euro area as a whole without the danger of being subject to possible inconsistencies that could arise if the different economies in the euro area were modelled separately. The effects of external shocks on the euro area are examined based on different simulations using generalised as well as structural impulse response functions. Compared to the previous version of the GVAR developed by PSW, this Mark II version, in addition to increasing the geographical coverage, also extends the estimation period, and includes long-term as well as short-term interest rates, thus allowing more fully for the possible effects of bond markets on output, inflation and equity prices.[4]

DYNAMIC PROPERTIES OF THE GLOBAL MODEL

The GVAR provides a general, yet practical, global modelling framework for a quantitative analysis of the relative importance of different shocks and channels of transmission mechanisms for the analysis of the co-movements of output, inflation, interest rates, exchange rates and equity prices. Using generalised impulse response functions, it is possible to estimate the effects of shocks to one variable in one country on the other variables in the same country and/or in the rest of the world. PSW illustrate the power of the analysis by focusing on the effects of a one standard error (unit) negative shock to US equity prices, oil prices and interest rates. DdPS provide further experiments in relation to the euro area.

As an example in Figure 12.1 we reproduce (from PSW) the time profiles of the effects of shocks to US equity market on equity prices worldwide. On impact, a fall in the US equity prices causes prices in all equity markets to fall as well but by smaller amounts: 3.5% in the UK, 4.5% in Germany, 2.4% in Japan, 2.6% in South East Asia, and 4.8% in Latin America, as compared to a fall of 6.4% in the US. However, the falls in equity prices across the regions generally start to catch up with the US over time, and even get amplified in the case of Italy and Latin America. While the precise values of the responses need to be treated with caution, the relative position and pattern of the impulse response functions confirm the pivotal role played by the US stock market in the global economy, for example, and suggest that in the longer run scope for geographic diversifications across equity market might be somewhat limited.

[4] DdPS also provide a theoretical framework where the GVAR is derived as an approximation to a global unobserved common factor model. Also using average pairwise cross-section error correlations, the GVAR approach is shown to be quite effective in dealing with the common factor interdependencies and international co-movements of business cycles.

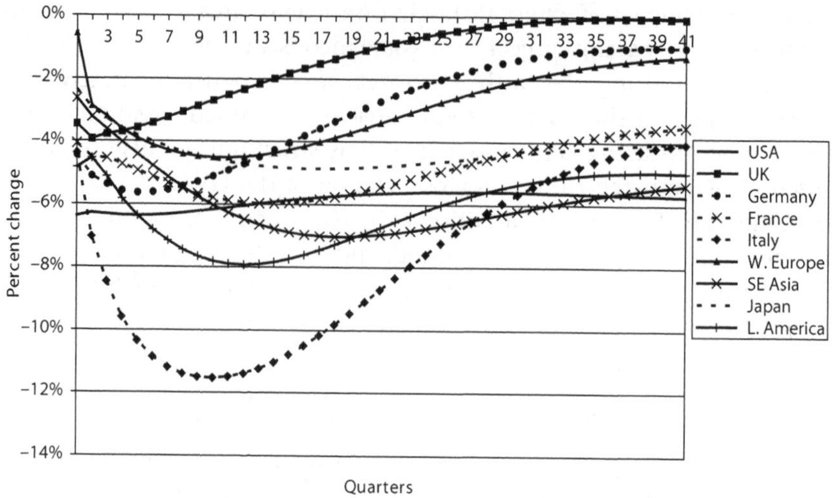

Figure 12.1 Impulse response of a negative one standard error shock to US real equity prices on real equity prices across regions.

The time profiles of the effects of the shock to the US equity market on real output across the different regions are shown in Figure 12.2.

The impact effects of the fall in the US equity market on real output are negative for most regions, but rather small in magnitude. After one year, real output shows falls of around 0.31% in the US, 0.25% in Germany, 0.29% in the UK, 0.26% in Latin America, and 0.12% in South East Asia, respectively. Japanese output only begins to be negatively affected by the adverse US stock market shock much later. The two regions without capital markets are either not affected by the shock (Middle East) or even show a rise in output (in the case of China). Once again, while these point estimates should be treated with caution, they provide a very useful indication of the likely dynamic effects of changes in the US equity market. Further exercises are provided in PSW to show the effects of a shock to the equity markets of South East Asia (providing useful insights with which to judge the experiences of the events surrounding the 1997 South East Asian crisis), and to derive a credit portfolio model based on forecasted default probabilities and loss distributions.

In PSW and elsewhere, the GVAR model has also been used as a global macroeconomic engine driving credit risk models. This is particularly relevant for policy analysis, where one would like to be able to examine how shocking a given macroeconomic variable in a given region could

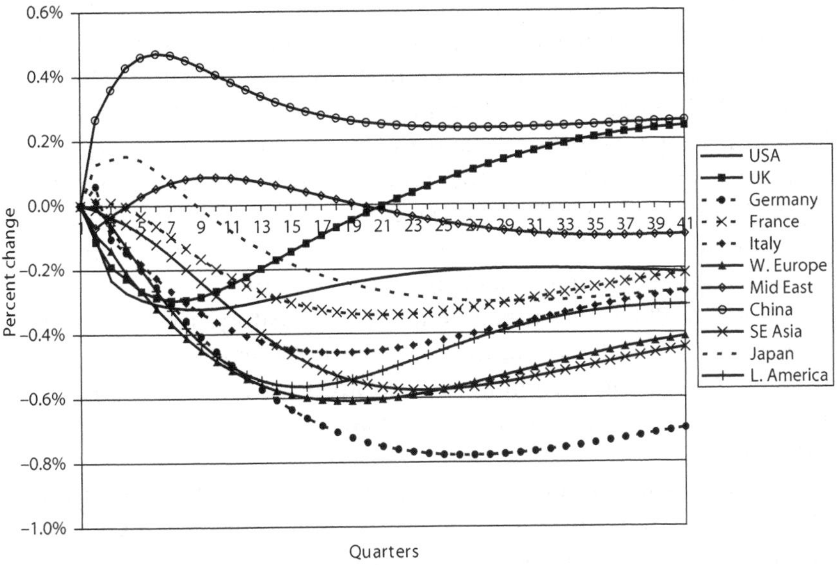

Figure 12.2 Impulse response of a negative one standard error shock to US real equity prices on real output across regions.

affect risk of a globally diversified credit portfolio. For example, it might be of interest to determine the effects of a contemporaneous 10% drop in the Japanese equity prices on other macroeconomic variables, and the effects that these have on the credit risk. As before, generalised impulse response functions can be used to carry out this type of analysis. For further details see Pesaran, Schuermann, Treutler and Weiner (2005) and Pesaran, Schuermann and Treutler (2005).

12.3 A monthly version of the core model

The interest in investigating structural cointegrating VAR models of the macroeconomy has been mirrored by a surge of interest in the use of impulse response analysis, work on the identification of trends and shocks and attempts to decompose the effects of these shocks. The analysis of the macroeconomic models of Canada, the US and the euro area described in the previous section, and the GVAR model, were all accompanied by impulse response analyses to interpret the implicit model properties. In a similar vein, there has been increased interest in obtaining economically meaningful shocks through the imposition of theory-based restrictions and the decomposition of trends. Hence, for example, Crowder *et al.* (1999) provide a decomposition of the effects of shocks to their four-variable cointegrating VAR model of the US to illustrate the historical importance of demand and supply shocks; Wickens and Motto (2001) illustrate the effects of money supply shocks in another four-variable model of the US through imposition of economically motivated restrictions on the cointegrating VAR; Mitchell (1999) examines the effects of monetary policy shocks in the G7 economies using models of a similar form to that of our core model; Ribba (2003) provides a permanent–transitory decomposition of measures of core inflation based for the US; Schumacher (2002) uses a permanent–transitory decomposition to investigate trend output in the euro zone which is, in turn, used to obtain measures of the output gap; and so on.

As the discussion of the earlier chapters made clear, the identification schemes of the short run used to identify economically meaningful shocks are frequently based on the timing of decisions and/or release of news. These identification schemes are often most easily motivated with reference to high frequency data, where temporal aggregation issues are less common. In this section, we briefly describe an application of the modelling techniques developed in the earlier chapters which constructs a monthly version of the core model of the UK, as discussed in Garratt, Lee and Pesaran (2005a). Such a model is particularly relevant for the conduct and the analysis of monetary policy, which is typically updated at a monthly frequency. It is particularly interesting to consider the impulse responses of a model, based on monthly observations that match more closely the decision-making frequency, and to contrast these with those obtained previously on quarterly data to gauge the robustness of the findings of the earlier modelling exercise.

THE STRUCTURE OF THE MONTHLY MODEL

The illustration below uses monthly data for the UK over the period 1965m1–2002m9 (453 observations). We undertake a modelling exercise of precisely the same form as in Chapter 9 and conduct an impulse response exercise, using the exact short-run identification scheme described in Chapter 10 to compute monetary policy and oil price shocks. Where possible, we collected the exact or near exact monthly equivalents of the quarterly measures used in the earlier chapters; see Garratt, Lee and Pesaran (2005a) for details. The variables available at the monthly frequency are p_t, $\widetilde{p}_t$, p_t^o, r_t, r_t^* and m_t. The remaining three variables, y_t, y_t^* and nominal domestic GDP are not directly observable on a monthly basis. We therefore use a linear exponential monthly interpolation method described in Dees, di Mauro, Pesaran and Smith (2004, appendix) for these variables.

The long-run structure we consider in the monthly model is identical to that described and estimated in Chapter 9, the lag length is six months (matching two quarters previously used). In this model, the long-run estimates obtained from the monthly model are given by:

$$(p_t - p_t^*) - e_t = \widehat{\xi}_{1,t+1}, \tag{12.2}$$

$$r_t - r_t^* = \widehat{\xi}_{2,t+1}, \tag{12.3}$$

$$y_t - y_t^* = \widehat{\xi}_{3,t+1}, \tag{12.4}$$

$$h_t - y_t = -\underset{(33.44)}{134.72}\, r_t - \underset{(0.00028)}{0.0021}\, t + \widehat{\xi}_{4,t+1}, \tag{12.5}$$

$$r_t - \Delta\widetilde{p}_t = \widehat{\xi}_{5,t+1}. \tag{12.6}$$

It is worth recalling that the estimates of the coefficients in the money demand equation based on the quarterly model were 56.10 and 0.0073, as compared to the above estimates of 134.72 and 0.0021, respectively. To ensure that the two estimates of the interest rate effects are comparable the one based on the monthly model should be divided by 3, which yields the estimate of 33.7 which is only somewhat lower than the estimate of 56.10 obtained from the quarterly model.[5] The estimate of the trend coefficient is also lower using the monthly model, partly reflecting the more recent sample that underlies the monthly model. As noted before it is unlikely that the downward trend in real money balances observed pre-1999 should continue into the future. The log-likelihood ratio statistic for testing the 23 over-identifying restrictions is 71.73, which is again in line with the results obtained for the quarterly model.

Table 12.1 reports the estimates of the loading matrix $\boldsymbol{\alpha}$ for the co-integrating terms in the error correction specification, along with various diagnostic test statistics.

The estimates of the loading coefficients show that the long-run relations make an important contribution in most equations and that the error correction terms provide for a complex and statistically significant set of interactions and feedbacks across commodity, money and foreign

[5] Note r_t is measured on a per annum basis and hence an approximate comparison with the quarterly coefficient would be the number is $134.72/4 = 33.7$.

Table 12.1 Reduced form error correction equations of the monthly model.

Eq	$\Delta(p_t - p_t^*)$	Δe_t	Δr_t	Δr_t^*	Δy_t	Δy_t^*	$\Delta(h_t - y_t)$	$\Delta(\Delta\tilde{p}_t)$
$\widehat{\xi}_{1,t}$	−0.009*	0.0263*	0.0002	−0.0002	0.007*	0.0109*	−0.0093	−0.0055
	(0.0027)	(0.011)	(0.0002)	(−0.0002)	(0.003)	(0.0019)	(0.0056)	(0.003)
$\widehat{\xi}_{2,t}$	−0.878*	1.433	0.007	0.0493*	1.187*	1.101*	−1.045	−1.237*
	(0.296)	(1.229)	(0.03)	(0.0171)	(0.341)	(0.210)	(0.622)	(0.342)
$\widehat{\xi}_{3,t}$	0.0157	−0.0623	−0.0015*	−0.00065	−0.0473*	−0.0108	0.0491*	0.0177
	(0.0085)	(0.035)	(0.0009)	(0.0101)	(0.009)	(0.006)	(0.0178)	(0.0098)
$\widehat{\xi}_{4,t}$	0.009*	−0.0152	−0.00024	−0.00002	−0.0097*	−0.0071*	−0.0020	0.0056
	(0.002)	(0.0084)	(0.0002)	(0.0001)	(0.0023)	(0.001)	(0.0043)	(0.0023)
$\widehat{\xi}_{5,t}$	0.052	−0.185	−0.0235*	−0.0152	−0.1984*	−0.1659*	0.5063*	0.700*
	(0.085)	(0.352)	(0.0086)	(0.0049)	(0.0976)	(0.0602)	(0.178)	(0.0981)
$\bar{R}^2$	0.2210	0.0697	0.0811	0.2689	0.2606	0.2401	0.2736	0.4682
$\hat{\sigma}$	0.0043	0.0179	0.00044	0.0003	0.0049	0.00308	0.0091	0.005
$\chi^2_{SC}[12]$	15.998	10.39	17.51	28.68	36.73	38.15	34.48	116.57
$\chi^2_{A}[12]$	22.008	3.31	62.63	1.511	116.14	24.91	23.30	9.17
$\chi^2_{N}[2]$	329.31	1804.3	295.2	522.7	262.16	117.23	231.99	305.74
$\chi^2_{H}[1]$	34.33	17.12	68.17	58.48	7.19	40.56	1.56	39.22

Note: To save space only the error correction coefficients are reported, with their standard errors given in parentheses.

exchange markets. The results in Table 12.1 also show that the core model fits the data well and the diagnostic statistics of the equations are generally satisfactory as far as the tests of the residual serial correlation, functional form and heteroscedasticity are concerned.[6]

IMPULSE RESPONSE ANALYSIS FOR THE MONTHLY MODEL

Figures 12.3 and 12.4 plot the monthly impulse responses of the variables to a monetary policy and oil price shock corresponding to the impulse responses described for the quarterly model in Section 10.2.

The shape and timing of the monthly and quarterly impulses are very similar. Focusing on the monetary policy shock, for example, the sign of the impact effects is the same in the quarterly and monthly models across all of the endogenous variables, and the shapes of the impulse responses are the same in monthly and quarterly versions for all the series too.[7] Moreover, the timing of the responses is very similar: domestic interest rates settle to their long-run levels after around 30 months in the monthly plots compared to around 12 quarters in the quarterly plot of Figure 10.4;

[6] The normality of the errors is rejected in all of the error correction regressions, and is almost certainly due to the three major oil price hikes experienced during the estimation period.

[7] There is, however, a minor exception in the core of the impulse responses for the effects of the monetary policy shock on the exchange rate. Unlike the quarterly model the monetary policy shock shows a brief (two month) period of depreciation in the monthly model.

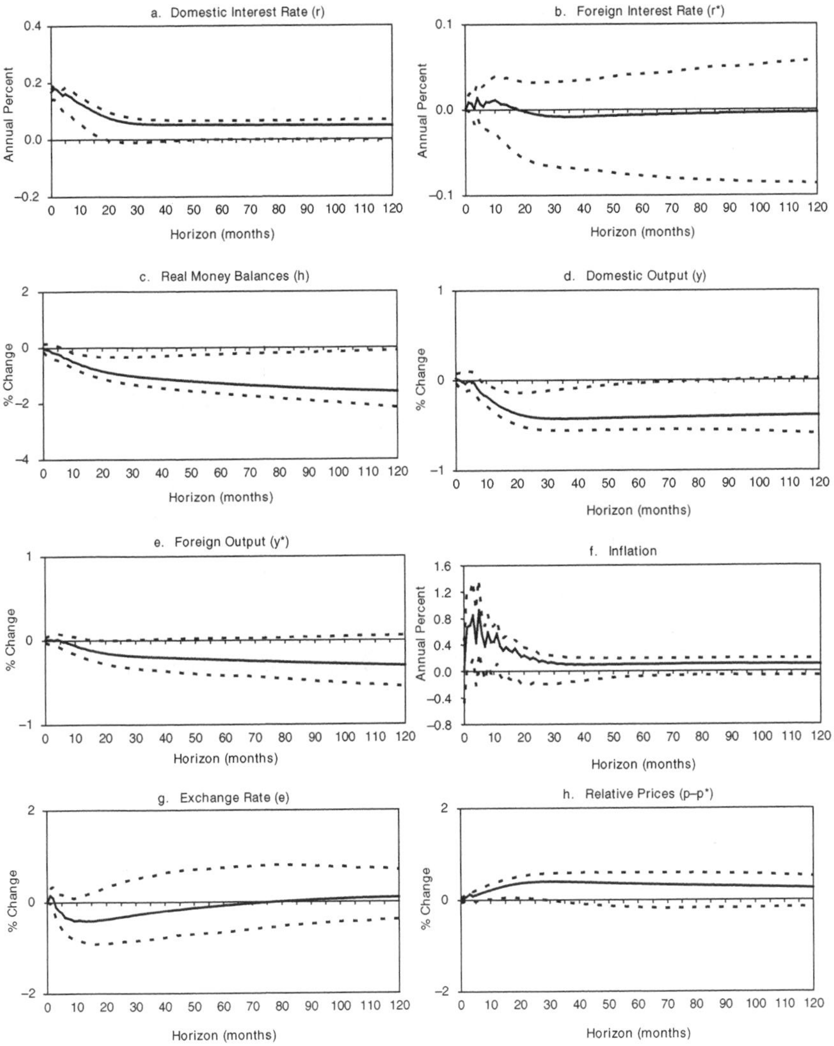

Note: The solid and dashed lines plot the point estimates and 95% confidence intervals of the impulse responses, which are generated from the bootstrap procedure using 2000 replications.

Figure 12.3 Monthly generalised impulse responses to a positive unit shock to monetary policy.

the initial upward impact on domestic output is reversed after six months in the monthly plot compared to two quarters in the quarterly plots; the puzzling rise in inflation in response to the contractionary shock shows in the monthly model as in the quarterly model, but the effects are relatively

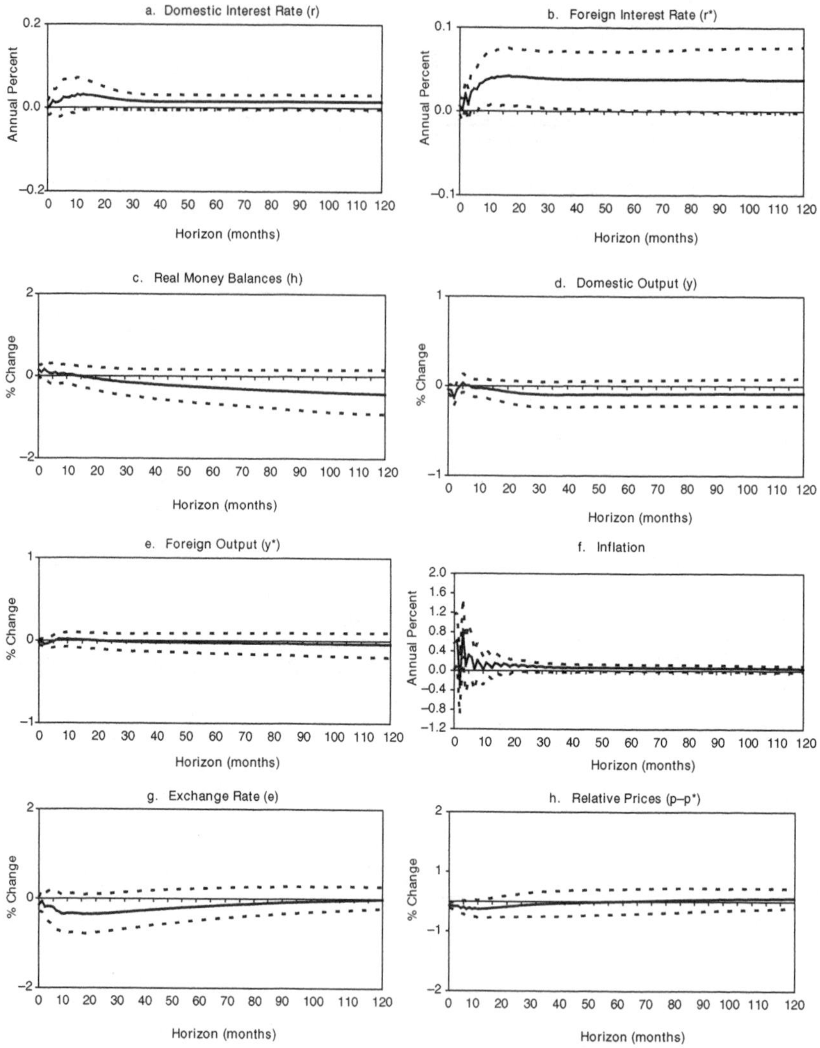

Note: The solid and dashed lines plot the point estimates and 95% confidence intervals of the impulse responses, which are generated from the bootstrap procedure using 2000 replications.

Figure 12.4 Monthly generalised impulse responses to a positive unit shock to the oil price.

short-lived and effectively disappear after 12 months (*cf.* four quarters in Figure 10.4). Similar comments apply to the impulse responses arising from the oil price shock. Again the responses from the monthly model are very similar to those obtained in the quarterly model, shown in Figure 10.6, both in terms of the sign of the impact effects and the shape and timing of the subsequent responses. (Perhaps the only notable feature that is distinctive is the higher volatility of the inflation response in the monthly plots compared to those in the quarterly plots.)

12.4 Probability forecasting and measuring financial distress in the UK

The material of Chapter 11 showed that probability forecasting is an extremely useful means of providing information on the properties of a model and conveying the uncertainty that surrounds the predictor of future events of particular interest. This type of analysis is also becoming increasingly popular, particularly as investigators recognise the ease with which the probability forecasts can be produced with the small and flexible models of the type we have promoted in our work. This is especially true for analyses of inflation forecasts and monetary policy formulation; see, for example, Diebold *et al.* (1999), Ehrmann and Smets (2003), and Hall and Mitchell (2005). In the illustration below, we consider the recent work of Lee and Mizen (2005) who focus on the use of the probabilistic statement as a macroeconomic indicator. The illustration is also of interest because it provides an example of the use of a satellite model, supplementing the core, as described in Section 3.3.2.

12.4.1 *A satellite model of the UK financial sector*

The extension of the model considered here concerns the measurement of 'financial distress' at the macroeconomic level. Financial distress relates to the vulnerability of individuals in their financial decision-making and is reflected in periods of high levels of defaults on loan repayments and bankruptcies. This has become a topic of some interest in recent years as the levels of credit card debt, in the UK, the US and elsewhere, have risen to unprecedented levels. There is widespread anxiety that this could generate financial instability if there were to be an adverse macroeconomic shock in the form of higher interest rates or low growth. Indeed, current levels of the 'debt burden' (showing debt interest payments on repayments based on unsecured debt relative to income) are, in 2005, at their highest ever level in the UK and have recently exceeded those observed in the early 1990s when many households experienced considerable financial hardship, personal bankruptcies were widespread and loan repayment defaults were extremely high.

Lee and Mizen (2005) consider this problem using the long-run structural modelling approach developed in the earlier chapters applied to the core macroeconomic model and to a satellite model of UK households' portfolio and expenditure decisions. Economic theory is used to motivate the long-run relations that are likely to hold between household consumption expenditure (c_t), money deposits (m_t) and borrowing (l_t) where a household can consume more than current income and money balances by borrowing at a 'credit card' interest rate r_t^l. The long-run relationships of the satellite model suggested by the theory relating to household portfolio and expenditure decisions can be written as

$$c_t = b_{10} + b_{11}t + \widetilde{y}_t + b_{12}r_t + \xi_{c,t+1}, \tag{12.7}$$

$$m_t = b_{20} + b_{21}t + \widetilde{y}_t + b_{22}r_t + \xi_{m,t+1}, \tag{12.8}$$

$$l_t = b_{30} + b_{31}t + \widetilde{y}_t + b_{32}r_t^l + \xi_{l,t+1}, \tag{12.9}$$

$$r_t^l = b_{40} + b_{41}t + r_t + \xi_{r,t+1}, \tag{12.10}$$

where $\widetilde{y}_t$ refers to real net labour income. This can be written more compactly as

$$\boldsymbol{\xi}_{bt} = \boldsymbol{\beta}_b'(\mathbf{w}_{t-1}, r_{t-1}) - \mathbf{b}_0 - \mathbf{b}_1(t-1),$$

where

$$\mathbf{w}_t = \left(c_t - \widetilde{y}_t, m_t - \widetilde{y}_t, l_t - \widetilde{y}_t, r_t^l\right)'.$$

$$\mathbf{b}_0 = (b_{10}, b_{20}, b_{30}, b_{40})', \ \mathbf{b}_1 = (b_{11}, b_{21}, b_{31}, b_{41})',$$

$$\boldsymbol{\xi}_{bt} = (\xi_{ct}, \xi_{mt}, \xi_{lt}, \xi_{rt})',$$

and

$$\boldsymbol{\beta}_b' = \begin{pmatrix} 1 & 0 & 0 & 0 & -b_{12} \\ 0 & 1 & 0 & 0 & -b_{22} \\ 0 & 0 & 1 & -b_{32} & 0 \\ 0 & 0 & 0 & 1 & -1 \end{pmatrix}. \tag{12.11}$$

A simplifying assumption is that the household portfolio and expenditure decisions are made taking into account the macroeconomic context, but that these household allocation decisions do not impact on the evolution of the national macroeconomic aggregates. In this case, the set of sectoral variables in $\mathbf{w}_t$ are influenced by the core macroeconomic variables of our core model (including the interest rate r_t) but not *vice versa*, and the modelling framework between a core and a satellite model described in Section 3.3.2 is appropriate. In particular, in these circumstances, the estimation of the core model can be conducted without reference to the satellite model (so that the model of Chapter 9 remains relevant), while the model of the household expenditure and portfolio decisions can be estimated taking the macroeconomic interest rate r_t as an exogenous $I(1)$ variable.

12.4.2 *UK financial distress in the early 1990s and early 2000s*

The estimation of the above model is discussed in Lee and Mizen (2005). The model provided an extremely useful vehicle with which to forecast future events relating to the macroeconomy and/or household portfolio and expenditure decisions. It is argued in Lee and Mizen (2005) that financial distress is associated with particular conjunctions of events involving the disequilibria in the credit market as reflected in the estimated values of ξ_{lt} in (12.9) and the economy's growth prospects. In this case, forecasts of the probability of the occurrence of these events provide useful indicators of financial distress at the macroeconomic level. With this in mind, Lee and Mizen calculate forecasts of various probabilities involving excess credit holdings (*i.e.* $\xi_{lt} > c_1$ for various threshold values, c_1) and recession or slow growth (defined where a four-quarter moving average falls below zero or 1% respectively; *i.e.* $\widehat{\Delta y_t^{MA}} < c_2$, for $c_2 = 0$ or 0.01). The exercise is conducted using the core and satellite models estimated over the period 1965q1–2001q1 and then again, using exactly the same methods, on the data ending in 1990q1 (just prior to the previous period of financial distress). Representative results are provided in Table 12.2.

These show that the estimated probability of excess credit holdings or slow growth occurring were very high in the early 1990s, so that the high levels of financial distress that were experienced would have been reflected in these forecast figures. In contrast, the corresponding probabilities observed for 2001–2002 were very much lower.[8] Despite the very high debt burden levels observed at this time, the point forecasts of excess credit

[8] The fact that the successive columns of the table relating to 2001q1–2003q1 are the same reflects the fact that the joint probability relates exclusively to the probability of slow growth; the probability of excess credit holdings was found to be zero for $c_1 = 0.2$, 0.3 and 0.4.

Table 12.2 Probability forecasts involving credit–income disequilibria and low growth 1990q2–1992q1 and 2001q2–2003q1

Forecast Horizon	$\Pr(A \cup B)$ $c_1 = 0.20$ $c_2 = 0.01$	$\Pr(A \cup B)$ $c_1 = 0.30$ $c_2 = 0.01$	$\Pr(A \cup B)$ $c_1 = 0.40$ $c_2 = 0.01$
1990q2	1.00	0.97	0.49
1990q3	1.00	0.92	0.45
1990q4	1.00	0.66	0.40
1991q1	1.00	0.74	0.46
1991q2	1.00	0.82	0.46
1991q3	1.00	0.84	0.44
1991q4	1.00	0.80	0.42
1992q1	1.00	0.83	0.40
Forecast Horizon	$\Pr(A \cup B)$ $c_1 = 0.20$ $c_2 = 0.01$	$\Pr(A \cup B)$ $c_1 = 0.30$ $c_2 = 0.01$	$\Pr(A \cup B)$ $c_1 = 0.40$ $c_2 = 0.01$
2001q2	0.21	0.21	0.21
2001q3	0.33	0.33	0.33
2001q4	0.38	0.38	0.38
2002q1	0.43	0.43	0.43
2002q2	0.36	0.36	0.36
2002q3	0.32	0.32	0.32
2002q4	0.30	0.30	0.30
2003q1	0.29	0.29	0.29

Note: The probability estimates relate to the quarter-on-quarter forecasts of the credit–income disequilibria and the four-quarter moving average of output growth (denoted Δy_t^{MA}). Slow growth is defined to occur when the latter falls below 1%. Event $A = \{\widehat{\xi}_{lt} > c_1\}$ and $B = \{\Delta y_t^{MA} < c_2\}$. $A \cup B$ means 'disequilibrium exceeds a critical value or slow growth occurs'.

holdings were low (and well below the threshold values for c_1 that were considered to relate to financial distress). Financial distress would be driven by the probability of recession or poor growth in these circumstances, but this seemed relatively unlikely in 2001–2003 also. Hence, the probability forecasts provided in Table 12.2 indicate low levels of financial distress and, as it turned out, this was not a period in which either high levels of loan default or bankruptcy actually occurred.

12.5 Directions for future research

This chapter provides an overview of the various applications and extensions of the long-run structural modelling strategy advanced in this volume, namely the rigorous use of long-run economic theory in the context of an econometrically coherent time series framework. We are confident that many of the areas that we have highlighted will be adapted or extended to initiate new research avenues in due course. In particular, we believe there to be considerable scope for the further development and use of the techniques in the sphere of global macroeconometric modelling. This chapter briefly discusses the evidence obtained so far in the literature on global VAR modelling. Here, the individual national economy models are combined in a feasible and consistent manner into a global macroeconometric model for use in policy analysis and risk management, very much reminiscent of the pioneering work of the Project Link under the leadership of Lawrence Klein. The GVAR models developed so far impose cointegrating rank restrictions on the individual economy models. The next stage would be to consider the imposition of over-identifying long-run theory restrictions on the cointegrating relations of the individual economies, very much along the lines implemented in this volume for the UK economy, before combining them into a global model. Preliminary analysis suggests that this could indeed be a promising line for future research.

13

Concluding remarks

In this book, our aim has been to provide a reasonably comprehensive account of the cointegrating VAR analysis of national and global macroeconomic modelling with a solid underlying long-run economic theory. We have compared our approach to other alternatives, particularly where either little economic theory is used in the modelling process or, where the economic theory is allowed to dominate the empirical evidence. We view both of these strands as valuable from a pedagogical viewpoint. For the modelling exercise to be useful and relevant to a better understanding of the macroeconomic processes and public debates about macroeconomic policy, a middle ground is needed. This book presents such an approach where implications of the long-run economic theory are combined with short-run dynamics within a cointegrating VAR framework. Contemporaneous restrictions from economic theory are imposed subsequently as a means of identification of the monetary policy shock and its impulse responses.

The book also addresses one of the important limitations of VAR for the analysis of relatively large system of equations that arise particularly in the case of global modelling. This is done by means of VARX or VARX* specifications where the familiar VAR model is augmented with $I(1)$ weakly exogenous (or long-run forcing) variables so that the 'core' variables are distinguished from the variables in the satellite sub-models. In the case of national macroeconometric modelling, core variables would typically include real output, inflation, interest rates and exchange rates, whilst the variables in satellite models could be consumption, investment, employment, real wages, imports or exports. At the national level, the core variables would be long-run forcing for the satellite variables, whilst within a global context the foreign variables, denoted as * variables, will be long-run forcing for the core national variables. The resultant modular structure is eminently suitable for a cointegrating analysis of large (log) linear systems.

In combining the long-run theory with empirically based short-run dynamics, particular attention is also paid to a simultaneous treatment of trends and cycles. This contrasts with much of the empirical implementation of the DSGE modelling where individual series are de-trended first, often with the help of Hodrick–Prescott filter, before modelling the relationships that might exist amongst the de-trended series. By building on long-run economic relations that are widely held as providing a solid economic foundation, and by allowing for unit roots and deterministic trends simultaneously, we believe that our modelling framework would be a suitable starting point for the analysis of short-run economic restrictions such as those implied by intertemporal optimisation, learning and expectations formation.

The long-run structural approach is illustrated with an application to the UK macroeconomy. Careful attention is paid to the different stages of the modelling exercise and, in the interest of ready replications of our results by other researchers, data and programs used are supplied with detailed accounts of their implementation. Further applications are considered and recent extensions of the modelling strategy to a global context (namely the GVAR modelling) are also discussed.

To summarise in more detail the book serves to

- explain and promote the long-run structural modelling approach as a way of undertaking macroeconometric research;
- provide a comprehensive illustration of the approach through a description of each stage of the development of the core model of the UK economy; and
- demonstrate how a model obtained following this approach can be used in real-world decision-making.

On the issue of promoting the long-run structural modelling approach, our aim throughout has been to present a fully transparent approach to macroeconomic modelling in which there is a clear statement of the economic theory and the associated econometric methodology. Our explicit description of a macroeconomic theory of the long run aims to highlight the level of abstraction at which an analyst might work in building a model that can be confronted with the data. Similarly, our description of the theory of the short run also exposes the extent to which economic theory might realistically inform our attempts to interpret macroeconomic dynamics. And our comprehensive description of the econometric methods underlying the long-run structural modelling approach showed how the insights obtained from an explicit statement on the long-run theory (and, if available, on the short-run theory) can be embedded, and tested, within a statistical model that can both possess economically reasonable properties and reflect the characteristics of the data. In brief, the intention is that the economic theory and the econometric methods complement and enhance each other.

We have been keen to compare and contrast our approach to modelling with other popular approaches not just to highlight its transparency and ease of implementation, but also to draw out those areas on which there is consensus in macroeconomics and those areas that are subject to controversy. Our approach emphasises the use of long-run theory on the grounds that this is the area in which there is most agreement. But we acknowledge that some questions require more detailed short-run analysis and so we explain how such an analysis can be undertaken and the assumptions that are required. Our discussion of these issues emphasises the difficulties in identifying economically meaningful shocks on the basis of the identification schemes currently employed in the literature, casting doubt on the ability of the current generation of theories of macroeconomic dynamics to deliver an all-encompassing description of the short run or one that is consistent with the data. However, even if we doubt the validity of some of the currently employed identification schemes, we hope that our work will contribute to what is an ongoing debate and, through our discussion of models employing higher frequency data, hope to focus modellers' attention on more reasonable identification schemes that can be defended with reference to information flows and the precise timing of decisions.

The second aim of the book is to provide an illustration of the entire process of building a model, from the description of the underlying economic theory and its empirical counterpart, through the collection of data and its initial characterisation, through the estimation and testing of the model, to its final use in interpreting the macroeconomy and its use in decision-making. Of course, we hope that the core model of the UK economy that we have obtained is useful in its own right, and we have provided full details of the data and the model estimation in Appendix C for this reason. But the primary purpose of this description is to illustrate the steps and decisions that have to be taken in building a macroeconomic model. The construction and maintenance of a model typically requires a sustained research effort. Our hope is that the description of our modelling activities for the UK economy can provide a blueprint for model construction in a variety of different (global and/or national) contexts so that the first stages of the modelling activity are more easily addressed, and we have provided details of our programs so that these can be readily adapted for the use of others.

The third objective of the book is that the work will be useful to practitioners. As can be seen from the discussion of the previous chapters, many of the methods that we have described are already being applied both inside and outside academia. Practitioners, who need manageable and interpretable models to answer specific questions, appreciate the transparency and pragmatism of the modelling approach so that the methods are already in increasingly widespread use in the policy-making and decision-making communities. Of course, it is true that our core model could not be used to answer questions on the impact of particular tax changes or other very detailed policy effects, which would require a large-scale macroeconomic model. But financial institutions and decision-makers in industry need to answer a large variety of questions and make use of a range of macroeconomic models to address these questions. Some of these models will be more complex than ours and some of them will be less complex. But in any event, the ease of construction of a model following our approach means that such models can be obtained easily either to stand in their own right or as a complementary view to other models. Moreover, as we have noted, a model obtained following our approach can be readily extended either by its inclusion within a broader framework (as in the GVAR model, for example), or by linking it to a more detailed 'satellite' model of the market of interest. In all cases, the relative simplicity and flexibility of the models that are obtained means that they are well-suited for use in simulation and other counter-factual exercises so that we believe they provide an extremely valuable tool for decision-making.

The research reported in this volume also points to a number of important extensions, and suggests a number of new applications that might be pursued. For example, alternative sets of short-run restrictions, motivated by macroeconomic theory, can be imposed and tested using the core long-run structural model; satellite models of labour market and foreign trade can be developed and tested; the global modelling framework can be utilised for identification of long-run theory relations in the world economy; and it can be used to investigate the extent to which business cycles are synchronised across different economies using the permanent/transitory decomposition of the variables in the cointegrating country-specific models; and so on. In each case, we believe the methods described in the book will contribute to a theoretically informed and evidence-based analysis of important macroeconomic phenomena.

APPENDIX A

Derivation of the interest rate rule

Recall from Chapter 5 that, in our model, we distinguish between three classes of variable: the first set consists of the four variables determined contemporaneously with r_t^b (namely, p_t^o, e_t, r_t^*, and r_t); the second set, denoted $\mathbf{w}_t$ contains output and inflation, which we shall assume are the variables of direct concern to the monetary authorities; and the third set, denoted $\mathbf{q}_t$, consists of the remaining variables. Hence, we have

$$\mathbf{z}_t = \begin{pmatrix} p_t^o \\ \mathbf{y}_t \end{pmatrix}, \quad \mathbf{y}_t = \begin{pmatrix} e_t \\ r_t^* \\ r_t \\ \mathbf{w}_t \\ \mathbf{q}_t \end{pmatrix}, \quad \mathbf{w}_t = \begin{pmatrix} y_t \\ \Delta p_t \end{pmatrix}, \quad \mathbf{q}_t = \begin{pmatrix} p_t - p_t^* \\ h_t - y_t \\ y_t^* \end{pmatrix}.$$

The assumptions discussed in Section 5.1 of the text imposes a structure on the parameter matrices of (5.2),

$$\mathbf{A}\,\Delta\mathbf{z}_t = \widetilde{\mathbf{a}} - \widetilde{\boldsymbol{\alpha}}\left[\boldsymbol{\beta}'\mathbf{z}_{t-1} - \mathbf{b}_1(t-1)\right] + \sum_{i=1}^{p-1}\widetilde{\boldsymbol{\Gamma}}_i\Delta\mathbf{z}_{t-i} + \boldsymbol{\varepsilon}_t, \tag{A.1}$$

as follows:[1]

$$\widetilde{\mathbf{a}} = \begin{pmatrix} \delta_o \\ \widetilde{a}_e \\ \widetilde{a}_{r^*} \\ \widetilde{a}_r \\ \widetilde{\mathbf{a}}_w \\ \widetilde{\mathbf{a}}_q \end{pmatrix}, \quad \widetilde{\boldsymbol{\alpha}} = \begin{pmatrix} 0 \\ \widetilde{\alpha}_e \\ \widetilde{\alpha}_{r^*} \\ \widetilde{\alpha}_r \\ \widetilde{\boldsymbol{\alpha}}_w \\ \widetilde{\boldsymbol{\alpha}}_q \end{pmatrix}, \quad \widetilde{\boldsymbol{\Gamma}}_i = \begin{pmatrix} \delta_{i,o} \\ \widetilde{\boldsymbol{\Gamma}}_{e,i} \\ \widetilde{\boldsymbol{\Gamma}}_{r^*,i} \\ \widetilde{\boldsymbol{\Gamma}}_{r,i} \\ \widetilde{\boldsymbol{\Gamma}}_{w,i} \\ \widetilde{\boldsymbol{\Gamma}}_{q,i} \end{pmatrix}, \quad \boldsymbol{\varepsilon}_t = \begin{pmatrix} \varepsilon_{o,t} \\ \varepsilon_{e,t} \\ \varepsilon_{r^*,t} \\ \varepsilon_{r,t} \\ \boldsymbol{\varepsilon}_{w,t} \\ \boldsymbol{\varepsilon}_{q,t} \end{pmatrix}$$

[1] In fact, for expositional purposes, we make the further assumption that exchange rates are determined prior to foreign interest rates in what follows.

and

$$\mathrm{A} = \begin{pmatrix} 1 & 0 & 0 & 0 & 0 & 0 \\ -\widetilde{\psi}_e & 1 & 0 & 0 & 0 & 0 \\ -\widetilde{\psi}_{r^*} & a_{r^*e} & 1 & 0 & 0 & 0 \\ -\widetilde{\psi}_r & a_{re} & a_{rr^*} & 1 & 0 & 0 \\ -\widetilde{\boldsymbol{\psi}}_w & \mathbf{A}_{we} & \mathbf{A}_{wr^*} & \mathbf{A}_{wr} & \mathbf{A}_{ww} & \mathbf{A}_{wq} \\ -\widetilde{\boldsymbol{\psi}}_q & \mathbf{A}_{qe} & \mathbf{A}_{qr^*} & \mathbf{A}_{qr} & \mathbf{A}_{qw} & \mathbf{A}_{qq} \end{pmatrix}.$$

The corresponding reduced form equation, given in (5.1), is

$$\Delta \mathbf{z}_t = \mathbf{a} - \boldsymbol{\alpha}\left[\boldsymbol{\beta}' \mathbf{z}_{t-1} - \mathbf{b}_1(t-1)\right] + \sum_{i=1}^{s-1} \boldsymbol{\Gamma}_i \Delta \mathbf{z}_{t-i} + \mathbf{v}_t, \tag{A.2}$$

where $\widetilde{\mathbf{a}} = \mathbf{A}\mathbf{a}$, $\widetilde{\boldsymbol{\alpha}} = \mathbf{A}\boldsymbol{\alpha}$, $\widetilde{\boldsymbol{\Gamma}}_i = \mathbf{A}\boldsymbol{\Gamma}_i$, $\boldsymbol{\varepsilon}_t = \mathbf{A}\mathbf{v}_t$ and

$$\mathbf{a} = \begin{pmatrix} \delta_o \\ a_e \\ a_{r^*} \\ a_r \\ \mathbf{a}_w \\ \mathbf{a}_q \end{pmatrix}, \quad \boldsymbol{\alpha} = \begin{pmatrix} 0 \\ \alpha_e \\ \alpha_{r^*} \\ \alpha_r \\ \boldsymbol{\alpha}_w \\ \boldsymbol{\alpha}_q \end{pmatrix}, \quad \boldsymbol{\Gamma}_i = \begin{pmatrix} \delta_{o,i} \\ \boldsymbol{\Gamma}_{e,i} \\ \boldsymbol{\Gamma}_{r^*,i} \\ \boldsymbol{\Gamma}_{r,i} \\ \boldsymbol{\Gamma}_{w,i} \\ \boldsymbol{\Gamma}_{q,i} \end{pmatrix}, \quad \mathbf{v}_t = \begin{pmatrix} v_{o,t} \\ v_{e,t} \\ v_{r^*,t} \\ v_{r,t} \\ \mathbf{v}_{w,t} \\ \mathbf{v}_{q,t} \end{pmatrix}.$$

A.1 The relationship between policy instruments and targets

To derive the monetary authorities' reaction function, we need an expression that explains the consequences of changes in the policy instrument, r_t^b, on the target variables, $\Delta \mathbf{w}_t$. The policy instrument affects the targets via the market interest rate, r_t, so we first focus attention on the block in the structural model of (A.1) relating the targets to the market interest rate. This block is given by the rows of (A.1) concerned with the determination of $\Delta \mathbf{w}_t$:

$$\begin{aligned} &- \widetilde{\boldsymbol{\psi}}_w \Delta p_t^o + \mathbf{A}_{we}\Delta e_t + \mathbf{A}_{wr^*}\Delta r_t^* + \mathbf{A}_{wr}\Delta r_t + \mathbf{A}_{ww}\Delta \mathbf{w}_t + \mathbf{A}_{wq}\Delta \mathbf{q}_t \\ &= \widetilde{\mathbf{a}}_w - \widetilde{\boldsymbol{\alpha}}_w\left[\boldsymbol{\beta}' \mathbf{z}_{t-1} - \mathbf{b}_1(t-1)\right] + \sum_{i=1}^{s-1} \widetilde{\boldsymbol{\Gamma}}_{w,i} \Delta \mathbf{z}_{t-i} + \boldsymbol{\varepsilon}_{w,t}. \end{aligned} \tag{A.3}$$

Using the reduced form model of (A.2), we can replace the terms involving Δp_t^o, Δe_t, Δr_t^*, and $\Delta \mathbf{q}_t$ in (A.3) to obtain an expression relating the targets to the market interest rate which involves only lagged information and news becoming available at time t in the form of structural shocks. Specifically, the reduced form model of (A.2) provides expressions for the oil price, exchange rate, foreign interest rate and variables in $\mathbf{q}_t$ as follows:

$$\Delta p_t^o = \delta_o + \sum_{i=1}^{p-1} \delta_{o,i}\Delta \mathbf{z}_{t-i} + v_{o,t}, \tag{A.4}$$

$$\Delta e_t = a_e - \alpha_e \left[\boldsymbol{\beta}' \mathbf{z}_{t-1} - \mathbf{b}_1(t-1)\right] + \sum_{i=1}^{p-1} \boldsymbol{\Gamma}_{e,i}\Delta \mathbf{z}_{t-i} + v_{e,t} \tag{A.5}$$

$$\Delta r_t^* = a_{r^*} - \alpha_{r^*} \left[\boldsymbol{\beta}' \mathbf{z}_{t-1} - \mathbf{b}_1(t-1)\right] + \sum_{i=1}^{p-1} \boldsymbol{\Gamma}_{r^*,i}\Delta \mathbf{z}_{t-i} + v_{r^*,t} \tag{A.6}$$

and

$$\Delta \mathbf{q}_t = \mathbf{a}_q - \boldsymbol{\alpha}_q \left[\boldsymbol{\beta}' \mathbf{z}_{t-1} - \mathbf{b}_1(t-1)\right] + \sum_{i=1}^{p-1} \boldsymbol{\Gamma}_{q,i}\Delta \mathbf{z}_{t-i} + \mathbf{v}_{q,t}. \tag{A.7}$$

Substituting (A.4)–(A.7) into (A.3) yields the structural relationship between the targets and the market rate:

$$\mathbf{A}_{wr}\Delta r_t + \mathbf{A}_{ww}\Delta \mathbf{w}_t = \mathbf{a}_{ww} + \boldsymbol{\alpha}_{w\xi} \left[\boldsymbol{\beta}' \mathbf{z}_{t-1} - \mathbf{b}_1(t-1)\right] + \sum_{i=1}^{p-1} \boldsymbol{\Gamma}_{wz,i}\mathbf{z}_{t-i} + \boldsymbol{\varepsilon}_{ww,t}, \tag{A.8}$$

where

$$\begin{aligned}
\mathbf{a}_{ww} &= \widetilde{\mathbf{a}}_w + \boldsymbol{\psi}_w\delta_o - \mathbf{A}_{we}a_e - \mathbf{A}_{we}a_{r^*} - \mathbf{A}_{wq}\mathbf{a}_q \\
\boldsymbol{\alpha}_{w\xi} &= -\widetilde{\boldsymbol{\alpha}}_w + \mathbf{A}_{we}\boldsymbol{\alpha}_e + \mathbf{A}_{wr^*}\boldsymbol{\alpha}_{r^*} + \mathbf{A}_{wq}\boldsymbol{\alpha}_q \\
\boldsymbol{\Gamma}_{wz,i} &= \widetilde{\boldsymbol{\Gamma}}_{w,i} + \boldsymbol{\psi}_w\delta_{o,i} - \mathbf{A}_{we}\boldsymbol{\Gamma}_{e,i} - \mathbf{A}_{wr^*}\boldsymbol{\Gamma}_{r^*,i} - \mathbf{A}_{wq}\boldsymbol{\Gamma}_{q,i} \\
\boldsymbol{\varepsilon}_{ww,t} &= \boldsymbol{\varepsilon}_{w,t} + \boldsymbol{\psi}_w v_{o,t} - \mathbf{A}_{we}v_{e,t} - \mathbf{A}_{wr^*}v_{r^*,t} - \mathbf{A}_{wq}\mathbf{v}_{q,t}.
\end{aligned}$$

The 'quasi' reduced form linking targets to the market rate, to be used subsequently in the optimisation problem, is then given by

$$\Delta \mathbf{w}_t = \boldsymbol{\Pi}_{wr}\Delta r_t + \boldsymbol{\Pi}_{ww} + \boldsymbol{\Pi}_{w\xi} \left[\boldsymbol{\beta}' \mathbf{z}_{t-1} - \mathbf{b}_1(t-1)\right] + \sum_{i=1}^{p-1} \boldsymbol{\Pi}_{wz,i}\Delta \mathbf{z}_{t-i} + \mathbf{v}_{ww,t}, \tag{A.9}$$

where $\boldsymbol{\Pi}_{ww} = \mathbf{A}_{ww}^{-1}\mathbf{a}_{ww}$, $\boldsymbol{\Pi}_{wr} = -\mathbf{A}_{ww}^{-1}\mathbf{A}_{wr}$, $\boldsymbol{\Pi}_{w\xi} = \mathbf{A}_{ww}^{-1}\boldsymbol{\alpha}_{w\xi}$, $\boldsymbol{\Pi}_{wz,i} = \mathbf{A}_{ww}^{-1}\boldsymbol{\Gamma}_{wz,i}$, and $\mathbf{v}_{ww,t} = \mathbf{A}_{ww}^{-1}\boldsymbol{\varepsilon}_{ww,t}$. Expression (A.9) can also be written as

$$\Delta \mathbf{w}_t = \boldsymbol{\Pi}_{wr}\Delta r_t + E\left[\Delta \mathbf{w}_t | \Im_{t-1}, \Delta r_t^b = 0\right] + \mathbf{v}_{ww,t}, \tag{A.10}$$

where

$$E\left[\Delta \mathbf{w}_t \mid \Im_{t-1}, \Delta r_t^b = 0\right] = \mathbf{\Pi}_{ww} + \mathbf{\Pi}_{w\xi}\left[\boldsymbol{\beta}' \mathbf{z}_{t-1} - \mathbf{b}_1(t-1)\right] + \sum_{i=1}^{p-1} \mathbf{\Pi}_{wz,i} \Delta \mathbf{z}_{t-i},$$

and represents the growth in the target variables that would occur in time t in the absence of any adjustment to the base interest rate $\left(\Delta r_t^b = 0\right)$ and in the absence of any structural innovations to the system ($\mathbf{v}_{ww,t} = 0$).

A.2 Deriving the monetary authority's reaction function

The first-order condition for the minimisation of (5.6) in the text, subject to (A.9), is given by

$$E\left[\left(\frac{\partial r_t}{\partial r_t^b}\right)\left(\frac{\partial \mathbf{w}_t}{\partial r_t}\right)' \mathbf{Q}\left(\mathbf{w}_t - \mathbf{w}_t^{\dagger}\right) + \theta\left(\frac{\partial r_t}{\partial r_t^b}\right) \Delta r_t \mid \Im_{t-1}\right] = 0. \tag{A.11}$$

Noting from the term structure relationship of (5.4) in the text that $\partial r_t / \partial r_t^b = 1$, and from (A.9) that

$$\frac{\partial \Delta \mathbf{w}_t}{\partial r_t} = \frac{\partial \mathbf{w}_t}{\partial r_t} = \mathbf{\Pi}_{wr},$$

(A.11) provides

$$E\left[\mathbf{\Pi}_{wr}' \mathbf{Q}\left(\mathbf{\Pi}_{wr} \Delta r_t + E\left[\mathbf{w}_t | \Im_{t-1}, \Delta r_t^b = 0\right] + \mathbf{v}_{ww,t} - \mathbf{w}_t^{\dagger}\right) + \theta \Delta r_t | \Im_{t-1}\right] = 0.$$

Rearranging, and noting from (5.4) that $E\left[\Delta r_t | \Im_{t-1}\right] = r_t^b - r_{t-1} + \rho_{b,t-1}$, we have

$$\left(\theta + \mathbf{\Pi}_{wr}' \mathbf{Q} \mathbf{\Pi}_{wr}\right)\left(r_t^b - r_{t-1} + \rho_{b,t-1}\right) = -\mathbf{\Pi}_{wr}' \mathbf{Q}\left(E\left[\mathbf{w}_t | \Im_{t-1}, \Delta r_t^b = 0\right] - \mathbf{w}_t^{\dagger}\right),$$

and the systematic component of the interest rate rule denoted by r_t^b is given by

$$r_t^b = r_{t-1} - \rho_{b,t-1} + \mathbf{\Upsilon}'\left(E\left[\mathbf{w}_t | \Im_{t-1}, \Delta r_t^b = 0\right] - \mathbf{w}_t^{\dagger}\right), \tag{A.12}$$

where

$$\mathbf{\Upsilon}' = -\left(\theta + \mathbf{\Pi}_{wr}' \mathbf{Q} \mathbf{\Pi}_{wr}\right)^{-1} \mathbf{\Pi}_{wr}' \mathbf{Q},$$

or, more fully,

$$r_t^b = r_{t-1} - \rho_{b,t-1} + \boldsymbol{\phi}^{\diamond} - \mathbf{\Upsilon}'\left(\mathbf{w}_t^{\dagger} - \mathbf{w}_{t-1}\right) + \boldsymbol{\phi}_r^{\diamond}\left[\boldsymbol{\beta}' \mathbf{z}_{t-1} - \mathbf{b}_1(t-1)\right] + \sum_{i=1}^{p-1} \boldsymbol{\phi}_{zi}^{\diamond} \Delta \mathbf{z}_{t-i}, \tag{A.13}$$

where

$$\boldsymbol{\phi}^{\diamond} = \boldsymbol{\Upsilon}'\boldsymbol{\Pi}_{ww}, \quad \boldsymbol{\phi}_{r}^{\diamond} = \boldsymbol{\Upsilon}'\boldsymbol{\Pi}_{w\xi},$$
$$\boldsymbol{\phi}_{zi}^{\diamond} = \boldsymbol{\Upsilon}'\boldsymbol{\Pi}_{wz,i}, \quad i = 1, 2, \ldots, s-1.$$

Expressions (A.12) and (A.13) are those given for r_t^b in the text.

A.3 Inflation targeting and the base rate reaction function

From equation (5.3) of the text, the relation between the market and base interest rates is given by

$$r_t - r_t^b = \rho_{b,t-1} + a_{rr^*}\left[r_t^* - E\left(r_t^* \mid \Im_{t-1}\right)\right] + a_{re}\left[e_t - E\left(e_t \mid \Im_{t-1}\right)\right]$$
$$+ \widetilde{\psi}_r\left[p_t^o - E\left(p_t^o \mid \Im_{t-1}\right)\right] + \varepsilon_{rt}. \tag{A.14}$$

Rearranging and substituting out r_t^b from the monetary authorities' reaction function in (A.12), we obtain

$$\Delta r_t = \boldsymbol{\Upsilon}'\left(E\left[\mathbf{w}_t \mid \Im_{t-1}, \Delta r_t^b = 0\right] - \mathbf{w}_t^{\dagger}\right) + a_{rr^*}\left[r_t^* - E\left(r_t^* \mid \Im_{t-1}\right)\right]$$
$$+ a_{re}\left[e_t - E\left(e_t \mid \Im_{t-1}\right)\right] + \widetilde{\psi}_r\left[p_t^o - E\left(p_t^o \mid \Im_{t-1}\right)\right] + \varepsilon_{rt}. \tag{A.15}$$

Taking this expression back to the quasi-reduced form expression for $\Delta\mathbf{w}_t$ in (A.10), we obtain

$$\mathbf{w}_t = (\mathbf{I} - \boldsymbol{\Lambda})\, E\left[\mathbf{w}_t \mid \Im_{t-1}, \Delta r_t^b = 0\right] + \boldsymbol{\Lambda}\mathbf{w}_t^{\dagger} + \mathbf{v}_{ww,t}^{\diamond},$$

where

$$\boldsymbol{\Lambda} = -\boldsymbol{\Pi}_{wr}'\boldsymbol{\Upsilon}' = \boldsymbol{\Pi}_{wr}'\left(\theta + \boldsymbol{\Pi}_{wr}'\mathbf{Q}\boldsymbol{\Pi}_{wr}\right)^{-1}\boldsymbol{\Pi}_{wr}'\mathbf{Q},$$

and

$$\mathbf{v}_{ww,t}^{\diamond} = \boldsymbol{\Pi}_{wr}'\left\{a_{rr^*}\left[r_t^* - E\left(r_t^* \mid \Im_{t-1}\right)\right] + a_{re}\left[e_t - E\left(e_t \mid \Im_{t-1}\right)\right]\right.$$
$$\left. + \widetilde{\psi}_r\left[p_t^o - E\left(p_t^o \mid \Im_{t-1}\right)\right] + \varepsilon_{rt}\right\} + \mathbf{v}_{ww,t}.$$

This shows that the value of the target variables achieved when the authorities pursue their optimal policy is a weighted average of the level that would be achieved if the base rate is left unchanged and the desired level, plus a random element generated by the structural shocks impacting on the p_t^o, e_t, r_t^* and target variables in time t. The weights on the expected target variable and the desired target variable terms are $(\mathbf{I} - \boldsymbol{\Lambda})$ and $\boldsymbol{\Lambda}$, respectively. In the simple case where there is only one target variable (say inflation), so that $\mathbf{A}'_{wr}$, $\mathbf{A}'_{ww}$ and $\mathbf{Q}$ are scalars in (A.1) and (5.7), and equal to a_{wr}, 1, and q respectively then the weights are simply

$$(\mathbf{I}-\mathbf{\Lambda}) = 1 - \frac{a_{wr}^2 q}{a_{wr}^2 q + \theta} \quad \text{and} \quad \mathbf{\Lambda} = \frac{a_{wr}^2 q}{a_{wr}^2 q + \theta}.$$

In particular, as $q/\theta \to \infty$, so that the cost of the target deviating from its desired level rises relative to the cost of changing the base rate in (5.7) in the text, we have

$$\frac{a_{wr}^2 q}{a_{wr}^2 q + \theta} \to 1$$

and

$$\mathbf{w}_t = \mathbf{w}_t^{\dagger} + \mathbf{v}_{ww,t}^{\diamond}.$$

Hence, abstracting from the unpredictable structural shocks, the target variable tracks the desired level precisely.

A.4 Reaction functions and targeting future values of variables

In the text, we consider the case where *future* values of target variables might be the concept of interest to monetary authorities. Consider the simple case in which the monetary authorities care about just one future period, $t+h$ say, and face the optimisation problem

$$\min_{r_t^b} \left\{ E\left[C(\mathbf{w}_{t+h}, r_t) \mid \Im_{t-1} \right] \right\}, \tag{A.16}$$

with

$$C(\mathbf{w}_{t+h}, r_t) = \tfrac{1}{2}\left(\mathbf{w}_{t+h} - \mathbf{w}_{t+h}^{\dagger}\right)' \mathbf{Q} \left(\mathbf{w}_{t+h} - \mathbf{w}_{t+h}^{\dagger}\right) + \tfrac{1}{2}\theta\left(r_t - r_{t-1}\right)^2.$$

Identification of the monetary policy shocks is obtained following the steps described in the previous section. Hence, derivation of the base rate decision rule first requires an expression linking the base rate to the target variable. This is readily obtained on the basis of (A.2), from which we can obtain a model of $\Delta\mathbf{z}_{t+h}$ in terms of $\mathbf{z}_{t+h-1}$, $s-1$ lagged values of $\Delta\mathbf{z}_{t+h}$ and $\mathbf{v}_{t+h}$. Recursive substitution of (A.2) can be used to generate a complex expression expressing $\Delta\mathbf{z}_{t+h}$ in terms of $\mathbf{v}_{t+h}, \mathbf{v}_{t+h-1}, \ldots, \mathbf{v}_{t+1}, \Delta\mathbf{z}_t, \mathbf{z}_{t-1}$, and $s-1$ lagged values of $\Delta\mathbf{z}_t$. Substituting out all of the elements of $\Delta\mathbf{z}_t$ other than Δr_t using the relevant rows of (A.1), we obtain an expression relating $\Delta\mathbf{z}_{t+h}$ to Δr_t along with lagged values of $\mathbf{z}_t$ and combinations of structural shocks dated at time t up to time $t+h$. Finally, we can premultiply $\Delta\mathbf{z}_{t+h}$ and the corresponding expression involving Δr_t by a selection vector choosing the target variables from within $\Delta\mathbf{z}_{t+h}$. This provides a relationship of the form:

$$\Delta\mathbf{w}_{t+h} = \mathbf{\Pi}_{wrh}\Delta r_t + E[\mathbf{w}_{t+h} \mid \Im_{t-1}, \Delta r_t^b = 0] + \mathbf{v}_{wwh,t},$$

where $\mathbf{\Pi}_{wrh}$ is a matrix of parameters capturing the effects of Δr_t on the target variables h periods ahead, $E\left[\mathbf{w}_{t+h} \mid \Im_{t-1}, \Delta r_t^b = 0\right]$ indicates the value of the target variables that would occur in time $t+h$ in the absence of any interest rate adjustment at t and in the absence of any structural innovations to system between t and $t+h$, and $\mathbf{v}_{wwh,t}$ summarises the effects of the structural innovations that do occur.

Given this expression describing the relationship between $\Delta \mathbf{w}_{t+h}$ and Δr_t, minimisation of (A.16) provides the first-order condition

$$E\left[\mathbf{\Pi}'_{wrh}\mathbf{Q}\left(\mathbf{\Pi}_{wrh}\Delta r_t + E\left[\mathbf{w}_{t+h} \mid \Im_{t-1}, \Delta r_t^b = 0\right] + \mathbf{v}_{wwh,t} - \mathbf{w}^{\dagger}_{t+h}\right) + \theta \Delta r_t \mid \Im_{t-1}\right] = 0,$$

and this provides a reaction function of the form

$$r_t^b = r_{t-1} - \rho_{b,t-1} + \mathbf{\Upsilon}'_h\left(E\left[\mathbf{w}_{t+h} \mid \Im_{t-1}, \Delta r_t^b = 0\right] - \mathbf{w}^{\dagger}_{t+h}\right),$$

where $\mathbf{\Upsilon}'_h$ is a function of the parameters of the econometric model and of the preference parameters of the monetary authorities (and $\mathbf{w}^{\dagger}_{t+h}$ is assumed known at time $t-1$). Substitution of the reaction function into the quasi-reduced form expression for $\Delta \mathbf{w}_{t+h}$ provides an expression for $\Delta \mathbf{w}_{t+h}$ as a weighted average of $E\left[\mathbf{w}_{t+h} \mid \Im_{t-1}, \Delta r_t^b = 0\right]$ and $\mathbf{w}^{\dagger}_{t+h}$ plus the effects of structural shocks experienced between t and $t+h$. Further, having derived the base rate reaction function, the structural interest rate equation is derived as in (A.15) above, and monetary policy shocks are identified as changes in the interest rate not explained by unanticipated movements in oil prices, exchange rates and foreign interest rates.

APPENDIX B

Invariance properties of the impulse responses with respect to monetary policy shocks

In this appendix, we provide a proof for footnote 4 of Chapter 10 that, once the position of the monetary policy variable in $\mathbf{z}_t$ is fixed (in our application as the fourth element of $\boldsymbol{\varepsilon}_t$), the impulse response functions of the monetary policy shocks will be invariant to the re-ordering of the variables before and after r_t in $\mathbf{z}_t$.

Since the proof becomes unduly complicated for the case where there are four or more variables in $\mathbf{z}_{1t}$, we consider the simpler case (without loss of generality) where there are only three variables in $\mathbf{z}_{1t}$. In particular, we consider the two different cases: (a) $\mathbf{z}_{1t}^{(a)} = (z_{1t}, z_{2t}, z_{3t})'$ and (b) $\mathbf{z}_{1t}^{(b)} = (z_{2t}, z_{1t}, z_{3t})'$, where z_{3t} is fixed at the last element of $\mathbf{z}_{1t}$, and $\mathbf{z}_{2t} = (z_{4t}, \ldots, z_{mt})'$. We then show that the impact impulse responses of ε_{3t} on $\mathbf{z}_{1t}$ and $\mathbf{z}_{2t}$ are the same under both cases.

Note that the impact impulse responses with respect to the third structural shocks are given by

$$\mathfrak{g}(0, \mathbf{z} : \varepsilon_3) = \frac{E(\varepsilon_{3t}\mathbf{u}_t)}{\sqrt{\omega_{33}}} = \frac{1}{\sqrt{\omega_{33}}}\begin{bmatrix} \mathbf{A}_{11}^{-1}E(\varepsilon_{3t}\boldsymbol{\varepsilon}_{1t}) \\ E(\varepsilon_{3t}\mathbf{u}_{2t}) \end{bmatrix} = \frac{1}{\sqrt{\omega_{33}}}\begin{bmatrix} \mathbf{A}_{11}^{-1}\boldsymbol{\Omega}_{11}\boldsymbol{\tau}_i \\ (\boldsymbol{\tau}_3'\mathbf{A}_{11}\boldsymbol{\Sigma}_{12})' \end{bmatrix}, \tag{B.1}$$

where $\boldsymbol{\varepsilon}_{1t} = (\varepsilon_{1t}, \varepsilon_{2t}, \varepsilon_{3t})'$ is a 3×1 vector of structural errors, the reduced form errors, $\mathbf{u}_t = (\mathbf{u}_{1t}', \mathbf{u}_{2t}')'$ are decomposed conformably with $\mathbf{z}_t = (\mathbf{z}_{1t}', \mathbf{z}_{2t}')'$, $\boldsymbol{\Omega}_{11} = \mathrm{Cov}(\boldsymbol{\varepsilon}_{1t})$, $\boldsymbol{\Sigma} = \mathrm{Cov}(\mathbf{u}_t) = \begin{bmatrix} \boldsymbol{\Sigma}_{11} & \boldsymbol{\Sigma}_{12} \\ \boldsymbol{\Sigma}_{12}' & \boldsymbol{\Sigma}_{22} \end{bmatrix}$, and $\boldsymbol{\tau}_3 = (0, 0, 1)'$ is a 3×1 selection vector.

Under this set-up we now have

$$\boldsymbol{\Sigma}_{11} = \mathbf{A}_{11}^{-1}\boldsymbol{\Omega}_{11}\mathbf{A}_{11}^{-1\prime} = \left(\mathbf{A}_{11}^{-1}\boldsymbol{\Omega}_{11}^{\frac{1}{2}}\right)\left(\boldsymbol{\Omega}_{11}^{\frac{1}{2}}\mathbf{A}_{11}^{-1\prime}\right) = \mathbf{PP}', \tag{B.2}$$

where

$$\mathbf{P} = \begin{bmatrix} p_{11} & 0 & 0 \\ p_{21} & p_{22} & 0 \\ p_{31} & p_{32} & p_{33} \end{bmatrix}$$

is the 3×3 lower-triangular matrix. Using (B.2), then $\boldsymbol{\Omega}_{11}$, $\mathbf{A}_{11}^{-1}$ and $\mathbf{A}_{11}$ can be obtained, respectively, as

$$\boldsymbol{\Omega}_{11} = \begin{bmatrix} \omega_{11} & 0 & 0 \\ 0 & \omega_{22} & 0 \\ 0 & 0 & \omega_{33} \end{bmatrix} = \begin{bmatrix} p_{11}^2 & 0 & 0 \\ 0 & p_{22}^2 & 0 \\ 0 & 0 & p_{33}^2 \end{bmatrix} \tag{B.3}$$

$$\mathbf{A}_{11}^{-1} = \mathbf{P} \times \begin{bmatrix} p_{11} & 0 & 0 \\ 0 & p_{22} & 0 \\ 0 & 0 & p_{33} \end{bmatrix}^{-1} = \begin{bmatrix} 1 & 0 & 0 \\ \frac{p_{21}}{p_{11}} & 1 & 0 \\ \frac{p_{31}}{p_{11}} & \frac{p_{32}}{p_{22}} & 1 \end{bmatrix} \tag{B.4}$$

$$\mathbf{A}_{11} = \begin{bmatrix} 1 & 0 & 0 \\ a_{21} & 1 & 0 \\ a_{31} & a_{32} & 1 \end{bmatrix} = \begin{bmatrix} 1 & 0 & 0 \\ -\frac{p_{21}}{p_{11}} & 1 & 0 \\ \frac{p_{21}p_{32}}{p_{11}p_{22}} - \frac{p_{31}}{p_{11}} & -\frac{p_{32}}{p_{22}} & 1 \end{bmatrix}. \tag{B.5}$$

Then, (B.1) simplifies to

$$\mathfrak{g}(0, \mathbf{z} : \varepsilon_3) = \frac{1}{\sqrt{\omega_{33}}} \begin{bmatrix} \begin{pmatrix} 0 \\ 0 \\ \omega_{33} \end{pmatrix} \\ E(\varepsilon_{3t}\mathbf{u}_{2t}) \end{bmatrix}.$$

Furthermore, in the absence of any over-identifying restrictions on the system of equations for $\mathbf{z}_{2t}$, $E(\varepsilon_{3t}\mathbf{u}_{2t})$ can be consistently estimated by

$$T^{-1}\sum_{t=1}^{T} \hat{\varepsilon}_{3t}\hat{\mathbf{u}}_{2t}',$$

where $\hat{\mathbf{u}}_{2t}$ are the reduced form residuals associated with $\mathbf{z}_{2t}$, and

$$\hat{\varepsilon}_{3t} = a_{31}\hat{u}_{1t} + a_{32}\hat{u}_{2t} + \hat{u}_{3t},$$

where $\hat{u}_{1t}$, $\hat{u}_{2t}$, and u_{3t} are the reduced form residuals associated with z_{1t}, z_{2t}, z_{3t} in $\mathbf{z}_{1t}$, respectively. Thus,

$$T^{-1}\sum_{t=1}^{T} \hat{\varepsilon}_{3t}\hat{\mathbf{u}}_{2t}' = a_{31}\left(T^{-1}\sum_{t=1}^{T} \hat{u}_{1t}\hat{\mathbf{u}}_{2t}'\right) + a_{32}\left(T^{-1}\sum_{t=1}^{T} \hat{u}_{2t}\hat{\mathbf{u}}_{2t}'\right) + \left(T^{-1}\sum_{t=1}^{T} \hat{u}_{3t}\hat{\mathbf{u}}_{2t}'\right). \tag{B.6}$$

Hence to prove that the invariance of the (structural) impulse responses of ε_{3t} on $\mathbf{z}_{1t}$ and $\mathbf{z}_{2t}$ to changing the order of z_{1t} and z_{2t} in $\mathbf{z}_{1t}$ as well as to changing the order of variables in in $\mathbf{z}_{2t}$, we *first* need to establish that p_{33}^2's obtained for cases (a) $\mathbf{z}_{1t} = (z_{1t}, z_{2t}, z_{3t})'$ and (b) $\mathbf{z}_{1t} = (z_{2t}, z_{1t}, z_{3t})'$, are identical, and *then* that $a_{31}^{(a)} = a_{32}^{(b)}$ and $a_{32}^{(a)} = a_{31}^{(b)}$, where superscripts '$(a)$' and '$(b)$' refer to cases (a) and (b), respectively.

First, consider the case (a) with $\mathbf{z}_{1t} = (z_{1t}, z_{2t}, z_{3t})'$. Here we have

$$\boldsymbol{\Sigma}_{11}^{(a)} = \begin{bmatrix} \sigma_{11} & \sigma_{12} & \sigma_{13} \\ \sigma_{12} & \sigma_{22} & \sigma_{23} \\ \sigma_{13} & \sigma_{23} & \sigma_{33} \end{bmatrix}.$$

Using the relationship in (B.2), it is straightforward to show

$$p_{11}^{(a)} = \sqrt{\sigma_{11}};\ p_{21}^{(a)} = \frac{\sigma_{12}}{\sqrt{\sigma_{11}}};\ p_{31}^{(a)} = \frac{\sigma_{13}}{\sqrt{\sigma_{11}}};$$

$$p_{22}^{(a)} = \sqrt{\frac{\sigma_{11}\sigma_{22} - \sigma_{12}^2}{\sigma_{11}}};\ p_{32}^{(a)} = \sqrt{\frac{\sigma_{11}\sigma_{23} - \sigma_{12}\sigma_{13}}{\sigma_{11}\left(\sigma_{11}\sigma_{22} - \sigma_{12}^2\right)}};$$

$$p_{33}^{(a)} = \sqrt{\frac{\sigma_{11}\sigma_{22}\sigma_{33} - \sigma_{11}\sigma_{23}^2 - \sigma_{22}\sigma_{13}^2 - \sigma_{33}\sigma_{12}^2 + 2\sigma_{12}\sigma_{13}\sigma_{23}}{\sigma_{11}\sigma_{22} - \sigma_{12}^2}}. \tag{B.7}$$

Turning to $\mathbf{A}_{11}$, and using the above results, we have

$$p_{21}^{(a)}p_{32}^{(a)} = \frac{\sigma_{12}}{\sqrt{\sigma_{11}}} \times \sqrt{\frac{\sigma_{11}\sigma_{23} - \sigma_{12}\sigma_{13}}{\sigma_{11}\left(\sigma_{11}\sigma_{22} - \sigma_{12}^2\right)}} = \frac{\sigma_{12}}{\sigma_{11}}\sqrt{\frac{\sigma_{11}\sigma_{23} - \sigma_{12}\sigma_{13}}{\sigma_{11}\sigma_{22} - \sigma_{12}^2}}$$

$$p_{11}^{(a)}p_{22}^{(a)} = \sqrt{\sigma_{11}} \times \sqrt{\frac{\sigma_{11}\sigma_{22} - \sigma_{12}^2}{\sigma_{11}}} = \sqrt{\sigma_{11}\sigma_{12} - \sigma_{12}^2}$$

$$\frac{p_{31}}{p_{11}} = \frac{\sigma_{13}}{\sigma_{11}}$$

so that

$$a_{31}^{(a)} = \frac{p_{21}^{(a)}p_{32}^{(a)}}{p_{11}^{(a)}p_{22}^{(a)}} - \frac{p_{31}^{(a)}}{p_{11}^{(a)}} = \frac{\sigma_{12}\sigma_{23} - \sigma_{13}\sigma_{22}}{\sigma_{11}\sigma_{22} - \sigma_{12}^2}, \tag{B.8}$$

and

$$a_{32}^{(a)} = -\frac{p_{32}^{(a)}}{p_{22}^{(a)}} = \frac{\sigma_{12}\sigma_{13} - \sigma_{11}\sigma_{23}}{\sigma_{11}\sigma_{22} - \sigma_{12}^2}. \tag{B.9}$$

Second, consider the case (b) of $\mathbf{z}_{1t} = (z_{2t}, z_{1t}, z_{3t})'$. Now we have

$$\boldsymbol{\Sigma}_1^{(b)} = \begin{bmatrix} \sigma_{22} & \sigma_{12} & \sigma_{23} \\ \sigma_{12} & \sigma_{11} & \sigma_{13} \\ \sigma_{23} & \sigma_{13} & \sigma_{33} \end{bmatrix},$$

and similarly,

$$p_{11}^{(b)} = \sqrt{\sigma_{22}};\ p_{21}^{(b)} = \frac{\sigma_{12}}{\sqrt{\sigma_{22}}};\ p_{31}^{(b)} = \frac{\sigma_{23}}{\sqrt{\sigma_{22}}};$$

$$p_{22}^{(b)} = \sqrt{\frac{\sigma_{11}\sigma_{22} - \sigma_{12}^2}{\sigma_{22}}};\ p_{32}^{(b)} = \sqrt{\frac{\sigma_{22}\sigma_{13} - \sigma_{12}\sigma_{23}}{\sigma_{22}\left(\sigma_{11}\sigma_{22} - \sigma_{12}^2\right)}};$$

$$p_{33}^{(b)} = \sqrt{\frac{\sigma_{11}\sigma_{22}\sigma_{33} - \sigma_{11}\sigma_{23}^2 - \sigma_{22}\sigma_{13}^2 - \sigma_{33}\sigma_{12}^2 + 2\sigma_{12}\sigma_{13}\sigma_{23}}{\sigma_{11}\sigma_{22} - \sigma_{12}^2}}. \tag{B.10}$$

Therefore, we now have

$$a_{31}^{(b)} = \frac{p_{21}^{(b)}p_{32}^{(b)}}{p_{11}^{(b)}p_{22}^{(b)}} - \frac{p_{31}^{(b)}}{p_{11}^{(b)}} = \frac{\sigma_{12}\sigma_{13} - \sigma_{11}\sigma_{23}}{\sigma_{11}\sigma_{22} - \sigma_{12}^2}, \tag{B.11}$$

$$a_{32}^{(b)} = -\frac{p_{32}^{(b)}}{p_{22}^{(b)}} = \frac{\sigma_{12}\sigma_{23} - \sigma_{13}\sigma_{22}}{\sigma_{11}\sigma_{22} - \sigma_{12}^2}. \tag{B.12}$$

Comparing (B.7), (B.8) and (B.9) with (B.10), (B.11) and (B.12), we find that

$$p_{33}^{2\,(a)} = p_{33}^{2\,(b)};\ a_{31}^{(a)} = a_{32}^{(b)};\ a_{32}^{(a)} = a_{31}^{(b)},$$

as desired.

This result clearly shows that once the order of the particular structural shock is determined, their impulse responses on the variables in the system are invariant to reordering of other variables before the specific equation of interest.

Finally, from (B.6) it is trivial to show that the structural impulse responses of the shocks to ε_{3t} on the variables in the system are also invariant to reordering of variables in $\mathbf{z}_{2t}$, since if their order is changed, then all the associated VAR parameter estimates are changed such that the structural impulse responses are intact.

APPENDIX C

Data for the UK model

Here we describe the definitions and sources of the variables used to estimate the core model of the UK economy. Our intention is to enable the user to use this appendix in combination with the information provided on the authors' web pages (which contains all the necessary files and data used in the estimation and construction of the core variables) to reproduce our results. The appendix also provides a brief guide on how to construct the *Microfit 4.0* file *ukmod.fit*, which contains all the variables used in the estimation and outlines the steps required to be performed in *Microfit 4.0* to reproduce our estimates.

C.1 Definitions and sources of the core model variables

The core UK model variables are as follows:

[1] y_t: the natural logarithm of UK real per capita domestic output, defined as $[\widetilde{Y}_t/(P_t \times POP_t)]$ in Chapter 4, is computed as:

$$\ln(GDP_t/POP_t),$$

where GDP_t is real gross domestic product, at 1995 market prices (index numbers, 1995 = 100), seasonally adjusted, source: Office of National Statistics (ONS) Economic Trends, code YBEZ. POP_t is total UK population in thousands, source: ONS, Monthly Digest of Statistics, code DYAY, which at the time of collection of the data was available up to 1998. For the 1999 number we extrapolated the 1998 annual number using the average annual growth rate for the period 1993–1997. For the population variable we constructed a quarterly series through linear interpolation of the annual numbers and then converted the quarterly population series to an index number.

[2] p_t: the natural logarithm of the domestic price level is computed as:

$$\ln(P_t),$$

where P_t is the UK Producer Price Index: Output of Manufactured Products (1995 = 100), source: ONS, Economic Trends, code PLLU.

The data used in the estimation are seasonally adjusted versions of p_t or $\ln(P_t)$, where the adjustment is performed using the *Stamp* package (see Harvey, Koopman, Doornik and Shephard, 1995). This involved using a Structural Time Series approach on the first difference of p_t, Δp_t (as we observed a seasonal pattern in the spectral density of Δp_t rather p_t) and then integrating the seasonally adjusted first difference up to compute the seasonally adjusted level. We adopted the *Stamp* manual's recommended version (p. 88) of the basic structural model of a stochastic trend with a stochastic slope, a trigonometric seasonal and an irregular component. A cyclical component was not included in the adjustment procedure. It is worth noting the *Stamp* manual's comment (p. 88) that in practice seasonal components seem to be insensitive to the specification of the trend and the inclusion of a cycle.

[3] $\Delta\widetilde{p}_t$: the UK inflation rate is computed as:

$$\ln(P_t^R) - \ln(P_{t-1}^R),$$

where P_t^R is the UK Retail Price Index, All Items (1995 = 100, rebased from 1987 = 100), source: ONS, Economic Trends, code CHAW. As with the Producer Price Index, in the estimation we use a seasonally adjusted version of $\ln(P_t^R)$, where the adjustment is performed using the Structural Time Series procedure described above.

[4] r_t: the domestic nominal interest rate, measured as a quarterly rate is computed as:

$$0.25 \times \ln\left[1 + (R_t/100)\right],$$

where R_t is the 90 day Treasury Bill average discount rate, at an annualised rate, source: ONS, Financial Statistics, code AJNB.

[5] $h_t - y_t$: the natural logarithm of real per capita money stock expressed as a proportion of real per capita income is computed as:

$$\ln(\widetilde{H}_t/\widetilde{Y}_t),$$

where $\widetilde{H}_t$ is the M0 definition of the money stock (end period, £ Million) seasonally adjusted, source: ONS, Financial Statistics and Bank of England. For the period 1969q2–1999q4 we use M0 money stock source: ONS, Financial Statistics, code AVAE. Prior to this period, where no M0 money stock data is available, we project the AVAE series backwards using the quarterly percentage change (where the quarterly data is the average of the monthly data) of estimated circulation of notes and coins with the public as documented in the Bank of England Abstract 1970. Nominal income $\widetilde{Y}_t$, is measured using gross domestic product at market prices (£ Million) and is seasonally adjusted, source: ONS, Economic Trends, code YBHA. Note that

$\ln(\widetilde{H}_t/\widetilde{Y}_t) = \ln(h_t/y_t)$ given that P_t and POP_t appear in both the numerator and denominator (see the definitions in Chapter 4).

[6] e_t: the natural logarithm of the UK nominal effective exchange rate is computed as:

$$-\ln(E_t),$$

where E_t is the Sterling Effective Exchange Rate (1995 = 100, rebased from 1990 = 100), source: ONS, Financial Statistics, code AJHX. The ONS define E_t as the foreign price of domestic currency (a rise represents a UK currency appreciation) hence we take minus the logarithm of E_t redefining e_t as the domestic price of foreign currency, as defined in the text.

[7] y_t^*: the natural logarithm of real per capita foreign output, defined as $[\widetilde{Y}_t^*/(P_t^* \times POP_t^*)]$ in Chapter 4 is computed as:

$$\ln(GDP_t^*/POP_t^*),$$

where GDP_t^* is a total OECD Gross Domestic Product Volume Index (1995 = 100), at 1995 market prices, seasonally adjusted, source: OECD, Main Economic Indicators (MEI), code Q00100319. POP_t^* is total OECD population (adjusted by subtracting the populations of Mexico, Poland, Hungary and Czech Republic), source: OECD, Labour Force Statistics, 1967–1987 and 1974–1996. For 1997–1999 we extrapolated the 1996 annual number using the average annual growth rate for the period 1992–1996. For the population variable we constructed a quarterly series through linear interpolation of the annual numbers and then converted the quarterly population series to an index number.

[8] p_t^*: the natural logarithm of the foreign price index is computed as:

$$p_t^* = \ln(P_t^*),$$

where P_t^* is the total OECD Producer Price Index, 1995 = 100, source: OECD, MEI, code Q005045k. Data was available on this series from 1982q1. The data prior to 1982q1 was constructed by backwardly imposing the percentage changes of a separately constructed weighted average index of OECD consumer and producer prices on the 1982q1 figure. As with the previous two price measures, in the estimation we used a seasonally adjusted version of the foreign price variable, where the adjustment is performed using the Structural Time Series procedure described above.

[9] r_t^*: the foreign nominal interest rate, measured as a quarterly rate is computed as:

$$r_t^* = 0.25 \times \ln\left[1 + \left(R_t^*/100\right)\right],$$

where R_t^* is a weighted average of foreign annualised interest rates computed as:

$$R_t^* = \sum_{j=1}^{m_r} w_j^r R_{jt},$$

where w_j^r are fixed weights and $m_r = 4$. The countries and weights in brackets are the United States (0.4382), Germany (0.236), Japan (0.2022) and France (0.1236). The weights are taken from the IMFs International Financial Statistics Yearbook 1998, pages x and xi which report Special Deposits Rights (SDR) weights for five countries which in 1996 were for the US 0.39, Germany 0.21, France 0.11, Japan 0.18 and the UK 0.11. Excluding the UK we the recompute the weights to get those reported above.

The annualised interest rates used in the calculation, R_{jt}, are all from the IMFs International Financial Statistics (IFS). For the US we use the three-month Treasury Bill rate (IFS Code Q11160C), for Germany the Money Market Rate (IFS Code Q13460B), for Japan the Money Market Rate (IFS Code Q15860B) and for France the three-month Treasury Bill Rate (IFS Code Q13260C).

[10] p_t^o: the natural logarithm of the oil price is computed as:

$$\ln(POIL),$$

where *POIL* is the Average Price of Crude Oil, in terms of US Dollars per Barrel, source: IMF, IFS, code Q00176AAZ, converted into a 1995 = 100 index.

To construct the *Microfit 4.0* file *ukmod.fit* read in the file *core.fit* into *Microfit 4.0* and run *core.bat*. The resulting file is *ukmod.fit*, which must be saved, where the names used in file, which correspond to the model variables defined above, are the following: $y = y_t$, $p = p_t$, $dpr = \Delta\tilde{p}_t$, $r = r_t$, $hy = (h_t - y_t)$, $e = e_t$, $ys = y_t^*$, $ps = p_t^*$, $rs = r_t^*$, $po = p_t^o$, $pps = (p_t - p_t^*)$, $dpo = p_t^o - p_{t-1}^o$.

All the estimation reported in Chapter 9 is performed in *Microfit 4.0* (the impulse responses, persistence profiles and probability forecasts can be computed using the *Gauss* files provided, see the next appendix describing the *Gauss* files). The results in the paper may be reproduced, using the file *ukmod.fit* in *Microfit 4.0*, through the execution of the following steps:

(i) Choose the multivariate estimation option, select the cointegrating VAR menu and choose option 4, unrestricted intercepts restricted trends.

(ii) Read in the *ukmod.lst*, set the period to be 1965q1–1999q4 and the order of the VAR to be two and estimate.

(iii) Set number of cointegrating vectors to be five ($r = 5$, option 2) and in the following menu select option 6, long-run structural modelling.

(iv) Choose option 4, likelihood ratio test, exactly identify the system by reading in *exiden.equ* and then estimate the cointegrating VAR model subject to the exact identifying restrictions.

(v) Then choose to impose and test the over-identifying restrictions. First using the restrictions contained in *oviden1.equ*, second using *oviden2.equ*.

APPENDIX D

Gauss programs and result files

Much of the estimation and analysis of the UK core model was carried out using Pesaran and Pesaran's (1997) econometric software package *Microfit 4.0*, and *Microfit 4.11*. However, a number of the calculations and computations reported in the book were conducted using a series of *Gauss* programs. For users who prefer the flexibility such programs allow and for those who wish to perform (and adapt) the range of estimation and computations reported in the book, we are making available, through our webpages, the *Gauss* programs we have used in the analysis of the core model in a sequence of files. The content and operation of these files is described below. Note that an updated version of microfit, *Microfit 5.0* (to be published by Oxford University Press in 2006), will be able to compute all the impulse responses and persistence profiles described below.

In total there are eight programs. The first two relate to impulse responses and persistence profiles:

- *GLPS-GIR.g* computes Generalised Impulse Responses (GIRs), Orthogonalised Impulse Responses (OIRs), Persistence Profiles (PPs), and VECM estimation results (with diagnostics), and examines the stability of the VECM system.
- *GLPS-SIR.g* computes impulse responses which result from (exogenous) oil price shocks and (unanticipated) monetary policy shocks, where monetary policy shocks are defined according to the short-run identification scheme developed in Chapter 5.

The next five programs compute and evaluate probability event forecasts. Two are concerned with out-of-sample probability events:

- *GLPS-PFS.g* computes out-of-sample probability event forecasts, h-steps ahead, taking into account future uncertainty only.
- *GLPS-PFB.g* computes out-of-sample probability event forecasts, h-steps ahead, taking into account future and parameter uncertainty.

The next three programs conduct in-sample forecast evaluation using one-step ahead recursive probability forecasts of directional-changes and events used in the calculation of probability integral transforms over the period 1999q1–2001q1 (nine quarters).

- *GLPS-EVS.g* computes in-sample one-step ahead probability event forecasts taking into account future uncertainty only.
- *GLPS-EVB.g* computes in-sample one-step ahead probability event forecasts taking into account future and parameter uncertainty.
- *GLPS-EV.g* computes forecast evaluation statistics for one-step ahead probability event forecasts: hit ratios, Kuipers Score, Pesaran–Timmermann, Kolmogorov–Smirnov test statistics for probability integral transform. To obtain the results reported in the book, you run this program using as inputs the files produced by first running the two programs above, *GLPS-EVS.g* and *GLPS-EVB.g*.

Finally the eighth program computes the trend decomposition in cointegrating VARs described in Section 10.3.

- *GLPS-DEC.g* computes the permanent and transitory decomposition of all the endogenous variables in the vector $\mathbf{z}_t$ using the estimated VECM core model and estimates of the restricted growth rates, $\mathbf{g}$.

D.1 General comments on the *Gauss* programs

All the programs presuppose that certain results have been obtained already (*e.g.* by *Microfit*, as described at the end of Appendix C). Specifically, they take as inputs: the ML estimates of the long-run cointegrating relationships subject to general linear non-homogeneous restrictions (and their rank); and the estimation results for the exogenous $I(1)$ variable(s) (here an oil price equation).

The initial step in each program loads and defines the data. It also specifies some initial information which is needed for the rest of the program, such as the VAR lag order, the rank and the estimates of cointegrating vectors. Given the estimates of the cointegrating vectors, the program estimates the dynamic short-run parameters. It then combines these results with the estimation results for the exogenous $I(1)$ variable(s), to provide the full system VAR estimation results. These form the basis for an analysis of further short-run dynamics such as impulse responses and forecasts. For the underlying econometric theory, see Chapters 6 and 7 and the related papers by Pesaran, Shin and Smith (2000) and Pesaran and Shin (2002).

D.2 Impulse response and persistence profile programs

The impulse response results for the UK described in Chapter 10 were obtained using the two programs *GLPS-GIR.g* and *GLPS-SIR.g* and reading in the UK dataset given in *ukmod99.dat*. The dataset has the dimension of 148×10 and the variables are saved in the column order: y_t, y_t^*, r_t, r_t^*, e_t, $h_t - y_t$, p_t^o, Δp_t^o, Δp_t and $p_t - p_t^*$ (see Appendix C for details). The full data period is 1963q1–1999q4 (148 observations), but the program estimates the cointegrating VAR(2) model over the period 1965q1–1999q4 (140 observations) using the Cointegrating VAR Option 4 with unrestricted intercepts and restricted trends.

GLPS-GIR.g

This program computes GIRs, OIRs, PPs, and the estimation results, and analyses stability of the VECM. It also provides an option to compute the empirical confidence intervals for PPs, GIRs and OIRs with respect to reduced form errors, based on the bootstrap re-sampling techniques. In our work, we employ non-parametric re-sampling methods with 2000 replications to allow for parameter uncertainty (see Section 6.4 for further details).

The estimation results in Sections 10.2.2 and 10.2.3, and also those reported in Garratt, Lee, Pesaran and Shin (2000) can be generated using this program. The results reported in Figures 10.3, 10.4, 10.5, 10.6, 10.9 and 10.10 are also computed using this file. The program requires the user to select the shock (to an equation) by specifying the number defining the order of the variable in the $\mathbf{z}_t$ vector (see below for the order). The program assumes the size of the shock is equal to the standard deviation of the selected equation error, and that all the results (except for OIR) are invariant to re-ordering of the variables in the VAR.

After running the program, you will obtain the following five *Gauss* data files (with an *fmt* extension) which contain the results for PPs, GIRs and OIRs. The saved files are: *PPOUT.fmt*, *GIRZOUT.fmt*, *OIRZOUT.fmt*, *GIROUT.fmt*, and *OIROUT.fmt*, respectively.

PPOUT.fmt contains the results for the scaled PPs of the cointegrating relations, which take the value of unity on impact of the shock and tend to zero as the time horizon tends to infinity. The dimensions are $(h + 1)$ by $7r$, where h is the number of horizon and r is the number of cointegrating vectors ($= 5$ in the case of the core UK model). The first r columns (1 to r) are point estimates of the PPs of the $1, \ldots, r$ cointegrating vectors; the next r columns ($r+1$ to $2r$) are empirical means; the next r columns ($2r + 1$ to $3r$) are empirical medians; the next r columns ($3r + 1$ to $4r$) are empirical 90% lower confidence intervals (CIs); the next r columns ($4r + 1$ to $5r$) are empirical 90% upper CIs; and finally, the next r columns ($5r + 1$ to $6r$) are empirical 95% lower CIs, whereas the final r columns ($6r+1$ to $7r$) are empirical 95% upper CIs. Note the order of the cointegrating relations for each block (containing r columns) is *PPP*, *IRP*, *OG*, *MME* and *FIP*.

GIRZOUT.fmt (*OIRZOUT.fmt*) contains the GIRs (OIRs) of the r cointegrating relations with respect to selected shocks, referred to as PPs in the text. These are the files which contain the results, when the foreign interest rate, foreign output and domestic interest rate are selected, which are plotted in Figures 10.3, 10.5 and 10.9, respectively. The dimensions and ordering of these result files are exactly the same as those of *PPOUT.fmt*.

The files *GIROUT.fmt* (*OIROUT.fmt*) contain results for GIRs (OIRs) of the m exogenous and endogenous $I(1)$ variables in the system with respect to selected shocks ($m = 9$ in the core UK model). The dimensions are $(h+1)$ by $7m$, where m is number of variables. The first m columns (1 to m) are point estimates of GIRs (OIRs) of $1, \ldots, m$ variables; the next m columns ($m+1$ to $2m$) are empirical means; the next m columns ($2m+1$ to $3m$) are empirical medians; the next m columns ($3m+1$ to $4m$) are empirical 90% lower CIs; and the next m columns ($4m+1$ to $5m$) are empirical 90% upper CIs. The next m columns ($5m+1$ to $6m$) are empirical 95% lower CIs, whereas the final m columns ($6m+1$ to $7m$) are empirical 95% upper CIs. Note the order of the variables for each block (containing m columns) is: p_t^o, e_t, r_t, r_t^*, Δp_t, y_t, $p_t - p_t^*$, $h_t - y_t$ and y_t^* (the numbering for the selection of the shock follows this order).

GLPS-SIR.g

This program computes the Structural Impulse Responses and PPs reported in Figures 10.1, 10.2, 10.7, 10.8, 12.3 and 12.4. For this purpose we decompose variables as $\mathbf{z}_t = (\mathbf{z}_{1t}, \mathbf{z}_{2t})$, where $\mathbf{z}_{1t} = (p_t^o, e_t, r_t^*, r_t)$ and $\mathbf{z}_{2t} = (\Delta p_t, y_t, p_t - p_t^*, h_t - y_t, y_t^*)$. Note the position of the variable, r_t, determined by the short-run identification scheme, is important for an analysis of monetary policy shocks. Once its position is determined, the impulse responses are invariant to the change of ordering of other variables in the system before and after r_t; see Appendix B for a proof.

As an additional option the program can examine the impact of an (exogenous) intercept shift in the interest rate equation, as an alternative autonomous or exogenous monetary policy shock. The program also provides the empirical mean and confidence intervals for generalised impulse response functions with respect to structural shocks to the oil price, exchange rate, foreign interest rate and domestic interest rate equations as well as an intercept shift in the interest rate equation, based on the bootstrap re-sampling techniques with 2000 replications to allow for parameter uncertainty (see Section 6.4 for further details). In all cases the size of the shock is equal to the standard deviation of the selected equation error. For the case of the intercept shift in the domestic interest equation, the size of the shock is equal to the standard deviation of the domestic interest equation error.

After running the program, you will obtain 10 *Gauss* result files (with an fmt extension). The saved files are *POGIR.fmt, POGIRZ.fmt, EXGIR.fmt, EXGIRZ.fmt, RSGIR.fmt, RSGIRZ.fmt, MPGIR.fmt, MPGIRZ.fmt, INTIR.fmt* and *INTIRZ.fmt*, respectively. We have then provided estimation results in Sections 10.2.1 and 10.2.4.

The files *POGIRZ.fmt, EXGIRZ.fmt, RSGIRZ.fmt* and *MPGIRZ.fmt* contain the results for the GIRs of the r cointegrating relations with respect to oil price shocks, exchange rate shocks, foreign interest rate shocks and monetary policy shocks, respectively. The file *INTIRZ.fmt* contains the results for impulse responses of the r cointegrating relations with respect to the autonomous intercept shift in the domestic interest equation. Their dimensions are $(h+1)$ by $7r$. The first r ($= 5$ here) columns (1 to r) are point estimates of the GIRs of $1, \ldots, r$ cointegrating vectors;

the next r columns ($r + 1$ to $2r$) are empirical means; the next r columns ($2r + 1$ to $3r$) are empirical medians; the next r columns ($3r + 1$ to $4r$) are empirical 90% lower CIs; the next r columns ($4r + 1$ to $5r$) are empirical 90% upper CIs; the next r columns ($5r + 1$ to $6r$) are empirical 95% lower CIs; and the final r columns ($6r + 1$ to $7r$) are empirical 95% upper CIs. Note the order of the cointegrating relations for each block (containing r columns) is *PPP*, *IRP*, *OG*, *MME* and *FIP*.

POGIR.fmt, *EXGIR.fmt*, *RSGIR.fmt* and *MPGIR.fmt* contain the results for the GIRs of the m variables with respect to oil price shocks, exchange rate shocks, foreign interest rate shocks and monetary policy shocks, respectively. The file *INTIR.fmt* contains the results for the impulse responses of the m variables with respect to the autonomous intercept shift in the domestic interest equation. Their dimensions are $(h + 1)$ by $7m$. The first m columns (1 to m) are the empirical means of the GIRs of $1, \ldots, m$ variables; the next m columns ($m + 1$ to $2m$) are the empirical means; the next m columns ($2m + 1$ to $3m$) are the empirical medians; the next m columns ($3m + 1$ to $4m$) are the empirical 90% lower CIs; the next m columns ($4m + 1$ to $5m$) are the empirical 90% upper CIs; the next m columns ($5m + 1$ to $6m$) are the empirical 95% lower CIs; and the final m columns ($6m + 1$ to $7m$) are the empirical 95% upper CIs. Note the order of the impulse responses for each block (containing m columns) is: p^o, e, r^*, r, Δp, y, $p - p^*$, $h - y$ and y^*.

D.3 Programs for computing probability forecasts

The probability forecast programs use the data file, *ukmod01.dat*. This is a 153×9 file which contains data for the extended period 1963q1–2001q1 (153 observations), saved in the column order of y, r, r^*, e, $h - y$, p^o, Δp, $p - p^*$, y^* (the change in oil prices, Δp^o, is defined in the program). We estimate the ML cointegrating vectors for the period 1965q1–2001q1, but estimate the short-run dynamic parameters of the vector error correction model over the shorter sample 1985q1–2001q1.

We allow for future and parameter uncertainty separately and jointly and in addition we allow for model uncertainty. We focus on uncertainty regarding the rank of the cointegrating vectors, so we consider the six cases with rank = 0,1,2,3,4,5 where we use exactly identified cointegrating vectors. We also consider our core model, *i.e.* the case where we have five cointegrating relationships which impose the theory based over-identifying restrictions described and tested in Chapter 9. This makes for seven models. For each of the seven models, we examine exogenous uncertainty through the consideration of two different oil price equations, based on (A) the simple random walk with a drift model and (B) the unrestricted VAR(2) specification. Hence in total 14 models are considered.

These models are denoted by OV5A and OV5B for the five cointegrating vectors obtained subject to the theory based over-identifying restrictions, combined with the oil price equations A and B, respectively. Similarly we denote EX5A and EX5B as being five cointegrating vectors obtained subject to the exactly identifying restrictions combined with an oil price equations A and B, respectively. Following this use of notation the remaining 10 models are denoted: EX4A, EX4B, EX3A, EX3B, EX2A, EX2B, EX1A, EX1B, EX0A, EX0B. Note that the models, EX0A and EX0B, have zero cointegrating relations.

The program computes the weights for these models according to the AIC weight scheme described in Chapter 7, but also considers weights based on SBC, HQ, and equal weights of 1/14. See Section 7.3 for more details.

D.3.1 *Programs for computing out-of-sample probability event forecasts*

The two programs, *GLPS-PFS.g* and *GLPS-PFB.g*, compute out-of-sample probability event forecasts based on the h-step ahead forecasts of the nine variables in $\mathbf{z}_t$ and their four-quarter moving averages with $h = 1, \ldots, 24$. Note that the computation algorithms for *GLPS-PFS.g* and *GLPS-PFB.g* are basically the same, where only future uncertainty is allowed for in *GLPS-PFS.g,* whereas both future and parameter uncertainties are allowed for in *GLPS-PFB.g*.

In our UK application, we consider the following seven events:

$E1$: A single event: Pr(four-quarter moving average of inflation $< a\%$), where a is per cent per annum and we use 10 threshold values of $a = (0, 0.5, 1, 1.5, 2, 2.5, 3, 3.5, 4, 5)$.

$E2$: A single event: Pr(four-quarter moving average of the gross output growth $< a\%$), where gross output growth is the sum of output growth and deterministic population growth, a is per cent per annum and we use 10 threshold values of $a = (-1.5, 0, 0.5, 1, 1.5, 2, 2.5, 3, 3.5, 5)$.

$E3$: A single event: BofE target met, Pr(1.5% < four-quarter moving average of inflation < 3.5%).

$E4$: A single event: recession, Pr(quarterly output growths < 0% for two consecutive quarters).

$E5$: A single event: low growth, Pr(four-quarter moving average of gross output growth < 1%)

$E6$: A joint event: Pr(no recession and BofE target met).

$E7$: A joint event: Pr(high growth and BofE target met).

GLPS-PFS.g (with future uncertainty only)

After running the program, you will obtain the following 18 *Gauss* result files (with an fmt extension). They contain the results of the Probability Event Forecasts based on future uncertainty only, which we have used in obtaining the tables and figures reported in Chapter 11 and Garratt, Lee, Pesaran and Shin (2003, *Journal of American Statistical Association*).

The saved files are *OV5ASPE.fmt, OV5BSPE.fmt, EX5ASPE.fmt, EX5BSPE.fmt, EX4ASPE.fmt, EX4BSPE.fmt, EX3ASPE.fmt, EX3BSPE.fmt,EX2ASPE.fmt, EX2BSPE.fmt, EX1ASPE.fmt, EX1BSPE.fmt, EX0ASPE.fmt, EX0BSPE.fmt, AVGSPE.fmt, AICSPE.fmt, SBCSPE.fmt*and *HQSPE.fmt*, respectively.

The dimensions of these *Gauss* result files is the number of horizons (= 24 here) by 25. The first 10 columns (1 to 10) are probability forecasts for event $E1$ for the

10 thresholds; the next 10 columns (11 to 20) are probability forecasts for event $E2$ with 10 thresholds; the 21st column is probability forecasts for event $E3$; the 22nd column is the probability forecasts for event $E4$; the 23rd column is the probability forecasts for event $E5$; the 24th column is the probability forecasts for event $E6$; and, finally, the 25th column is the probability forecasts for event $E7$.

GLPS-PFB.g (with future and parameter uncertainty)
This program is as above but where the Probability Event Forecasts are based on both future and parameter uncertainty. The saved files are *OV5ABPE.fmt*, *OV5BBPE.fmt*, *EX5ABPE.fmt*, *EX5BBPE.fmt*, *EX4ABPE.fmt*, *EX4BBPE.fmt*, *EX3ABPE.fmt*, *EX3BBPE.fmt*, *EX2ABPE.fmt*, *EX2BBPE.fmt*, *EX1ABPE.fmt*, *EX1BBPE.fmt*, *EX0ABPE.fmt*, *EX0BBPE.fmt*, *AVGBPE.fmt*, *AICBPE.fmt*, *SBCBPE.fmt* and *HQBPE.fmt*.

D.3.2 *Programs for computing in-sample probability event forecast evaluation*

The three programs, *GLPS-EVS.g*, *GLPS-EVB.g* and *GLPS-EV.g*, are used to evaluate the probability event forecasts. They compute in-sample forecast evaluation using one-step ahead probability forecasts of directional-change and events used in calculating probability integral transforms, which are obtained using recursive point forecasts over 1999q1–2001q1 (nine quarters).

To replicate the results reported in Chapter 11, first run the programs *GLPS-EVS.g* and *GLPS-EVB.g* and save the output *Gauss* results files. Then run the program *GLPS-EV.g*. The algorithms used in *GLPS-EVS.g* and *GLPS-EVB.g* are essentially the same, although only future uncertainty is allowed in *GLPS-EVS.g* whereas both future and parameter uncertainties are allowed in *GLPS-EVB.g*.

Here we consider the following nine single event probability of directional changes:

$$E1: \Pr\left(\Delta^2 p^o_{T+1} > 0\right) \qquad E2: \Pr\left(\Delta e_{T+1} > 0\right)$$
$$E3: \Pr\left(\Delta r^*_{T+1} > 0\right) \qquad E4: \Pr\left(\Delta r_{T+1} > 0\right)$$
$$E5: \Pr\left(\Delta^2 p_{T+1} > 0\right) \qquad E6: \Pr\left(\Delta^2 y_{T+1} > 0\right)$$
$$E7: \Pr\left(\Delta(p_{T+1} - p^*_{T+1}) > 0\right) \qquad E8: \Pr\left(\Delta^2(h_{T+1} - y_{T+1}) > 0\right)$$
$$E9: \Pr\left(\Delta^2 y^*_{T+1} > 0\right).$$

We also consider the following nine single events for the probability integral transform, which will be used in computing the Kolmogorov–Smirnov test statistic:

$$I1: \Pr\left(\text{forecast of } \Delta^2 p^o_{T+1} > \text{actual } \Delta^2 p^o_{T+1}\right)$$
$$I2: \Pr\left(\text{forecast of } \Delta e_{T+1} > \text{actual } \Delta e_{T+1}\right)$$
$$I3: \Pr\left(\text{forecast of } \Delta r^*_{T+1} > \text{actual } \Delta r^*_{T+1}\right)$$
$$I4: \Pr\left(\text{forecast of } \Delta r_{T+1} > \text{actual } \Delta r_{T+1}\right)$$
$$I5: \Pr\left(\text{forecast of } \Delta^2 p_{T+1} > \text{actual } \Delta^2 p_{T+1}\right)$$
$$I6: \Pr\left(\text{forecast of } \Delta^2 y_{T+1} > \text{actual } \Delta^2 y_{T+1}\right)$$

$I7$: $\Pr\left(\text{forecast of } \Delta(p_{T+1} - p^*_{T+1}) > \text{actual } \Delta(p_{T+1} - p^*_{T+1})\right)$
$I8$: $\Pr\left(\text{forecast of } \Delta^2(h_{T+1} - y_{T+1}) > \text{actual } \Delta^2(h_{T+1} - y_{T+1})\right)$
$I9$: $\Pr\left(\text{forecast of } \Delta^2 y^*_{T+1} > \text{actual } \Delta^2 y^*_{T+1}\right)$.

GLPS-EVS.g (with future uncertainty only)

After running the program, you will obtain the following 50 *Gauss* data files (with an fmt extension). They contain the results for (i) the one-step ahead central forecasts (18 files), (ii) root mean square errors (RMSEs) (14 files), (iii) the in-sample Probability Event Forecasts (18 files):

(i) The 18 files for one-step ahead central forecasts with no future and no parameter uncertainties are: *OV5AFOR.fmt, OV5BFOR.fmt, EX5AFOR.fmt, EX5BFOR.fmt, EX4AFOR.fmt, EX4BFOR.fmt, EX3AFOR.fmt, EX3BFOR.fmt, EX2AFOR.fmt, EX2BFOR.fmt, EX1AFOR.fmt, EX1BFOR.fmt, EX0AFOR.fmt, EX0BFOR.fmt, AVGFOR.fmt, AICFOR.fmt, SBCFOR.fmt* and *HQFOR.fmt*. Here the first four letters refer to individual models, and AVG, AIC, SBC and HQ indicate the equal weights, the AIC weights, the SBC weights and the HQ weights, respectively, used in pooling the forecasts.

The dimensions of all the above *Gauss* result matrices are the same, the number of in-sample horizons (here nine quarters over 1999q1–2001q1) by 54. The first nine columns (1 to 9) are one-step ahead central forecasts of the level of the nine variables (in the order of $p^o, e, r^*, r, \Delta p, y, p-p^*, h-y, y^*$); the next nine columns (10 to 18) are one-step ahead central forecasts of the four-quarter moving averages of the levels of the nine variables; the columns from 19 to 27 are one-step ahead central forecasts of the first differences; the next nine columns (28 to 36) are one-step ahead central forecasts of the four-quarter moving average of the first differences; columns 37 to 45 are one-step ahead central forecasts of the second differences; and the next nine columns (46 to 54) are one-step ahead central forecasts of the four-quarter moving average of the second differences.

(ii) The 14 files for RMSEs of the one-step ahead central forecasts with no future and no parameter uncertainties are: *OV5ARMSE.fmt, OV5BRMSE.fmt, EX5ARMSE.fmt, EX5BRMSE.fmt, EX4ARMSE.fmt, EX4BRMSE.fmt, EX3ARMSE.fmt, EX3BRMSE.fmt, EX2ARMSE.fmt, EX2BRMSE.fmt, EX1ARMSE.fmt, EX1BRMSE.fmt, EX0ARMSE.fmt* and *EX0BRMSE.fmt*.

The dimensions of all the above *Gauss* result files are the same, the number of in-sample horizon (here nine quarters over 1999q1–2001q1) by 27. The first nine columns (1 to 9) are RMSEs of the one-step ahead central forecasts of the level of the nine variables (in the order of p^o, e, r^*, r, Δp, y, $p - p^*$, $h - y$, y^*); the next 9 columns (10 to 18) are RMSEs of the one-step ahead central forecasts of the first diferences; and the next columns from 19 to 27 are RMSEs of the one-step ahead central forecasts of the second differences.

(iii) The 18 files for the probabilities of directional changes and probability integral transform with future uncertainty only are: *OV5ASPR.fmt, OV5BSPR.fmt,*

EX5ASPR.fmt, EX5BSPR.fmt, EX4ASPR.fmt, EX4BSPR.fmt, EX3ASPR.fmt, EX3BSPR.fmt, EX2ASPR.fmt, EX2BSPR.fmt, EX1ASPR.fmt, EX1BSPR.fmt, EX0ASPR.fmt, EX0BSPR.fmt, AVGSPR.fmt, AICSPR.fmt, SBCSPR.fmt and *HQSPR.fmt*.

The dimensions of all the above *Gauss* data files are the same: the number of in-sample horizon (here nine quarters over 1999q1–2001q1) by 36. The first nine columns (1 to 9) are the probabilities of directional changes (see definitions of the events given above and denoted by $E1, \ldots, E9$) for the nine variables (in the order of p^o, e, r^*, r, Δp, y, $p - p^*$, $h - y$, y^*), using one-step ahead central forecasts of the first and second differences; the next nine columns (10 to 18) are the probabilities of directional changes for the nine variables using one-step ahead central forecasts of the four-quarter moving average of the first and second differences; the nine columns (19 to 27) are the probabilities of integral transforms (see definitions of the events given above and denoted by $I1, \ldots, I9$) for the nine variables, using one-step ahead central forecasts of the first and second differences; and the final nine columns (28 to 36) are the probabilities of integral transforms for the nine variables using one-step ahead central forecasts of the four-quarter moving average of the first and second differences.

Finally, we have also saved the two additional data files, *actdat.fmt* and *a4actdat.fmt*, which contain in-sample actual data observations for the first differences and the second differences of the data, and which will be used for comparison with one-step ahead forecasts of directional changes in the program *GLPS-EV.g*.

GLPS-EVB.g (with both future and parameter uncertainties)

After running the program, you will obtain the following 18 *Gauss* result files (with an fmt extension). They contain the results for Probability Event Forecasts for directional changes and probability integral transform with both future and parameter uncertainties. These will be used in the companion file *GLPS-EV.g* to compute various test statistics reported in the tables of Chapter 11.

The 18 files are *OV5ABPR.fmt, OV5BBPR.fmt, EX5ABPR.fmt, EX5BBPR.fmt, EX4ABPR.fmt, EX4BBPR.fmt, EX3ABPR.fmt, EX3BBPR.fmt, EX2ABPR.fmt, EX2BBPR.fmt, EX1ABPR.fmt, EX1BBPR.fmt, EX0ABPR.fmt, EX0BBPR.fmt, AVGBPR.fmt, AICBPR.fmt, SBCBPR.fmt* and *HQBPR.fmt*. The dimensions and ordering of the *Gauss* result files are as described in probability event matrices for *GLPS-EVS.g*.

GLPS-EV.g

This program computes the in-sample forecast evaluation test statistics using the *Gauss* result files saved after running the companion programs, *GLPS-EVS.g* and *GLPS-EVB.g*. The program computes the following statistics:

(i) *UD*, *DD*, *DU* and *UU*, where the first letter denotes the direction of forecasts (*D* for down, *U* for up) and the second the direction of actual outcome.

(ii) The hit ratio defined as: $(DD + UU) / (UD + DD + DU + UU)$.

(iii) The Kuipers Score statistic given by $H - F$, where $H = UU/(UU + UD)$ is the proportion of ups that were correctly predicted to occur, and $F = DU/(DU + DD)$ is the proportion of downs that were incorrectly predicted.

(iv) The Pesaran–Timmerman, test statistic.

(v) The Kolmogorov–Smirnov test statistic.

D.4 Program for computing the decomposition of trends in cointegrating VARs

GLPS-DEC.g

This program provides the decomposition of the underlying $I(1)$ variables into permanent and transitory components as described in Section 10.3. This decomposition can be viewed as a (generalised) multivariate BN decomposition but has an advantage that it is characterised fully in terms of observables and estimated parameters. See also Garratt, Robertson and Wright (2005). The program also computes the more conventional multivariate Beveridge–Nelson trends of the system.

As in the case of the programs for GIRs and PPs, we use the data file, *ukmod99.dat* and the ML estimates of the cointegrating VAR(2) model over 1965q1–1999q4 (140 observations) using the Cointegrating VAR Option 4 with unrestricted intercepts and restricted trends. The program requires as an input estimates of the vector **g**, the trend growth rates (these are computed using a restricted SURE procedure in Chapter 10; see Section 10.3). After running the program, you will obtain nine ASCII files with txt extensions: *po.txt, ex.txt, rs.txt, r.txt, dp.txt, y.txt, pps.txt, hy.txt* and *ys.txt*. They contain summary results for each of the variables (in the order of $p^o, e, r^*, r, \Delta p, y, p - p^*, h - y, y^*$). These files can be easily be read into the *Excel* program for constructing tables and figures. The dimensions of the result files are 140 (the sample size) by 6. In each case, the first column contains the actual data, the second column the permanent component, the third column the transitory component, the fourth column the de-trended data, the fifth column the deterministic (permanent) trend and the sixth column the stochastic (permanent) trends.

Bibliography

Abadir, K. M., K. Hadri and E. Tzavalis (1999), 'The Influence of VAR Dimensions on Estimator Biases', *Econometrica*, 67, 163–181.

Abbot, A. J. and G. De Vita (2002), 'Long-Run Price and Income Elasticities of Demand for Hong Kong Exports: A Structural Cointegrating VAR Approach', *Applied Economics*, 34, 1025–132.

Adolfson, M., S. Laseen, J. Linde and M. Villani (2005), 'Bayesian Estimation of an Open Economy DSGE Model with Incomplete Pass-Through', *Sveriges Riksbank Working Paper Series*, no 179.

Akerlof, G., W. Dickens and G. Perry (1996), 'The Macroeconomics of Low Inflation', *Brookings Papers on Economic Activity*, 1, 1–76.

Akusuwan, M. (2005), *A Small Quarterly Macroeconometric Model for the Thai Economy: A Structural Cointegrating VAR Approach*. PhD. Thesis, Faculty of Economics, University of Cambridge.

Allen, C., S. G. Hall and J. Nixon (1994), 'The New London Business School Model of the UK Economy', *Center for Economic Forecasting Discussion Paper* No. 18–94.

Anderson, R. G., D. L. Hoffman and R. H. Rasche (2002), 'A Vector Error-Correction Forecasting Model of the US Economy', *Journal of Macroeconomics*, 24, 569–598.

Ando, A. and F. Modigliani (1969), 'Econometric Evaluation of Stabilisation Policies', *American Economic Review*, 59, 296–314.

Astley, M. and A. Garratt (1996), 'Interpreting Sterling Exchange Rate Movements', *Bank of England Quarterly Bulletin*, November, 394–404.

Baillie, R. and P. McMahon (1989), *The Foreign Exchange Market: Theory and Econometric Evidence*. Cambridge University Press: Cambridge.

Bakhshi, H., A. Haldane and N. Hatch (1997), 'Some Costs and Benefits of Price Stability in the UK', *Bank of England Working Paper* No. 97.

Banerjee, A., J. Dolado, J. W. Galbraith and D. F. Hendry (eds.) (1993), *Co-integration, Error Correction and the Econometric Analysis of Non-Stationary Data*. Oxford University Press: Oxford.

Barassi, M. R., G. M. Caporale and S. G. Hall (2001), 'Testing for Changes in the Long-Run Causal Structure of Cointegrated Vector Auto Regressions', *Imperial College Discussion Paper*, ICMS13.

Barrell, R., K. Dury, I. Hurst and N. Pain (2001), 'Modelling the World Economy: The National Institute's Global Econometric Model, NiGEM', Paper presented at the workshop organised by the European Network of Economic Policy Research Institutes (ENEPRI) on *Simulation Properties of Macroeconometric Models* in Paris, July.

Barro, R. and D. Gordon (1983), 'A Positive Theory of Monetary Policy in a Natural Rate Model', *Journal of Political Economy*, 91, 589–610.

Barro, R. J. (ed.) (1989), *Modern Business Cycle Theory*. Basil Blackwell: Oxford.

—— and X. Sala-i-Martin (1995), *Economic Growth*, Advanced Series in Economics. McGraw-Hill: New York, London and Montreal.

Bernanke, B. S. (1986), 'Alternative Exploration of the Money-Income Correlation', *Carnegie-Rochester Conference Series on Public Policy*, 25, 49–100.

—— and A. S. Blinder (1992), 'The Federal Funds Rate and the Channels of Monetary Transmission', *American Economic Review*, 82, 901–921.

——, M. Gertler and M. W. Watson (1997), 'Systematic Monetary Policy and the Effects of Oil Price Shocks', *Brookings Papers on Economic Activity*, 1, 91–142.

——, T. Laubach, F. S. Mishkin and A. S. Posen (1999), *Inflation Targeting: Lessons from the International Experience*. Princeton University Press: Princeton.

—— and I. Mihov (1998), 'Measuring Monetary Policy', *Quarterly Journal of Economics*, 113, 869–902.

Beveridge, S. and C. R. Nelson (1981), 'A New Approach to the Decomposition of Economic Time Series into Permanent and Transitory Components with Particular Attention to Measurement of the "Business Cycle"', *Journal of Monetary Economics*, 7, 151–174.

Bernard, A. B. and S. N. Durlauf (1995), 'Convergence in International Output', *Journal of Applied Econometrics*, 10, 97–108.

Binder, M. and M. H. Pesaran (1995), 'Multivariate Rational Expectations Models and Macroeconometric Modelling: A Review and Some New Results', in M. H. Pesaran and M. R. Wickens (eds.), *Handbook of Applied Econometrics Volume 1—Macroeconomics*, 139–187. Basil Blackwell: Oxford.

—— and —— (1999), 'Stochastic Growth Models and Their Econometric Implications', *Journal of Economic Growth*, 4, 139–183.

Bjørnstad, J. F. (1990), 'Predictive Likelihood: A Review', *Statistical Science*, 5, 242–265.

—— (1998), 'Predictive Likelihood', *Encyclopedia of Statistical Science*, 2, 539–545.

Blake, A. P. (1996), 'Forecast Error Bounds By Stochastic Simulation', *National Institute Economic Review*, 72–79.

Blanchard, O. J. (1989), 'A Traditional Interpretation of Macroeconomic Fluctuations', *American Economic Review*, 79, 1146–1164.

—— and S. Fischer (1989), *Lectures on Macroeconomics*. MIT Press: Cambridge, Mass.

—— and D. Quah (1989), 'The Dynamic Effects of Aggregate Demand and Supply Disturbances', *American Economic Review*, 79, 655–673.

——and M. Watson (1986), 'Are Business Cycles Alike?', in R. J. Gordon (ed.), *The American Business Cycle: Continuity and Change*. University of Chicago Press: Chicago.

Blinder, A. S. (1998), *Central Banking in Theory and Practice*. MIT Press: Cambridge, Mass.

Blundell, R., S. Bond, M. Devereux and C. Meghir (1992), 'Investment and Tobin's Q: Evidence from Company Panel Data', *Journal of Econometrics*, 151, 233–257.

Bodkin, R. G., L. R. Klein and K. Marwah (eds.) (1991), *A History of Macroeconometric Model Building*. Edward Elgar: Aldershot.

Brand, C. and N. Cassola (2004), 'A Money Demand System for Euro Area M3', *Applied Economics*, 36, 817–838.

Branson, W. H. (1977) 'Asset Markets and Relative Prices in Exchange Rate Determination', *Sozialwissenschaftliche Annalen*, 1, 69–89.

Brayton, F., A. Levin, R. Tryon and J. C. Williams (1997), 'The Evolution of Macro Models at the Federal Reserve Board', *Finance and Economics Discussion Series* 1997–29, Board of Governors of the Federal Reserve System: Washington D.C.

——and E. Mauskopf (1985), 'The Federal Reserve Board MPS Quarterly Econometric Model of the U.S. Economy', *Economic Modelling*, 2, 170–292.

——and P. Tinsley (1996), 'A Guide to FRB/US: A Macroeconomic Model of the United States', *Finance and Economics Discussion Series* 1996–42, Board of Governors of the Federal Reserve System: Washington D.C.

Breedon, F. J. and P. G. Fisher (1996), 'M0: Causes and Consequences', *Manchester School*, 64, 371–387.

Breeson, G., F. Kramarz and P. Sevestre (1992), 'Dynamic Labour Demand Models', in L. Mátyás and P. Sevestre (eds.), *The Econometrics of Panel Data*, 360–387. Kluwer: Boston.

Britton, E., P. Fisher and J. Whitley (1998), 'The Inflation Report Projections: Understanding the Fan Chart', *Bank of England Quarterly Bulletin*, 38, 30–37.

Britton, A. and P. Westaway (1998), 'On the Equilibrium Properties of Macroeconomic Models', Chapter 10 in I. Begg and B. Henry (eds.), *Applied Economics and Public Policy*. Cambridge University Press: Cambridge.

Brunner, A. D. (2000), 'On the Derivation of Monetary Policy Shocks: Should We Throw the VAR Out with the Bath Water', *Journal of Money, Credit and Banking*, 32, 254–279.

Bruno, M. and J. Sachs (1984), *The Economics of Worldwide Stagflation*. Basil Blackwell: Oxford.

Buiter, W. (1980), 'The Macroeconomics of Dr. Pangloss: A Critical Survey of the New Classical Macroeconomics', *Economic Journal*, 90, 34–50.

Bullard, J. and J. W. Keating (1995), 'The Long-Run Relationship Between Inflation and Output in Postwar Economies', *Journal of Monetary Economics*, 36, 477–496.

Burnham, K. P. and D. R. Anderson (1998), *Model Selection and Inference: A Practical Information-Theoretic Approach*. Springer-Verlag: New York.

Busetti, F. and R. Taylor (2004), 'Tests of Stationarity Against a Change in Persistence', *Journal of Econometrics*, 123, 33–66.

Bühlmann, P. (1997), 'Sieve Bootstrap for Time Series', *Bernoulli*, 3, 123–148.

Calvo, G. (1978a), 'On the Indeterminacy of Interest Rates and Wages with Perfect Foresight', *Journal of Economic Theory*, 19, 321–337.

——(1978b), 'On the Time Consistency of Optimal Policy in a Monetary Economy', *Econometrica*, 46, 1411–1428.

——(1983), 'Staggered Prices in a Utility Maximising Framework', *Journal of Monetary Economics*, 12, 383–398.

Campbell, J. Y. and N. G. Mankiw (1989), 'International Evidence of the Persistence of Economic Fluctuations', *Journal of Monetary Economics*, 23, 319–333.

Cayen, J-P., A. Corbett and P. Perrier (2005), 'An Optimised Monetary Policy Rule for TOTEM', *mimeo*, Bank of Canada.

Canova, F. (1998), 'Detrending and Business Cycle Facts', *Journal of Monetary Economics*, 41, 475–512.

Champernowne, D. G. (1960), 'An Experimental Investigation of the Robustness of Certain Procedures for Estimating Means and Regressions Coefficients', *Journal of the Royal Statistical Society*, Series A, 123, 398–412.

Chatfield, C. (1995), 'Model Uncertainty, Data Mining and Statistical Inference', *Journal of the Royal Statistical Society*, Series A, 158, 419–466.

Chauduri, K. and B. C. Daniel (1998), 'Long-run Equilibrium Real Exchange Rates and Oil Prices', *Economics Letters*, 58, 231–238.

Cheung, Y. W. and K. S. Lai (1993), 'Finite-Sample Sizes of Johansen's Likelihood Ratio Tests for Cointegration', *Oxford Bulletin of Economics and Statistics*, 55, 313–328.

Choi, E. and P. Hall (2000), 'Bootstrap Confidence Regions Computed from Autoregressions of Arbitrary Order', *Journal of the Royal Statistical Society*, Series B, 62, 461–477.

Christiano, L. and M. Eichenbaum (1992a), 'Liquidity Effects and the Monetary Transmission Mechanism', *American Economic Review*, 82, 346–353.

——and—— (1992b), 'Current Real Business Cycle Theories and Aggregate Labour Market Fluctuations', *American Economic Review*, 82, 432–450.

—— and —— (1995), 'Liquidity Effects, Monetary Policy and the Business Cycle', *Journal of Money, Credit and Banking*, 27, 1113–1136.

Christiano, L. J., M. Eichenbaum and C. Evans (1996), 'The Effects of Monetary Policy Shocks: Some Evidence from the Flow of Funds', *Review of Economics and Statistics*, 96, 16–34.

——, —— and ——C. L. Evans (1998), 'Modeling Money?' *NBER Working Paper* No. 3916, 98/1.

——, —— and ——(1999), 'Monetary Policy Shocks: What Have We Learned and to What End?', Chapter 2 in J. B Taylor and M. Woodford (eds.), *Handbook of Macroeconomics*, Volume 1A. North-Holland, Elsevier: Amsterdam.

——, —— and —— (2005), 'Nominal Rigidities and the Dynamic Effects of a Shock to Monetary Policy', *Journal of Political Economy*, 113, 1–45.

——, —— and D. Marshall (1991), 'The Permanent Income Hypothesis Revisited', *Econometrica*, 59, 397–423.

Clarida, R. and J. Gali (1994), 'Sources of Real Exchange Rate Fluctuations: How Important are Nominal Shocks?' *Carnegie-Rochester Conference Series on Public Policy*, 41, 1–56.

——, J. Gali and M. Gertler (1999), 'The Science of Monetary Policy: A New Keynesian Perspective', *Journal of Economic Literature*, 37, 1661–1707.

——, —— and M. Gertler (2000), 'Monetary Policy Rules and Macroeconomic Stability Evidence and Some Theory', *Quarterly Journal of Economics*, 115, 147–180.

Clarke, P. (1987), 'The Cyclical Component of U.S. Economic Activity', *Quarterly Journal of Economics*, 102, 797–814.

Clemen, R. T. (1989), 'Combining Forecasts: A Review and Annotated Bibliography', *International Journal of Forecasting*, 5, 559–583.

Clements, M. P. and D. F. Hendry (2002), 'Explaining Forecast Failure in Macroeconomics', in M. P. Clements and D. F. Hendry (eds.), *A Companion to Economic Forecasting*. Blackwell Publishing: Oxford.

Cochrane, J. H. (1998), 'What do VARs Mean? Measuring the Output Effects of Monetary Policy', *Journal of Monetary Economics*, 41, 277–300.

Cogley, J. (1990), 'International Evidence on the Size of the Random Walk in Output', *Journal of Political Economy*, 98, 501–18.

Cogley, T., S. Morozov and T. J. Sargent (2005), 'Bayesian Fan Charts for UK Inflation: Forecasting and Sources of Uncertainty in an Evolving Monetary System', *Journal of Economic Dynamics and Control*, 29, 1893–1925.

—— and J. M. Nason (1995), 'Output Dynamics in Real Business Cycle Models', *American Economic Review*, 85, 492–511.

—— and T. J. Sargent (2001), 'Evolving Post-World War II US Inflation Dynamics', in B. Bernanke and K. Rogoff (eds.), *NBER Macroeconomics Annual*, MIT: Cambridge, MA.

—— and —— (2005), 'The Conquest of US Inflation: Learning and Robustness to Model Uncertainty', *Review of Economic Dynamics*, 8, 528–563.

Cooley, T. (ed.) (1995), *Frontiers of Business Cycle Research*. Princeton University Press: Princeton.

Cooley, T. F., J. Greenwood and M. Yorukoghu (1997), 'The Replacement Problem', *Journal of Monetary Economics*, 40, 457–499.

—— and G. D. Hansen (1989), 'The Inflation Tax in a Real Business Cycle Model', *American Economic Review*, 79, 733–748.

—— and —— (1995), 'Money and the Business Cycle', Chapter 4 in T. F. Cooley (ed.), *Frontiers of Business Cycle Research*. Princeton University Press: Princeton.

Cooley, T. and S. LeRoy (1985), 'Atheoretical Macroeconometrics: A Critique', *Journal of Monetary Economics*, 16, 283–308.

Crowder, W. J., D. L. Hoffman and R. H. Rasche (1999), 'Identification, Long-Run Relations, and Fundamental Innovations in a Simple Cointegrated System', *Review of Economics and Statistics*, 81, 109–121.

—— and M. E. Wohar (2004), 'A Cointegrated Structural VAR Model of the Canadian Economy', *Applied Economics*, 36, 195–213.

Darby, M. R. (1983), 'Movements in Purchasing Power Parity: The Short and Long Runs', in M. R. Darby and J. R. Lothian (eds.), *The International Transmission of Inflation*. University of Chicago Press: Chicago.

Davidson, J. E. H., D. F. Hendry, F. Srba and S. Yeo (1978), 'Econometric Modelling of the Aggregate Time-series Relationship between Consumers Expenditure and Income in the United Kingdom', *Economic Journal*, 88, 661–692.

Dawid, A. P. (1984), 'Present Position and Potential Developments: Some Personal Views—Statistical Theory, The Prequential Approach', *Journal of the Royal Statistical Society*, Series A, 147, 278–292.

Dees, S., F. di Mauro, M. H. Pesaran and L. V. Smith (2005), 'Exploring the International Linkages of the Euro Area: A Global VAR Analysis', *CESifo Working Paper* No. 1425. Presented at CESifo Area Conference on Macro, Money and International Finance, February 2005.

DeJong, D., D. Ingham and C. Whiteman (1993), 'Analysing VARs with Monetary Business Cycle Model Priors', *Proceedings of the American Statistical Association, Bayesian Section*, 160–169.

Del Negro, M. and F. Schorfheide (2004), 'Priors from Equilibrium Models for VARs', *International Economic Review*, 45, 643–673.

——, ——, F. Smets and R. Wouters (2005), 'On the Fit and Forecasting Performance of New Keynesian Models', *European Central Bank Working Paper No 491*.

Dickey, D. A. and W. A. Fuller (1979), 'Distribution of the Estimators for Autoregressive Time Series With a Unit Root', *Journal of the American Statistical Association*, 74, 427–431.

—— and —— (1981), 'Likelihood Ratio Statistics for Autoregressive Time Series With a Unit Root', *Econometrica*, 49, 1057–1072.

Diebold, F. X., T. A. Gunther and A. S. Tay (1998), 'Evaluating Density Forecasts with Applications to Financial Risk Management', *International Economic Review*, 39, 863–884.

——, J. Hahn and A. S. Tay (1999), 'Multivariate Density Forecast Evaluation and Calibration in Financial Risk Management: High Frequency Returns on Foreign Exchange', *Review of Economics and Statistics*, 81, 661–673.

—— and J. A. Lopez (1996), 'Forecast Evaluation and Combination', in G. S. Maddala and C. R. Rao (eds.), *Handbook of Statistics*, Volume 14, 241–268. North-Holland, Elsevier: Amsterdam.

——, A. S. Tay and K. F. Wallis (1999), 'Evaluating Density Forecasts of Inflation: the Survey of Professional Forecasters', in R. Engle and H. White (eds.), *Cointegration, Causality and Forecasting: A Festschrift in Honour of Clive Granger*, Oxford University Press.

Doan, T., R. Litterman and C. Sims (1984), 'Forecasting and Conditional Projections Using Realistic Prior Distributions', *Econometric Reviews*, 3, 1–100.

Dornbusch, R. (1976), 'Expectations and Exchange Rate Dynamics', *Journal of Political Economy*, 84, 1161–1176.

Draper, D. (1995), 'Assessment and Propagation of Model Uncertainty', *Journal of the Royal Statistical Society*, Series B, 58, 45–97.

Dryhmes, P. (1971), *Distributed Lags: Problems of Estimation and Formulation*. Holden Day: San Francisco.

Ehrmann, M. and F. Smets (2003), 'Uncertain Potential Output: Implications for Monetary Policy', *Journal of Economic Dynamics and Control*, 27, 1611–1638.

Eichenbaum, M. and C. L. Evans (1995), 'Some Empirical Evidence on the Effects of Shocks to Monetary Policy on Exchange Rates', *Quarterly Journal of Economics*, 110, 975–1010.

Engle, R. and G. Granger (1987), 'Cointegration and Error-Correction: Representation, Estimation and Testing', *Econometrica*, 55, 251–276.

Evans, G. and L. Reichlin (1994), 'Information, Forecasts and Measurement of the Business Cycle', *Journal of Monetary Economics*, 33, 234–254.

Fabiani, S. (1996), *Technological Change and Output Fluctuations: An Empirical Analysis for the G7 Countries*. PhD thesis. University of Cambridge.

Fair, R. C. (1980), 'Estimating the Expected Predictive Accuracy of Econometric Models', *International Economic Review*, 21, 355–378.

—— (1994), *Testing Macroeconometric Models*. Harvard University Press: London.

Feldstein, M. (1998), 'The Costs and Benefits of Going from Low Inflation to Price Stability', in C. Romer and D. Romer (eds.), *Monetary Policy and Inflation*. University of Chicago Press: Chicago.

Favero, C. and R. Rovelli (2003), 'Macroeconomic Stability and the Preferences of the Fed: A Formal Analysis 1981–98', *Journal of Money, Credit and Banking*, 35, 545–556.

Fernandez, C., E. Ley and M. F. J. Steel (2001a), 'Benchmark Priors for Bayesian Model Averaging', *Journal of Econometrics*, 100, 381–427.

——, —— and —— (2001b), 'Model Uncertainty in Cross-Country Growth Regressions', *Journal of Applied Econometrics*, 16, 563–576.

Fisher, P. G. (1992), *Rational Expectations in Macroeconomic Models*. Advanced Studies in Theoretical and Applied Econometrics, 26. Kluwer Academic Publishers: Dordrecht.

——, S. K. Tanna, D. S. Turner, K. F. Wallis and J. D. Whitley (1990), 'Econometric Evaluation of the Exchange Rate in Models of the U.K. Economy', *Economic Journal*, 100, 1230–1244.

——, D. S. Turner and K. F. Wallis (1992), 'Forward Unit Root Exchange-Rate Dynamics and the Properties of Large-Scale Macroeconometric Models', in C. Hargreaves (ed.), *Macroeconomic Modelling of the Long Run*. Edward Elgar: Aldershot.

Frankel, J. A. and A. K. Rose (1995), 'Empirical Research on Nominal Exchange Rates', in G. M. Grosman and K. Rogoff (eds.), *Handbook of International Economics*, Volume 3. North-Holland Elsevier: Amsterdam.

Froot, K. A. and K. Rogoff (1995), 'Perspectives on PPP and Long-Run Real Exchange Rates', in G. M. Grosman and K. Rogoff (eds.), *Handbook of International Economics*, Volume 3. North-Holland Elsevier: Amsterdam.

Fuhrer, J. C. and C. H. Bleakley (1996), 'Computationally Efficient Solution and Maximum Likelihood Estimation of Nonlinear Rational Expectations Models', *Federal Reserve Bank of Boston Working Paper* No. 96-2.

Gali, J. (1992), 'How Well Does the IS-LM Model Fit Postwar US Data', *Quarterly Journal of Economics*, 107, 709–738.

—— and M. Gertler (1999), 'Inflation Dynamics: A Structural Econometric Analysis', *Journal of Monetary Economics*, 44, 195–222.

—— and T. Monacelli (2005), 'Monetary Policy and Exchange Rate Volatility in a Small Open Economy', *Review of Economic Studies*, 72, 707–734.

Garratt, A., K. Lee, M. H. Pesaran and Y. Shin (2000), 'The Structural Cointegrating VAR Approach to Macroeconometric Modelling', Chapter 5 in S. Holly and M. Weale (eds.), *Econometric Modelling: Techniques and Applications*. Cambridge University Press: Cambridge.

——, ——, —— and —— (2003a), 'A Long Run Structural Macroeconometric Model of the UK', *Economic Journal*, 113, 487, 412–455.

——, ——, —— and —— (2003b), 'Forecast Uncertainty in Macroeconometric Modelling: An Application to the UK Economy', *Journal of the American Statistical Association*, 98, 464, 829–838.

——, —— and —— (2005a), 'Identifying Short-Run Impulse Response Functions in Long-Run Structural Models', under preparation.

——, —— and —— (2005b), 'Cointegrating Rank Tests in the Presence of Multivariate GARCH Errors in Macroeconomic Data', under preparation.

——, D. Robertson and S. Wright (2005), 'Permanent vs Transitory Components and Economic Fundamentals', forthcoming in *Journal of Applied Econometrics*.

Gerrard, W. J. and L. G. Godfrey (1998), 'Diagnostic Checks for Single-Equation Error-Correction and Autoregressive Distributed Lag Models', *Manchester School*, 66, 222–237.

Gertler, M. and S. Gilchrist (1994), 'Monetary Policy, Business Cycles, and the Behavior of Small Manufacturing Firms', *Quarterly Journal of Economics*, 109, 309–340.

Giles, C. (2001), 'Bamboozled by Statistics', *Financial Times*, December 18th.

Giannone, D., L. Reichlin and L. Sala (2005), 'VARs, Common Factors and the Empirical Validation of Equilibrium Business Cycle Models', forthcoming in *Journal of Econometrics*.

Goffe, W. L., G. D. Ferrier and J. Rodgers (1994), 'Global Optimisation of Statistical Functions with Simulated Annealing', *Journal of Econometrics*, 60, 65–99.

Gonzalo, J. (1994), 'Five Alternative Methods of Estimating Long-Run Equilibrium Relationships', *Journal of Econometrics*, 60, 203–233.

—— and C. Granger (1995), 'Estimation of Common Long-Memory Components in Cointegrated Systems', *Journal of Business and Economic Statistics*, 13, 27–35.

—— and S. Ng (2001), 'A Systematic Framework for Analysing the Dynamic Effects of Permanent and Transitory Shocks', *Journal of Economic Dynamics and Control*, 25, 1527–1546.

Gordon, D. B. and E. M. Leeper (1994), 'The Dynamic Impacts of Monetary Policy: An Exercise in Tentative Identification', *Journal of Political Economy*, 102, 1228–1247.

Granger, C. W. J. (1981), 'Some Properties of Time Series Data and their Use in Econometric Model Specification', *Journal of Econometrics*, 16, 121–30.

—— (1986), 'Developments in the Study of Co-Integrated Economic Variables', *Oxford Bulletin of Economics and Statistics*, 48, 213–228.

—— (1989), 'Combining Forecasts—Twenty Years Later', *Journal of Forecasting*, 8, 167–173.

Granger, C. and Y. Jeon (2004), 'Thick Modelling', *Economic Modelling*, 21, 323–343.

Granger, C. W. J. and J. L. Lin (1995), 'Causality in the Long-Run', *Econometric Theory*, 11, 530–536.

—— and P. Newbold (1974), 'Spurious Regressions in Econometrics', *Journal of Econometrics*, 2, 111–120.

—— and M. H. Pesaran (2000a), 'A Decision Theoretic Approach to Forecast Evaluation', in W. S. Chan, W. K. Li and H. Tong (eds.), *Statistics and Finance: An Interface*, 261–278. Imperial College Press: London.

—— and —— (2000b), 'Economic and Statistical Measures of Forecast Accuracy', *Journal of Forecasting*, 19, 537–560.

Gredenhoff, M. and T. Jacobson (2001), 'Bootstrap Testing Linear Restrictions on Cointegrating Vectors', *Journal of Business and Economic Statistics*, 19, 63–72.

Griffin, J. M., F. Nardari and R. Stulz (2004), 'Stock Market Trading and Market Conditions', *NBER Working Paper 10719*, 1–48.

Griliches, Z. (1967), 'Distributed Lags: A Survey', *Econometrica*, 26, 16–49.

Grilli V. and G. Kaminsky (1991), 'Nominal Exchange Rate Regimes and the Real Exchange Rate: Evidence from the United States and Great Britain, 1885–1986', *Journal of Monetary Economics*, 27, 191–212.

Grossman, G. M. and E. Helpman (1991), *Innovation and Growth in the Global Economy*. MIT Press: Cambridge, Mass.

Haldrup, N. (1998), 'A Review of the Econometric Analysis of I(2) Variables', *Journal of Economic Surveys*, 12, 595–650.

Hall, P. (1992), *The Bootstrap and Edgeworth Expansion*. Springer-Verlag: New York.

Hall, S. G. (1987), 'A Forward Looking Model of the Exchange Rate', *Journal of Applied Econometrics*, 2, 47–60.

Hall, S. G. (1995), 'Macroeconomics and a Bit More Reality', *Economic Journal*, 105, 974–988.

Hall, S. and J. Mitchell, (2005), 'Evaluating, Comparing and Combining Density Forecasts using the KLIC with an Application to the Bank of England and NIESR Fancharts of Inflation', *NIESR Working Paper* No. 253.

Hamilton, J. D. (1994), *Time Series Analysis*. Princeton University Press: Princeton.

Hansen, L. P. and T. J. Sargent (1991), 'Two Difficulties in Interpreting Vector Autoregressions', in L. P. Hansen and T. J. Sargent (eds.), *Rational Expectations Economics*. Westview Press: London.

—— and —— (1995), 'Discounted Linear Exponential Quadratic Gaussian Control', *IEEE Transactions on Automatic Control*, 40, 968–971.

Harbo, I., S. Johansen, B. Nielsen and A. Rahbek (1998), 'Asymptotic Inference on Cointegrating Rank in Partial Systems', *Journal of Business and Economic Statistics*, 16, 388–399.

Harding, D. and A. Pagan (2002), 'Dissecting The Cycle: A Methodological Investigation', *Journal of Monetary Economics*, 49, 365–381.

Harris, I. R. (1989), 'Predictive Fit for Natural Exponential Functions', *Biometrika*, 76, 675–684.

Harvey, A. C. (1985), 'Trends and Cycles in Macroeconomic Time Series', *Journal of Business and Economic Statistics*, 3, 216–247.

—— and A. Jaeger (1993), 'Detrending, Stylised Facts and the Business Cycle', *Journal of Applied Econometrics*, 8, 231–247.

Haug, A. A. (1996), 'Tests for Cointegration: a Monte Carlo Comparison', *Journal of Econometrics*, 71, 89–115.

—— (2002), 'Temporal Aggregation and the Power of Cointegration Tests: A Monte Carlo Study', *Oxford Bulletin of Economics and Statistics*, 64, 399–412.

——, O. Karagedikli and S. Ranchhod (2005), 'Monetary Policy Transmission Mechanisms and Currency Unions—A Vector Error Correction Approach to a Trans-Tasman Currency Union', *Journal of Policy Modelling*, 27, 55–74.

Hecq, A., F. C. Palm and J. Urbain (2000), 'Permanent and Transitory Decomposition in VAR Models with Cointegration and Common Cycles', *Oxford Bulletin of Economics and Statistics*, 62, 511–532.

Hendry, D. and M. Clements (2004), 'Pooling of Forecasts', *Econometrics Journal*, 7, 1–31.

Henry, S. G. B. and B. Pesaran (1993), 'VAR Models of Inflation', *Bank of England Quarterly Bulletin*, 33, 231–239.

Hercowitz, Z. and M. Sampson (1991), 'Output Growth, the Real Wage and Employment Fluctuations', *American Economic Review*, 81, 1215–1237.

Hoeting, J. A., D. Madigan, A. E. Raftery and C. T. Volinsky (1999), 'Bayesian Model Averaging: A Tutorial', *Statistical Science*, 14, 382–417.

Hodrick, R. J. and E. C. Prescott (1997). 'Postwar U.S. Business Cycles: An Empirical Investigation', *Journal of Money, Credit and Banking*, 29, 1–16.

Hondroyiannis, G. (2004), 'Estimating Residential Demand for Electricity in Greece', *Energy Economics*, 26, 319–334.

Huizinga, J. (1988), 'An Empirical Investigation of the Long-Run Behavior of Real Exchange Rates', *Carnegie-Rochester Conference Series on Public Policy*, 27, 149–214.

Ireland, P. (2004), 'A Method for Taking Models to the Data', *Journal of Economic Dynamics and Control*, 28, 1205–1226.

Ismihan, M., K. Metin-Ozcan and A. Tansel (2005), 'The Role of Macroeconomic Instability in Public and Private Capital Accumulation and Growth: The Case of Turkey 1963–1999', *Applied Economics*, 37, 239–251.

Jacobs, J. P. A. M. and K. W. Wallis (2005), 'Comparing SVARs and SEMs: Two Models of the UK Economy', *Journal of Applied Econometrics*, 20, 209–228.

Janssen, N. (1996), 'Can We Explain the Shift in M0 Velocity? Some Time Series and Cross-Sectional Evidence', *Bank of England Quarterly Bulletin*, February, 39–50.

Johansen, S. (1988), 'Statistical Analysis of Cointegration Vectors', *Journal of Economic Dynamics and Control*, 12, 231–254.

—— (1991), 'Estimation and Hypothesis Testing of Cointegrating Vectors in Gaussian Vector Autoregressive Models', *Econometrica*, 59, 1551–1580.

—— (1995), *Likelihood-Based Inference in Cointegrated Vector Autoregressive Models*. Oxford University Press: Oxford.

—— (2000), 'A Bartlett Correction Factor for Tests on the Cointegrating Relations', *Econometric Theory*, 16, 740–778.

—— and K. Juselius (1990), 'Maximum Likelihood Estimation and Inference on Cointegration—with Applications to the Demand for Money', *Oxford Bulletin of Economics and Statistics*, 52, 169–210.

—— and —— (1992), 'Testing Structural Hypotheses in a Multivariate Cointegration Analysis of the PPP and UIP for UK', *Journal of Econometrics*, 53, 211–244.

Jorgenson, D. (1966), 'Rational Distributed Lag Functions', *Econometrica*, 34, 135–149.

Kapetanios, G., A. Pagan and A. Scott (2005), 'Making a Match: Combining Theory and Evidence in Policy-Oriented Macroeconomic Modelling', *Centre for Applied Macroeconomic Analysis Working Paper* (http://econrsss.anu.edu.au/~arpagan/).

Kasa, K. (2000), 'Forecasting the Forecasts of Others', *Review of Economic Dynamics*, 3, 726–756.

Kilian, L. (1998), 'Small-Sample Confidence Intervals For Impulse Response Functions', *Review of Economics and Statistics*, 80, 186–201.

—— (1999), 'Finite-Sample Properties of Percentile and Percentile-t Bootstrap Confidence Intervals for Impulse Responses', *Review of Economics and Statistics*, 81, 652–660.

—— (2002), 'Impulse Response Analysis in Vector Autoregressions with Unknown Lag Order', *Journal of Forecasting*, 20, 161–179.

Kim, K. and A. R. Pagan (1995), 'The Econometric Analysis of Calibrated Macroeconomic Models', Chapter 7 in M. H. Pesaran and M. Wickens (eds.), *Handbook of Applied Econometrics: Macroeconomics*. Basil Blackwell: Oxford.

Kim, S. and N. Roubini (2000), 'Exchange Rate Anomalies in the Industrial Countries: A Solution with a Structural VAR Approach', *Journal of Monetary Economics*, 45, 561–586.

King, M. (1994), 'Monetary Policy in the UK', *Fiscal Studies*, 15, 109–128.

—— (1999), 'Challenges for Monetary Policy: New and Old', *Symposium Proceedings* sponsored by the Federal Reserve Bank of Kansas City, Jackson Hole, Wyoming August 26–28.

King, R. G., C. I. Plosser, J. H. Stock, and M. W. Watson (1991), 'Stochastic Trends and Economic Fluctuations', *American Economic Review*, 81, 819–840.

Koop, G., M. H. Pesaran and S. M. Potter (1996), 'Impulse Response Analysis in Nonlinear Multivariate Models', *Journal of Econometrics*, 74, 119–47.

Koopman, S. J., A. C. Harvey, J. A. Doornik and N. Shephard (1995), *STAMP 5.0: Structural Time Series Analyser, Modeller and Predictor*. Chapman and Hall: London.

Kydland, F. and E. Prescott (1982), 'Time to Build and Aggregate Fluctuations', *Econometrica*, 50, 1345–1370.

La Cour, L. and R. MacDonald (2000), 'Modeling the ECU against the Dollar: A Structural Monetary Interpretation', *Journal of Business and Economic Statistics*, 18, 436–450.

Lastrapes, W. D. and G. Selgin (1994), 'Buffer-Stock Money: Interpreting Short-Run Dynamics Using Long-Run Restrictions', *Journal of Money, Credit and Banking*, 26, 34–54.

—— and —— (1995), 'The Liquidity Effect: Identifying Short-Run Interest Rate Dynamics Using Long-Run Restrictions', *Journal of Macroeconomics*, 17, 387–404.

Lawson, N. (1992), *The View From No. 11: Memoirs of a Tory Radical*. Bantam Press: London.

Laxton, D., P. Isard, H. Faruqee, E. Prasad and B. Turtleboom (1998), 'MULTIMOD Mark III The Core Dynamic and Steady-State Models', IMF Occasional Papers 164.

Lee, K. C. (1998), 'Cross-Country Interdependence in Growth Dynamics: A Model of Output Growth in the G7 Economies, 1960–1994', *Weltwirtschaftliches Archiv*, 134, 367–403.

—— and P. Mizen (2005), 'Indicating Financial Distress Using Probability Forecasts: An Application to the UK Unsecured Credit Market', *mimeo*, University of Leicester (www.le.ac.uk/economics/kcl2/).

—— and M. H. Pesaran (1993), 'Persistence Profiles and Business Cycle Fluctuations in a Disaggregated Model of UK Output Growth', *Ricerche Economiche*, 47, 293–322.

——, —— and R. G. Pierse (1992), 'Persistence of Shocks and their Sources in a Multisectoral Model of UK Output Growth', *Economic Journal*, 102, 342–356.

——, —— and —— (1993), 'Persistence, Cointegration and Aggregation: A Disaggregated Analysis of Output Fluctuations in the US Economy', *Journal of Econometrics*, 56, 57–88.

——, —— and R. P. Smith (1997), 'Growth and Convergence in a Multi-Country Empirical Stochastic Solow Model', *Journal of Applied Econometrics*, 12, 357–392.

——, —— and —— (1998), 'Growth Empirics: A Panel Approach—A Comment', *Quarterly Journal of Economics*, 113, 319–323.

Levtchenkova S., A. R. Pagan and J. C. Robertson (1998), 'Shocking Stories', *Journal of Economic Surveys*, 12, 507–532.

Levy, M. S. and S. K. Perng (1986), 'An Optimal Prediction Function for the Normal Linear Model', *Journal of the American Statistical Association*, 81, 196–98.

L'horty, Y. and C. Rault (2004), 'Inflation, Minimum Wage and Other Wages: An Econometric Study on French Macroeconomic Data', *Applied Economics*, 36, 277–290.

Litterman, R. (1986), 'Forecasting with Bayesian Vector Autoregressions – Five Years of Experience', *Journal of Business and Economic Statistics*, 4, 25–38.

—— and L. Weiss (1985), 'Money, Real Interest Rates and Output: A Reinterpretation of Postwar US Data', *Econometrica*, 53, 129–156.

Long, J. B. and C. Plosser (1983), 'Real Business Cycles', *Journal of Political Economy*, 91, 39–69.

Lothian, J. R. and M. P. Taylor (1996), 'Real Exchange Rate Behavior: The Recent Float from the Perspective of the Last Two Centuries', *Journal of Political Economy*, 104, 488–509.

Lucas, R. E. (1976), 'Econometric Policy Evaluation: A Critique', in K. Brunner and A.H. Meltzer (eds.), *The Phillips Curve and Labour Markets, Carnegie-Rochester Series on Public Policy*, Volume 1, 19–46.

Lütkepohl, H. (1991), *Introduction to Multiple Time Series Analysis*. Berlin: Springer-Verlag.

MacDonald, R. (1995), 'Long-Run Exchange Rate Modeling: A Survey of the Recent Evidence', *International Monetary Fund Working Paper*, No. WP/95/14.

—— and P. D. Murphy (1989), 'Testing for the Long Run Relationship Between Nominal Interest Rates and Inflation using Cointegration Techniques', *Applied Economics*, 21, 439–447.

Magnus, J. R. and H. Neudecker (1988), *Matrix Differential Calculus with Applications in Statistics and Econometrics*. John Wiley and Sons: Chichester, UK.

Mark, N. C. (1990), 'Real and Nominal Exchange Rates in the Long Run: An Empirical Investigation', *Journal of International Economics*, 28, 115–136.

McCallum, B. T. (1989), 'Real Business Cycle Models', Chapter 2 in R. J. Barro (ed.), *Modern Business Cycle Theory*. Basil Blackwell: Oxford.

MacKinnon, J. G (1996), 'Numerical Distribution Functions for Unit Root and Cointegration Tests', *Journal of Applied Econometrics*, 11, 601–618.

Meese, R. A. and K. Rogoff (1983), 'Empirical Exchange Rate Models of the Seventies', *Journal of International Economics*, 14, 3–24.

Mellander, E., A. Vredin and A. Warne (1992), 'Stochastic Trends and Economic Fluctuations in a Small Open Economy', *Journal of Applied Econometrics*, 7, 369–394.

Mills, T. (1991), 'Are Fluctuations in UK Output Transitory or Permanent?', *Manchester School*, 59, 1–11.

Minford, A. P. L., K. G. P. Matthews and S. S. Marwaha (1979), 'Terminal Conditions as a Means of Ensuring Unique Solutions for Rational Expectations Models with Forward Expectations', *Economics Letters*, 4, 117–20.

Mishkin, F. S. (1992), 'Is the Fisher Effect For Real?' *Journal of Monetary Economics*, 30, 195–215.

Mitchell, J. (1999), *Identification and Estimation of Impulse Response Functions in VAR Models: Analysing Monetary Shocks in the G7 Economies*. PhD Thesis. University of Cambridge.

Morley, J. C., C. R. Nelson and E. Zivot (2003), 'Why Are the Beveridge-Nelson and Unobserved-Components Decompositions of GDP so Different?, *Review of Economics and Statistics*, 85, 235–243.

Murphy, C. W. (1988), 'An Overview of the Murphy Model', *Australian Economic Papers*, 27 (Supp.), 175–99.

—— (1992), 'The Steady-State Properties of a Macroeconometric Model', in C. Hargreaves (ed.), *Macroeconomic Modelling of the Long Run*. Edward Elgar: Aldershot.

Muscatelli, V. A. and A. S. Hurn (1995), 'Econometric Modelling Using Cointegrated Time Series', in L. T. Oxley, D. A. R. George, C. J. Roberts and S. T. Sayer (eds.), *Surveys in Econometrics*. Blackwell Publishers: Oxford.

Mussa, M. (1976), 'The Exchange Rate, the Balance of Payments, and Monetary and Fiscal Policy under a Regime of Controlled Floating', *Scandinavian Journal of Economics*, 78, 229–48.

Neave, H. R. and P. L. Worthington (1992), *Distribution-Free Tests*. Routledge: London.

Nelson, C. R. and C. I. Plosser (1982), 'Trends and Random Walks in Macro-Economic Time Series', *Journal of Monetary Economics*, 10, 139–162.

Nerlove, M. (1958), 'Distributed Lags and Demand Analysis for Agricultural and Other Commodities', *Agricultural Handbook*, No. 141, U.S. Department of Agriculture.

Newbold, P. and D. I. Harvey (2002),'Forecasting Combination and Encompassing', in M. P. Clements and D. F. Hendry (eds.), *A Companion to Economic Forecasting*. Blackwell Publishing: Oxford.

Nickell, S. (1985), 'Error Correction, Partial Adjustment and All That: An Expository Note', *Oxford Bulletin of Economics and Statistics*, 47, 119–129.

—— (1990), 'Unemployment: A Survey', *Economic Journal*, 100, 391–439.

Obstfeld, M. and K. Rogoff (1996), *Foundations of International Macroeconomics*. MIT Press: Cambridge.

Okun, A. (1962), 'Potential GNP: Its Measurement and Significance', *American Statistical Association, Proceedings of the Business and Economics Section*, 98–104.

Oxley, L. and M. McAleer (eds.) (1998), Special Issue of *Journal of Economic Surveys*, **12**.

Pagan, A. R. (1987), 'Three Econometric Methodologies: A Critical Appraisal', *Journal of Economic Surveys*, 1, 3–24.

—— (1999), 'The Getting of Macroeconomic Wisdom', ANU. CEPR Discussion Paper No. 412, Australian National University (http://econrsss.anu.edu.au/˜arpagan/).

—— and J. C. Robertson (1998), 'Structural Models of the Liquidity Effect', *Review of Economics and Statistics*, 80, 202–217.

—— and M. H. Pesaran (2005), 'On Econometric Analysis of Structural Systems with Permanent and Transitory Shocks' *mimeo*, University of Cambridge.

Peel, D. A. and R. A. Nobay, (2000), 'Optimal Monetary Policy with a Nonlinear Phillips Curve', *Economics Letters*, 67, 159–164.

Perron, P. (1989), 'The Great Crash, The Oil Price Shock, and the Unit Root Hypothesis', *Econometrica*, 57, 1361–1401.

Pesaran, M. H. (1991), 'Costly Adjustment under Rational Expectations: A Generalisation', *Review of Economics and Statistics*, 73, 353–358.

—— (1997), 'The Role of Economic Theory in Modelling the Long Run', *Economic Journal*, 107, 178–91.

—— (2004a), 'A Pair-Wise Approach to Testing for Output and Growth Convergence', http://www.econ.cam.ac.uk/faculty/pesaran/, revised November 2005.

—— (2004b), 'Estimation and Inference in Large Heterogenous Panels with a Multifactor Error Structure', http://www.econ.cam.ac.uk/faculty/pesaran/, revised version of *CESifo Working Paper No.869*, October 2002.

—— and B. Pesaran (1997), *Working with Microfit 4.0: An Interactive Introduction to Econometrics*. Oxford University Press: Oxford.

—— and —— (2006), *Microfit 5.0*, forthcoming Oxford University Press: Oxford.

——, T. Schuermann and S. M. Weiner (2004). 'Modeling Regional Interdependencies using a Global Error-Correcting Macroeconometric Model', (with discussion), *Journal of Business and Economic Statistics*, 22, 129–162 and 175–181.

——, —— and B. J. Treutler (2005), 'Global Business Cycles and Credit Risk', NBER Working Paper 11493 (http://www.nber.org/papers/w11493), forthcoming in M. Carey and R. Stulz (eds.), *Risks of Financial Institutions*, University of Chicago Press: Chicago.

——, ——, —— and S. M. Weiner (2005), 'Macroeconomics and Credit Risk: A Global Perspective', forthcoming, *Journal of Money, Credit and Banking*, available as Wharton Financial Institutions Center Working Paper #03–13B.

—— and Y. Shin (1996), 'Cointegration and Speed of Convergence to Equilibrium', *Journal of Econometrics*, 71, 117–143.

—— and —— (1998), 'Generalized Impulse Response Analysis in Linear Multivariate Models', *Economics Letters*, 58, 17–29.

—— and —— (1999), 'An Autoregressive Distributed Lag Modelling Approach to Cointegration Analysis', Chapter 11 in S. Strom (ed.), *Econometrics and Economic*

Theory in the 20th Century: The Ragnar Frisch Centennial Symposium. Cambridge University Press: Cambridge.

Pesaran, M. H. and Y. Shin (2002), 'Long-Run Structural Modelling', *Econometric Reviews*, 21, 49–87.

——, —— and R. J. Smith (2000), 'Structural Analysis of Vector Error Correction Models with Exogenous I(1) Variables', *Journal of Econometrics*, 97, 293–343.

——, —— and —— (2001), 'Bounds Testing Approaches to the Analysis of Level Relationships', *Journal of Applied Econometrics* Special Issue in honour of J.D. Sargan on the Theme *Studies in Empirical Macroeconometrics*, D. F. Hendry and M. H. Pesaran (eds.), 16, 289–326.

—— and S. Skouras (2002), 'Decision-Based Methods for Forecast Evaluation', in M. P. Clements and D. F. Hendry (eds.), *A Companion to Economic Forecasting*. Blackwell Publishing: Oxford.

—— and R. P. Smith (1985), 'Evaluation of Macroeconometric Models', *Economic Modelling*, 2, 125–134.

—— and —— (1995), 'Role of Theory in Econometrics', *Journal of Econometrics*, 67, 61–79.

—— and —— (1997), 'New Directions in Applied Dynamic Macroeconomic Modelling', in R. Dahel and I. Sirageldin (eds.), *Models for Economic Policy Evaluation Theory and Practice: An International Experience*. JAE Press Inc: Greenwich.

—— and —— (1998), 'Structural Analysis of Cointegrating VARs', *Journal of Economic Surveys*, 12, 471–506. Also Chapter 3 in L. Oxley and M. McAleer (eds.), *Practical Issues in Cointegration Analysis*, 1999. Basil Blackwell: Oxford.

—— and —— (2005), 'Macroeconometric Modelling with a Global Perspective', Unpublished manuscript, Cambridge University.

——, —— and V. Smith (2005), 'What if the UK had Joined the Euro in 1999? An Empirical Evaluation using a Global VAR', CESifo Working Paper No.1477.

—— and L. W. Taylor (1999), 'Diagnostics for IV Regressions', *Oxford Bulletin of Economics and Statistics*, 61, 255–281.

—— and A. Timmermann (1992), 'A Simple Nonparametric Test of Predictive Performance', *Journal of Business and Economic Statistics*, 10, 461–465.

——, —— and D. Pettenuzzo (2004), 'Forecasting Time Series Subject to Multiple Structural Breaks', http://www.econ.cam.ac.uk/faculty/pesaran/HMC_29Aug_2005.pdf

—— and P. Zaffaroni (2005), 'Model Averaging and Value-at-Risk Based Evaluation of Large Multi Asset Volatility Models for Risk Management', CESifo Working Paper No.1358.

Phillips, P. C. B. (1986), 'Understanding Spurious Regressions in Econometrics', *Journal of Econometrics*, 33, 311–340.

—— (1991), 'Optimal Inference in Cointegrated Systems', *Econometrica*, 59, 283–306.

—— and P. Perron (1988), 'Testing For Unit Roots in Time Series Regression', *Biometrika*, 75, 335–346.

Plosser, C. I. (1989), 'Understanding Real Business Cycles', *Journal of Economic Perspectives*, 3, 51–77.

Poulizac, D., M. Weale and G. Young (1996), 'The Performance of National Institute Economic Forecasts', *National Institute Economic Review*, 55–62.

Proietti, T. (1997), 'Short Run Dynamics in Cointegrated Systems', *Oxford Bulletin of Economics and Statistics*, 59, 405–422.

Ribba, A. (2003), 'Permanent-Transitory Decompositions and Traditional Measures of Core Inflation', *Economics Letters*, 81, 109–116.

Ríos-Rull, J. (1995), 'Models with Heterogenous Agents', Chapter 4 in T. F. Cooley (ed.), *Frontiers of Business Cycle Research*. Princeton University Press: Princeton.

Rogoff, K. (1985), 'The Optimal Degree of Commitment to an Intermediate Monetary Target', *Quarterly Journal of Economics*, 100, 1169–1190.

—— (1996), 'The Purchasing Power Parity Puzzle', *Journal of Economic Literature*, 34, 647–668.

Rosenblatt, M. (1952), 'Remarks on a Multivariate Transformation', *Annals of Mathematical Statistics*, 23, 470–472.

Rotemberg, J. and M. Woodford (1999), 'Interest Rate Rules in an Estimated Sticky Price Model', in J. B. Taylor (ed.), *Monetary Policy Rules*, 57–119. University of Chicago Press: Chicago.

Roy, S. D. (2004), 'Employment Dynamics in Indian Industry: Adjustment Lags and the Impact of Job Security Regulations', *Journal of Development Economics*, 73, 233–256.

Sargan, J. D. (1964), 'Wages and Prices in the United Kingdom: A Study in Econometric Methodology', in P. E. Hart, G. Mills and J. K. Whitaker (eds.), *Econometric Analysis for National Economic Planning*. Butterworth: London.

Schumacher, C. (2002), 'Forecasting Trend Output in the Euro Area', *Journal of Forecasting*, 8, 543–558.

Schwarz, G. (1978), 'Estimating the Dimension of a Model', *Annals of Statistics*, 6, 461–464.

Sims, C. (1980), 'Macroeconomics and Reality', *Econometrica*, 48, 1–48.

—— (1981), 'An Autoregressive Index Model for the US 1948–1975', in J. Kmenta and J.B. Ramsey (eds.), *Large-Scale Macro-econometric Models: Theory and Practice, Contributions to Economic Analysis*. North-Holland: Amsterdam.

—— (1986), 'Are Forecasting Models Usable for Policy Analysis?', *Quarterly Review, Federal Reserve Bank of Minneapolis*, 10, 2–16.

—— (1992), 'Interpreting the Macroeconomic Time Series Facts: The Effects of Monetary Policy', *European Economic Review*, 36, 975–1000.

—— and T. Zha (1998), 'Bayesian Methods for Dynamic Multivariate Models', *International Economic Review*, 39, 949–968.

Smets, F. and R. Wouters (2003), 'An Estimated Stochastic Dynamic General Equilibrium Model of the Euro Area', *Journal of the European Economic Association*, 1, 1123–1175.

Stadler, G. W. (1990), 'Business Cycle Models with Endogenous Technology', *American Economic Review*, 80, 763–778.

Summers, L. (1991), 'How Should Long Term Monetary Policy be Determined?', *Journal of Money, Credit and Banking*, 123, 625–631.

Smith, R. P. (1994), 'The Macromodelling Industry: Structure, Conduct and Performance', in S. G. Hall (ed.), *Applied Economic Forecasting Techniques*. Harvester Wheatsheaf: London.

Smith, J. and K. F. Wallis (2005), 'Combining Point Forecasts: The Simple Average Rules, OK?', *mimeo*, Department of Economics, University of Warwick.

Stock, J. H. and M. W. Watson (1988), 'Testing for Common Trends', *Journal of the American Statistical Association*, 83, 1097–1107.

Strachan, R. W. and H. K. van Dijk (2004), 'Valuing Structure, Model Uncertainty and Model Averaging in Vector Autoregressions', *Econometrics Institute Report*, EI 2004–23, Erasmus University Rotterdam.

Strongin, S. (1995), 'The Identification of Monetary Policy Disturbances: Explaining the Liquidity Puzzle', *Journal of Monetary Economics*, 34, 463–497.

Svensson, L. E. O. (1997), 'Optimal Inflation Targets, Conservative Central Banks, and Linear Inflation Contracts', *American Economic Review*, 87, 98–114.

—— (1999), 'Price Level Targeting versus Inflation Targeting', *Journal of Money, Credit and Banking*, 31, 277–295.

—— (2001), 'Inflation Targeting: Should It be Modelled as an Instrument Rule or a Target Rule?', *European Economic Review*, 46, 771–780.

—— (2002), 'What is Wrong with Taylor Rules? Using Judgement in Monetary Policy through Targeting Rules', *Journal of Economic Literature*, 41, 426–477.

Tang, T. C. (2004), 'Do Financial Variables Explain Aggregate Japanese Import Demand? A Cointegration Analysis', *Applied Economics Letters*, 11, 775–780.

Taylor, J. B. (1993), 'Discretion Versus Policy Rules in Practice', *Carnegie-Rochester Conference Series on Public Policy*, 39, 195–214.

Taylor, M. P. (1988), 'An Empirical Examination of Long Run Purchasing Power Parity Using Cointegration Techniques', *Applied Economics*, 20, 1369–1381.

Tiffin, R. and P. J. Dawson (2002), 'The Demand for Calories: Some Further Estimates from Zimbabwe', *Journal of Agricultural Economics*, 53, 221–232.

Turner, D. S. (1991), 'The Determinants of the NAIRU Response in Simulations on the Treasury Model', *Oxford Bulletin of Economics and Statistics*, 53, 223–242.

——, K. F. Wallis and J. D. Whitley (1989), 'Differences in the Properties of Large-Scale Macroeconometric Models: The Role of Labour Market Specifications', *Journal of Applied Econometrics*, 4, 317–344.

Turner, P. M. (1993), 'A Structural Vector Auto Regression Model of the UK Business Cycle', *Scottish Journal of Political Economy*, 40, 143–164.

Vlaar, P. J. G. (2004), 'Shocking the Eurozone', *European Economic Review*, 48, 109–131.

Wallis, K. F. (1995), 'Large-Scale Macroeconometric Modelling', Chapter 6 in M. H. Pesaran and M. R. Wickens (eds.), *Handbook of Applied Econometrics Volume 1: Macroeconomics*. Basil Blackwell: Oxford.

—— (1999), 'Asymmetric Density Forecasts of Inflation and the Bank of England's Fan Chart', *National Institute Economic Review*, 106–112.

——, P. G. Fisher, J. A. Longbottom, D. S. Turner and J. D. Whitley (1987), *Models of the UK Economy: A Fourth Review by the ESRC Macroeconomic Modelling Bureau*. Oxford University Press: Oxford.

—— and J. D. Whitley (1987), 'Long-run Properties of Large-Scale Macro-econometric Models', *Annales d'Economie et de Statistique*, 6/7, 207–224.

Watson, M. W. (1986), 'Univariate Detrending Methods with Stochastic Trends', *Journal of Monetary Economics*, 18, 49–75.

—— (1994), 'Vector Autoregressions and Cointegration', Chapter 47 in R. F. Engle and D. L McFadden (eds.), *Handbook of Econometrics,* Volume 4. North Holland Elsevier: Amsterdam.

West, K. D. (1995), 'Inventory Models', Chapter 4 in M. H. Pesaran and M. R. Wickens (eds.), *Handbook of Applied Econometrics Volume 1: Macroeconomics*. Basil Blackwell: Oxford.

Whitley, J. D. (1997), 'Economic Models and Policy-Making', *Bank of England Quarterly Bulletin*, May, 163–72.

Wickens, M. R. (1995), 'Real Business Cycle Analysis: A Needed Revolution in Macroeconometrics', *Economic Journal*, 105, 1637–1680.

—— (1996), 'Interpreting Cointegrating Vectors and Common Stochastic Trends', *Journal of Econometrics*, 74, 255–271.

—— and R. Motto (2001), 'Estimating Shocks and Impulse Response Functions', *Journal of Applied Econometrics*, 16, 371–387.

Woodford, M. (2002), 'Inflation Stabilization and Welfare', *Contributions to Macro-economics*, 2, Article 1.

—— (2003), *Interest and Prices: Foundations of a Theory of Monetary Policy*, Princeton University Press.

Wren-Lewis, S., J. Darby, J. Ireland and O. Ricchi (1996), 'The Macroeconomic Effects of Fiscal Policy: Linking an Econometric Model with Theory', *Economic Journal*, 106, 543–559.

Yang, J., C. Hsiao, Q. Li and Z. Wang (2005), 'The Emerging Market Crisis and Stock Market Linkage: Further Evidence', forthcoming in *Journal of Applied Econometrics*.

Yates, A. (1995), 'On the Design of Inflation Targets', in A. G. Haldane (ed.), *Targeting Inflation*, Bank of England, 135–169.

Yazgan, M. E. (2003), 'The Purchasing Power Parity Hypothesis for a High-Inflation Country: A Re-examination of the case of Turkey', *Applied Economics Letters*, 10, 143–147.

Yule, G. U. (1926), 'Why Do We Sometimes Get Nonsense-Correlations between Time-series? A Study in Sampling and the Nature of Time Series', *Journal of the Royal Statistical Society*, 89, 1–64.

Index